THE EVOLUTION OF THE
GLOBAL TERRORIST THREAT

Columbia Studies in Terrorism and Irregular Warfare

THE
EVOLUTION
OF THE
GLOBAL
TERRORIST
THREAT

From 9/11 to Osama bin Laden's Death

EDITED BY
BRUCE HOFFMAN
AND FERNANDO REINARES

Columbia University Press
New York

Columbia University Press
Publishers Since 1893
New York   Chichester, West Sussex
cup.columbia.edu
Copyright © 2014 Columbia University Press
All rights reserved

Scholarly research for this volume was made possible with a generous grant from the Real
Instituto Elcano, Madrid, and the Center for Security Studies and Security Studies Program,
Edmund A. Walsh School of Foreign Service at Georgetown University.

Library of Congress Cataloging-in-Publication Data
The Evolution of the global terrorist threat : from 9/11 to Osama bin Laden's death /
edited by Bruce Hoffman and Fernando Reinares.
pages cm. — (Columbia studies in terrorism and irregular warfare)
Includes bibliographical references and index.
ISBN 978-0-231-16898-4 (cloth : alk. paper) — ISBN 978-0-231-53743-8 (e-book)
1. Terrorism—History—21st century. 2. Jihad—History—21st century. I. Hoffman, Bruce, 1954–
editor of compilation. II. Reinares, Fernando, 1960– editor of compilation.
HV6431.E934 2014
363.32509'0511—dc23
2014008127

11-2014

Columbia University Press books are printed on permanent and durable acid-free paper.
This book is printed on paper with recycled content.
Printed in the United States of America

c 10 9 8 7 6 5 4 3 2 1

COVER DESIGN: Elliot Strunk/Fifth Letter
COVER IMAGE: © Getty Images

References to websites (URLs) were accurate at the time of writing. Neither the
author nor Columbia University Press is responsible for URLs that may have expired
or changed since the manuscript was prepared.

Contents

CONTENTS

CONTENTS

Introduction

BRUCE HOFFMAN AND FERNANDO REINARES

On September 11, 2001, nineteen terrorists hijacked four airplanes and changed the course of history. What followed was no less consequential: a global war on terrorism led by the United States that resulted in al-Qaeda's expulsion from Afghanistan; the loss of its training camps, operational bases, and command headquarters in that country; and the killing or capture of hundreds of al-Qaeda leaders and operatives, which has continued to this day. More than a decade after the 9/11 attacks, it remains clear that even if we always knew *why* we were fighting this war, we arguably were never entirely certain *whom* we were fighting. When the enemy appeared to be exclusively the core al-Qaeda organization, founded and led by Osama bin Laden, the answer was obvious. But when it involved the multiplicity of actual, putative, or suspected al-Qaeda branches or so-called franchises, its affiliates and associates, casual hangers-on, or the array of wannabe jihadists and lone wolves, the answer was often less clear.

The purpose of this book is to provide that answer. In the decade since the September 11 attacks, disagreement in academic as well as government circles has persisted over the nature of the threat, al-Qaeda itself, bin Laden's authority over the movement after its expulsion from Afghanistan, and whether a leader*less* process of terrorist radicalization and violence had superseded a leader-*led* one. Arguments were often voiced that al-Qaeda had ceased to be an organized entity; that it had practically disappeared as a hierarchical structure; and that the movement that existed at the time of the attacks on New York City and Washington, D.C., had disintegrated into an ideology and an amorphous phenomenon devoid of leadership and strategy. The main terrorist threat, some claimed, no longer came from distinct jihadist groups and organizations but rather from independent, self-constituted local cells or from isolated, self-recruited individuals.

A countervailing view throughout this period challenged these same assumptions. It held that al-Qaeda persisted as an articulate and active terrorist organization and that bin Laden continued to exercise an important degree of command and charismatic influence over both al-Qaeda and the global jihadi movement allied or associated with it. Far from being an amorphous phenomenon, the al-Qaeda global terrorist threat was seen as a polymorphous phenomenon, composed of an admittedly heterogeneous collection of like-minded groups led by a variety of leaders who embraced the same strategy and conformed to observable patterns of organizational conduct.

These divergent interpretations of both the jihadi threat and the nature and organization of the al-Qaeda movement became the subject of an intense debate that appeared in the pages of the May/June and July/August 2008 issues of *Foreign Affairs*.[1] In a review of Marc Sageman's *Leaderless Jihad: Terror Networks in the Twenty-First Century*, one of this volume's editors challenged the book's core thesis that terrorism in the twenty-first century had drifted from the provenance of top-down direction and implementation provided by established, existing organizations to an entirely bottom-up, loosely networked phenomenon of radicalized individuals gravitating toward one another and sharing a penchant for violence.[2] This "bunch of guys" theory of leaderless jihad defined these collections of individuals as the new threat we all had to prepare for: self-selected, self-radicalized, and mostly self-trained wannabes with a limited capacity for violence who were allegedly multiplying and spreading to challenge both the more traditional conceptions of terrorism and the attendant countermeasures and security responses based upon this anachronistically organized style of terrorism. Indeed, with the rise of the leaderless jihad, it was argued, organizations had become as immaterial as they were superfluous. In response, Hoffman addressed the accumulating evidence attesting to al-Qaeda's planning and oversight of all of the most consequential terrorist attacks and plots since September 11 and argued that rather than solely the product of radicalization, the terrorist threat actually represented the fruition of strategic, organizational decisions made by al-Qaeda years before.

Now that this first phase of the war on terrorism is over—demarcated by the killing of bin Laden in 2011 by U.S. Navy SEALS—it is possible to look back at its first decade and reflect on the contours of this debate and more clearly assess which interpretation of al-Qaeda was more accurate. To do so, this volume gathers twenty-five case studies that analyze the most significant terrorist attacks and plots that occurred between September 11, 2001, and May 1, 2011, in the West, along with some of the most serious and protracted campaigns of terrorism in countries and regions beset with conflict, such as Afghanistan and Pakistan, as well as Southeast Asia, East Africa, and North Africa. The editors included acts of violence committed by lone individuals, such as the 2004 murder of the controversial Dutch filmmaker Theo Van Gogh, that would appear to substantiate the "bunch of guys" theory along with terrorist acts with clear al-Qaeda pedigrees, such as the 2005 suicide bombings on London public transport and the 2006 plot to bomb seven commercial airliners in flight from London's Heathrow Airport to a variety of American and Canadian destinations. It also considers incidents such as the 2004 Madrid commuter-train bombings and the "Sauerland" plot in Germany where al-Qaeda played a different role, in combination with other jihadist organizations such as the Islamic Jihad Union or the now extinct Moroccan Islamic Combatant Group. In addition, the editors included studies focusing on the al-Qaeda terrorist campaigns in countries as diverse as Afghanistan and Iraq and in such regions as South Asia.

To assess the part that al-Qaeda may or may not have played throughout the war on terrorism's first ten years, this book considers the following pressing questions: Did al-Qaeda in fact virtually cease to exist following Operation Enduring Freedom, the invasion of Afghanistan, and the subsequent U.S.-led global counterterrorism campaign, or did it adapt and persist as a distinctive terrorist organizational entity? Had Osama bin Laden been reduced to a mere figurehead in the years preceding his death, or had he continued to provide strategic guidance and exercise continuing command and control over worldwide al-Qaeda operations up until the end? Did the global al-Qaeda, as it existed following the expulsion from Afghanistan, evidence the attributes of an articulated, transnationally connected structure, or was it nothing more than a loose collection of individuals and ideas amorphously arrayed around a decaying ideology? Depending on the answers to these questions, what is the preeminent terrorist threat today, and what will it likely be in the future? As 9/11 fades further into the past, should the world, particularly the West, anticipate and confront the terrorist threat as emerging from independent, self-constituted cells or from larger groups and organizations?

To answer these questions and test the various hypotheses put forward over the years about the al-Qaeda movement, we embraced the traditional case study. It is reasonable to assume that a significant number of relevant cases, covering the corpus of al-Qaeda activity over the past decade, would evidence the attributes and behavioral characteristics needed to assess both of these contrasting interpretations. Given the wealth of empirical material and data now available from this enormously important period, we, as the editors, were convinced that it was now possible to render this judgment. Moreover, in addition to the empirical evidence presented throughout this volume, we hoped to indicate critical theoretical implications for further study and research of the al-Qaeda and global jihadism phenomenon. We believe that an intellectual and practical effort of this magnitude would yield a great amount of substantive knowledge on jihadist terrorism generally, which remains as poorly documented as it is understood. As editors, we hope that having this material collected in one volume will benefit fellow scholars, students, policy makers, and counterterrorism practitioners alike.

In order to intellectually bound this examination of relevant cases, we decided to focus, on the one hand, on most of the post-9/11 jihadist attacks and foiled attempts that occurred in Western countries since 2002 and, on the other hand, on events outside the West until the killing of Osama bin Laden, particularly in countries with predominantly Muslim populations, including those immersed in profound conflict.

To provide these in-depth analyses on the selected terrorist cases and campaigns, we assembled an international collection of renowned experts from academia, think tanks, and media. This was possible thanks to the generous financial support offered by Elcano Royal Institute and Universidad Rey Juan Carlos in Spain as well as the Center for Security Studies in Georgetown University's Edmund A. Walsh School of Foreign Service in the United States. We would also be remiss not to acknowledge the absolutely invaluable assistance provided in the course of this project by Amy Buenning Sturm and, later, by Caitlyn Turgeon and Christopher Wall, of Georgetown University's Security Studies Program, and by Carola García-Calvo, of Elcano Royal Institute and Universidad Rey Juan Carlos.

The book is divided in two parts. The first examines jihadist terrorist attacks and foiled plots in the West between the September 11 attacks and bin Laden's killing. These include chapters on the evolution of the al-Qaeda terrorist threat in the United States following the September 11 attacks by Lorenzo Vidino; Fernando Reinares on the 2004 Madrid train bombings; Lindsay Clutterbuck on the case of Dhiren Barot, a Hindu convert to Islam and al-Qaeda operative, which British police refer to as Operation "Rhyme"; Peter R. Neumann and Ryan Evans on Operation "Crevice," another British counterterrorism effort against a homegrown cell led by a U.K. citizen named Omay Khayam; Beatrice de Graaf's examination of the murder of the controversial Dutch artist Theo Van Gogh; Stewart Bell on the case of the Toronto 18; Sally Neighbour's study of the Australian counterterrorist investigation, known as Operation "Pendennis"; Bruce Hoffman on the July 7, 2005, bombings of London transportation targets; Javier Jordán on the series of foiled attacks in Italy; Guido Steinberg analyzing Germany's "Sauerland" plot; Michael Taarnby on the Danish Glasvej Case and its connections to Pakistani jihadists; Fernadno Reinares on the 2008 plot to attack the Barcelona subway; and, finally, Jean-Pierre Filiu on the Iraq-related jihadist networks active in France after 2003.

The second part of the book is concerned with jihadist terrorism attacks and campaigns conducted outside the West during the same time frame. Seth Jones begins this part with a study of al-Qaeda operations in Afghanistan; the Southeast Asia jihadist terrorist organization known as al-Jemaah al-Islamiyah (or Jemaah Islamiyah) is the subject of Rohan Gunaratna's chapter; Jonathan Fighel examines the 2002 Mombassa attacks; al-Qaeda's Iraqi affiliate is analyzed by Mohammed M. Hafez; the series of suicide bomb attacks in Istanbul in November 2003 is addressed by Guido Steinberg and Philipp Holtmann; Holly L. McCarthy and Ami Pedahzur provide a case study of the mysterious series of terrorist attacks in the Sinai Peninsula; Jack Kalpakian examines al-Qaeda's operations in Morocco; Anneli Botha considers the 2007 suicide attacks in Algeria; Thomas Hegghammer examines the 2003 and 2008 al-Qaeda bombing campaigns in Saudi Arabia; C. Christine Fair addresses al-Qaeda-related or -inspired terrorism in Pakistan; and Anneli Botha examines the 2010 suicide bomb attacks in Kampala.

Our conclusions, as editors, on the nature of the global jihadist phenomenon and on the evolving global terrorism threat complete this volume.

NOTES

1. Bruce Hoffman, "They Myth of Grass-Roots Terrorism: Why Osama bin Laden Still Matters," *Foreign Affairs* 87, no. 3 (May/June 2008): 133–38; and Marc Sageman, "The Reality of Grass-Roots Terrorism" and Bruce Hoffman, "Hoffman Replies," in "Does Osama Still Call the Shots: Debating the Containment of al Qaeda's Leadership," *Foreign Affairs* 87, no. 4 (July/August 2008): 163–66.

2. Marc Sageman, *Leaderless Jihad: Terror Networks in the Twenty-First Century* (Philadelphia: University of Pennsylvania Press, 2008).

THE EVOLUTION OF THE
GLOBAL TERRORIST THREAT

[1]

In the West

The Evolution of the Post-9/11 Threat
to the U.S. Homeland

LORENZO VIDINO

On March 10, 2007, Khalid Sheikh Mohammed, the man the United States government accused of masterminding the September 11 attacks, finally stood before a military panel convened to judge him at the Guantánamo Bay detention facility. Before closing the introductory procedures, the presiding judge asked KSM, the acronym under which most Westerners know the man, if he wished to make a statement. KSM's legal representative informed the panel that the detainee had written a statement that KSM wanted him to read. "I was a member of the Al Qaeda Council," he began, "[and] I was the Operational Director for Sheikh Osama Bin Laden for the organizing, planning, follow-up, and execution of the 9/11 Operation."[1] KSM's admission confirmed a fact that few had doubted. For years American authorities had divulged ample evidence pointing to KSM's key role in the attacks, and KSM had boasted about it when al-Jazeera reporter Yosri Fouda secretly interviewed him in 2002 in his Karachi hideout.[2]

What came as a surprise was the rest of the statement. It detailed thirty-one terrorist plots, some of which were previously undisclosed to the public, that KSM claimed full or partial involvement in planning. The attacks, some carried out, some simply planned, spanned four continents and more than a decade. Among them, KSM indicated his role in "planning, training, surveying, and financing the New (or Second) Wave of attacks against the following skyscrapers after 9/11: a. Library Tower, California b. Sears Tower, Chicago c. Plaza Bank, Washington State d. The

Empire State Building, New York City."[3] The "Second Wave" was not the only attack KSM claimed to have planned against the U.S. mainland after 9/11. He added that he plotted an attack against the New York Stock Exchange and other financial targets, a "shoe bomber operation" to down two U.S.-bound airplanes, and entirely different plots (separate from the Second Wave) to destroy the Sears Tower in Chicago using tanker trucks and to bomb suspension bridges in New York.

Puzzled by the breadth of such a confession, intelligence analysts, terrorism experts, and forensic psychiatrists have debated both the validity of KSM's claims and the reasons behind them.[4] Some believe that KSM simply wished to take advantage of the opportunity to spread misinformation in order to intimidate the public and increase his stature as a terror mastermind. Others maintain that his confession should be attributed to the alleged torture he suffered while in captivity, and they question the confession's veracity. KSM, in fact, later told the International Committee of the Red Cross that while subjected to harsh interrogation techniques, he gave "a lot of false information in order to satisfy what I believed the interrogators wished to hear in order to make the ill-treatment stop."[5] Yet many believe that KSM was, for the most part, telling the truth.[6] Stressing that most of his claims are corroborated by information obtained from related investigations and other detainees' statements, many analysts are convinced that KSM was indeed a central figure in the terrorism world for more than a decade and that his involvement in thirty-one plots is not far-fetched and epitomizes the evolution and increased complexity of al-Qaeda's planning.

Of particular interest for this chapter is KSM's involvement in planning operations against the American homeland after 9/11. Since that tragic day in 2001, American authorities have thwarted dozens of attacks planned by terrorists of Islamist inspiration against various targets throughout the country. The characteristics of each plot, from the sophistication to the profile of the individuals involved, vary significantly. An analysis of the plots allegedly hatched by KSM is extremely useful to highlight these differences and to identify long-term trends in al-Qaeda's evolution and the post-9/11 terrorist threat to the American homeland. In particular, this chapter aims to show that the shift from sophisticated and remotely controlled operations to homegrown and inevitably amateurish efforts, though particularly evident over the last couple of years, began in the immediate aftermath of the 9/11 attacks as KSM struggled to follow up on his terrorist masterpiece.

Before analyzing the plots, it is necessary to address the sources used for this chapter. Despite being a key player in terrorist networks for more than a decade and having been in custody since March 2003, KSM managed to hide many aspects of his life and activities. Information on his background was gained from some journalistic sources and his extensive profile in the *9/11 Commission Report*. More problematic was the collection of detailed and corroborated information on the plots masterminded by KSM. Some of the foiled plots resulted in trials in U.S. federal courts, generating ample information and allowing defendants to challenge the prosecution's arguments according to the standards of due process. For other plots, however, the only available sources are declassified and highly redacted portions of U.S. government reports originating from interrogations of detainees held at Guantánamo Bay. This information inevitably raises doubts about completeness and reliability.

It is unclear, at the time of this writing, whether U.S. authorities have the full picture of KSM's plots and whether they ever will. Assuming they do, a large amount of information on them is still classified and, therefore, not publicly available. Accordingly, this chapter cannot and does not claim to provide the definitive account of all the post-9/11 plots orchestrated by KSM. Its aim, rather, is to describe such plots with as much accuracy as possible given the limitations of the sources and to draw conclusions based on the analysis of their known characteristics.

A GLOBAL TERROR ENTREPRENEUR

KSM was born in 1965 in Kuwait, one of the five children of a family of Baluchi immigrants who, like many others, had moved to the small Gulf emirate attracted by the oil boom.[7] KSM's family was known to be quite religious. His father was the imam of a local mosque, and in the early 1980s, his older brother Zahid became one of the leaders of the local branch of the Muslim Brotherhood while attending Kuwait University.[8] KSM himself joined the Brotherhood while a teenager and became immersed in Islamist ideology, along with his brothers and his nephew

Ramzi Youssef, who would later gain worldwide notoriety for master-minding the 1993 bombing of New York City's World Trade Center.

Upon graduation from secondary school, KSM traveled to the United States, where he attended college in North Carolina. Fellow students remember him as religious but not fanatical: an intelligent but unre-markable student who socialized mostly with fellow Muslims.[9] According to the memoirs he wrote during his detention in Guantánamo, KSM did not enjoy his experience in the United States. He was briefly detained for unpaid bills, and his limited contacts with Americans confirmed his views of America as a "debauched and racist country."[10] In 1986, upon obtaining his degree in mechanical engineering from North Carolina Agricultural and Technical State University, KSM left the United States but, instead of returning to Kuwait, joined his brother Zahid in Peshawar. At the time Peshawar was the gateway to Afghanistan, and Arab charities such as the Kuwaiti Lajnat al-Dawa al-Islamiya, of which Zahid was regional manager, provided aid to Afghan refugees and support to foreign volunteers who wanted to join the mujaheddin to fight against Soviet forces.

Thanks to his brother's influential position, KSM established connections with important leaders of the Afghan jihad. Like most non-Afghans, KSM joined the forces led by Abdul Rasul Sayyaf, an Afghan who headed one of the most ideological factions fighting the Soviets. Fluent in Arabic and a strict Salafist, Sayyaf was the natural point of contact for most foreign muja-heddin and one of the favored recipients of financial aid flowing in from the Arab Gulf. After a period with Sayyaf, KSM returned to Peshawar and took up various administrative jobs working for Abdullah Azzam, the spiritual leader of the "Afghan Arabs." As the war ended, KSM reportedly left for a short stint in Bosnia but soon returned to Pakistan to continue his work for the network set up by Azzam, who had been assassinated in 1989, and Sayyaf.

During that time, he reunited with his nephew Ramzi Youssef, who had traveled to Afghanistan to receive training in explosives. Youssef allegedly told KSM about his intention to use his newly acquired skills to attack the United States. The two relatives kept in contact after Youssef left for America and KSM moved to Qatar to work as an engineer at the Ministry of Electricity and Water. According to U.S. authorities, KSM wired Youssef a small amount of money from Qatar to fund the attacks.[11] But if KSM's support for attacks against America was until then limited to a negligible money transfer, the relative success of Youssef's bombing of the World Trade Center galvanized him. It was, in fact, after the attack that KSM began to build his career as a freelancer and entrepreneur of terrorism. Working independently of any organization, KSM began to travel around the world under dozens of aliases to build a network of contacts; acquire expertise in document forgery, explosives, and money transfer; and, finally, carry out terrorist operations.

In 1994 KSM joined Youssef in Manila. There, his enterprising nephew had established a cell of Arab militants, most of them veterans of the Afghan camps or childhood friends from Kuwait, who were planning various terrorist operations. KSM began to hone his skills as a terrorist mastermind during his time in the Philippine capital. The men bombed a local movie theater and made plans to kill the pope and President Bill Clinton during their visits to that country. In January 1995, Youssef inadvertently set fire to an apartment used by the cell to mix chemicals for homemade explosives. Because of the blaze the Philippine authorities stumbled onto the cell and arrested some of its members.[12] KSM and Youssef, however, managed to flee the country. But while KSM returned safely to Qatar, Youssef was apprehended a few weeks later in Pakistan. Among the documents found in the Manila apartment, authorities were shocked to see sketches for a sophisticated plan to detonate explosives on twelve U.S.-bound commercial jetliners over the Pacific. The operation, which the men had called "Bojinka," had already proceeded beyond the planning phase, and the men had successfully detonated a homemade explosive prototype on a Tokyo-bound flight, killing one Japanese passenger. The idea conceived in Manila would linger in KSM's mind for years to come.

While still working for the Qatari government, KSM continued to travel around the world building ties with like-minded Islamist extremists, operating as a freelancer with a surfeit of ideas but limited means. Things began to change in 1996, when KSM was tipped off by friends inside the Qatari government about the possibility of a "snatch and grab" rendition by U.S. authorities.[13] KSM immediately left Qatar and returned to Afghanistan. After having reconnected with his old mentor, Sayyaf, KSM established contact with another veteran of the war against the Soviets who had recently returned to Afghanistan: Osama bin Laden. The two men had reportedly met during the 1980s but were not close. KSM had a good relationship with Mohammed Atef, then al-Qaeda's military chief, and Atef reportedly organized the meeting.[14]

Years later KSM told American interrogators that during the meeting with bin Laden and al-Qaeda's leadership, he had pitched various ideas for attacks, including a grandiose operation that entailed hijacking ten airplanes inside the United States. Nine, recounted KSM, would have been crashed into landmark buildings on both coasts. Then KSM himself would have landed in the tenth airplane at a U.S. airport and, after having killed all male passengers, delivered a speech in front of the cameras condemning U.S. foreign policies.[15] Bin Laden opposed such a theatrical plot, but the idea of crashing airplanes into buildings was something the al-Qaeda leadership had toyed with since its days in Sudan. By the first months of 1999, after some initial hesitations, bin Laden approved a more modest version of the plan, and KSM was asked to lead what came to be known within al-Qaeda as the Planes Operation.[16] In order to oversee the operation, KSM moved to Kandahar and began to head some of al-Qaeda's most important internal committees.[17]

Al-Qaeda's leadership provided KSM with a group of Yemeni militants who should have been used for the Planes Operation. But the Yemenis' inability to obtain visas to enter the United States forced KSM to split the operation in two.[18] Saudi members of al-Qaeda, who could more easily get U.S. visas, were tasked to crash the hijacked planes into buildings on the East Coast along with an Egyptian national, Mohammed Atta, and the other members of a Hamburg cell who had joined al-Qaeda. The Yemenis were assigned to execute a new Bojinka plot and blow up U.S.-bound commercial planes in midair over the Pacific Ocean. The two operations were scheduled simultaneously in order to maximize their psychological impact. With planning and training for both operations under way in the spring of 2000, bin Laden decided that the two plots were too difficult to coordinate and canceled the Bojinka portion.[19] KSM reluctantly but obediently focused on the other part of the remaining but greatly scaled down plot, which was masterfully executed on September 11, 2001.

PLANNING THE SECOND WAVE

In his interrogations KSM admitted that while the meticulous planning for the 9/11 attacks consumed most of his time, he kept thinking about a possible second wave of attacks against the United States throughout

2000 and in the early months of 2001.[20] Al-Qaeda planners had debated among themselves whether a second wave should consist of more hijackings or entail some other form of attack.[21] Hijackings seemed to be the prevailing choice, and a handful of operatives were selected in late 2000 and early 2001 to receive the same training as the 9/11 hijackers. KSM predicted that security would improve after the execution of the Planes Operation and decided that the operatives involved in the Second Wave should hold non-Arab passports in order to attract less attention.[22]

One of these operatives was a French national named Zacarias Moussaoui. Despite being dubbed "the twentieth hijacker" by the media, Moussaoui apparently was never meant to participate in the 9/11 attacks but, rather, was supposed to be one of the pilots of the Second Wave.[23] Selected because of his French passport, Moussaoui was first sent to Malaysia to attend a flight school under the supervision of operatives from Jemaah Islamiyah (JI), al-Qaeda's Southeast Asian affiliate. After JI leaders complained about the Frenchman's behavior, KSM sent him to the United States to continue his training. Moussaoui's erratic behavior attracted the attention of personnel at the Minnesota flying school he had enrolled in, and FBI agents arrested him in August 2001.[24] In 2006, after a long and dramatic trial, Moussaoui was sentenced to life in prison without parole by a federal court. According to U.S. authorities, the Canadian national Abderraouf Jdey (a.k.a. Faruq al-Tunisi), was the second al-Qaeda operative assigned to take part in the Second Wave as a pilot, but he decided to back out of the plot in the summer of 2001.[25] As of 2013, Jdey is wanted by U.S. authorities, who are offering a $5 million reward for information leading to his capture.[26]

Moussaoui's arrest and Jdey's renunciation led KSM to scratch the plans for the Second Wave, albeit only temporarily. Reflecting his seemingly insatiable obsession with planning potential attacks, KSM continued to work on other plots. Between August 2000 and April 2001, for example, he dispatched the al-Qaeda operative Dhiren Barot, a British-born convert to Islam, to surveil various targets on the East Coast.[27] Along with two British accomplishes, Barot traveled to the United States on various occasions posing as a student and conducted detailed surveillance of several financial institutions and Jewish targets throughout the eastern seaboard.[28] Barot wrote extensive reports about the buildings' vulnerabilities, exploring possible methods of attack and suggesting in some cases the use of limousines packed with explosives. The plan to strike these targets was shelved after 9/11 as the cell turned to carrying out attacks inside Great Britain, but it was never completely abandoned even after KSM's capture.[29]

Other British operatives were supposed to execute the first operation KSM planned immediately after 9/11. Having escaped the American attack on Taliban-controlled Afghanistan, KSM settled in Karachi. The suburbs of the sprawling Pakistani metropolis offered a perfect refuge for the ingenious mastermind, who tasked his nephew (and Ramzi Youssef's cousin), Ali Abdal Aziz Ali (a.k.a. Ammar al-Baluchi) to keep open lines of communication with al-Qaeda leaders and operatives throughout the world using the Internet and personal couriers.[30]

Per KSM's instructions, in late 2001 al-Baluchi began to impart operational instructions to two recent graduates of al-Qaeda's training camps in Afghanistan—British nationals Richard Reid and Saajid Badat.[31] Reid, the son of an English mother and a Jamaican father, was a petty criminal who had converted to Islam while serving in a youth prison and had then fallen under the spell of Abu Qatada (Omar Mahmoud Othman) and Abu Hamza al-Masri, two of the most radical imams in London's Salafist scene at the end of the 1990s. Initially tapped for the Second Wave, Reid was soon dispatched to carry out a less ambitious plan.[32] Traveling throughout Europe and the Middle East, Reid tested security procedures at various airports. According to his own account, it was after flying to Israel that Reid conceived the idea of hiding explosives in his shoes to detonate in midair. Reid later recounted in a detailed report he wrote for al-Qaeda leaders that, having undergone El Al's strict security controls, he had noticed that personnel had not checked the insides of his shoes.[33]

Acting on instructions from al-Baluchi, Reid boarded an American Airlines flight from Paris to Miami on December 22, 2001, with the intention of downing it over the Atlantic by detonating explosives he had hidden in his shoes.[34] His clumsy attempt to light a fuse dangling from his sneakers with a match attracted the attention of the flight crew and other passengers, who immobilized him until the plane crossed the Atlantic and landed safely in Boston. Interrogated by FBI agents after his arrest, Reid stated that he wanted to down an airplane during the holiday season because he wanted to "cause the American public to lose confidence in airline security and stop traveling, leading to a substantial loss of revenue which would in turn hurt the American economy."[35] Reid's thinking closely reflected KSM's, who since the 1993 World Trade Center bombing had decided attacks on financial targets best exploited the vulnerabilities of the United States.[36]

Where Reid failed, Badat did not even try. Born in Gloucester to a pious Muslim family originally from Malawi, Badat was a quiet, studious, and deeply religious boy who had studied to become an imam.[37] In September 2001 Badat traveled to Pakistan and Afghanistan, where he was given explosives and custom-made shoes similar to those given to Reid.[38] Once back in Europe, Badat began having second thoughts and sent e-mails to his handlers indicating a newfound reluctance to carry out the attack. He finally wrote, "You will have to tell Van Damme [an obvious reference to Reid's hulking figure] that he could be on his own."[39] Badat never purchased his ticket to fly to the United States, but he kept the explosive kit he had been given in Afghanistan. He admitted to being part of the plot when, in November 2003, British authorities raided his home and found the shoe bombs.[40]

The shoe-bomb operation's failure seems inevitable in retrospect. Badat, for example, had not undergone the same operational and psychological training that KSM had imposed on the core 9/11 hijackers and other trusted operatives like Barot. Similarly, Reid hardly possessed the intelligence and operational skills of a Mohammed Atta. In hindsight, the whole operation seems a rushed attempt on KSM's behalf to strike a blow while al-Qaeda was reeling under the pressure of the opening salvo of the U.S.-led global war on terrorism. KSM, in fact, admitted to his interrogators that while he expected the Plane Operation to be a historic success, he and the rest of al-Qaeda's leadership were stunned by the catastrophic impact of their actions and, consequently, by the severity of the U.S. response.[41] Determined to carry out any sort of follow-up operation in the immediate aftermath of 9/11, KSM appeared to be forced to rely on Reid and Badat given the absence of any concrete plan for an attack of greater complexity.

Yet shortly after the U.S. invasion of Afghanistan, KSM did begin to put together a more meticulous new plan for more attacks on the U.S. homeland. Picking up from where he had left off in the summer of 2001 after Moussaoui's arrest, KSM's plan once again involved crashing hijacked airplanes into high-rise buildings.[42] But by this time KSM, admitting he was "impressed by the security measures implemented in the U.S. in the immediate aftermath of the attacks," decided that the hijackers could not be Arabs and instead employed Southeast Asian operatives.[43]

In October 2001, KSM contacted Riduan Isamuddin (a.k.a. Hambali), Jemaah Islamiyah's operational leader, to ask for his help.[44] Hambali, who at the time was planning a series of attacks throughout Southeast Asia, reportedly selected a group of seventeen Southeast Asian operatives for what was supposed to be the new Second Wave.[45] Central to the group, which was dubbed the Guraba Cell, were four Malaysian men. One of them was Mohammed Nazir Bin Lep (a.k.a. Lillie), one of Hambali's top lieutenants who was later involved in the 2003 bombing of the Jakarta Marriott Hotel.[46] Hambali also tasked another of his lieutenants, Mod Farik Bin Amin (a.k.a. Zubair), to participate in the operation. Zubair had met Lillie in college in the 1990s and had later trained in the Afghan camps.[47] Upon his return to Southeast Asia he had become one of Hambali's most trusted couriers, carrying messages and money to and from al-Qaeda's leadership.[48] Zakaria Zeini, an engineer, and Masran bin Arshad, the alleged cell leader, completed the team put together by Hambali.

According to U.S. authorities, once selected, the four Malaysians traveled to Afghanistan to meet bin Laden, as the pilots of the 9/11 plot had, to swear their personal allegiance (bayat).[49] Reportedly, the men were told they had been chosen for a suicide operation against the United States but were not informed of any operational details. But KSM had a plan in mind. He envisioned an operation that combined the shoe-bomb plot with 9/11. The Southeast Asian operatives, whom KSM personally trained in the use of explosives, were to detonate a shoe bomb in midair. But unlike Reid and Badat, they would not seek to down the plane but rather to blow up the reinforced doors that had been introduced after 9/11 to prevent access to the cockpits.[50] The men would have then stormed the cockpit, and Zeini, who had trained as a pilot, would have crashed the plane into its intended target.

In his statement before the military panel at Guantánamo, KSM listed a series of buildings located throughout the United States that were initially selected as targets for the Second Wave. In reality, KSM soon understood that the list was too long. First, he could not count on having the services of so many trained pilots. Second, having evaluated the enhanced security measures put in place after 9/11, he assessed the chances of another successful wave of synchronized hijackings inside the United States as "dismal."[51] He decided instead to focus on one target, which authorities believe was the Los Angeles Library Tower (which President Bush in a 2006 speech mistakenly called the Liberty Tower).[52] An iconic seventy-three-story high-rise in the heart of downtown Los Angeles, the Library Tower is the tallest skyscraper west of the Mississippi. In KSM's calculations, its destruction would have brought to the West Coast the pain and disruption that the eastern part of the country had suffered on 9/11.[53]

But this time KSM's plan did not work, and, upon returning to Southeast Asia, the cell tasked for the Second Wave fell apart. Zeini, the only trained pilot, backed out, saying that he did not want to die, and he surrendered to Malaysian authorities.[54] In February 2002, bin Arshad, the commandos' leader, was arrested, and the remaining members of the cell concluded that the plot had been canceled.[55] Finally, in the summer of 2003, Thai authorities arrested Lillie, Zubair, and Hambali, who were later transferred to Guantánamo. According to U.S. authorities, the arrests were triggered by the confessions made by KSM to CIA interrogators. Initially uncooperative, after being subjected to enhanced interrogation techniques KSM reportedly told interrogators about the Los Angeles plot and revealed the names of some of the people involved in it. That information proved crucial in arresting Zubair, who, in turn, led authorities to Hambali. According to U.S. officials, the interrogation of Hambali and other members of the Guraba Cell confirmed KSM's words.[56]

THE "THIRD WAVE"

The failure of the Second Wave led KSM to reassess his strategy to carry out attacks against the U.S. homeland. Security constraints forced him to abandon the possibility of hijackings and other grandiose operations, leading him to focus instead on less ambitious plans. Moreover, he understood the need to rely on operatives who would attract the least amount of attention. He came to see American citizens or individuals who had long-established ties to the country as the only perpetrators who could enter and travel throughout the United States without raising suspicion.

One operative who fit these criteria was Jose Padilla, a New York–born former gang member who had converted to Islam in Florida and had been shuttling between various al-Qaeda training camps since at least 2000.[57] Padilla had pitched various ideas for catastrophic attacks against the United States, including a plot involving detonating nuclear material, to senior al-Qaeda leaders. In March 2002, he was sent to Karachi to discuss his proposals with KSM. KSM was skeptical about the dirty-bomb plot but suggested that Padilla and an accomplice, the Ethiopian native Binyam Mohamed, travel to the United States. They were instructed to rent several apartments in high-rise buildings that had gas stoves.[58] The plan was for the men to detonate bombs in the buildings after having left the gas on in order to enhance the explosions that would follow. After receiving extensive training in communication security from KSM, al-Baluchi, and the 9/11 planner Ramzi Binalshibh, Padilla and Mohamed were reportedly given $20,000 each and dispatched to the United States. Mohamed was arrested in Pakistan and later transferred to Guantánamo, where he remained until February 2009, when he was repatriated to the United Kingdom without being charged. Padilla was arrested upon entering the United States at Chicago's O'Hare airport in May 2002. Initially accused of planning to carry out a dirty-bomb attack inside the country, Padilla was detained as an enemy combatant. After extensive legal vicissitudes, in 2007 Padilla was tried in a civilian court and convicted of material support charges.[59]

KSM also established a network of sleepers—trained operatives waiting for an activation order—throughout the United States before 2001. After 9/11 and the failure of the Second Wave, the network was mobilized.[60] U.S. authorities stumbled upon one of the alleged key members, Ali Saleh Kahlah al-Marri, immediately after 9/11. Al-Marri was a dual Saudi and Qatari national who had lived in Peoria, Illinois, from 1983 to 1991 and had obtained a science degree from a local university.[61] He had returned to Peoria on September 10, 2001, allegedly to obtain a graduate degree. In the wake of the 9/11 attacks, U.S. authorities discovered that al-Marri had placed several phone calls to Mustafa al-Hawsawi, a close collaborator of KSM who had served as the principal financier for the 9/11 hijackers. Questioned by FBI agents, al-Marri denied making such calls. Convinced that he was part of an al-Qaeda network inside the country, U.S. authorities arrested him in December 2001 for lying under interrogation and for providing a false name and a stolen Social Security number to obtain a bank account.[62] During the search of his home, officials found large amounts of jihadi literature and almost a thousand credit card numbers and information on how to forge documents and credit cards on his computer. Al-Marri was then classified as an enemy combatant and detained in a navy brig in South Carolina.[63]

Al-Marri later confirmed his role in KSM's U.S. network. In April 2009, in fact, al-Marri pleaded guilty to one count of conspiracy to provide material support to al-Qaeda in a federal court. He stated that he had attended al-Qaeda training camps between 1998 and 2001 and that he had been ordered by KSM to reach Peoria by September 10 in order to "plan and prepare for future acts of terrorism within the United States."[64] Al-Marri recounted the details of how he had kept in close contact with the terror mastermind using prearranged codes in e-mail conversations and public payphones miles from his home. He also admitted to researching chemical weapons and potential targets during his sojourn in Illinois. In his interrogations, KSM, who identified al-Marri as "the point of contact for AQ operatives arriving in the US for September 11 follow-on operations," described him as "the perfect sleeper agent" because he had "studied in the United States, had no criminal record, and had a family with whom he could travel."[65]

Another recruit possessing similarly attractive characteristics was Majid Khan, a Pakistani native who in 1996, when still a teenager, had immigrated to the suburbs of Baltimore.[66] Upon graduation from high school, Khan's political and religious views had reportedly grown increasingly radical. He traveled to Pakistan, and there, according to U.S. authorities, he was introduced by his uncle and cousin, who were al-Qaeda operatives, to KSM. KSM, impressed by Khan's knowledge of the United States and the English language, immediately recruited him.[67]

According to U.S. authorities, while in Pakistan, Khan assisted al-Baluchi in smuggling al-Qaeda operatives across the Afghan border and funneling funds to Jemaah Islamiyah for attacks against U.S. and Israeli targets in Southeast Asia.[68] But Khan's American ties were what attracted KSM. The mastermind began training Khan on how to build timing devices and tested his commitment to becoming a suicide bomber.[69] Once he completed the training, Khan was tasked to return to the United States to plan a series of attacks.[70] KSM asked Khan, whose family owned a gas station in the Baltimore area, to research the feasibility of blowing up gas stations by detonating explosives in the underground storage tanks.[71] He also instructed him to study the possibility of poisoning U.S. water reservoirs.[72] Neither of these plots seems to have gone beyond the research phase. Khan was arrested in Karachi on March 5, 2003, just four days after KSM's capture. He was later moved to Guantánamo, where he became one of the base's high-value detainees.[73]

Khan kept in contact with a number of al-Qaeda operatives and sympathizers inside the United States. According to U.S. authorities, Khan developed a relationship with two New York–based Pakistani nationals, Saifullah and Uzair Paracha.[74] The father and son allegedly helped hide Khan from U.S. authorities during his travels to Pakistan and launder money for attacks through their textile import/export business. Uzair was later sentenced to thirty years in prison for providing material support to al-Qaeda, and his father, Saifullah, has been detained as an enemy combatant in Guantánamo.[75] Khan was also in touch with Aafia Siddiqui, a long-time Boston resident and MIT graduate who had been involved in militant activities for more than fifteen years.[76]

The Parachas and Aafia Siddiqui, however, only provided logistical support. Khan recommended to KSM another of his associates, Iyman Faris, as the executor of an attack.[77] Faris was a Kashmir-born naturalized U.S. citizen and a longtime resident of Columbus, Ohio, who had visited Khan's residence in Baltimore in mid-2001.[78] During the visit, Faris would later tell investigators, Khan had told him about the fighting in Afghanistan, his involvement with KSM, and his desire to martyr himself in an operation against then-Pakistani president Pervez Musharraf.[79] Faris had already been involved with al-Qaeda, having allegedly met bin Laden while training at an Afghan camp in 2000.[80] Faris's American passport and Khan's intercession led KSM to task Faris with planning attacks inside the United States.[81]

Faris and KSM discussed several options. Faris, a licensed truck driver, said he could penetrate security at airports and drive a truck laden with explosives under a plane as it sat on the tarmac.[82] KSM expressed an interest in the idea but in the end tasked Faris with planning two simultaneous attacks in Washington and New York.[83] The former involved derailing trains by sabotaging railroad tracks. In New York, on the other hand, KSM aimed to destroy the iconic Brooklyn Bridge by severing the suspension bridge's cables. KSM tasked Faris with obtaining the means and tools with which to carry out both operations. Faris did extensive Internet searches and even traveled from Columbus to New York to surveil the bridge. Unable to obtain the necessary tools and discouraged by the security surrounding the iconic structure, Faris began sending coded e-mails to KSM and al-Baluchi indicating his inability to carry out the attacks.[84]

At this point Faris began to plot an attack of his own. Apparently without KSM's knowledge, in the summer of 2002, Faris discussed various ideas about attacks inside the United States with a small group of like-minded individuals in the Columbus area. The apparent leader of the cluster was Christopher Paul, an African American convert to Islam who had first attended al-Qaeda training camps in Afghanistan and Pakistan in the early 1990s.[85] Since then, Paul had been immersed in militant activities. He had traveled several times to Afghanistan, Pakistan, Bosnia, and Western Europe, where he had developed a network of contacts, but he had also spent extensive time in his native Columbus, where he had built a network of local jihad enthusiasts.[86]

Paul, Faris, and Nuradin Abdi, a Somali national who had received training in Ogaden, began talking about possible attacks throughout the country, finally settling on a vague plan to blow up a shopping mall in the Columbus area.[87] Once again, the plot did not go beyond the initial stages of planning as authorities, who had kept the men under close surveillance, swooped in on the cell. Faris was later sentenced to twenty years in prison for material support to al-Qaeda.[88] Abdi pleaded guilty to material support charges and was sentenced to ten years incarceration.[89] Paul was arrested in 2007 for his involvement in an unrelated plot to attack American tourists in cooperation with Europe-based al-Qaeda operatives.[90] Tried in 2009 in a federal court, he was sentenced to twenty years.[91]

FROM KSM'S GENIUS TO HOMEGROWN JIHAD

According to his confession and information released by U.S. authorities, KSM planned six terrorist attacks against the American homeland between the 9/11 attacks and his capture in Rawalpindi in March

2003. None of these plans, except Reid's attempt to blow up the Paris–Miami flight, went beyond the planning phase. In some cases, individuals decided to abandon the plots for personal reasons, such as second thoughts about participating in a suicide mission. But, for the most part, the common denominator of KSM's repeated failures is the markedly aggressive counterterrorism posture adopted by the United States and its partners worldwide after 9/11.

The Planes Operation of September 11 was unquestionably a remarkable display of organizational ability on al-Qaeda's part. The inefficiencies of the American security apparatus before 9/11, however, doubtlessly contributed to the success of the attacks. The intelligence agencies' inability to aggressively pursue al-Qaeda and more generally, the widespread "failure of imagination" that prevented most American policy makers from grasping the severity of the threat posed by the organization contributed to the success of the attacks no less than KSM's operational genius. The 9/11 hijackers behaved quite professionally but did commit several mistakes that would have allowed U.S. authorities, had they been more alert, to uncover at least parts of the plot. Limited interagency and international cooperation, poor enforcement of immigration rules, and lax airport security are just some of the factors that allowed KSM's plan to become a terrorism masterpiece.

Most of these conditions, as KSM himself claimed to have noticed, were removed immediately after 9/11. Preventing terrorist attacks and dismantling al-Qaeda cells became the priority of the U.S. government and of many of its allies throughout the world. The failures of KSM's post-9/11 plots are a direct consequence of this shift. The improvement of immigration and airport security forced KSM to scale back the Second Wave to just one aircraft. Newly enhanced intelligence cooperation with U.S. allies led to the definitive disruption of the plot, just as the capture of Hambali, Lillie, and Zubair took place thanks to the close partnership among American, Thai, and other Southeast Asian intelligence agencies. Close interagency cooperation and the use of counterterrorism tools introduced after 9/11 led to the arrest of many of KSM's U.S.-based associates, such as al-Marri, Faris, and the Parachas.

These new security measures, combined with the loss of al-Qaeda's Afghan sanctuary, created almost insurmountable challenges to KSM's ability to plan large-scale, sophisticated operations. Interrogated by

CIA officials after his capture, the terror mastermind confirmed this view and called his post-9/11 operations "opportunistic and limited."[92] KSM's inability to make any Second Wave attempt progress beyond the planning and training stage is indeed telling. He consequently decided to resort to smaller operations involving either operatives he had personally trained and dispatched to the United States or others who were selected later because of their unique characteristics. The former, such as Richard Reid and Jose Padilla, headed operations in which KSM's participation seems almost half-hearted, characterized by a limited investment of time and resources and dictated mostly by his understanding that al-Qaeda needed any kind of follow-up operation to the 9/11 attacks, even one of limited sophistication.

As for the U.S.-based operatives, KSM found increasing difficulties in coordinating their activities. The actions of Iyman Faris upon his return to the United States from Pakistan perfectly illustrate the deterioration of al-Qaeda's centralized planning. Having received only limited training and vague instructions from KSM, Faris returned to Columbus with ample discretion on how to implement the plan to destroy the Brooklyn Bridge and derail trains. But Faris appeared to lack the discipline and smarts of other KSM-trained operatives. Unable to obtain the tools necessary for the attacks and discouraged by the high security surrounding the bridge, he decided to abandon the plan and hatch one of his own. Then, with a group of local like-minded individuals who had ties to al-Qaeda but were acting in complete operational independence, he began drawing up vague plans for an unsophisticated plan against a local target.

The shift in Faris's plans seems to epitomize the evolution of the terrorist threat facing the U.S. homeland after 2001. Until mid-2003 virtually all of the terrorist conspiracies intended to strike against American soil had been planned, albeit with varying degrees of involvement, by KSM and al-Qaeda's central leadership. The arrest of most of the known U.S.-based associates of KSM and of the terrorist mastermind himself seems to mark the end of this phase. Except for the 2006 transatlantic plot, a plan by U.K.-based militants apparently directed by al-Qaeda members in Pakistan to detonate liquid explosives on board several U.S.-bound flights, and the 2009 attempt by Umar Farouk Abdulmutallab to blow up an Amsterdam to Detroit flight with explosives provided to him by al-Qaeda in the Arabian Peninsula (AQAP), every single attack against the American homeland thwarted by U.S. authorities from 2003 to the summer of 2013 appears to have been conceived by individuals acting independently of al-Qaeda's leadership.[93]

The Columbus mall plot seems consistent with the characteristics of many of these plots. The individuals involved often are an odd mix of low-ranking al-Qaeda members such as Faris and Paul and jihad enthusiasts like Abdi. Most other plots were conceived by individuals who never had any contact with al-Qaeda or other established organizations. All of them, however, have been characterized by the absolute operational independence of the planners. Rather than a voluntary decision, such autonomy seems to have been caused by the difficulty that U.S.-based al-Qaeda sympathizers appear to have experienced after 9/11 in establishing contacts with foreign-based al-Qaeda leaders. It seems evident that the immediate result of the shift from leader-led to homegrown terrorist cells has been a remarkable decrease in the sophistication of the operations planned in the United States.

The 9/11 Commission outlined six characteristics that a terrorist organization should possess in order to carry out an operation of that complexity.[94] A leadership "able to evaluate, approve, and supervise the planning and direction of the operation" seems to be personified by KSM, whose meticulous planning skills prompted a senior Pakistani intelligence official to comment he is "not an ordinary man."[95] KSM's obsession with constant yet secure contact with his operatives assured the second characteristic, "communications sufficient to enable planning and direction of the operatives," and KSM's trusted lieutenants and the al-Qaeda training camps provided the third, "a personnel system that could recruit candidates, vet them, indoctrinate them, and give them necessary training."[96] Al-Qaeda's extensive intelligence-gathering apparatus and ability to move people and money, the remaining three characteristics, were also demonstrated in all the operations masterminded by KSM.

Although none of the six operations planned by KSM succeeded, most were characterized by a level of sophistication that few operations against the American homeland planned after 9/11 possessed. Not only were most of the "post-KSM" plots less ambitious, often involving relatively unsophisticated actions such as a mall shooting or placing small amounts of explosives in public places, but the modus operandi of most American homegrown jihadists involved in them was, for the most part, quite amateurish. The fact that U.S. authorities were able to thwart all the attacks planned by KSM and his network after 9/11 makes it unsurprising that these less-professional jihadists also failed.

FUTURE TRENDS

The KSM plots offer valuable lessons on the post-9/11 evolution of al-Qaeda and American counterterrorism efforts. Moreover, they seem to provide possible scenarios for future attacks against the U.S. homeland. Two alternative forms of attack are represented by variations of the homegrown model. One possibility is that a homegrown network, while retaining its operational independence, would acquire a certain level of professionalism or manage to operate undetected and carry out an attack. This dynamic seems to be behind the April 2013 Boston Marathon bombings. Even though the older of the Tsarnaev brothers, Tamerlan, did attempt to link up with jihadists in the Caucasus, it appears that he and his brother, Dzhokhar, acquired bomb-making skills and carried out the attacks in complete independence. Over the last few years U.S. authorities have arrested dozens of self-radicalized and operationally independent individuals throughout the country. While many of these individuals were little more than naïve "jihadist wannabes" arrested through the use of aggressive "agent provocateur" investigative techniques, there is no question that the U.S. is home to a small yet disturbing number of individuals willing to commit acts of violence in furtherance of jihadist ideology.

Equally plausible is the scenario in which a homegrown network manages to establish, via the Internet or other ways, some sort of contact with al-Qaeda or other structured groups in its orbit. Several investigations conducted by U.S. authorities since 2009 seem to show that this is becoming more likely. The cases of Bryant Neal Vinas, a twenty-six-year-old Long Island native who was captured in Pakistan after training with al-Qaeda; Najibullah Zazi, a Denver resident and al-Qaeda camp graduate who was convicted in 2010 for planning a bombing campaign in the New York City area; the failed 2010 Times Square bomber, Faisal Shahzad; and David Coleman Headley, a Chicago resident who for years scouted terrorist targets throughout the world for Lashkar-e-Taiba are just some of the latest examples of American-based militants linking up with the upper echelons of al-Qaeda and affiliated groups in Pakistan.[97]

Although only Zazi and Shahzad were apparently planning attacks against the U.S. homeland, this trend has potentially severe repercussions for U.S. domestic security. In all these cases, in fact, authorities have noticed with apprehension that American militants returning from Pakistan were significantly better trained and organized than the homegrown jihadists who had been operating in the country in the previous years. Moreover, if authorities traditionally estimated that al-Qaeda's leadership intended to strike inside the United States only with a mass-casualty attack that would at least rival the actions of 9/11, lately this assessment has been revised.[98] Recent cases have shown that not only independent clusters but also American networks operating in cooperation with Afghanistan/Pakistan-based groups are focusing on less grandiose plans, considering that even a less ambitious attack would be a success.

Finally, the threat of pure, externally led attacks is hardly over. Unquestionably, the capture of KSM and most known members of his American network, together with the relentless hunt for al-Qaeda leaders in the tribal areas of Pakistan, has kept America safe from the most direct threat of attacks planned by al-Qaeda's central leadership. Nevertheless, al-Qaeda and some of its affiliates worldwide have demonstrated a remarkable ability to generate new and competent operational leadership capable of centrally planning relatively sophisticated attacks in various parts of the world. It would be naïve to think that the organization would not aim, despite the difficulties in doing so, at carrying out similar operations against its most precious target, the U.S. homeland.

Evidence supporting this hypothesis came on December 25, 2009, when Umar Farouk Abdulmutallab attempted to blow up Northwest flight 253 from Amsterdam to Detroit by detonating in midair explosives he had hidden in his underpants.[99] According to information released by U.S. and Yemeni authorities, Abdulmutallab had been trained by and supplied the explosives from operatives of al-Qaeda in the Arabian Peninsula. A few days after the failed attack, AQAP claimed responsibility for the action in a public message.[100] The failed Christmas bombing appears to be, therefore, an externally planned plot, even though, for the first time since 9/11, the organization behind it is not the Afghanistan/

Pakistan-based al-Qaeda central but, rather, one of its franchises around the world. In any case, the plot underscores the heterogeneity and constant evolution of the threats facing the U.S. homeland and provides a stark reminder of the challenges facing U.S. authorities.

NOTES

1. Verbatim Transcript, Combatant Status Review Tribunal hearing for ISN 10024, March 10, 2007.

2. Yosri Fouda and Nick Fielding, *Masterminds of Terror: The Truth Behind the Most Devastating Attack the World Has Ever Seen* (New York: Arcade, 2003).

3. Verbatim Transcript for ISN 10024.

4. See, for example, "Khalid Sheikh Mohammed's Own Words Provide Glimpse Into the Mind of a Terrorist," Associated Press, March 15, 2007.

5. International Committee of the Red Cross, *Report on the Treatment of Fourteen "High Value Detainees" in CIA Custody* (Washington, D.C.: February 2007), 37.

6. The most authoritative voice endorsing this view is that of the Central Intelligence Agency. A 2004 CIA memorandum, titled "Khalid Shaykh Muhammad: Preeminent Source on Al-Qa'ida," states that since his March 2003 capture, KSM "has become one of the US Government's key sources on Al-Qa'ida" and "has provided [redacted] reports that have shed light on Al-Qa'ida's strategic doctrine, plots and probable targets, key operatives, and the likely methods for attacks in the US homeland, leading to the disruption of several plots against the United States." The memorandum judged the information to be mostly "accurate" and "consistent." Interviewed by the *Washington Post* in 2009, a CIA official familiar with the interrogations described how KSM "seemed to relish the opportunity, sometimes for hours on end, to discuss the inner workings of al-Qaeda and the group's plans, ideology and operatives. He'd even use a chalkboard at times" (Peter Finn, Joby Warrick, and Julie Tate, "How a Detainee Became an Asset," *Washington Post*, August 29, 2009).

7. Extensive profiles of KSM, from which most of the information used here is taken, have been made in the *Final Report of the National Commission on Terrorist Attacks Upon the United States* (New York: Norton, 2004), 145–50; *Khalid Shaykh Muhammad: Preeminent Source on Al-Qa'ida*, declassified Central Intelligence Agency memorandum, July 13, 2004, http://www.washingtonpost.com/wp-srv/nation/documents/Khalid _Shayhk_Muhammad.pdf; Fouda and Fielding, *Masterminds of Terror*, 88–102; Patrick J. McDonnell, Terry McDermott, and Josh Meyer, "The Plots and Designs of Al Qaeda's Engineer," *Los Angeles Times*, December 22, 2002.

8. Kuwait University was, at the time, a particularly fertile ground for Islamist activities. In the late 1970s and early 1980s, Khaled Meshal and other Palestinian students founded the Islamic Bloc, a Muslim Brotherhood–inspired group that would

be central to the creation of Hamas in 1987. See Azzam Tamimi, *Hamas: A History from Within* (Northampton, Mass.: Olive Branch Press, 2007); and Matthew Levitt, *Hamas: Politics, Charity, and Terrorism in the Service of Jihad* (New Haven, Conn.: Yale University Press, 2006).

9. McDonnell, McDermott, and Meyer, "The Plots and Designs of Al Qaeda's Engineer."

10. *Khalid Shaykh Muhammad*, CIA memorandum, 12.

11. Ibid., 20.

12. Fouda and Fielding, *Masterminds of Terror*, 90; Robert Walker, Affidavit in Support of Complaint Against Benevolence International Foundation, Inc., United States of American v. Benevolence International Foundation Inc., Case No. 02CR0410 (E.D. Ill.), April 29, 2002.

13. James Risen and Benjamin Weiser, "U.S. Officials Say Aid for Terrorists Came Through Two Persian Gulf Nations," *New York Times*, July 8, 1999.

14. *Final Report of the National Commission on Terrorist Attacks Upon the United States*, 148.

15. Ibid., 149.

16. Ibid.; Substitution for the Testimony of Khalid Sheikh Mohammed, exhibit in U.S. v. Zacarias Moussaoui, Cr. No. 01-455-A (E.D. Va.).

17. *Final Report of the National Commission on Terrorist Attacks Upon the United States*, 154. *Khalid Shaykh Muhammad*, CIA memorandum, 2.

18. Substitution for the Testimony of Khalid Sheikh Mohammed, exhibit in U.S. v. Zacarias Moussaoui.

19. *Final Report of the National Commission on Terrorist Attacks Upon the United States*, 159.

20. Substitution for the Testimony of Khalid Sheikh Mohammed, exhibit in U.S. v. Zacarias Moussaoui; *Khalid Shaykh Muhammad*, CIA memorandum, 20.

21. Substitution for the Testimony of Khalid Sheikh Mohammed, exhibit in U.S. v. Zacarias Moussaoui.

22. Ibid.

23. Ibid.

24. U.S. v. Zacarias Moussaoui, Cr. No. 01-455-A, Indictment, December 11, 2001 (E.D. Va.).

25. *Final Report of the National Commission on Terrorist Attacks Upon the United States*, 527.

26. FBI's Reward for Justice website, http://www.fbi.gov/wanted/terrorinfo/abderraouf-jdey (accessed July 4, 2013).

27. *Final Report of the National Commission on Terrorist Attacks Upon the United States*, 150; Verbatim Transcript of Combatant Status Review Tribunal hearing for ISN 10024; "Dhiren Barot, an Immigrant Who Converted to Islam Under the Spell of Muslim Radicals," *International Herald Tribune*, November 7, 2006.

28. U.S. v. Dhiren Barot, 05-CRIM-311, Indictment, April 12, 2005 (S.D. N.Y.); also see documents released by the Metropolitan Police and available at the NEFA Foundation's website: http://www.nefafoundation.org/miscellaneous/East_Coast_Buildings _Plot.pdf; "Prosecution Case Against Al Qaeda Briton," *BBC*, November 6, 2006.

29. Metropolitan Police Service, press release, November 7, 2006; "Prosecution Case Against Al Qaeda Briton." Barot and his accomplices were arrested in Great Britain in 2004 along with five other British men and charged with planning terrorist operations in both the United Kingdom and the United States. Barot later pleaded guilty and was sentenced to life in prison.

30. Phone interview with U.S. official, February 2009; Director of National Intelligence report on Ali Abdal Aziz Ali, undated.

31. Director of National Intelligence report on Ali Abdal Aziz Ali.

32. Phone interview with U.S. official, February 2009.

33. U.S. v. Richard Colvin Reid, 02-CR-10013-WGY, Government's Sentencing Memorandum, January 17, 2003 (Mass.); Olga Craig, "From Tearaway to Terrorist: The Story of Richard Reid," *Telegraph*, December 30, 2001.

34. U.S. v. Richard Colvin Reid.

35. U.S. v. Richard Colvin Reid.

36. *Final Report of the National Commission on Terrorist Attacks Upon the United States*, 153.

37. Philippe Naughton, "Profile: Friendly, Popular, Badat Hid Dark Secret," *Times* (London), February 28, 2005.

38. U.S. v. Saajid Mohammed Badat, 04-10223-GAO, Superseding Indictment, September 2004 (Mass.).

39. Jenny Booth, "Gloucester Shoebomber Jailed for Thirteen Years," *Times* (London), April 22, 2005.

40. For a complete analysis of the timeline and the plot, see *KSM's Transatlantic Shoe Bomb Plot*, report by the NEFA Foundation, available at http://nefafoundation .org/miscellaneous/shoebombplot.pdf.

41. Substitution for the Testimony of Khalid Sheikh Mohammed, exhibit in U.S. v. Zacarias Moussaoui.

42. Ibid.

43. Ibid.

44. Substitution for the Testimony of Khalid Sheikh Mohammed, exhibit in U.S. v. Zacarias Moussaoui; an extensive profile of Hambali is in *Final Report of the National Commission on Terrorist Attacks Upon the United States*, 150–52; *Khalid Shaykh Muhammad*, CIA memorandum, 5.

45. Memorandum written by Principal Deputy Attorney General Steven G. Bradbury to CIA Senior Deputy General Counsel John A. Rizzo, May 30, 2005.

46. Director of National Intelligence report on Mohammed Nazir Bin Lep, undated.

47. Director of National Intelligence report on Mod Farik Bin Amin, undated.

48. Director of National Intelligence report on Mod Farik Bin Amin.

49. Frances Fragos Townsend, Press Briefing on the West Coast Terrorist Plot, February 9, 2006; Simon Elegant, "The Terrorist Talks," *Time*, October 5, 2003.

50. Townsend, Press Briefing; "President Discusses Progress in War on Terror to National Guard," February 9, 2006, www.whitehouse.gov/news/releases/2006/02/20060209-2.html.

51. Substitution for the Testimony of Khalid Sheikh Mohammed, exhibit in U.S. v. Zacarias Moussaoui.

52. "President Discusses Progress in War on Terror to National Guard."

53. Phone interview with U.S. official, February 2009.

54. "Malaysian Said Involved in '02 Terror Plot," *USA Today*, February 10, 2006; also see *KSM's West Coast Airline Plot*, report by the NEFA Foundation, http://www.nefafoundation.org/miscellaneous/WestCoastAirline_Plot.pdf.

55. Townsend, Press Briefing; Elegant, "The Terrorist Talks."

56. Bradbury to Rizzo, memorandum; *Khalid Shaykh Muhammad*, CIA memorandum, 5.

57. Summary of Jose Padilla's Activities with Al Qaeda, Department of Defense Memorandum, May 28, 2004; Declaration of Jeffrey N. Rapp, Director of the Joint Intelligence Task Force for Combating Terrorism, filed in the Padilla case, August 30, 2004; U.S. v. Adham Amin Hassoun et al., , 04-60001-CR-Cooke, Indictment, November 17, 2005 (S.D. Fla.).

58. Department of Defense Summary of Padilla's Activities, May 28, 2004.

59. Department of Justice, "Jose Padilla and Co-Defendants Sentenced on Terrorism Charges," press release, January 22, 2008.

60. U.S. authorities openly acknowledge the existence of such a network. Interviewed by *Newsweek*, senior U.S. officials stated that "it was organized, [and] it was being directed by the leaders of Al Qaeda." See Daniel Klaidman, Mark Hosenball, Michael Isikoff, and Evan Thomas, "Al Qaeda in America: The Enemy Within," *Newsweek*, June 23, 2003.

61. Deposition of FBI Special Agent Nicolas A. Zambeck in U.S. v. Ali Saleh Kahlah al-Marri, December 2002 (S.D. N.Y.); Klaidman, Hosenball, Isikoff and Thomas, "Al Qaeda in America."

62. Deposition of Nicolas A. Zambeck in U.S. v. Ali Saleh Kahlah al-Marri.

63. Al-Marri v. Pucciarelli, 534 F.3d 213, 217 (4th Cir. 2008).

64. U.S. Attorney's Office, Central District of Illinois, "Ali Al-Marri Pleads Guilty to Conspiracy to Provide Material Support to Al-Qaeda," press release, April 30, 2009, http://www.usdoj.gov/opa/pr/2009/April/09-nsd-415.html.

65. Klaidman, Hosenball, Isikoff, and Thomas, "Al Qaeda in America."

66. Summary of Evidence for Combatant Status Review Tribunal: Majid Khan, Department of Defense, Office for the Administrative Review of the Detention of Enemy Combatants, March 28, 2007; Summary of Evidence for Combatant Status Review Tribunal: Khalid Shaykh Muhammad, Department of Defense, Office for the

Administrative Review of the Detention of Enemy Combatants, date unknown; Eric Rich and Dan Eggen, "From Baltimore Suburbs to a Secret CIA Prison," *Washington Post*, September 10, 2006; Katherine Shrader, "An Immigrant's Journey from Maryland to Gitmo," Associated Press, March 22, 2007: 5.

67. Summary of Evidence for Combatant Status Review Tribunal: Majid Khan.

68. Director of National Intelligence report on Ali Abdal Aziz Ali; Summary of Evidence for Combatant Status Review Tribunal: Majid Khan; *Khalid Shaykh Muhammad*, CIA memorandum, 9.

69. Director of National Intelligence report on Majid Khan, undated.

70. Director of National Intelligence report on Ali Abdal Aziz Ali.

71. Director of National Intelligence report on Majid Khan; interview with U.S. official, Washington, D.C., May 2008.

72. Director of National Intelligence report on Majid Khan.

73. Verbatim Transcript of Combatant Status Review Tribunal hearing for ISN 10020, April 15, 2007.

74. Summary of Evidence for Combatant Status Review Tribunal: Majid Khan; Director of National Intelligence report on Majid Khan; Verbatim Transcript of Combatant Status Review Tribunal hearing for ISN 10020; Rich and Eggen, "From Baltimore Suburbs to a Secret CIA Prison."

75. Department of Justice press release regarding Uzair Paracha's sentencing, July 20, 2006; Saifullah Paracha v. George W. Bush, 04-CV-2022.

76. Director of National Intelligence report on Majid Khan; U.S. v. Aafia Siddiqui, 1:08-cr-00826-RMB, September 2, 2008 (S.D. N.Y.).

77. Director of National Intelligence report on Majid Khan.

78. Summary of Evidence for Combatant Status Review Tribunal: Majid Khan.

79. Ibid.

80. Department of Justice, "Iyman Faris Sentenced for Providing Material Support to Al Qaeda," press release, October 28, 2003, http://www.usdoj.gov/opa/pr/2003/October/03_crm_589.htm.

81. Department of Justice, "Ohio Truck Driver Pleads Guilty to Providing Material Support to Al Qaeda," press release, June 19, 2003; Summary of Evidence for Combatant Status Review Tribunal: Majid Khan, Department of Defense; Director of National Intelligence report on Majid Khan.

82. U.S. v. Iyman Faris, 03-189-A, Statement of Facts, June 19, 2003 (E.D. Va.); Klaidman, Hosenball, Isikoff, and Thomas, "Al Qaeda in America."

83. U.S. v. Iyman Faris; Director of National Intelligence report on Majid Khan.

84. U.S. v. Iyman Faris; Department of Justice, "Iyman Faris Sentenced."

85. U.S. v. Christopher Paul, 2:07-cr-00087-GLF, Statement of Facts, undated (S.D. Ohio).

86. U.S. v. Christopher Paul; Kevin Mayhood, Jodi Andes, and John Futty, "Muslim Convert Plotted with Foreigners in Town, Unsealed Indictment Says," *Columbus Dispatch*, April 13, 2007.

87. U.S. v. Nuradin M. Abdi, Indictment, June 14, 2004 (S.D. Ohio); U.S. v. Abdi, No. 2:04 CR88 (S.D. Ohio), Opposition of the United States to Defendant's Motions In Limine (#104) to Exclude Computer Images, Dissertation Text "Pillar of the Preparing for Jihad."

88. Department of Justice, "Iyman Faris Sentenced."

89. U.S. Immigration and Customs Enforcement, "Ohio Man Sentenced to Ten Years Imprisonment for Conspiracy to Provide Material Support to Terrorists," November 27, 2007.

90. U.S. v. Christopher Paul, 2:07-cr-00087-GLF, Indictment, April 11, 2007 (S.D. Ohio).

91. U.S. Attorney, Southern District of Ohio, "Ohio Man Sentenced to Twenty Years for Terrorism Conspiracy to Bomb Targets in Europe and the United States," February 26, 2009, http://cincinnati.fbi.gov/doj/pressrel/2009/ci022609.htm.

92. *Khalid Shaykh Muhammad*, CIA memorandum, 15.

93. For an overview of homegrown networks in the United States, see Lorenzo Vidino, "Homegrown Jihadist Terrorism in the United States: A New and Occasional Phenomenon?" *Studies in Conflict and Terrorism* 32, no. 1 (2009): 1–17.

94. *Final Report of the National Commission on Terrorist Attacks Upon the United States*, 172–73.

95. McDonnell, McDermott, and Meyer, "The Plots and Designs of Al Qaeda's Engineer."

96. *Final Report of the National Commission on Terrorist Attacks Upon the United States*, 172–73.

97. For Vinas, see US v. Bryant Neal Vinas, Superseding Indictment, 08-823 (NGG) (S-1), January 28, 2009 (E.D. N.Y.); for Zazi, see U.S. Department of Justice press release, February 22, 2010, http://www.fbi.gov/newyork/press-releases/2010/nyfo022210 .htm; Kevin Johnson, "Alleged Terror Threat Seen as 'Most Serious' Since 9/11 Attacks," *USA Today*, September 25, 2009; for Shahzad, see U.S. v. Faisal Shahzad, Indictment (S.D. N.Y.), available at http://www.cbsnews.com/htdocs/pdf/Shahzad_Faisal_Indictment .pdf; for Headley, see U.S. Department of Justice, press release, December 7, 2009, http://www.justice.gov/opa/pr/2009/December/09-nsd-1304.html

98. David Johnston and Eric Schmitt, "Smaller-Scale Terrorism Plots Pose New and Worrisome Threats, Officials Say," *New York Times*, December 31, 2009.

99. U.S. v. Umar Farouk Abdulmutallab, Case 2:10-cr-20005, Indictment, January 6, 2010 (E.D. Mich.).

100. See, for example, President Barack Obama, Weekly Address, January 2, 2010, http://www.whitehouse.gov/the-press-office/weekly-address-president-obama-outlines-steps-taken-protect-safety-and-security-ame; White House, "Release of the Security Review Conducted After the Failed Christmas Terrorist Attack," January 7, 2010, http://www.whitehouse.gov/blog/2010/01/07/release-security-review-conducted -after-failed-christmas-terrorist-attack-0; Eileen Sullivan and Lolita C. Baldor, "Al-Qaida Group Says It Was Behind Jetliner Attack," Associated Press, December 28, 2009.

The 2004 Madrid Train Bombings

FERNANDO REINARES

Since the attacks of September 11, 2001, on New York and Washington, D.C., there has been an ongoing controversy about whether the real threat of global terrorism is posed by al-Qaeda, its burgeoning decentralized territorial extensions and affiliated organizations, or by independent individual and collective actors inspired by, but unconnected to, such entities. The March 11, 2004, Madrid train bombings are often held up as the archetype of an independent local cell at work, the perpetrators depicted as self-recruited leaderless terrorists only aroused by the propaganda of al-Qaeda.[1] However, evidence connecting some of the most notorious members of the Madrid bombing network with al-Qaeda's senior leadership, along with features of the terrorist network itself, the characteristics of its components, and distinctive elements of the likely strategy behind the blasts, imply these assumptions are misleading.

The extensive criminal proceedings on the Madrid attacks, as well as other relevant primary and secondary sources, including not only complementary judicial documents but also intelligence collected since the main sentence on these train bombings was pronounced by Spain's National Court in 2007, refute the leaderless hypothesis. They also reveal that al-Qaeda's senior leadership approved, facilitated, and even supervised the operation through a key intermediary connecting its central command in Pakistan with the terrorist network in Spain. In addition, the accumulated evidence helps us better understand what the Madrid train bombings told us about al-Qaeda and global terrorism in transition, as well as the changing nature of the threat to open societies in general and to Western European countries in particular.[2]

911 DAYS BETWEEN

On March 11, 2004, two and a half years after 9/11, exactly 911 days between these two dates, another spectacular act of mass-casualty terrorism took place, but on the other side of the Atlantic and against a much softer target: commuter trains on the railway line connecting the historical town of Alcalá de Henares with Madrid's downtown Atocha station. On that day, thirteen bombs, each containing no less than 10 kilograms of dynamite and about 650 grams of ironmongery, were placed inside plastic bags and backpacks in twelve different carriages on four trains filled to rush-hour capacity.[3] Some of the ten to thirteen terrorists who placed the bombs arrived in two vehicles. One vehicle, a van, was found by the national police on the morning of the attacks and the other, a car, was discovered three months later, both parked in Alcalá de Henares, where terrorists boarded the trains. In the former, detonators and traces of explosives were found next to audiocassettes with recordings of Quranic recitations, and in the latter, there was a suitcase with more tapes exalting a bellicose notion of jihad.[4]

Ten of the bombs exploded almost simultaneously between 7:37 and 7:41 a.m. They were detonated by means of the synchronized alarms of cellular phones. Incidentally, the same brand and model of cellular phone had been used in a similar way in the November 2002 bombings in Bali.[5] Three other devices placed in the rail carriages failed to explode. Disposal experts successfully defused one of these bombs in the early hours of March 12, providing crucial evidence for the police investigation of the attacks.

The blasts in the commuter trains killed 191 people and injured 1,841.[6] Though the attacks caused immediate material damages calculated at some 17.62 million euros, the minimum direct economic cost has been estimated at more than 211.58 million euros.[7] The Madrid train bombings were the most devastating act of insurgent terrorism in contemporary Spain. Moreover, for Western Europe they were second in lethality only to the midair bombing of Pan Am flight 103 over the Scottish town of Lockerbie in December 1988, which killed the 259 passengers and crew on board and 11 people on the ground.

The Madrid bombings were not the only attacks intended by their perpetrators. On April 2, making use of similar explosive substances and detonators, individuals belonging to the same terrorist network prepared to derail a Seville-bound high-speed train in transit through the province of Toledo. The subsequent police investigation found that they had accumulated information on new targets in and around Madrid, such as a Jewish recreational facility, a Jewish school, British educational centers and national public institutions.[8] The terrorists had stored weapons and explosives in abundance. They had formally rented their rural operational base in the municipality of Chinchón, on January 28, 2004, though it had been in use by cell members since no later than October 2002. On March 4, they had rented a safe house close to the emblematic city of Granada, in southern Spain, and on March 8, a hideout in the commuter city of Leganés, near Madrid, where several terrorists thought to remain for about a month after the commuter trains attacks.[9] They also retained a financial reserve of almost 1.5 million euros. By comparison, the overall cost of the March 11 train attacks was estimated by the authorities at no less than 105,000 euros, although not every possible expense is included in this calculation.[10] The Madrid bombing network was largely financed through trafficking in illegal drugs, which were also traded for industrial explosives stolen from a mine in Asturias in northern Spain by a criminal band of native Spaniards.[11]

Further terrorist plans were disrupted on April 3, when experts from the national police intelligence unit devoted to international terrorism (at the time rather small) discovered the operational cell's hideout in Leganés. Of the eight terrorists present, one managed to escape on foot, and the remaining seven, all cornered in the same flat, fired shots and shouted Islamic slogans before blowing themselves up after 9:00 p.m. A special-operations agent was killed and several others were injured by the explosion, and an entire apartment complex, previously evacuated by the security forces, was destroyed. This may well be considered the first suicide explosion in Western Europe related to the current web of global terrorism.[12] Even if this was a reactive incident prompted by the police operation, among those who perpetrated the commuter-train blasts were individuals willing to become suicide bombers at any time. This is suggested by the farewell letters left behind, at least one of which was written before the Madrid attacks. "This is my testament," wrote a member of the local cell to his close relatives in this second letter. He insists on jihad as "an obligation for the faithful," adding, "I cannot live in this world, humiliated and weakened before the eyes of infidels and tyrants." He concludes, "I have chosen death as the path for life."[13]

The bombings of March 11, 2004, had other serious domestic consequences, both political and social. They occurred three days before the Spanish general elections on Sunday, March 14. Prime Minister José María Aznar's incumbent liberal-conservative Partido Popular (Popular Party, or PP) had sound reasons to believe it would retain its majority in Spain's bicameral parliament and control over the central government. Reliable surveys conducted in the weeks before polling day, however, registered a gradually narrowing gap and indicated that the PP's support was statistically close to that of the moderate left-wing Partido Socialista Obrero Español (Spanish Socialist Workers' Party, or PSOE). Nevertheless, there is little doubt that the mobilization of a significant segment of the electorate, spurred by the terrorist massacre and its aftermath, secured the Socialist victory.[14] The government's insistence that the Basque terrorist group ETA was behind the attacks, when emerging evidence clearly pointed toward jihadist terrorism, also proved counterproductive to the ruling party. After the election, Spanish society became deeply divided over whom to blame for the train blasts.

Yet on the day of the bombings, at around 7:30 p.m. local time in London and 8:30 p.m. in Madrid, *Al-Quds al-Arabi*, a well-known Arabic-language daily published in the British capital, received an e-mail claiming responsibility for the attacks. Earlier that evening, the editor was told over the phone by someone in a country in the Gulf to expect this special e-mail. Like other messages sent by Osama bin Laden's organization to the newspaper since the late 1990s, it was seen as a genuine al-Qaeda communiqué and immediately made public.[15] It was signed by the Abu Hafs al-Masri Brigade (al-Qaeda). This same designation, referring to Mohamed Atef, a former head of al-Qaeda's military committee who was killed in 2001 in Afghanistan, had been used before to claim responsibility for attacks such as those of November 2003 in Nasiriya and Istanbul.

Moreover, two days later, on March 13, at around 7:30 p.m., an individual, speaking in Spanish but with a noticeable Arab accent called the regional broadcasting corporation Telemadrid to let its executives know of a videocassette left inside a waste container near the so-called M-30 mosque, Madrid's largest Islamic place of worship and community center. The improvised tape was recorded minutes after 5:00 p.m. that same day by train bombers. In the tape, a hooded terrorist, dressed in white and holding a Sterling assault rifle, read a statement that insisted, probably because of the ongoing dispute over who was to blame for the attacks hours before election day, on "our responsibility for what occurred in Madrid, just two-and-a-half years after the attacks in New York and Washington" and featured as an announcement signed by "Abu Dujan al-Afghani," literally presented as "military spokesman for al-Qaeda in Europe."[16]

Outside Spain, the issue is not whether the Madrid bombings were an expression of jihadist terrorism or the indiscriminate manifestation of Basque ethno-nationalist terrorism. There is an overwhelming consensus attributing the commuter-train blasts to individuals associated with a radical Islamist orientation. The issue is rather the characteristics of those individuals and whether they are part of an amorphous and leaderless phenomenon or part of a polymorphous and still often centrally led web of global terrorism. Were the Madrid bombings a case of homegrown, al-Qaeda-inspired terrorism, or did those who prepared and executed the blasts have international connections with al-Qaeda or any of its affiliated organizations? Analysis of the Madrid bombing network and its integrants, evidence now available about its ties with al-Qaeda's command structures in North Waziristan, and an assessment of the strategy behind the commuter-train blasts support the second of these propositions.

ANALYZING THE NETWORK

The terrorist network behind the 2004 Madrid train bombings came together between March 2002 and August 2003.[17] The desire and decision to perpetrate a terrorist attack in Spain led three relatively small, separate, and partially overlapping clusters of people to coalesce.[18] The first of these had evolved from the remnants of an important al-Qaeda cell established in Spain in or shortly before 1994.[19] This cell had important connections in several countries from the Middle East to Southeast Asia. In the aftermath of 9/11, international security and intelligence investigations revealed that its leader, the Syrian-born Imad Eddin Barakat Yarkas, better known as Abu Dahdah, had a direct link to the Hamburg cell led by Muhammad Atta that carried out the attacks on the World Trade Center and Pentagon in 2001.

Atta traveled to Spain twice in 2001. During his second trip, between July 8 and 19, 2001, Atta met with the al-Qaeda operative Ramzi Binalshibh—the so-called twentieth hijacker—and one or two unidentified individuals involved in the 9/11 attacks. The meeting took place in two municipalities in the Catalonian coastal province of Tarragona. Based on detailed analysis of the physical movements and phone activity in the area among Abu Dahdah cell members, Spanish security services are convinced that the cell, including Amer Azizi (also known as Othman al-Andalusi, Jaffar al-Maghrebi, and, occasionally, Othman al-Faruq and Ilyas), facilitated the meeting between Binalshibh and Atta—although it cannot be established with certainty whether any of the Abu Dahdah cell members actually attended the gathering.[20] However, Abu Dahdah had previous knowledge of Atta's plans to carry out a strike on U.S. soil and was informed about ongoing preparations.[21] Evidence of the connection between the Hamburg and Abu Dahdah cells led Spanish security services to dismantle the latter. Operation Dátil was launched in November 2001, and most of the Abu Dahdah cell's core members—though not all cell members—were detained.

A second cluster within the Madrid bombing network was linked to the structure established by the Moroccan Islamist Combatant Group (MICG) across Western Europe, particularly in France and Belgium.[22] The third cluster, and the last to be incorporated, brought to the terrorist network a bunch of former delinquents active throughout Spain who specialized in the trafficking of illegal drugs and stolen vehicles.[23]

Although the number of people directly or indirectly connected to the network may be larger, there are twenty-seven individuals based in Western Europe for whom there is both empirical evidence and legal grounds to implicate them in the preparation or execution of the March 11 attacks.[24] These include the sixteen tried and convicted (twelve in

Spain, three in Morocco, and one in Italy) in relation to the blasts on the commuter trains; the seven who committed suicide on April 3 in Leganés; and four known fugitives, all of whom died in Iraq during 2005 and 2006—three of them when perpetrating suicide attacks and the remaining one in the course of an armed confrontation.

Three of these twenty-seven individuals were affiliated with the earlier al-Qaeda cell in Spain but not arrested because of a lack of evidence according to the judicial knowledge and legal standards in effect at the time of the cell's dismantlement in November 2001. These three, actually latecomers to the Abu Dahdah cell, were Sarhane ben Abdelmajid Fakhet (better known as "the Tunisian" because of his country of origin) and Jamal Zougam, both of whom played key roles in the attacks, plus Said Berraj, a prominent member of the network.[25] The owner of the property in Chinchón that the terrorists used as their base of operations was Mohamed Needel Acaid, a Syrian detained in November 2001 for his involvement in the same al-Qaeda cell and who was convicted in 2005.[26]

Allekema Lamari, one of the Leganés suicides, had indirect ties with the same cell. Initially arrested in Valencia in 1997 for membership in the Armed Islamic Group of Algeria (GIA) and later sentenced to fourteen years in prison for terrorism offenses,[27] he was released from prison in early 2002 because of a judicial error and went into hiding. Two leaders of his GIA cell in Spain, Nouredine Abdoumalou and Abdelkrim Bensmail, were close to Abu Dahdah in those years. These former bonds facilitated Lamari's insertion into the Madrid bombing network. A classified report from Spain's Centro Nacional de Inteligencia (CNI, the National Intelligence Center) dated November 6, 2003, referred to his suspicious behavior and mentioned reliable informants who believed he was likely to organize and execute an imminent act of terrorism in the country.[28] Another classified CNI note, dated March 15, 2004, commented that after his release from the penitentiary, he had "sworn that Spain would pay very dearly for his arrest" and that "he even declared that he would commit acts involving arson or derailment." The note also stressed that he knew "Valencia, Tudela, Madrid and Alcalá de Henares" well.[29]

Hassan el-Haski and Youssef Belhadj, two prominent members of the MICG based in Belgium, were also among the no less than twenty-seven individuals involved in the Madrid bombing network. The former was close to Abdelkader Hakimi, head of the MICG in Europe, and was acquaintanted with Jamal Zougam, making him knowledgeable about the terrorist plans in Spain.[30] Youssef Belhadj was, according to his nephew, also a member of al-Qaeda.[31] He frequently traveled to Madrid to meet his associates who had joined the local jihadist cell.[32] On March 3, 2004, at 8:35 p.m., just eight days before the attacks, Belhadj boarded flight number TV861 back to Brussels from Madrid, where he had been the previous month.[33]

Indeed, when the Belgian police arrested Belhadj, initially for his belonging to an MICG cell in Belgium that had been dismantled shortly after the Madrid train bombings, they found two cellular phones in his Brussels bedroom. The one he regularly used operated with a prepaid card acquired on October 19, 2003, the day after Osama bin Laden threatened Spain in a message aired on the Qatari-based television channel al-Jazeera. Belhadj had obtained the phone using a false identity, claiming that his birthday was March 11, 1921.[34] The second phone, commonly used by his brother Mimoun, operated with another prepaid card purchased shortly after the first and again was obtained using a false identity, with May 16 as the fictitious date of birth. It may not have been coincidence that May 16 and March 11 were the dates of the 2003 Casablanca attacks—when terrorists targeted a Spanish restaurant and social club—and the planned date for the Madrid bombings, respectively.[35] Similarly, 1921 may have been chosen as a reference to sura 21 of the Quran, which alludes to the time when unbelievers "will not be able to ward off the fire from their faces, nor yet from their backs, and no help can reach them!"

Also embedded in the Madrid bombing network was Rabei Osman el-Sayed Ahmed, known as "Mohamed the Egyptian," a former member of the Egyptian Islamic Jihad Group, which had merged with al-Qaeda in 2001. He spent at least five years in the Egyptian army and served in a brigade based in Port Said that specialized in explosives. Confidential sources indicated to Spanish authorities that Rabei Osman spent time in the maximum-security penitentiary of Abu Zaa Abal, where those suspected or convicted of terrorist activities were usually imprisoned. He was an active al-Qaeda recruiter of likely suicide terrorists in Western Europe. Italian security forces secretly taped and filmed him doing just that in the flat where he lived in Milan before his close links with some of the commuter-train bombers detained in Spain led to his arrest in June 2004. Rabei Osman lived in Spain from 2002 to February 2003, a period during which, together with Fakhet, he actively radicalized youngsters in and around mosques.[36] One of the Italian films clearly shows Rabei Osman claiming involvement in the Madrid bombings. A recording from May 26, 2004, captures him, while indoctrinating a young acolyte in his Milan apartment, saying: "Listen, Yahya, be careful and do not speak. The whole Madrid operation was an idea of mine. They were among my most loved friends, fallen as martyrs, may Allah have mercy on them. . . . This operation required many lessons and lots of patience over two and a half years."[37] Indeed, Rabei Osman also knew in advance about the March 11 date. On February 4, 2004, following his return to Italy after his last trip to Spain before the attacks, he opened and activated an e-mail account in a Yahoo server, using fictitious personal data, including March 11, 1970, as his date of birth.[38]

In addition to the individuals already mentioned and the associates whom they mobilized in turn, the Madrid bombing network included several former delinquents who had been part of a gang regularly engaged in trafficking drugs and stolen cars before joining the jihadist network in summer 2003. Their boss, Jamal Ahmidan, also known as "the Chinese," was not a newcomer to jihadist circles, however. His radicalization process started in 1996, after four years of internment under a false identity in the Spanish penitentiary of Valdemoro, near Madrid, following his conviction for drug offenses. His radicalism intensified during another stint in prison in Morocco between 2000 and June 2003.[39] Before this, in 1999, Ahmidan met with Abu Dahdah, then leader of Spain's al-Qaeda cell in the Netherlands and expressed the desire to go and fight in Chechnya.[40] Loyalty toward "the Chinese," as the band's linchpin, seems to have been the key factor in the involvement of this group of petty criminals in the commuter-train plot. This last cluster was introduced mainly for operational and financial purposes.[41]

MOBILIZED FOR JIHAD

Not surprisingly, all those who were a part of the Madrid bombing network were men, and all were born between 1960 and 1983. More than half were between twenty-three and thirty-three years old at the time of the train bombings. Most were native Moroccans, except for three Algerians, an Egyptian, and a Tunisian.[42] All but three were living in Spain, most of them in or around Madrid when the attacks took place. Two, however, lived in Brussels and one in Milan. Typically, although not exclusively, they were economic migrants, some residing legally and others illegally. Many were single, although a considerable number were married, with a few even having children. Although their sociological profiles were quite diverse, they showed, in general, relatively low levels of both formal education and employment. Those mobilized in the Madrid bombing network, however, did not all adopt jihadist ideology or become radicalized and recruited in the same place, at the same time, or through the same processes.[43]

At least twenty of the twenty-seven in the terrorist network adopted a jihadist ideology while in Spain, with temporary stays abroad reinforcing their extremist views. At least four internalized an extremist set of attitudes and beliefs outside of Spain. Hassan el-Haski, already a leading member of the MICG by March 11, 2004, radicalized in Morocco and Syria. Youssef Belhadj, who joined the same organization, likely radicalized in Morocco. Rabei Osman espoused jihadism in Egypt, his native country, leading him to join the Egyptian Islamic Jihad, which merged with al-Qaeda in 2001. Allekema Lamari was a member of the GIA by 1996, before arriving in Spain from Algeria. Doubts remain about Daoud Ouhnane, born in Algeria, who may well have radicalized before his arrival in Spain in the 1990s.

That the majority adopted a jihadist ideology while in Spain is not necessarily suggestive that the Madrid bombing network was a case of "homegrown terrorism" sensu stricto or of a "homegrown network" of mere al-Qaeda sympathizers. The network included individuals linked to cross-border international terrorist organizations, such as the MICG, or to the previous al-Qaeda cell in Spain. Two of those who radicalized abroad, Rabei Osman and Youssef Belhadj, came to act as radicalizing agents for others living in or near Madrid who later participated in the Madrid bombings network. In addition, none of the twenty-seven individuals was born or naturalized in Spain or in any other European Union member state. Most of them arrived in Spain between 1990 and 2001 as immigrants in their late teens and mid-twenties. While in Spain, their daily lives placed them in constant interaction with people of similar origin. Rachid Aglif is the only one who could be considered a "homegrown" terrorist since he settled in Spain with his father and other close Moroccan relatives as a ten-year-old child. Aglif attended public schools in the Madrid region and started working at his family's shop when he was sixteen years old.

The 2003 invasion of Iraq is often referred to as a causal factor in the 2004 Madrid train bombings.[44] Yet less than half of the network members internalized a jihadist ideology after the invasion of Iraq. At least five of those who radicalized after the invasion of Iraq belonged to the previously existing gang of delinquents, under the direction of Jamal Ahmidan. Another three became involved with that gang, which placed them on the periphery of the Spanish al-Qaeda cell. On the other hand, twelve or thirteen members of the Madrid bombing network radicalized before the invasion of Iraq. Of these, five to six did so after 9/11 and the subsequent military intervention in Afghanistan, and eight became prone to terrorism before the 9/11 attacks.

Three of these last eight members had strong links to the al-Qaeda cell led in Spain by Abu Dahdah before 9/11. As mentioned previously, these were Jamal Zougam, Said Berraj, and Sarhane ben Abdelmajid Fakhet, "the Tunisian." This subset of network members also includes Hassan el-Haski, Rabei Osman, Youssef Belhadj, and Allekema Lamari, all of whom had been or were part of jihadist entities by 9/11. Jamal Ahmidan ("the Chinese")—linchpin of the criminal gang that morphed into a terrorist outfit in the summer of 2003—began radicalizing around 1996, as noted earlier, with his views hardening during a further period of imprisonment in Morocco. The individuals who radicalized before 9/11 were the most notorious members of the Madrid bombing network, including those who acted as radicalizing agents for the rest and as local operational ringleaders.

The members of the Madrid bombings network who became jihadists in Spain before 9/11 and were in contact with Abu Dahdah and his cell attended the city's main Islamic worship places, such as the Abu Bakr mosque and the M-30 mosque, where they were initially spotted as possible candidates for recruitment.[45] In addition to indoctrination in these places of worship, where books and pamphlets were disseminated, they were usually invited to countryside gatherings located next to the Alberche River close to the rural town of Navalcarnero. In these informal meetings, recreational activities mixed with proselytizing sessions on religion, jihad, and open conflicts involving large Muslim communities like Bosnia. Those who attended the meetings were persuaded to donate money for the mujaheddin in these conflicts and often were invited to undergo military training in Afghan camps. Said Berraj, for example, was on his way to Afghanistan in 2000 when he was arrested in Turkey.[46] Eventually, some individuals were selected and secluded in private residences to foster indoctrination by watching videos on Bosnia or Chechnya. They also listened to taped sermons from jihadist preachers.

Following the dismantling of Abu Dahdah's al-Qaeda cell in Spain weeks after 9/11, parties on the riverbank ceased and contacts in worship places decreased or moved to less notorious ones. Meetings became more discreet and were held behind closed doors in city apartments and storefronts, such as a barber shop located in Lavapiés, a quarter of Madrid where Maghrebi and other immigrant populations are concentrated. During this period, influential people arriving from abroad, such as Mimoum Belhadj and his brother Youssef Belhadj, already members of the MICG, often socialized individuals into jihad. Abdelmajid Bouchar was radicalized in this way. Others who later became part of this network, such as Fouad el-Morabit Anghar, were seen in 2002 outside worship places in Madrid and were subjected to proselytizing by Rabei Osman. Others, like Mohamed Bouharrat, radicalized in prison in Spain during the same year.[47]

Members the Madrid bombing network who radicalized after the invasion of Iraq generally did so more rapidly than the others, although with varying degrees of intensity. Countryside gatherings resumed on an ad hoc basis since the planning of the attacks was already under way by the summer of 2003 under the joint guidance of "the Tunisian" and "the Chinese." Some of those who attended these gatherings became actual bombers on 3/11. The Internet also played a limited role in the radicalization of this subset of the network, but never to the point of self-radicalization. The Internet was absent in the case of those who adopted a violent ideology before 9/11 and of limited influence for those radicalized between September 2001 and February 2003. Judicial documentation of the case provides valuable information, based on police investigations, about the Internet sites visited by those involved in the attacks and the indoctrination materials used.

Of particular interest are the files recovered from a hard disk and some USB devices found in the debris of the Leganés apartment rented as a safe house. The files were created between July 1997 and February 2004. Before 9/11, leading members of the Madrid network paid special attention to texts by Abdullah Azzam and Abu Qatada (Omar Mahmoud Othman). Between 9/11 and February 2003, they went to webpages such as www.jehad.net and extracted writings in Arabic by Sayyid Qutb or downloaded audiovisual postings produced by al-Sahab, al-Qaeda's media production house. After March 2003, they visited, among others, www.tawhed.ws, www.almaqdese.com, www.alsunnah .info, or the Global Islamic Media Center website. They focused on texts by Abu Qatada, Ibn Taymiyya—quoted in the letter left before the train bombings by Abdenabi Kounjaa and by "the Tunisian" in a draft communiqué written afterward—Ayman al-Zawahiri, Abu Mohammed al-Maqdisi, Nasir bin Hamad al-Fahd, Abdul Munim Mustafa Halima, and Hamed al-Ali, or Mohammed Fizazi.[48]

Previous affective ties between individuals contributed to the adoption of jihadism among those involved in the Madrid bombings but also led directly to their actual inclusion in the terrorist network. These relationships are usually based on kinship, friendship, and neighborhood links. That eleven out of the twenty-seven individuals were born in Tétouan and Tangiers is an indicative but not definitive variable in their mobilization. Militating against direct correlation is the fact that more than 20 percent of the several tens of thousands of Moroccans living in Madrid and in the nearby region come from these two cities in northwest Morocco.[49] There are cases, however, in which interaction within the same city quarter between members of the same jihadist cell dates back to childhood or youth, as is the case with Jamal Zougam and Said Berraj in Tangiers. In these cases, affective ties based on neighborhood become much more significant, particularly if they recur during occasional stays in the city of origin.

However, it is not always easy to distinguish between the likely impact on terrorist radicalization of locality of birth or residence and other variables, such as kinship. Jamal Ahmidan, Hicham Ahmidan, and Hamid Ahmidan not only came from Tétouan but also shared family bonds. Mohamed and Rachif Oulad Akcha were brothers and were born in Tétouan. A quarter of the Madrid bombing network had at least one relative inside the same network. Concerning ties of friendship, it is difficult to make important analytical distinctions between those relationships that existed before individual socialization into jihadism and those forged within the four clusters after adopting extremist ideas and before network formation. Nevertheless, concerning individuals engaged in delinquent activities headed by "the Chinese," loyalty to the criminal band and its kingpin seems to have been the key factor for involvement in the plot.

AL-QAEDA CONNECTION

The clue that connects the Madrid bombing network to the al-Qaeda hierarchy appeared late in 2005, although it was only confirmed to the author over the last two months of 2009. It emerged in a remote mountainous location in northwestern Pakistan, not far from the Afghan border. In the early hours of December 1, 2005, a Hellfire missile hit a compound in the village of Haisori, close to Miran Shah, the administrative capital of Northern Waziristan, one of the seven agencies that form the Federally Administered Tribal Areas (FATA). The core of al-Qaeda's leadership and most of its commanders, as well as many of its members and affiliated groups, had relocated to the FATA and the adjacent North West Frontier Province between late 2001 and the beginning of 2002. Al-Qaeda also relocated a large number of its active militants and most of its training infrastructure to North Waziristan between the middle of 2004 and the beginning of 2005,[50] and it has since benefited from the protection afforded by Talibanized sectors of the indigenous Pashtun communities.

The Hellfire, launched by one of the unmanned Predator drones used by the U.S. Central Intelligence Agency to target al-Qaeda leaders and commanders, killed five people near the Afghan-Pakistani border. Among them was the main target of the strike, the Egyptian Abu Hamza Rabia, then head of al-Qaeda's external operations command and responsible for the organization's plots in North America and Western Europe. At the time of his death, Rabia was regarded as one of the top five people in al-Qaeda's core. Early in 2002, Osama bin Laden had split al-Qaeda's operational structure into two commands.

The internal operations command belonged to Mustafa al-Uzayti (also known as Abu Faraj al-Libi), focusing on Afghanistan and Pakistan. Leadership of the external operations command initially belonged to Khalid Sheikh Mohammed, who masterminded the September 11 attacks in the United States. When KSM was arrested in Rawalpindi in March 2003, al-Libi likewise became engaged in external operations, but Rabia assumed command.[51]

U.S. intelligence identified one of the four men who died with Rabia some weeks later as Amer Azizi.[52] A Moroccan born in the town of Hedami in 1968, Azizi migrated to Spain in the early 1990s. Once settled in Madrid, he married a native Spaniard, Raquel Burgos, who converted to Islam. Azizi began to attend Tablighi Jamaat gatherings in the capital, and by the middle of the decade Abu Dahdah radicalized and recruited him into his recently established al-Qaeda cell in Spain. Abu Dahdah soon sent him to a military training facility in Zenica, Bosnia. By 2000, Azizi had also received military training in Afghanistan camps managed by al-Qaeda and its North African affiliates.[53] Azizi's training experience made him a respected member of the Abu Dahdah cell, within which he became prominent and a leading recruiter.[54] Azizi was formally prosecuted in absentia by Spain's National Court for terrorist offenses attributed to that cell after he managed to escape following the police operation that substantially dismantled the cell in November 2001. When Operación Dátil was launched, Azizi was in Iran, coordinating the route to Afghanistan for jihadists recruited in Spain. He evaded arrest and made his way to Pakistan by November or December 2001. Once in Pakistan, Azizi joined al-Qaeda central and moved up the ranks, becoming a key facilitator for the Madrid attacks.

Inside al-Qaeda central, Azizi operated alongside Abd al-Hadi al-Iraqi, a senior al-Qaeda member who directed incursions into Afghanistan.[55] Azizi was also linked to Mustafa Abu'l Yazid, also known as Said al-Masri, a historical leader of al-Qaeda and the former head of its financial committee, as well as to the al-Qaeda operative Khalid Habib. Azizi's trajectory in al-Qaeda since 2002 suggests he was an important and highly valued senior member with the experience and knowledge to direct terrorist operations in the West in general and in Western Europe in particular. Interestingly, a 2005 European Union intelligence report on al-Qaeda's leadership mentioned an unidentified al-Qaeda operative of Moroccan origin, based in the Afghanistan-Pakistan area and considered one of the main al-Qaeda chiefs in that zone, who "formerly acted as intermediary between Abu Faraj al-Libi and Western Europe, where he resided."[56]

Many of the details on Azizi's activities also appeared in a biography published by Tauhid Press as part of a series on "Martyrs of Maghreb al-Aqsa in the Land of the Hindu Kush," disseminated on jihadist websites in 2009.[57] The biography referred to Azizi by name and described his "military activities" and role as "administration responsible" in al-Qaeda before "the amir" entrusted him to other important duties, first in "the information team" and, subsequently, "to lead one of the military sections." Azizi, as the document asserted, finally "assumed the function of adjunct to the commander for external action" and was involved, among other tasks, in instructing "the lions that came from far away with the end of preparing them to transform the tranquility of the crusaders into a hell."[58] The biography noted that Azizi's intention to target Spain predated 9/11. According to the story presented in the biography, in 2001 he returned to Spain from Afghanistan with the idea of executing an act of jihad on these "usurped lands."[59] Yet his attack plans were frustrated because, as the document explained, "most members of the jihadist cell" were arrested because of the "blessed attacks of New York and Washington." This statement obviously referred to the dismantling of the Abu Dahdah cell two months after 9/11.

The initial groundwork for the Madrid attacks began with a meeting in Karachi in December 2001 between Amer Azizi and Abdelatif Mourafik.[60] Mourafik, though also Moroccan, was then an operative of the Libyan Islamic Fighting Group (LIFG).[61] The two individuals met initially in Afghanistan at some point during or before 2000, when Azizi received military training at the Shahid Abu Yahya Camp operated by the LIFG, then about thirty kilometers from Kabul. In addition to LIFG members, recruits for the MICG were indoctrinated and trained there as well. Later investigations into the Madrid bombing cell revealed that some of its members were affiliated with the MICG.[62] Toward the end of the 1990s, both the LIFG and the MICG agreed to coordinate activities.[63] After 9/11, this agreement became relevant for the Madrid attacks as senior members of the LIFG and MICG were involved not only in the strategic-operational decision to attack targets in Spain but also in the actual configuration of the network behind the Madrid blasts.

Moreover, Fakhet, as ringleader of the local cell, had cell phone exchanges with Abu Abdullah al-Sadeq (the alias of Abdelhakim Belhaj), then emir of the LIFG, a few months before the Madrid attacks when Fakhet was in Madrid and al-Sadeq was in Hong Kong.[64] Furthermore, on the evening of March 24, 2010, the day after al-Sadeq was released from jail in Libya, I had the opportunity to meet him for a brief interview at the home of his siblings in Tripoli. In the course of the exchange, the former emir of the LIFG acknowledged having had what he termed "social relations" with Fakhet.[65] Separately, on April 3, 2004, minutes before Fakhet and six other members of the Madrid bombing cell blew themselves up in Leganés, Fakhet made a cell phone call to a prominent LIFG member in London.[66]

The meeting in Karachi in December 2001 led to a more formal gathering in Istanbul in February 2002. In Istanbul, delegates from the LIFG and the MICG, as well as from the Tunisian Combatant Group, agreed that they should not limit jihad to conflict zones and should conduct it in countries where their members originated or resided.[67] This argument was subsequently disseminated in Madrid by August 2002 in the early meetings of what would become the Madrid bombing network.[68] In March 2002, at the instigation of Mourafik, Mustafa Maymouni, another Moroccan, initiated the formation of the local cell that would eventually prepare and execute the Madrid attacks.[69] Maymouni had been a friend of Azizi since at least 1999, when the two attended the same Tablighi congregations in Madrid.[70] Azizi recruited his friend into the Abu Dahdah cell by 2001, and Maymouni became his closest collaborator.[71] Indeed, Mourafik found Maymouni through Azizi.

In 2002, Maymouni first rented the rural house Morata de Tajuña in Chinchón that subsequently served as the base of operations for the bombers.[72] As mentioned, he rented the house from the wife of Mohamed Needel Acaid, who was at the time incarcerated in Spain for his membership in the Abu Dahdah cell. In May 2003, however, Maymouni was imprisoned in Morocco after being arrested in the aftermath of the Casablanca attacks, the same charge that moved Turkish police to almost simultaneously arrest Mourafik and extradite him to the Moroccan authorities.[73] Because of Maymouni's arrest, another Moroccan, Driss Chebli, and Sarhane ben Abdelmajid Fakhet ("the Tunisian") came to jointly lead the Madrid cell. Yet, a few months later, Chebli was arrested in Spain, also accused of belonging to the Abu Dahdah cell.[74] Fakhet, who had close ties to Azizi, became the sole local organizer. The continuity between the remains of the Abu Dahdah cell and the Madrid bombing network is so evident that Fakhet himself might have conferred with Abu Dahdah on the plot through a close friend and coworker who regularly visited the latter in prison, including a visit only five days before the March 11 attacks.[75]

Azizi radicalized and recruited Fakhet into Abu Dahdah's al-Qaeda cell in the late 1990s.[76] They met each other frequently until the summer of 2001 and communicated by e-mail through 2002 and 2003, although they left no electronic traffic since they saved the e-mails in the draft folder of an e-mail account they shared.[77] Azizi, to complete the local operational cell, likely suggested engaging Jamal Zougam, a Moroccan whom the Spanish national police had investigated for his links to the Abu Dahdah case and in connection with the Casablanca attacks in 2003.[78] Azizi had been in contact with Zougam before escaping to Pakistan in 2001.[79] Azizi's connections to the bombing network did not end there. Said Berraj, who remains a fugitive for his role in the Madrid attacks, also had close ties to Azizi. On October 10, 2000, both Azizi and Berraj were temporarily arrested in Turkey on their way to Afghanistan.[80] Azizi was then found in possession of five false Pakistani visas.

The senior al-Qaeda operative who had ties to most, if not all, key members of the Madrid bombing network was Amer Azizi. Not surprisingly, Azizi is repeatedly mentioned in no less than 141 of the 241 volumes on the Madrid bombings compiled by the National Court in Spain. His name is also referred to in eight of the thirty supplementary volumes that make up the vast judicial documentation on the case. Taken together, these documents, the result of specialized law-enforcement investigations and international police exchanges, reveal, on the one hand, the close ties between Azizi and the individuals who played pivotal roles in the formation and subsequent development of the local terrorist cell that prepared and placed the March 11 bombs and, on the other hand, his links with individuals and groups from North Africa involved in the web of global terrorism.

By all accounts, Azizi traveled from Pakistan to Spain at the end of 2003, likely to convey the approval of al-Qaeda's senior leadership for the Madrid attack and to finalize the bombing preparations. This momentous detail and other crucial pieces of information were acquired by at least three Western intelligence services between 2008 and 2010 and shared with this author.[81]

AN UNDERLYING STRATEGY

The will to perpetrate an act of jihadist terrorism in Spain that materialized in the attacks of March 11, 2004, dates to late 2001 and early 2002.[82] It was initially motivated by revenge following a major police operation, which dismantled and incarcerated most of the members of the al-Qaeda cell led by Abu Dahdah. It is no coincidence that three prominent members of the Madrid bombing network and their intermediary with al-Qaeda central were strongly tied to that cell. Soon afterward, the desire to attack was enhanced by the joint strategic decision adopted at the meeting in Istanbul in February 2002. The invasion of Iraq added a further motivation and provided a particularly favorable opportunity for those wishing to perpetrate a terrorist attack in Madrid to converge and for al-Qaeda senior leadership to approve.

A good starting point for assessing the organizational strategy underlying the 2004 Madrid bombings is the audio recording by Osama bin Laden aired by al-Jazeera in October 2003, in which he threatens Spain and five other countries (in addition to the United States) for having deployed soldiers in Iraq.[83] On October 26, an e-mail sent to the London-based *al-Majallah* weekly by Abu Muhammad al-Ablaj, referred to by the paper as an important al-Qaeda figure, announced: "We are preparing for a great day" in "a place in the Western countries" mentioned by Osama bin Laden in his message, excluding the United States.

A number of observers have been inclined to view the commuter-train blasts as inspired by two jihadist documents. One, "Jihad in Iraq: Hopes and Dangers," contains a sophisticated argument on how to induce the coalition partners of the United States, in particular Spain, then a major European contributor, to pull their troops out of Iraq by striking at their soldiers so that other countries might be expected to follow. The other document, "A Message to the Spanish People," hinted at the possibility of an attack within Spain.[84] However, by the time the former was promulgated in September 2003 and both were published on the Global

Islamic Media Centre website in December, the Madrid bombing network was complete, and the decision to perpetrate a major attack was already made. There are, moreover, no traces of either document having been viewed or downloaded through any of the computers used by the terrorists.

The timing, sequence, and contents of the communiqués claiming responsibility for the attacks are interesting. Besides those issued on March 11 and 13, a communiqué from the Abu Hafs al-Masri Brigades (al-Qaeda) appeared on March 15 (the day after the general election), and a second message from the local terrorist cell, whose members also recorded some unreleased videos on March 27, was broadcast on April 3.

As already mentioned, the March 11 communiqué by the Abu Hafs al-Masri Brigades (al-Qaeda) was sent by e-mail to the editor of *Al-Quds al-Arabi* who, based on experience with other al-Qaeda claims, considered it authentic. The Spanish national police, who rated the communiqué as "relatively trustworthy," corroborated that the e-mail was forwarded from Iran, though technically it could have originated in Yemen, Egypt, or Libya.[85] The text, written in Arabic, said, among other things:

> The death squad has managed to penetrate the bowels of Crusading Europe, striking one of the pillars of the Crusader alliance, Spain, with a painful blow. This is part of the settling of old scores with the Crusading Spain, the ally of America in its war against Islam. Where is America, Aznar? Who will protect you, Great Britain, Italy, Japan, and other agents? When we struck against the Italian troops in Nasiriya we already sent a warning to America's agents: withdraw from the alliance against Islam.

It thus claimed responsibility for the attacks and justified them by referring to Spain both as an ally of the United States and as a country with which there were scores to settle. This might well allude to the Muslim territory on the Iberian Peninsula lost to the Christians in the fifteenth century, to the persecution and imprisonment of many al-Qaeda members and followers in Spain since fall 2001, or both. The issue of Iraq is framed in the broader terms of armed religious confrontation, and the Spanish prime minister is mentioned as the personification of that policy. The Nasiriya attacks of November 12, 2003, were also attributed to al-Qaeda by Abu Muhammad al-Ablaj in an e-mail sent nine days later to *al-Majallah*. One of the bombers in those attacks was recruited and traveled to Iraq through the same transnational network that helped some of those implicated in the Madrid blasts escape from Spain.[86]

However, there appeared to be no implicit or explicit allusion in this initial communiqué to the general elections scheduled for March 14. The message does include a clear demand, reiterating the notion of a clash between religions, to citizens of the West as opposed to their ruling elites: "The people of the allies of the United States should force their governments to end this alliance in the war against terrorism, which means the war against Islam. If you stop the war, we shall stop ours." Although the invasion and occupation of Iraq were overwhelmingly unpopular in Spain and had became a major electoral issue, the terrorists might have been seeking, in addition to revenge, to affect Spanish public opinion in general, to influence governmental foreign-policy decisions, rather than voting behavior in particular.[87]

The videotape released on March 13 by the local cell included statements such as, "We declare our responsibility for what happened in Madrid exactly two and a half years after the attacks on New York and Washington," and, "We swear by the Almighty that if you do not halt in your injustice and in the deaths of Muslims with the excuse of combating terrorism, we shall blow your houses up in the air and spill your blood as if it were a river. We are prepared for what will fill your hearts with terror." Although the terrorists did not refer to the general elections, the tape was hurriedly recorded at around 5:00 p.m. on the eve of election day and delivered in time for nationwide release by the media.

After the March 14 election, the extent to which the local cell in Madrid followed the directives issued by the Abu Hafs al-Masri Brigades (al-Qaeda) from the Gulf became clear. On March 17, a fax signed by the latter organization and dated March 15 was received in another London-based Arabic-language newspaper, *Al-Hayat*, and sent by e-mail to *Al-Quds al-Arabi*. This communiqué mentioned both the elections and the electoral outcome when explaining why the initial claim of responsibility had appeared with unusual speed: "In the case of the battle of Madrid, the time factor was very important to finish with the government of the contemptible Aznar," and it added that "we have given the Spanish people the choice between war and peace, and they have chosen peace by voting for the party that stood up against the American alliance in its war against Islam." Clearly alluding, once again, to Spain's Islamic past, as well as to the incoming government, it announced that

> our leadership has decided to halt all operations on the soil of al-Andalus against what are known as civilian targets until we are sure of the direction the new government will take, that has promised to withdraw Spanish troops from Iraq, and thereby make sure that there is no interference by the new executive in matters concerning Muslims. For this reason we reiterate the decision to all battalions on European soil to cease operations.

This communiqué was posted on the Global Islamic Media Centre website on March 18, as "Notification for the Nation regarding the suspension of operations in the land of al-Andalus." It was downloaded the following morning at 10:16 a.m. to a portable computer found by the Spanish police in the home of Jamal Ahmidan, "the Chinese."[88] This explains the second message from the local cell (once more presented as coming from Abu Dujan al-Afghani) on April 3, hours before the suicide explosion in Leganés. This message was handwritten by "the Tunisian"[89] and faxed to the national newspaper *ABC* in Madrid with the warning that "we, the Death Battalion, announce the annulment of our previous truce," threatening Spaniards with "making your country an inferno and making your blood flow like rivers" unless certain demands, including the withdrawal of troops from Iraq and Afghanistan, were met within twenty-four hours by the "people and government of Spain."[90]

However, it was not the local cell but rather the Abu Hafs al-Masri Brigades (al-Qaeda) that had declared the truce this message was now terminating. The local cell in Madrid seems always to have accepted the premises transmitted in advance by the Abu Hafs al-Masri Brigade (al-Qaeda) from the Gulf.[91] Whether they directed the local cell to end the truce or the decision was adopted autonomously (though in line with the March 15 communiqué) is uncertain. However, in the message faxed April 3, the local cell leader established a twenty-four-hour deadline, whereas in a video he and other terrorists recorded on March 27 that was never released the deadline was fixed at eight days. So at least as early as March 27, days after the new government expressed its intention to withdraw Spanish troops from Iraq but increase the number of soldiers in Afghanistan, the Madrid bombers clearly had it in mind to perpetrate a new act of terrorism on or after April 4.

Al-Qaeda's leaders seem to have been more restrained than other global terrorists in exploiting the 2004 Madrid bombings for propaganda purposes.[92] Osama bin Laden first mentioned them a month later in an audio recording broadcast by al-Jazeera and al-Arabiya on April 15, in which he offered a peace treaty to the Europeans. In this message, the commuter-train blasts were interpreted as acts of revenge: "There is a lesson regarding what happens in occupied Palestine and what happened on September 11 and March 11. These are your goods returned to you."[93] On November 16, 2005, the top al-Qaeda leader Ayman al-Zawahiri alluded to the March 11 attacks in a video praising the suicide bombings of July 7, 2005, in London as "the blessed raid which, like its illustrious predecessors in New York, Washington, and Madrid, took the battle to the enemy's own soil."[94] Not until January 19, 2006, when a new video recording was aired by al-Jazeera, did bin Laden again refer to the case, this time indirectly and in conjunction with the London bombings: "The war against America and its allies has not remained limited to Iraq, as Bush claims. Evidence of this is the explosions you have witnessed in the capitals of the most important European countries that are members of this hostile coalition."[95] But bin Laden reiterated once more an explicit allusion to past bombings in Madrid and London in a September 25, 2009, message to Europeans urging withdrawal from Afghanistan.[96] In addition, al-Qaeda has frequently introduced graphic material from the commuter-train blasts to illustrate the actions of its global jihad. These images are now being reproduced in propaganda videos by al-Qaeda in the Islamic Maghreb as well.

CONCLUSION

Both the decision to attack Spain and the mobilization of a terrorist network to accomplish this objective were top-down processes. The groundwork started on December 2001 in Pakistan and extended until February 2002, involving al-Qaeda's North African associate organizations whose delegates gathered in Turkey that same month. The track record of Amer Azizi, from prominent member of the al-Qaeda cell established in Spain by the middle 1990s to adjunct of al-Qaeda's head of external-operations command, suggests he favored the subsequent approval and facilitation of the plot by al-Qaeda's senior leadership. Soon, in 2002, Azizi had instructed his LIFG associate Abdelatif Mourafik to place Mustafa Maymouni—already one of Azizi's closest collaborators—in charge of articulating the terrorist network. The process included interaction among key local organizers, including main members of the operational cell who were previously linked to the Spanish al-Qaeda cell dismantled in November 2001 and to Azizi before and after he was appointed adjunct to Hamza Rabia.

The 2004 Madrid train bombings were not the product of an independent cell. It is no accident that the National Court sentence in the case refers to all those individuals prosecuted and convicted for the attacks as "members of terrorist cells and groups of jihadist type."[97] On the contrary, those attacks were an early and complex manifestation of al-Qaeda's capabilities in Western Europe after 9/11. The coordinated explosions of March 11, 2004, made clear the existence, within Western Europe, of jihadist networks or cells prone to direction, support, and even supervision from al-Qaeda's external-operations command through intermediaries with firsthand knowledge of the concrete operational scenario and ties to local operatives. Networks and cells able to eventually incorporate individuals ascribed to al-Qaeda's affiliated entities, which also had a significant presence in Western Europe. On March 11, 2004, two and a half years after September 11, 2001, they were able to perpetrate sophisticated, coordinated, and highly lethal attacks in the region explicitly following al-Qaeda's general strategy.

While in U.S. custody at Guantánamo Bay after his arrest in May 2005, Abu Faraj al-Libi, the overall manager of al-Qaeda's operations at the time of the Madrid attacks, declared that Abu Hamza Rabia, then the chief external-operations planner, "wanted strongly to attack passenger trains in the US or UK following the March 2004 bombing of commuter trains in Madrid."[98] On July 7, 2005, one year and almost four months later, suicide bombers struck the London Underground system. The role of the alleged al-Qaeda mastermind behind this plot, Abu Ubaydah al-Masri, could be compared to that of Azizi in the Madrid attacks. In December 2005, when a U.S. drone killed Amer Azizi and Hamza Rabia in a North Waziristan home, they were both preparing operatives for a similar strike on the continental United States.[99]

Overall, the Madrid train bombings revealed much about global terrorism. Terrorism is a polymorphous phenomenon, with diverse and heterogeneous interacting components whose leaders recognize a top-down hierarchy of command and control, but this structure is flexible and adapted to specific circumstances, producing extraordinary combinations when necessary and allowing the strategies of international actors and the aspirations of local activists to converge at the operational level. Further, the attacks of March 11, 2004, illuminate the changing nature of the threat. Al-Qaeda did not plan, prepare, and execute the attacks on its own. Neither were they the product of autonomous, self-constituted cells. The Madrid bombing network speaks for itself as a composite source of threat, where individuals from different groups and organizations converge. The blasts also point to the terrorists' lasting predilection for public-transport systems as soft targets, their preference for the use of improvised explosive devices, and their suicidal determination. Finally, the Madrid attacks reveal much about terrorist strategy. Al-Qaeda's broad guidelines, decisions adopted by associated organizations, and the subordinate vision of local cells can converge to make the best of favorable opportunities.

NOTES

1. Marc Sageman, *Leaderless Jihad: Terror Networks in the Twenty-First Century* (Philadelphia: University of Pennsylvania Press, 2008); a similar interpretation can be found in Mitchell D. Silber, *The Al Qaeda Factor: Plots Against the West* (Philadelphia: University of Pennsylvania Press, 2012), 184–205.

2. The criminal proceedings over the Madrid train bombings fill 241 volumes and 30 separate pieces, including previously secret records and reserved documents, comprising 93,226 pages of files. Available judicial documentation on the case includes sentences handed down by the National Court and the Supreme Court in Spain, as well as data from related criminal proceedings and sentences delivered in Milan, Italy, and Salé, Morocco. In addition, this chapter also relies on personal interviews with knowledgeable police and intelligence officers from various Western nations between 2007 and 2012, as well as related relevant official documents to which the author was granted access.

3. Audiencia Nacional, Juzgado Central de Instrucción no. 6, *Sumario 20/2004*, vol. 161: 60,764, 60,771.

4. Ibid., vol. 68: 20,629 and vol. 161: 60,767.

5. Ibid., vol. 161: 60,858.

6. Audiencia Nacional, Sala de lo Penal, Sección Segunda, *Sentencia 65/2007*, 229–422.

7. On the immediate material damages, see *Sumario 20/2004*, vol. 216: 84,062. On the direct economic costs, see Mikel Buesa, Aurelia Vilariño, Joost Heijs, Thomas Baumert and Javier González, "The Economic Cost of March 11: Measuring the Direct Economic Cost of the Terrorist Attack on March 11, 2004 in Madrid," *Terrorism and Political Violence* 19, 4 (Winter 2007): 489–509.

8. *Sumario 20/2004*, vol. 162: 61,522–24.

9. Ibid., separate piece 29, annex II, document 8, and annex IV, document 2; Comisaría General de Información, Unidad Central de Información Exterior, "Acta de declaración de Hassan Bel Hadj," Diligencias 8,470, April 14, 2004, 3, in *Sumario 20/2004*, pieza separada 5, 8,276.

10. *Sumario 20/2004*, separate piece 29, annex II, documents 15 and 16.

11. On the financing of the Madrid train bombings, see *Sumario 20/2004*, separate piece 10.

12. Rogelio Alonso and Fernando Reinares, "Maghreb Immigrants Becoming Suicide Terrorists: A Case Study of Religious Radicalization Processes In Spain," in Ami Pedahzur, ed., *Root Causes of Suicide Terrorism: The Globalization of Martyrdom* (London: Routledge, 2006), 179–97.

13. *Sumario 20/2004*, vol. 61: 18,591; vol. 81: 18,634 and 25,176; and vol. 162: 61,529–30, 61,556–8.

14. Ignacio Lago and José R. Montero, *The 2004 Election in Spain: Terrorism, Accountability, and Voting*, working paper no. 253 (Barcelona: Institut de Ciències Polítiques i Socials, 2006).

15. Abdel Bari Atwan, *The Secret History of Al-Qa'ida* (London: Abacus, 2007), 116.

16. See http://elpais.com/diario/2004/03/14/espana/1079218802_850215.html; http://www.elmundo.es/elmundo/2004/03/14/espana/1079223918.html; http://www.cnn.com/2004/WORLD/europe/03/13/spain.blasts/index.html.

17. *Sumario 20/2004*, vol. 97: 31,840. Also see Fernando Reinares, *¡Matadlos! Quién estuvo detrás del 11-M y por qué se atentó en España* (Barcelona: Galaxia Gutenberg, 2014), 114–17.

18. Fernando Reinares, "The Madrid Bombings and Global Jihadism," *Survival* 52, no. 2 (2010): 83–104.

19. This cell was detected by the police at the end of 1994. Among its founding members were Anwar Adnan Mohamed Saleh, also known as Chej Salah, who moved from Madrid to Peshawar in October 1995, and Mustafa Setmarian Nasar, better known as Abu Musab al-Suri, who relocated to London four months earlier and then settled close to Osama bin Laden in Afghanistan. Abu Dahdah and seventeen other individuals were convicted of terrorism-related offenses by the National Court on September 26, 2005. Fifteen of these convictions were confirmed by the Supreme Court on May 31, 2006.

20. For details, see Audiencia Nacional, Sala de lo Penal, Sección Tercera, *Sentencia 36/2005*, 203–211; "Informe ampliatorio de las investigaciones realizadas en torno a las visitas a España de Mohamed Atta y Ramzi Binalshibh [*sic*]," Dirección General de la Policía, Comisaría General de Información, Unidad Central de Información Exterior, October 16, 2002; *Sumario 35/2001*, vol. 6, 1,823–1,869, vol. 53, 16, 614–616, 625, in particular the report "Informe sobre Mohamed Belfatmi, sus relaciones con Amer Azizi y la célula de Abu Dahdah," Dirección General de la Policía, Comisaría General de Información, April 16, 2004. Also see "Informe sobre estado de las Diligencias Previas 367/01 y solicitud de comisión rogatoria internacional," Dirección General de la Guardia Civil, Jefatura del Servicio de Información, September 16, 2002.

21. Audiencia Nacional, Sala de lo Penal, Sección Tercera, *Sentencia 36/2005*, 203–211.

22. On the MICG and its links with the Madrid train bombings, see the comprehensive police report in *Sumario 20/2004*, vol. 97, 31,838–72. Also see Reinares, *¡Matadlos!*, 69–84.

23. *Sumario 20/2004*, vol. 17, 4,426–7 and vol. 191, 74,612–13. Also see Reinares, *¡Matadlos!*, 97–111.

24. No mention is made here of people who were detained following the attacks but never charged or who were prosecuted but absolved of all charges. Others, for instance a person convicted for providing false documents and a few more convicted for dealing with stolen explosives that ended up in the hands of the terrorists, were not part of the jihadist network as such and are excluded from this analysis.

25. Fakhet, Zougam, and Berraj were all investigated by the National Court in connection with the al-Qaeda cell led by Abu Dahdah. See *Sumario 20/2004*, vol. 163: 61,694–700, 61,735–44, and 61,781–801. Also see Reinares, *¡Matadlos!*, 33–51.

26. The property was registered under the name of his wife. See *Sumario 20/2004*, vol. 161: 60,823.

27. Audiencia Nacional, Juzgado Central de Instrucción no. 5, *Sumario 9/1997*; Sala de lo Penal, Sección Tercera, *Sentencia 14/2001*.

28. *Sumario 20/2004*, separate piece 11, 790–93.

29. Ibid., 793–94.

30. Ibid., vol. 97: 31,898–9, and vol. 163: 61,580–608. The Madrid bombing sentencing document refers to Hassan el-Haski as a "leader of the Moroccan Islamic Combattant Group." See *Sentencia 65/2007*, 217 and 218. See also Tribunal de grande Instance de Paris, 16eme chamber/1, no. d'affaire 0313739016, jugement 11 July 2007, 55 and 73.

31. *Sumario 20/2004*, vol. 163: 61,627. Youssef Belhadj is defined in one document as a "member of one of the groups which form the al-Qaeda network." *Sentencia 65/2007*, 215.

32. 28 *Sumario 20/2004*, vol. 106: 35,601–14; vol. 115: 39,970–73; vol. 133: 48,728–33; and vol. 163: 61,608–24.

33. Ibid., vol. 180: 69,863.

34. Ibid., vol. 163: 61,622–23; see also *Sentencia 65/2007*, 216–17. Also see Reinares, *¡Matadlos!*, 76-81.

IN THE WEST

35. *Sumario 20/2004*, vol. 163: 61,621–22.

36. Rabei Osman el-Sayed Ahmed had been investigated by the national police's antiterrorism branch in 2002. *Sumario 20/2004*, vol. 17: 4,412; vol. 79: 24,154; vol. 81: 25,039, and vol. 163: 61,643–63.

37. During the same radicalizing speech, Rabei Osman asserted, "You have to join the al-Qaeda ranks. This is the solution, since the doors of al-Qaeda are open." *Sumario 20/2004*, vol. 163: 61,650. Also see Corte d'Assise di Milano, *Sentenza 10/2006*, 44.

38. *Sumario 20/2004*, vol. 79,24,191; vol. 163: 61,654. Also see Corte d'Assise di Milano, *Sentenza 10/2006*, 21–22.

39. *Sumario 20/2004*, vol. 14,3,632.

40. Audiencia Nacional, Sala de lo Penal, Sección Segunda, *Sentencia 65/2007*,201

41. See *Sumario 20/2004*, separate piece no. 11. Separately, at least three other members of the Madrid bombing network were also in contact with a cell of Pakistani men detained in Barcelona in September 2004 and afterward convicted of sending funds to al-Qaeda's senior members in Pakistan. See Audiencia Nacional, Juzgado Central de Instrucción no. 2, *Auto* of April 11, 2005,6; Audiencia Nacional, Sala de lo Penal, Sección Primera, *Sentencia 39/2007*, 4–5.

42. The Moroccans were Mohamed Afalah, Rachid Aglif, Hamid Ahmidan, Hicham Ahmidan. Jamal Ahmidan, Mohamed Oulad Akcha, Rachid Oulad Akcha, Fouad el-Morabit Anghar, Rifaat Anouar Asrih, Mohamed (Mimoum) Belhadj, Youssef Belhadj, Said Berraj, Abdelmajid Bouchar, Mohamed Bouharrat, Othman el-Gnaoui, Saed el-Harrak, Hassan el-Haski, Abdelilah Hriz, Abdenabi Kounjaa, Othman el-Mouib, Mohamed Larbi ben Sellam, and Jamal Zougam. The Algerians were Nasreddine Bousbaa, Allekema Lamari, and Daoud Ouhnane. The Egyptian was Rabei Osman el-Sayed Ahmed. The Tunisian was Serhane ben Abdelmajid Fakhet.

43. For a preliminary approach to this subject see Fernando Reinares, "Jihadist Radicalization and the 2004 Madrid Bombing Network," *CTC Sentinel* 2, no. 11 (2009): 16–19.

44. One individual in the Madrid bombings network, Mohamed Larbi ben Sellam, subsequently engaged, from Spain as well as Turkey and Syria, in activities that sought to bring to Iraq Muslim extremists who had radicalized in Europe and wanted to join the terrorist campaigns of al-Qaeda-related organizations. Some of the fugitives, such as Mohamed Belhadj and Abdelilah Hriz, were arrested in Syria, but four others actually made it to Iraq. Also see Reinares, *¡Matadlos!*, 215–25.

45. It is worth mentioning that, before he was radicalized into a jihadist ideology, Sarhane ben Abdelmajid Fakhet had joined the Tablighi Jamaat. Also see Reinares, *¡Matadlos!*, 38.

46. Said Berraj was traveling in the company of other three followers of Abu Dahdah, Amer Azizi, Salaheddin Benyaich (also known as Abu Muhgen), and Lahcen Ikassrien, who was captured by the U.S. military in Afghanistan after 9/11, imprisoned for a few years in Guantánamo, and finally extradited to Spain in 2005, where he was released. They managed to arrive in Afghanistan.

47. Rachid Aglif and Othman el-Gnaoui, both of whom radicalized into violence as from March 2003, also had experience in prison during the 1990s, but apparently this did not result in the adoption of extremist attitudes.

48. See Comisaría General de Información, "Informe general de conclusiones, atentados del 11 de marzo, Sumario 20/2004," July 3, 2006, 31–62.

49. Bernabé López García and Mohamed Berriane, eds., *Atlas de la inmigración Marroquí en España* (Madrid: Universidad Autónoma de Madrid, 2005), 499–500.

50. Rohan Gunaratna and Anders Nielsen, "Al Qaeda in the Tribal Areas of Pakistan and Beyond," *Studies in Conflict and Terrorism*, 31, no. 9 (September 2008): 786–88.

51. Ibid., 780, 783.

52. Oral confirmation to author by CIA sources present in Pakistan during the Haisori strike, and written confirmation from Spain's police intelligence in November and December 2009. Spain's authorities were informed by their American counterparts, in writing, in 2006 and 2007. Also see Reinares, *¡Matadlos!*, 133–38.

53. Audiencia Nacional, Juzgado Central de Instrucción no. 5, *Sumario 35/2001*, vol. 57: 18,322–69; Audiencia of September 19, 2003. Also, Audiencia Nacional, Juzgado Central de Instrucción no. 5, "Declaración judicial. Abdula Jayata Kattan @Abu Ibrahim," February 4–5, 2004, 19.

54. Late in 2001, British soldiers found in al-Qaeda's camps in Afghanistan the files of several Moroccans, residents of Spain, in which they stated that it was Othman al-Andalusi (Amer Azizi) who sent them there for training. See *Sumario 35/2001*, 35, 668–75, 679.

55. Personal interview, senior antiterrorism officer in the Spanish national police, November 2009; personal interviews, senior intelligence officers from two Western governments, including one European country, December 2011, and, for further documented confirmation, February 2012.

56. Personal interview, intelligence liaison officer based in Brussels, then working in the framework of the European Union Common Foreign and Security Policy, October 2007.

57. See, for instance, www.alqimmah.net/showthread.php?t=9752 (accessed June 11, 2010).

58. Ibid.

59. This refers to the jihadist idea that non-Muslims currently inhabiting Spain are occupying al-Andalus, the historical denomination for the Moorish dominion that extended over most of the Iberian Peninsula between the eighth and fifteenth centuries.

60. Personal interviews, senior intelligence officers from two Western governments, including one European country, December 2011, and, for further documented confirmation, February 2012. Spain's authorities were informed by U.S. intelligence on these facts, which included data from services of other countries, in writing, in 2009. At the meetings, Azizi and Mourafik also probably planned attacks in Morocco. Some of those involved in planning the Madrid attacks were later arrested after the

2003 Casablanca suicide bombings in Morocco. Mourafik is also known as Malek el-Andalusi and Malek al-Maghrebi. Further details are offered in Reinares, ¡Matadlos!, 145–47.

61. "Informe general sobre conclusiones de la investigación de los atentados terroristas del 11 de marzo de 2004," Dirección General de la Policía, Comisaría General de Información, Unidad Central de Información Exterior, July 3, 2006, 67, 70–74; Audiencia Nacional, Juzgado Central de Instrucción no. 6, Sumario 20/2004, vol. 234: 91, 130–191, 134.

62. The GICM became affiliated with and supported by al-Qaeda beginning in 2001, when its founder, Nafia Noureddine, met, first, with Osama bin Laden and Ayman al-Zawahiri and, then, with Mohammed Atef (Abu Hafs al-Masri). For details, see Peter L. Bergen, The Osama bin Laden I Know (New York: Free Press, 2006), 279.

63. Evan F. Kohlmann, "Dossier: Libyan Islamic Fighting Group," NEFA Foundation, 2007, 13–15.

64. The content of these phone calls is not known. On these exchanges there is a Spanish police report dated June 7, 2005, elaborated with the help of friendly services—presumably British—included in Sumario 20/2004, vol. 233: 90, 730–790, 734.

65. I was in the company of Rohan Gunaratna, head of the International Centre for Political Violence and Terrorism Research at Singapore's Nanyang Technological University.

66. In a personal communication on March 22, 2010, also in Tripoli, and reiterated during a meeting in Madrid in November the same year, Noman Benotman, a former high-ranking LIFG member, confirmed this to the author. According to Benotman, he was in London with the man who received the call at the time it was made.

67. An intelligence note of December 17, 2004, about this meeting and the strategic decision adopted is incorporated in the criminal proceedings for the Madrid bombings. See Sumario 20/2004, vol. 97: 31,848 and 32,316.

68. Audiencia Nacional, Juzgado Central de Instrucción no. 6, Auto of July 5, 2006, 64–65.

69. At the same time, Mourafik instructed Maymouni to create another operational cell in Kenitra, Morocco, a task in which the latter was assisted by Jamal Zougam. The Kenitra cell was dismantled after the 2003 Casablanca attacks. See Sumario 20/2004, vol. 97: 31,840, and the secret police intelligence report providing those details, included in vol. 191: 74,588–615.

70. Dirección General de la Policía, Comisaría General de Información, Unidad Central de Información Exterior, "Informe general sobre conclusiones de la investigación de los atentados terroristas del 11 de marzo de 2004," 73. From at least 2000, Fakhet also frequented these congregations.

71. When Azizi escaped, Maymouni was ordered by Mourafik to go to Morocco, where Azizi's wife had moved shortly after the disappearance of her husband, and he helped her rejoin him, first in Turkey and then in Pakistan. See Sumario 20/2004, vol. 191: 74,600–674. During its fall 2009 offensive in South Waziristan, the Pakistani

Army found and exhibited to the international press a passport belonging to Raquel Burgos, recovered from the debris of a house, next to the passport of Said Bahaji, a German citizen and associate of the lead 9/11 hijacker, Mohammed Atta. See Katherine Tiedemann, "Passports Linked to 9/11 Found in Northwest Pakistan Military Operations," *The AfPak Channel*, October 30, 2009.

72. *Sumario 20/2004*, vol. 21: 5,583.

73. Maymouni was also investigated by the Spanish police in 2003, following the Casablanca attacks, under *Sumario 9/2003*. See *Sumario 20/2004*, vol. 17: 4,423, and vol. 21: 5,583.

74. Details are included in the court indictment of Amer Azizi, where he was charged with terrorist offenses related to his membership in the Abu Dahdah cell as a "lieutenant" of the cell leader. See Audiencia Nacional, Juzgado Central de Instrucción no. 5, *Sumario 35/2001*, Audiencia of September 19, 2003, 15, 17–18.

75. Personal interview, senior Spanish police officer charged in the past with the criminal investigation of the Abu Dahdah cell, November 2008. Also, *Sumario 20/2004*, vol. 99: 32,907–911.

76. *Sumario 20/2004*, vol. 163: 61,740.

77. The testimony of a protected witness, a person who lived with Fakhet during 2002 and 2003, was fundamental in knowing about these exchanges, as documented in *Sumario 20/2004*, vol. 114: 39,154, and vol. 163: 61,923–961.

78. *Sumario 20/2004*, vol. 17: 4,411. A 2005 report from Spain's central police intelligence unit stated that "it is true that Amer Azizi was a friend of Sarhane ben Abdelmajid Fakhet, and it is possible that he provided advice through the Internet and even interceded in favor of the terrorist project being prepared in Madrid." See *Sumario 20/2004*, vol. 161: 60,875.

79. For instance, following a formal request from the French authorities, specifically judge Jean-Louis Bruguiére, concerning Zougam—who was already suspected of jihadist terrorism activities by 2000—the Spanish national police searched his home in Madrid and found, in addition to al-Qaeda propaganda, written contact details for Azizi. See *Sumario 35/2001*, 28, 477–428, 588; *Sumario 20/2004*, vol. 163: 61,679, 61,785.

80. *Sumario 20/2004*, vol. 17: 4, 414, and vol. 163: 61,684–85.

81. Personal interviews, senior intelligence officers of two Western governments, one of them European, December 2011, and, for further documented confirmation, February 2012. Spain's authorities received a U.S. intelligence report on this, including information provided by security services of at least a third country, by 2010. Further details are offered in Reinares, *¡Matadlos!*, 175 and 289.

82. This idea was also stressed by the public prosecutor's office during the Madrid bombings case, as reflected in its final report submitted on June 4, 2007, by the public prosecutor to the Sala de lo Penal (Criminal Hall) at the National Court, 12 and 13.

83. The other five countries were the United Kingdom, Australia, Poland, Japan, and Italy.

84. Brynjar Lia and Thomas Hegghammer, "Jihadi Strategic Studies: The Alleged Al Qaeda Policy Study Preceding the Madrid Bombings," *Studies in Conflict and Terrorism* 27, no. 5 (September–October 2004): 355–75.

85. *Sumario 20/2004*, vol. 17: 4,405.

86. See Audiencia Nacional, Sala de lo Penal, Sección Primera, *Sentencia 3/2010*, 7.

87. According to surveys conducted by Elcano Royal Institute in November 2002 and February 2003, between six and seven out of every ten adult Spaniards opposed the U.S.-led invasion of Iraq. See http://www.realinstitutoelcano.org/wps/portal /rielcano_eng/Content?WCM_GLOBAL_CONTEXT=/elcano/elcano_in/barometer /barometer+1; and http://www.realinstitutoelcano.org/wps/portal/rielcano_eng /Content?WCM_GLOBAL_CONTEXT=/elcano/elcano_in/barometer/barometer2.

88. Ibid., vol. 13: 59,062; vol. 149: 56,763; vol. 156: 9,062; and vol. 161: 61,016.

89. Ibid., vol. 161: 60,872.

90. It also explains the contents of several video recordings made by the local cell on March 27 but not made public, where its ringleader announced the ending of the truce. See ibid., vol. 161: 60,873; and vol. 162: 61,538–40.

91. In their general report on the Madrid bombings, the Spanish police state: "There is an assumed relationship between the Abu Hafs al-Masri Brigades and the terrorist commando itself which acted in Madrid" since there is an observable coincidence in "the form they called the operative group" and because in ending the truce "the terrorist commando of Madrid acted in consonance" with the March 17 communiqué. *Sumario 20/2004*, vol. 161: 60,920.

92. Manuel R. Torres, "Spain as an Object of Jihadist Propaganda," *Studies in Conflict and Terrorism* 32, no. 11 (November 2009): 940–41.

93. A translation of this audio recording is available at http://www.memri.org /bin/articles.cgi?Area=sd&ID=SP69504.

94. See http://news.bbc.co.uk/2/hi/middle_east/4443364.stm.

95. A translation of this audio recording is available at http://memri.org/bin /latestnews.cgi?ID=SD107406.

96. See http://www.nytimes.com/2009/09/26/world/europe/26germany.html.

97. *Sentencia 65/2007*, 172. In this important judicial document there is not a single mention of "local cell," "independent cell," "independent local cell," or any similar notion.

98. The Joint Task Force Guantánamo assessment on Abu Faraj al-Libi, September 10, 2008, http://projects.nytimes.com/guantanamo/detainees/10017-abu-faraj-al -libi, esp. page 11.

99. Personal oral communications with senior intelligence officers of two Western states, one of them European, December 2011 and, for further documented confirmation, February 2012. Further details are offered in Reinares, *¡Matadlos!*, 137 and 282.

[3]

Operation Crevice in London

PETER R. NEUMANN AND RYAN EVANS

In 2004, Operation Crevice, a codename used by the British Security Service (MI5) and the London Metropolitan Police, became the most extensive counterterrorism operation ever to have taken place in the United Kingdom, involving 34,000 man-hours of surveillance and 45,000 hours of monitoring and transcription over the course of a year.[1] It was directed against a group of (mostly) British Muslims of Pakistani descent who were plotting to carry out bomb attacks against targets in Britain, including the Bluewater shopping center in Kent, the Ministry of Sound nightclub in London, and utilities across the country. Fearing that the plotters were about to turn their plans into reality, the police moved against the cell on March 30, 2004. The subsequent year-long trial in London resulted in five life sentences and two acquittals for the suspected terrorists. In a separate trial in Ottawa, a Canadian member of the cell was sentenced to ten and a half years in prison.

The aim of this chapter is to examine the Crevice plot and determine to what extent it was supported or directed by al-Qaeda. As will be shown, while the Crevice conspirators enjoyed a degree of independence and initiative, links into al-Qaeda structures clearly existed, and these links were significant at every stage of the plot. Of particular importance were al-Qaeda's "middle managers," which represented the operational link between the Crevice cell and the al-Qaeda leadership. It is they who made the plot *leader-led* rather than *leaderless*.

It would be wrong, of course, to imagine the relationship between the plotters and al-Qaeda in traditional command and control terms. Al-Qaeda's influence manifested itself in more subtle—yet no less important—ways: during the cell's formation; in the provision of resources, especially training; and through guidance and direction at key moments in the plot's evolution. In our judgment, had the cell been truly leaderless, members would have failed to gain access to essential resources and direction, and the plot would never have progressed to become a potentially devastating conspiracy.[2]

THE PLOT

Among the many uncertainties surrounding Crevice is the question of who exactly belonged to the cell. Peter Clarke, the former head of the London Metropolitan Police's Counter-Terrorism Command, who led the Crevice investigation, commented that the idea of membership has to be used cautiously because "dozens if not hundreds of people [were coming] in and out of the picture."[3] In fact, the court documents and media reports mention numerous associates, acquaintances, and contacts in the Islamist militant milieu but often fail to make it clear to what extent they were involved or had any knowledge of the plot.

This chapter will focus on the seven core members of the so-called Crawley group (named after the small town in Sussex in which many of them lived) as well as two associates who were based in North America: Jawad Akbar, 20, from Crawley; Salahuddin Amin, 29, from Luton; Mohammed Junaid Babar, 28, from New York; Anthony Garcia, 21, from east London; Nabeel Hussain, 19, from Horle; Mohammed Momin Khawaja, 24, from Ottawa, Canada; Omar Khyam, 23, from Crawley; Shujah Mahmood, 18, from Crawley; and Waheed Mahmood, 32, from Crawley.[4]

Several members of the cell had been involved in jihadist support activities—mostly supplying money and equipment—for some years. According to the British Intelligence and Security Committee's report, MI5 received intelligence in early 2003 about a person named Mohammed Qayum Khan, who was said to be the leader of an "Al Qaeda facilitation network . . . providing financial and logistical support" to the terrorist organization in Afghanistan and Pakistan.[5] The resulting investigation was codenamed Crevice and—almost exactly one year later—led to the identification of a "further key member of the [al-Qaeda facilitation] network," Omar Khyam, who "appeared to be acting as a courier" and later emerged as the ringleader of the plot.[6] In other words, the Crevice investigation had been about al-Qaeda from its inception.

In the course of the British trial, it emerged that some members had gone through training camps in Pakistan before joining the cell, but there is no evidence to suggest that any had been actively involved in military or terrorist operations in Pakistan or anywhere else. This changed during the run-up to the Iraq war, when members of the cell decided that they wanted to carry out acts of terrorism in Britain. In February 2003, Waheed Mahmood—the eldest and perhaps most action-hungry member of the cell—related to Babar that he could not understand why people insisted on coming to Pakistan and Afghanistan for jihad when it could also be done in Britain.[7] Khyam expressed similar sentiments and asked Amin—who had good connections with al-Qaeda—to arrange for him to receive explosives training. According to information provided by Amin when questioned by police, Khyam wanted "to get trained to come back to the UK to do like, you know, eh. I didn't know what their intention was, what they were up to, what they were exactly gonna do in the UK, but I knew that they wanted to get explosives training to do something in the UK."[8]

The cell never agreed on a set of targets, despite having gathered all the materials that were needed to assemble and detonate explosive devices. Initially, Waheed Mahmood suggested poisoning beer at football stadiums.[9] In June 2003, Khyam revealed to Babar that he aspired to launch near-simultaneous attacks against pubs, nightclubs, and trains, but he never went beyond stating general principles.[10] Even eight months later, in February 2004, no firm decisions had been taken. At a meeting in Crawley, Khyam spoke about the idea of attacking utilities, and Akbar raised the possibility of targeting a nightclub, such as the Ministry of Sound in London.[11] Following the Madrid train bombings on March 11, 2004, it seemed clear that members of the cell were yearning to take action sooner rather than later. Waheed Mahmood, who described the Madrid attacks as "absolutely beautiful" in a conversation with Khyam then offered to set off "a little explosion at Bluewater [shopping center in Kent]—tomorrow if you want."[12]

The renewed sense of urgency following the Madrid attacks indicates that the members clearly wanted their actions to have strategic impact and that—contrary to public perception—they had a good idea of how this could be achieved. For example, Akbar's justification for attacking the Ministry of Sound nightclub, as portrayed by the media, was based on his comment that "no one can even turn around and say 'oh they were innocent' those slags dancing around." Numerous reports concluded that he and, by implication, other members of the cell must have been driven by a profound sense of alienation, if not perhaps by some subliminal sexual frustration that additionally manifested itself in the intended violence.[13]

In reality, however, Akbar's rant about "those slags dancing around" was followed by a lengthy and fairly sophisticated explanation of how attacks against places such as Ministry of Sound would meet the cell's strategic objectives. He explained that it was essential for all their actions to "put terror in their hearts . . . put fear in their hearts," and claimed that this could best be accomplished by going "for the social structure." In Akbar's view, a nightclub was the ideal target because it was this kind of place "where every Tom, Dick and Harry goes on a Saturday night," thereby communicating a sense of fear and terror to a much wider audience.[14]

Members of the cell were not sophisticated ideologues, but they clearly had a basic grasp of what the movement was about and how their actions would advance its aims. Khawaja, for example, was familiar with the writings of prominent jihadist thinkers, such as Osama bin Laden's mentor, Abdullah Azzam, and frequently referenced them in his e-mail correspondence and public blog.[15] The underlying motive of the plot appears to have been identical to what Khawaja described as the goal of his own involvement in the jihadist movement, namely, to "[deter] those who wish to destroy Islam and the Muslims."[16] It may be no coincidence, therefore, that the plotters' attention shifted from supporting the jihad in Pakistan and Afghanistan toward carrying out attacks in Britain precisely when tensions over the invasion of Iraq had reached their peak. Britain's participation in what they interpreted as America's latest attempt to subjugate the Muslim world led Khyam and other members of the cell to conclude that "whereas before myself and others made excuses, now we believe the UK and America need to be attacked."[17]

None of the core members of the cell was planning to get involved in suicide attacks. Indeed, the security services decided to move against the cell when it was discovered that members were booking flights for a trip to Pakistan in early April 2004, which was thought to indicate an imminent timeline for the attacks.[18] Around this time, Khyam also visited a storage facility in West London, where 600 kilograms of ammonium nitrate fertilizer had been stockpiled, stating that this would be the final month they needed the storage space.[19] This explains why Crevice is often referred to as "the fertiliser plot."[20]

CELL FORMATION

The cell and the nature of its relationship with al-Qaeda cannot be understood outside the context of jihadist milieus or subcultures, which were thriving in London and Pakistan at the time and facilitated members' association with al-Qaeda's network.

At the beginning of the 2000s, London had come to be known as "Londonistan" for the range and extent of jihadist activities that were tolerated by the British government.[21] It is impossible to say how many groups and networks existed, but it seems clear that the majority of aspiring jihadists gravitated around three individuals: Abu Qatada (Omar Mahmoud Othman), who acted as the spiritual leader for a number of al-Qaeda affiliated groups; Abu Hamza, whose Supporters of the Shariah attracted hundreds of young British Muslims to the Finsbury Park mosque (where he served as imam); and Omar Bakri Mohammed, the leader of al-Muhajiroun, a splinter of the radical group Hizb-ut Tahrir, which emerged in 1996.

The groups that made up the jihadist milieu in London differed in size and outlook, yet they all performed similar functions: they provided individuals or groups with entry points into the organized jihadist scene; they enabled jihadists of different persuasions to connect with one another; and they offered opportunities to establish links to the violent jihad. Al-Qaeda associates were part of this milieu, and while it would be mistaken to label the entire jihadist milieu as al-Qaeda, it seems obvious that being associated with any of the groups significantly shortened the distance between a potential recruit and al-Qaeda.

In some cases, the leaders of these groups might have gone as far as providing formal introductions to al-Qaeda.[22] For the Crevice plotters, however, the primary function of the milieu was to socialize them into the jihadist scene. Khyam's involvement began in 1998, when—as a seventeen-year-old—he started attending events organized by Bakri's al-Muhajiroun, which had been targeting the Langley Green mosque in his hometown, Crawley.[23] It is unlikely that Khyam ever became a full member of al-Muhajiroun—of which there were only 160—but he initially took full advantage of the group's activities and would have counted as one of the 7,000 or so "contacts" that Bakri boasted he had made as a result of al-Muhajiroun's events and other recruitment activities.[24] Indeed, it was through his participation in al-Muhajiroun's activities that he met the much older Waheed Mahmood and became acquainted with other jihadists across the greater London area.[25]

By 1999, Khyam had decided that he wanted to take action. After Waheed Mahmood returned from a brief stay in Pakistan in early 2000, where he mixed with militant groups and received basic weapons training, he introduced Khyam to a group of jihadist activists in Luton.[26] Led by two al-Qaeda associates, Abu Munthir and Qayum Khan, the group was involved in running a logistical support network for violent jihadists. One of its members was Salahuddin Amin, who became part of the Crevice plot. Khyam, in turn, agreed to join the Luton group and started acting as a courier for the network.[27] It was Khyam's involvement in this support network—described by the British authorities as an "Al Qaeda facilitation network"—which led to the discovery of the Crevice cell.

The September 11 attacks and the subsequent Western intervention in Afghanistan prompted many British jihadists to "migrate" from London to Pakistan. Publicly, Bakri rejected any involvement with or support for violence, insisting that his references to jihad had been "taken . . . out of context" and that he could not be held "responsible for everything these people do."[28] In reality, he had initiated the setting up of an office in Pakistan through which British recruits were channeled to the front lines of the confrontation between the American-led coalition and the alliance of al-Qaeda and the Taliban.[29] It is impossible to say precisely how many of Bakri's followers managed to make their way to Afghanistan via Pakistan, but several are reliably known to have died fighting—including one of Khyam's acquaintances from Crawley, Yasir Khan.[30]

Among the Crevice plotters who went to Pakistan during that period was Mohammed Junaid Babar from New York, who left the United States only days after September 11. He was a member of al-Muhajiroun's New York branch and wanted to help with the setting up of that group's Pakistan office.[31] Khyam's friend from Crawley, Waheed Mahmood, moved to Pakistan in October and was followed by Amin in November. In January 2002, Mohammed Momin Khawaja—one of Babar's acquaintances—arrived in Pakistan as well. All were part of the same jihadist circles and had been looking for ways to support al-Qaeda and the Taliban, which meant that they mixed with one another and got to know jihadists from across the world. Indeed, the connection between the North American (Babar and Khawaja) and British plotters (Mahmood and Amin) was made in April 2002, when Babar met Waheed Mahmood.[32]

The remaining members of the Crevice cell were recruited in London between 2002 and 2003. Akbar and Garcia, who were responsible for the plot's finances, were close acquaintances of Khyam. Nabeel Hussain was Akbar's step-cousin, and Shujah Mahmood was Waheed's younger brother.[33] The two youngest members of the cell, Shujah Mahmood and Hussain, played only minor roles in the preparation of the plot. They convinced the jury in the British trial that they had been misled about Khyam's intentions, claiming not to know that his plan had been to carry out terrorist attacks in Britain.[34]

Overall, it seems clear that the cell was the product of a milieu in which ostensibly nonviolent groups such as al-Muhajiroun provided entry points into organized jihadist structures.[35] Being associated with al-Muhajiroun did not limit their contacts to members of that group, nor did it constrain their activism to nonviolent means. On the contrary, it significantly improved their chances of connecting to individuals linked with al-Qaeda, even if the group's leadership played no active role in facilitating such links. Indeed, Khyam's ability to connect with an al-Qaeda support network after becoming involved with al-Muhajiroun and meeting Waheed Mahmood is an excellent illustration of the how the milieu worked.

Khyam and the other members of the Crevice cell would not refer to themselves as "members of al-Qaeda." Nor did al-Qaeda central direct the process of cell formation or its members' deliberations or everyday activities. But, as will be shown in the following sections, the cell's association with—and integration into—the al-Qaeda network proved critical at several key junctures of the plot's evolution.

RESOURCES

This section focuses on the resources that were required to make the plot viable. By resources, we mean not only finance (all of the money was raised by the plotters themselves) but, more importantly, expertise, skills, and less tangible factors such as motivation, focus, and group cohesion. We will argue that al-Qaeda played a critical role in providing resources necessary to advance the plot. Although al-Qaeda's approach was "hands-off," the plot could not have progressed as far as it did without al-Qaeda's facilitation, in particular, the provision of training-camp places.

Khyam received paramilitary training with militants in Pakistan and Afghanistan in the summer of 2001, before the formation of the Crevice cell. Most of the other plotters, however, had never been formally trained and lacked even the most basic knowledge of weapons and explosives. Indeed, most had come to Pakistan precisely because they wanted to acquire this kind of knowledge. Hence, when the decision was taken in early 2003 to carry out operations in Britain, Khyam approached Amin, who—among all the members of the cell—had the best connections into the al-Qaeda network, in order to facilitate access to training camps.[36]

Amin conveyed the request to his superiors, who approved the cell's plans and permitted members to attend two camps in the summer of 2003. The first was held in Kohat in Pakistan's Northwest Frontier Province in May or June 2003. Over the course of two days, Khyam and Amin—together with another man who had no relation with the Crevice cell—received comprehensive training in the use of explosives. Their instructor was a jihadist named Tarik, who taught his students not only about explosive materials and how to turn them into functioning devices but also how to source materials for explosives in a country like Britain, where—he claimed—most of the necessary ingredients could be bought for completely innocent reasons in hardware and paint shops.[37]

The second training camp was held in Malakand in the Northwest Frontier Province of Pakistan in July or August 2003. Amin and Khyam were provided basic military training and taught to handle weaponry, such as light machine guns and rocket-propelled grenade launchers. Undoubtedly less specialized than the camp Khyam and Amin had attended two months earlier, this course was open to a wider range of recruits. With the exception of Amin, Hussain, and Waheed Mahmood, all the members of the Crevice cell were present.[38] It was also at this camp that members of the Crevice plot connected with Mohammed Siddique Khan, the ringleader of the cell that carried out the transit bombings in London on July 7, 2005.[39]

A request by Babar for further training was turned down by Amin's al-Qaeda superiors.[40] Al-Qaeda also did not help with the sourcing of the materials or the construction of the explosive device directly. Indeed, much of the cell members' time during the autumn of 2003 was taken up by attempts to find the right ingredients, experiment with various explosive material, and construct the remote detonators that were needed to launch the bombs.

While al-Qaeda was not directly involved in any of these tasks, there clearly existed a willingness to provide advice when preparations for the plot appeared to have become stuck. In February 2004, for example, Khyam wrote an e-mail to Amin, stating that he had managed to buy the aluminum nitrate (fertilizer) but did not remember what ratios to use when combining it with other ingredients. Amin responded: "You learned it. Why are you asking me? You already learned it." Khyam admitted that he had "forgot[ten] already."[41] As it turned out, Amin had forgotten, too—he asked one of his al-Qaeda superiors, Abu Munthir, who sent an e-mail with the needed information, which was intercepted by the U.S. National Security Agency—prompting the British authorities to step up surveillance and, two months later, break up the cell.[42]

The technical training and oversight provided by al-Qaeda was critical to converting a group of (mostly) clueless young activists into halfway competent operators. The connection with al-Qaeda—and the kind of instruction and training that it facilitated—may not have transformed them into professional terrorists, but it provided the Crevice plotters with just enough technical knowledge and confidence to turn their ideas into a viable plot. In that sense, it was al-Qaeda's training and support that made the difference between mere talk and the ability to carry out a terrorist operation.

The training camps were important in other respects, too. From a purely technical perspective, the training camp in Malakand, in which six of the nine Crevice plotters participated, provided the recruits with no useful skills or expertise. After all, neither machine guns nor grenade launchers were to be used during the planned attacks in England, nor did any member of the cell seek to acquire such weapons after they returned to their home countries. But the experience of the training camp brought together the various individuals as a group, sharpened their focus, and spurred their efforts to put their ideas into practice. According to Babar, for example, what had been a fairly loose group of young men who were joking around and using slang words suddenly turned into a serious and determined conspiracy; after the training-camp indoctrination, "the guys were talking jihad, praying and quoting the Quran. They were saying, 'Let's go kill the kufr [infidel].'"[43] In an e-mail to his fiancée, Khawaja confirmed Babar's description of the camaraderie generated at training: "It was . . . amazing, the best experience in my whole life, cuz u know the . . . hardship purifies the nafs [soul] [sic]."[44]

The training-camp experience also gave the members of the cell a sense that they had become part of something larger and that—like other "graduates" of the camps—they were expected to make good on the investment that had been made in them. In other words, instead of being mere observers, the training camp had made them "foreign mujaheddin"—soldiers of Islam—who had an obligation to carry the struggle forward. Khawaja's e-mails to his fiancée illustrate this transformation. He described in great detail—and with great admiration—the way in which the camp was run and how "some of the bros were kept in Pakistan for specialized . . . training [whereas others were] sent to different part of the world . . . to help out in the jihad worldwide."[45] In another e-mail that was written shortly after he had returned from the camp, he impressed upon his future wife that "you're seeking to marry a guy who is in the J[ihad]. . . . The J is more important to him than anything and everything."[46]

In judging the importance of the training camps, it is essential, therefore, to consider not just the transfer of technical skills but also their social and psychological impact. In this particular case, the plotters' stay at the Malakand camp represented a watershed. It allowed individuals to get to know one another and form a cohesive unit; it imbued them with a sense of mission, drive, and purpose; and it created an unspoken obligation to act. It is, of course, impossible to say what might have happened had they been unable to attend the training camps, but it seems evident that—in addition to the technical skills that were acquired—the training-camp experience significantly reduced the risk of the cell's losing focus or interest or even breaking up by providing the social glue to bind the group together.

GUIDANCE

On paper, the cell's position within the al-Qaeda network was clear. The transcripts from the Canadian trial, which led to the conviction of Khawaja, provide a summary of Babar's assessment, which can be said to reflect the settled consensus of prosecutors and intelligence agencies on both sides of the Atlantic:

> Khyam worked for a man named Q[ayum Khan] who lived in Luton, near London. Q . . . had ties to al Qa'eda. . . . Salahuddin Amin also worked under Q insofar as UK matters were concerned, but under Abu Munthir as concerned Pakistani operations. Munthir [on the other hand] was a leader in Pakistan, who responded to al Qa'eda higher up, Sheikh Abdul Hadi.[47]

Abd al-Hadi al-Iraqi (real name: Nashwan Abdulbaki) was thought to be al-Qaeda's "number three" and the group's main liaison with al-Qaeda in Iraq. Born in Iraq in 1961, he had a long history with al-Qaeda: in the 1990s, he served as a commander and accountant for the group and also ran one of its "guest houses"; in December 2001, he commanded the so-called Arab Brigade, which fought the Northern Alliance and the Western Coalition just outside of Kabul. Following its defeat, al-Hadi managed to escape to Pakistan and was captured in 2006 or 2007, as he tried to make his way to Iraq.[48] In Babar's view, Abdul Hadi was "the ultimate emir on top. . . . But underneath him, there were multiple emirs, three or four . . . and Q was one of those emirs."[49] In that sense, the Crevice plotters represented one of several cells, which—in theory—were fully integrated into al-Qaeda's chain of command.

In practice, of course, the relationship between al-Qaeda central and the Crevice cell was not nearly as clear-cut as Babar's description suggests. Even so, there were at least three occasions on which members of the Crevice cell—principally Khyam and Amin—consulted with their immediate superiors in al-Qaeda, Qayum Khan and Abu Munthir, in order to receive guidance and direction. In February 2003, when members of the cell had decided that they wanted to attack targets in Britain, Amin reported their intention to Abu Munthir who, in turn, consulted with al-Hadi. Munthir reported back to Amin, saying that the priorities were for money and equipment, but that "if they really wanted to . . . go back to the UK and do something there," the leadership would approve it.[50] Several months later, al-Qaeda arranged for members of the cell to participate in the two training camps in Pakistan. In the summer of 2003, Munthir invited Khyam to see him in the tribal areas of Pakistan to discuss their plans. According to Babar, Khyam "didn't have any . . . specific targets, he just had general ideas. So, the plan was to . . . discuss specific targets, how they would be carried out, every—like, just everything like that with Abu Munthir."[51] Khyam returned from the meeting convinced that they had to do multiple bombings, "simultaneous or one after the other on the same day."[52] In a later conversation with Akbar about targeting utilities, Khyam said, "You have to understand it has to be a simultaneous operation to be of effect . . . you have to all be co-ordinated."[53] In February 2004, following Amin's admission that both he and Khyam had forgotten some of the lessons they had learned at the training camp, Abu Munthir advised Amin on how to combine the fertilizer with other bomb-making ingredients in order to produce a functioning explosive device.

More conversations and meetings are likely to have taken place, but the small sample provided here shows that even the most sporadic communication could be of great strategic significance.[54] The Crevice plotters may not have, at any time, received daily orders from their al-Qaeda superiors, but guidance was sought and given at several key junctures of the plot's evolution: at its inception, during the process of target selection, and in the course of its implementation.[55]

Equally important is the degree to which members of the cell believed they were part of the al-Qaeda network and the extent to which they regarded themselves as bound by—and dependent upon—the kind of direction that was given. Several of the communications that were recorded by the British security services when the plot was discovered demonstrate that leading members of the cell clearly saw themselves as part of a chain of command, which meant that—despite the considerable independence and initiative the cell had enjoyed in putting together the plot—nothing was likely to happen unless they received their superiors' go ahead.

A revealing conversation took place between Khyam and the ring-leader of the London transport attacks, Mohammed Siddique Khan, in early 2004. According to the British authorities, members of the Crevice cell met Khan five times in February and March, discussing a wide range of issues, including various scams to raise money for the jihad.[56] It continues to be unclear how much Khan knew about the Crevice plot, but statements in which he advised Khyam to "rip the country apart economically" clearly indicate that he was conscious that they were planning something.[57] Indeed, at one point, Khan confronts Khyam by asking, "You're seriously, basically a terrorist?" Khyam's reply is ambiguous but provides a good idea of how he thought about his own role and that of his cell: "I'm not a terrorist. They're working through us."[58]

By February, it had become obvious to the plotters that their operation was not progressing as smoothly as they had anticipated. Nevertheless, in discussing the plot with Akbar, Khyam issued a strong warning against acting on one's own initiative. Their cell, Khyam pointed out, was just one of several, and it was impossible for them to know how their operation was to be coordinated with the actions of others. He explained: "So now in England, imagine you do something and there's brothers here, you could jeopardize them." He concluded by telling Akbar to be patient and disciplined: "It's better to consult those who are running the jihad. There's a structure so work within the structure."[59]

In a separate conversation with Akbar, which took place at around the same time, Khyam vented his frustration about the lack of progress. In spite of many discussions and the progress that had been made in putting together the bomb, a firm set of targets still had not been agreed upon, nor had they received any clear instructions from their superiors about when to move ahead. The plot, it seemed, was "all over the place," and one of the key missing ingredients—Khyam believed—was the input from the "emirs." Referring to a conversation he had recently had with another member of the cell, Khyam said: "All it needs right now is coordination, back up plans, emirs, all this needs to be put in place, cause right now he's pretty right, nobody knows what's really going on, it's just ideas coming out."[60]

It would be mistaken to interpret the lack of clear guidance in early 2004 as evidence that the cell was leaderless. The opposite is true. If the cell had been truly leaderless, the lack of direction would not have presented an obstacle to moving ahead. It is *precisely because* the Crevice plotters had a longstanding relationship with al-Qaeda, and because they saw themselves as part of a network and structure within which they could operate, that the temporary lack of guidance produced confusion and dithering and deprived them of the confidence they had gained at earlier stages of the plot's evolution.

The Crevice plot was to be carried out by a group of young men who showed considerable initiative and determination in putting together a viable terrorist operation, which—if successful—would have killed hundreds of innocent people and created enormous political, economic, and social costs. However, simply because the plot was conceived of by a group of local men who showed initiative and determination does not imply that they were acting on their own, or leaderless. As this chapter has shown, the Crevice cell had an active relationship with al-Qaeda operatives from the very beginning; it was recruited from milieus of which al-Qaeda was an integral part; it drew on al-Qaeda's resources; it followed al-Qaeda's instruction and guidance; and it consciously regarded itself as part of the wider al-Qaeda network. After all, it was the cell's connection to al-Qaeda that led to the discovery of the plot.

Furthermore, it seems clear that the plot would have followed an entirely different trajectory had al-Qaeda not been part of the equation. Al-Qaeda sanctioned attacks against Britain and prescribed the format—simultaneous attacks—in which they were to be carried out. It facilitated the plotters' participation in training camps, providing them with bomb-making skills, and formed them into a cohesive unit that had the drive, focus, and sense of mission that were needed in order for their plans to be realized. It helped members overcome difficulties in constructing the explosive device that was going to be used in the attacks. It failed to provide clear guidance during the implementation phase and, thus, prevented the attacks from being carried out.

It seems obvious, therefore, that it was al-Qaeda's actions—or, in the last case, its lack thereof—which determined the plot's trajectory. The story of Crevice is not one of leaderless jihad. Rather, al-Qaeda played a critical role in the plot's formation to its near execution. There are numerous policy implications and strategic recommendations that follow from this analysis. Three are particularly important.

First, governments must pay more attention to jihadist milieus. In the Crevice case, the process of cell formation relied on the existence of a jihadist subculture in which boundaries between violent and ostensibly nonviolent organizations were fluid. As a result, members of the cell encountered few obstacles in connecting to al-Qaeda and integrating into its network. There can be no doubt that the British authorities' tolerance of these subcultures until the mid-2000s is one of the reasons the country has been faced with a consistent challenge from al-Qaeda-related and -inspired terrorism. The priority for any government must be to prevent these subcultures from emerging as a precursor to more violent tendencies. Where they already exist, security forces need to understand, monitor, and aim to disrupt the milieu as a whole rather than separating and concentrating exclusively on its al-Qaeda component.

Second, security forces need to focus on al-Qaeda's middle management. The Crevice plot demonstrates that it was not al-Hadi or other members of the al-Qaeda leadership who forged the relationship with the plotters, but middle managers such as Abu Munthir and Qayum Khan. In this case, it was the middle managers who were the organization's center of gravity because they maintained the operational link between the leadership and the grassroots members. Arguably, if the middle managers—rather than al-Qaeda's top leadership—had been removed, the plot would have come to a standstill. For policy makers and security forces, it is essential, therefore, to conceive of al-Qaeda as a multilayered organization in which middle managers can have an important role in running the everyday business of terrorist operations. To disregard them and concentrate on the top leadership alone would be to misunderstand the dynamics of al-Qaeda as an organization.

Third, the disruption of training camps should remain a strategic priority. The Crevice case demonstrates how important the training-camp experience was in the plot's evolution. Not only did it provide essential technical skills without which the members would have been unable to produce a functioning explosive device, it also represented an important psychological watershed. Bonding at the camp helped members of the cell connect to one another and develop a strong sense that they were now soldiers of Islam who had an obligation to take their mission forward. These observations echo other accounts of jihadist training-camp experiences and underline the need to keep disrupting the camp structures in Pakistan and prevent them from emerging or reemerging in places like Yemen, Somalia, and Afghanistan.[61]

The Crevice case also reminds us how vital it is to keep monitoring the evolution of al-Qaeda's structures, which have undoubtedly changed over the course of the group's existence. There can be no question that the relationship between the plotters and al-Qaeda would have been vastly different had the plot taken place just five years earlier. The Crevice cell enjoyed a degree of freedom and initiative that might have been inconceivable in an earlier period. But to say that it was leaderless would be a profound misrepresentation of the subtle dynamics that we have described.

NOTES

1. Intelligence and Security Committee (ISC), *Could 7/7 Have Been Prevented? Review of the Intelligence on the London Terrorist Attacks on 7 July 2005* (London: HMSO, 2009), 9.

2. In arriving at this conclusion, the authors sifted through all publicly available materials and statements dealing with Crevice, which included—but were by no means limited to—trial exhibits and court records from the United Kingdom and Canada. Other important sources were a 2009 report of the British Parliament's Intelligence and Security Committee, which provided additional information on Crevice and its relationships with other Islamist militant cells, as well as credible and well-sourced media reports. In addition, a first draft of this chapter was reviewed by Peter Clarke, the former head of the London Metropolitan Police's Counter-Terrorism Command, who led the Crevice investigation. Clarke's comments and insights were enormously helpful in making sure that the information provided in the chapter provides an accurate reflection of the full spectrum of evidence that was available to the police and intelligence services at the time. Readers, however, should be under no illusion. Even authoritative sources, such as court documents, have inconsistencies and contradictions and sometimes offer no more than snapshots of the cell's connections and relationships. The full story of Operation Crevice may not be told for many years—if ever. In the meantime, this chapter represents our best possible account.

3. Peter Clarke, correspondence with authors, September 2009. Clarke's successor, Andy Hayman, confirmed this impression in his recently published memoirs. See Andy Hayman and Margaret Gilmore, *The Terrorist Hunters* (London: Bantam Press, 2009), 284.

4. All ages are of the time of the arrests in 2004. The British trial resulted in five life sentences. Khawaja was sentenced to ten and a half years in a Canadian court. Nabeel Hussain and Shujah Mahmood were found not guilty, and Babar turned against his former comrades and served as the prosecution's "star witness" in both the Canadian and British trials. See R v. Khyam et al., Judgement, Supreme Court of Judicature, Court of Appeal (Criminal Division), July 23, 2008, 3, 28.

5. ISC, *Could 7/7 Have Been Prevented?*, 7.

6. ISC, *Could 7/7 Have Been Prevented?*, 7; also R v. Khyam, 2–3. According to the prosecution in the British trial, the network funneled funds and supplies such as winter gear to the terrorist group; see HMG v. Khyam et al., Opening Note, March 21, 2006, 23, 60–61.

7. HMG v. Khyam et al., 11.

8. Extracts of police interview, Salahuddin Amin, Paddington Green Police Station, February 8, 2005.

9. "Operation Crevice Timeline," *Ottawa Citizen,* June 24, 2008.

10. HMG v. Khyam et al., 13–14.

11. Extracts of listening devices placed at Colley House, February 22, 2004.

12. HMG v. Khyam et al., 32.

13. See, for example, Rosie Cowan, "British Suspects Considered Blowing Up Club, Court Told," *Guardian*, March 23, 2006.

14. Extracts of listening devices placed at Colley House.

15. Ian Macleod, "Khawaja Awaits Fate. Verdict Today in U.K.-Related Terror Case," *Canwest News Service*, October 29, 2008.

16. Khawaja, quoted in HM v. Mohammad Momin Khawaja, Reasons for Judgment, Ontario Superior Court of Justice, October 29, 2008, 7, 16.

17. Khyam, quoted in Sarah Knapton, "Dateline London: Operation Crevice," *Canwest News Service*, June 24, 2008.

18. The prosecution in the British trial claimed that the trip was to precede the attacks, but the Intelligence and Security Committee concludes that the plotters' intention had been to go to Pakistan after the attacks. See HMG v. Khyam et al., 54; ISC, *Could 7/7 Have Been Prevented?*, 18. The appeal court found that the "implementation of the project was delayed" for reasons that have not yet been made public. See R v. Khyam, 3.

19. HMG v. Khyam et al, 53.

20. See, for example, "Fertiliser Plot Suspect Refuses to Give Evidence," *Daily Telegraph*, September 18, 2006.

21. "What's the Risk to London?," *BBC News*, September 8, 2009, http://www.bbc .co.uk/london/content/articles/2005/09/08/kurtbarling_londonrisk_feature.shtml.

22. Abu Hamza, for example, frequently bragged that his "letter of recommendation" could guarantee acceptance at al-Qaeda's notorious Khalden training camp. Bakri repeatedly stated that his organization had created a "Jihad Network" through which people could gain access to training camps all over the Middle East and Asia. Abu Qatada was considered a senior figure in the al-Qaeda movement and has often been referred to by security services and the media as "Osama bin Laden's Ambassador to Europe." See Sean O'Neill and Daniel McGrory, *The Suicide Factory: Abu Hamza and the Finsbury Park Mosque* (London: Harper Collins, 2006), 97–98; Mike Whine, "Will the Ban on the Al Muhajiroun Successor Organisations Work?," *ICT Brief*, August 8, 2006, http://www.ict.org.il/Articles/tabid/66/Articlsid/224/currentpage/9/Default.aspx; "Britain "Sheltering Al-Qaeda Leader," *BBC News*, July 8, 2002, http://news.bbc.co.uk/1/hi/uk/2115371.stm.

23. Nicola Woodcock, "The Schoolboy Cricketer Who Converted to a Deadly New Game," *Times* (London), May 1, 2007.

24. Quintan Wiktorowicz, *Radical Islam Rising: Muslim Extremism in the West* (Boulder, Colo.: Rowman and Littlefield, 2005), 10.

25. See Jeevan Vasagar, "The Five Who Planned to Bomb UK Targets," *Guardian*, April 20, 2007; Knapton, "Dateline London: Operation Crevice."

26. Knapton, "Dateline London: Operation Crevice"; also see "Profile: Omar Khyam," *BBC News*, April 20, 2007, http://news.bbc.co.uk/1/hi/uk/6149794.stm.

27. ISC, *Could 7/7 Have Been Prevented?*, 7; HM v. Mohammad Momin Khawaja, 11.

28. Bakri, quoted in Jamie Doward and Andrew Wander, "The Network," *Observer* (London), May 6, 2007.

29. Whine, "Will the Ban on the Al Muhajiroun Successor Organisations Work?"

30. John Steele and Stewart Payne, "More British Muslims 'Missing in Action,'" *Daily Telegraph* (London), October 31, 2001.

31. HMG v. Khyam et al., 7–8; HM v. Mohammad Momin Khawaja, 8.

32. HMG v. Khyam et al., 5, 10, 35–36; Vasagar, "The Five Who Planned to Bomb UK Targets."

33. R v. Khyam, 35, 36.

34. See Vasagar, "The Five Who Planned to Bomb UK Targets"; "Five Get Life Over UK Bomb Plot," *BBC News*, April 30, 2007, http://news.bbc.co.uk/1/hi/uk/6195914.stm; also see "Profile: Shujah Mahmood," *BBC News*, April 30, 2007, http://news.bbc.co.uk/1/hi/uk/6149796.stm.

35. Just how tightly knit the jihadist milieu in London had been can also be seen in the number of terrorist investigations that were launched *as a result* of Operation Crevice. The British Intelligence and Security Committee's report lists four major investigations, including one in which the main suspect "was assessed to be a significant Al-Qaida-linked facilitator and radicaliser who tried to supply Al-Qaida with funds." Another contact of the Crevice cell was Mohammed Siddique Khan, the ringleader of the terrorist attacks in London on July 7, 2005, who first came to the

attention of the British authorities as a result of his meetings with Khyam and others in Crawley in February and March 2004. See ISC, *Could 7/7 Have Been Prevented?*, 13.

36. Extracts of police interview, Salahuddin Amin; HM v. Mohammad Momin Khawaja, 11.

37. HMG v. Khyam et al., 14–15, 37–38; extracts of police interview, Salahuddin Amin.

38. HMG v. Khyam et al., 13, 43, 49; HM v. Mohammad Momin Khawaja, 9–10; Knapton, "Dateline London: Operation Crevice"; Jim Brown, "Ties Alleged Between Khawaja and UK Terror Cell," *Waterloo Region Record*, July 2, 2008.

39. Jim Brown, "London Suicide Bomber Went to Same Training Camp as Khawaja," *Canadian Press*, June 30, 2008. They also met another young man from England, Zeeshan Siddiqui—better known as Imran—who was regarded as mentally unstable and put forward by Khyam as a suitable candidate for "martyrdom" operations. Upon his return to Britain, Siddiqui was put under house arrest but managed to escape. He continues to be on the run. See Matthew Taylor, "Man on the Run from Control Order 'Was Asked to Bomb Underground,'" *Guardian*, June 15, 2007.

40. HMG v. Khyam et al., 16.

41. Extracts of police interview, Salahuddin Amin; HMG v. Khyam et al., 39–40.

42. HMG v. Khyam et al., 40; ISC, *Could 7/7 Have Been Prevented?*, 7; Macleod, "Khawaja Awaits Fate."

43. Knapton, "Dateline London: Operation Crevice."

44. HM v. Mohammad Momin Khawaja, 10.

45. Ibid.

46. Donna Casery, "A Case of 'Undue Haste,'" *Ottawa Sun*, October 30, 2008.

47. HM v. Mohammad Momin Khawaja, 11.

48. At the time of this writing, al-Hadi is detained at Guantánamo Bay. See "Unclassified Summary of Evidence for Administrative Review Board in the Case of Salem al Hadi," Office for the Administrative Review of the Detention of Enemy Combatants at U.S. Naval Base at Guantanamo Bay, August 22, 2007, http://www.dod.gov/pubs/foi /detainees/csrt_arb/08-F-0481_FactorsDocsBates101-200.pdf, 41.

49. Ian Cobain and Jeevan Vasagar, "Free—the Man Accused of Being an Al Qaida Leader, aka 'Q,'" *Guardian*, May 1, 2007.

50. Extracts of police interview, Salahuddin Amin.

51. HM v. Mohammad Momin Khawaja, 11.

52. Knapton, "Dateline London: Operation Crevice."

53. Extracts of listening devices placed at Colley House, March 10, 2004, 6.

54. This includes one in which Abu Munthir is alleged to have approached Amin with the request to buy a so-called "dirty bomb" from mafia elements in Belgium. See HMG v. Khyam et al., 38–39.

55. It is worth noting that when the plotter's homes were raided, the authorities found winter and outdoor gear, indicating that—even while they were plotting to

launch attacks in the UK—they continued to collect and direct supplies to al-Qaeda overseas. See HMG v. Khyam et al., 60–61.

56. ISC, *Could 7/7 Have Been Prevented?*, 22.

57. Knapton, "Dateline London: Operation Crevice."

58. The conversation continues with Khan saying, "Who are? There's no one higher than you." Unfortunately, Khyam's response to this comment has not been made available. See Knapton, "Dateline London: Operation Crevice."

59. Duncan Gardham, "The Crawley Targets," *Daily Telegraph* (London), May 1, 2007.

60. Extracts of listening devices placed at Colley House, March 10, 2004.

61. See, for example, Omar Nasiri, *Inside the Jihad: My Life with Al Qaeda* (London: Basic Books, 2008).

[4]

Dhiren Barot and Operation Rhyme

LINDSAY CLUTTERBUCK

The investigation into the activities of Dhiren Barot and his fellow conspirators, generally known in the United Kingdom by its police codename of "Operation Rhyme," lasted just under seven weeks. Dhiren Barot, a Hindu convert to Islam brought up in the U.K. since he was a small child, was a key figure in Operation Rhyme because of both his involvement as their leader and his past terrorist-related activities and long-standing connections to al-Qaeda in Pakistan. These links stretched back to the mid-1990s, and during early 2004 he intended to put the knowledge and experience he gained since then to full use in the new environment created by the events of 9/11. He is therefore a transitional figure, linking the "old," centralized al-Qaeda before 9/11 with its more diffuse counterpart of 2001 and onward.

Barot acknowledged the debt he owed to al-Qaeda. In a document setting out his concept of how to carry out terrorist attacks, he observed that "it was selected by applying methods and parameters [that he] learnt from observing senior planners."[1] These planners included Khalid Sheikh Mohammed, believed to have been the main inspiration behind the 9/11 plot, and Riduan Ibn Isamuddin ("Hambali") from Jemaah Islamiyah, the al-Qaeda-linked group that instigated the bomb attacks in Bali in 2002 that led to the deaths of 202 victims.[2]

Barot was to make good use of the skills he had learned and the contacts he had made in his preparations to carry out a series of terrorist attacks in the U.K., probably scheduled to occur toward the end of 2004. Operation Rhyme commenced earlier in the year, on June 15, when Barot first came under surveillance in the U.K., and it ended on August 3 when he and twelve others were arrested. Two weeks later, eight people were charged with a number of offenses related to terrorist activity, including conspiracy to commit murder. Of the remainder, two were released without being charged, two were rearrested and charged with possessing forged documents, and one was charged with possessing a prohibited weapon.

In November 2006, Barot pleaded guilty at the Central Criminal Court and was sentenced to forty years in prison (later reduced on appeal to thirty years). Six of his coconspirators followed the same course in 2007 and pleaded guilty: Nadeem Tarmohamed, Abdul Aziz Jalil, Junade Feroze, Omar Abdul Rahman, Mohammed Naveed Bhati, and Zia ul-Haq. A seventh individual arrested at the same time, Qaisar Shaffi, was found guilty at a separate trial in June 2007. Of these conspirators, Barot, Tarmohamed, and Shaffi were also indicted in the United States on charges related to an earlier terrorist conspiracy.[3] There is little doubt that Barot was the principal plotter, and in court he was characterized as the "general," with Feroze, Jalil, and Tarmohamed acting as his "lieutenants" and the remainder of the conspirators presumably filling the role of foot soldiers.[4] It was also alleged in court that there were others involved in the plot but that the defendants were "the most prominent among that team."[5]

In terms of their backgrounds, the plotters' ages ranged from twenty-one to thirty-one. Most were born in the U.K. of Pakistani descent, and most lived in west London (Feroze lived in Blackburn, Lancashire).[6] They were also well educated: four held degrees, one was studying for a degree, and another was a postgraduate student. The subjects they studied encompassed architecture and planning, graphical information design, information systems, manufacturing engineering, and modeling and analysis. Clearly, Barot had assembled a team with the intelligence and skills required to help him achieve his objective. Junade Feroze appeared to be the exception, but his utility lay elsewhere. His family business was a workshop and garage, giving Barot "a mechanic on my team" and access to tools and equipment.[7]

At first glance, Operation Rhyme appears to be a straightforward security operation against a conspiracy headed by Dhiren Barot, whose terrorist activities in the U.K. did not progress beyond the initial research phase. However, by placing the plot within the historical context of how terrorist cells and violent jihadist activities developed in the U.K. between 1995 and 2008, Operation Rhyme can be seen to be indicative of a number of trends in the evolution of British terrorist plots. At the same time, the operation, which spanned three countries to identify and target Barot and his team, can now be better assessed to elucidate its lessons for future international counterterrorism operations.

Operation Rhyme is important for three main reasons. First, it revealed the existence of a local violent jihadist group within the U.K. whose intention was to carry out mass-casualty attacks, and it provided chilling insights into how they intended to achieve it. Second, in hindsight, the foiled plot was an early clue to an emerging pattern wherein active preparations for terrorism in the U.K. became closely interlinked with terrorist activity in Pakistan. From at least mid-2004, the planning and preparation of terrorist attacks in the U.K. was encouraged, aided, and abetted by violent jihadist groups and individuals in Pakistan, many connected to al-Qaeda.

By December 2008, the pattern had become apparent enough for the then prime minister of the U.K., Gordon Brown, to state publicly, "Three quarters of the most serious plots investigated by the British authorities have links to Al Qaeda in Pakistan."[8] A pattern had become clear. Over time, a mechanism had arisen in Pakistan that enabled those residents and citizens of the U.K. eager to partake in violent jihad and who had traveled to Pakistan in order to carry it out in Afghanistan and Kashmir, to come directly under the influence of others there who were steeped in the global jihadist ideology of al-Qaeda. They had practical skills in explosives and bomb making, and these were passed on to selected individuals. In turn, they were encouraged to return home to the U.K. to put these skills to use to attack targets within the U.K. rather than in the countries they originally intended. The consequence of this combination of factors was the production of real plans and real preparations to mount terrorist attacks within the U.K. and against its inhabitants.

Finally, this plot is important because it shows clearly that al-Qaeda was instrumental in developing Dhiren Barot into a competent and trusted terrorist-operations planner. Barot believed he was acting on its behalf and demonstrated confidence that his proposed attacks in the

U.K. would at least meet with the approval of al-Qaeda and additionally attract its support and assistance. Operation Rhyme also revealed that during the planning and preparation phases for the attacks by al-Qaeda in the United States on September 11, 2001, Barot conducted surveillance and reconnaissance on its behalf on a variety of other targets in New York and Washington.

Operation Rhyme showed that both the U.K. and United States were under active assessment as targets for mass-casualty terrorist attacks and that one of the methods being considered was a radioactive "dirty bomb." It also demonstrated that the leader of the conspiracy, Dhiren Barot, was meticulous in his targeting and planning activities and had long-standing connections to al-Qaeda. Moreover, he was actively seeking the approval and support of al-Qaeda as a prelude to carrying out the attacks. Consequently, Rhyme revealed a significant plot, and—if it had come to fruition in any of the ways envisaged by its chief planner—it would have resulted in great destruction and many casualties.

OPERATION RHYME IN CONTEXT

From the early 1990s onward, an increasing number of citizens and residents of the U.K. involved themselves in violent jihad and terrorism. Initially, they traveled to other countries and regions to do so, including Bosnia, Chechnya, and Kashmir. For example, Andrew Rowe, a London-born convert to Islam of Jamaican descent who had fought in Chechnya and Bosnia, was convicted in September 2004 of possessing material for terrorist purposes.[9] In August 1999, a new development emerged when eight Britons and two Algerians were convicted in Yemen of planning a campaign of terrorism against Western targets.[10] By the end of the 1990s, the number of U.K. "jihadis" had increased, and their destination of choice became Pakistan, where they hoped to receive military training from al-Qaeda and other similar groups. Throughout this period, the U.K. was not targeted for attack by violent jihadists from within or outside. With the arrival of the new millennium, the situation changed yet again.

In November 2000, two men were arrested in Manchester. They were accused of conspiring to cause explosions and possessing explosive material. One suspect, Moinul Abedin, was convicted and sentenced to twenty years imprisonment for possessing a substantial quantity of HMTD explosives, detonators, and electrical timers. Moinul Abedin was a U.K. resident who had lived in Birmingham since his parents had moved from Bangladesh when he was two years old. At the time, there was no evidence indicating his potential target or targets, nor of any link between Abedin and any terrorist organization.[11] By 2003, a much clearer picture had emerged, prompting the director of the U.K. Security Service (MI5) to state, "It is not known for what purpose they intended this explosive but it is certain that it was for use in the UK."[12] In August 2006, the home secretary, John Reid, went even further, stating publicly that this was the first "Al Qaeda plot" planned in and targeted against the U.K.[13] If it was the first plot to target the U.K. that originated with al-Qaeda, it was certainly not the last.

By the time Operation Rhyme commenced, the police and Security Service had dealt with a number of terrorist conspiracies aimed at initiating attacks in the U.K. The first significant plot resulted in eight individuals charged in January 2002 in connection with a conspiracy to manufacture and use the poison ricin on the public (Operation Springbourne).[14] Another seven individuals were charged in March 2004 with conspiring to cause explosions after 600 kg of ammonium nitrate fertilizer and other bomb-making materials were seized from a self-storage depot in West London (Operation Crevice).[15]

At the subsequent trials, seven suspects were acquitted of the ricin conspiracy and one, Kamal Bourgas, an Algerian believed to have strong links to al-Qaeda, was found guilty. At a previous trial he was also found guilty of the murder of a police Special Branch officer, whom he stabbed to death during his arrest at a house in Manchester.[16] Five individuals from Operation Crevice were found guilty of possessing ammonium nitrate and conspiracy to cause explosions. They were led by Omar Khyam, a U.K. citizen of Pakistani descent with strong links to al-Qaeda dating back over several years.[17] These two cases show not only how the threat to the U.K. from terrorists driven by violent jihadist ideology began to manifest itself but also how the threat evolved in the aftermath of 9/11. Up to and including Operation Springbourne, almost all the most serious conspiracies in the U.K. seemed to emanate from groups and individuals who either were from or closely linked to North Africa, particularly Algeria. With the advent of Operation Crevice, the center of gravity of the threat changed, with a steep decline in the involvement of groups focused on North Africa (although individuals still continued to feature in conspiracies). At the same time, there was a rapid expansion of involvement by groups and individuals of Pakistani origin or descent. Operation Rhyme quickly demonstrated to the police and Security Service that the change in the origins of the conspirators was an emerging trend and that al-Qaeda was indeed actively trying to carry out attacks in the U.K.

DHIREN BAROT AND HIS EARLY CONNECTIONS TO AL-QAEDA

Barot was born in India in 1972, emigrating to the U.K. with his parents a year later.[18] Brought up as a Hindu, he converted to Islam sometime before September 1995, when he left the U.K. to undertake paramilitary and terrorist training in Pakistan.[19] At some stage after this, he appears to have taken part in paramilitary actions in Kotti, Kashmir, and in 1998 served as "a lead instructor at a jihadi training camp in Afghanistan."[20] As a consequence of his actions in Pakistan and Kashmir, Barot became a protégé of Khalid Sheikh Mohammed, a man described by the *9/11 Commission Report* as a "terrorist entrepreneur" and "the principal architect of the 9/11 attacks."[21]

In 1998 or 1999, Barot spent some time in Kuala Lumpur, Malaysia. with Riduan Ibn Isamuddin, better known as "Hambali." Hambali was a key figure in Jemaah Islamiyah (JI), a group closely associated with al-Qaeda, and his specific role was to coordinate terrorism in Southeast Asia by acting in concert with al-Qaeda.[22] Hambali had close operational connections to Khalid Sheikh Mohammed, which were revealed in early 2002 when a plot to crash an airliner into the tallest skyscraper in Los Angeles was thwarted. Khalid Sheikh Mohammed had devised it, and Hambali was to provide the operatives from within JI to carry it out.[23] In 1999, Barot attended Camp Hudaybiyah, a terrorist training camp in the Philippines run by the Egyptian group al-Jamaah al-Islamiyah.[24] It is reasonable to speculate that this training opportunity was the result of the connections he made with Khalid Sheikh Mohammed and that Barot became known to KSM's nephew, Musaad Aruchi, a man who also appeared to be well connected within the al-Qaeda "operational planning" network.

Barot then began to operationalize his training in terrorism on behalf of al-Qaeda, and in June 2000 he applied for and received admission to a college in New York. On August 17, 2000, he traveled from the United Kingdom to the United States with Nadeem Tarmohamed, a long-standing friend and a coconspirator in Operation Rhyme. They visited New York City and Washington, D.C., and on September 5 Tarmohammed returned to the U.K. Barot remained in the United States for a number of weeks, eventually returning to the U.K. on November 14. Whatever else he did in this period, he did not attend the college in New York.[25]

On March 11, 2001, Barot returned to the United States, arriving once again in New York. This time Qaisar Shaffi accompanied him, another future Rhyme conspirator. Shaffi became ill on April 3 and went to a hospital in New York. He returned to the U.K. the same day, leaving Barot behind. The next day, Nadeem Tarmohamed arrived once more in New York. Barot and Tarmohamed then returned together to the U.K. on April 8.[26]

There is every possibility that the information gathering and surveillance needed for the U.S. target selection were carried out by these three individuals during this period. However, five months later the plans they were preparing were made redundant by the events of September 11. It is reasonable to assume that some time after 9/11, Barot turned his attention to the U.K. and decided that he was not only going to research and plan a terrorist attack operation against targets there, he was going to put it into action as well.

EVENTS UNFOLD

The first critical juncture for Operation Rhyme occurred in Karachi, Pakistan, with the arrest of Musaad Aruchi on June 12, 2004. Aruchi is the nephew of Khalid Sheikh Mohammad and a cousin of Ramzi Yousef, the main instigator of the first World Trade Center bomb attack in 1993.[27] It appears that despite his extensive high-level connections, Aruchi was quick to cooperate with his captors because on June 15, Dhiren Barot was "first identified and placed under surveillance in the UK."[28] However, it was another arrest in Lahore on July 13, occurring as a consequence of Aruchi's arrest, that brought Barot under close scrutiny from the U.K. authorities.

On July 13, Mohammed Naeem Noor Khan, a key figure linked to al-Qaeda, which valued him for his technological expertise with the Internet and World Wide Web, was arrested in Lahore, Pakistan.[29] He worked for al-Qaeda as "a key communications facilitator for the network, transmitting important information from Al Qaeda members in Afghanistan and the Pakistani tribal areas to operatives around the world."[30] An analysis of the material found on a laptop computer in his possession revealed a large amount of data relating to terrorism. On it were several files that laid out in meticulous detail how and where a series of mass-casualty terrorist attacks could be undertaken against a wide variety of targets in the United States and the United Kingdom.[31]

Targets in the United States had been both extensively researched and closely examined on the ground by an individual known as "E a B," the author of these so-called research reports. The targets included the New York Stock Exchange; the main offices of Citigroup in New York; the Prudential World Headquarters in Newark, New Jersey; and, in Washington, D.C, the International Monetary Fund (IMF) and the International Bank for Reconstruction and Development (IBRD).[32]

Perhaps the most worrying file concerned information on the means to acquire, construct, and use a radiological dispersal device (RDD), a weapon otherwise known as a "dirty bomb." Al-Qaeda's interest in radiological and nuclear weapons had been made clear by Osama bin Laden in a November 2001 interview and in a number of documents and other evidence that began to surface in the aftermath of the coalition invasion of Afghanistan later that month.[33] The author of all of the recently discovered computer files was Esa al-Britani (hence "E a B"), but in reality he was Dhiren Barot. He also called himself Issa al-Hindi, although it is not clear how and when the authorities knew that all these names referred to the same individual.

By the time that the files surfaced after the arrest of Mohammed Naeem Noor Khan, Barot had been under active surveillance in the U.K. for a month in a joint police and Security Service operation. During that period, it quickly became apparent that Barot and some of his regular contacts were not only knowledgeable of antisurveillance measures but were constantly putting them into practice in their daily life.[34] On one occasion, Barot and Abdul Aziz Jalil made a four-hour journey to use an Internet café in Swansea, South Wales, returning to the London area after less than an hour there.[35]

Furthermore, Barot appeared to be at the head of a group of other individuals, some of them with specialized skills and knowledge in their own right, who actively supported his activities and carried out his instructions. The most senior members were his three lieutenants, Junade Feroze, Abdul Aziz Jalil, and Nadeem Tarmohamed. Four other members played more specialized roles: Omar Abdul Rahman, Qaisar Shaffi, Naveed Bhatti, and Zia ul-Haq. At their trial, the prosecution alleged that there may have been others who were involved but these seven represented "the most prominent among that team."[36]

Barot was an extremely difficult surveillance subject, and on July 28, 2004, he disappeared from the radar of both the police and Security Service.[37] A decision was made that the risk to the public of allowing Barot to remain at large was too great and that as soon as he was relocated, he would be arrested. He resurfaced on August 3 and was arrested while having his hair cut in Willesden, North London.[38] His network was then quickly rounded up, with thirteen arrests made in London, Luton, Blackburn, and Watford. Under the authority of the Terrorism Act 2000, investigators had fourteen days to charge or release the Rhyme conspirators.

Investigating detectives raced against time to ensure that enough primary evidence was accumulated to charge as many of the suspects as possible. An intensive, international effort began to turn intelligence and information into evidence sufficient to bring substantive criminal charges reflecting the gravity of the suspected offences. Barot and seven coconspirators were charged with conspiracy to murder and other offences almost as the deadline was reached.[39] One additional conspirator was charged with possessing a prohibited weapon; two were released under the Terrorism Act and rearrested for possessing forged documents; and two more were released without charge.[40]

THE "E A B" COMPUTER FILES

The computer documents produced in evidence at the trial of Dhiren Barot fall into two categories: the selection of potential targets in the United States and potential attack methods against targets in the U.K.[41] A further document referred specifically to radioactivity and its potential use in a radiological dispersed device (RDD). Besides the different target areas, there is a significant difference between the four U.S.-related documents and the U.K. ones.[42] The U.S. documents, dating from 2000, form a series focused on specific buildings and localities as potential targets for attack. They present a range of information to assist in the further selection of a target and form the basis on which a plan of attack could be developed. They all follow a similar format, consisting of basic geographic and architectural features, times of opening and public access, and the overt security measures observed. Finally, a section entitled "Vital Statistics" covers twenty-six subtopics on further planning that would be needed to determine how a terrorist attack could effectively be carried out. The collection is best characterized as target research documents, put together using open-source research plus surveillance and reconnaissance carried out on the ground at each site, with the aim of using them to inform any future operational planning.

The U.K.-related document signed by "E a B" is entitled "Rough Presentation for Gas Limos Project," and it differs greatly from the U.S. target research documents in structure, content, and aim. The goal of the document is to present a workable methodology for terrorist attacks using vehicle-borne improvised explosive devices (VBIED). It presents a series of detailed options on how (and to a much lesser extent where) mass-casualty attacks could be most effectively carried out. In contrast to the U.S. documents, it is not intended to help identify targets where an attack may best be carried out. The author points out that it is "a very small summarised account of a project" and that it has taken a year to complete the work as "the details have been checked multiple times." It is part of a plan for action.

In the document, "E a B" makes his overall aim very clear when presenting his final conclusions for all the projects he suggests: to carry out "synchronised, concurrent execution on the same day at the same time." In his view, they "are all realistic projects" that can be executed "if the go ahead is given and the resources made available." He ends the report by summarizing the next steps as "to simply prepare and be involved 'in the completion of the job' if it is accepted and approved."

The existence of the "Rough Presentation" document does not just imply a higher authority whose approval to go ahead was sought by Barot; it demonstrates Barot's belief that this authority had the financial resources to make his plan a reality. In the chapter of the "Rough

Presentation" devoted to "Manpower and Costs," he sets out a requirement for a substantial sum of money, "£60,000 (minimum)" in order to carry out the operation. He must have therefore been expecting to put his proposal to an audience that could grant him this level of funding. A second financial implication arises because Barot is not considering suicide attacks. This is clear as he makes various references to a "getaway" and recommends that a "withdrawal plan should be devised." More money would need to be allocated for this "additional expense" on top of the £60,000 already required.

With hindsight, a tentative timescale for Barot's activities can be constructed. After the his conviction, the police national coordinator for terrorist investigations, Deputy Assistant Commissioner Peter Clarke, stated, "We believe that early in 2004 he presented his plans to AQ leadership with the intention of getting permission and the resources to mount attacks in the UK."[43] As Barot is known to have traveled to Pakistan in February 2004, using the false name of Haris Feroze, this must have been when he gave his presentation to al-Qaeda.[44] Barot states in the "Rough Presentation" document it had taken him "one year" to complete it, so it can be inferred that he must have commenced work on it at least a year before, i.e., in early 2003. Interestingly, Mohammed Naeem Noor Khan is alleged to have been in the U.K. during at least January 2003, enrolling in a "human resource management course at City University in central London." After four lectures, he ceased to attend.[45] It is conceivable that his presence in the U.K. at the same time that Barot began his research work means his involvement had begun by this initial stage.

It is clear from the surveillance evidence that on his return to the U.K. from Pakistan, Barot and his team were actively engaged in trying to implement at least some elements of his proposal. In the proposal itself, he refers to the best time to launch an attack as being "around autumn time, when the days are short (daylight factor) but the weather is not freezing (because it could harm the IED)." This could have been the timeframe he was working toward. The police assessment was that in their "best estimate . . . the autumn of 2004 is when he was planning to carry out his attacks."[46]

Given Barot's terrorist experience, his specialized role as a planner, and his long-standing connections to al-Qaeda, his intention must have been to seek their endorsement and support to move his research and planning into preparations to carry out a series of terrorist attacks in the U.K. The response to his proposition from al-Qaeda is unknown, but the continuing high tempo of activity from Barot and his group until the moment of their arrest indicates they fully expected the attacks to happen.

THE PAKISTAN CONNECTIONS

To place the events of Operation Rhyme in context, it is necessary to look back to early 2004 and, more specifically, to the month of March. In August 2004, just over a week after the arrest of Dhiren Barot, the president of Pakistan, Pervez Musharraf, stated to a reporter from *Time* magazine that a "terrorist summit" had taken place in Waziristan in March. After his comment had been "expounded on by US officials," the names of "Abu Issa al-Hindi" and "Mohammed Junaid Babar" were given by *Time* as being present at this "summit."[47] If this was so, there existed a connection of time and place between two of the leading conspirators of Operation Rhyme (Musa al-Hindi is an alias of Dhiren Barot) and Operation Crevice (Mohammed Junaid Babar is a U.S. citizen who was to give prosecution evidence in trials in the U.K. and Canada against his coconspirators).

However, following the publication of the report, a spokesman for the Pakistan military denied there had been any "summit meeting." He went on to state that *Time* had been told that "Mohammed Naeem Noor Khan, caught last month, met 'discreetly' in Lahore with Musa al Hindi, arrested this month in Britain."[48] He made no mention of the presence of Mohammed Babar, although he had been arrested in New York on his return from Pakistan in early April. If these are the facts, they serve to confirm the connection between Barot and Khan, an active member of al-Qaeda in Pakistan.

In addition, they dispel the idea of any connection between Barot and the Operation Crevice team. Any connection to Crevice would be important as it is well established that Omar Khyam, the leader of the Crevice group, also had contacts with Mohammed Siddique Khan and Shezad Tanweer, the key members of the "7/7" cell. These two individuals, along with two others, carried out the four suicide attacks that killed fifty-two people on the London Underground and on a local bus on July 7, 2005.[49] However, there appears to be no visible connection between Rhyme and the other two U.K. terrorist attack conspiracies, Crevice and 7/7.[50] What is known is that active planning was under way in Rhyme from at least July 2003 and in Crevice from February 2004. Therefore, the conspiracies were planned and prepared in parallel, with the roots of both plots leading back to Pakistan and al-Qaeda.

Another sequence of events relates to the aftermath of the arrest of Mohammed Naeem Noor Khan. It is reported that he agreed to work with his captors on a plan to identify and exploit the individuals involved in terrorism whom he was in contact with.[51] He allegedly agreed to send e-mails to al-Qaeda operatives in a variety of countries, urgently asking them to contact him. This "double-cross" operation may have resulted in the arrest of a significant al-Qaeda figure when Ahmed Khalfan Ghailani, a Tanzanian indicted by the United States for his alleged role in the East Africa embassy bomb attacks in 1998, was captured on July 24 in Gujarat, Pakistan.[52]

Ghailani was found to have information concerning attack planning in the United Kingdom and the United States stored on his computer, although the latter appeared to predate the 9/11 attacks. It is reasonable to assume that these were the same "E a B" research files, particularly as another file found with them named "Eminem2.doc" (but also signed by E a B) appeared to be a detailed proposal on how a series of mass-casualty attacks could be carried out against a variety of targets in London.[53] So both Mohammed Naeem Noor Khan and Ahmed Khalfan Ghailani are connected, in different ways, to the "terrorist operations" network of al-Qaeda, and both were found to have the files prepared by Dhiren Barot on their computers.

Finally, the primary role played by Barot tends to overshadow the links of other team members to Pakistan and to violent jihadism. Both Abdul Aziz Jalil and Junade Feroze were known to have attended al-Qaeda training camps in Pakistan some years before their involvement in Rhyme, Jalil in 1997, when he attended a camp at Tank, and Feroze in October 2001 (when Jalil was also issued with an entry visa for Pakistan). Zia ul-Haq was a regular traveler to Pakistan, for unknown reasons, from 1995 onward. In 1998 he remained there for over nine months.[54]

IMPACT OF U.S. COUNTERTERRORISM ON OPERATION RHYME

The main activities associated with Operation Rhyme that unfolded from early 2004 onward took place in Pakistan and the U.K. However, authorities in the United States undertook several actions that had a significant and adverse effect in the U.K. on the counterterrorism aspects of Rhyme. U.S. and Pakistani intelligence agencies also carried out further operations that compromised the Rhyme investigations in the U.K. [55]

On August 1, 2004, the U.S. Homeland Security threat level was raised to "Orange" for New York City, Newark, and Washington, D.C., apparently in response to a heightened threat from al-Qaeda. The director of Homeland Security, Tom Ridge, justified raising the alert level by stating, "Al Qaeda is targeting several specific buildings." He named the same four locations that were set out in the "E a B" computer files.[56]

The following day, the U.S. media published the name of Mohammed Naeem Noor Khan and details of his arrest, linking him to the raising of the alert state. It now appears the news of the arrest had been released by the White House in a background briefing, and it was then immediately published. If, as alleged, Mohammed Naeem Noor Khan had been used since his arrest on July 13 by Pakistan and the United States to run a "double-cross operation," these revelations must have compromised it.[57] This also caused operational difficulties for Operation Rhyme. When the arrest of Khan was made public, it was almost certain that Barot would discover that one of his key contacts with al-Qaeda was now cooperating with the authorities. To compound the problem, Dhiren Barot was not under the direct operational control of the U.K. authorities when the revelation was made and had in fact been missing since surveillance of him was lost on July 28.

The police and Security Service were left with no choice but to arrest Barot as soon as he was relocated, followed by the arrest his support team. To delay would have risked Barot's fleeing or, even more worryingly, accelerating his attack preparations. Concerns over operational compromise were not misplaced; the computer used by Zia ul-Haq at his workplace showed that on the day of his arrest, August 3, he had been viewing news stories on the Internet concerning the recovery of Barot's U.S. plans from a computer seized in Pakistan.[58] The arrests went ahead, even though at that time there was little hard evidence to put before a court. Fortunately, sufficient evidence came to light just before the time it was required to either charge or release him. A few months later, on a visit to the U.K., Tom Ridge publicly expressed his regret over the impact the U.S. leaks had on Operation Rhyme.[59]

Dhiren Barot had been involved in violent jihadism and terrorism for almost a decade before his arrest in 2004. He had been working on behalf of al-Qaeda or individuals closely involved with it before 9/11 as a planner and a trusted functionary. It is likely that it was in this capacity that he had made two trips to the United States, in 2000 and 2001. The intention was to carry out surveillance and reconnaissance on four targets for potential attacks by al-Qaeda. As a result of these visits, he produced thorough and methodical reports concerning each target and presumably submitted them to the al-Qaeda operatives that had tasked him to carry out the mission.

However, Barot seems to have had ambitions beyond working to advance the plans of others. By the beginning of 2003, he was developing his own concept of how to carry out an "internationally applicable (transferable)" mass-casualty terrorist attack using vehicle-borne IEDs.[60] Over the next year, he continued to research and refine the concept into a blueprint. By early 2004 Barot had put together a thorough and sophisticated plan to construct, deliver, and detonate a vehicle-borne, flammable-gas-based IED.

The next stage as envisaged by Barot was to present his core plan to elements in Pakistan in order to win their approval and gain the financial resources to execute it. With his background and connections, it is natural he would have sought out al-Qaeda as his potential sponsor, using either Musaad Aruchi or Mohammed Naeem Noor Khan as his contacts. Exactly what transpired between Barot and al-Qaeda is not publicly known, but the outcome was a renewed outburst of activity from Barot on his return to the U.K. from his final trip to Pakistan in February 2004. Barot also assembled a cell of long-standing friends and trusted individuals whom he had gathered about him from 2000 onward. Whether Barot and his coconspirators could have put into place all the elements required for a successful series of attacks in autumn of 2004 in the way they envisaged them is still an open question.

Where there is no doubt is that if they had been left undisturbed, at some stage they would have attempted to carry out an attack in the U.K. using at least one vehicle-borne IED. The "E a B" computer files clearly indicate that they planned more than this single attack and that they aspired to use a radiological dispersal device in the future. Operation Rhyme ensured this threat was nullified.

Countering this type of threat cannot be dealt with solely by one country, and, conversely, no country can rely solely on the efforts of its international partners. Both elements are required. Perhaps most crucial is the international dimension; success in the U.K. has relied on the assistance, cooperation, and coordination of many other countries. Success can only occur if trust is maintained, and there is no quicker way to erode this than for one country to compromise sensitive operational details by revealing them to the media. Operation Rhyme gives a clear indication of how internal political considerations in the United States negatively affected an extensive, ongoing counterterrorism operation in the U.K. These ripples may well have spread into other covert operations and perhaps other countries. It is to be hoped a lesson has been learned for the future.

Operation Rhyme also sheds light on two central developments in the evolution of violent jihadist plots in the U.K. First, Dhiren Barot and his cell were not just trying to emulate al-Qaeda; they were intimately connected to it, primarily but not exclusively through the person of Dhiren Barot. Barot was clearly an al-Qaeda operative from at least 1998 onward, when he acted as their liaison with Jemaah Islamiyah in Kuala Lumpur. Working for al-Qaeda for so long had shaped him and given him the knowledge and expertise he intended to use to carry out attacks in the U.K. on their behalf.

As a consequence, Barot sought al-Qaeda's approval and support as an integral part of the planning process. In fact, of all the terrorist attacks and major conspiracies in the U.K. since 2000 where there are proven links to al-Qaeda, the Barot conspiracy probably has the best claim to be categorized as an al-Qaeda operation. At the very least, the "hidden hand" of al-Qaeda was instrumental over many years in bringing together at a particular time and place the actors needed to shape and drive subsequent events.

Second, the activities of the Barot cell illustrate a key point that has been borne out in connection with almost every significant case in the U.K. since. The terrorist attacks and conspiracies in the U.K. after 2000 are not examples of "domestic terrorism," i.e., terrorism generated within and confined to one country. The driving ideological and motivating force behind them is firmly seated in another country, Pakistan.

Moreover, to successfully carry out a terrorist attack using any form of IED requires a level of practical skill that cannot be obtained from documents available on the Internet. It is in Pakistan that these skills are available and where they can be taught to others who have traveled there in pursuit of the opportunity to carry out violent jihad. Once willing recruits reach Pakistan, al-Qaeda is able to influence, instruct, and train them. They are persuaded to abandon their original idea of "fighting jihad" in Afghanistan, Kashmir, or Pakistan and prevailed upon to return to the U.K. instead to carry out attacks. Prime examples since April 2004 are the thwarted conspiracy of Operation Crevice, the four suicide attacks on 7/7, the five failed suicide attacks on 21/7, and the thwarted conspiracy in August 2006 against U.S.-bound airliners leaving Heathrow.

Each one of these was a plot targeted against the U.K. by U.K. residents, but each plot also revealed the strong presence of al-Qaeda's hidden hand, acting as a catalyst and a facilitator. As a consequence, while the terrorism in the U.K. may seem at first sight to arise from the actions of "homegrown terrorists," it is not purely domestic terrorism. The continuing activities of al-Qaeda in Pakistan ensure that it is an international phenomenon requiring an international response.

NOTES

1. Dhiren Barot, "Rough Presentation for Gas Limos Project," available at www .nefafoundation.org/documents-intlegal.html1#barot.

2. Thomas H. Kean et al., *The 9/11 Commission Report: Final Report of the National Commission on Terrorist Attacks Upon the United States* (New York: Norton, 2004), 145, 150–51.

3. USA v. Dhiren Barot, Nadeem Tarmohamed and Qaisar Shaffi, Grand Jury Indictment (S.D. N.Y.), available at www.foxnews.com/projects/pdf/hindi.pdf.

4. USA v. Dhiren Barot, Nadeem Tarmohamed and Qaisar Shaffi; *Times* (London), June 16, 2007.

5. USA v. Dhiren Barot, Nadeem Tarmohamed and Qaisar Shaffi.

6. It has not been possible to ascertain with any accuracy many aspects of their backgrounds and upbringing.

7. Barot, "Rough Presentation for Gas Limos Project," 56.

8. Gaby Hinsliff, "PM Offers Pact to Stop Pakistan Exporting Terror," *Guardian*, December 15, 2008.

9. Sean O'Neill, "International Warrior of al-Qaeda Dedicated His Life to Waging Jihad," *Times* (London), September 4, 2005.

10. "Middle East Britons Convicted of Yemen Bomb Plot," *BBC Online Network*, August 9, 1999.

11. "Abedin Team May Go Abroad," *BBC News*, February 27, 2002.

12. Eliza Manningham-Buller, director general of the Security Service, "Global Terrorism: Are We Meeting the Challenge?," James Smart Memorial Lecture, October 16, 2003, available at www.homeoffice.gov.uk/docs2/james_smart_lecture2003 .html.

13. "Reid Tells of 'Four Terror Plots,'" *BBC News*, August 13, 2006.

14. For a summary of these events, see "The Ricin Case Timeline," *BBC News*, April 14, 2005.

15. For a summary of the conspiracy as outlined by the prosecution, see Rosie Cowan, "Seven with Alleged al-Qaida Links Deny Plotting Terror Bomb Campaign," *Guardian*, March 22, 2006; also see this volume, chapter 3.

16. Duncan Campbell, Vikram Dodd, Richard Norton, "Police Killer Gets Seventeen Years for Poison Plot," *Guardian*, April 14, 2005.

17. "Profile: Omar Khyam," *BBC News*, April 30, 2007.

18. Paul Cheston, "He Plotted Carnage on Scale of 9/11 in London," *Evening Standard* (London), November 6, 2006, available at http://www.highbeam.com /doc/1P2-1394655.html.

19. "Muslim Convert Who Plotted Terror," *BBC News*, November 6, 2007.

20. USA v. Dhiren Barot, Nadeem Tarmohamed and Qaisar Shaffi, 2.

21. Kean et al. *The 9/11 Commission Report*, 145.

22. Ibid., 150–51.

23. Gerry J. Gilmore, "Los Angeles Skyscraper Was Terrorist Target Says Bush," American Forces Press Service, U.S. Department of Defense, February 9, 2006, http:// www.defenselink.mil/news/newsarticle.aspx?id=14900.

24. "Plotter Received Terror Training Overseas," *Metro* (London), November 6, 2006, http://www.metro.co.uk/news/article.html?in_article_id=24020&in_page_id=34.

25. USA v. Dhiren Barot, Nadeem Tarmohamed, and Qaisar Shaffi.

26. Ibid.

27. Jarret M. Brachman, *Global Jihadism: Theory and Practice* (London: Routledge, 2009), 161.

28. "Police Terror Probe of Vast Scale," *BBC News*, November 7, 2006, http://news .bbc.co.uk/go/pr/fr/-/1/hi/uk/6125338.stm.

29. "Profile: Muhammed Naeem Noor Khan," Centre for Grassroots Oversight, http://www.historycommons.org/entity.jsp?entity=muhammad_naeem_noor_khan_1.

30. Brachman, *Global Jihadism*, 162.

31. "Profile: Muhammed Naeem Noor Khan."

32. Ibid.

33. Hamid Mir, "Osama Claims He Has Nukes: If the US Uses N-Arms, It Will Get the Same Response," available at http://www.dawn.com/archive, November 9, 2001, quoted in Robert O. Marlin, *What Does Al-Qaeda Want? Unedited Communiqués* (Berkeley: North Atlantic Books), 40.

34. Metropolitan Police Press Bureau, "Operation Rhyme; Defendants—Abdul Aziz Jalil."

35. "Prosecution Case Against Al Qaeda Briton," *BBC News*, November 6, 2006, http://news.bbc.co.uk/2/hi/uk_news/6122270.stm.

36. "Al-Qaeda Bomb Plot Commander's Team Follow Him to Prison," *Times* (London), June 16, 2007.

37. Rosie Cowan, "Buried Inside a Bruce Willis Video, the Evidence of a Plot to Kill Thousands," *Guardian*, November 7, 2006.

38. "Police Terror Probe of Vast Scale."

39. David Pallister, "Seven Linked to Al-Qaeda are Jailed for Terror Plot," *Guardian*, June 16, 2007.

40. "Suspect Linked to Terror Alert Charged," NewsMax.com Wires, August 17, 2004, www.newsmax.com/archives/articles/2004/8/17/120342.shtml.

41. The documents were heavily redacted before their public release, and there may be others that have not been made available publicly.

42. The four U.S.-related documents are available at www.nefafoundation.org/miscellaneous/Barot/Citigroup.pdf; www.nefafoundation.org/miscellaneous/Barot/IMF_WorldBank.pdf; www.nefafoundation.org/miscellaneous/Barot/NYSE.pdf; and www.nefafoundation.org/miscellaneous/Barot/Prudential.pdf.

43. "Muslim Convert Who Plotted Terror."

44. Metropolitan Police Press Bureau, "Operation Rhyme; Defendants—Abdul Aziz Jalil".

45. Brachman, *Global Jihadism*, 162.

46. "Target: The Twin Towers," *Daily Mail* (London), November 8, 2006.

47. Elaine Shannon and Tim McGurk, "What Is This Man Plotting?," *Time*, August 15, 2004, http://www.time.com/time/magazine/article/0,9171,682236,00.html.

48. "Report on 'Terror Summit' Denied," www.dawn.com/2004/08/17/top5.htm.

49. See MI5 website at https://www.mi5.gov.uk/.

50. "7/7 Bombers Stay Free Because of US Outing of Al-Qaeda Operative," *Times* (London), August 3, 2004, quoted in "Profile: Muhammed Naeem Noor Khan."

51. "Profile: Muhammed Naeem Noor Khan."

52. Brachman, *Global Jihadism*, 162.

53. Ibid.

54. Metropolitan Police Press Bureau, "Operation Rhyme; Defendants—Abdul Aziz Jalil."

55. "Profile: Muhammed Naeem Noor Khan."

56. Ibid.

57. Ibid.

58. Metropolitan Police Press Bureau, "Operation Rhyme; Defendants—Zia ul Haq."

59. "US 'Regrets' Anti-Terror News Leaks," *Guardian*, September 17, 2004.

60. "Rough Presentation for Gas Limos Project."

[5]

The Van Gogh Murder and Beyond

BEATRICE DE GRAAF

In 2007, the Dutch General Intelligence and Security Service (Algemene Inlichtingen- en Veiligheidsdienst, AIVD) defined a jihadist network as "a fluid, dynamic, vaguely bounded structure, consisting of a number of individuals (radical Muslims). They are inter-related at both individual and aggregated level (cells/groups) and are at least temporarily linked by a common interest. That interest is the striving towards an objective that can be related to jihadism (including terrorism)."[1] In the Netherlands, such networks manifested themselves with different degrees of national versus international embeddedness. In this chapter, I will submit these purported compositions and the shifts between them to a historicizing analysis.

This chapter discusses the shifting nature of jihadist networks in the Netherlands as attributed to them by the AIVD and counter-terrorist organizations, with a special focus on the network dubbed the "Hofstad Group," which was identified and manifested itself in 2003. Other authors, notably Lorenzo Vidino in his seminal text on the Hofstad Group, have argued that these groups were strictly homegrown.[2] Vidino's description and many of his conclusions still stand. However, upon closer examination, the definitions and boundaries proposed by intelligence officials and academics between internationally organized terrorist attacks by existent terrorist groups with top-down command structures, on the one hand, and the "new," loosely knit, bottom-up terror cells that have emerged in Europe since 2002, on the other, seem to be much more fluid. The gradual shift from internationally organized plots to more localized plots and back again appears, in the Dutch case, to be a result, first, of the urgency to map this new phenomenon and to attribute meaning to it in order to politicize, institutionalize, and enable new policy approaches to tackle this threat. On the other hand, the framing and defining of a trend from the international to the homegrown (and vice versa) seems to depend on the counterterrorism measures employed, rather than solely on a shift in the make-up or motivational background of the jihadists involved.

The chapter starts with a discussion of the murder of Theodoor (Theo) Van Gogh on November 2, 2004, and the nature of the Hofstad Group, the network to which the perpetrator, Mohammed Bouyeri, belonged. It will then, drawing on assessments of the group's background and command structure as presented by the Dutch intelligence services, embed this plot within the broader context of the emergence of Dutch jihadism, in both its transnational and national manifestations since the late 1990s. It addresses how the perception of homegrown jihadism became fixed around 2004. Finally, it concludes with a brief introduction to the current trend—back to internationally led jihadist plots. The discussion draws from a list of terrorism arrests, releases, convictions, acquittals, and other outcomes composed by the author based on public reports, newspaper articles, and some interviews conducted with intelligence and counterterrorism employees (see table 5.1 at the end of this chapter). The table builds on an overview compiled by the Dutch newspaper *NRC Handelsblad*.

As the Dutch case illustrates, the division between international and homegrown jihadism, as made by the counterterrorism agencies, is largely semantic and artificial. The true threat to the Netherlands, and to Europe as a whole, does not depend on whether jihadist activity fits neatly into a "foreign" or "domestic" frame, nor in a "leader-led" or "leaderless" framework. Rather, at any given point the established networks and radicalization patterns have the potential to spurn both internationally directed and locally grown plots, based on a variety of internal and external pressures. In other words, Dutch terrorism—and European terrorism writ large—takes the form most expedient to the needs and origins of the plotters. Having said this, it remains rather hazardous to draw positive conclusions about trends and currents based on only a handful of incidents and arrests.[3] A caveat thus should stay in place while discussing the threat assessments made by security agencies.

THE ASSASSINATION OF VAN GOGH: A SINGLE ACT OF A RELIGIOUS FANATIC OR PART OF THE GLOBAL JIHAD?

On the early morning of November 2, 2004, Mohammed Bouyeri, a twenty-six-year old Dutch Moroccan born and raised in Amsterdam, awaited publicist Theo Van Gogh in an Amsterdam street, shot him off his bicycle, and slaughtered him with a knife in the middle of the street in front of many witnesses.[4] Under the new Dutch antiterror laws passed in August 2004, Bouyeri was arrested and tried for murder with "terrorist intent."[5] On July 26, 2005, he received a life sentence without parole— unusually harsh in Dutch judicial history.[6]

Bouyeri's action took the security services by surprise. From 2002, the AIVD had monitored a group of some jihadi radicals whom Bouyeri was acquainted with, a network the service internally dubbed the "Hofstad Group," since it operated in the governmental residence city the Hague (Hofstad translates as "court city").[7] Its core members were under surveillance, but Bouyeri was not one of them. He did not take part in the foreign trips some of the members made and was not considered a main actor in the Netherlands jihadi scene.[8] Bouyeri's radical texts calling for violent jihad, disseminated under the name "Abu Zubair," were only noticed after the police and the AIVD stepped up their investigation into the Hofstad Group after the murder of Van Gogh on November 2, 2004, when the service discovered that Bouyeri and Abu Zubair were the same person.[9]

The central question for the judiciary (and the police and security services) was simple: did Bouyeri commit this attack on his own, or did other members of the group assist him as part of a wider jihadist campaign? Similarly, it was important to ascertain if this target selection was a new development for jihad in the Netherlands. Answers to the first question came immediately after Bouyeri's arrest, but they were not conclusive.

First of all, Bouyeri's radicalization process had taken some time, and he did not radicalize on his own. He grew up in a dreary area in Amsterdam-West as the eldest son (after his sister Saïda) of eight children, but he was able to attend high school and engaged in community development. From 1999, he rented his own flat at the Marianne Philipsstraat and studied business informatics. His behavior became more radical and aggressive; for example, he held his sister prisoner for having a boyfriend.[10] In the summer of 2000, he was involved in a pub brawl, an attempt to stab police officers, and in the spring of 2001, he attacked his sister's boyfriend. In October, he was sentenced to twelve weeks in prison, where he intensively studied the Quran.

At the end of 2001, when he was released, his father was declared disabled, and his mother died of cancer. In 2002, Bouyeri's plans to set up a youth center in his neighborhood stalled. He quit college and started to live on social security. He now completely devoted his time to studying radical Islamic texts and started wearing fundamentalist clothes. In the el-Tawheed mosque, which he frequently visited, he met with similarly radicalizing Muslim youngsters and a self-proclaimed jihadi veteran of Syrian descent, Redouan al-Issa, or Abu Khaled, an opaque figure.[11]

Bouyeri invited his new soulmates to his house, where he organized living-room meetings and listened to lectures by Abu Khaled. He also accommodated one of the leaders of this Hofstad Group, Nouredine el-Fatmi, and two other members. His mentor, Abu Khaled, taught him and the other members of the Hofstad Group about "tawheed" (the unity of Allah) and instructed them in how to live as radical salafist Muslims and oppose the Western lifestyle. Bouyeri embraced these ideas.[12] After Abu Khaled was expelled from the Netherlands as an illegal immigrant in October 2003, Bouyeri tried to take over Khaled's role as spiritual leader. As the ideologue of the Hofstad Group, Bouyeri wrote, translated, and disseminated via the Internet more than fifty texts in which he increasingly called his brothers to arms against Dutch society rather than on behalf of international jihad elsewhere.[13]

In May 2004, he abused an employer at the Social Service, and on September 29, 2004, the police arrested him because he refused being fined for fare dodging. The officers found notes with telephone numbers and e-mail addresses of Hofstad Group members with him and a paper bearing similarities to a last will, which they sent to the AIVD. Bouyeri was released since he had committed only a minor offense, and he was not on the list of approximately 150 jihadi radicals that the AIVD had identified as security risks. Neither the police nor the AIVD judged Bouyeri to be a grave danger at that time, nor did they take his participation in the jihadi network of the Hofstad Group seriously enough.[14]

Second, although Bouyeri carried out the immediate preparations for his attack on his own initiative, he was surrounded all the time during this preparatory stage by his jihadi comrades, who must have supported him one way or another. On May 19, 2004, Bouyeri received his last social security check. Between May 19 and October 28, he withdrew only €200, not an amount someone can live on for five months. On October 28, he withdrew his last money, €930, and reached his maximum overdraft. That same day, he handed Rachid Bousana an envelope with €1650, intended for his family. Where did he find the additional €720, and how could he have afforded his firearm, a HS 2000 pistol, which probably cost a €1,000 to €1,500? It is therefore hard to accept that the other defendants were not involved in one way or another, although the prosecution could prove no concrete evidence for his support.[15]

On Monday evening, November 1, 2004, during Ramadan, Bouyeri had a late supper together with his friends from the Hofstad Group. He also left behind some letters—later to be discovered as his will. Early in the morning, Bouyeri prayed with his comrades, had breakfast with them, and left the house on his bike with his pistol, a ritual kukri (a Nepalese dagger), and a fillet knife in his rucksack. His housemate, Bousana, denied having known anything about these weapons, although they lived together in his cramped two-room flat (the living room measured fifteen square meters, the single bed room only ten). Nor did he explain how Bouyeri could have purchased it.[16]

According to the public prosecutor, Bouyeri carefully planned the attack on his victim, the controversial publicist and filmmaker Theo Van Gogh. Van Gogh was known, among other things, for his anti-Islamist feelings, and he produced the provocative documentary *Submission* (an attempt to liberate Muslim women from oppression, broadcast in August 2004) with the Somali-born Dutch representative Ayaan Hirsi Ali. Hirsi Ali was well protected at that time, but Van Gogh rejected protection and seemed a good second choice. For weeks, Bouyeri observed Van Gogh's house and daily cycling route, and he picked the place, in one of the most crowded streets on the route, where he would slay his target. At 8:40, on Tuesday morning, November 2, Bouyeri overhauled Van Gogh on the Linnaeusstraat, shot him from his bike, followed him to the other side of the street, fired another salvo of bullets (eight in total) and then cut his throat with the kukri, in front of fifty-three witnesses. With the smaller knife, he pinned an "Open letter to Hirsi Ali" to Van Gogh's chest and then fled, fruitlessly shooting at some passersby before engaging in gunfire with the police. He tried to kill the officers that pursued him, planning to be killed in the process and become a martyr, but he was shot in the leg and overpowered.[17]

Bouyeri had a farewell letter with him titled "Drenched in Blood." This verse-form text read as an incitement to holy war and was signed "Saifu Deen al-Muwahhied," which, according to Ruud Peters, a Dutch Islam expert and witness for the prosecution, is a combination of two Arabic terms: "sword of religion" (*saif al-din*) and "confessor of *tawheed*" (*al-muwahhid*).[18] In the "Open Letter" he directly threatened Ayaan Hirsi Ali and blamed politicians for allowing Jewish influences in politics. According to the Norwegian researcher Petter Nesser, the conclusion of the letter shows "the essence of al-Qaidaism," by prophesying the defeat of the enemy on the individual, local, regional, and global levels in order of priority:

> And like a great prophet once said: "I deem thee lost, O Pharaoh." (17:102) And so we want to use similar words and send these before us, so that the heavens and the stars will gather this news and spread it over the corners of the universe like a tidal wave. "I deem thee lost, O America." "I deem thee lost, O Europe." "I deem thee lost, O Holland." "I deem thee lost, O Hirshi Ali" "I deem thee lost, O unbelieving fundamentalist."[19]

These two texts showed that Bouyeri's attack was the outcome of an ideological turn to violent jihad against the Netherlands that evolved from the Hofstad Group since Bouyeri wrote these texts as spiritual support for this network.[20] In one of Bouyeri's last writings, "Open Letter to the Dutch Population," dated August 12, 2004 (which he left on a USB stick for other Hofstad Group members to disseminate within "the Umma"), he announced attacks against Dutch public places, justifying the attacks because of the support of the Dutch government for the United States and Israel.[21] His argument echoed a fatwa announced by the dissident Saudi sheikh Hamoud bin Oqlaa' al-Sjou'abi that legitimized the September 11 attacks.[22] A translation of this and other texts was found on the computers of other Hofstad Group members.[23]

The public prosecutor charged him on November 11 with murder, attempted murder (of a police officer), attempted manslaughter (of bystanders and police officers), violation of gun-control laws, suspicion of participation in a criminal organization with terrorist aims, and conspiracy to murder with a terrorist purpose Van Gogh, Hirsi Ali, and others who were mentioned in his open letter. The prosecutor demanded a life sentence.[24] The public prosecutor also set out to detain the other members of the Hofstad Group for taking part in a conspiracy to commit terrorism in the Netherlands.

The nature and character of the terrorist threat captured Dutch public debate for many months. The attacks by al-Qaeda in New York and Washington, D.C., had, of course, already shocked the Dutch government and awoken a public that had been rather indifferent to international terrorism until that time. The murder of Van Gogh, however, triggered public and political vigilance vis-à-vis the terrorist threat within Dutch society. For example, the Dutch minister of economic affairs, Gerrit Zalm, declared "war" on Muslim terrorists.[25] Fear of the terrorist threat was enhanced by emerging concerns about globalization, immigration, and Islam and transformed these fears into a state of moral panic. From that moment, policy efforts, research projects, and public debate centered on whether Bouyeri was a lone wolf or one of many radicalized Muslim youths in the Netherlands who were being recruited and organized to inflict more damage to Dutch society.[26]

JIHADISM IN THE NETHERLANDS:
THREE TRANSNATIONAL NETWORKS

Indeed, Bouyeri was not the first jihadi terrorist arrested in the Netherlands, nor was the Hofstad Group the first network to surface, as table 5.1 shows. Although it is hard to estimate since terrorism was only made a punishable offence in August 2004, between September 2001 and November 2, 2004, at least seventy-four people were apprehended based on suspicion of terrorism-related activities (twelve were convicted). Between August 2004, after the new terrorism law was adopted, and

December 2005, the Office of National Prosecution counted fifty-seven arrests of terrorist suspects. In fourteen of these cases the public prosecutor achieved convictions. The other suspects were released immediately or acquitted in court. Some suspects were expelled from the country because they turned out to be illegal immigrants (see table 5.1). This relatively low conviction percentage does not mean, however, that no "real" terrorist plots were uncovered and thwarted. Some acquittals are attributable to the absence of a Dutch terrorism law before 2004. But even before 2004, the AIVD and the police did uncover and disrupt various jihadist activities.[27]

From the late 1990s, the AIVD firstly identified so-called jihadist transnational networks, composed of immigrant jihadist mujaheddin who supported international jihad (MI5's al-Qaeda "facilitation networks").[28] Around 1999 or 2000, the AIVD identified "internationally-oriented local networks," the product of successful radicalization and recruitment efforts through the transnational networks of Muslims raised or born in the West. These new groups undertook the same activities as the original transnational networks but included more native members. Finally, the AIVD recognized "local-autonomous networks" made up entirely of young Muslim immigrants who were radicalized or radicalized themselves under the influence of various sources. These jihadists still viewed their activities as part of the international jihad but directed them against their country of residence.[29]

This endogenous shift took place, according to another AIVD report, from 2003 onward, when radical Islamic groups started operating inside the Netherlands but outside existing structures. The networks no longer sought shelter in mosques, where radical Muslims had found inspiration up until 2003. Instead, they looked for inspiration from veterans of the jihad who had fought in places such as Afghanistan and Chechnya or from foreign preachers. The command structures of the groups that were formed in this stage were spontaneous and local. At the same time, according to the AIVD and the Dutch National Coordinator for Counterterrorism (Nationaal Coördinator Terrorismebestrijding, NCTb), the role of the Internet increased within these groups from 2003 on—in terms of both the process of radicalization and maintaining internal communication—while the part played by mosques dwindled.[30]

In December 2002 the AIVD for the first time publicly warned in a report that "recruitment for the jihad in the Netherlands" had developed "from incident to trend." The service saw "some dozens of young Muslims . . . being prepared for the jihad, the holy Islamic war. This recruitment is an expression of a violent radical-Islamic (Islamistic) movement that has crept into the Dutch society." Most of the youths that were recruited were of Moroccan descent, and their recruiters generally were "immigrants who are either legally or illegally resident in the Netherlands" and had "a mujahedeen background." According to the report,

> most of them underwent religious-ideological and military training, mostly in Al-Qaeda training camps in Afghanistan, and some of them actually participated in the Islamistic war. They approach the young Muslims while visiting, for example, orthodox mosques. Islamic centres, coffee shops and especially prisons have also turned out to be suitable places for making contacts. Following a successful approach, the recruited youths are isolated from their environment and subjected to indoctrination. The recruitment process is completed by a testimony for posterity and a paramilitary training.[31]

Between 2001 and 2004 the service uncovered three transnational jihadist networks in the Netherlands that seemed to follow this pattern to some extent and that I will discuss below: the Eik case, the Jihad case, and the case of the Hofstad Group.[32]

THE EIK CASE, 2001

On July 28, 2001, a Frenchman of Algerian descent, Djamel Beghal, or Abu Hamza, was arrested in Dubai for preparing an attack against the U.S. embassy in Paris and the U.S. Army base at Kleine Brogel in Belgium.[33] Beghal had close contacts with the al-Qaeda leadership.[34] Through this arrest, four members of the radical self-proclaimed Takfir wal-Hijra group living in Rotterdam were arrested as well. Among those four were the French Algerian Jerome Courtailler (27) and the Algerian Abdelghani Rabia (30). Their apartments turned out to be "safe houses" or transit stations belonging or connected to an international al-Qaeda network, according to police sources.[35] In one Rotterdam safe house, the police retrieved stolen and forged travel documents and identity cards.[36] In Belgium, the police found an Uzi submachinegun, 220 pounds of sulfur, and around 50 liters acetone. [37] Courtailler and Rabia were involved in the planned attack against the American embassy in Paris and pivotal figures in Takfir wal-Hijra. The "delivery area" for their forged documents extended throughout Europe, demonstrated by the numerous rendition requests that the Belgian, German, British, and Spanish governments submitted to the Dutch Ministry of Justice. Both Courtaller and Rabia had close contact with the former professional soccer player Nizar Trabelsi, who had traveled from an al-Qaeda training camp to the Netherlands in June 2001. Abu Hamza had charged Trabelsi with carrying out the attack on the American embassy, and Courtailler and Rabia were to assist him with the preparations.[38]

Courtailler was a pivotal figure in the Takfir wal-Hijra network in Europe as he was heavily involved in credit-card fraud and supplying radical members with false passports, identity cards, mobile phones, and safe houses. Interestingly, no Dutch citizens were involved, and no evidence was found that the network was planning attacks on Dutch soil or against Dutch targets. The Algerian and French terrorists appeared to be using Rotterdam only as a safe haven, not as a recruiting base. As a result, the court acquitted Courtailler and Rabia of all charges and released them because the whole case had been built on inadmissible AIVD reports—the two suspects had not carried out punishable offences after the police started to monitor them.[39] The acquittal was upheld on appeal in June 2004 and confirmed by the Supreme Court of the Netherlands in 2006.[40] As illegal residents, Courtailler and Rabia were deported to France and Algeria.[41]

THE JIHAD CASE, 2002

On August 27, 2002, the intelligence service alerted the national counter-terrorism prosecutor to an active network of extremist Muslims that committed crimes (such as forgery and passport fraud) with the intent of materially, financially, and otherwise supporting and facilitating a terrorist organization in the Netherlands.[42] According to the AIVD report to the National Prosecution Office, the network furthermore "supported or participated in the al-Qaeda organization of Osama bin Laden."[43] Three days later, the police arrested twelve suspects and conducted several raids on apartments in Rotterdam. Numerous recordings of Salafist texts and two martyr's wills were found in the safe houses.[44]

Moreover, the police and AIVD discovered that this network had close links to yet another network, which the AIVD had kept under surveillance since April 2002. The two networks, according to the Dutch security forces, were closely joined and displayed strong international links to al-Qaeda training camps, functioning as an al-Qaeda "facilitation network."[45] One member, the Belgian citizen Jawad M., was extradited to Belgium for taking part in the murder of an Afghan warlord, Ahmad Shah Massoud, commander of the United Front opposition to the Taliban regime, on September 9, 2001.[46] This fear was enhanced by the discovery of the telephone number of one of the arrested suspects, Anwar al-M., among the possessions of three Saudi jihadists who had been planning an attack on British and American vessels in the Strait of Gibraltar in 2002 (which was thwarted by Moroccan authorities).[47]

Apart from these international connections to al-Qaeda, the "Jihad case" also revealed new characteristics in the emergent Dutch threat: this time, Dutch citizens, of Moroccan descent, were involved in supporting terrorist activity.[48] A twenty-five-year old Algerian named Rodoin Daoud had used his religious knowledge and charisma to recruit and indoctrinate Dutch Muslims to wage jihad abroad. As a result, two young Dutch citizens from Eindhoven, Khariq el-Hassnoui and Ahmed el-Bakiouli went to Kashmir to take part in global jihad, but were shot dead by the Indian Border Security Forces in January 2002.[49]

The suspects arrested in August 2002 were tried in Rotterdam. Again, the verdict proved a defeat for the prosecution: all twelve suspects were acquitted of the principal charges (human trafficking, illegal possession of firearms, handling stolen goods, and "assisting enemies of the Dutch state and/or its allies during armed conflict"). One French suspect was sentenced to three months in prison for possessing a false passport, and an Algerian received a four-month sentence for forgery.[50] Dutch law was not prepared yet to address terrorism offenses: preparatory activities and recruiting or training on behalf of violent jihad were still not punishable under the law. Moreover, the investigation team had messed up the evidence, mislabeling the Arabic documents and recordings.[51] However, according to Bart Nieuwenhuizen, head of the National Prosecutor's Office, while the case might have been lost, the network was disrupted. A signal had also been sent to the legislative power that new legal measures against terrorism were urgently needed.[52]

THE CASE OF THE HOFSTAD GROUP, 2002–2004: A TURN TO HOMEGROWN, LOCALLY ORGANIZED TERRORISM?

The network in the Eik case had an international command structure (Abu Hamza instructed the members), was linked to al-Qaeda, operated on a transnational basis, and did not include Dutch citizens nor direct its actions against Dutch targets. The Jihad case involved Dutch citizens but still was oriented outward (jihadists targeting the Afghan warlord Massoud) and seemed to use the Netherlands only as a safe haven. Only in 2003, when the Hofstad Group surfaced, were homegrown jihadists identified.[53]

However, the same AIVD reports, court cases, and media sources can lead to another conclusion: that amorphous transnational networks, emerging after 9/11, employed both foreign and indigenous Islamists, operated both in the Netherlands and abroad, directed their activities against a wide range of targets (Kashmir, Chechnya, Paris), and carried out a broad scope of criminal activities. The command structures of these networks precludes division into the distinct categories that the AIVD typology suggests.[54] The Eik case was the only network that featured a hierarchical command structure and involved international al-Qaeda connections. But even this network was already rather autonomous in 2001 and 2002, as were the others that were uncovered in subsequent years. This amorphous character and the parallelism of both foreign inspiration and local activity become more clear if we take a closer look at the Hofstad Group network.

From December 2001, the AIVD had been monitoring the radical Salafist el-Tawheed mosque in the north of Amsterdam for suspicion of Egyptian and Saudi influences (the mosque had financial relations to a Saudi nongovernmental organization, al-Haramein).[55] In the summer of 2002, the service identified a group of Muslim youth that met in or near the mosque and gravitated around Redouan al-Issa (43), also known as "Abu Khaled" or "the Sheikh," who had ties to radical Muslims in Spain and Belgium. Abu Khaled was an illegal immigrant from Syria, a former member of the Syrian Muslim Brotherhood, and—according to the Dutch police and AIVD—a Takfir wal-Hijra adherent who came to the Netherlands in 1995. He became a mentor for a number of radical muslims.[56]

He inspired, among others, the seventeen-year-old high school student Samir Azzouz, of Moroccan origin but born and raised in the Netherlands. Samir Azzouz came to the notice of the AIVD in January 2003, when he took a train to Berlin, bound for Chechnya to join local jihadists in their fight against the Russian forces; he was accompanied by his friend Khalid (or Hussam, age seventeen). They brought luggage with them, including dried fruits, energy drinks, lots of clothes, cooking gear, a laptop, and a map, under the cover story of being tourists traveling to the Ukraine. At the Ukrainian border, they were arrested and put back on a train to Western Europe. The media described their adventurous journey as an amateurish endeavor, but the two young Islamists had prepared for their trip thoroughly. The police found night-vision goggles and a GPS system (which turned out to have been used in Russia) at Samir's residence after their return. The police suspect the two students were recruited by Redouan al-Issa. After his return, Azzouz's status rose; he started his own Islamic book company and began associating only with Moroccan youths.[57]

Ismail Aknikh was another Hofstad Group member with international aspirations. Aknikh, born in Amsterdam in 1982 to Moroccan immigrants, regularly attended the el-Tawheed mosque in Amsterdam, where he became acquainted with Azzouz and helped form the Hofstad Group in the fall of 2002. In the summer of 2003, he traveled with Azzouz to Barcelona to meet with Abdeladim Akoudad for guidance and instructions. Akoudad (or "Naoufel"), a Moroccan living in Spain, was suspected by the Moroccan security services of involvement in the Casablanca attacks of March 16, 2003.[58]

In October 2003, Akoudad and Azzouz discussed over the phone "shoes, first and second rate, coming from Greece or Italy and that will do well in Spain," and "documents." At this point, the Spanish authorities intervened and arrested Akoudad on October 14.[59] Two days later, the AIVD alerted the national prosecutor that Azzouz and other members of the Hofstad Group, all regular visitors to the el-Tawheed mosque and a phone shop in Schiedam that functioned as a meeting point, were probably preparing a terrorist attack. On October 17, arrests were made in the Hague, Schiedam, and Amsterdam: Samir Azzouz, Redouan al-Issa, Jason Walters, Ismail Akhnikh, and Mohamed Fahmi Boughaba were apprehended. Apartments were raided, including the house of Mohammed Bouyeri in Amsterdam.[60]

However, the authorities could not substantiate the allegation of terrorism and released the Hofstad Group members after only eleven days. Even the retrieval of a supermarket bag filled with goods resembling ingredients for constructing explosive devices, including six security glasses, fertilizer, power tape, distilled water, liquid ammonia, hydrochloric acid, batteries, a timer, kitchen gloves, halogen bulbs, and chemical cleaner kept by Mohamed Fahmi Boughaba on Azzouz's instructions was not enough evidence to keep the men in custody. The bag did not suffice in establishing a direct link to a terrorist organization or individual terrorist intent.[61]

After their temporary detainment in October 2003, Akhnikh, Azzouz, and Walters further developed their skills as jihadists and urged other Muslims to go abroad to wage jihad.[62] Aknikh already went to Pakistan earlier that year, as did Zakaria Taybi and Jason Walters (who went twice, in July and December 2003). Walters and Akhnikh even bragged about contacts with Maulana Masood Azhar, a core al-Qaeda member—something they later downplayed in court. In June 2004, Nouredine el-Fatmi went to Portugal with three friends. The AIVD warned the Portugese authorities, out of fear that the members were planning to kill José Manuel Durao Barroso (then president-designate of the European Commission) and other guests during a reception in Oporto within the context of the European Soccer Championship that was taking place in Portugal. The four were arrested and sent back to the Netherlands, where the AIVD and the special antiterrorism unit of the KLPD interrogated them. No evidence of concrete preparations was found, not even an indication of terrorist activity. Again, the men walked free.[63] Only then, when they felt the security forces in Pakistan, Portugal, and the Netherlands were closing in on them did they start conspiring at home and confine their scope to their local environment. The next time the security forces intervened to arrest them was after the murder of Van Gogh in November 2004.

The foreign inspiration and organizational impulse of the Hofstad Group came mainly from Redouan al-Issa, who also acted as Bouyeri's mentor until October 2003. With his alleged experience as a jihadist, he seemed to function as the charismatic "magnet" that bound the group together from 2002 onward. In his seminal study *Leaderless Jihad*, Marc Sageman dismisses the role of al-Issa because "he seemed to have simply disappeared from his group" and "the remaining members of the Hofstad Group rarely mentioned him."[64] Sageman correctly warns against viewing types like al-Issa as hierarchical leaders or recruiters in the traditional sense of the word. However, precisely because terrorist networks are not static organizations, we should be careful not to dismiss him too soon from the picture.

Moreover, it is only logical that the remaining Hofstad Group members did not mention al-Issa *after their arrests in 2004*, since they all tried to escape conviction and did not plead guilty to terrorism charges. On the contrary, they denied being part of a terrorist organization altogether.[65] It would have been foolish to admit their attachment to al-Issa or dwell on his role as inspiration of the group. There is another explanation for his disappearance from the scene: after the first arrests in October 2003, al-Issa, as an illegal immigrant, was expelled from the country and declared an "unwanted alien." His role as inspirer, ideologist, and proselytizer was taken over by other leader personalities, such as Azzouz and Bouyeri.[66] Al-Issa did return in the course of 2004 (and had contact with Mohammed Bouyeri) but had too little time to regain his former position or build another network because he fled the country again on the morning of the November 2, when Bouyeri committed his assassination.

Al-Issa's real role within the network still remains vague (because of the group members' silence) and fluctuated over time (because of counterterrorist pressure). He should not be underestimated, however. He brought the Hofstad Group members together, first through meetings in the el-Tawheed mosque in Amsterdam and later, on a more informal basis, at Mohammed Bouyeri's place, where he inspired them with stories of international jihad, taught them radical Takfir wal-Hijra ideology, and conducted Islamic marriages.[67] After his apprehension in October 2003, al-Issa compared himself to a "Christian evangelist." A witness in court, who attended the living-room meetings at Bouyeri's place, saw him as a "priest" and the youngsters surrounding him as "disciples."[68]

Only in the course of 2004 did the remaining Dutch members of the network take over his role.[69]

In short, the Hofstad Group was organized locally, without any demonstrable direction from an al-Qaeda command center or from any other identifiable, preexisting terrorist organisation.[70] It started with some individuals prone to radical jihadist philosophy who actively sought inspiration from international contacts, from a foreign preacher and whom they viewed as a jihadi veteran, and from international Salafist texts. They subsequently actively supported and subscribed to international jihad in Chechnya and established contact with terrorists abroad. Only after these attempts in 2002 and 2003 were thwarted by the intelligence services and their mentor was expelled did they start conspiring against Dutch targets in 2004.[71]

THE HOFSTAD GROUP DISSOLVED, 2004–2006

After the murder of Van Gogh, the national prosecutor decided to round up again the other Hofstad Group members. Most of the arrests went smoothly, but on November 10, 2004, an arrest squad entered the apartment in The Hague where Aknikh and Jason Walters resided. They threw a hand grenade, wounding five police officers and turning the arrest into a fourteen-hour siege and a national spectacle.[72] In the meantime, two other leaders, al-Issa (who had illegally entered the country again) and Noureddine el-Fatmi, fled the country. In June 2005, when el-Fatmi returned, he was arrested together with his wife, Soumaya Sahla, and friend Martine van den Oever (a Dutch Islamist convert), while trying to pull an automatic weapon (a Croatian Agram 2000) from his rucksack.[73] A few months later, on October 14, 2005, Azzouz and Jermaine Walters (the brother of Jason Walters), who were suspects in the first Hofstad case but not incarcerated, and five other coconspirators were arrested on suspicion of preparing an attack against unnamed national politicians, the AIVD, and other targets.[74]

On December 5, 2005, the case against the fourteen Hofstad Group members started under overwhelming media presence. The court dealt with the defendants one at a time, starting with Bouyeri, whom the prosecution identified as the leader of the group. Bouyeri had remained silent during his first trial in July 2005. This time, he delivered a three-hour-long speech where he confessed that he was filled with "joy and pride" that the prosecution compared him to Osama bin Laden. He also explained that he had killed Theo Van Gogh because he had insulted "the Prophet."[75] The other suspects, however, denied being real terrorists. Jason Walters defended himself by explaining that he only acted along with the Hofstad Group to "look cool."[76]

On March 10, 2006, Jason Walters, Aknikh, and el-Fatmi were convicted and sentenced to fifteen, thirteen, and five years in prison, respectively. Nine other suspects were convicted of being members of a criminal terrorist organization. The other five suspected members were acquitted of this charge. The Hofstad Group was also placed on the EU blacklist of terrorist organizations.[77] A second group, including Azzouz, named the "Piranha case," was convicted on December 1, 2006. Azzouz received a sentence of eight years, the others sentences of four and three years.[78]

However, on January 23, 2008 the Court of Appeal in the Hague overturned the sentences in the Hofstad case, judging that there was too little evidence to define the Hofstad Group as a terrorist organization whose members shared an ideological viewpoint and conspired and associated on a regular basis.[79] According to the judge, "the Hofstad Group displayed insufficient organizational substance to conclude the existence of an organization as laid out in the paragraphs 140 and 140a of the Penal Law."[80] The court upheld only the sentences of Jason Walters (fifteen years for attempted murder for throwing the hand grenade), Aknikh (fifteen months for possession of illegal firearms and munitions), el-Fatmi (five years for possession of illegal firearms), and his wife (nine months, same charge).[81]

In the Piranha case, the suspects also filed for appeal, and the Hague court upheld its decision on October 2, 2008. Moreover, they received even higher sentences since the prosecutor proved their involvement in concrete criminal acts (possession of firearms, etc.), rather than charging them with membership of an terrorist organization or possessing terrorist intentions, which is more difficult to substantiate.[82] Azzouz was sentenced to nine years imprisonment, Noureddine el-Fatmi to eight years, Mohammed Chentouf to six years, Soumaya Sahla to four years, and Mohammed Hamid to three months.

The Hofstad Group won their acquittals in Dutch court in reference to articles 9 and 10 of the European Treaty on Human Rights (freedom of religion and freedom of speech). In the Piranha case, the prosecution could prove that the suspects possessed illegal firearms and munitions and had collected the names and addresses of politicians and were therefore in a much later stage of preparations than the Hofstad Group suspects.[83] The Hofstad Group case depended heavily on ideological writing, which according to the judge did not provide sufficient evidence for labeling the Hofstad Group as a terrorist organization. The court emphasized that it attached great importance to religious pluralism and freedom of speech, even if this pluralism included fundamentalist and antidemocratic opinions, such as those expressed by the members of the Hofstad Group.[84]

This ruling, however, did not mark the end of the Hofstad Group saga. The public prosecutor filed for cassation, and on February 2, 2010, the Dutch Supreme Court ordered a retrial.[85] The Supreme Court rejected the argument that the suspects' organization was too loosely structured to merit the conviction. According to the Supreme Court, the Hague court had too narrowly applied the legal definition of what constitutes a terrorist organization and should bring the definition more in line with other cases of criminal organizations that specialized in stock fraud or money laundering.[86] The case was referred to the Amsterdam court again.[87] In December 2010, the court again ruled the terrorist paragraph admissible and sentenced seven defendants for participating in a terrorist and criminal organization; five of them received a sentence of fifteen months, one thirty-eight months, and one thirteen years.[88] The Hofstad Group network was defined as an organization aimed at inciting to hatred, violence, and intimidation, partly with a terrorist intent.[89] Six of the seven defendants lodged a cassation appeal and are awaiting a response.[90] The ruling of the Amsterdam court of appeal nevertheless had a large impact on legal counterterrorism instruments since it lowered the standards for defining a group as a terrorist organization.

PRELIMINARY LESSONS FOR COUNTERTERRORISM, 2004–2008

Although the AIVD had been perspicacious in identifying homegrown domestic threats by organizationally unaffiliated militants as early as

1998 and 2002,[91] antiterrorism legislation was only adopted in August 2004. This meant many cases failed for procedural reasons (see table 5.1). Only under the influence of the Madrid bombings of March 2004 and the European Framework Decision of 2002,[92] did the Dutch parliament agree to new counterterrorism laws that made it possible to prosecute and arrest suspects for terrorist offences such as taking part in preparations for terrorist attacks, recruitment, receiving training, or being a member of a terrorist organization.[93]

In 2004, the "comprehensive approach to terrorism" propagated by the AIVD and the National Coordinator for Counterterrorism found enough political and public support.[94] This approach entailed appeals to school teachers, youth workers, and imams to report radicalization signs to the police.[95] The NCTb also initiated a number of publicity campaigns and advertisements appealing to the population to exercise vigilance against possible terrorism.[96]

From the failures to get convictions in the Eik, Jihad, and Hofstad cases, the prosecution learned that vague allusions to international terrorism did not hold up in court. Nor was it easy to convince the court of the existence of a terrorist organization according to the new Law on Terrorist Crimes adopted in August 2004.[97] Therefore, the prosecution after 2004 concentrated more on hard evidence (such as possession of firearms) than on trying to demonstrate wider but vaguer connections to terrorist networks or trying to prove (ideological) terrorist intentions.[98] This new approach was more fruitful, as with the Piranha case (whereas the prosecution lost the first rounds of appeals in the Hofstad Group case because the evidence relied too heavily on ideological semantics).[99]

Moreover, because of intelligence efforts, the Hofstad Group network and other similar homegrown networks seem defeated, disrupted, or divided from within.[100] The AIVD's close tail on jihadists like Samir Azzouz, for example, prevented him from developing extensive professional skills or international terrorist contacts. Intelligence services frustrated his early trip to Chechnya in 2003 and his contacts with Mohammed Achraf (an Algerian arrested in Switzerland in 2004) and Abdeladim Akoudad (which proved that Azzouz had been serious about soliciting more international contacts and experience).[101]

According to the AIVD, the activities of homegrown radicals have been disrupted. Even if it could not arrest suspects for terrorism, it could expel them from the country, according to AIVD official reports ("*ambts-berichten*") to the IND. This procedure was deployed against three immigrants, of Algerian, Moroccan and Turkish origin, who were consequently declared "unwanted aliens"[102]—a procedure that has earned criticism on human rights grounds because neither the immigrants nor their lawyers are entitled to study the evidence (since the expelled immigrants were not arrested for terrorism, they do not feature on table 5.1).[103]

The radicalization of Moroccan youngsters continued, according to the AIVD. Young Muslims met on the Internet or while attending the sermons of traveling youth preachers. However, this radicalization trend should be viewed more as part of an Islamist youth counterculture that uses radicalism as a way to express a separate identity within the Dutch context. Moreover, the scale of radicalization has been reduced. On the contrary, the AIVD noticed that Dutch Moroccan Muslims increasingly found ways of articulating their grievances and frustrations through democratic and activist channels. The Israeli bombing of Gaza, in December 2007/January 2008, for example, led to an explosion of nonviolent initiatives, such as demonstrations, petitions, fund-raising activities, and appeals to boycott certain products. In comparison, the movies of Geert Wilders (*Fitna*) and Ehsan Jami attracted much less response and indignation than suspected. Within the Dutch salafist milieu, the AIVD therefore noted a "self-cleansing power" and an increased resilience against (violent) radical tendencies within the Muslim community, an estimate confirmed by newspaper reports.[104]

A RETURN TO THE INTERNATIONAL, 2008–2011

Since 2008, both the NCTb, or National Coordinator for Terrorism and Security (formerly the Nationaal Coördinator Terrorisme en Veiligheid, NCTV; renamed in 2011) and the AIVD have claimed to have these home-grown networks under control.[105] In its 2008 annual report, the AIVD concluded, "The terrorist threat increasingly emanates from transnational and local networks with an international orientation, but less from local-autonomous networks." The transnational or international threat, in the form of returning trainees from the Afghanistan/Pakistan regions or from Somalia and Yemen is therefore back on the national counterterrorist agenda.[106] This international turn showed itself in at least three concrete ways in 2008 and 2009.

First, Dutch authorities identified direct links between networks or individuals operating on Dutch soil and networks and organizations in Pakistan or Afghanistan. In May 2008, a Dutch citizen of Turkish descent was apprehended and extradited to France for taking part in the Islamic Movement of Uzbekistan (IMU), a terrorist organization that had been operating in the Pakistan-Afghanistan border region since 2001. In August 2008, a Pakistani known as Aqeel A., who resided in the Netherlands on a student visa, was handed over to the Spanish authorities under a European arrest warrant. According to the Spanish authorities, he was part of a jihadist network of fourteen people (almost all of Pakistani origin) that they arrested in January 2008 in Barcelona that planned suicide attacks in Western Europe. Aqeel was designated for a suicide mission in Germany. Unlike in the United Kingdom or Germany, where similar networks with Pakistani or Afghan links were uncovered, this "Barcelona case" showed no homegrown component. The network consisted of "Pakistani-born, long-term residents of Europe," who acted primarily as facilitators for younger "operatives," also from Pakistan, who had been radicalized and trained there before being sent to Europe specifically to carry out suicide attacks.[107] In December 2008, the first national coordinator for counterterrorism, Tjibbe Joustra, warned against a "substantial" terrorism threat (he even added to that in defining the threat as "substantial with a little plus"), he meant exactly this kind of international terrorism, triggered by the notoriety the Dutch had gained through anti-Islam movies like Geert Wilders's *Fitna*, Ayaan Hirsi Ali's *Submission*, and Ehsan Jami's *An Interview with Muhammed*.[108]

Second, in late July 2009 three Dutch youngsters of Moroccan descent and one Moroccan citizen with a residence permit (all aged twenty-one) were arrested in Kenya, while allegedly trying to join the Islamist movement al-Shabaab in Somalia.[109] These arrests coincided with the exposure of an al-Shabaab plot involving four Australian citizens the same month and the heightened awareness of the FBI vis-à-vis the threat of Somali recruiters in the United States. It showed that al-Qaeda-affiliated groups elsewhere, but especially in the Horn of Africa, were regrouping and recruiting young supporters through the Somali diaspora in the West, thus creating a safe haven for jihadists from all over the world.[110]

Third, on Christmas Day 2009, an attack by the twenty-three-year old Nigerian Umar Farouk Abdulmutallab, who intended to blow up a plane with high explosives sewn into his underwear, was foiled at the last minute. Abdulmutallab arrived from Yemen and transferred at Schiphol Airport to a flight to Detroit. The Nigerian claimed to have been trained by al-Qaeda.[111] The attack demonstrated that even although the level of the terrorism alert in the Netherlands had been lowered to "restricted" only a few weeks before, the country could still be used as a transit point for international terrorism. The National Coordinator for Counterterrorism immediately started an investigation into security checks at Schiphol; moreover, the ministry for Home Affairs announced the introduction of body scans.[112]

In addition to these solid cases based on material evidEnce, a series of arrests based on preliminary AIVD warnings and alerts from foreign agencies failed to achieve convictions. Between 2008 and 2011, thirty-seven arrests were made, involving alleged hijacking plots in August 2008, fake warnings about Moroccan jihadist attacks in March 2009, purported "dry runs" for terrorist attacks carried out by Yemenis en, culminating in the arrest of twelve Somali men suspected of preparing terrorist attacks on behalf of al-Shabaab (see table 5.1). All suspects were released within a couple of days. The rise in arrests shows the enhanced legal and operational competence and increased alertness by the Dutch security services, police, and judicial authorities. They also displayed the focus on foreign threats, immigrant networks, and new centers of disturbance in the Horn of Africa, especially Somalia.

In sum, according to the AIVD and the National Coordinator for Counterterrorism, the development of jihadism in the Netherlands had again become international, including jihadists being flown in from outside Europe expressly to commit acts of terror here,[113] Dutch citizens being recruited for jihad abroad, or terrorists using Dutch airport Schiphol as a transit. This lead the NCTb to raise intermittently the alert level from "restricted" to "substantial" in March 2008 (which it had also been from May 2005 until April 2007).[114] This level was confirmed in the Sixteenth Terrorist Threat Assessment, issued in April 2009, and in the Tenth Anti-Terrorism Progress Report, published two months later.[115] It was lowered to "restricted" again in December 2009 since jihadist attacks against targeting the Netherlands no longer seemed to be imminent, a status that was confirmed in December 2011.[116] However, the Christmas Day plot of 2009 and a number of foreign alerts showed that the Netherlands, with Schiphol as a global airport, could still function as a transit site for international terrorism.

It is difficult to assess clearly the extent to which the jihadist plots, notably the assassination of Theo Van Gogh, were leader-led or leaderless and—correspondingly—whether they were internationally, transnationally, or locally oriented. As demonstrated by the most important cases of jihadist networks in the Netherlands since 2001, it is impossible to strictly divide the terrorist threat in the Netherlands along a pre-2004 international/transnational, leader-led and a post-2004 homegrown and leaderless line, as argued by the AVID.

First, the numbers are too low to derive statistically convincing trends from them. Second, and more important, the different jihadist networks uncovered in 2001 and 2002 displayed a mixture of both indigenous, spontaneous activities and an international orientation and inspiration. The Jihad case revealed both transnational links and domestic activities. And, in addition to its local center of gravity, the Hofstad Group demonstrated an international orientation as well, demonstrated by visits to training camps, participation in international jihad, contacts with terrorist suspects in other countries, preparation for terrorist attacks abroad, and inspiration by a foreign mentor. The Hofstad Group was built on the foundation of its predecessors, proving that terrorism does not emerge from a vacuum. In almost all cases, an amalgam of domestic, transnational, and international activities and actors could be identified, brought together by means of the Internet and facilitated by various personal circumstances.[117] The homegrown jihadists of the Hofstad Group and the alleged al-Shabaab recruits from the Hague arrested in July 2009 did not spontaneously radicalize:[118] they needed real-life jihadist veterans, preachers, or inspirers who could offer them leadership, ideology, connections, and instruments, at least in the initial stages, as Redouan al-Issa offered to the Hofstad Group.

In 2004, Dutch political and public debate focused on the supposedly new threat of homegrown jihadism. This resulted in new counterterrorism measures, the expansion of existing security forces, and the adoption of a range of national and local deradicalization programs. Through these initiatives, the AIVD, NCTb, and other security organs claim to have effectively contained or disrupted the threat of locally organized jihadi networks in the Netherlands.

Given the warnings against a new international terrorism threat after 2008, we should however be careful to identify this as a new type of terrorism. Rather than focusing again strictly on the division between leader-led and leaderless jihad, we should see this development as underlining the fact that jihadists also learn from the past and adapt to circumstances in a gradual and organic way. Terrorist strategies and organization forms are often determined by the security measures undertaken by their counterparts.[119] In the Netherlands, an increase in security measures and disruptive efforts partly caused the transformation of internationally organized groups into local networks, which gave way to a new international jihadist threat again in 2008 and 2009—a trend that persisted after 2011 and transformed into a wave of Dutch youngsters joining the "foreign fight" in Syria. In 2013, the National Coordinator for Security and Counterterrorism counted more than one hundred "foreign fighters" and increased the national threat level to "substantial." Based on this acceleration of events, it should be stressed that terrorism is also a highly reactive phenomenon. Radicals are adaptive to counterterrorism measures and are able to switch quickly among local, national, and international structures than general trend assessments and strict definitions might suggest.

A final remark and caution is called for here. Since 2009, the increased number of dead-end arrests under the 2004 laws has sparked serious criticism in the media and among suspected and targeted minority communities (Moroccans, Somalis, and Yemenis).[120] Moreover, the latest terrorist attacks in the Netherlands involved lone white male operators, a tendency mirrored by the attacks of Anders Breivik on July 22, 2011, in Norway.[121] Thus, authorities were pressed to shift their attention to other types of violent extremist behavior. Notwithstanding the value of disturbance and preventative arrests, counterterrorism focused on jihadist terrorism needs to be calibrated and put into perspective against other types of threats in order to be perceived as legitimate by (targeted) minority groups and society as a whole.

TABLE 5.1

Terrorism arrests in the Netherlands, September 13, 2001–December 2011

Date	Place	Reason for Arrest	Arrested	Released	Convicted	Acquitted	Expelled	Extradited	Escaped
September 13, 2001	Rotterdam	Eik case, suspicion of preparation for terrorist attack	4		2	1	1		
September 24, 2001	Rotterdam	"Eik case	1	1					
November 2001	Amsterdam	Primary school janitor arrested for lack of identification	1	1					
December 22, 2001	Eindhoven	Involvement in attack on Afghan warlord Massoud	1					1	
February 22, 2002	Schiphol	As above	1					1	
April 24, 2002	Bergen op Zoom / Groningen / Eindhoven	Recruiting on behalf of "jihad" (the jihad case)	10	5	2[a]	1		1	1
June 24, 2002	Canada	Involvement in preparations for terrorist attacks (Eik case)	1		1				

(continued)

TABLE 5.1
(Continued)

Date	Place	Reason for Arrest	Arrested	Released	Convicted	Acquitted	Expelled	Extradited	Escaped
August 30, 2002	Den Bosch, Den Helder, Eindhoven, Rotterdam, Roosendaal	Recruiting on behalf of "jihad" (the Jihad case)	12	5		7	2		
November 4, 2002	Eindhoven	Recruiting on behalf of "jihad" (the Jihad case)	2	1		1			
March 2003	Germany	Involvement in preparations for terrorist attacks (Eik case)	1		1		1		
September 2003	Amsterdam	Rendition request from the U.S., based on charges of telecom fraud and support for al-Qaeda	3	1			1	1	
October 2003	Amersfoort, Amsterdam, The Hague, Schiedam	Preparation of terrorist attacks (first arrest of Hofstad Group members)	5	5					
November 2003	Schiedam	ThreateningMember of Parliament Geert Wilders	1		1				
December 7, 2003	Schiphol	Jihadist recruitment	1					1	

Date	Location	Description					
January 27, 2004	North Limburg	Arrested during traffic stop for involvement in Casablanca bombings	1				1
June 30, 2004	The Hague	Preparing terrorist attacks (second arrest of Samir Azzouz)	1			1	
July 17, 2004	Nijmegen	Preparing terrorist attacks during the Nijmegen "Avondvierdaagse" (a national walking event)	2	1			1
July 2004	Rotterdam	Preparing terrorist attacks against the Efteling (theme park) and Diergaarde Blijdorp (zoo)	4	1	3[a]		
August 19, 2004	Roosendaal	Involvement in Madrid bombings	9	2			7
September 21, 2004	Brunssum	Behaving suspiciously around NATO Headquarters	4	4			
September 26, 2004	Utrecht	AIVD indications that explosives were hidden at an address in Buchelius Street	4	4			

(continued)

TABLE 5.1
(Continued)

Date	Place	Reason for Arrest	Arrested	Released	Convicted	Acquitted	Expelled	Extradited	Escaped
September 24, 2004	Sas van Gent	Threatening MP Geert Wilders	1		1				
September 30, 2004	Leidschendam	AIVD employee (interpreter, Moroccan origin) arrested for leaking state secrets to members of the Hofstad Group, among others	1		1				
October 1, 2004	Utrecht	Handling state secrets	1	1					
October 2, 2004	Utrecht	Transporting explosives	1	1					
October 4, 2004	Utrecht	Handling state secrets	1	1					
November 2, 2004	Amsterdam	Assassination of Van Gogh (Mohammed Bouyeri)	1		1				
November 2–3, 2004	Amsterdam	Involvement in assassination of Van Gogh (Hofstad Group)	7	2		5		1	
November 5, 2004	Amsterdam	As above	1			1			

Date	Location	Description					
November 5 and 8, 2004	The Hague	Threatening MP Geert Wilders	4	3	1		
November 10, 2004	The Hague	Arrested in Antheunis Street for involvement in Van Gogh assassination (Hofstad Group: Jason Walters and Ismail Akhnikh)	2		2		
November 10, 2004	Amersfoort, Amsterdam	Involvement in Van Gogh assassination (Hofstad Group)	5			5	
March 24, 2005	Amsterdam	Jihadist recruitment	1		1		
April 15, 2005	Schiedam	Involvement in Van Gogh assassination	1	1			
May 18, 2005	Tours (France)	As above	1	1			
June 9, 2005	Amersfoort	Involvement in jihadist travels to Iraq (Wesam al D.)	4	3			1
June 15, 2005	Amsterdam	Connections to Hofstad Group	1	1			
June 22, 2005	Amsterdam	Automatic weapon ("Piranha" case: Noureddine el-Fatmi, Martine van den Oever, Soumaya Sahla)	3	1	2		

(continued)

TABLE 5.1
(Continued)

Date	Place	Reason for Arrest	Arrested	Released	Convicted	Acquitted	Expelled	Extradited	Escaped
July 11, 2005	Amsterdam	Threatening MP Geert Wilders and possession of homemade explosives	1		1				
July 11, 2005	Dordrecht	Preparing a terrorist attack against Schiphol	3	1	2[a]				
July 29, 2005	Rotterdam	Anonymous phone call	7	7				2	
October 14, 2005	Leiden, Almere, Amsterdam, The Hague	Preparing terrorist attacks ("Piranha" case)	7	2	5				
October 28, 2005	Rotterdam	Preparing attacks	1	1					
November 1, 2005	Amsterdam	Suspicious behaviour on international train	2	2					
November 5, 2005	Rijswijk	Preparing attacks	1	1					
December 14, 2005	Schiphol	Possession of suspicious handbag on Schiphol regional train	1	1					

Late December 2005	Azerbaijan	Arrested in Azerbaijan for allegedly trying to join international jihad; claimed to be "on holiday"	3	3	
April 7, 2006	Schiphol	Making threats in an airplane	5	5	
No date	Leiden	Suspicion of being terrorists ("Nooitgedagt" case)	6	6	
October 3, 2007	Rotterdam	Hiding explosives	2	2	
December 31, 2007	Rotterdam	Preparing terrorist attacks against the Erasmus Bridge	3	3	
August 2008	Rotterdam	False reporting of an airplane hijacking by al-Qaeda	3	2	1
March 12, 2009	Amsterdam	Anonymous phone call about an imminent terrorist threat against IKEA and other stores in Amsterdam South East	7	7	
May 4, 2009	Amsterdam	Maker of the anonymous phone call that resulted in the arrests of March 12	1	1	

(continued)

TABLE 5.1
(Continued)

Date	Place	Reason for Arrest	Arrested	Released	Convicted	Acquitted	Expelled	Extradited	Escaped
July 30, 2009	Kenya	Trying to join a jihadist training camp of al-Shabaab in Somalia[b]	4	4					
September 19, 2009	The Hague	Director of the TodaysArt festival arrested for showing movies about terrorist attacks in The Hague that could lead to copy-cat behavior; released the same day	1	1					
November 8, 2009	Dronten	Request by the United States because of involvement and support of the international jihad	1					1	
August 30, 2010	Amsterdam	Dry run and preparation for terrorist attacks[c]	2	2					
September 19, 2010	Amsterdam	Tip from the British authorities[d]	1	1					
November 23, 2010	Amsterdam	Request of Belgian government	3	1					

Date	City	Charge							
December 24, 2010	Rotterdam	Preparing terrorist attacks and involvement with al-Shabaab[e]	12	12					1
February 22, 2011	Rotterdam	Human trafficking and preparing attacks on oil pipelines in Nigeria	1	1					
April 2011		Suspicion of trying to kill American soldiers in Afghanistan and al-Qaeda[f]	1						
Total			184	112	28	22	5	19	1

[a] Not for terrorist-related activities.

[b] Four suspects (three Dutch citizens of Moroccan descent and one Moroccan with a residence permit) arrested in Kenya, transported to Brussels, extradited to the Netherlands; inquiry is still pending.

[c] Two Yemeni men arrested at Schiphol Airport. Several suspicious objects had been found in their luggage in the United States. Nothing illegal is found, and the men are released a day after their arrest.

[d] A British citizen of Somali descent is arrested on Schiphol Airport after a tip from British authorities that he might be involved in foreign terrorist activities; released for lack of evidence.

[e] Twelve men from Somali descent are arrested in Rotterdam after the Dutch Intelligence Agency (AIVD) tips the police; all suspects are released within a couple of days.

[f] A Dutch citizen of Moroccan descent was arrested in Pakistan in 2010 and extradited to the Netherlands in April 2011. A district court ruled in November that he could be extradited to the United States, case sent to the Court of Appeals.

Source: Based on research conducted by *NRC Weekblad*, "'Vals alarm," June 6, 2009; numbers provided by the Dutch Dutch Public Prosecution Office. Terrorism (and terrorism-related activities such as recruitment, training, and preparation) was defined as a punishable offence only in August 2004. Before that date, terrorism as such could not be prosecuted; the arrests listed before 2004 were based on other grounds (e.g., possession of firearms, lack of identification). Also based on research conducted by *Onderzoeksjournalistiek van de Publieke Omroep*, "Overzicht van aan terrorisme gerelateerde arrestaties in Nederland sinds 11 september 2011," September 10, 2011, http://www.onjo.nl/Item.2558.0.html?&no_cache=1&tx_ttnews%5Btt_news%5D=49511.

NOTES

The author wishes to express her sincere thanks to Bart Schuurman, Quirine Eijkman, Liesbeth van der Heide, Edwin Bakker (Centre for Terrorism and Counterterrorism, the Hague/Leiden Univeristy) and the editors of this volume for their contributions and comments.

1. Roel Willemse, senior policy adviser with the Dutch General Intelligence and Security Service (AIVD), "Terrorism and Radicalisation, a Study in the Dutch Context," in *Radicalisation in Broader Perspective*, ed. The National Coordinator for Counterterrorism (NCTb) (The Hague: NCTb, 2007), 25. Cf. also General Intelligence and Security Service (AIVD), *Violent Jihad in the Netherlands: Current Trends in the Islamist Terrorist Threat* (The Hague: AIVD, 2006), 13–14.

2. Lorenzo Vidino, "The Hofstad Group: The New Face of Terrorist Networks in Europe," *Studies in Conflict and Terrorism* 30, no. 7 (2007): 579–92; Lorenzo Vidino, *Al Qaeda in Europe: The New Battleground of International Jihad* (New York: Prometheus Books, 2006), esp. chapter 12, "The Van Gogh Assassination." See also Bart Schuurman, Quirine Eijkman, and Edwin Bakker, "The Hofstadgroup Revisited: Questioning the Status of a 'Quintessential' Homegrown Jihadist Network," *Terrorism and Political Violence* 25 (2014, forthcoming): 1–23.

3. Cf. the discussion by Nassim Taleb on the danger of measuring the risk of rare events, making society dependent on spurious measurements: Nassim Nicholas Taleb, *The Black Swan: The Impact of the Highly Improbable* (New York: Random House, 2007).

4. A highly informative account of the assassination of Van Gogh and the development of the Hofstad Group can be found in Albert Benschop, "Jihad in the Netherlands: Chronicle of a Political Murder Foretold," http://www.sociosite.org/jihad_nl_en.php (accessed June 2009).

5. Verdict against Bouyeri, District Court of Amsterdam, Case Number LJN: AU0025, Rechtbank Amsterdam, 13/129227-04, July 26, 2005.

6. In the Netherlands, life sentences are rare. Bouyeri was the twenty-eighth person to receive such a sentence since 1945, war criminals included. Capital felonies, such as murder, usually result in sentences of ten to fifteen years. The new terrorism law, however, states that if there is a terrorist motive for a crime, the sentence can be increased by half. Imprisonments ordinarily in excess of fifteen years can be upgraded to life imprisonment, as was the case with Bouyeri.

7. Description of this case is based, among others, on the records of the national prosecutor in the Hofstad Group case: National Prosecutor's Office, *Requisitoir van de officier van Justitie*, part 1, January 23, 2006, and part 2, January 25, 2006; verdict in the Hofstad Group Case, District Court of Rotterdam, March 10, 2006; verdict against Bouyeri, District Court of Amsterdam; also see http://zoeken.rechtspraak.nl /resultpage.aspx?snelzoeken=true&searchtype=ljn&ljn=AU0025&u_ljn=AU0025;

verdict in the Hofstad Group case; Appeal Court; "The 'Hofstadgroep,'" *Transnational Terrorism, Security, and the Rule of Law*, Working Paper, April 2008, available at www .transnationalterrorism.eu.

8. The Review Committee on the Intelligence and Security Services officially established in March 2008 that this had been a serious intelligence failure as evidence surfaced before the attack that Bouyeri was at least affiliated with Dutch jihadist groups. See the official report by the Review Committee on the Intelligence and Security Services, "Toezichtsrapport inzake de afwegingsprocessen van de AIVD met betrekking tot Mohammed B.," *Commissie van Toezicht betreffende de Inlichtingen- en Veiligheidsdiensten (CTIVD)*, no. 17 (March 2008).

9. Siem Eikelenboom, *Niet bang om te sterven. Dertig jaar terrorisme in Nederland* (Amsterdam: Nieuw Amsterdam, 2007), 23–27; see also National Prosecutor's Office (Landelijk Parket), "Repliek van de officier van justitie in de strafzaken tegen Nadir A. etc.," Amsterdam, February 6, 2005, 4–5, 9–10, 17–23.

10. *Trouw*, July 9, 2005.

11. Jutta Chorus and Ahmet Olgun, *In godsnaam. Het jaar van Theo van Gogh* (Amsterdam: Contact, 2005), 64, 200.

12. Ruud Peters, "De ideologische en religieuze ontwikkeling van Mohammed B. Deskundigenrapport in de strafzaak tegen Mohammed B. in opdracht van het Openbaar Ministerie opgesteld voor de arrondissementsrechtbank Amsterdam," (2005), http://www.sociosite.org/jihad/peters_rapport.pdf, 8; Peters was an expert witness for the prosecution in the trial. Also see Verdict in the Hofstad Group case, paragraph 109, 116.

13. For his religious and ideological ideas and their development, see Peters, "De ideologische en religieuze ontwikkeling."

14. Statement of Interior Minister Johan Remkes during the parliamentary debate on the murder, Handelingen Tweede Kamer, November 11, 2004, No. 22-1303; Chorus and Olgun, *In godsnaam*, 200.

15. National Prosecutor's Office, *Requisitoir van de officier van Justitie in de strafzaak tegen Mohammed B.*, Amsterdam, July 12, 2005, 7–8.

16. Ibid., 7.

17. Ibid., 10–26.

18. Ruud Peters, "Dutch Extremist Islamism: Van Gogh's Murderer and His Ideas," in *Jihadi Terrorism and the Radicalisation Challenge in Europe*, ed. Rik Coolsaet (London: Ashgate, 2008) 115–30.

19. Petter Nesser, "The Slaying of the Dutch Filmmaker: Religiously Motivated Violence or Islamist Terrorism in the Name of Global Jihad?," FFI/Rapport-2005/0376 (Kjeller, Norway, 2005), 25.

20. National Prosecutor's Office, *Requisitoir van de officier van Justitie in de strafzaak tegen Mohammed B.*, 29.

21. National Prosecutor's Office, *Repliek van de officier van justitie in de strafzaken tegen Nadir A.*, 31–32.

22. A Dutch biography of this sheikh is available on the website of the "Marokko Community," in which references to the September 11 fatwa are found: "Sheikh Hamoud bin Uqla as-Shu'aybi. De levensloop van een groot geleerde," posted July 24, 2008, http://forums.marokko.nl/showthread.php?t=2092457 (accessed July 11, 2009).

23. National Prosecutor's Office, *Requisitoir van de officier van Justitie in de strafzaak tegen Mohammed B.*, 43.

24. Ibid., 49; District Court of Amsterdam, *Verdict against Bouyeri*, LJN AU0025, 13/129227–04, July 26, 2005.

25. "Zalm: we zijn in oorlog! Regering: terrorisme met wortel en tak uitroeien," *Algemeen Dagblad*, November 6, 2004; "Terroristen met dubbele nationaliteit raken Nederlands paspoort kwijt. Kabinet verklaart de oorlog aan terreur," *Het Parool*, November 6, 2004; "Overheid wil meer armslag: anti-terreurmaatregelen," *Trouw*, November 6, 2004.

26. See, for example, Ron Eyerman, *The Assassination of Theo van Gogh: From Social Drama to Cultural Trauma* (Durham, N.C.: Duke University Press, 2008); Ian Buruma, *Murder in Amsterdam: The Death of Theo van Gogh and the Limits of Tolerance* (New York: Penguin, 2006).

27. Interview with an AIVD official, the Hague, October 10, 2008.

28. This term is used by MI5 to "refer to groups of extremists who support the Al-Qaida cause and who are involved in providing financial and logistical support, rather than being directly involved in terrorist attack planning" (Intelligence and Security Committee [ISC], *Could 7/7 Have Been Prevented? Review of the Intelligence on the London Terrorist Attacks on 7 July 2005* [London: HMSO, 2009], 7).

29. AIVD, *Violent Jihad in the Netherlands*, 17–26.

30. Ibid., 29, 37, 43–50.

31. AIVD, "Recruitment for the Jihad in the Netherlands: From Incident to Trend," press release, December 9, 2002.

32. C. J. De Poot and A. Sonnenschein published a highly interesting description of the general characteristics of jihadist networks that were active between 2001 and 2005 in the Netherlands. However, since they based their research on police records, they had to anonymize their text and combined the data from the different networks into one account. That still makes the report crucial in understanding the nature and dynamics of jihadi networks in the Netherlands, but it (intentionally) does not offer concrete information on separate networks, cases, or individuals. See C. J. de Poot and A. Sonnenschein, *Jihadistisch terrorisme in Nederland. Een beschrijving op basis van afgesloten opsporingsonderzoeken* (The Hague: WODC, 2010).

33. "Threats and Responses: The Trail in Europe: Four Suspected of Dutch Plot Go on Trial," *New York Times*, December 3, 2002, http://www.nytimes.com/2002/12/03/world/threats-and-responses-the-trail-in-europe-4-suspected-of-dutch-plot-go-on-trial.html.

34. Chris Marsden, "Why Did It Take So Long to Bring Abu Hamza to Trial?," *Global Research*, February 20, 2006. http://www.globalresearch.ca/index.php?context=va&aid=2014 (accessed December 28, 2009).

35. Police records on the "Eik zaak," Criminal Investigation, Rotterdam; paraphrased in Eikelenboom, *Niet bang om te sterven*, 66–73.

36. LJN AP3601, Hoger beroep, 2200071203, June 21, 2004, http://www.wetboek-online .nl/jurisprudentie/ljnAP3601.html.

37. "Thwarting Terror Cells in Europe," CNN, January 23, 2002; "In Paris, a Frightening Look at Terror's Inconspicuous Face," *Los Angeles Times*, October 21, 2001.

38. LJN AP3601, Hoger beroep, 2200071203, Gerechtshof 's-Gravenhage, June 21, 2004, http://www.wetboek-online.nl/jurisprudentie/ljnAP3601.html.

39. LJN AF2141, Rechtbank Rotterdam, 10/150080/01, December 18, 2002, http:// zoeken.rechtspraak.nl/detailpage.aspx?ljn=af2141; Polyan Spoon, national prosecutor for terrorism affairs, interview Rotterdam, September 7, 2009.

40. Verdict, LJN AP3601, Gerechtshof 's-Gravenhage , 2200071203, June 21, 2004, http://jure.nl/ljn%20ap3601, point 11; verdict, LJN AP2058, Gerechtshof 's-Gravenhage, 2200071403, June 21, 2004, http://jure.nl/ap2058; verdict, LJN AV4122, Hoge Raad, 01422/05, September 5, 2006, http://jure.nl/av4122.

41. Eikelenboom, *Niet bang om te sterven*, 72–73.

42. Verdict of the Hague Court of appeal, June 12, 2004, No. 1015008001.

43. Cf. "Echte terreur of een hetze," *Trouw*, August 15, 2005; legal file on the "Jihad" case, Rotterdam police; Eikelenboom, *Niet bang om te sterven*, 73–74.

44. National Prosecutor's Office, "Requisitoir in de strafzaak tegen Jerome Courtailler en Abdelghani Rabia," December 4, 2002.

45. ISC, *Could 7/7 Have Been Prevented?*, 7.

46. For an account of Massoud's assassination, see Jon Lee Anderson, *The Lion's Grave: Dispatches from Afghanistan* (New York: Grove Press, 2002); see also "Major Terror Trial in Belgium," CNN, May 21, 2003.

47. Lorenzo Vidino and Erick Stakelbeck, "Dutch Lessons," *Wall Street Journal Europe*, August 7, 2003, http://www.investigativeproject.org/169/dutch-lessons.

48. AIVD, "Recruitment for the Jihad in the Netherlands," 8.

49. "Herdenking in kaftans en jeans," *NRC Handelsblad*, January 23, 2002; AIVD, "Recruitment for the Jihad in the Netherlands."

50. Verdict by the Court of Rotterdam, December 18, 2002, No. 10/150080/01.

51. Ibid.

52. Eikelenboom, *Niet bang om te sterven*, 78–81.

53. See Rick Coolsaet and Teun van de Voorde, "The Evolution of Terrorism in 2005: A Statistical Assessment," University of Gent Research Paper, February 2006.

54. Spoon, interview.

55. NCTb, *Salafisme in Nederland* (The Hague: NCTb, 2008), 25; "De omstreden El Tawheed-Moskee," NOVA broadcast, November 9, 2004, http://www.novatv.nl/page /detail/uitzendingen/3011 (accessed June 2009). According to NOVA, the Saudi businessman Aqeel Alaqeel financed the el-Tawheed mosque with 1.3 million euros. Al-Haramein was blacklisted as an al-Qaeda charity, but the accusations were not substantiated and the mosque continued to operate. I am grateful to Dennis de Widt for these references.

56. Ministers of the interior and justice, "Feitenrelaas," attachment to Letter to Parliament, November 10, 2004, Handelingen van de Tweede Kamer, No. 29854.

57. For an account of this story, see "Samir A. Staatsvijand nr.één," *KRO Reporter*, October 1, 2006; the documentary includes interviews with Azzouz and his wife. Also see Eric Vrijsen, "Van Samir A tot Marad J," *Elsevier*, December 1, 2005; Arjan Erkel, *Samir* (Amsterdam: Uitgeverij Balans, 2007).

58. Nesser, "The Slaying of the Dutch Filmmaker," 17–19.

59. Ibid.; "Spanish Link to Dutch Film-Maker's Killing Is Probed," *El País*, November 9, 2004; Craig S. Smith, "Dutch Look for Qaeda Link After Killing of Filmmaker," *New York Times*, November 6, 2004; "Muslims Arrested in Van Gogh Murder Belong to Militant Group," *Haaretz*, November 13, 2004.

60. Emerson Vermaat, *De Hofstadgroep. Portret van een radicaal-islamitisch netwerk* (Soesterberg: Uitgeverij Aksent, 2005), 76–77.

61. Eikelenboom, *Niet bang om te sterven*, 81–83; National Prosecutor's Office, *Requisitoir in de strafzaak tegen de verdachten van de Hofstadgroep*, part 1; Spoon, interview.

62. National Prosecutor's Office (Landelijk Parket), *Repliek van de officier van justitie in de strafzaken tegen Nadir A.*, 7, 13.

63. "Dutch Radical Islamic Group Planned Euro 2004 Attack in Portugal," Agence France-Presse, November 15, 2004; "Dutch Islamists Planned Barroso Attack," Reuters, November 15, 2004; Ministry of Justice, Letter to Parliament, with a Report on the Assassination of Theo van Gogh, November 10, 2004, Handelingen van de Tweede Kamer (HTK) 2004–2005, 29,854, No. 3. Also see the parliamentary debate on this report on November 11, 2004; HTK 2004–2005, No. 22, 1,278–1,332.

64. Marc Sageman, *Leaderless Jihad: Terror Networks in the Twenty-First Century* (Philadelphia: University of Pennsylvania Press, 2008), 79; also see Vidino, "The Hofstad Group," 585–87; Marc Sageman, "Hofstad Case and The Blob Theory," in *Theoretical Frames on Pathways to Violent Radicalization* (Artis Research and Risk Modelling, August 2009), http://www.artisresearch.com/articles/ARTIS_Theoretical_Frames _August_2009.pdf, 14.

65. See their defense in the court cases in Rotterdam and Amsterdam, 2006; "Hofstadgroep bestaat helemaal niet," *NRC Handelsblad*, February 1, 2006.

66. National Prosecutor's Office, *Requisitoir van de officier van Justitie*, 44–45. For the role of al-Issar also see Vermaat, *De Hofstadgroep*, 69–74.

67. Peters, "Dutch Extremist Islamism," 118.

68. Verdict in the case of the Hofstad Group, paragraph 109.

69. At present, al-Issar is supposedly arrested and detained in Syria.

70. See also Vidino, "The Hofstad Group," 585;

71. National Prosecutor's Office, *Requisitoir van de officier van Justitie*; verdict in the Hofstad Group case; "The 'Hofstadgroep,'" *Transnational Terrorism, Security, and the Rule of Law*, Working Paper.

72. "Gewonden bij politieactie in Den Haag," *De Telegraaf*, November 10, 2004.

73. Verdict in the Hofstad Group case. For the story of female radicalization around the Hofstad Group, also see Beatrice de Graaf, *Gevaarlijke vrouwen. Tien militante vrouwen in het vizier* (Amsterdam: Boom, 2012) 249–89.

74. Verdict on appeal, Court of the Hague, October 2, 2008, No. 2200734906.

75. "Bouyeri: Vergelijking met Bin Laden te veel eer," *Elsevier*, February 2, 2006.

76. "Jason W.: Ik wilde interessant doen," *Elsevier*, December 9, 2005.

77. Verdict, LJN AV5108, Rechtbank Rotterdam, 10/000322-04; 10/000328-04; 10/000396-04; 10/000393-04; 10000325-04; 10/000323-04; 10/000395-04, March 10, 2006, http://jure.nl/av5108.

78. Verdict in the Piranha case, Court of Rotterdam, December 1, 2006; "Samir A.: acht jaar cel voor terreurplannen," *Elsevier*, December 1, 2006.

79. "Hofstadgroep vrijgesproken van terrorisme," *De Volkskrant*, January 23, 2008.

80. The Hague Court of Appeals, decision in the appeal of Jason Walters, LJN: BC2576, Gerechtshof 's-Gravenhage, 2200189706, January 23, 2008.

81. Spoon, interview.

82. The Hague Court of Appeals, decision in the appeal in the Piranha case, October 2, 2008, No. 2200734906.

83. Ibid.

84. Verdict in the Piranha case, LJN: AZ3589, 10/600052-05, 10/600108-05, 10/600134-05, 10/600109-05, 10/600122-05, 10/600023-06, 10/600100-06.

85. "Hoge Raad vernietigt vrijspraken in de Hofstadgroep zaken," *Hoge Raad*, February 2, 2010.

86. Verdict, LJN BK5196, Supreme Court of the Netherlands, 08/00740, February 2, 2010, http://jure.nl/bk5196.

87. "Hoge Raad vernietigt vrijspraak Hofstadgroep," *NRC Handelsblad*, February 2, 2010.

88. Verdict, LJN: BO7690, Court of Amsterdam, nr. 2300075110, December 17, 2010, http://jure.nl/bo7690.

89. Verdict, LJN: BO9018, BO9017, BO9016, BO9015, BO9014, Gerechtshof Amsterdam, 23-000748-10, December 17, 2010; LJN: BO8032, Gerechtshof Amsterdam, 23-000747-10; 17 December 2010, http://jure.nl/bo8032; LJN: BO7690, Gerechtshof Amsterdam, 23-000751-10; December 17, 2010, http://jure.nl/bo7690.

90. Federal Prosecutor (Openbaar Ministerie), "Evaluatie Perspectief op 2010," May 19, 2011, http://www.om.nl/publish/pages/137849/evaluatie_perspectief_op_2010.pdf, 23.

91. AIVD, De politieke Islam in Nederland, May 1998; Ministry of Interior and Kingdom Relations (BZK), "BVD Focuses on Forces Against Integration," May 22, 2001; AIVD, "Recruitment for the Jihad in the Netherlands."

92. "Kaderbesluit van de Raad van 13 juni 2002 (2002/475/JBZ) inzake terrorismebestrijding," Publicatieblad van de Europese Gemeenschappen, L164/3, June 22, 2002.

93. W. Koopstra and P. Ende, *Wettelijk kader terrorismebestrijding* (The Hague: Sdu, 2007); M. J Borgers, *De vlucht naar voren* (The Hague: Boom Juridische uitgevers, 2007); T. Roos, "Terrorisme en strafrecht in Nederland," in *Hedendaags radicalisme. Verklaringen & aanpak*, ed. S. Harchaoui (Apeldoorn/Antwerp: Het Spinhuis, 2006), 81–113; see also B. de Graaf and B. de Graaff, "Counterterrorism in the Netherlands: The 'Dutch Approach,'" in *Intelligence, Security, and Policing Post-9/11: The UK's Response to the War on Terror*, ed. Jon Moran and Mark Phythian (London: Palgrave Macmillan, 2008), 183–202.

94. The Netherlands Counterterrorism Coordinator, "Comprehensive Approach to Radicalism and Radicalisation Required," press release, October 3, 2005, available at http://english.minbzk.nl//news-and-press/@63738/comprehensive_0; Monica den Boer, "Wake-up Call for the Lowlands: Dutch Counterterrorism from a Comparative Perspective," *Cambridge Review of International Affairs* 20, no. 2 (2007): 285–302. This support for new, sometimes rather intrusive measures also inspired criticism. See Herman van Gunsteren, *Gevaarlijk veilig* (Amsterdam: Van Gennep, 2004); the Wiardi Beckman Stichting criticized the fact that the social-democrats (the PvDA) took part in this antiterrorism hype: WBS, ed., *De bedreigde rechtsstaat. Sociaal-democratie, terrorismebestrijding en burgerschap* (Amsterdam: Wiardi Beckman Stichting, 2007), 53–60.

95. See, for example, the more than 200 research projects initiated in the Netherlands since 2004 that deal with Muslim radicalization and deradicalization. Such projects have received the bulk of government research funds, even if the violence perpetrated by Muslim extremists has resulted in only one victim so far, Theo Van Gogh. See http://www.terrorismdata.leiden.edu/, a project coordinated by the Centre for Terrorism and Counterterrorism/the Hague. A detailed and interesting example of such research projects on radicalization is made by Frank Buijs, Froukje Demant, and Atef Hamdy, *Strijders van eigen bodem. Radicale en democratische moslims in Nederland* (Amsterdam: Amsterdam University Press, 2006).

96. "Campagne 'Nederland tegen terrorisme' legt nadruk op voorkomen radicalisering," *Persbericht NCTb*, November 19, 2007; "Minder privacy, makkelijker straffen," *NRC Handelsblad*, September 8, 2007; E. Bakker, "Contraterrorismebeleid: mag het een onsje minder?," *Internationale Spectator* 62, no. 2 (2008): 61–62.

97. See "Dutch Struggle to Prevent Terror and Protect Rights," *New York Times*, December 25, 2005.

98. Spoon, interview.

99. "Terror Plot Trial Opens," *Radio Netherlands*, February 24, 2005. This article described the second trial of Samir Azzouz, who was arrested in June 2004 for alleged robbery of a supermarket but was released in April 2005—only to be arrested for the third time in October 2005 (and convicted in December 2006).

100. "The 'Hofstadgroep,'" *Transnational Terrorism, Security, and the Rule of Law*, Working Paper 16; AIVD, *Annual Report 2006* (The Hague: AIVD, 2007), 33 (in Dutch).

101. "AIVD zoekt link met aanslag Casablanca," *De Volkskrant*, July 25, 2004; "Terror Plot Trial Opens," *Radio Netherlands*.

102. AIVD, *Annual Report 2008* (The Hague: AIVD, April 2009), 20–22.

103. "Ministerie knoeit met ambtsberichten," *De Volkskrant*, April 18, 2005.

104. AIVD, *Annual Report 2008*, 27–29; A. Olgun, "Nuance keert terug in Nederland," *NRC Handelsblad*, February 13, 2008; "Bijna 3000 digitale knuffels voor PVV-voorman Wilders," *Metro*, January 30, 2008; B. Heijne, "Waarom ik Geert Wilders dankbaar ben," *NRC Handelsblad*, January 26 , 2008.

105. AIVD, *Annual Report 2008*, 20–22; NCTb, "Samenvatting Dreigingsbeeld Terrorisme Nederland," September 2011 (DTN26), p. 2.

106. AIVD, *Annual Report 2008*, 20–22.

107. Ibid.,, 17–19, 23–24.

108. *Submission*, dir. Theo van Gogh, written by Ayaan Hirsi Ali, 10 mins., in English. The movie was broadcast on August 29, 2004, and caused considerable uproar in the Muslim world. See "Ex-Muslim Turns Her Lens on a Taboo," *New York Times*, September 27, 2004. *Submission* was allegedly one of the reasons Bouyeri selected Theo van Gogh as his victim. Ehsan Jami, *An Interview with Muhammed*, in English, December 9, 2008. On *Fitna*, see "Fitna belangrijkste reden dreiging," *De Volkskrant*, December 3, 2008.

Joustra's warnings did not cause much upheaval. Instead, fear of terrorism began to fade, which is also apparent elsewhere in Europe. See "Fears of an Islamic Revolt in Europe Begin to Fade," *Observer* (London), July 26, 2009.

109. "Strijd in Somalië lokt jongeren," *De Volkskrant*, July 31, 2009.

110. The NCTb had already warned against these recruiting efforts within the Somali community in the Netherlands in June. See NCTb, Letter to Parliament with the Tenth counterterrorism Progress Report, June 22, 2009, http://english.nctb.nl /current_topics/Anti_terrorism_progress_report (accessed August 3, 2009); also see "Police Swoop on Melbourne Homes After Somali Islamists' Terror Plot Exposed," *Australian*, August 4, 2009; "Minnesota Men Charged in Somali Recruiting," CNN, July 16, 2009.

111. "Terror Suspect Umar Farouk Abdulmutallab Faces Twenty Years, $250,000 Fine for Attack on Flight 253," *New York Daily News*, December 26, 2009.

112. "Onderzoek naar veiligheid Schiphol," *De Pers*, December 26, 2009; "Nederland loopt voor de troepen uit met bodyscan," *De Volkskrant*, December 30, 2009.

113. See also Bruce Hoffman, "Covering the Waterfront: The Continuing, Myriad Threats From Both Leader-Led and Leader-Less Terrorism," *SITE* 2, no. 6 (June 2009): 3–6. The Dutch prosecutor for terrorist affairs, Polyan Spoon, however warns correctly that the number of incidents is rather low for identifying and defining a real trend with any certainty yet (Spoon, interview).

114. NCTb, Letter to Parliament with a Summary of the Twelfth Threat Report, March 6, 2008.

115. NCTb, Letter to Parliament with a Summary of the Sixteenth Terrorist Threat Assessment Netherlands, April 6, 2009; NCTb, Letter to Parliament with the Tenth

Counterterrorism Progress Report, June 22, 2009, http://english.nctb.nl/current _topics/Anti_terrorism_progress_report (accessed July 3, 2009).

116. NCTb, Letter to Parliament with the Eleventh Counterterrorism Progress Report, December 15, 2009; NCTV, DTN 27, 12 December 2011.

117. NCTb, *Jihadisten en het internet* (The Hague: NCTb, December 2006).

118. "Kenya Arrests Dutchmen Headed for Somalia," *NRC Handelsblad*, July 30, 2009. The suspects had to be released for lack of evidence.

119. See also Bob de Graaff, "Winnen de dark mobs het van hun bestrijders?," *Beleid, Politiek en Maatschappij* 36, no. 2 (2009): 132–239.

120. Cf. news item by *Onderzoeksjournalistiek van de Publieke Omroep*, "Overzicht van aan terrorisme gerelateerde arrestaties in Nederland sinds 11 september 2011," http:// www.onjo.nl/Item.2558.0.html?&no_cache=1&tx_ttnews%5Btt_news%5D=49511, September 10, 2011; cf. also B. A. de Graaf and Quirine Eijkman, "Terrorismebestrijding & securitisering: een rechtssociologische verkenning van de neveneffecten," *Justitiële Verkenningen* 37, no. 8 (2011): 33–52.

121. On April 30, 2009, thirty-eight-year-old Karst Tates drove a car into a crowd celebrating Queen's Day in Apeldoorn, killing eight, including himself. His intentions remain unclear; he was possibly driven by antimonarchical resentment. Cf. www. Karsttates.com; "Karst T. had hekel aan koningshuis," *NU.nl*, 16 May 2009. On April 9, 2011, twenty-four-year-old Tristan van der Vlis went on a shooting spree in a local mall in Alphen aan de Rijn, killing six beforfe shooting himself. He had a history of psychiatric problems. See "Netherlands Shooting Kills Six," *BBC News*, April 9, 2011.

[6]

Leadership and the Toronto 18

STEWART BELL

The world awoke to the threat of al-Qaeda terrorism on the morning of September 11, 2001, but for Canada, that moment came almost two years earlier. On December 14, 1999, Ahmed Ressam loaded explosives and detonators into the trunk of a rented Chrysler sedan and left Vancouver, British Columbia, to bomb Los Angeles International Airport. Ressam was an Algerian who had been living in Montreal since 1994, despite his lack of refugee status, and supporting himself with petty crime. He befriended a group of North African extremists who had fought in Bosnia and Afghanistan and, in 1998, trained at Abu Zubaydah's camps in eastern Afghanistan. At the Khalden and Darunta camps, Ressam learned "how to blow up the infrastructure of a country" and returned to Canada in 1999 with $12,000, precursor chemicals, and a notebook full of bomb-making instructions.[1] As he made the final preparations for the attack in a Vancouver motel room, Ressam phoned Afghanistan to ask whether Osama bin Laden wanted to take credit for the attack, but he received no reply.

Ressam took a car ferry to Port Angeles, Washington, and attempted to cross the border, but he behaved erratically and U.S. customs officers searched his vehicle. They found the components of the bomb in the spare tire compartment. Ressam fled on foot but was tackled and caught. He was dubbed the Millennium Bomber because he had planned the attack for January 1, 2000. After a Los Angeles jury convicted Ressam, he acknowledged that Abu Zubaydah had provided encouragement and facilitation and that bin Laden was aware of the operation.[2] A White House memo written in the summer of 2001 said the United States had received intelligence indicating that bin Laden intended to retaliate for the 1998 U.S. missile strike on an al-Qaeda base in Afghanistan and that the Ressam plot was a possible "first serious attempt to implement a terrorist strike in the U.S."[3]

By the time of the Ressam plot, Canada already had a long history of political violence. Aside from domestic extremists such as the separatist Front de Libération du Quebec and the leftist Squamish Five, most major foreign terrorist groups operated in Canada, where they were engaged in fund raising, propaganda, recruitment, procurement, and collection of intelligence. Further, they generally tried to harness diaspora communities to support homeland causes, resulting in a "spillover effect" in which foreign conflicts were imported into Canada. Rarely but devastatingly, they engaged in mass-casualty violence, the most notorious example being the 1985 bombing of Air India Flight 182, which was outbound from Toronto. Canadian Sikh terrorists were responsible for the attack, which killed 329 and until 9/11 was the deadliest terrorist incident in modern history. More recently, Sri Lanka's Tamil Tigers have conducted fund-raising, propaganda, and weapons procurement in Toronto and Montreal.[4]

Sunni Islamist extremists have also operated in Canada since early in the 1990s. A central figure was Ahmed "al-Kanadi" Khadr, an Egyptian-born engineer who was close to Osama bin Laden, Ayman al-Zawahiri, and Gulbuddin Hekmatyar and who used Canada as a base for financing paramilitary training camps in Afghanistan.[5] Other Islamist extremists active in Canada included Essam Marzouk, a training-camp instructor who played a behind-the-scenes role in the 1998 bombings of the U.S. embassies in Kenya and Tanzania. However, for Canada, the Ressam case was a "watershed event in the evolution of the Sunni Islamic threat."[6] Until then, Islamist terrorists were using Canada primarily as a safe haven. The Ressam case signaled that Canada had become "an active operational environment."[7]

The 9/11 attacks were therefore seen by the Canadian intelligence community not as the arrival of a new threat but as a symbol of "the failure of Western governments to adapt to a threat environment that had already changed."[8] After 9/11, Canada and its allies continued to monitor, disrupt, and arrest Canada-based Sunni Islamist extremists who had participated in terrorist training or operations abroad, but the profile of counterterrorism targets began to change. Whereas previously they had been foreigners whose radicalization had begun overseas, increasingly they were young Canadian citizens whose radicalization had occurred at least partly within Canada. For example, Mohammed Mansour Jabarah, after graduating from a Catholic high school in southern Ontario, traveled to Afghanistan for training and attended several camps, including the al-Farooq camp near Kandahar. He fought with the Taliban, met bin Laden, and formally joined al-Qaeda by pledging the oath known as *bayat*. Apparently seeing leadership potential in Jabarah, bin Laden sent him to Karachi to train under Khalid Sheikh Mohammed, who assigned him to oversee a joint al Qaeda–Jemaah Islamiyah plot to bomb the American and Israeli embassies in Singapore.[9] Using money supplied by al-Qaeda, Jabarah scouted the targets and was in the planning stages of the operation when the Singaporean authorities discovered the plot. Jabarah fled to Malaysia and Thailand before al-Qaeda assigned him to travel to Oman, where authorities caught him in 2002. After confessing to Canadian intelligence, Jabarah surrendered to the FBI and provided information about al-Qaeda and its central figures. He is now serving a life sentence.[10]

The influence of al-Qaeda was also a factor in the next major investigation of a Canadian Sunni Islamist extremist. Early in 2003, Britain's MI5 launched Operation Crevice to investigate an al-Qaeda "facilitation network" in the United Kingdom.[11] In February 2004, a twenty-four-year-old Canadian named Mohammad Momin Khawaja arrived in the United Kingdom and showed the subjects of the investigation, who were under surveillance, a remote-detonation device he was building; he called it the "hifidigimonster." They asked him to build about thirty of them, and he agreed. Although the Canadian judge ruled that Khawaja did not know specifically how the detonators were to be used, British police found 600 kilograms of ammonium nitrate in a locker rented by the group and overheard them discussing mass-casualty attacks against such targets as the Bluewater shopping mall and Ministry of Sound nightclub. After UK authorities arrested five suspects in March 2004, Khawaja was arrested in Ottawa. The police search of Khawaja's home turned up not only assault rifles, ammunition, and detonators but also jihadist literature, some of it by bin Laden's late partner in jihad, Abdullah Azzam. A web of ties among the British group and al-Qaeda figures was uncovered, although the Canadian judge said there was no evidence Khawaja knew of these connections. The members of the group, including Khawaja, had trained in Pakistan. In an e-mail, Khawaja called bin Laden "the most beloved person to me."[12]

Khawaja was the first person charged under the Anti-Terrorism Act passed by Canada's parliament in response to the 9/11 attacks. The legislation explicitly criminalized terrorism and terrorist financing for the first time. The fact that Khawaja was Canadian-born further stoked concerns about "homegrown" radicalization and recruitment. Analysts with the Canadian Security Intelligence Service (CSIS) began reporting the emergence of a new generation of extremists who were long-time residents or citizens of Western countries but had nonetheless embraced the al-Qaeda philosophy.[13] The CSIS Intelligence Analysis Branch assessed that young, committed Canadian jihadists had become a significant threat to national security and that their familiarity with Canada and Canadian customs, fluent English, and legitimate Canadian passports allowed them to evade scrutiny. "For terrorist recruiters, these young men's idealism, hatred, language skills and cultural familiarity with the West renders them valuable potential resources in the international Islamic extremist movement."[14] While CSIS considered the process of radicalization to be highly individual, common factors included the influence of extremist fathers and spiritual advisers and the perception, often fed by heavy Internet use, that Islam was under attack from the West. "You can become radicalized and committed to the Al Qaeda ideology without ever having been to an Al Qaeda training camp in Pakistan or Afghanistan. You can do all of that over the Internet. You can learn techniques and acquire materials over the Internet. You can assemble an operational cell over the Internet," Jack Hooper, the CSIS deputy director, operations, said in testimony to the Standing Senate Committee on National Security and Defence.[15]

CSIS launched Operation Claymore to investigate an amorphous group of Toronto-based youths active on extremist Web forums. The group had two leaders who were high school friends. Zakaria Amara was a young gas jockey who was born in Jordan and lived in Saudi Arabia and Cyprus before immigrating to Canada with his Christian mother and Muslim father. Amara's online activities included posting poetry in which he complained that Westerners called him "Osama" and "extreme" and looked at him in a "funny" way. The other leader, Fahim Ahmad, was born in Afghanistan in 1984 and fled with his parents to Pakistan until he was ten years old, at which point he moved to Canada. His mother was a teacher, his father a civil engineer. After 9/11, he began spending more time at the mosque, where

> he began to interact with individuals who believed Islam was under attack and that Muslims everywhere needed to stand up for their faith and for those Muslims whose countries were being attacked by the United States and its allies. . . . At the same time Mr. Ahmad began to spend more time on the Internet, including sites making claims that atrocities were being committed against Muslims by Western forces overseas. He became convinced it was his duty to assist the Afghani people and his faith by becoming involved in the conflict.[16]

In his online postings, he talked about the Taliban and complained that his parents were not religious and had disapproved when he told them he wanted to "fight for Allah."[17] Both leaders were consumers of al-Qaeda propaganda, which clearly shaped their ideology, motivation, and tactics, and, to that extent, the Toronto 18 group could be described as al-Qaeda led.

Much of the early discussion concerned training. Typically, at least one member of an al-Qaeda-inspired terrorist group has trained at a foreign camp. Such camps not only provide weapons and tactical training but also allow trainees to network and strengthen their ideological beliefs. Camp graduates often go on to become leaders of al-Qaeda-inspired cells and train their colleagues.[18] A British extremist named Aabid Khan, a.k.a. Abu Umar, led the Toronto group's online discussions about how to train, where, with whom, and how to finance it. Although not a member of al-Qaeda, Abu Umar was a committed peddler of al-Qaeda ideology and a recruiter for Pakistani terrorist groups. Evidence seized from his computer revealed that he was in contact with Lashkar-e-Taiba (LeT) and Jaish-e-Mohammed (JeM).[19] "He preyed on vulnerable young people and turned them into recruits to his cause, using Internet chat to lure them in then incite them to fight," the British Crown Prosecution Service said in a press release following his conviction. "He arranged their passage to

Pakistan for terrorism training, and talked about 'a worldwide battle.' "[20] A resident of the British city of Bradford and the son of Pakistani immigrants, Abu Umar traveled repeatedly to Pakistan, staying for up to six months, and described himself as an "orthodox Muslim" with "strong Islamic beliefs."[21] He had been fascinated with computers from an early age and, at age twelve, began using the Internet to follow the struggles of armed Islamist groups in Chechnya and elsewhere. He visited Internet newsgroups and forums to discuss jihad and contemporary Muslim issues, as well as the military weapons and tactics of mujaheddin groups. Abu Umar wanted to use Toronto as a base where recruits would assemble before and after their training in Pakistan, and he discussed renting basement apartments around the city for that purpose. "He was always spoken of in the sense of one who could facilitate travel to places for training and was particularly hopeful of having a place near Toronto, where his wife lived," said Mubin Shaikh, a police agent who infiltrated the group.[22] Abu Umar wrote about recruiting for "commando training" and said his purpose was to "cause trouble for kuffar . . . cause fear and panic in their countries."

Despite the increased role of the Internet in extremist radicalization and recruitment, "real-world social relationships continue to be pivotal . . . the Internet can support and facilitate but never completely replace direct human contact and the ties of friendship and kinship through which intense personal loyalties form."[23] The virtual relationship that the Toronto group had developed with Abu Umar progressed to a face-to-face meeting early in 2005. Abu Umar traveled to Toronto and met members of the extremist group. One of Abu Umar's online contacts from Atlanta also visited Toronto with an associate. Syed Haris Ahmed and Ehsanul Islam Sadequee met members of the Canadian group and "discussed strategic locations in the United States suitable for a terrorist strike, to include oil refineries and military bases," according to the Federal Bureau of Investigation. "They also plotted how to disable the Global Positioning System in an effort to disrupt military and commercial communications and traffic. Finally, the assembled group developed a plan for traveling to Pakistan, where they would attempt to receive military training at one of the several terrorist-sponsored camps."[24] Shortly after the Toronto meeting, the Atlanta men drove to Washington, D.C., where they recorded casing videos of potential targets including the Capitol, the Pentagon, the World Bank, the Department of Energy, a Masonic Temple in Alexandria, Virginia, and fuel storage tanks near Interstate 95 in northern Virginia. Sadequee then sent two of the video clips to Abu Umar. In the summer of 2005, Abu Umar traveled to Pakistan. Ahmed did the same, intending to train with the LeT. One of the Toronto group followed in November, but he was too ill to train.

Although in the short term it focused on training in Pakistan, the Toronto group's goal was to conduct terrorist operations within Canada. They were "motivated by an interpretation of Islam which required an attack upon the near enemy, including the Canadian military and Parliament."[25] The targeting of Canada is consistent with al-Qaeda strategy. Bin Laden named Canada as a target country in a 2002 audio address in which he condemned Western countries for their military involvement in Afghanistan and security cooperation with the United States. Subsequently, Canada was mentioned increasingly as a target country. In 2004, the online jihadist manual *Al-Battar* listed Canada as the fifth most important "Christian" country to be attacked, following the United States, the United Kingdom, Spain, and Australia.[26] An article posted on a password-protected Islamist extremist forum in December 2005 urged Muslim terrorist cells in Canada to attack the Trans-Alaska Pipeline.[27] At the same time, there were increased reports of suspicious behavior such as videotaping or photographing subway stations, ports, tourist sites, government and financial buildings, shopping malls, and nuclear and electrical plants. Some of these incidents were consistent with pre-operational attack planning.[28]

The Toronto group is an example of how terrorist propaganda can constitute a form of leadership. Al-Qaeda did not direct the operation in Toronto. None of the members of the Toronto group belonged to a foreign terrorist organization, but that does not mean al-Qaeda played no role in the plot. It arguably played the most important part. The question at the root of the conspiracy is: Why would a group of Muslims from Toronto form a terrorist group to attack Canada? CSIS partially answered that question when it described the Toronto group as al-Qaeda inspired.[29] While there is no indication that al-Qaeda exercised command and control over the Toronto group, there is considerable evidence that its key members were followers of al-Qaeda. They spoke frequently about al-Qaeda, exchanged videos featuring al-Qaeda leader Osama bin Laden, and intended to flee to Afghanistan following their operation in Canada. "We're not officially Al Qaeda," one of the ringleaders said, "but we share their principles."[30] The co-leader compared the group to al-Qaeda.[31] During searches, police found photos and videos of bin Laden. Ahmad, the driving force behind the recruitment and indoctrination, also produced and distributed videos that glorified al-Qaeda and its ideology. They advocated "violence towards and hatred of non-believers in Islam, and depicting atrocities against Muslims and retaliating violence against western forces in Iraq and Afghanistan. Some of the material he distributed called for violence in North America."[32] In a monitored conversation, one of the ringleaders described jihad as the view of al-Qaeda.[33] Another suspect suggested claiming responsibility for the attacks under the name al-Qaeda Organization in Canada.[34] "Al Qaeda created an ideology and an operational doctrine upon which disparate activists have seized," Hooper said in his testimony. "We have a bifurcated threat at this point—the threat that comes to Canada from the outside as well as a homegrown threat, and the homegrown variants look to Canada to execute their targeting."[35]

Canada's participation in the conflict in Afghanistan had made Canadians legitimate targets in the eyes of the Toronto group. The group interpreted the NATO mission as an attack on Islam and said that if Canada suffered a terrorist attack the government would withdraw its troops because it was "not tough like Britain or the United States."[36] Saad Khalid, who was selected to drive one of the truck bombs, said during his sentencing that he "was not motivated by a hate of Canada, Canadians, democracy or Canadian values of freedom, civil liberties, and women's rights . . . [but] was instead motivated by issues of disagreement on Canadian foreign policy, specifically Canada's involvement in Afghanistan and [he] had thought that [he] could make a difference."[37] Khalid was born in Saudi Arabia to parents of Pakistani origin and later moved to Canada and attended high school with Amara. A psychiatrist who examined him said while he had been raised in a moderate Muslim household he became increasingly religious in his later high school years and developed narcissistic features, "including the need to emulate powerful and influential leaders."[38] His "sense of religiously condoned behavior superseded his perceived need to abide by secular laws." Saad Gaya, a Montreal-born university student who was also chosen to drive a truck bomb to its target,[39] said during his postarrest interview with police that it was Amara who had revealed to him that Canada had sent troops to Afghanistan, "like 3,000 of them, like [he] didn't know that." Amara told Gaya he was "special," that he had been chosen by God to participate and that he would be a hero in the eyes of God. The purpose of the terrorist plot was to "fix the situation in Afghanistan" and to tell Canadians "it's not their job, they should leave," Gaya explained.[40] At other times, however, the group talked about its hatred for non-Muslims and spoke about a "global fight," defeating "Rome" and establishing the religion of Allah.[41]

As part of its preparations, the Toronto group began to acquire firearms. On August 13, 2005, Ali Dirie was attempting to cross the border into Canada when his rented car was searched. Both he and his passenger were caught with concealed, loaded handguns taped to their legs and ammunition stuffed in their socks. Police determined their vehicle had been rented using a credit card registered to one of the leaders of the Toronto terrorist group, who later told the undercover agent Mubin Shaikh that two of his associates had been arrested at the border and that they were supposed to bring back assault rifles but had deviated from the plan.[42] Dirie was a Somali with a troubled past. His father died in the Somali conflict. He immigrated to Canada with his mother at a young age, but in his teenage years, he was convicted of seven offences. He said he was passionately opposed to Canada's involvement in Afghanistan.[43] His arrest at the border did not dampen his fervency. Even after he was imprisoned for gun smuggling, Dirie continued to consider himself part of the terrorist group. He made connections with other inmates in an attempt to purchase firearms and tried to recruit fellow prisoners into the group. During phone calls with the co-leader of the group, Dirie provided direction and advice on recruiting, acquiring guns, and planning.[44] The co-leader attempted to send a package to Dirie at his prison address, but it was seized after corrections officials found it included videos of bin Laden.

Late in 2005, the Toronto group "accepted their obligation to jihad" because of the influence of radical preachers, the Internet, and the echo chamber of their self-reinforcing views. "Rapidly, they shifted from talking and debating towards action."[45] Khalid said he "began to believe that he had to be part of making a difference, feeling a religious obligation as something bad was happening to Muslims. Since Muslims were in

Afghanistan and the land was being invaded, Muslims had a responsibility to help out."[46] The nature of the counterterrorism investigation changed accordingly. What had been an intelligence operation became a criminal case. CSIS is a civilian security intelligence service, not a law enforcement agency. Its mandate is to advise the government on matters of national security. It does not collect evidence for criminal prosecutions. When CSIS comes across what may be evidence of a crime, it is required to notify the Royal Canadian Mounted Police, which is responsible for investigating national security crimes. As the Operation Claymore targets appeared to stray into criminality, CSIS informed the RCMP, which launched its own parallel investigation, Project Osage. The lead agency was the Integrated National Security Enforcement Team in Ontario, known as O-INSET. INSETs are headed by the RCMP but include other agencies such as CSIS, Canada Border Services Agency, and local and provincial police departments, in this case the Toronto, York, Peel, and Durham police departments and the Ontario Provincial Police. On November 27, 2005, the police agent Mubin Shaikh was tasked to visit a banquet hall to make contact with the two leaders of the Toronto group. Shaikh was a former Canadian cadet, a self-described fundamentalist Muslim, and the administrator at a small neighborhood mosque in Toronto. He had once wanted to fight in Chechnya or Afghanistan but came to realize his mistake. Following the arrest of Khawaja, whom he had known, Shaikh offered his services to CSIS because he believed a terrorist attack would be devastating for Canada, particularly for Canadian Muslims. After meeting Shaikh, the suspects began to recruit him by speaking about the oppression of Muslims.[47] They referred to Canada as an enemy because of its close ties to the United States. Amara showed the agent a map and mentioned that he had already scouted locations for training.[48]

The training began on December 18 on a wooded property two hours north of Toronto. Nine adults and four youths attended. Although some present were told the camp was a religious retreat, its purpose was to train and screen potential recruits for a terrorist group that would conduct attacks against Canada's parliament and infrastructure. Only the leaders of the group were aware of the details. Amara did not want everyone knowing the plans. A handwritten note found in his car before the camp read: "Dealing with new recruits: do not tell them anything—just give them jihadi da'wah; give false name; keep them on down low."[49] That remained the case throughout the conspiracy; only a handful of people knew the full picture. The strategy was apparently adopted from al-Qaeda. One of the suspects said the group subscribed to the teachings of "El Ariri who advocates that, in planning an attack, only the centre man should know the entire plan."[50] No such name exists in al-Qaeda, but he may have been referring to Yusuf al-Ayiri, the al-Qaeda ideologue and media coordinator who urged Muslims in the West to "start forest fires," a euphemism for homegrown attacks.[51]

The training camp was in a secluded softwood forest. It was bitterly cold, and deep snowdrifts covered the property. Dressed in camouflage fatigues and checkered kaffiyehs, the trainees marched, ran obstacle courses, wrestled, and took turns firing at barren trees and pictures of Hindu gods. A video filmed at the camp shows men scrambling over a snowbank waving a black flag and yelling "God is great." A man is shown leaning the barrel of a rifle against a tree limb and firing.[52] At night, they sat and listened to one of the leaders talking into a video camera about the tough times ahead. "We're here to kick it off, man," the boyish militant said, addressing his cadres inside a dimly lit tent. "We're here to get the rewards of everybody that's gonna come after us, God willing." He added: "Whether we get arrested, whether we get killed, we get tortured, our mission's greater than just individuals. It's not about you or I or this Emir or that Emir, it's not about that. It's about the fact that this has to get done. Rome has to be defeated. And we have to be the ones that do it, no holding back, whether it's one man that survives, you have to do it."[53] Ahmad "told those assembled that they were like Al Qaeda; not part of that group but that they held the same beliefs."[54] The camp lasted until December 30, when the last of the trainees returned to Toronto, leaving shell casings scattered in the snow.

Amara and his co-leader wanted to purchase a property in northern Ontario to use as a base of operations for their terrorist group, so on February 4, 2006, a carload drove north to Opasatika, a rural town near Timmins, Ontario, the hometown of the country singer Shania Twain. Shaikh said the plan was

a Chechnya style resistance in northern Ontario and in the bushes in, you know, in the back forty, if you will. And that to have guys up there and we would fortify ourselves and that if they came looking for us, we were going to, you know, we were going to take them on. And we looked at the roads and we, you know, we were saying, okay, we're going to booby-trap this, we're going to have snipers over here. It was like, it was planned out.[55]

They inspected a property but felt it was not secure and that their activities might attract the attention of neighbors and police. During the long drive back to Toronto, they discussed Operation Badr, a plot that involved storming the Parliament Buildings in Ottawa and holding members of parliament hostage. They would demand that Canada pull its troops out of Afghanistan and release Muslim prisoners. If their demands were not met, they intended to kill the politicians using a tactic popularized by al-Qaeda: beheadings.

Homegrown cells often seek to emulate al-Qaeda, but on a smaller scale. They begin with grandiose plans but typically end up selecting soft targets with undefended and exploitable vulnerabilities, and often ones that they know.[56] In some ways, however, the Toronto group's plans grew more elaborate over time. The day after they returned to Toronto from Opasatika, police monitored a meeting during which Amara explained he had built a "radio frequency remote control detonator" but that he was not satisfied with the range. Amara continued to work on the detonator and used a public library computer to research explosives. "This is to establish the religion of Allah and to get rid of the oppressors," one of the suspects said in a March 5 meeting to discuss raising money to buy military assault rifles. "It's a global fight. It's not just a specific country and a specific battlefield. . . . Like, it's an obligation to attack them here." The suspect said the Toronto attacks would be greater than the London transit bombings of 2005.[57] The exchange highlights one of the underlying assumptions of the plotters, that Muslims were everywhere suffering under the boot of the Western world and that terrorist violence was a justified response to defend Islam from this perceived assault. The Toronto group could not have developed this mindset in isolation. Like-minded extremists and the propaganda of the leaders of global jihad influenced it.

Three months after the training camp, the terrorist group splintered. Amara was upset to learn that Ahmad had lied when he had said he had traveled to Iraq and that fighters there had told him to return to Canada. Amara was also angry that Ahmad had sent a video showing Amara's face overseas.[58] Amara and his group, which numbered five or six, formally broke away from Ahmad and pushed ahead with the bombing operation. A police agent, Shaher Elsohemy, was present when Amara revealed his plans for the first time on April 7. The plot involved renting three U-Haul vans and packing them with explosives. They would park the vans at the Toronto Stock Exchange, the CSIS regional office in downtown Toronto, and a military base between Toronto and Ottawa, and detonate the bombs remotely. Amara told the agent he had already built and tested the electronic detonators. He then asked the agent to help him obtain 2 gallons of nitric acid and 1.5 tons of ammonium nitrate, which were required to produce the bombs. He told an accomplice he wanted to place metal chips around the bombs to harm more civilians. He calculated the plan would cost $20,000 for the bomb plot and $10,000 to finance his escape to Afghanistan. Two days after Amara outlined his plan, police observed him entering a Canadian Tire garden center and looking at bags of fertilizer.

The members of the Toronto group knew they were under surveillance. A member of the group found and removed a covert camera placed inside an exit sign at one of the leader's homes. They believed they were followed constantly and that their phones were monitored. They videotaped vehicles they thought were tailing them. One conspirator talked about getting caught but figured he would only serve ten years and that the Muslims at the prison would consider him a leader. Amara said he would not "feel sorry" if he were arrested as long as he had tried his best. The members of the group were also undeterred by the arrests of their associates in Atlanta, Ahmed and Sadequee. The Toronto suspects read about the arrests in the newspaper. Dirie said he "kind of shook for a sec you know," but their plotting continued regardless.[59]

The bomb plotters met at restaurants, coffee shops, mosques, the gas station where Amara worked, and at the Mississauga campus of the University of Toronto. Amara communicated with the others in messages stored on computer flash drives, which they exchanged at school or mosque. Their plan was to leave Canada immediately after the bombings except for Amara, who wanted to leave either the day before or immediately afterward. Amara intended to travel to Pakistan and then cross into

Afghanistan, where he thought he would be considered a leader. One of the central figures wanted to leave two weeks before the bombing and return two weeks after it happened. He then hoped to carry out attacks at the Sears Building in Chicago or the United Nations in New York. He said he would bring the chemicals across the border, even if he had to do it cup by cup. Amara continued refining his cell-phone-activated detonators and tasked two members of the group, Gaya and Khalid, to rent a warehouse to store the chemicals. To disguise their intensions, they printed shirts and business cards that read "Student Farmers."

The bombing was initially to take place on September 11, 2006, "to teach the world to be aware of this date forever," Amara said, but it was pushed back to November. One of the suspects said he hoped the attack would happen at night or early morning when there would be fewer people around, but he then said that "casualties would be good as it will show that we are not afraid," and the time of the attack was finally set for nine a.m. [60] They expected the bombing to be devastating and make the London transit attacks seem small by comparison. One suspect compared it to bomb attacks in Saudi Arabia and told the police agent "glass will be shattered on the streets, cars will be flipped and streets will be damaged."[61] He added the attack would "screw" Prime Minister Stephen Harper, the Canadian government, and the military and that "as a result of the bombings, Canada might withdraw its troops from Afghanistan." He called the attacks the "Battle of Toronto" and said there "will be blood, glass and debris everywhere." He add further that he wanted to make a video of the attack "as if Al Qaeda was the one who did it" and said the video should depict that "this is the Al Qaeda Organization in Canada." RCMP explosives experts later built and detonated a replica of the bomb using Amara's formula. The blast caused a 2,230-kilogram steel shipping container 20 meters away to flip 360 degrees.[62] Such a bombing "would have caused catastrophic damage to a multi-storey glass and steel frame building 35 metres from the bomb site, as well as killing or causing serious injuries to people in the path of the blast waves and force."[63]

While the Amara faction was planning the bombings, Ahmad continued preparations for a military-style firearms assault. He held another training camp on May 20, 2006, at the Rockwood Conservation Area. They wore hooded camouflage, conducted "clandestine exercises," and videotaped their activities. One of the participants later told investigators that the camp leader had spoken about the oppression of Muslims and the need to prepare for jihad and had promised to show him recorded lectures of bin Laden,[64] but two weeks later, police put the whole operation to rest. On June 2, 2006, Gaya and Khalid drove to an industrial warehouse north of Toronto to receive a shipment of chemicals that Amara wanted for his bombs. At 5:38 p.m., the delivery truck arrived, and the two men began unloading its contents: 120 bags labeled ammonium nitrate and a box containing 15 liters of nitric acid. A video recorded using a camera hidden inside the truck shows Gaya and Khalid at work, looking over their shoulders frequently. After twenty minutes, one of them looks up and recoils in shock, and his partner backs into a wall and raises his hands in surrender. A four-member police tactical team dressed in black descends upon them, laying them spread-eagled on the floor of the warehouse and cuffing their hands behind their backs before one of the officers gives the thumbs up signal.[65] During a search of Amara's residence, police found $12,000 cash, electronic components, bomb-making instructions, maps, satellite photos of the Parliament Buildings, and extremist literature such as *The Fundamental Concepts of Al Jihad*, *Islamic Ruling on the Permissibility of Self-Sacrifice Operations: Suicide or Martyrdom*, *The Clarification Regarding Intentionally Killing Women and Children*, *The Tawhid of Action*, *The Book of Jihad*, and chapters from *The Urban Guerrilla*.

By morning, seventeen suspects were in police custody, ranging in age from fifteen to forty-three, although most were in their early twenties. Five were juveniles under the age of eighteen. All twelve adults were Canadian citizens, although most were born abroad.[66] At a news conference, the RCMP said the arrests had prevented the assembly of explosive devices that would have been three times as powerful as the Oklahoma City bombing. "These individuals were allegedly intent on committing acts of terrorism against their own country and their own people," Prime Minister Harper said. Four days later, Abu Umar was arrested as he was returning to Britain from Pakistan. One more arrest followed in Canada in August. The press referred to the group as the "Toronto 18," but investigators said the actual target group was about fifty. Seven of those arrested were eventually released on peace bonds, or the Crown stayed their charges. The first conviction came in September 2008. Justice John Sproat wrote that there was overwhelming evidence of the existence of a terrorist group and rejected the claim that the group had done no more than fantasize.[67] Since then, all have pleaded guilty or been convicted. "Democracy flourishes because it tolerates and values a diversity of views and protects the rights of those who hold views at odds with the views of the majority," the judge said at Ahmad's sentencing. He continued:

> Such tolerance and recognition of the value of diversity is founded on the principle that members of our society will not seek to effect change by violent means. Those who turn to terrorism to effect change break this fundamental compact. They are not only a threat to the physical safety of the populace but to the foundational principles of our civil society. Those who pursue terrorism seek to make all of us less free.[68]

To lead is to influence others to action. The leaders of the global jihadist movement once did this predominantly in foreign camps, where they would indoctrinate and train recruits and dispatch them to conduct terrorist operations. That continues to some extent. Even though al-Qaeda's network of camps in Afghanistan has been destroyed, similar sites have emerged in Pakistan's tribal areas and Kashmir. Terrorist operations against the West, including the Toronto 18 case, are almost invariably traceable to such camps.[69] At the same time, terrorist leaders have harnessed technology to lead indirectly, exercising what some call transcendent leadership. Although al-Zawahiri and, until his death, bin Laden, were not "managing Al Qaeda's operations on a daily basis they guide the overall direction of the jihadist movement around the world, even while they are in hiding."[70]

The leaders of global jihad are not only masterminds of operational terrorism; they are also framers of perception. Through their propaganda, they "construct an ultra-conservative ideological frame from which violence against non-Muslims, or other Muslims, is a logical progression."[71] Since 9/11, they have done this increasingly through video and audio statements delivered to broadcasters or to jihadist media outlets that package them for Internet consumption. "An indicator of Al Qaeda's renewed vitality lies in its growing propaganda operation. While it has long understood that propaganda is a key to its success, its output has been increasing at a significant rate," reads a study by Ottawa's Carleton University.[72] If these propaganda materials are not produced in English, they are translated almost instantaneously, which indicates that they target Western audiences. Zawahiri has been particularly pro-lific in this regard, apparently believing his broadcasts are "important in encouraging the trend towards locally-organized attacks."[73] The purpose of this propaganda is to incite terrorist violence, and to the extent that homegrown groups are responding to this incitement, the global jihadist movement leads them. The Toronto 18 group bought into this violent, radical worldview. They "followed an extremist interpretation of Islam and intended to commit violent acts in pursuit of their religious beliefs."[74] There could not have been a Toronto 18 without the leadership provided by global jihad in general and al-Qaeda in particular. The Toronto 18 never met bin Laden or any other al-Qaeda leaders, but these Canadian terrorists were nonetheless a product of their distant leadership.

NOTES

1. "A Terrorist Testimony," *Frontline*, PBS, available at http://www.pbs.org/wgbh/pages/frontline/shows/trail/inside/testimony.html.

2. Thomas H. Kean et al., *The 9/11 Commission Report: Final Report of the National Commission on Terrorist Attacks Upon the United States* (New York: Norton, 2004), 176.

3. "Text of White House Memo on Al Qaeda," *ABC News Online*, http://www.abc.net.au/news/2004-04-11/text-of-white-house-memo-on-al-qaeda/168278 (accessed April 11, 2004).

4. Stewart Bell, *Cold Terror: How Canada Nurtures and Exports Terrorism Around the World* (Toronto: Wiley, 2006); Integrated Threat Assessment Centre, *Terrorist Threats to Canada and North America* (Ottawa: Government of Canada, 2006).

5. Integrated Threat Assessment Centre, *Is Canada Next?* (Ottawa: Government of Canada, 2006), 3.

6. Canadian Security Intelligence Service, *Sunni Islamic Extremism and the Threat to Canadian Maritime Security* (Ottawa: Government of Canada, 2004).

7. Ibid.

8. Andy Ellis, assistant director policy and strategic partnerships, Canadian Security Intelligence Service, speaking notes, 2011 CASIS International Conference, November 10, 2011, Ottawa.

9. Stewart Bell, *The Martyr's Oath: The Apprenticeship of a Homegrown Terrorist* (Toronto: Wiley, 2005); Canadian Security Intelligence Service, *Mohammed Mansour Jabarah* (Ottawa: Government of Canada, 2002);.Federal Bureau of Investigation, "Information Derived from Mohammed Mansour Jabarah," U.S. Department of Justice, August 21, 2002.

10. USA v. Mohammed Jabarah, January 18, 2008, (S.D. N.Y.).

11. Intelligence and Security Committee, *Could 7/7 Have Been Prevented? Review of the Intelligence on the London Terrorist Attacks of 7 July 2005* (London: HMSO, 2009), 7, 10.

12. R. v. Mohammad Momin Khawaja, Reasons for Judgment, Ontario Superior Court of Justice, October 29, 2008.

13. Integrated Threat Assessment Centre, *Canada: The Threat from Terrorism and Extremism* (Ottawa: Government of Canada, 2007).

14. Canadian Security Intelligence Service, *Sons of the Father: The Next Generation of Islamic Extremists in Canada* (Ottawa: Government of Canada, 2004); and Integrated National Security Threat Assessment Centre, *Al Qaeda Attack Planning Against North American Targets* (Ottawa: Government of Canada, 2004).

15. Jack Hooper, in "Proceedings of the Standing Senate Committee on National Security and Defence," Ottawa: Government of Canada, May 29, 2006, available at http://parl.gc.ca/39/1/parlbus/commbus/senate/Com-e/defe-e/02ev-e.htm?Language=E&Parl=39&Ses=1&comm_id=76.

16. R. v. Fahim Ahmad, Sentencing, Justice F. Dawson, Ontario Superior Court of Justice, October 25, 2010, Brampton.

17. Omar El Akkad and Greg McArthur, "A Grand Existence Among Muslims Online," *Globe and Mail* (Toronto), August 19, 2006.

18. Integrated Threat Assessment Centre, *Acquisition of Paramilitary Skills by Al Qaeda Inspired Extremists in Western Countries* (Ottawa: Government of Canada, 2008).

19. United States of America v. Syed Haris Ahmed, Specific Findings of Fact, United States District Court of Atlanta (June 10, 2009).

20. Crown Prosecution Service, "Terrorist 'Mr. Fix-It' Convicted with Two Others of Terrorism Offences," press release, London, August 18, 2008.

21. Evan Kohlmann, *Anatomy of a Modern Homegrown Terror Cell* (New York: NEFA Foundation, 2008).

22. Interview with Mubin Shaikh, Toronto.

23. Tim Stevens and Peter R. Neumann, "Countering Online Radicalisation: A Strategy for Action," International Centre for the Study of Radicalisation and Political Violence, London, 2009, http://icsr.info/wp-content/uploads/2012/10/12367684 91ICSROnlineRadicalisationReport.pdf.

24. USA v. Ehsanul Islam Sadequee, Affidavit in Support of Arrest Warrant, New York, United States District Court, 2006. Sadequee and Ahmed were both convicted in the summer of 2009.

25. "A Twenty-Year-Old Toronto Man Has Been Found Guilty of Participating in a Homegrown Terror Cell," *National Post* (Toronto), September 25, 2008.

26. Integrated Threat Assessment Centre, *Al Qaeda: Potential Threats to North American Targets* (Ottawa: Government of Canada, 2004).

27. Integrated Threat Assessment Centre, *Is Canada Next?*, 3.

28. Ibid., 1.

29. Canadian Security intelligence Service, "Statement by Assistant Director, Operations, at Press Conference, Saturday, June 3, 2006," available at http://www .csis-scrs.gc.ca/nwsrm/spchs/spch03062006-eng.asp.

30. Melissa Leong, "Toronto Eighteen Youth Guilty of Terrorism," *National Post* (Toronto), September 26, 2008.

31. R v. Zakaria Amara, Agreed Statement of Facts, Ontario Superior Court of Justice, October 8, 2009, Brampton.

32. R. v. Ahmad, Sentencing.

33. R v. N.Y., Summary of the Crown's Anticipated Evidence, Ontario Superior Court of Justice, March 25, 2008, Brampton.

34. R v. Saad Khalid, Agreed Statement of Facts, Ontario Superior Court of Justice, 2009, Brampton.

35. Jack Hooper, in "Proceedings of the Standing Senate Committee on National Security and Defence."

36. R v. Saad Khalid, Agreed Statement of Facts.

37. "Toronto Eighteen Member Sentenced to Fourteen Years in Prison," *National Post* (Toronto), September 3, 2009.

38. R v. Saad Khalid, Reasons for Sentence, Ontario Superior Court of Justice, September 3, 2009, Brampton.

39. R v. Saad Gaya, Agreed Statement of Facts, Ontario Superior Court of Justice, September 28, 2009, Brampton.

40. Transcript of interview with Saad Gaya, conducted by Detective Blaise Doherty, Ontario Superior Court of Justice, June 2, 2006, Brampton.

41. R. v. Ali Dirie, Agreed Statement of Facts, Ontario Superior Court of Justice, September 21, 2009, Brampton.

42. R. v. Ali Dirie, Agreed Statement of Facts.

43. R. v. Ali Dirie, Reasons for Sentence, Ontario Superior Court, October 2, 2009, Brampton.

44. R. v. Ali Dirie, Agreed Statement of Facts.

45. Mitchell D. Silber and Arvin Bhatt, *Radicalization in the West: The Homegrown Threat* (New York: NYPD Intelligence Division, 2007).

46. R. v. Saad Khalid, Reasons for Sentence.

47. R. v. Ansari, Reasons for Ruling, Ontario Superior Court of Justice, October 19,2006, Toronto, http://www.canlii.org/en/on/onsc/doc/2006/2006canlii42261 /2006canlii42261.html.

48. R. v. Zakaria Amara, Agreed Statement of Facts.

49. Ibid.

50. R. v. Saad Khalid, Reasons for Sentence.

51. Jonathan Fighel, "The Forest Jihad," International Institute for Counter-Terrorism, October 28, 2008, http://www.ict.org.il/Articles/tabid/66/Articlsid/506 /currentpage/3/Default.aspx.

52. NEFA, "Toronto 18 Training Camp," YouTube, available at http://www.youtube.com/watch?v=yVAKhQ5OCvg.

53. R. v. N.Y., Factum of the Applicant, Ontario Superior Court of Justice, 2008, Toronto.

54. R. v. Ahmad, Sentencing.

55. "Canada: The Cell Next Door," *Frontline*, PBS, January 30, 2007.

56. Integrated Threat Assessment Centre, *Canada: The Threat from Terrorism and Extremism*.

57. R v N.Y., Summary of the Crown's Anticipated Evidence.

58. R v. Ahmad, Sentencing; R. v. N.Y., Factum of the Applicant.

59. R. v. Ali Dirie, Agreed Statement of Facts.

60. R. v. Saad Khalid, Agreed Statement of Facts.

61. Ibid.

62. The author viewed a video of the test explosion, 2010, Toronto.

63. R v. Saad Khalid, Agreed Statement of Facts.

64. R. v. N.Y., Summary of the Crown's Anticipated Evidence.

65. The author has viewed the video of the arrest.

66. Privy Council Office, "Arrests of Terrorism Suspects in Toronto," Ottawa: Government of Canada, June 5, 2006.

67. *National Post* (Toronto), September 25, 2008.

68. R. v. Ahmad, Sentencing.

69. Integrated Threat Assessment Centre, *Acquisition of Paramilitary Skills by Al Qaeda Inspired Extremists in Western Countries* (Ottawa: Government of Canada, 2008).

70. Peter Bergen, "Commentary: Where's Osama bin Laden?," CNN, September 11, 2009.

71. Integrated Threat Assessment Centre, *The Problem of Radicalization* (Ottawa: Government of Canada, 2007).

72. Angela Gendron, "Al Qaeda: Propaganda and Media Strategy," Integrated Threat Assessment Centre, Ottawa, 2007, http://www.itac.gc.ca/pblctns/tc_prsnts/2007-2-eng.asp.

73. Integrated Threat Assessment Centre, "Al-Jazeera Broadcast, 2005 08 04," Government of Canada, Ottawa, August 5, 2005.

74. R. v. Ali Dirie, Agreed Statement of Facts.

[7]

Operation Pendennis in Australia

SALLY NEIGHBOUR

In September 2004, agents monitoring a suspected terrorist cell in Melbourne, Australia, intercepted a chilling conversation between two of their targets. The discussion was between the cell leader, an Algerian-born cleric, Abdul Nacer Benbrika, and one of his followers, a nineteen-year-old named Abdullah Merhi, who was later accused of volunteering to be Australia's first suicide bomber.[1]

"You shouldn't just do, kill one or two or three, you need some good . . . like close to the station, the train . . . Do a big thing!" Benbrika urged his young associate.

"Yeah . . . like Spain." Merhi replied.

The conversation turned to the involvement of Australian troops in the U.S.-led wars in Afghanistan and Iraq, as Benbrika continued: "When you in here, in Australia, when you do something, they stop to send the troops. If you kill, we kill, here a thousand, the government is going to think . . ."

Merhi finished the sentence for him: "Bring the troops home, because if you get large numbers here, a thousand, the government will listen."[2] The exchange was a signal point in Australia's largest counterterrorism investigation, code-named Operation Pendennis, which culminated fourteen months later in raids across two states, Victoria and New South Wales, which led to the arrest of twenty-two men identified as members of two separate cells in Melbourne and Sydney.

Police said they had thwarted a potentially "catastrophic" act of terror.[3] The men had stockpiled chemicals, weapons, ammunition, and a huge cache of extremist material, including al-Qaeda literature and bomb-making instructions. A cell member told police they had planned to attack Australia's premier sports stadium, the Melbourne Cricket Ground, on the day of the country's biggest sporting event, the Australian Football Rules Grand Final, or to bomb Melbourne's Crown Casino.[4] One of the accused men had obtained five military rocket launchers stolen from the Australian Defence Force and was overheard in an intercepted phone conversation telling an associate, "I am going to blow up the nuclear place," referring to the Lucas Heights nuclear reactor in Sydney.[5] During 16,400 hours of covertly recorded conversations, Benbrika said: "If we want to die for jihad, we do maximum damage, maximum damage. Damage to their buildings with everything and damage to their lives, just to show them."[6]

It was Australia's first homegrown terrorist conspiracy, though certainly not the first time Australia had been targeted by al-Qaeda, its affiliated groups, or individuals who shared their ideology. Australia had been identified as a target by the global jihadist movement numerous times before, but on each previous occasion, the plots had been closely linked to and directed by senior al-Qaeda figures or by allied organizations such as the Pakistani Lashkar-e-Taiba or the Indonesian-based Jemaah Islamiyah. The first of these was in 2000, when a British-born Australian JI member, Jack Roche, was seconded from JI's Australian branch by the group's Malaysia-based operations chief, Hambali (Riduan Isamuddin), and dispatched for training in Afghanistan's al-Farouk camp. Roche later described how he discussed with senior al-Qaeda figures, including Mohammed Atef and Saif al-Adel plans to attack targets in Australia.[7] Roche pleaded guilty in 2004 to having conspired to bomb the Israeli embassy in Canberra and was sentenced to nine years in jail.[8] The second such case involved the Australian Muslim convert Jack Thomas, who was invited by al-Qaeda operative Khalid bin Attash to carry out an attack in Australia similar to al-Qaeda's 1998 bombings of the U.S. embassies in Kenya and Tanzania.[9]

Only four years later, the Pendennis plot signaled an entirely new type of threat for Australia. While newspaper headlines branded the accused men "Osama's Aussie Offspring,"[10] in truth their connections with al-Qaeda central were minimal. For the first time, an independent cohort of Australian citizens, most of them locally born and raised, had formed a group of their own and conspired to launch an attack on Australian soil. They were certainly part of the global jihadist movement; they were undoubtedly motivated by al-Qaeda's ideology and reliant on training manuals and instructional guides obtained through the Internet; three of them had trained in al-Qaeda or LeT camps; and they had been nurtured by an established Islamist community with strong historical connections to al-Qaeda and its associated groups. They were acting entirely on their own, however. As the head of the Australia Security Intelligence Organisation, Paul O'Sullivan, stated in March 2006: "There is no evidence . . . of any link so far to an outside controller or outside direction."[11]

THE ORIGINS OF THE MELBOURNE CELL

The leader of the two cells was an Algerian-born, self-taught Muslim cleric, Abdul Nacer Benbrika, known to his followers as Abu Bakr. Benbrika had arrived in Australia in 1989 at the age of twenty-nine as a refugee from his native Algeria, which was then in the grip of an Islamist uprising and on the brink of civil war.[12] A former electrical technician with Algerian airlines, Benbrika was apparently at this stage neither a political nor a religious activist. He told Australia's Immigration Review Tribunal that he feared for his life if he returned to the "dangers" of his homeland and assured them of his "love of the Australian lifestyle."[13] Benbrika settled in Melbourne's multicultural working-class northern suburbs and married a twenty-year-old Lebanese woman who had Australian residency. They ultimately had seven children, and he obtained Australian citizenship in 1998. Benbrika was the president of the local Algerian Society, which provided services to Algerian refugees, and a regular speaker at the Preston mosque in Melbourne's northern suburbs.[14]

In the 1990s, Benbrika joined the Islamic Information and Support Centre of Australia (IISCA),[15] a community group based at Melbourne's Brunswick mosque and formed by Australia's largest Salafist organization, the Ahlus Sunnah Wal Jamaah Association (referred to by the authorities as ASJA, although it uses the acronym ASWJ).[16] Both ASJA and IISCA are headed by a Jordanian-born cleric, Mohammed Jamal Omran,

known among his followers as Abu Ayman, who is the preeminent author-
ity in Salafist circles in Australia. Australian police describe Omran as
Benbrika's mentor,[17] and a 2007 report by the New York Police Depart-
ment Intelligence Division, "Radicalization in the West: The Homegrown
Threat," labeled Omran "the extremist incubator, who paved the way for
(Benbrika's) radicalization."[18]

After migrating to Australia in the 1980s, Omran maintained contact
with a cohort of militant Islamists overseas, including his old friend from
Jordan, Omar Mahmoud Othman, more widely known as Abu Qatada,
often described as "Osama bin Laden's right-hand man in Europe."[19]
In 1994, Sheikh Omran hosted Abu Qatada on a visit to Australia and
took him on a speaking tour of Sydney and Melbourne, later defending
his "personal friendship" with the foreign cleric.[20] In 2003, Omran was
named during a Spanish court case over contacts with another senior
al-Qaeda figure, Imad Eddin Barakat Yarkas, better known as Abu Dahdah, the accused senior operative of al-Qaeda in Spain. A court document filed in the case against Abu Dahdah documented phone contacts
between the two men and said Sheikh Omran had attempted to visit
Abu Dahdah in 2001 but was not successful.[21] Omran denied any connection with Abu Dahdah.[22]

Abu Qatada's 1994 visit, hosted by Sheikh Omran, was a pivotal event
in the emergence of the jihadist movement in Australia and the radicalization of Benbrika. By one account, Omran "took Abu Qatada to an
area of woodlands north of Melbourne where Qatada gave a sermon to
devotees from the Preston and Brunswick mosques."[23] One man who witnessed it described it as a seminal moment in the evolution of the radical
Islamist milieu in Australia:

> His emphasis was on politics. It was about what was going on in Saudi
> Arabia, Jordan, and how Arab governments were selling out their reli-
> gion. He spoke out against Arab governments for not being Islamic
> enough, for not adhering to pure Sharia law. He was radical and politi-
> cised—we had never heard this stuff before. His impact was enormous
> and that is where it all began.[24]

Abu Qatada's tirade evidently struck a powerful chord with the
Algerian-born Benbrika. As spiritual leader of the Armed Islamic Group

(GIA) and the Salafist Group for Preaching and Combat, Abu Qatada was violently opposed to the infidels who had prevented the Islamic Salvation Front (FIS) taking power in Algeria and imposing sharia law. By this account, Benbrika was in awe of the visiting preacher and was "both energised and transformed by Abu Qatada's radical and pure doctrinal approach to Islam."[25]

After his encounter with Abu Qatada, Benbrika immersed himself in Islamic study and received an appointment as a teacher at IISCA, despite his lack of formal qualifications.[26] His wife later noted "he hasn't studied religion and nor is he a cleric, he is self-taught."[27] The NYPD analysts observed, "Rather than studying jurisprudence at a recognized Islamic university, Benbrika taught himself Islam, largely cut off from the wider community. This absence of a classical background contributed to Benbrika's adoption of the jihadi-Salafi interpretation of Islam and only enabled him to teach the younger group members a 'cut and paste' version of Islam."[28] In 1999 and 2000, under the leadership of Omran and Benbrika, the Brunswick mosque became the hub for a group of would-be jihadists who embraced al-Qaeda's ideology via their imams' sermons and literature and audio-visual material accessed via the Internet. According to Omran's estranged former son-in-law, Ali Kassae, the young men who attended were "taught to hate" by being subjected to virulently anti-Western, anti-Christian, and anti-Jewish sermons and propaganda.[29] A DVD distributed among the group incited viewers: "You should hate them as they hate you, invade them as they invade you, fight them as they fight you. Whoever dies will be granted the mercy of God and paradise. Jews should die. We should proclaim jihad until they all die, until every single one of them is dead."[30]

In 1999 and 2000, a succession of young men from the Salafist *ummah* in Australia headed off for military training in foreign jihadist camps. Some traveled to Pakistan to train with Lashkar-e-Taiba, and others went to Afghanistan to train in al-Qaeda camps such as al-Farouk camp near Kandahar. Benbrika believed that undergoing military training was a religious obligation and said later he would be "betraying my religion" if he stopped them.[31] Three of the men who undertook this training would later be identified as members of the Pendennis cells. One was the Melbourne Muslim convert Shane Kent, who trained in al-Farouk.[32] The other two were the Lebanese Australian Khaled Cheikho and his nephew

Moustafa Cheikho, members of the Sydney cell, who witnesses said trained with LeT in Pakistan.[33] The roles of these individuals and the significance of their training and foreign links will be examined later in this chapter.

Over time, Benbrika's increasingly virulent views caused a falling out with the more mainstream Muslim community. The imam at the Preston mosque, Sheikh Fehmi Naji el-Imam, recalled, "We did not see eye to eye with him, he took a hardline opinion on religion."[34] Another Muslim elder said, "He made a lot of trouble at the Preston mosque. He was associated with a small group of extremists. He was not a stable man and he did a lot of damage to the community."[35] He also parted ways with Sheikh Omran, whom he reportedly deemed to be "not radical enough."[36]

Benbrika retreated to his home, where he held prayer sessions and talks with a small group of loyal followers. He did not work but relied on unemployment benefits paid by the Australian government to support his wife and seven children, living largely cut off from mainstream society. A neighbor said of Benbrika's family: "We don't know them, if we saw them on the street we'd say 'hello' but that's all. They are very close people. We never saw the kids."[37]

Benbrika preached that his *jemaah* (community) should follow Islamic law and, where it conflicted with Australian law, sharia should prevail. In an interview with the Australian Broadcasting Corporation in August 2004, three months before his arrest, Benbrika said, "I don't accept all other religion except religion of Islam. . . . My religion doesn't tolerate other religion, it doesn't tolerate. The only one law which needs to spread, it can be here or anywhere else, has to be Islam."[38] Benbrika told his followers Australia is a "land of war" because of the involvement of Australian troops in the wars in Afghanistan and Iraq,[39] and that no distinction should be made between the government of Prime Minister John Howard and the people who elected it. In his ABC interview, he appeared to condone Australian Muslims going to fight against Australian forces in those countries.

> You may find many Muslims fighting in Iraq and Afghanistan, which [is] because they believe they are a brother. As John Howard is helping Bush in his war, then the people they do the same. . . . According to my religion, jihad is a part of my religion and what you have to understand,

that anyone who fights for the sake of Allah, the first, when he dies, the first drop of blood that comes from him out, all his sin will be forgiven.[40]

Benbrika was the subject of three psychiatric reports while he was in prison. The psychiatrist who examined him judged that he was a zealot who embraced a "persecutory interpretation" of local and international events but exhibited "no significant personality disturbance, cognitive impairment or other psychological defect."[41] The judge who sentenced Benbrika found that "the essence of [his] criminality lies in his exercising an enormous influence over the young men who followed him, and imbuing, or seeking to imbue in them, a fanatical hatred of non-Muslims."[42]

BENBRIKA'S CELL

Benbrika's group in Melbourne numbered about a dozen young men, aged in their twenties and hailing from the city's poorer northern suburbs. Press reports described them as a "cult-like following" of "young hotheads and small-time criminals . . . hardened street boys armed with attitude and the Koran, who saw in Benbrika a father figure and a way to re-claim their lost souls."[43] They were mostly manual laborers and tradesmen, and a few had prior convictions for property crimes such as theft and credit card fraud. Benbrika's wife said: "They used to go out and get drunk and not follow religion. . . . He took them in and changed them into better people. . . . They all love him and swear by him. Some of them would give him their eyes if he asked for them."[44]

The key feature the men in Melbourne cell had in common was that they were all the sons of Lebanese families who had immigrated to Australia during the Lebanese civil war and formed close-knit diaspora communities in their adopted land. They were either Australian born or had come to Australia as children. They had grown up in a transplanted milieu, alienated by virtue of distance from the culture of their parents and grandparents and, by virtue of their upbringing and strong cultural heritage, from the broader mainstream of Australian society. They bring to mind the "de-territorialized" terrorists described by Olivier Roy in his book *Globalised Islam: The Search for a New Umma*.[45] The Australian scholar

Anthony Bubalo notes that "Al Qaeda's ideology was one designed by people who had lost contact with their original political and social milieus";[46] the Melbourne cell suggests the ideology continues to resonate with a younger generation that has experienced a similar disconnect. It also seems to fit the pattern observed by Marc Sageman of the archetypal homegrown terrorists as "socially alienated young men" who "become embedded in a socially disembedded network, which, precisely because of its lack of any anchor to any society, is free to follow abstract and apocalyptic notions of a global war between good and evil."[47]

THE "LEADERSHIP COMMITTEE"

The terrorist organization that Benbrika was ultimately found guilty of leading consisted of a *jemaah* of some one dozen men, most of whom swore the *bayat* to Benbrika.[48] The judge who presided over their trial found that the *jemaah* had no formal structure, although it had a *sandooq* (literally "box") to which members made financial contributions.[49] The prosecutor asserted that the core of the *jemaah* was a "leadership committee" comprising Benbrika and his three most staunch loyalists, although the evidence showed they only met once in the sixteen months they were under surveillance.

Chief among Benbrika's lieutenants was the twenty-one-year-old Aimen Joud, the second youngest of the group, described by the prosecution as Benbrika's "right-hand man."[50] Joud was the eldest of eight children in a Lebanese family that migrated to Australia in 1980, four years before his birth. His father was a typical hard-working migrant who went from driving taxis to running an investment company that built suburban shopping strips. Enrolled by his father in a local Catholic college, Joud was expelled over the theft of laptop computers and transferred to an Islamic school whose principal described him as a loner who "disappeared" without sitting his final exams.[51] Joud worked in a fruit shop, a computer shop, and his parents' café before his father appointed him as a construction supervisor in the family company. Like many Lebanese émigré families, the Jouds maintained strong contacts with homeland. Joud was photographed in 2002 near his father's village proudly brandishing an AK-47.[52] Covertly recorded conversations revealed Joud as a brash, defiant young man who seemed to relish the role of "enforcer," enthusiastically suggesting that associates suspected of informing on the cell should be bashed. In the midst of Operation Pendennis, Joud was convicted and sentenced to one month in jail for dismantling stolen cars and reselling them as parts, a racket sanctioned by Benbrika as *halal* because "when you fight the *kufr*, their blood and money is lawful."[53]

The second member of Benbrika's so-called leadership committee was Fadl Sayadi, twenty-five, described by prosecutors as Benbrika's "left hand man."[54] Sayadi was born in Tripoli and migrated as a toddler with his family to Melbourne, where he attended high school, worked as a hotel attendant and concrete layer, and reportedly lived at home with his parents until he married a few months before his arrest. Neighbors said the family had lived on the street for twenty years and "never caused any trouble" and Sayadi "seemed to be a very peaceful, quiet young man . . . who minded his own business and didn't say much."[55] Underneath the mild exterior lay a fiercely committed jihadist, who in an intercepted conversation defended the Chechen rebels who held schoolchildren hostage in the Beslan siege in 2004 where 334 people died.[56]

The final member of the "leadership committee" was twenty-two-year-old Ahmed Raad, described by the prosecutor as the Melbourne cell's "treasurer."[57] Raad attended the same high school as Sayadi, left in year eleven to become a plumbing apprentice, drifted into alcohol and substance abuse after the death of an older brother, and finally turned for spiritual guidance to the mosque where he met Benbrika.[58]

THE FOLLOWERS

The remaining cell members were brothers, cousins, friends, former schoolmates, or fellow Muslims who had met at the mosque. Ezzit Raad was the twenty-three-year-old elder brother of "treasurer" Ahmed. He was married with a toddler daughter and described as a "quiet" man who liked playing cards with his brother.[59] The evidence suggested he was a somewhat reluctant recruit who repeatedly expressed qualms over the group's car-theft racket and objected to stolen vehicles stored in his garage.[60] However, he had no such reservations over atrocities like the

July 2005 London bombings in which fifty-two people died, commenting afterward "[although] terrible, [it] should have been more."[61]

Amer Haddara was another second-generation Lebanese Australian, described as a "determined business minded man."[62] He had an advanced diploma in computer systems engineering from Victoria University and a job with a recruitment firm and had started his own travel company running hajj tours to Mecca.[63] Haddara reportedly volunteered as a computer technician at the Royal Institute for the Blind[64] and visited Benbrika's house regularly, mainly to help him fix his computer. Despite his apparently seamless integration into Australian society, Haddara was a committed jihadist who told police after his arrest that he would join any group that advocated a Muslim uprising and he supported violent jihad "just as much as Americans support their own militants." He said he observed sharia ahead of Australian law and volunteered that it was "unfortunate" Australia's foreign policy "followed the same oppressive lines as America's."[65]

The youngest member of the Melbourne cell was twenty-year-old Abdullah Merhi, referred to in the group as "Abdullah the young one," an apprentice electrician whose eighteen-year-old wife was about to give birth to their first child when he was arrested. Merhi's family came to Australia from Lebanon in 1971, and his father died suddenly when Merhi was eighteen years old.[66] His lawyer argued that Merhi was "young, impressionable and naïve" and for a period of nine weeks in 2004 had fallen under "Benbrika's spell."[67] It was during that period that Merhi and Benbrika were heard discussing killing "a thousand in an attack like Spain." There was also the following exchange:

MERHI: "If for example John Howard kills innocent family, Muslim . . . Do we, we will make transgress back to him? Do we have to kill him and his family or can we just kill his people, like people at the football?"
BENBRIKA: "If they kill our kids, we kill (inaudible) kids."
MERHI: "The innocent ones?"
BENBRIKA: "The innocent ones. Because he kills our innocent ones."[68]

Police claimed the conversations, combined with a hand-written will and notes he made about "paradise" and "hellfire," were evidence of Merhi's intent. "It was quite clear that he wanted to go the way of a suicide bomber," Det. Sgt. Chris Murray told the Melbourne Magistrates

Court.[69] The jury ultimately rejected this assertion, acquitting Merhi on the charge of providing himself as a resource to a terrorist organization while convicting him of belonging to a terrorist organization. Despite his lawyer's assertion, Merhi remained unrepentant, leading his fellow defendants in defying an order to stand in court and telling the magistrate: "We stand only to God."[70]

The only Caucasian in the Melbourne group was a twenty-eight-year-old Australian convert, Shane Kent, who went by the Muslim name Yassin. He was pale-skinned and red-headed and enjoyed heavy metal music, played Australian rules football, and studied multimedia in a one-year diploma course at a tertiary college in Melbourne, emerging "highly competent" in Web programming and development.[71] He converted to Islam in his early twenties and married a Turkish woman with whom he had four children.

Kent was the only member of the Melbourne cell who had undertaken military training overseas. In 2001, he traveled to Pakistan and Afghanistan, accompanied by a friend whom he had met at IISCA and facilitated by a Pakistani man associated with ASJA who organized their tickets and travel.[72] They spent three days in an orientation camp run by the Jaish-e-Mohammed group in Pakistan then traveled on to Afghanistan to al-Qaeda's Camp Faruq, where they spent two months training in firearms, topography, tactics, and explosives. Kent's companion described later how they met Osama bin Laden, who "asked who we were, where we were from [and] how the Muslims in Australia were going." By this account, Kent described bin Laden as a "heroic fighter."[73] Kent returned to Australia with a large amount of jihadist literature including an al-Qaeda training manual and a photo of himself armed with an automatic weapon, labeled "al Faruqi."[74] In 2005 he helped make a video extolling the virtues of martyrdom for the al-Qaeda-connected At-Tibyan Publications.[75]

Despite being the only trained mujaheddin in Benbrika's Melbourne cell, the evidence did not indicate nor did the prosecutor assert that Kent played a central role in the group or that his training or overseas connections was crucial to its activities. The only evidence of Kent's having shared his expertise with the others was a conversation in which he suggested to Joud that it would be useful for one of the group to study topography as he had done in Camp Faruq. Another exchange recorded Benbrika and Joud agreeing that "the other brothers" needed to undertake the type of training Kent had done. Kent was clearly a respected figure and known hardliner in the Islamist community; he held a position on Sheikh Omran's *shura* but fell out with him after Omran threatened to report to the security services one of his students, who was talking about doing a terrorist act in Australia "to avenge Muslim brethren." Kent believed Sheik Omran was "betraying Muslims" and "aiding the enemy" by threatening to hand his student over to the security services.[76] However, there was nothing to implicate Kent in planning for a terrorist act, and he appears to have kept himself somewhat aloof from the group. There was no evidence that he gave the *bayat* to Benbrika, contributed to the *sandooq*, or attended group "bonding trips" or *dars* classes.[77] At one point Benbrika complained that he had not seen much of him and that Kent had not been attending classes.[78] The jury at his trial was unable to reach a verdict on whether Kent was a member of Benbrika's organization and was ordered to stand trial again. In 2009, rather than face a retrial, Kent pleaded guilty to two charges and received a relatively light prison term, a minimum of three years and nine months. The judge found that Kent's fervor for the group and its cause had "waxed and waned" and that his criminality should be regarded as "mid-range." As for Kent's al-Qaeda training, the judge ruled that while this was "undoubtedly relevant" to Kent's membership of the cell, it "should not be overemphasized [because] he did so before 11 September 2001 and in circumstances of some ambiguity as to the purpose of the camp and the ideology behind its establishment and operation.[79]

The final member of the Melbourne cell was a twenty-five-year-old maverick named Izzydeen Atik, a serial fraudster who earned thousands of dollars a week from credit card fraud, which enabled him to rent a luxury townhouse, employ a butler, drive a BMW, and make hundreds of calls to telephone sex lines.[80] He also had a history of mental illness, including hallucinations, a diagnosis of schizophrenia, and psychiatric reports recording that he heard the voices of birds and demons. Atik's role in the group was principally to obtain free airline tickets and mobile phone accounts using fraudulent credit cards. Atik ultimately pleaded guilty and agreed to testify against the others, claiming, among other things, that Benbrika had told him the group planned to attack the Melbourne Cricket Ground during the Australian Football Rules grand final. However, the judge dismissed Atik as "a liar, cheat and fraudster of significant accomplishment" whose evidence, including his account of the targets conversation with Benbrika, was mostly untrue and unsafe to rely on.[81]

The dynamics within the Melbourne cell were examined by a Victoria Police intelligence analyst, Dr. Gaetano Joe Ilardi, who was a senior analyst on Operation Pendennis and later appointed to head counter-radicalization and deradicalization strategy for the Victoria Police. His paper titled "Home-Grown Terrorism and Radicalisation Activities: More Than Meets the Eye" provides some useful insights into the appeal and impact of joining a jihadist cell:

> Belonging to a jihadi group can instill in its members a sense of empowerment, control and purpose few experience outside this collective. . . . The belief that one is performing God's work, in which one has a unique insight into what it means to be a 'true Muslim' . . . serves to elevate the individual's sense of confidence and self-worth. . . . [T]his sense of exclusivity can be added to by the belief perpetuated by jihadi literature that one is involved in, and able to exert influence over, grand events both of the terrestrial and religious type. The life of a jihadi allows the individual to form a perception of their new self, frequently in contrast to their previous existence, as someone of importance and influence. . . . The appeal of this new identity, frequently linked as it is to a glorious past and an elitist interpretation of Islam, is that it can restore an individual's pride and dignity by vilifying that identity group which was the source of the individual's earlier feelings of inadequacy and impotence.

Ilardi noted that access to jihadist websites and propaganda, which featured heavily in the Melbourne cell's activities, is a crucial facet of such a group and contributes to "a cognitive transformation" that is central to the radicalization process:

> Firstly, it instills a sense of outrage and creates a perception of Islam in crisis [which] is central to the thinking and motivation of jihadists, providing a reference and rallying point around which their new identity can crystallize and their perceptions of individual victimization and exclusion can take on a more obvious and outward-appearing form. This perception of a common identity serves to create a bond which legitimizes and inspires the individual's sense of enmity.

Ilardi says the constant exposure to jihadist material and imagery serves to both desensitize and empower, thereby "facilitating the individual's journey from unremarkable citizen to someone who has internalised a belief system which makes violence a duty of the highest order."[82]

THE MELBOURNE CASE

The investigation into the Melbourne cell began in July 2004 when police received a tip that Benbrika's group was talking about an attack in Australia. Telephone intercepts and listening devices were installed and surveillance begun on Benbrika and his cohorts and continued for sixteen months. The evidence ultimately presented against them relied principally on 482 covertly recorded conversations, the case against them "encapsulated in the words of the accused themselves," as the prosecutor noted.[83] The most damning evidence were the conversations in which Benbrika discussed doing "a big thing . . . like Spain." He was also heard saying, "We will do damage, blast things," and asking Abdullah Merhi, "Are you ready to give your life to get the paradise maidens?"—to which in response, Merhi replied, "No comment."[84] Benbrika told his followers the "treaty" forbidding Muslims from attacking their host country had been broken by the Australian government's sending its troops to Muslim lands. "They killing our brothers, or sisters, it's enough," Benbrika said.[85]

The Melbourne cell, notably Joud, amassed a "vast library" of jihadist literature via the Internet, including *The Terrorists Handbook*, *The Car Bomb Recognition Guide*, *The White Resistance Manual*, writings by Abdullah Azzam and Abu Qatada, and numerous instructional guides on manufacturing explosives.[86] They made inquiries about obtaining high-powered weapons and went on bush camping trips to "do a bit of, you know, terrorist training," one of them joked to his wife.[87] In mid-2004, an undercover police operative posing as a Turkish Muslim infiltrated the group and told Benbrika he knew how to blow up tree stumps using explosives made from ammonium-nitrate-based garden fertilizer. Benbrika asked the operative, code-named SIO39, to teach him how to do so and asked how much ammonium nitrate was necessary to destroy a house. SIO39 told him 50 to 75 kilograms for a house, 200 to 250 kilos for a larger building. Benbrika then asked if he could obtain 500 kilograms of the explosive. Police later filmed covertly as the two traveled to a mountaintop near Melbourne and SIO39 demonstrated a test bomb made from ammonium nitrate in an ice cream container.[88]

The Melbourne cell took precautions against detection, with Benbrika using ten different mobile phones, eight of them registered in false names, while his right-hand man, Joud, used at least thirteen phones in twelve names.[89] Benbrika told his followers he expected his arrest at any time and that the *jemaah* would continue its activities in prison. Despite their attempts at countersurveillance, the cell was brazenly contemptuous of the authorities' interest, and their intentions were an open secret in their community. At one point, the father of one of Benbrika's followers rang to quiz his son about rumors that he and his friends were going to "blow up Australia."[90] Later a Muslim cleric confronted Benbrika and threatened to report him after hearing he was "teaching the boys to do something violent in this country."[91]

Despite their enthusiasm for jihad, the Melbourne cell did not make much concrete progress. The sentencing judge, Bernard Bongiorno, concluded it was "an embryonic terrorist organization" and "although it had encouraged them to perform a terrorist act or acts in the future and had taken steps towards that end, no target or targets had been selected and no explosives or other material had been obtained to carry out such an attack." Nonetheless, he found "the existence of the *jemaah* as a terrorist organisation constituted a significant threat that a terrorist act would be committed in Melbourne."[92]

As the judge noted, it was possible the Melbourne cell would never have got to the point of carrying out a terrorist act. A far more imminent danger was posed by Australia's second jihadist cell based in Sydney, whose activities, by the time Operation Pendennis reached its climax in November 2005, had taken a more sinister and concrete turn. It was when these two groups began to merge, under the guidance of Benbrika, and the Sydney group began stockpiling weapons and chemicals that the authorities feared a "catastrophic" attack.

THE ORIGINS OF THE SYDNEY CELL

The Sydney cell was an altogether more resolute group that demonstrated not only the desire but also the capacity and determination to execute a terrorist attack. Unlike their Melbourne counterparts who, with the exception of Benbrika, were neophytes in the jihadist movement, the nine men arrested in Sydney included several seasoned veterans of the Islamist cause who had been under ASIO (Australian Security Intelligence Organisation) surveillance for some years. They were part of a hardened core of Salafi jihadists based at the notorious Haldon Street *musollah* in suburban Lakemba, Sydney's Muslim heartland, with strong historical and personal links to al-Qaeda, LeT, and Indonesia's JI.

This cohort first garnered attention in mid-2000 in the lead-up to the Sydney Olympic Games, when residents reported hearing automatic-weapons fire at a remote bush property in New South Wales and saw a crowd of bearded men unloading weapons from a car.[93] When police inspected the property, they found an abandoned campsite littered with casings from military assault weapons and the remnants of an improvised explosive device in a campfire. The head of the Olympic Intelligence Unit, former ASIO officer Neil Fergus, who had identified radical Islamists as the major threat to Olympic security, said the site had "all the hallmarks of a full-blown terrorist training camp."[94] The property was owned by three brothers from Lebanon by the name of Elomar, who ran a large engineering and construction company in Sydney. They reportedly told police the property was sometimes used for hunting trips by the Lakemba-based Islamic Youth Movement, a community group in which another brother, Mohammed Ali Elomar, was involved.[95]

The 2000 incident placed the so-called Islamic Youth Movement (IYM), based at the Haldon Street *musollah*, firmly on ASIO's radar. The IYM was established under the auspices of Sheikh Omran's ASJA by one of Omran's followers, a Lebanese-born immigrant, Bilal Khazal, who arrived in Australia in 1987.[96] In Lebanon Khazal had been a significant figure in the Islamic Tawhid movement, an al-Qaeda linked group based at the Ein al-Hilweh Palestinian refugee camp, of which Khazal was reportedly a financier.[97] A CIA assessment obtained by the author in 2003 reported that Khazal, known by his *kuniyah* Abu Suhaib, had met Osama bin Laden and Ayman al-Zawahiri in Afghanistan in 1998 and had been made al-Qaeda's representative in Sydney. "Al Qaeda has reportedly become very active in Australia and there are rank and file and leadership elements heading to Australia with forged passports. The Al Qaeda leadership has allegedly delegated responsibility to Abu Suhaib." The report asserted that Khazal was "reportedly planning an explosives attack against some US embassies [and] also has plans to attack with explosives US interests in the Philippines."[98] Khazal was convicted in absentia in Lebanon in 2003 for being the "chief financier"[99] of the bombing of a Beirut McDonald's in April of that year. He was also named in documents filed in the Central Court of Instruction in Madrid as a key contact of both Abu Dahdah and Abu Qatada and described as being "implicated in recruiting mujahidin whose destination are training camps controlled by Osama bin Laden."[100] In September 2009, Khazal was sentenced by a Sydney court to nine years in prison over the publication of a document he posted on the Internet, which contained instructions on how to shoot down planes, attack motorcades, and assassinate government leaders in the United States, Britain, and Australia.[101]

Khazal was a dominant authority at the *musollah* where members of the Sydney cell prayed. Another key figure there was a Palestinian-born cleric, Abdul Salam Zoud, who was named in a dossier compiled by the French counterterrorism judge Jean-Louis Bruguière as "the recruiter in Australia of volunteers for the jihad."[102] Most of the individuals caught up in the global jihadist movement in Australia have shared the Haldon Street prayer room as their spiritual home, including Mamdouh Habib, who was arrested in 2001 in Pakistan and "rendered" to Egypt and Guantánamo Bay; Jack Roche, jailed for plotting to bomb the Israeli embassy; and the Frenchman Willie Brigitte, an LeT-trained militant who traveled to Australia in 2003 to carry out "a large-scale terrorist action," in the words of Judge Bruguière.[103] Members of the Australian branch of Indonesia's JI, who held joint training camps with ASJA followers under the tutelage of a JI trainer sent to Australia for the purpose in 1999, also frequented the prayer room.[104]

THE SYDNEY CELL

Police characterized the Sydney cell as an extreme "sub-group" within Sheikh Omran's Ahlus Sunnah Wal Jemaah Association. A police report tendered in court stated:

The ASJA is an Australian-based Sunni Islamic group which follows a fundamentalist Salafi/jihadist ideology. The sub-group within ASJA is composed of Islamic extremists who adhere to a hardline takfiri inter-pretation of Islam and support the use of militant jihad against those it perceives as enemies of Islam. . . . Similarly, sub-group members have no respect for Australian society, including Australian laws.[105]

The leader and financier of the cell, according to the evidence ulti-mately presented against them, was forty-year-old Mohammed Ali Elo-mar,[106] whose family owned the NSW property where the abandoned "terrorist training camp" was discovered in 2000. The Elomar family had seemed like the archetypal Australian multicultural success story. The parents migrated from Lebanon in the 1970s and started a family of boil-ermakers, riggers, and welders who established a sprawling corporate empire in construction, real estate, engineering, steel fabrication, and security. Elomar was an engineering consultant with a comfortable home in suburban Bankstown, and press reports described him as a "devout Muslim and dedicated family man" whose wife was pregnant with his sixth child at the time of his arrest.[107] However, Elomar had been under close surveillance since at least 2000, and security agencies regarded him as a dangerous fanatic. In 2003, according to evidence presented in a sep-arate criminal trial in Sydney, Elomar bought five military rocket launch-ers stolen from the Australian army and told an associate he was "going to blow up the nuclear place," referring to the Lucas Heights nuclear reactor in Sydney.[108]

The second-most seasoned member of the Sydney cell was Abdul Rakib Hasan, a Bangladeshi migrant in his thirties who first came to the attention of ASIO for his involvement with the Australian branch of JI. Hasan worked at a halal butchery on Haldon Street owned by another ASIO target, Kusmir Nesirwan, the Indonesian-born deputy emir of JI in Australia.[109] The JI trainer Asman Hashim told Malaysian Special Branch police when he was arrested that Hasan had been a regular attendant at his bush training camps in NSW.[110] Hasan was also investigated over his links to the French terrorist Willie Brigitte, who was dispatched to Australia by LeT in 2003 to coordinate a terrorist attack. Phone taps at Nesirwan's butcher shop revealed that Brigitte rang the shop forty-two times to speak to Hasan, and that Hasan arranged three safe houses for Brigitte during his stay in Australia. Hasan was charged with making false statements to ASIO after admitting to only three conversations with Brigitte when the phone tap records revealed they had spoken twenty-three times.[111]

Another veteran was Khaled Cheikho, thirty-two, a loyal ASJA member and follower of Sheikh Omran who was sent for training with LeT in Pakistan in 1999.[112] Cheikho was also on ASIO's watch list because of his marriage to the daughter of the Australian Muslim convert Rabiah Hutchinson, described by the U.S. counterterrorism analyst Marc Sageman as "the matriarch of radical Islam." Hutchinson is the former wife of JI's Australian emir, Abdul Rahim Ayub, and of the senior al-Qaeda strategist and *shura* member Mustafa Hamid, a.k.a. Abu Walid el-Masri, whom she wed in Afghanistan in 2001.[113] Lebanese-born Cheikho was described by the prosecutor in the Pendennis case as "one of the leaders, thinkers and co-ordinators" of the Sydney cell.[114]

Moustafa Cheikho, the twenty-eight-year-old Australian-born son of Lebanese parents, is Khaled Cheikho's nephew. He worked as a security guard in Sydney and underwent training with LeT in Pakistan a year after his uncle, according to a fellow militant who testified at their trial.[115] French authorities reportedly believe that Cheikho trained alongside Willie Brigitte.[116] An intercepted phone call recorded Cheikho telling a friend he still had a robe owned by the British militant Abu Qatada, which the cleric had left behind after his visit to Australia in 1994. Cheikho described Abu Qatada as a "religious fighter" and "probably the highest scholar in the world."[117]

Despite the two Cheikhos being the only Sydney cell members to have received foreign training, there has been no evidence produced to suggest this afforded them an elevated position in the group or an enhanced role in its activities. The two men may have passed on elements of their training during the bush camping trips they took part in, but there was no evidence presented at their trial indicating they did so. Rather, the evidence overwhelmingly indicated that the group relied for practical advice and assistance on material obtained over the Internet. While prosecutors described Khaled Cheikho as a "leader and coordinator," and it seems logical to assume this may have derived from his LeT training, there was no evidence provided to the court to support this. Khaled Cheikho's training was not part of the case against him, presumably because there was no witness willing to testify on it.

Mohammed Omar Jamal was the youngest member of the Sydney cell, aged twenty-one at the time of his arrest. He was also of keen interest to the security agencies, mainly because of the activities of his elder brothers. Jamal's most notorious sibling was Saleh Jamal, a former criminal turned fanatical Islamist who was convicted in Lebanon of terrorism charges, which were later overturned. He was subsequently extradited to Australia, convicted of knee-capping an associate and shooting at a suburban police station, and sentenced in 2010 to up to nineteen years in prison.[118] The Patriotic Union of Kurdistan in northern Iraq detained another Jamal brother, Ahmad, for "security reasons," as they believed him to be fighting with Islamic militants.[119] Mohammed Jamal (known by his middle name, Omar) was the most junior of the Sydney cell, an amateur IT buff whose role was principally that of "computer person" and gofer for the group.[120]

The remaining four members of the Sydney cell were relative newcomers to the jihadist scene. Three were troubled young men with a history of family violence or drug abuse and delinquency, who had turned to religion and found solace in the aggressive brand of Islam preached at the Haldon Street *musholla*. Bradley Omar Baladjam, twenty-seven, was the son of an Indonesian father and Australian mother; he was abused as a child, indulged in heavy drug use as a teenager, and became a "born again" Muslim in his twenties.[121] Mazen Touma, twenty-five, was a similarly rebellious teenager with juvenile convictions for assault and drug possession.[122] Khaled Sharrouf, forty, was brutalized as a child by a violent father, expelled from school at sixteen, developed an amphetamines habit, and by the age of twenty was diagnosed with schizophrenia.[123] His lawyer described him as "a troubled young man suffering physical and emotional problems [who] could be unduly influenced by people."[124] The last of the Sydney cell members was Mirsad Mulahalilovic, twenty-nine, a Bosnian who arrived in Australia in 1996 as a refugee from the civil war in the former Yugoslavia. He was now an Australian citizen, self-employed as a painter and handyman, and lived with his pregnant wife in a granny flat at the rear of his parents' home.[125]

While continuing to attend the Lakemba *musollah*, the nine Sydney men looked to Benbrika in Melbourne for spiritual guidance, often driving the 1,000 kilometers to the Victorian capital to visit him or hosting his frequent visits to Sydney. Benbrika played the role of "spiritual sanctioner" for the conspiracy that unfolded in 2005.[126]

THE CONSPIRACY

In April 2005, while the Melbourne cell was still talking the talk about jihad, members of the Sydney cell began acquiring large amounts of weapons and ammunition and placing orders for laboratory equipment and chemicals. Touma and Baladjam were heard in an intercepted conversation talking about how they needed to get fit to "shoot some motherfuckers," and later took delivery of 15 boxes of ammunition containing 7,500 rounds.[127] Touma was also heard discussing his attempts to make an improvised explosive device using copper pipe. Elomar and Hasan traveled to Melbourne to meet Benbrika and Joud, with whom they wrote a list of fifty-five items of laboratory equipment that they later ordered from a Melbourne supplier. When searching Elomar's home in a preemptive raid, police found 12 firearms and 28,000 rounds of ammunition, including more than 11,000 rounds suitable for use in a semiautomatic weapon like an AK-47; his arsenal was enough for 38 hours of continuous firing using a conventional gun.[128]

In June, the Sydney cell started buying bulk loads of chemicals that are known precursors for high-powered explosives favored by terrorists such as HMTD and TATP, known as "the mother of Satan." Twenty-four bottles of hydrogen peroxide were bought and hidden behind Khaled Sharrouf's home.[129] More hydrogen peroxide was bought by Omar Baladjam after he learned it was used in the London bombings of July 7, 2005. Baladjam later told a prison psychologist, "He thought if he could do something similar in Australia without hurting people, it would extend awareness of aggression against Muslims and alert Australians to oppose the government and stop the nation's alliance with the United States."[130] In an alarming spike of activity in September and October 2005, Hasan and Jamal ordered 200 liters of sulphuric acid, 400 liters of methylated spirits, 50 liters of hydrochloric acid, 25 kilograms of citric acid, 20 liters of glycerine, and 120 liters of acetone from different Sydney suppliers.[131] They placed the orders using aliases and mobile phones registered in false names. Khaled Sharrouf visited a Big W supermarket with Touma and Khaled Cheikho, where Sharrouf was caught stealing 6 clocks and 140 batteries, which he later confessed were part of the preparations for a terrorist act.[132]

Convinced that the Sydney cell was on the verge of attacking, on November 8, 2005, police and federal agents staged raids across NSW and Victoria, eventually arresting twenty-two men. They were tried in separate trials in Melbourne and Sydney in 2008 and 2009. Benbrika was sentenced to at least twelve years in jail, and seven of his followers were convicted and given prison terms of between three and eight years.[133] The Sydney trial concluded in October 2009 with five men convicted of conspiring to do acts in preparation for a terrorist act. The other four had already pleaded guilty and been sentenced to between three and fourteen years in jail.[134]

The Pendennis case illustrates the evolution of the global terrorist threat since it first materialized in the Australian public consciousness with the attacks of September 11 and the Bali bombings of October 2002, which killed 202 people, including 88 Australians. In the words of Agent Kemuel Lam Paktsun of the Australian Federal Police Joint Counter Terrorism Team: "The terrorist threat in Australia has changed significantly in the past seven years. . . . Today, home-grown terrorists are the biggest threat faced by Australian law enforcement." Often, "these extremists are previously unknown to authorities, exhibit no prior extremist tendencies publicly, do not associate with known extremists and are assimilated into the greater community."[135]

Their embeddedness in the mainstream creates particular difficulties for the authorities, as Victoria Police analyst Gaetano Ilardi concurs:

> These individuals are also likely to be organizationally unaligned with the broader jihadi community, and as a result, trained, funded and tasked with little or no outside assistance. Self-contained and with few or no links to more formal groups and networks, home-grown terrorists have proven particularly difficult to detect, depriving counter-terrorist agencies of investigative starting points from which it becomes possible to identify individuals or groups of interest.[136]

The Pendennis case equally demonstrates the enduring potency and reach of the al-Qaeda philosophy, which provided the ideological underpinning and impetus for the Australian cells. For while the individuals were mostly self-recruited and self-indoctrinated, there was nothing "homegrown" about the credo that impelled them. Even as al-Qaeda's ability to exert command and control diminishes because of global counterterrorism efforts, the al-Qaeda philosophy flourishes, its headquarters now comfortably ensconced in cyberspace, where it enjoys virtual immunity from the terrestrial war on terror. As Lam Paktsun notes:

> To a large extent the internet has replaced actual training camps as a source of instruction and inspiration for militant Muslims. In the West, including Australia, terrorist ideology and instructions are disseminated mostly through the internet. The virtual space has been the greatest enabler of teaching, nurturing and sustenance of extremist jihadi ideology and how-to training manuals spread in mass diffusion throughout the world.[137]

In Australia, as elsewhere, ready access to the jihadists' simplistic ideology provides an instant way to empower and galvanize young men in search of a cause:

> An opinion that one is protecting victimized Muslims throughout the world can instill a feeling of exclusivity, elevating one's own sense of self-importance and purpose. The process of arriving at this point can create a sense of elitism among jihadists [and] a perception that one forms part of the crème de la creme . . . in which jihadis perceive themselves as the most spiritually advanced and righteous of all Muslims.[138]

Some heart may be taken from the success of Australian counterterrorism authorities in exposing, investigating, dismantling, and prosecuting the Pendennis cells. However, the practical and logistical tasks of surveillance, intelligence gathering, and policing are the easy part of the modern counterterrorism challenge. The more daunting aspect is countering the jihadist narrative online, where it continues to hold mesmerizing appeal for disaffected young men who yearn to be part of an exalted elite, unbound by the strictures of democratic, secular law.

NOTES

1. The Queen v. Abdul Nacer Benbrika, Aimen Joud, Shane Kent, Fadl Sayadi, Hany Taha, Abdullah Merhi, Bassam Raad, Ahmed Raad, Shoue Hammoud, Ezzit Raad, Majed Raad, Amer Haddara, Transcript of Proceedings, Supreme Court of Victoria, Criminal Jurisdiction, Melbourne (February 25, 2008).

2. Transcript of conversation tendered as evidence in the Queen v. Benbrika et al. (February 13, 2008).

3. Comment by NSW Police Commissioner Ken Maroney, quoted in Cameron Stewart and Nick Leys, "Osama's Aussie Offspring: Terror Plot Foiled After Seventeen Arrested," *Australian* (Sydney), November 9, 2005.

4. The Queen v. Benbrika et al., Transcript of Proceedings.

5. Police statement tendered as evidence in Central Local Court, Sydney, quoted in James Madden and Natalie O'Brien, "Rocket Launchers Part of War Plan," *Australian* (Sydney), January 11, 2007; Les Kennedy, "Launchers Bought After War Talk, Court Told," *Sydney Morning Herald*, January 11, 2007.

6. Regina v. Mohamed Ali Elomar, Abdul Rakib Hasan, Khaled CHeikho, Moustafa Cheikho and Mohammed Omar Jamal, transcript of conversation tendered as evidence, Supreme Court of NSW Common Law Division, Criminal List, Sydney, Friday July 17, 2009.

7. Record of interview with Jack Roche, Australian Federal Police, November 2002, Perth; interviews with Jack Roche, Perth, May 2003 and November 2007.

8. A full account of the Roche case is included in Sally Neighbour, *In the Shadow of Swords: On the Trail of Terrorism from Afghanistan to Australia* (Sydney: Harper Collins Australia, 2004), 228.

9. Record of interview with Jack Thomas, Australian Federal Police, Pakistan, March 8, 2003; interview with Jack Thomas, Melbourne, April and December 2005; Sally Neighbour, "The Convert," *Four Corners*, ABC TV, February 27, 2002.

10. Stewart and Leys, "Osama's Aussie Offspring."

11. Patrick Walters, "Suspects Have No Links to Terror Groups," *Australian* (Sydney), March 3, 2006.

12. The Queen v. Benbrika et al., opening submission by Remy Van de Weil, defence counsel for Abdul Nacer Benbrika, Supreme Court of Victoria (February 27, 2008).

13. Cameron Stewart, "Refuge of a Radical Scoundrel," *Australian* (Sydney), August 6, 2005.

14. The Queen v. Benbrika et al., sentencing judgment by Justice Bernard Bongiorno, Supreme Court of Victoria Criminal Division, Melbourne, (February 3, 2009).

15. Ibid.

16. Neighbour, *In the Shadow of Swords*, 145; Sally Neighbour, *The Mother of Mohammed: An Australian Woman's Extraordinary Journey into Jihad* (Melbourne: Melbourne University, 2009), 155. Also see http://aswj.com.au.

17. Kemuel Lam Paktsun, Australian Federal Police Joint Counter Terrorism Team, "The Changing Face of Terrorism in Australia," presentation to Terrorism, Trade, and Security Winter School, 2007, University of Sydney, Centre for International Security Studies, July 2007.

18. Mitchell D. Silber and Arvin Bhatt, *Radicalization in the West: The Homegrown Threat* (New York: NYPD Intelligence Division, 2007).

19. "Profile: Abu Qatada," *BBC News*, February 26, 2007, http://news.bbc.co.uk/2 /hi/uk_news/4141594.stm.

20. Rafael Epstein, "Federal Police Person of Interest Denies Terrorist Involvement," *ABC Radio PM program*, September 3, 2003, http://www.abc.net.au/pm/content /2003/s938431.htm.

21. Central Court of Instruction, Madrid, Folio 11811, 76, translation obtained by the author, August 2003.

22. Epstein, "Federal Police Person of Interest Denies Terrorist Involvement."

23. Martin Chulov, *Australian Jihad: The Battle Against Terrorism from Within and Without* (Sydney: Pan McMillan Australia, 2006), 22.

24. Cameron Stewart, "The Day One Man Infected a Community with Hatred," *Australian* (Sydney), November 12, 2005.

25. Ibid.

26. The Queen v. Benbrika et al., sentencing judgment.

27. Richard Kerbaj, "Suspect Turned His Followers to Faith," *Australian* (Sydney), November 16, 2005.

28. Silber and Bhatt, *Radicalization in the West.*

29. Interview with Ali Kassae, Sydney, September 2007, quoted in Sally Neighbour, "Islamic Cleric Preaching Extremism Hate," *Australian* (Sydney), October 2, 2007.

30. Translation from the Arabic, jihadist DVD, copy obtained by the author, Sydney, September 2007.

31. Nick McKenzie, "Suspect Claims ASIO Surveillance Unjust," interview with Abdul Nacer Benbrika, August 4, 2005, *7.30 Report*, ABC TV, available at http://www .abc.net.au/7.30/content/2005/s1430601.htm.

32. Police statement by Ahmad Kalek, January 9, 2004. Kalek traveled with Kent to Afghanistan and trained at Camp Faruq.

33. Sworn evidence of Moustafa Cheikho's LeT training was provided by a Korean American LeT recruit, Yong Ki Kwon, who testified in the Supreme Court of NSW to having trained alongside Cheikho. Accounts of Khaled Cheikho's LeT training were provided to the author in confidential interviews in Sydney with fellow LeT trainees.

34. Stewart, "The Day One Man Infected a Community with Hatred."

35. Stewart, "Refuge of a Radical Scoundrel."

36. Cameron Stewart, "Terror Link to Radical Sheiks," *Australian* (Sydney), November 11, 2005.

37. Susie O'Brien and Kate Ross, "Extremist Gathers Fans in Suburbs," *Melbourne Herald-Sun*, August 6, 2005.

38. McKenzie, "Suspect Claims ASIO Surveillance Unjust."

39. The Queen v. Benbrika et al., transcript of intercepted conversations tendered as evidence in Supreme Court of Victoria, February 13, 2008.

40. McKenzie, "Suspect Claims ASIO Surveillance Unjust."

41. Report of Dr. Danny Sullivan, consultant psychiatrist, October 10, 2008, cited in the Queen v. Benbrika et al., sentencing judgment.

42. The Queen v. Benbrika et al., sentencing judgment.

43. Stewart, "The Day One Man Infected a Community with Hatred."

44. Kerbaj, "Suspect Turned His Followers to Faith."

45. "Globalised Islam," interview with Olivier Roy, *Religioscope*, November 8, 2004, available at http://www.religion.info/english/interviews/article_117.shtml.

46. Anthony Bubalo, program director for West Asia, Lowy Institute for International Policy, Sydney. Analysis posted on the TIN (Trusted Information Network) 2 Web forum, quoted in "The Power of Outreach: Leveraging Expertise on Threats in Southeast Asia: A Report of the CSIS Transnational Threats Project," Center for Strategic and International Studies, Washington D.C., April 2009.

47. Marc Sageman, *Understanding Terror Networks* (Philadelphia: University of Pennsylvania Press, 2004), 151.

48. The Queen v. Benbrika et al., Supreme Court of Victoria, February 14, 2008.

49. The Queen v. Benbrika et al., sentencing judgment.

50. The Queen v. Benbrika et al., opening submission by crown prosecutor Richard Maidment, Supreme Court of Victoria, February 13, 2008.

51. Stuart Rintoul, "Principal's Jaundiced View of Angel Joud," *Australian* (Sydney), November 11, 2005.

52. Natasha Robinson, "Just a Regular Guy on Hols, Says Terror Accused," *Australian* (Sydney), August 15, 2006.

53. The Queen v. Benbrika et al., transcript of recorded conversation tendered as evidence, Supreme Court of Victoria, February 20, 2008.

54. The Queen v. Benbrika et al., opening submission.

55. James Madden and Padraic Murphy, "Suspect Wanted to Be a Bomber," *Australian* (Sydney), November 9, 2005.

56. The Queen v. Benbrika et al., transcript of conversation tendered as evidence.

57. The Queen v. Benbrika et al., opening submission.

58. The Queen v. Benbrika et al., sentencing judgment.

59. Marian Wilkinson and Matthew Moore, "Patient Hunters Wait to Spring the Trap," *Sydney Morning Herald*, November 12, 2005.

60. The Queen v. Benbrika et al., Evidence in Supreme Court of Victoria.

61. The Queen v. Benbrika et al., transcript of recorded conversation cited in opening submission, Supreme Court of Victoria.

62. Wilkinson and Moore, "Patient Hunters Wait to Spring the Trap."

63. The Queen v. Benbrika et al., sentencing judgment.

64. Wilkinson and Moore, "Patient Hunters Wait to Spring the Trap."

65. The Queen v. Benbrika et al., Amer Haddara, record of interview, tendered as evidence in Supreme Court of Victoria.

66. The Queen v. Benbrika et al., sentencing judgment.

67. The Queen v. Benbrika et al., submission by defence counsel Mark Taft, Supreme Court of Victoria.

68. Transcript of recorded conversation tendered in evidence, Supreme Court of Victoria.

69. Madden and Murphy, "Suspect Wanted to Be a Bomber."

70. Luke McIlveen and Elissa Hunt, "Holy War on Australia: Seventeen Arrested as Terror Network Smashed," *Daily Telegraph* (Sydney), November 9, 2005.

71. Natasha Robinson, "Caucasian Accused a Student of Jihad," *Australian* (Sydney), November 10, 2005.

72. Police statement by Ahmad Kalek.

73. Ibid.

74. Regina v. Kent, Supreme Court of Victoria, sentencing judgment by Justice Bernard Bongiorno, September 2, 2009.

75. Regina v. Kent, sentencing judgment.

76. The Queen v. Benbrika et al., transcript of conversation, February 20, 2008.

77. Regina v. Kent, sentencing judgment.

78. The Queen v. Benbrika et al., transcript of conversation, February 20, 2008.

79. Regina v. Kent, sentencing judgment.

80. The Queen v. Benbrika et al., sentencing judgment.

81. The Queen v. Benbrika et al., sentencing judgment.

82. Gaetano Joe Illardi, "Home-Grown Terrorism and Radicalisation Activities: More Than Meets the Eye," Victoria Police and Global Terrorism Research Centre, Monash University, March 2009.

83. The Queen v. Benbrika et al., opening submission.

84. The Queen v. Benbrika et al., transcript of conversation tendered in evidence, February 15, 2008.

85. The Queen v. Benbrika et al., transcript of conversation tendered in evidence, March 1, 2005.

86. Evidence tendered in the Queen v. Benbrika et al.

87. The Queen v. Benbrika et al., transcript of conversation tendered in evidence, February 14, 2008.

88. The Queen v. Benbrika et al., transcripts of conversations and police surveillance video tendered in evidence, February 13, 2008.

89. The Queen v. Benbrika et al., opening submission.

90. The Queen v. Benbrika et al., opening submission.

91. The Queen v. Benbrika et al., testimony of Samir Mohtada.

92. The Queen v. Benbrika et al., sentencing judgment.

93. Interview with Archie Brown, resident of Braidwood, NSW, quoted in Sally Neighbour, "The Australian Connections," *Four Corners*, ABC TV, June 9, 2003, available at http://www.abc.net.au/4corners/content/2003/20030609_australian_connections /default.htm.

94. Interview with Neil Fergus, quoted in Neighbour, "The Australian Connections."

95. Paul Daley, "The Terror Trail," *The Bulletin* (Sydney), November 22, 2005, 17.

96. Interview with Bilal Khazal, Sydney, May 9, 2003.

97. Classified assessment by the U.S. Central Intelligence Agency, obtained by the author from a confidential source in 2003.

98. Ibid.

99. Regina v. Bilal Saadallah Khazaal, Supreme Court of New South Wales, Common Law Division, bail judgment by Justice Greg James, June 22, 2004.

100. Central Court of Instruction, Madrid, Folio 11811, 76, translation obtained by the author, August 2003.

101. Lindy Kerin, "DIY Terrorist Author Sentenced to Twelve Years Jail," *ABC Radio PM Program*, September 25, 2009, available at http://www.abc.net.au/pm/content /2009/s2696878.htm.

102. "Presentation of the Facts" by Jean-Louis Bruguiere, deputy presiding judge in charge of the investigation, and Jean-Francois Ricard, chief examining magistrate, Paris Court of Appeal, Civil Trial Court of General Jurisdiction, November 3, 2003.

103. Ibid.

104. Sally Neighbour, *In the Shadow of Swords*, 219.

105. Police statement tendered in Central Local Court, Sydney, November 14, 2005, quoted in Kelly Burke, "Police Allege Link to Imam," *Sydney Morning Herald*, November 15, 2005.

106. Regina v. Elomar et al., evidence tendered in Supreme Court of NSW Common Law Division, Criminal List, Sydney, Friday July 17, 2009.

107. Marian Wilkinson and Tom Allard, "Shadowy Links Start to Emerge," *Sydney Morning Herald*, November 10, 2005.

108. Police statement and transcript of intercepted conversation, tendered in the Central Local Court, Sydney, January 10, 2007.

109. Neighbour, *In the Shadow of Swords*.

110. Confidential briefing to author by Australian security agency officer, May 2004.

111. Martin Chulov, *Australian Jihad*.

112. Confidential author interviews with fellow LeT trainees, Sydney, 2008.

113. Sally Neighbour, *The Mother of Mohammed: An Australian Woman's Extraordinary Journey Into Jihad* (Melbourne: Melbourne University Publishing, 2009).

114. Regina v. Elomar et al., closing submission by crown prosecutor, Supreme Court of New South Wales, July 10, 2009.

115. Regina v. Elomar et al., testimony of Yong Ki Kwon, Supreme Court of NSW.

116. Stewart, "Terror Link to Radical Sheiks."

117. Regina v. Elomar et al., transcript of recorded conversation July 17, 2009.

118. Janet Fife-Yeomans, "Saleh Jamal Jailed for Lakemba Police Station Shooting," *Daily Telegraph* (Sydney), May 29, 2010.

119. Natalie O'Brien, "Aussie Tortured in Iraqi Prison," *Australian* (Sydney), March 10, 2006.

120. Regina v. Elomar et al., evidence tendered in Supreme Court of NSW.

121. Regina v. Omar Baladjam, Supreme Court of New South Wales, Common Law Division Criminal List, Parramatta, sentencing judgment by Justice James Whealy, April 7, 2009.

122. Regina v. Mazen Touma, Supreme Court of New South Wales, Common Law Division Criminal List, Parramatta, sentencing judgment by Justice James Whealy, October 24, 2008.

123. Regina v. Khaled Sharrouf, Supreme Court of New South Wales, Common Law Division Criminal List, Parramatta, sentencing judgment by Justice James Whealy, September 24, 2009.

124. Wilkinson and Allard, "Shadowy Links Start to Emerge."

125. Regina v. Mirsad Mulahalilovic, Supreme Court of New South Wales, Common Law Division Criminal List, Parramatta., sentencing judgment by Justice James Whealy, January 30, 2009.

126. Silber and Bhatt, *Radicalization in the West.*

127. Regina v. Elomar et al., transcripts of intercepted conversations, police video surveillance, police witness statements tendered in Supreme Court of NSW.

128. Regina v. Elomar et al., chronology of crown allegations, exhibit MF14, Supreme Court of NSW.

129. Regina v. Elomar et al., evidence tendered in Supreme Court of NSW.

130. Regina v. Baladjam, sentencing judgment, Justice James Whealy, April 7, 2009.

131. Regina v. Elomar et al., evidence tendered in Supreme Court of NSW.

132. Regina v. Sharrouf, sentencing judgment, Justice James Whealy, September 24, 2009.

133. The Queen v. Benbrika et al., sentencing judgment.

134. Regina v. Elomar et al., jury verdict in Supreme Court of NSW, September 16, 2009; also see James Madden and Angus Thompson, "Terror Quintet Facing Life in Jail for Plotting Murder on a Massive Scale," *Australian* (Sydney), September 17, 2009.

135. Lam Paktsun, "The Changing Face of Terrorism in Australia."

136. Ilardi, "Home-Grown Terrorism and Radicalization."

137. Lam Paktsun, "The Changing Face of Terrorism in Australia."

138. Ilardi, "Home-Grown Terrorism and Radicalization."

[8]

The 7 July 2005 London Bombings

BRUCE HOFFMAN

Both at the time of the July 7, 2005, London bombing attacks and since then, a misconception has often been perpetuated that this was entirely an organic or homegrown phenomenon of self-radicalized, self-selected terrorists.[1] Indeed, British authorities initially believed that the attacks were the work of disaffected British Muslims: self-radicalized and self-selected, operating only within the United Kingdom and entirely on their own.[2] Newspaper accounts repeatedly quoted unnamed security sources using the term "clean skins" to describe the bombers: a shorthand of sorts meaning that they had no prior convictions or known terrorist involvement.[3] In the Cabinet Office on the day of the bombing, a senior intelligence officer's suggestion that al-Qaeda was behind the attacks was reportedly "laughed at" and dismissed as "absurd."[4] That morning, Scotland Yard's deputy assistant commissioner, Brian Paddick, told a press conference, "As far as I am concerned, Islam and terrorists are two words that do not go together."[5] And in an interview on BBC Radio 4 on the morning after the bombings, Home Secretary Charles Clarke stated that the attacks had come "out of the blue," suggesting that the bombings were some spontaneous outburst of rage and anger manifested in an act of extreme violence that could not have been anticipated or prevented.[6]

Such arguments were widely cited in support of the then-fashionable contention that entirely homegrown threats had superseded those posed by al-Qaeda and that al-Qaeda was no longer a consequential, active terrorist force. Accordingly, many analysts and government officials concluded that the threat from al-Qaeda had in fact receded and that the main security challenge emanated completely from unaffiliated, self-selected, and self-radicalized individuals. The evidence that has come to light since the 2005 London attacks, however, points to precisely the opposite conclusion: that al-Qaeda was and is alive and kicking and that it has been actively planning, supporting, and directing terrorist attacks on a global canvas since at least 2004 and was certainly behind the 2005 London bombings.[7] Hence, rather than an organic, entirely homegrown plot perpetrated by "clean skins" acting entirely on their own, al-Qaeda's involvement—and that of other terrorist organizations—is crystal clear.

THE BOMBINGS

At 8:50 a.m. on Thursday morning, July 7, 2005, three bombs exploded within fifty seconds of one another on three different London Underground (subway) trains.[8] One explosion occurred on an eastbound Circle line train traveling from Liverpool Street to Aldgate Station. The bomb had been placed on the floor of the third carriage. Seven people were killed, and at least ninety others were injured in the blast. A second bomb was on a westbound Circle line train that had just left the Edgware Road station bound for Paddington. The train was one hundred meters into the tunnel when a bomb located on the floor exploded in the second carriage. At the same moment, another train happened to be passing headed in the opposite direction.[9] Its driver later described how the force of the explosion lifted his own train completely off the track.[10] In the second explosion, eight people were killed and another 185 injured. The third device detonated in the first carriage of a westbound Piccadilly line train between Kings Cross and Russell Square stations, killing fourteen people and injuring seventy-three. Nearly an hour later, at 9:47 a.m., a fourth bomb detonated on the upper deck of one of London's famed red double-decker buses. The blast tore the roof off the route 30 bus as it crossed the junction of Tavistock Square and Upper Woburn Place. Twenty-seven people died in the bus attack, and another 180 were injured. A total of fifty-six people perished that morning, including the four bombers. More than 500 were injured.[11]

London's long experience with Irish terrorism coupled with extensive planning, drills, and other exercises ensured that the city's emergency services responded quickly and effectively in a highly coordinated manner. The initial deployment of emergency service personnel to the four blast sites entailed seventy-three ambulances and twelve response units, with many additional vehicles drawn from other sources. According to the official lessons learned report,

> all five London Strategic Health Authorities played a part in the response and all London hospitals were placed on major incident alert, with 1,200 beds rapidly made available for more than 700 casualties arriving at accident and emergency departments over a period of several hours. The vast majority (more than 80%) were fit for discharge on the same day. Of the 103 casualties admitted to hospital, including 21 critically injured, three were to die of their injuries.[12]

In the two hours following the explosions, some 200,000 people were evacuated from more than 500 trains as the entire London Underground was shut down while a network-wide security inspection was conducted.[13]

The nearly simultaneous blasts, their horrific casualty toll, and the prospect that this was the opening salvo in a sustained terrorist campaign stunned the United Kingdom. Indeed, only weeks earlier, on June 2, the Joint Terrorism Assessment Center (JTAC), Britain's principal governmental counterterrorism coordinating body, had concluded that "at present there is not a group with both the current intent and the capability to attack in the UK" and consequently downgraded the overall countrywide terrorism threat level.[14] That the four bombers had deliberately killed themselves to ensure both the attack's success and its lethal outcome further exacerbated the fear and alarm pervading the country.[15] On this score as well, the authorities had been shown grievously complacent. A report issued in March 2005 by the Joint Intelligence Committee (JIC), Britain's most senior intelligence assessment and evaluation body, had determined that suicide "attacks would not become the norm within Europe."[16] This judgment, coupled with the testimony of Dame Eliza Manningham-Buller, then director-general of the Security Service (MI5), prompted the parliamentary committee investigating the 2005 London bombings to conclude, "The fact that there were suicide attacks in the UK on 7 July [2005] was clearly unexpected: the Director General of the Security Service said it was a surprise that the first big attack in the UK for ten years was a suicide attack."[17]

THE BOMBERS

From personal documents found at the attack sites, British authorities quickly established the bombers' identities.[18] They were Mohammed Siddique Khan, age thirty, who was responsible for the Edgware Road blast; Shezad Tanweer, age twenty-two, who blew himself up at Aldgate; Jermaine Lindsay, age nineteen, who perpetrated the Russell Square explosion; and, Hasib Hussain, age eighteen, whose bomb detonated on the number 30 bus. The four men were all British citizens and, with the exception of Lindsay, had been born in the U.K.[19] Although British authorities were aware of the potential that British nationals might commit terrorist acts within the U.K., the attacks nonetheless took the government and the public by surprise.[20] "We were working off a script which actually has been completely discounted from what we know as reality," Andy Hayman, then the assistant commissioner for specialist operations at Scotland Yard, told the parliamentary committee investigating the bombings.[21] Indeed, on the morning of July 6, 2005, at a private security briefing for senior Labour Party members of parliament, Manningham-Buller had assured them that there was no identifiably imminent terrorist threat either to London or, for that matter, anywhere in the U.K.[22] However, just weeks earlier, a senior-level U.S. government delegation led by the U.S. National Security Council's top counterterrorism official had reportedly arrived in London to warn their British counterparts of the danger of just such an attack. Their visit had been prompted by what the Americans regarded as a dangerous complacency on the part of the U.K. government.[23]

Mohammed Siddique Khan (MSK), the oldest of the group, was also its leader. There is nothing in his background that would necessarily suggest the trajectory into terrorism that his life followed. He was born in Leeds on October 20, 1974, the youngest of six children. Described as "quiet, studious and never in trouble," his background and profile hardly fits the stereotype of the deranged, homicidally fanatical suicide terrorist. MSK was from a solidly middle-class background, held a university degree, was gainfully employed, had married, and had a daughter who was then eighteen months old. His wife, Hasina, was pregnant and miscarried the day of the bombing.[24]

A graduate of Leeds Metropolitan University with a degree in business studies, MSK had been employed as a community worker, focusing on troubled and disadvantaged youth. Between 2001 and 2004, he was a teaching assistant at a local primary school, working with special-needs children and other students who had either behavioral problems or difficulties with learning the English language. Based on the evidence gathered about MSK, the parliamentary committee investigating the bombings observed that "Khan, known widely as 'Sid,' had a real talent and vocation for working with young people. He was highly regarded by teachers and parents, and had a real empathy with difficult children. Children saw him as a role model."[25] Similarly, MSK's mentoring role in the local community had attracted positive attention and considerable praise. He reportedly was especially effective at gaining the trust of troubled youths and helping them deal with personal problems. A fellow community youth worker lauded MSK as "a sharp, switched-on professional . . . a tower of strength within the community."[26] Another profile explained how Khan's "peers admired his focus on family, work, working out, and Islam."[27]

Although he claims not to have been observant in his youth, MSK was noticeably religious by 2001. However, the parliamentary investigative report noted that MSK "was not aggressive, extreme or politicized in the way he spoke about religion to colleagues. He had spoken out against the 9/11 attacks at school." What stood out more, however, were increasing absences from work that eventually led to his going on sick leave from September 20 to November 19, 2004. MSK was subsequently dismissed after the school administration concluded he was not in fact ill but was claiming medical leave nonetheless; at about the same time MSK gave notice he was quitting anyway.[28]

Shezad Tanweer was closest to MSK both in age and in their relationship, compared to the other two bombers. Born on December 15, 1982, he was the second of four children and the eldest son. A good student and excellent sportsman, Tanweer's passion in life appeared to be cricket. He also practiced the martial art jujitsu. Tanweer attended

Leeds Metropolitan University, where he studied sports science. He left university after only two years and then worked part-time in a fish-and-chips takeaway shop owned by his father. Unlike MSK, Tanweer had been religiously observant from a young age, although those who knew him state that he never expressed extremist views. Like MSK, however, Tanweer also defies the stereotypical image of the suicide terrorist as either a wild-eyed fanatic or someone uneducated or from an economically deprived background. People who knew him when he was a boy described his demeanor "as calm, friendly, mature and modest" and observed that he "was popular with his peers." Tanweer also dressed fashionably and drove a red Mercedes that was a gift from his father, a prominent local businessman who drove a silver Mercedes and owned a profitable abattoir, a video rental store, and fish-and-chips shops. He in fact came from a family who appeared to epitomize the "classic immigrant success story, seeming proof of the multiculturalism that Britain often boasts is woven into its society."[29]

Tanweer reportedly became more devout when he was age sixteen or seventeen, and by mid-2002 religion had become the major focus of his life. Even so, on the eve of the bombings he was seen doing what he would have been doing on any other pleasant summer evening: playing cricket in the local park.[30] Tanweer's uncle, Bashir Ahmed, recalled that his nephew was "proud to be British. He had everything to live for. His parents were loving and supportive. He was a very kind and calm person." Neighbors agreed that was a "nice lad" with a friendly, outgoing personality.[31]

Hasib Hussain, the youngest member of the cell, had an undistinguished academic record and never completed his college course in business studies. However, according to the official parliamentary inquiry's report of the attacks, his family, like those of Tanweer and Khan, was "not poor by the standards of the area." The youngest of four children, Hussain was born on September 16, 1986. An indifferent student with few friends, he was mostly remembered for his large stature. In 2002, together with family, Hussain undertook the hajj—the pilgrimage to Mecca that is one of the pillars of Islam. Thereafter he become demonstrably more religious, wearing traditional clothing and a prayer cap. Hussain told one teacher that he intended to become an imam when he left school. Hussain also became more vocal in support of al-Qaeda, lauding the 9/11 terrorists as martyrs. In 2003, he suddenly began exercising regularly and watching what he ate, and he lost seventy pounds. Hussain's only apparent brush with police occurred in 2004, when he was arrested for shoplifting.[32]

MSK, Tanweer, and Hussain were all also second-generation British citizens whose parents had emigrated from Pakistan. They were Muslims by birth, grew up in stable households with their parents and siblings, and shared the same basic socioeconomic and demographic characteristics.[33]

Jermaine Lindsay, the cell's fourth member, was different in every sense from his cohorts. A convert to Islam who had emigrated from the Caribbean as an infant, Lindsay grew up in a broken and impoverished home. He was born in Jamaica on September 23, 1985, to a nineteen-year-old mother and a father who abandoned them. The following year, Lindsay left Jamaica with his mother and a man who was not his father and settled in Huddersfield, England. This stepfather reportedly treated Lindsay harshly. He had a better relationship with his second stepfather and a more stable family life, along with his younger half-sisters. Lindsay was perhaps the archetypal underachiever. Had he grown up perhaps in a household with his birth father or with a more consistent and less abusive father figure, in a better neighborhood and socioeconomic environment with less deprived schools, he might have made something of himself. Indeed, Lindsay was remembered as "artistic and musical . . . a bright child, successful academically and good at sport." As a teenager, he became interested in martial arts and kickboxing in addition to playing soccer and participating in track and field activities, particularly the long jump. Like the other three bombers, he regularly worked out and was physically fit.[34]

A turning point in Lindsay's life occurred when he and his mother converted to Islam in 2000. At this time, his behavior also changed. From someone who was "a very happy person, always telling jokes, always smiling," he suddenly became more serious and even solemn. Lindsay stopped smoking, listening to music, and playing soccer and instead changed his name to an Islamic one (Abdullah Shaheed Jamal), grew a beard, asked permission to pray at school, and started wearing Muslim attire.[35] Lindsay was disciplined at school for distributing leaflets supporting al-Qaeda and reportedly began hanging around with "troublemakers." He is also believed to have been strongly influenced by another Jamaican convert to Islam, Sheikh Abdallah al-Faisal, a cleric who was imprisoned for soliciting murder, incitement to murder, and incitement to racial hatred because of his febrile, anti-Semitic sermons.[36] Lindsay impressed other worshippers at his local mosque and members of the local Islamic study groups around Huddersfield with whom he prayed, both with how quickly he became fluent in the Arabic language and his ability to memorize and recite long passages from the Quran. In 2002, much to Lindsay's consternation, his mother moved to the United States to live with yet another man. This had a profoundly disruptive effect on Lindsay, who dropped out of school and went on welfare, occasionally doing odd jobs, such as selling mobile telephones and Islamic books. In 2002, he met his future wife, a Caucasian Christian convert to Islam named Samantha Lewthwaite, over the Internet. Their first date was at a "Stop the War" in Iraq rally in London on October 30, 2003. They moved to Aylesbury in September 2004, and their first child, a boy, was born the following year. His wife, who was eight months pregnant when the bombings occurred,[37] remembered him as "a loving husband and father."[38] Lindsay worked as a carpet fitter until early 2005 and then became involved in petty crime, such as burglary.[39] He was unemployed when he died. It is not known how or when Lindsay met MSK but the parliamentary report on the bombings states that they "were close associates by the latter half of 2004." Because of MSK's prominence in Islamic circles around the Huddersfield and Dewsbury areas, it is certainly likely they met there.[40]

With the exception of Lindsay, the three bombers all grew up in Beeston and the neighboring area of Holbeck, known as "gritty, working-class suburbs," just outside of Leeds. Tanweer and Hussain both still lived there, in their parents' homes, at the time of the bombings. MSK had moved a short distance away to Batley and then, following his marriage in 2001, to Dewsbury, a more upscale Leeds suburb.[41] Beeston is depicted as "largely residential, close-knit and densely populated with back-to-back terraced housing, much of which is in poor condition." An ethnically diverse neighborhood, it is also among the poorest communities in the U.K., with the living standards of nearly two-thirds of its 16,300 residents among the worst in the country.[42] People of Pakistani heritage make up 11 percent of Beeston's population and are the largest minority in the community. More than 40 percent have no job qualifications, and unemployment is thus twice that of the area's Caucasian population. The unemployment rate in Beeston is 7.8 percent, compared to Leeds's 3.3 percent.[43]

Three mosques in Beeston serve the community and all of south Leeds. In 2000, MSK obtained local government funds to establish a gym. Associated with the nearby mosque on Hardy Street, MSK reportedly conceived of the gym as a means to get young men off the streets by interesting them in weightlifting, thus helping local youth avoid the ever-present temptations of drugs, alcohol, and street fighting. These community activities for youth continued while MSK worked as a teaching assistant. MSK, Tanweer, Hasib, and Lindsay used to work out together at the gym.[44] After having reportedly been expelled from the Hardy Street mosque "on suspicion of preaching extreme interpretations of Islam to young people," in 2004 MSK opened another gym on Beeston's Lodge Lane under the aegis of the youth program at the nearby Hamara Centre and charitable foundation. Although the new facility was officially closed for renovations two months before the bombings, neighbors claim that MSK and others still used it regularly. All of the bombers worked out there,[45] and, according to some sources, locals referred to the facility as the "Al Qaeda gym."[46] Indeed, a friend of MSK told the BBC that MSK "used it, [Lodge Lane], as a [terrorist] recruitment centre."[47]

The bombers intersected in other ways as well. Tanweer and Hasib, for instance, lived about a half mile from each other, and Hasib's brother played cricket with Tanweer when they were children. Hussain likely encountered MSK because since at least 2001, he, too, had become involved in local community youth work. By 2004, MSK was a frequent visitor at Hussain's home. Tanweer, Hussain, and MSK were all known to frequent a local Islamic bookstore, the Iqra Learning Center, where MSK and Tanweer had volunteered to work in its youth drop-in program. Someone who knew MSK and Tanweer claims to have seen them watching a DVD at the bookstore depicting an Israeli soldier purportedly killing a Palestinian girl.[48] According to another account, MSK, Tanweer, and Hussain

> were part of a larger clique of British-raised South Asian men in Beeston . . . who turned their backs on what they came to see as a decadent, demoralizing Western culture. Instead, the group embraced an Islam whose practice was often far more fundamentalist than their

fathers', and always more political, focused passionately on Muslim suffering at Western hands.

The worldwide violence inflicted on Muslims in general, and Muslim women and children especially, was cited by Beeston locals as a salient motivating factor in the young men's politicization and radicalization.[49]

THE BOMBERS' AIMS AND MOTIVATIONS

The bombers' intellectual pathways to radicalization and violence have, of course, been the subject of considerable comment and speculation.[50] As noted above, Hussain was apparently the most outspoken in his praise for bin Laden and the nineteen terrorists responsible for the September 11, 2001, attacks. According to Tanweer's family, he, too, "idolized" bin Laden and was consumed by what he regarded as Britain's anti-Muslim policies pertaining to Kashmir, Iraq, and Afghanistan. Supposedly, Lindsay met MSK through their mutual association with and admiration of the firebrand preacher al-Faisal.[51] At the same time, however, one of MSK's relatives has claimed that he never heard the cell's ringleader ever talk about politics or radical Islam, much less Palestine or the invasion of Iraq. Indeed, while Lindsay's first date with his future wife was attending a protest against the impending American and British invasion of that country, MSK declined to join his cousin on a big London march against the invasion.[52]

Accordingly, perhaps the clearest indication of the bombers' motivation and the attack's purpose comes from the two so-called martyrdom videos recorded by MSK and Tanweer. The videos were released and broadcast, respectively, the following September and in July 2006, on the bombings' first anniversary. Both videos were made while the two bombers were in Pakistan between November 2004 and February 2005.[53] Like all Osama bin Laden's and Ayman al-Zawahiri's videotaped statements and appearances, the MSK and Tanweer tapes were both professionally produced and released by al-Qaeda's perennially active communications department, "Al-Sahab [the Clouds] for Media Production." The first of the two videos, MSK's, was broadcast on the Qatar-based Arabic-language news station, al-Jazeera, on September 1, 2005. The most relevant portions of his message are as follows:

I and thousands like me are forsaking everything for what we believe. Our driving motivation doesn't come from tangible commodities that this world has to offer. Our religion is Islam—obedience to the one true God. Allah, and following the footsteps of the final prophet and messenger Muhammad. . . . This is how our ethical stances are dictated.

Your democratically elected governments continuously perpetuate atrocities against my people all over the world. And your support of them makes you directly responsible, just as I am directly responsible for protecting and avenging my Muslim brothers and sisters.

Until we feel security, you will be our targets. And until you stop the bombing, gassing, imprisonment and torture of my people we will not stop this fight. We are at war and I am a soldier. Now you too will taste the reality of this situation. . . .

I myself, I make du'a [calling] to Allah . . . to raise me amongst those whom I love like the prophets, the messengers, the martyrs and today's heroes like our beloved Sheikh Osama bin Laden, Dr Ayman al-Zawahiri and Abu Musab al-Zarqawi and all the other brothers and sisters that are fighting in . . . this cause.[54]

Al-Zawahiri in fact appears at the end of the same tape, praising MSK for having brought the "blessed battle . . . to the enemy's land." In a subsequent video, aired on al-Jazeera on September 19, al-Zawahiri also claimed responsibility for the attacks in the name of al-Qaeda.[55]

MSK's video is noteworthy for the strident profession of his preeminent allegiance to and identification with his religion and the umma—the worldwide Muslim community. Hence, unlike most Western conceptions of identity and allegiance that are rooted in the nation or state, MSK's is exclusively rooted in theology. Further, like most terrorists, MSK frames his choice of tactic and justifies his actions in ineluctably defensive terms. He describes his struggle as intrinsically one of self-defense and his act as a response to the repeated depredations and unmitigated aggression of the West directed against Muslims worldwide. There is also a palpable sense of individual empowerment and catharsis evident in both MSK's words and demeanor on the tape. Indeed, his apparent intense desire for vengeance and martyrdom was cited by the official House of Commons report on the bombings as likely encapsulating for MSK "supreme evidence" of his fervent religious commitment and unswerving fidelity to his faith.[56] Finally, MSK's laudatory comments about bin Laden and his deputy, al-Zawahiri, are noteworthy in respect of al-Qaeda's role in the attacks.

On the first anniversary of the London bombings, a similar martyrdom tape made by MSK's traveling companion and fellow bomber, Tanweer, was released by al-Sahab. Titled "The Final Message of the Knights of the London Raid," it shows Tanweer expressing similar views to MSK. "To the non-Muslims of Britain," he begins,

> you may wonder what you have done to deserve this. You are those who have voted in your government, who in turn have, and still continue to this day, continue to oppress our mothers, children, brothers and sisters, from the east to the west, in Palestine, Afghanistan, Iraq, and Chechnya. Your government has openly supported the genocide of over 150,000 innocent Muslims in Falluja.
>
> You have offered financial and military support to the U.S. and Israel, in the massacre of our children in Palestine. You are directly responsible for the problems in Palestine, Afghanistan, and Iraq to this day. You have openly declared war on Islam, and are the forerunners in the crusade against the Muslims.

Al-Zawahiri then appears on the tape to explain that "what made Shehzad join the camps of Qaeda Al-Jihad was the oppression carried out by the British in Iraq, Afghanistan, and Palestine. He would often talk about Palestine, about the British support of the Jews, and about their clear injustice against the Muslims." An unidentified narrator then continues:

> In order to remove this injustice, Shehzad [sic] began training with all his might and devotion. Together with the martyr Siddiq Khan, he received practical and intensive training in how to produce and use explosives, in the camps of Qaeda Al-Jihad. The recruits who join these camps do not have to achieve high averages or to pass entrance exams. All they need is to be zealous for their religion and nation, and to love Jihad and martyrdom for the sake of Allah.[57]

The video continues with Tanweer warning "all you British citizens to stop your support to your lying British government, and to the so-called 'war on terror,' and ask yourselves why would thousands of men be willing to give their lives for the cause of Muslims." Al-Zawahiri also again appears to emphasize how both Khan and Tanweer were "striving for martyrdom, and were hoping to carry out a martyrdom operation. Both of them were very resolute in this." Tanweer then calls upon his fellow British Muslims to rise and fight the "disbelievers, for it is but an obligation made on you by Allah." A statement is then heard from the U.S.-born Muslim convert Adam Gadahn (also known as "Azzam the American") before concluding with Tanweer threatening:

> What you have witnessed now is only the beginning of a series of attacks, which, *inshallah*, will intensify and continue, until you pull all your troops out of Afghanistan and Iraq, until you stop all financial and military support to the U.S. and Israel, and until you release all Muslim prisoners from Belmarsh, and your other concentration camps. And know that if you fail to comply with this, then know that this war will never stop, and that we are ready to give our lives, one hundred times over, for the cause of Islam. You will never experience peace, until our children in Palestine, our mothers and sisters in Kashmir, and our brothers in Afghanistan and Iraq feel peace.[58]

THE ATTACK'S ORGANIZATIONAL DIMENSIONS:
A TOP-DOWN CONSPIRATORIAL WEB

In contrast to the initial assumptions and discredited conventional wisdom that attended the 7/7 bombings, it has now been established incontrovertibly that MSK and Tanweer were recruited by a fellow British national of Pakistani descent, a longtime al-Qaeda operative named Rashid Rauf. An al-Qaeda report written by Rauf and acquired by German intelligence in 2012 explains how he subsequently arranged for MSK and Tanweer to travel to Pakistan to obtain training in bomb making and the use of explosives. The two bombers, accordingly, arrived in Pakistan in November 2004. Rauf deliberately made no contact with them until he was certain that Pakistani authorities were not following them. Once he was convinced that they were not under surveillance, Rauf arranged to meet with MSK and Tanweer in Faisalabad. For a period, he observed the two men in order to assess their fitness and determination to undertake a suicide-bomb attack on al-Qaeda's behalf.[59] Rauf wrote in the report how he was impressed by MSK and Tanweer's "sound knowledge" of jihad and al-Qaeda's struggle, which they had derived from listening to tapes of radical clerics such as the late Anwar al-Awlaki, Abu Hamza al-Masri, and Abdullah al-Faisal. Rauf reported that both men were "ready for martyrdom operations."[60] Three potential targets were proposed to them: the Bank of England building, the forthcoming G-8 summit to be held from July 6–8, 2005, in Gleneagles, Scotland, or the London Underground. MSK determined that an attack on the G-8 summit would require too much explosives and instead choose London transport following a reconnaissance trip to the city in late June 2005.[61]

MSK and Tanweer were hosted by Pakistani jihadi terrorists during their visit and then were trained by al-Qaeda operatives in both bomb making and countersurveillance techniques and tradecraft.[62] They were provided with this instruction at an al-Qaeda camp in the Malakand Agency of Pakistan's North West Frontier Province. MSK and Tanweer were also told that when away from the camp and in public that they should behave in an "un-Islamic manner": going to the cinema and generally behaving boisterously. While at the al-Qaeda facility, they met with a senior al-Qaeda commander who used the name "Haji" as an alias. U.S. intelligence believes that this man was Abu Ubaydah al-Masri, the head of al-Qaeda's external operations at the time and the controller as well of the 2006 bombing plot of American and Canadian aircraft in flight from London. "Haji," Rauf wrote, "would guide us throughout. His experience in Europe and technical knowledge of explosives was important to the operation." "Haji" persuaded MSK and Tanweer to carry out a suicide-bomb attack in the U.K. He arranged for them to receive instruction by an expert al-Qaeda bomb maker named Marwan Suri. Under his tutelage, MSK and Tanweer learned to fabricate hexamine peroxide detonators and improvised explosives fashioned from hydrogen peroxide. MSK and Tanweer test-detonated a 300-gram explosive mixture using these ingredients. Once back in England, they would obtain hydrogen peroxide from gardening stores and hexamine from camping-stove fuel. The final ingredient, citric acid, was readily obtainable.[63]

Rauf's supervision of the two men was all encompassing. Indeed, he was responsible for the recording of their martyrdom video in a house that the trio had rented in Islamabad following their training at the Malakand camp. Plans for the attack were implemented shortly after their return to England on February 1, 2005. Rauf had instructed MSK and Tanweer to lay low for three weeks and not undertake anything connected with the plot until they were certain that British intelligence or police were not watching. MSK and other members of the terrorist cell were in contact with extremists and terrorists in Pakistan up until the attack, and the cell was in contact with other radicals and extremists in the U.K. both right up until and even during the attack. MSK in fact received several telephone calls from a phone box in Rawalpindi, Pakistan, in the weeks leading up to the July 7 attack. The final call was made five days before the bombings. MSK and Tanweer remained in regular contact with Rauf from the time they returned to Britain. They used a series of previously agreed upon code words. They used e-mail, telephone calls, and, most effectively, Yahoo Messenger. Both Rauf and MSK would change e-mail addresses and switch out their cell phones frequently, exchanging details of the changes in code. Shortly before the London bombings, Rauf provided MSK with critical technical advice on the correct strength of the hydrogen peroxide he was boiling in their subleased apartment-cum-bomb-factory at 18 Alexandra Grove in Leeds to make into high explosive.[64]

The aforementioned report by the Parliament's Intelligence and Security Committee, despite its constraints on the sharing of classified information and careful wording for legal reasons given the bombings' then-ongoing investigations, confirms many of the above points, noting, among its other conclusions: "Investigations since July [2005] have shown that the group [the four London bombers] was in contact with others involved in extremism in the UK"; "Siddique Khan is now known to have visited Pakistan in 2003 and to have spent several months there with Shazad Tanweer [another bomber] between November 2004 and February 2005. It has not yet been established who they met in Pakistan, but it is assessed as likely that they had some contact with Al Qaeda figures"; "The [British intelligence and security] Agencies believe that some form of operational training is likely to have taken place while Khan and Tanweer were in Pakistan. Contacts in the run-up to the attacks suggest they may have had advice or direction from individuals there."[65]

The evidence linking the July 2005 attacks to both al-Qaeda and other operational terrorist cells in the U.K., the nexus of these plots emanating from Pakistan, and the hitherto underappreciated organizational dimension behind them is both voluminous and compelling. Rather than the single, isolated outburst of anger and rage as originally depicted, the attacks actually had a direct conspiratorial link to the foiled 2004 jihadi attacks known as "Operation Crevice"; the aborted July 21, 2005, copycat attacks on London transport targets; the 2006 airliner-bombings plot; and even the 2003 suicide bombings carried out by two British Muslims in Israel. All of these plots have links to MSK, his fellow bombers, and the July 2005 attacks.

OPERATION CREVICE

The most authoritative investigation of the links between the July 2005 attacks and other U.K.-based terrorist networks is that of the House of Commons Intelligence and Security Committee (ISC) review of the intelligence pertaining to the bombings, titled *Could 7/7 Have Been Prevented?* It focuses on the connections between the London bombers and their would-be counterparts involved in the plot that British authorities dubbed "Operation Crevice": the planned terrorist operation to bomb a London nightclub (the Ministry of Sound) and a shopping mall in Kent (the Bluewater Shopping Center).

On April 30, 2007, one of the longest terrorist trials in British history concluded with the convictions of five British Muslims "charged with plotting to use an explosive device constructed of fertilizer to attack the nightclub and shopping center."[66] The authorities first became aware of the plot because of their 2003 identification of a British Muslim named Mohammed Qayum Khan (MQK) as an "Al Qaeda facilitator." MI5 concluded that Khan (who is not related to MSK) was a part-time taxi driver residing in Luton and the leader of a U.K.-based "Al-Qaida facilitation network"—the term that MI5 uses to "refer to groups of extremists who support the Al-Qaida cause and who are involved in providing financial and logistical support, rather than being directly involved in terrorist attack planning."[67] MI5 had also linked MQK to al-Qaeda networks in

Pakistan and to the Taliban as well: thus locking the security service's attention onto him.[68]

Testimony in the trial further revealed that MQK had been "in direct contact with one of Osama bin Laden's most senior lieutenants"—Abd al-Hadi al-Iraqi. A Kurd and former officer in Saddam's Hussein's army, Abdul Hadi was described in court as a bin Laden "confidant" and key liaison with the late Abu Musab al-Zarqawi, the commander of al-Qaeda in Iraq between 2003 and 2006.[69] According to Muhammed Junaid Babar, whom prosecutors termed a "junior Al Qaeda fixer" and who subsequently became an FBI informant, al-Hadi was the overall commander of al-Qaeda operations in Britain until his capture in 2007 by U.S. forces in Iraq.[70] Al-Hadi was the "ultimate emir on top" for the U.K. jihadis, Babar told court. "But underneath him there were multiple emirs, three or four emirs, before you reached Abdul Hadi, and [MQK] was one of those emirs."[71] It has been reported that in late 2004, al-Hadi met MSK and Tanweer in Pakistan and allegedly "retasked" them to undertake the suicide bombing attack on London's Underground.[72]

In January 2004, MI5 identified another British Muslim of Pakistani descent named Omar Khyam as the principal courier for MQK's network.[73] Within a month, however, as a result of continued surveillance of both MQK and Khyam, MI5 concluded, in the words of the ISC report, that they "were no longer looking at a facilitation network providing financial support to Al-Qaida overseas, but had instead found a bomb plot probably aimed at the UK. At this point," the report continues, "KHYAM became one of MI5's top targets and Operation CREVICE became their top priority."[74] MI5 obviously remained intensely interested in MQK as well, and he was now regarded as a "trusted member of the CREVICE network." Still another "significant Al-Qaida-linked facilitator," involved in fund raising, radicalization, and recruitment in the UK was also identified by the security service but as of yet has not been publicly named. These investigations further uncovered at least two other UK-based al-Qaeda networks with direct links back to the organization's senior command in Pakistan.[75]

Because of the surveillance mounted as part of Operation Crevice, MI5 had come across both MSK and Tanweer at least two years before the London bombings.[76] On April 14, 2003, a West Yorkshire Police surveillance team following someone identified only as a "known extremist" observed this person entering a car registered to MSK.[77] Further, data obtained from MQK's mobile telephone revealed several telephone conversations that he had with MSK on at least four occasions—July 13, 19, and 24 and August 17, 2003.

Meanwhile, on February 2, 2004, surveillance of Omar Khyam—who at this time was still considered an al-Qaeda courier-cum-facilitator and not the leader of an operational attack cell—separately led authorities to MSK, who was seen using his wife's green Honda Civic to meet with Khymam. Shortly afterward, MI5 concluded that Khyam was in fact planning to launch a terrorist attack in the U.K. and elevated the surveillance focused on him to "top priority." As a result of this intensified monitoring, on February 28, 2004, Khyam was observed meeting with both MQK *and* MSK, accompanied by Tanweer. MI5 watchers recorded a further meeting among Khyam, MSK, and Tanweer on March 23, 2004, where an eavesdropping device picked up their discussion of various financial fraud techniques but not attack planning.[78] Accordingly, MI5 drew the mistaken conclusion that MSK and Tanweer were more in the category of "petty fraudsters" than the leader and a key figure in an entirely separate operational terrorist cell.[79] Neither MSK nor Tanweer were therefore deemed "priority targets" and hence were not subjected to surveillance and investigation.[80] As the Intelligence and Security Committee report explains:

Both MI5 and the police therefore followed three unidentified men, one of whom we now know was Mohammed Siddique KHAN and another we now know to be Shazad TANWEER, after they were seen meeting the target of a surveillance operation. This did not mean that MI5 or the police had these UDMs [unidentified men] 'under surveillance.' It meant that they were 'housing' [i.e., establishing a link between people and addresses with which they appear to be connected] them to obtain a lead to run checks on if necessary or to come back to if they needed to in the future. . . .

[Tanweer and MSK] were of some interest to MI5 [e.g., as noted above, in 2003 and 2004] because they were seen meeting Omar KHYMAN, a known attack planner and were heard on 23 March [2004] talking about financial fraud and possible travel to Pakistan. . . .

So, on 23 March [2004], MI5 had heard [Tanweer and MSK] talking to KHYAM, but they did not mention the bomb plot. At no time during

Operation CREVICE did MI5 obtain any intelligence that indicated that [Tanweer and MSK] were involved in attack planning.[81]

Finally, the committee report reveals that MSK had attracted the attention of police on at least three occasions before the July 2005 attacks, once for an assault incident in 1993 that was described as a "routine police matter." Of greater relevance, however, was the West Yorkshire Police surveillance operation conducted in 2001 that monitored a group of some forty men at a rural jihadi training camp in Yorkshire. At the time only nine of the men photographed were identified by name; following the 7/7 attacks, however, MSK was identified as another of the participants.[82]

TRAINING TRIPS TO PAKISTAN

The Intelligence and Security Committee's May 2009 report also concluded unequivocally that MSK had traveled to Pakistan at least twice for the purposes of receiving training in terrorism and that he likely had previously visited Afghanistan for the same purpose. In April 2004, an unidentified terrorist detainee informed his interrogators that two men known as "Ibrahim" and "Zubair" had traveled to Pakistan in 2003 for training and met the other members the Operation Crevice cell. The two pseudonyms were later conclusively linked to MSK and another person from the Leeds area named Mohammed Shakil.[83] Hence, it is now clear that MSK made at least two trips to Pakistan for terrorist training: the one referred to previously between November 2004 and February 2005 and the one reported here between June and August 2003.[84]

MSK had previously also received "military training in a mujahiddin camp in Pakistan in early 2001."[85] According to Waheed Ali, one of three men charged with assisting the 7/7 bombers, he accompanied MSK on a July 2001 training trip to Pakistan. Upon their arrival in Islamabad, they were met by members of the Pakistani jihadi terrorist group Harakat ul-Mujahideen (HuM), who took them to a camp along the border with Kashmir, where they learned to shoot Kalashnikov AK-47s and light machine assault rifles and fire rocket-propelled grenades.[86] Their intention to fight alongside the Taliban near Bagram Airbase went awry when, because of their lack of combat experience, they were assigned to a nearby support base. While there, however, both men became so ill with diarrhea that they had to return to the U.K.[87] MSK boasted to friends that he traveled regularly to Pakistan and Afghanistan to attend military training camps—a claim borne out by this evidence.[88]

The aforementioned MQK was described in court documents as having been "instrumental" in arranging for MSK and Tanweer's first visit in 2003 to the al-Qaeda terrorist training camp in Pakistan's Malakand Agency.[89] Shortly before that trip, in April 2003, MSK and Tanweer reportedly attended a fund-raising barbecue for the camp, which was held near Leeds by a "long-standing activist of Al-Muhajiroun." Among the other guests, according to Babar, the previously cited FBI informant, were Hassan Butt, a former extremist who has since turned against violence, and "about 100 hardcore Islamists"—including MQK. Some £3,500 was raised for the camp and, according to one report, "Within weeks two of the most dangerous British-born jihadi terrorists—[Mohammed Siddique] Khan, and Omar Khyam, leader of the so-called Crevice gang— were learning to make bombs at Malakand."[90] Butt had first met MSK at a jihadi safe house in Pakistan in 2002. They had been introduced to one another by Babar.[91]

The most consequential trip, however, at least with respect to the 7/7 bombings, was the one that MSK and Tanweer took to Pakistan on November 19, 2004.[92] Tanweer told relatives that the trip was meant to enable him "to learn how to correctly pronounce readings from the Koran."[93] After arriving in Karachi, the pair reportedly visited Lahore and Faisalabad before traveling to Malakand.[94] Significantly, members of at least two other British Muslim terrorist cells were also present at the camp at the same time: Mukhtar Said Ibrahim (MSI), the leader of the failed July 21, 2005, suicide-bomb plot, and Abdulla Ahmed Ali, one of the leaders of the August 2006 airliner-bombing plot.[95] MSI and two of the other July 21 plotters were also photographed in Snowdonia National Park in Wales while on a team-building white-water rafting trip organized by MSK that included Tanweer and Hussain.[96]

The person who paid for MSI's ticket to Pakistan to attend the Malakand training course was identified in the London trial of the six British jihadis accused in the airliner-bombing plot as Mohammed al-Ghabra.[97] In December 2006, the U.S. Treasury designated al-Ghabra, a twenty-eight-year-old Syrian-born, naturalized British citizen who lives with his mother and sister in London's Forest Gate neighborhood, as an al-Qaeda agent and facilitator who had provided material and logistical support to al-Qaeda and other jihadi terrorist organizations. A statement issued by the Treasury's Office of Foreign Assets Control explained, "Mohammed Al-Ghabra has backed Al Qaeda and other violent jihadist groups, facilitating travel for recruits seeking to meet with Al Qaeda leaders and take part in terrorist training. We must act against those who fund and facilitate Al Qaeda's agenda of violence against innocents."[98] Among other crimes, al-Ghabra was accused by the Treasury Department of arranging for British militants to travel to Pakistan to receive training in "jihad" and to meet with senior al-Qaeda officials and then return to the U.K. to engage in "covert activity on behalf of Al Qaeda"; arranging for British militants to travel to Iraq "to support the insurgents' fight against coalition forces"; providing material and logistical support to terrorist organizations in Pakistan, such as Harakat ul-Jihad-I-Islami (HUJI) and the Pakistan Kashmiri jihadi group, Harakat ul-Mujahideen (HuM); undertaking training at a HuM training camp in Kashmir; consorting with al-Qaeda leaders such as Abu Faraj al-Libi and Haroon Rashid Aswat while on visits to Pakistan; and, radicalizing British Muslims through the distribution of "extremist media."[99]

The British press has openly described al-Ghabra as a "senior Al Qaeda operative." Following his designation by the U.S. Treasury, the Bank of England followed suit by freezing his bank accounts and other assets. Al-Ghabra was subsequently placed on the United Nations Security List of terrorist suspects linked to al-Qaeda and the Taliban, and his name was entered on terrorist watch lists maintained by Interpol and the European Union. Under the terms of British terrorism-financing laws, al-Ghabra and his attorneys are prohibited from reviewing it or knowing how that information was obtained. Press reports suggest that it includes sensitive intelligence, based on confidential sources and methods, including telephone intercepts and information believed to have been derived from the interrogation of al-Qaeda detainees.[100]

Additional links between the 7/7 bombers and other jihadi terrorist groups include the reports that Tanweer attended madrassas (religious schools) run by al-Qaeda; its Southeast Asian offshoot, Jemaah Islamiyah;

and Lashkar-e-Taiba (LeT), the Pakistani jihadi organization responsible for the November 2006 assault on Mumbai, India.[101]

In sum, rather than the isolated, unconnected outbursts of rage by entirely self-radicalized, self-selected, independently operating terrorists, as British authorities initially described the July 7, 2005, bombing, the failed July 21, 2005 attacks, and the August 2006 airliner-bombing plots, a connecting thread clearly links Britain to Pakistan and al-Qaeda to each of these incidents.[102] This evidence was doubtless what Manningham-Buller was referring to in her landmark November 2006 public address to a London audience. "We are aware of numerous plots to kill people and to damage our economy," the then-director-general explained. "What do I mean by numerous? Five? Ten? No, nearer 30 that we currently know of," she continued. "These plots often have linked back to Al Qaeda in Pakistan and through those links Al Qaeda gives guidance and training to its largely British foot soldiers here on an extensive and growing scale."[103]

Less clear, but potentially equally significant, are the mutual associations formed by all these plotters through participation in a variety of U.K.-based Tablighi Jamaat activities. Ali and at least two other people implicated in the 2006 airliner-bombing plot attended weekend camps hosted by the movement. Two of the July 7 suicide bombers, MSK and Tanweer, studied at a Tablighi Jamaat madrassa in Dewsbury, West Yorkshire (where the movement's European headquarters is located).[104] One of the Tablighi Jamaat's most popular preachers, Abdullah el-Faisal, was an important influence on Lindsay, a fellow Jamaican convert to Islam.[105] Ibrahim and another July 21, 2005, would-be bomber, Manfo Asiedu, worshipped at Tablighi Jamaat services and participated in other movement activities.[106]

PUTATIVE CONNECTION WITH BRITAIN'S
FIRST SUICIDE TERRORISTS

Finally, in addition to the links between the July 2005 bombers and other British terrorist cells, Pakistani jihadi terrorist cells, and, indeed, al-Qaeda, an intriguing connection reportedly exists between MSK and Asif Hanif and Omar Khan Sharif. Hanif and Sharif, both British Muslims of Pakistani heritage, staged the April 2003 suicide attack at Mike's Place,

a seaside pub in Tel Aviv, Israel. According to a Manchester businessman named Kursheed Fiaz, in July 2001 MSK, Hanif, and Khan met with
him four times in hopes of enlisting Fiaz's help to recruit young men
to travel to Pakistan, Syria, or Afghanistan in order "to reinvigorate the
youngsters with pure Islamic ways."[107] Less than two years later, Hanif
and Sharif would travel a similar route via Syria to stage their attack in
Israel. Intriguingly, MSK is believed to have followed an identical itinerary—through Syria before ending his journey in Israel—seven weeks
before the Mike's Place bombing.[108]

At least a year before the 7/7 attacks, a joint Home Office and Foreign
Office report prepared for the prime minister, titled "Young Muslims
and Extremism," had warned of a rising tide of extremism, radicalization, and subversion engulfing Britain's Muslim community. It concluded
that al-Qaeda was actively though secretly recruiting "affluent, middle-
class Muslims in British universities and colleges to carry out terrorist
attacks" in the U.K. The report went on to detail how an estimated 10,000
people attended Muslim extremist conferences in Britain. Given that the
police already knew that some 3,000 British Muslims had been trained in
al-Qaeda camps throughout the late 1990s, this new information should
have aroused sufficient alarm among the authorities and their political
masters.[109] That it did not led inevitably to tragedy.

It is thus all the more surprising to read the testimony of both Manningham-Buller, the director-general of the MI5, and Tom Dowse, chief of
the assessments staff, before the Parliament committee that investigated
the 7/7 attacks. "Could we, could others, could the police have done better? Could we with greater effort, greater imagination, have stopped it?"
Manningham-Buller asked rhetorically.

> We knew there were risks we were running. We were trying very hard
> and very fast to enhance our capacity, but even with the wisdom of
> hindsight I think it is unlikely that we would have done so, with the
> resources available to us at the time and the other demands placed
> upon us. I think that position will remain in the foreseeable future.
> We will continue to stop most of them, but we will not stop all of
> them.[110]

Similarly, Dowse averred, "I think the more we learned over this period of several years, the more we began to realize the limits of what we knew."[111] It may have been that, for too long, many British had consoled themselves that their country's increasingly fluid upward socioeconomic mobility, post-empire absorption of its former colonial subjects, and politically tolerant policy of offering sanctuary to dissidents from abroad provided a firewall that mitigated if not effectively countered the radicalization of Muslim youth that in recent years had plagued other European countries. Yet the dimensions of al-Qaeda's subversion of Britain, establishment of a terrorist infrastructure in that country, effective radicalization of a sizeable element of its young Muslim population, and seamless recruitment into its ranks underscore the perils of complacency in the face of an enemy that believes itself to have developed the ultimate "fifth column."

In this respect, al-Qaeda is like the archetypal shark that must keep moving forward—no matter how slowly or incrementally—or die. In al-Qaeda's context, this means adapting and adjusting to the environment in which it swims: cultivating new sources of support, developing new reservoirs of potential recruitments, and identifying new targets and vulnerabilities in enemy nations. Accordingly, because of the movement's operational durability or resiliency, al-Qaeda cannot be destroyed or defeated in a single tactical military engagement or series of engagements—much less ones exclusively dependent on the application of conventional forces and firepower. To a significant degree, therefore, al-Qaeda's defeat will depend on a dual effort. First, tactical military elements must be used to systematically destroy and weaken enemy capabilities. Second, the equally critical, broader nonkinetic strategic imperatives of countering the continued resonance of the al-Qaeda message must be seriously pursued to break the cycle of terrorist recruitment and replenishment that has sustained the movement.

Success in this struggle requires first and foremost that our assessments and analyses be anchored firmly in sound empirical judgment and not blinded by conjecture, mirror imaging, politically partisan prisms, and wishful thinking. Second, policy makers and academics must recognize that al-Qaeda cannot be defeated by military means alone. Al-Qaeda's capacity to continue to prosecute this struggle is a direct reflection of both the movement's resiliency and the continued resonance of its ideology. Finally, we must always bear in mind Manningham-Buller's final admonition, that "we will continue to stop most of them, but we will not stop all of them." She did not describe terrorism as a tactic that can be eliminated, an enemy that can be defeated, or a phenomenon that can be abolished. Rather, Manningham-Buller framed the struggle against terrorism in its proper context: we are neither defenseless nor powerless against this threat, but, at the same time, neither are we omnipotent nor omniscient. With patience and fortitude, however, and with a dynamic and evolutionary approach to counterterrorism, we can triumph.

NOTES

1. See, for instance, Fareed Zakaria, "Getting It Wrong on Security and the Surge," *Washington Post*, January 21, 2009.

2. See, for example, Jason Bennetto and Ian Herbert, "London Bombings: The Truth Emerges," *Independent* (London), August 13, 2005. See also the comment by Melanie Phillips, *Londonistan* (New York: Encounter, 2006), 7, 53; Bruce Riedel, *The Search for Al Qaeda: Its Leadership, Ideology, and Future* (Washington, D.C.: Brookings, 2008), 130.

3. Duncan Campbell and Sandra Laville, "British Suicide Bombers Carried Out London Attacks, Say Police," *Guardian*, July 13, 2005. It should be noted that the 2009 Intelligence and Security Committee report specifically addressed this issue and determined that MI5 neither called the bombers "clean skins" nor uses that term. See Intelligence and Security Committee (ISC), *Could 7/7 Have Been Prevented? Review of the Intelligence on the London Terrorist Attacks on 7 July 2005* (London: HMSO, 2009), 15–16, 67.

4. "When I suggested this at Cobra [Cabinet Office Briefing Room A], I was met with laughter. Someone senior from an intelligence organization said, 'Who are you and what possibly qualifies you to come out with such an absurd statement'" (Chris Driver-Williams, a expert on suicide terrorism then an analyst on the Defence Intelligence Staff, quoted in Duncan Gardham, "Intelligence Officials 'Laughed' at Al Qaeda 7/7 Bomb Link," *Telegraph* [London], May 19, 2009).

5. Quoted in Phillips, *Londonistan*, 53.

6. Quoted in ISC, *Could 7/7 Have Been Prevented?*, 67.

7. Riedel, *The Search for Al Qaeda*, 130.

8. The reason the attack occurred on that date has never been conclusively established. Hypotheses have ranged from the G8 summit that Britain was hosting in Gleneagles, Scotland, that same day; the previous day's announcement that London had been awarded the 2012 Summer Olympic games; or the trial of Abu Hamza al-Masri that was scheduled to commence around that same morning, on charges that the extremist imam's notorious Finsbury Mosque incited racial hatred and violence.

See Sean O'Neill and Daniel McGrory, *The Suicide Factory: Abu Hamza and the Finsbury Mosque* (London: Harper Perennial, 2006), 20–21.

9. "Operation Theseus (Leeds)," PowerPoint presentation by Metropolitan Police—SO13 and West Yorkshire Police, Homicide and Major Enquiry Team.

10. Peter Zimonjic, *Into the Darkness: An Account of 7/7* (London: Vintage, 2008), 9.

11. "Operation Theseus (Leeds)."

12. Quoted in Australian Government, Attorney-General's Department Emergency Management Australia, "Lessons from London and Considerations for Australia: London Terrorist Attacks, 7 July 2005," 2007, 6.

13. Zimonjic, *Into the Darkness*, 78–79.

14. Quoted in ISC, "Report into the London Terrorist Attacks on 7 July 2005: Presented to Parliament by the Prime Minister by Command of Her Majesty," May 2006, 23. Note should be taken, however, that although the threat level was reduced to "Substantial," this designation still "indicates a continued high level of threat and that an attack might well be mounted without warning" (as quoted in "Report into the London Terrorist Attacks on 7 July 2005"). Also see Crispin Black, *7-7: The London Bombings: What Went Wrong?* (London: Gibson Square, 2005), 23; Phillips, *Londonistan*, 37.

15. Honourable House of Commons, *Report of the Official Account of the Bombings in London on 7th July 2005* (London: The Stationery Office), HC 1087, May 11, 2006, section of the report specifically titled "Were They Directed From Abroad?," 27.

16. ISC, "Report into the London Terrorist Attacks on 7 July 2005," 27, 29.

17. Ibid., 28.

18. See ISC, *Could 7/7 Have Been Prevented?*, 15–16.

19. Campbell and Laville, "British Suicide Bombers"; "London Bombers Were All British," *BBC News*, July 12, 2005, available at http://news.bbc.co.uk/2/hi/uk_news/4676577.stm. Also see Alison Pargeter, *The New Frontiers of Jihad: Radical Islam in Europe* (Philadelphia: University of Pennsylvania Press, 2008), 140.

20. Pargeter, *The New Frontiers of Jihad*, 25–26, 29–30; Phillips, *Londonistan*, 7–8. Prime Minister Tony Blair was quoted as saying he was "shocked" to learn that the bombers were born and raised in Britain. Gethin Chamberlain, "Attacker 'Was Recruited' at Terror Group's Religious School," *Scotsman* (Edinburgh), July 14, 2005.

21. Quoted in ISC, "Report into the London Terrorist Attacks on 7 July 2005," 30.

22. Ian Cobain, David Hencke, and Richard Norton-Taylor, "MI5 Told MPs on Eve of 7/7/: No Imminent Terror Threat," *Guardian*, January 9, 2007.

23. Interview with senior U.S. National Security Council counterterrorism official, Washington, D.C., December 2006.

24. Sandra Laville, "Widow of July 7 Ringleader Tells of Miscarriage on Day of Bombings," *Guardian*, July 27, 2007; James Macintyre, "July 7 Bomber's Widow 'Has Lost Her Identity,'" *Independent* (London), July 27, 2007.

25. House of Commons, *Report of the Official Account of the Bombings in London*, 13–14.

26. Quoted in Shiv Malik, "My Brother the Bomber," *Prospect*, June 2007, http://www.prospectmagazine.co.uk/2007/06/mybrotherthebomber/.

27. Amy Waldman, "Seething Unease Shaped British Bombers' Newfound Zeal," *New York Times*, July 31, 2005; Sandra Laville, Audrey Gillian, and Dilpazier Aslam, "'Father Figure' Inspired Young Bombers," *Guardian*, July 15, 2005.

28. House of Commons, *Report of the Official Account of the Bombings in London*, 13–15; Lizette Alvarez, "Lives of Three Men Offer Little to Explain Attacks," *New York Times*, July 14, 2005; "Suicide Bombers' 'Ordinary Lives,'" *BBC News*, available at http://news .bbc.co.uk/2/hi/uk_news/4678837.stm.

29. Sudarsan Raghavan, "Friends Describe Bomber's Political, Religious Evolution," *Washington Post*, July 29, 2005.

30. Waheed Ali testified in court that the last time he saw Tanweer was when they played cricket together that evening: James Sturcke and agencies, "July 7 'Helper' Played Cricket with Aldgate Bomber," *Guardian*, May 21, 2008. See also House of Commons, *Report of the Official Account of the Bombings in London*, 13–15; Alvarez, "Lives of Three Men Offer Little to Explain Attacks,"; "Suicide Bombers' 'Ordinary Lives'"; Craig Whitlock, "Trail from London to Leeds Yields Portraits of Three Bombers: Identities Revealed, but Motives Still a Mystery," *Washington Post*, July 15, 2005.

31. Quoted in "Suicide Bombers' 'Ordinary Lives.'"

32. House of Commons, *Report of the Official Account of the Bombings in London*, 13–14; Alvarez, "Lives of Three Men Offer Little to Explain Attacks"; "Suicide Bombers' 'Ordinary Lives.'"

33. House of Commons, *Report of the Official Account of the Bombings in London*, 13.

34. House of Commons, *Report of the Official Account of the Bombings in London*, 17–18; Lizette Alvarez, "New Muslim at Fifteen, Terror Suspect at Nineteen," *New York Times*, July 18, 2005.

35. Alvarez, "New Muslim at Fifteen, Terror Suspect at Nineteen."

36. Faisal also advocated spreading Islam "by the Kalashnikov" and had declared that jihad's purpose in part is to "lessen the population of unbelievers." Quoted in Ali Hussain, "Focus: Undercover on Planet Beeston (UK In Danger)," *Sunday Times* (London), July 2, 2006.

37. Alvarez, "New Muslim at Fifteen, Terror Suspect at Nineteen." Samantha gave birth to a daughter weeks after the bombing (O'Neill and McGrory, *The Suicide Factory*, 276).

38. Quoted in "Suicide Bombers' 'Ordinary Lives.'"

39. O'Neill and McGrory, *The Suicide Factory*, 270. A Fiat Brava automobile registered to Lindsay left the scene of a robbery committed in Luton on May 27, 2005. See ISC, *Could 7/7 Have Been Prevented?*, 17.

40. House of Commons, *Report of the Official Account of the Bombings in London*, 18; Alvarez, "New Muslim at Fifteen, Terror Suspect at Nineteen"; "Suicide Bombers' 'Ordinary Lives.'"

41. Alvarez, "Lives of Three Men Offer Little to Explain Attacks." Also see Waldman, "Seething Unease Shaped British Bombers' Newfound Zeal."

42. House of Commons, *Report of the Official Account of the Bombings in London*, 13.

43. Paul Tumelty, "An In-Depth Look at the London Bombers," *Terrorism Monitor* (Jamestown Foundation) 3, no. 15 (July 28, 2005), available at http://www.jamestown .org/single/?no_cache=1&tx_ttnews%5Btt_news%5D=535.

44. Ibid.; Alvarez, "Lives of Three Men Offer Little to Explain Attacks"; O'Neill and McGrory, *The Suicide Factory*, 276.

45. O'Neill and McGrory, *The Suicide Factory*, 270. See also, Laville, Gillian, and Aslam, " 'Father Figure' Inspired Young Bombers"; Tumelty, "An In-Depth Look at the London Bombers."

46. Christopher Caldwell, "After Londonistan," *New York Times Magazine*, June 25, 2006, 43.

47. Quoted in Laville, Gillian, and Aslam, " 'Father Figure' Inspired Young Bombers."

48. "Suicide Bombers' 'Ordinary Lives' "; see also Raghavan, "Friends Describe Bomber's Political, Religious Evolution."

49. Waldman, "Seething Unease Shaped British Bombers' Newfound Zeal."

50. See Caldwell, "After Londonistan."

51. O'Neill and McGrory, *The Suicide Factory*, 270; Tumelty, "An In-Depth Look at the London Bombers."

52. Ian Cobain, " 'He Never Spoke of the Iraq War,' " *Guardian*, May 19, 2007.

53. House of Commons, *Report of the Official Account of the Bombings in London on 7th July 2005*, 20.

54. Ibid.

55. "London's blessed raid is one of the raids which Jama'at Qa'idat al-Jihad (Al Qaedah of Jihad Group) was honoured to launch" (ibid., 19). See also Gilles Kepel and Jean-Pierre Milelli, eds., *Al Qaeda in Its Own Words* (Cambridge, Mass.: Belknap Press of Harvard University Press, 2008), 162; Assaf Moghadam, *The Globalization of Martyrdom: Al Qaeda, Salafi Jihad, and the Diffusion of Suicide Attacks* (Baltimore, Md.: Johns Hopkins, 2008), 207; Riedel, *The Search for Al Qaeda*, 32.

56. House of Commons, *Report of the Official Account of the Bombings in London on 7th July 2005*, 19.

57. Quoted in MEMRI, Clip No. 1186, "Al Qaeda Film on the First Anniversary of the London Bombings Features Messages by Bomber Shehzad Tanweer, American Al Qaeda Member Adam Gadan and Al Qaeda Leader Ayman Al-Zawahiri, recorded message of London bomber Shehzad Tanweer and statements by Al Qaeda leaders Ayman Al-Zawahiri and Adam Gadahn, which were posted on www.tajdeed .net.tc on July 8, 2006," available at http://www.memrijttm.org/content/en/clip .htm?clip=1186&param=GJN (accessed February 27, 2013).

58. Ibid.

59. Nic Robertson, Paul Cruickshank, and Tim Lister, "Documents Give New Details on al Qaeda's London Bombings," CNN World, April 30, 2012, http://www.cnn .com/2012/04/30/world/al-qaeda-documents-london-bombings/index.html.

60. Quoted in ibid.

61. Ibid.

62. Ibid.; and interviews with a senior British Security Service officer, Washington, D.C., March and April 2008.

63. Quoted in Robertson, Cruickshank, and Lister, "Documents Give New Details on al Qaeda's London Bombings."

64. Ibid.

65. Ibid., 12. Also see House of Commons, *Report of the Official Account of the Bombings in London on 7th July 2005*, 20–21.

66. Eight people were initially arrested in the plot, of whom five were convicted (Omar Khyam, Jawad Akbar, Salahuddin Amin, Waheed Mahmood, and Anthony Garcia—all were British citizens except for Garcia, who was a dual British Algerian national residing in the U.K.). Two were acquitted (Shujah Mahmood and Nabeel Hussain), and another person (Mohammad Momin Khawaja) is being tried in Canada. Operation Crevice has been described as the "largest operation MI5 and the police had ever undertaken." Some thirty addresses were searched; 45,000 man-hours were consumed by monitoring and transcription; and 20 surveillance camera operations were mounted involving 34,000 man-hours. Specific information on the number of covert searches of the suspects' property and baggage and eavesdropping devices deployed remains classified. See ISC, *Could 7/7 Have Been Prevented?*, 11, 9.

67. Ibid., 7. Also see Ian Cobain and Jeevan Vasagar, "Free—the Man Accused of Being an Al Qaeda Leader, aka 'Q,'" *Guardian*, May 1, 2007; Shiv Malik, "The Jihadi House Parties of Hate," *Sunday Times* (London), May 6, 2007.

68. ISC, *Could 7/7 Have Been Prevented?*, 29; "Questions Over 'Plot Mastermind,'" *BBC News*, May 1, 2007, available at http://bbc.co.uk/go/pr/fr/-/1/hi/uk/6248803.stm.

69. Cobain and Vasagar, "Free"; Daniel McGrory et al., "Meeting of Murderous Minds on the Backstreets of Lahore," *Times* (London), May 1, 2007.

70. McGrory et al., "Meeting of Murderous Minds on the Backstreets of Lahore"; Rachel Williams, "July 7 Plot Accused Tell of Times with Taliban," *Guardian*, May 21, 2008; Cobain and Vasagar, "Free; Moghadam, *The Globalization of Martyrdom*, 206.

71. Cobain and Vasagar, "Free."

72. See Peter Bergen and Paul Cruickshank, "Al Qaeda-on-Thames: UK Plotters," *Washington Post*, April 30, 2007; Moghadam, *The Globalization of Martyrdom*, 206.

73. Cobain and Vasagar, "Free"; ISC, *Could 7/7 Have Been Prevented?*, 7.

74. ISC, *Could 7/7 Have Been Prevented?*, 7.

75. Ibid., 29, 13, 14.

76. See Security Service MI5, "The 7/7 Bombings: Rumours and Reality," available at http://www.mi5.gov.uk/output/the-7-7-bombings-rumours-and-reality.html (accessed June 17, 2009).

77. ISC, *Could 7/7 Have Been Prevented?*, 17.

78. Ibid., 19–23.

79. Explanation of John Reid, then home secretary. Quoted in David Batty, "MI5 Chief Denies Complacency Over July 7 Bombers," *Guardian*, April 30, 2007. Also see Security Service MI5, "Links Between the 7 July Bombers and the Fertiliser Plotters," available at http://www.mi5.gov.uk/output/links-between-the-7-july-bombers-and -the-fertiliser-plotters.html (accessed June 17, 2009).

80. Intelligence and Security Committee, *Could 7/7 Have Been Prevented?*, 23, 26, 48. See the transcript of the conversation at "Law & Order: MI5 Transcript of Bomber's Conversation," Channel 4 News, March 23, 2004, available at http://www.channel4 .com/news/articles/society/law_order/mi5+transcript+of+bombers+conversation /491157.

81. Intelligence and Security Committee, *Could 7/7 Have Been Prevented?*, 22–23, 27, 28. See also "Government Response to the Intelligence and Security Committee's Report Into the London Terrorist Attacks on 7 July 2005 Presented to Parliament by the Prime Minister by Command of Her Majesty," May 2006, 1.

82. Intelligence and Security Committee, *Could 7/7 Have Been Prevented?*, 17, 57. See also "Blow by Blow: How July 7 Mastermind Slipped Through Yorkshire Police Net," *Yorkshire Post*, May 19, 2009, available at http://www.yorkshirepost.co.uk/news /Blow-by-blow-How-July.5282166.jp.

83. Intelligence and Security Committee, *Could 7/7 Have Been Prevented?*, 37–39.

84. McGrory et al., "Meeting of Murderous Minds on the Backstreets of Lahore."

85. Intelligence and Security Committee, *Could 7/7 Have Been Prevented?*, 38

86. O'Neill and McGrory, *The Suicide Factory*, 274; Williams, "July 7 Plot Accused Tell of Times with Taliban"; Sheila MacVicar, "July 7 Bombers Tied to Al Qaeda," *CBS News*, August 18, 2005, available at http://www.cbsnews.com /stories/2005/08/18eveningnews/printable787072.shtml (accessed June 17, 2009).

87. Williams, "July 7 Plot Accused Tell of Times with Taliban."

88. Laville, Gillian, and Aslam, "'Father Figure' Inspired Young Bombers."

89. Cobain and Vasagar, "Free"; Malik, "My Brother the Bomber."

90. Malik, "The Jihadi House Parties of Hate." The diary of another British Muslim accused of terrorist training and activities, Zeeshan Siddiqui, identified Khan and Khyam as two other British nationals whom Siddiqui trained with at the camp. See Dominic Casciani, "Jihadi Diary: Inside the Mind," *BBC News*, June 14, 2007, available at http://bbc.co.uk/go/pr/fr/-/1/hi/magazine/6750911.stm.

91. Williams, "July 7 Plot Accused Tell of Times with Taliban."

92. Mark Kukis, "With Friends Like These . . . ," *New Republic*, February 20, 2006.

93. "Suicide Bombers' 'Ordinary Lives'"; Kukis, "With Friends Like These . . ."; Raghavan, "Friends Describe Bomber's Political, Religious Evolution."

94. "Suicide Bombers' 'Ordinary Lives.'"

95. Sean O'Neill, "Analysis: How the Plan Was Put Together; Little Did Ahmed Ali and His Cohorts Know That They Were Under Round-the-Clock Surveillance While Plotting Their Attacks," *Times* (London), September 9, 2008. Also see Gordon Corera,

"Bomb Plot—the Al Qaeda Connection," *BBC News*, September 9, 2008, available at http://bbc.co.uk/go/pr/fr/-/2/hi/uk_news/7606107.stm; Duncan Gardham, "Airliner Bomb Trial: George W. Bush Took Decision That Triggered Arrests," *Telegraph* (London), September 8, 2008; David Leppard, "Fixer for 21/7 Plot Free in London," *Sunday Times* (London), July 15, 2007.

96. "Operation Theseus (Leeds)."

97. Gardham, "Airliner Bomb Trial: George W. Bush Took Decision That Triggered Arrests." See also, Richard Greenberg, Paul Cruickshank, and Chris Hansen, "Inside the Terrorist Plot that 'Rivaled 9/11,'" *Dateline NBC: The Hansen Files with Chris Hansen*, September 16, 2008, available at http://www.msnbc.msn.com/id/26726987.

98. Quoted in "Treasury Designates Individual Supporting Al Qaeda, Other Terrorist Organizations," *States News Service*, December 19, 2006.

99. Ibid. Also see Sean O'Neill, "Terror Suspect Who Won Court Battle Is Named as a 'Top Al Qaeda Agent'; a 'Key Player' Accused of Radicalizing British Muslims Is Living Openly in the UK," *Times* (London), April 26, 2008.

100. See "Briton Denies Being 'Al Qaeda Banker,'" Agence France Presse, January 7, 2007; David Leppard and Robert Booth, "Londoner Named as Al Qaeda 'Banker'; Accounts Frozen as Suspect Accused Over Terror Pipeline," *Sunday Times* (London), January 7, 2007; O'Neill, "Terror Suspect Who Won Court Battle Is Named as a 'Top Al Qaeda Agent'"; "Bank Accounts of Key Al Qaeda Suspect Frozen," *Press Trust of India*, January 7, 2007; Jason Groves, "Fury as State Benefits Go to Suspects on UN Terror List," *Express on Sunday* (London), July 8, 2007.

101. Gethin Chamberlain, "Attacker 'Was Recruited' at Terror Group's Religious School," *Scotsman* (Edinburgh), July 14, 2005.

102. Also see Peter Bergen, "Where You Bin?," *New Republic*, January 29, 2007, available at http://www.lawandsecurity.org/get_article/?id=64; Bergen and Cruickshank, "Al Qaeda-on-Thames"; Steve Coll and Susan B. Glasser "In London, Islamic Radicals Found a Haven," *Washington Post*, July 10, 2005; Gordon Corera, "Were Bombers Linked to Al Qaeda?," *BBC News*, July 6, 2006, available at http://news.bbc.co.uk/2/hi/uk_news/5156592.stm; Rosie Cowan and Richard Norton-Taylor, "Britain Now No 1 Al-Qaida target—Anti-Terror Chiefs," *Guardian*, October 19, 2006; Margaret Gilmore and Gordon Corera, "UK 'Number One Al Qaeda Target,'" *BBC News*, October 19, 2006, available at http://news.bbc.co.uk/2/hi/uk_news/6065460.stm; Mohammed Khan and Carlotta Gall, "Accounts After 2005 London Bombings Point to Al Qaeda Role from Pakistan," *New York Times*, August 13, 2006; Moghadam, *The Globalization of Martyrdom*, 207.

103. "Extracts from MI5 Chief's Speech," *BBC News*, November 10, 2006, available at http://news.bbc.co.uk/2/hi/uk_news/6135000.stm.

104. Phillips, *Londonistan*, 8; Duncan Gardham, "Airliner Bomb Trial: Fears Raised Over Fundamentalist Islamic Group in Britain," *Telegraph* (London), September 9, 2008.

105. Convicted on charges related to terrorism incitement, el-Faisal was recently paroled from British prison and left the country.

106. Gardham, "Airliner Bomb Trial."

107. Malik, "My Brother the Bomber"; Crown v. Sharif, Sharif, and Tabassum, 2003, indictment and court transcripts, July 2004 and November 2004; "Britain's First Suicide Bombers," *Panorama*, BBC, July 11, 2006; "Links Uncovered Between Britain's First Suicide Bombers and 7/7 Bomber," *BBC News*, July 9, 2006, available at http://www .bbc.co.uk/pressoffice/pressreleases/stories/2006/07_july/09/bombers.shtml.

108. Malik, "My Brother the Bomber"; "Britain's First Suicide Bombers"; "Links Uncovered Between Britain's First Suicide Bombers and 7/7 Bomber."

109. Robert Winnett and David Leppard, "Leaked No 10 Dossier Reveals Al Qaeda's British Recruits," *Sunday Times* (London), July 10, 2005. This information has been personally verified by the author in discussion with senior British police and intelligence officials on numerous occasions since 1999.

110. ISC, "Report into the London Terrorist Attacks on 7 July 2005," 39.

111. Ibid., 10.

[9]

The 2006 Airline Plot

PAUL CRUICKSHANK

During the night of August 9, 2006, British police arrested two dozen individuals at addresses in and around London, suspected of being only weeks away from launching a plot to blow up more than half a dozen transatlantic airliners with liquid explosives. For authorities, who had been monitoring the cell for months, the stakes could not have been higher. By that time, six of the plotters had already recorded suicide tapes. Michael Chertoff, the former secretary of Homeland Security stated that if successful, the alleged plot "would have rivaled 9/11 in terms of the number of deaths and in terms of the impact on the international economy." The plot, which disrupted air travel at the time, led authorities to impose permanent restrictions on liquids and gels on airplanes.[1]

Twelve men, all British citizens, were charged with conspiracy to murder and conspiracy to blow up transatlantic airplanes. All have now been put on trial for a plot described by prosecutors as "an act of terrorism of international scale directed from abroad using homegrown terrorists."[2] Three individuals considered ringleaders in the plot—Abdulla Ahmed Ali, Assad Sarwar, and Tanvir Hussain, were convicted in September 2009 on all charges and one individual—Umar Islam—was found guilty of a general murder conspiracy charge. All four received life sentences. The guilty verdicts followed a six month retrial ordered by British authorities after a jury delivered mixed verdicts in an initial trial in 2008. Two men, Don Stewart Whyte and Mohammed Gulzar, a man accused of being a ringleader in the plot were acquitted of all charges. Although they were cleared of knowing the targets would be airliners, neither of the first two trials produced definitive verdicts on whether three of those charged—Ibrahim Savant, Arafat Waheed Khan, and Waheed Zaman—were guilty of the murder conspiracy charges. However, the trio were found guilty of that offence in a follow-up trial in 2010. In December 2009—in yet another trial—three others were convicted in relation to the plot: Osman Adam Khatib was found guilty of conspiring to detonate suicide bombs on board aircraft, Nabeel Hussain was found guilty of acts preparatory to terrorism, and Mohammed Uddin was found guilty of possessing a document likely to be useful to terrorists.[3]

TARGET AND TIMING

According to British authorities, the cell aimed to target commercial airliners departing Heathrow Airport for cities in the United States and Canada.[4] The terrorist plan, authorities say, was for a team of suicide bombers to board a number of transatlantic flights leaving London over an interval of several hours. They planned to bring on board explosive mixtures of hydrogen peroxide (a high explosive) and Tang, disguised as sports drinks, in their carry-on luggage in order to pass through airport security scanners.[5] They intended to detonate the bombs with hexamethylene triperoxide diamine (HMTD), a highly explosive mushy paste whose constituent parts they had purchased. The plotters planned to bring condoms and "dirty magazines" with them, so that they would arouse less suspicion when they went through security. The plan was for the suicide bombers to detonate their explosives while all the flights were midair. The plotters knew that once the flights took off, authorities would be powerless to act as planes dropped out of the sky.[6]

Authorities did not establish whether the terrorists intended to explode the planes over the Atlantic or over North American cities.[7] The al-Qaeda point person in the plot later revealed that nine suicide bombers in total had been recruited, suggesting that number of planes would be targeted, and also revealed that the plan was to bomb the flights at the same time, when they were all in the air.[8] British investigators only ascertained that the cell's target might be commercial aviation in late June 2006. On August 6, 2006, their suspicions were confirmed, when British agents observed Abdulla Ahmed Ali, the cell's U.K. ringleader, looking up timetables for transatlantic flights.[9]

When authorities arrested Ali three days later, they found a USB thumb drive in his jacket pocket with copies of timetables of North American bound flights departing between August and October 2006. No return flights had been pasted into the document. Seven flights by American and Canadian airliners to Chicago, New York, Washington, D.C., San Francisco, Toronto, and Montreal, all scheduled to depart Heathrow Terminal 3 during a two-and-a-half-hour period, were highlighted in bold—which gave authorities a sense of the scale of the terrorist cell's ambition. Prosecutors stated that "at the very least" these seven flights were targeted.[10] It would not have been unusual for more than 1,500 people to be on these flights.[11]

Authorities say that if the planes had been exploded over densely populated North American conurbations, the death toll would likely have been considerably higher—significantly worse than seven Lockerbie-type events. "I just dread to think [if the bombs had been detonated] coming into the approach to New York City, Los Angeles, whatever it might have been, the devastation and loss of life would've been dreadful," the then-serving assistant police commissioner, Andy Hayman, told Dateline NBC.[12]

Although no complete devices were recovered by police when they moved in to make arrests on August 9, authorities say that the bombers had acquired all the components and substances necessary to make twenty bombs.[13] In a bugged conversation hours before they were arrested on August 9, Ali was asked by another cell member how far from execution the operation was. His reply was, "A couple of weeks." This would suggest that the plan at that stage was to carry out the operation around the last week of August 2006, less than two weeks before the fifth anniversary of the 9/11 attacks.[14]

During the opening phase of the trial, it was revealed that the terrorist cell's targets and ambitions extended well beyond commercial aviation. They also conducted Internet research on other targets, which prosecutors suggested the cell hoped to hit as part of a second wave of attacks following the planes operation. The targets included power plants, nuclear power stations, gas and oil refineries, the country's national electricity grid, the U.K.'s major Internet service provider exchange, London's Canary Wharf office complex, Heathrow Airport's new control tower, and a gas pipeline between Britain and Belgium.[15]

AL-QAEDA DIRECTION

In early 2007, the U.S. government publicly stated that the plot was the work of al-Qaeda. Testifying before a Senate committee in January 2007, the director of the Defense Intelligence Agency, Lt. Gen. Michael D. Maples, described the plotters as "an al-Qaida cell, directed by al-Qaida leadership in Pakistan."[16]

Al-Qaeda leaders presumably hoped to inflict maximum economic damage on the United States and its allies by launching the airline operation. In a March 2006 videotape broadcast by al-Jazeera, Ayman al-Zawahiri called on Muslims to "inflict losses on the crusader West, especially to its economic infrastructure, with strikes that would make it bleed for years."[17] The launching of a spectacular attack around the fifth anniversary of 9/11 plot was also presumably intended to show the world that al-Qaeda was still in business. The targeting of Canadian as well as American airliners demonstrated al-Qaeda's determination to punish a key U.S. ally. At the trial, Ali testified that they targeted Canada because it was "involved hand-in-hand with America."[18]

Planning in one form or another for such an attack, however, had been in the works for more than a decade before 2003. The 2006 plot saw al-Qaeda adapt longstanding plans. The blueprint for the 2006 airline plot had strong similarities with "Operation Bojinka," a plot devised by Khalid Sheikh Mohammed (KSM) and Ramzi Youssef in the early 1990s to bomb a dozen U.S. commercial jumbo jets over the Pacific with liquid explosives over a two-day period. The Bojinka plot had involved the use of nitroglycerin rather than hydrogen peroxide as the liquid explosive and timers rather than suicide bombers.[19]

Youssef was arrested in February 1995, but his uncle, KSM, went on to become al-Qaeda's operational mastermind, orchestrating the 9/11 attacks.[20] The 2006 airline plot blended the Bojinka plot's use of liquid explosives with the 9/11 plot's use of suicide operatives.

THE AL-QAEDA POINT PERSON

According to counterterrorism officials, it was Rashid Rauf, a British Pakistani, who provided the link between the senior leadership of al-Qaeda and the British cell. Rauf wrote a detailed account of his role in the plot, including his recruitment of its ringleaders in Pakistan and communication with them as they prepared the attack, in an internal al-Qaeda report he wrote sometime before his reported death in a drone strike in 2008. The report and more than a hundred other documents were found embedded inside a pornographic movie on a memory disk belonging to a suspected al-Qaeda operative arrested in Berlin in May 2011.[21]

Rauf, who had grown up in Birmingham, fled to Pakistan from the U.K. in 2002 after being sought for questioning by police after his uncle was murdered. In Pakistan Rauf forged deep connections with the Kashmiri militant group Jaish-e-Mohammed (JeM) after marrying a relative by marriage of the group's leader, Masood Azhar.[22] It was presumably through JeM, a group with close ties to bin Laden's terrorist organization, that Rauf developed ties to senior al-Qaeda operatives in the tribal areas of Pakistan.[23]

By 2004 Rauf had become something of a point person for British wannabe jihadists seeking terrorist training in Pakistan to fight in Afghanistan. He was able to exploit this position to connect British militants to al-Qaeda operatives in the tribal areas of Pakistan, who in turn persuaded them to launch attacks back in the U.K. In his internal al-Qaeda report, Rauf described how he met the July 7, 2005, London bombing ringleaders, Mohammed Siddique Khan and Shezad Tanweer, shortly after they arrived in Pakistan in late 2004 and sent them onto al-Qaeda encampments in Pakistan's tribal areas. Rauf wrote he did the same for July 21, 2005, London ringleader, Mukhtar Said Ibrahim, and two other associates a few weeks later. Rauf housed both groups in Islamabad before dispatching them to see a senior al-Qaeda operative called "Haji." U.S. intelligence agencies believe this was Abu Ubaydah al-Masri, then a senior Egyptian member of al-Qaeda's external operation unit. He persuaded them to return to the U.K. to launch an attack and supervised their bomb-making training. Rauf, who spent time with the 7/7 ringleaders in the Federally Administered Tribal Areas (FATA), supervised the recording of Siddique Khan's, Tanweer, and Said Ibrahim's martyrdom tapes when they returned to Islamabad. After the 7/7 bombers returned to the U.K., Rauf communicated with Siddique Khan through e-mails, phone calls, and Yahoo messenger with a system of codes, which allowed Rauf to provide Siddique with technical guidance to ensure he got his bomb mixture right after the latter became unsure whether he had reduced the hydrogen peroxide to the required strength to make it explode. Rauf was not able to communicate with Said Ibrahim after his return, and he wrote that his inability to pass on technical guidance was one of the reasons the devices used in the 21/7 attack failed.[24]

In the same report, Rauf described also meeting with Ali, the future ringleader in the airline plot, in late 2004, and connecting him with Haji in the tribal areas of Pakistan. That winter the Egyptian arranged for Ali to receive weapons and explosives training, according to Rauf's account. Ali returned to Pakistan in June 2005 and was sent back to the U.K. late in 2005 tasked with putting together a plot to hit a wide range of targets. At this stage al-Qaeda had not yet come up with the plan to target airliners, wrote Rauf. He revealed that because al-Qaeda believed it would be difficult to purchase hydrogen peroxide in the U.K. in the wake of the London bombings that July, al-Qaeda taught Ali on this trip how to make explosive devices with gas.

Eventually, Rauf and others in al-Qaeda decided the best plan was to smuggle hydrogen peroxide, a liquid, from Pakistan to the U.K. in rosewater bottles, which would be packed to look unopened, Rauf wrote. "We then analyzed the various machines that were used for checking baggage and persons at airports. We found it was very difficult to detect liquids explosives," Rauf wrote. "After analysis that it would be possible to take concentrated hydrogen peroxide on board, the thought came to our mind: would it be possible to detonate the hydrogen aboard an airplane?" That was the moment when the liquid-bomb plot was conceived. "The way they progressed from London bomb plots to airline was very unexpected and brilliant," according to a senior U.S. counterterrorism official.

British counterterrorism officials now believe that all three conspiracies and a 2004 plot to blow up targets in the U.K. with fertilizer bombs were part of a coordinated campaign by al-Qaeda to target the United Kingdom with a rolling series of attacks.[25] Indeed, Ali may have been in communication with Said Ibrahim on his return to the U.K. in spring of

2005, according to British officials, who explain that a cell phone police recovered from Ali contained a number used by Said Ibrahim.[26]

Rauf's account revealed that like for the 7/7 and 21/7 plots, Abu Ubaydah al-Masri was the driving force within al-Qaeda behind the plan to target transatlantic aviation. He described how in the months after the airline plot was first conceived, Haji/al-Masri brainstormed about how such devices could be constructed and smuggled onto a plane undetected. Al-Masri decided they would convert AA batteries into detonators, Rauf wrote. "We also practiced how to open a drink bottles, empty it, and replace it with Hydrogen Peroxide, to make it seem unopened." Rauf wrote that al-Qaeda believed half a kilo of liquid explosive would without a doubt destroy an airplane, having noted that a similar amount of plastic explosive Semtex had destroyed Pan Am Flight103 over Lockerbie, Scotland, in 1988.

THE SENIOR AL-QAEDA MASTERMIND

Before Rauf's account emerged, British counterterrorism officials already believed that al-Masri was the senior al-Qaeda figure who oversaw the plot.[27] According to a U.S. counterterrorism source, al-Masri is thought to have been based near Mir Ali, the second largest town in North Waziristan.[28]

There is little open-source information on al-Masri. He is believed to be a veteran of the 1980s Afghan jihad who spent several years in Germany in the mid-1990s before returning to Afghanistan to become a terrorist trainer. He next surfaced as an al-Qaeda commander in Kunar province, Afghanistan—the most violent area of insurgent operations in that country, sitting astride Afghanistan's lawless border with Pakistan. Following Khalid Sheikh Mohammed's capture in 2003, al-Masri became part of a group of senior al-Qaeda operational planners who oversaw external operations against the West, and specifically against Britain. As well as overseeing the training of the July 7 and July 21, 2005, London bombers, al-Masri also reportedly trained a Danish al-Qaeda recruit, Hammad Khurshid, in Waziristan in the spring of 2007.[29]

Al-Masri ascended to the position of chief of al-Qaeda's external operations in late 2005, taking over a position previously held by Abu Faraj al-Libi (who was captured in June 2005) and his Egyptian compatriot Abu Hamza Rabia (who was killed in an airstrike in November 2005).[30] It is possible, therefore, that al-Masri, who died of hepatitis in December 2007, took over command of a plot that his predecessors in the post first signed off on.[31] Western counterterrorism officials have evidence that Rauf traveled to the tribal areas of Pakistan to brief al-Masri in the early summer of 2006 as the airline plotters made final preparations to launch their attack.[32]

Bin Laden's involvement in the plot remains difficult to untangle. Back in January 2006, bin Laden did warn Americans of major attacks in the works: "Operations are being prepared, and you will witness them in your own land, as soon as preparations are complete," but it was unclear whether he was referring to the airline plot.[33] "I can't tell you whether operationally it went up to bin Laden," Secretary of Homeland Security Michael Chertoff told NBC, "but I think the links to the al-Qaida network are, in my mind, pretty clear."[34] The fact that bin Laden has never explicitly mentioned the plot does not indicate he was out of the loop. Al-Qaeda leaders have seldom referred to failed plots. A plot of such ambition would presumably have required some sort of sign off from al-Qaeda's leader, but according to a senior U.S. counterterrorism official, documents recovered from bin Laden's Abottabad compound provided no conclusive indications that bin Laden knew about the plot.[35]

In his report on the plot, Rauf indicated that he arranged terrorist training for several others in Ali's U.K. circle in FATA in 2005 and 2006, including Assad Sarwar, the future bomb chemist. British investigators believe that Rauf provided bomb-making guidance to Sarwar in Pakistan and in e-mail communications back to Ali and Sarwar in the U.K.[36]

Rauf's role in the plot could not have been more hands-on. In the final months before the arrests, Rauf was in near constant communication by phone, e-mail, and text message with the U.K. cell's key leaders, suggesting an unprecedented level of micromanagement.[37] Peter Clarke, who as head of Scotland Yard's Counter-terrorism Command, led the Metropolitan Police investigation into the airline plot, says that it seems to have had a greater degree of continuous direction from Pakistan than any other plot he had investigated, including the 2004 fertilizer bomb plot broken up by Operation Crevice and the 2005 London bombings.[38] In his account of the plot, Rauf described how as the plotters prepared their attack, he was in extensive contact with Sarwar and Ali and another plotter through e-mails, text messages, phone calls, and instant messaging.[39]

THE U.K. CELL

Twelve British Muslim men, nine of them from east London, were charged in the U.K. with murder conspiracy charges in relation to the airline plot, the majority of them of Pakistani descent. Most were from what the British call lower-middle-class backgrounds. Few were in full-time employment, and some lived in council houses (British public housing). While they could not be described as more educated than the average citizen of the U.K., most at some point attended second-tier British universities, institutions that were once called polytechnics. Authorities believed they were savvy enough to undertake their mission.[40] As a group, they were also not young hormonal hotheads. The majority of them (eight) were married or engaged.[41]

Authorities described four men as "ringleaders" in the plot: Abdulla Ahmed Ali, 25 at the time of his arrest; Assad Sarwar, then 22; and Mohammed Gulzar, then 25; and Tanvir Hussain, then 25.[42] Eight others were described as having more junior roles in the conspiracy: Ibrahim Savant, 25; Arafat Waheed Khan, 25; Waheed Zaman, 22; Umar Islam (a.k.a Brian Young), 28; Nabeel Hussain, 22; Abdul Waheed (a.k.a Don Stewart-Whyte), 21; Osman Adam Khatib, 19; and Mohammed Uddin, 35.[43]

Eight of the alleged plotters (Ali, Tanvir Hussain, Savant, Khan, Zaman, Nabeel Hussain, Khatib, and Uddin) grew up in and around Walthamstow, east London, and three (Sarwar, Islam, and Stewart-Whyte) grew up in High Wycombe, a country town thirty miles west of London.[44] Gulzar, originally from Birmingham, allegedly flew in to the U.K. from South Africa to oversee final preparations for the plot.[45]

All of the group shared certain characteristics but could not be said to have a common profile. In total, nine of the alleged plotters were of Pakistani descent. Those who were not of Pakistani origin (Savant, Islam, and Stewart-Whyte) had converted to Islam several years previously. Several of the plotters had become born again into Islam after not taking their religion too seriously during their teenage years. Two of the born again (Tanvir Hussain and Khan) had drunk, taken drugs, and chased girls in their late teenage years.[46] In contrast, others had followed their religion more seriously during their youth. Several, including Ali and Gulzar, attended sessions run by the Muslim revivalist movement Tablighi Jamaat in their youth.[47] British authorities alleged the entire group had become highly radicalized. When police made the arrests, they found al-Qaeda propaganda materials in the residences of all twelve.[48] It is not clear in every case what caused their radicalization, but the suicide tapes of six of their number suggest that anger over Western foreign policy was a key factor.[49]

Abdulla Ahmed Ali was the UK cell leader. Described as intelligent, strong-willed, and charismatic, he would recruit a majority of the "foot soldiers" in the plot, liaise with al-Qaeda's point man in Pakistan, Rashid Rauf, and oversee the design mechanics of the liquid bombs.[50] Ali, a British citizen, was born in London in 1980 to parents who had settled in the U.K. in the 1960s, part of a wave of immigrants from Pakistani Kashmir. Shortly after his birth, the family moved back to Pakistan but returned to London when Ali, now fluent in Urdu and Punjabi, was seven years old.[51] His parents, despite settling in Walthamstow, one of London's poorer neighborhoods, were solidly middle class. His father was a businessman who owned factories in both Pakistan and England, and the family lived in a modern semidetached house.[52] Ali's siblings—five brothers and two sisters—did not find it difficult to integrate into mainstream society; one of his brothers was a successful entrepreneur and another a probation officer at Britain's Home Office.[53]

Classmates at the local state (public) school that Ali attended recall him as a devout but by no means radical Muslim who loved sports. "He always joined in and accepted Western society," one recalled.[54] At around the age of fifteen Ali became more religious. Encouraged by his parents, who had taught him some of the basics of Islam, Ali started attending sessions of the Islamic missionary organization Tablighi Jamaat, an organization that has attracted the attention of U.K. and U.S. authorities because some of its members have become involved in terrorist plots.[55] He testified in court that it was the first time he got to properly know his religion. In court, Ali described himself as becoming more politically conscious during this period, watching the evening news every night. He also testified that reports about Serbian oppression of Muslims in Bosnia particularly affected him.[56]

Ali's high-school religious education teacher, Mark Hough, noticed two sides of his pupil. On the one hand, Ali seemed a perfectly "ordinary lad," good at sports and especially basketball. On the other hand, Hough observed some radical views emerging in his pupil. Ali "thought the Taliban had created a model society in Afghanistan," Hough said, explaining that when Ali was around fifteen, he began to praise the Taliban, who were then in control of a number of Afghan provinces, and called for the introduction of strict Muslim sharia law to Britain. Hough believed some older college-age students whom the young Ali began to associate with after school influenced Ali. He said they watched videos depicting the killing and mistreatment of Muslims in Bosnia and Chechnya along with ones extolling the virtues of Taliban-ruled Afghanistan.[57] In his suicide tape, recovered by police after his arrest, Ali claimed to have long wished to die fighting jihad. "Thanks to God I Swear by Allah, I have the desire since the age of 15/16 to participate in jihad in the path of Allah. I had the desire since then to punish the Kuffar for the evil they are doing. I had the desire since then for Jannah [Paradise]."[58]

It is possible, however, that Ali was grandstanding in that tape. When Ali went to City University, a former polytechnic, in London in 1999 to take a course in computer engineering, little yet marked him as a future terrorist prepared to kill his fellow citizens.[59] To the contrary, many in the community saw Ali as a young man with bright prospects. Imtiaz Qadir, a friend of the family who had known Ali since childhood, says that the tall, smart, popular, and handsome young man seemed destined to follow in his father's footsteps and become a successful entrepreneur. He points out that while Ali may have held some trenchant views, they were hardly unusual among young Muslims growing up in the area.[60]

However, something appears to have snapped in Ali in the years after 9/11. After the U.S. invasion of Afghanistan, Ali started to do volunteer work in the east London offices of the Islamic Medical Association (IMA), a small charitable organization sending supplies to help victims of the U.S. bombing campaign in Afghanistan.[61] Although it is not clear how Ali became more radicalized, one of the regulars at the charity shop was Mohammed Hamid, a hard-line radical preacher who ran an Islamic bookshop across the road. It is certainly possible that Hamid had an influence on Ali during this period. In 2008, the fifty-year-old Hamid, who liked to style himself "Osama bin London," was convicted for organizing terrorist training in the British countryside for several of those plotting to bomb the London transport system on July 21, 2005.[62]

During the trial, it emerged that many of the plotters had connections to the IMA charity. In 2002, Ali persuaded three members of his east London circle—Savant, Khan, and Tanvir Hussain—to volunteer at the charity offices.[63] The head of the charity was also a close associate of Mohammed Gulzar, an alleged leading member of the conspiracy acquitted of all charges.[64]

In early March 2003, several months after graduating from university and two weeks after attending a million-person-strong protest against the war in Iraq on the streets of London, Ali traveled to Pakistan on behalf of his medical charity, the first time he had been back since he was seven years old.[65] It is unclear whether he met with Rashid Rauf or anybody from al-Qaeda during this trip, but, strikingly, his itinerary was exactly the same as a trip made by Mohammed Hamid, the terrorist cleric, the year before, transiting through Karachi to an Afghan refugee camp in Chaman, on the Afghanistan-Pakistan border.[66]

In Pakistan, Ali met two other IMA volunteers: Assad Sarwar, the future bomb chemist for the cell, and Sarwar's High Wycombe friend Umar Islam, a Rastafarian convert who would also become involved in the plot.[67] The British-born Sarwar had grown up in High Wycombe, the son of Kashmiri immigrants. His background was more working class than those of some of the other plotters. His father spoke no English and worked as a laborer. Although Sarwar was raised as a Muslim, Islam does not appear to have been especially emphasized within the family. Sarwar's younger brother Ajmar was an atheist.[68]

In court, Sarwar described himself as a very shy young man with low self-esteem who did not have girlfriends at school. In September 2001, he enrolled at Brunel University but quit the course because he found the work too difficult. Back at home, and working as a supermarket stock clerk, he started attending an Islamic education center, where he met Umar Islam. What he learned there made him increasingly religious. It is unclear what specifically radicalized Sarwar, but a trip he took with Umar Islam at the end of 2002 to work in the Chaman refugee camp in Pakistan on behalf of the IMA may have played a role. In court he said it was there that he got to know Ali, whose strong and persuasive character turned him into a somewhat of a follower. Sarwar returned to the U.K. in 2003 and worked for stints at the Royal Mail and British Telecom.[69]

Ali, for his part, testified that the suffering he saw in the refugee camps, much of which he claimed was the result of the American bombing campaign in Afghanistan, contributed to his radicalization. He claimed that one woman, when she found out he was from England, blamed him for the suffering: "You've done this," she told him. Ali also testified that, above all, the Iraq war turned him against the United States and Britain. After the invasion, which he described as a "criminal act," he became convinced that the "root problem" of Muslim suffering around the world was the "foreign policy [of America and Britain] . . . and that should be tackled." The failure of the million-strong "Stop the War" march to prevent the Iraq War left him disillusioned with the power of protest, he testified. He recalled how he also began to become frustrated with aid work, which he felt could have little effect on the suffering caused by the wars launched by the United States and its allies.[70] Reinforcing his increasingly militant views, Ali at some point read *Signposts*, a 1963 book by the Egyptian militant Sayyid Qutb that later became a manifesto for al-Qaeda and other militant Islamist groups. In court, Ali described the book, which authorities found in his home, as a "must read."[71]

In July 2003, after his return from Pakistan, Ali married a British woman of Pakistani descent whom his mother had selected as his bride.[72] Cossar Ali, his wife, would be charged three years later for failing to alert authorities about the plot, but she was cleared in a 2010 trial.[73] After getting married, the couple moved into a council estate in Walthamstow, where Cossar soon became pregnant. Ali supported her by doing odd jobs for his brothers. In late 2003, Ali traveled to Saudi Arabia to make the hajj with a future fellow conspirator, Tanvir Hussain. Tragically, shortly after he returned, his wife gave birth to a child with serious birth defects who died soon afterward.[74]

THE BEGINNINGS OF THE PLOT

In the fall of 2004, Ali made a second trip to Pakistan, accompanied by his wife. He again visited the refugee camp in Chaman, his anger growing at the conditions there.[75] It was on this trip that he met Rashid Rauf.

According to Rauf, Ali told him he never wanted to return home and instead wanted training to wage jihad in Afghanistan. Rauf connected Ali with al-Masri, who arranged for him to receive weapons and explosives training. From then on, "a big change came over his temperament when he first came and when he left," Rauf wrote. "He was a very clever, patient brother and a natural leader," Rauf wrote.[76]

When he returned to the U.K. in January 2005 from his second trip to Pakistan, Ali started up a business selling mobile-phone contracts with Tanvir Hussain.[77] His views had hardened. An acquaintance recalls that Ali could no longer stand the sight of people who disagreed with him, viewing them as unbelievers.[78] When terror hit London's streets on July 7, 2005, Ali was in Pakistan again on a third trip to the country, accompanied by Adam Khatib, the younger brother of his best friend.[79] Sometime during the fall the duo is suspected of having linked up with Assad Sarwar, the future bomb chemist, who traveled back to Pakistan in October that year.[80]

It was during this trip that Ali received training on how to make explosives out of gas, according to Rauf. Rauf recounted how Assad Sarwar and other future members of the U.K. cell traveled to Pakistan between the closing months of 2005 and early 2006, and how some, but not Sarwar, volunteered to become suicide bombers for whatever plot was finalized by al-Qaeda.[81]

Sarwar obliquely acknowledged his contact with Rauf in court. He testified that during this trip he first met a Kashmiri militant called Jamil, who in the future would help with bomb design. He stopped short of revealing the individual's true identity.[82] British investigators established that the individual Sarwar called Jamil was in reality Rashid Rauf, the al-Qaeda point man in the terrorist conspiracy, who used the name as an alias, but prosecutors were prevented from mentioning Rauf by name at any point in court.[83] Although Sarwar denied meeting other plotters during this trip, his fingerprints and those of Ali and Khatib were found on a tourist map of Lahore later seized by police. Investigators believe that the trio may have met up in Lahore to receive bomb-making instruction somewhere in Pakistan. A handwritten formula for concentrating chemicals was later found in a book belonging to Khatib, who only made one trip to Pakistan.[84] Al-Qaeda at the time was moving toward more quickly training European recruits. "We would now send back brothers quickly and not keep them for a long time," Rauf wrote. "This was largely due to the fact that (after July 7) we knew there would be intelligence monitoring of people travelling from the UK to Pakistan."[85]

Planning for some sort of terrorist attack against the U.K. appears to have commenced in January 2006, shortly after Ali and Sarwar returned from Pakistan. Ali at trial acknowledged meeting Sarwar several times in east London to discuss exploding a device to draw attention to the suffering of Muslims in Iraq and Afghanistan. The jury did not believe his claim that the plan they settled on was to set off liquid bomb devices in a Heathrow terminal to scare people rather than kill them. He claimed they aimed the stunt at bringing publicity to a documentary on the suffering of Muslims that they intended to film and post on YouTube.[86] During this time, Ali increasingly cropped up on the radar screens of British security services, according to counterterrorism sources, because of his contacts with individuals suspected of terrorist activity in the U.K. Authorities did not yet know, however, what, if anything, he was planning.[87]

In February and March, according to retrieved computer documents, Sarwar conducted online research on a variety of targets in the U.K., including oil and gas terminals, the national grid, and nuclear power stations.[88] Prosecutors maintain that Sarwar, who did not record a suicide tape, was not selected to become a suicide bomber in the airline plot operation and suggested that that was because he had been tasked with scoping out targets for a second wave of attacks.[89] Rauf's account, which emerged after the trials for the airline conspirators were completed, suggested, however, that in early 2006 al-Qaeda had yet to settle on attacking planes, only deciding to attack transatlantic aviation a bit later that year.[90]

Early preparations for this new plan may have gotten going in April, when, unknown to police at the time, Sarwar purchased the first small batch of hydrogen peroxide, the main ingredient of the liquid explosives, from a health-products supplier in Wales.[91] Something about a fourth trip Ali made to Pakistan in May 2006—officials will not disclose exactly what—heightened their suspicion. Rauf wrote he had been recalled so al-Qaeda could train him on how to make the new devices its bomb makers, under the supervision of al-Masri, had designed. Rauf wrote that Ali was instructed to target flights heading towards the United States.[92]

In setting off on this trip, Ali was questioned at Heathrow on departure and tracked by Pakistan's military intelligence—the ISI—when he arrived, Rauf wrote. The ISI requested local police in the Islamabad area stop Ali and search his baggage, but they were friends of his family and tipped him off about the ISI's interest. "We trained (him) quickly, and wanted him to leave ASAP. He was also told to do anti-surveillance measures when he got back and only start work when he was comfortable that everything was clear," wrote Rauf.[93]

When Ali arrived back in London on June 24, 2006, British agents "were waiting at Heathrow to secretly open his baggage in a back room."[94] British counterterrorism sources say that the first clues that Ali might be planning an attack on commercial aviation came to their attention in June 2006, though a more complete picture emerged only several weeks later, in mid-July.[95]

Days before Ali returned to the U.K., his accomplice, Assad Sarwar, set off again for Pakistan. At trial Sarwar admitted that the purpose of this third trip was to receive bomb-making instruction. Sarwar testified that this instruction came from "Jamil," the Kashmiri militant he had met the previous year, who British investigators believe was actually Rauf.[96] Sarwar testified that when he again met Jamil/Rauf in June 2006 in Islamabad, he asked him how to make HMTD-based detonators and hydrogen-peroxide-based explosives. At trial Sarwar explained that a note, "Make 80HP," found in his notebook referred to these lessons. According to Sarwar's testimony, Jamil/Rauf taught him that the hydrogen peroxide would need to be at 80 percent concentration by volume to make a bomb.[97] Rauf wrote that when he met Sarwar on this trip it was decided his role would be to support Ali in putting together a plot and continue al-Qaeda's work in the U.K. after the operation.[98]

Sarwar, however, did not reveal the full extent of the U.K. cell's training in Pakistan in his court testimony. U.S. officials have stated, without going into names and dates, that several other members of the cell were trained by al-Qaeda operatives in the tribal areas of Pakistan.[99] Eight of the twelve men charged in relation to the plot were in Pakistan at some point between 2003 and 2006.[100] In late 2005, six were there at the same time, and three—Ali, Sarwar, and Khatib—were present in the same city, Lahore, during that period.[101] Rauf in his account of the plot recounted that in the closing months of 2005 and early 2006, a number of other cell members, besides Ali and Sarwar, were trained by al-Qaeda in Pakistan and expressed their wish to become martyrs.[102] This indicates that Tanvir Hussain, who traveled to Pakistan in early 2006, also received bomb-making training. In 2006 the three individuals eventually involved most closely with making the bombs, Ali, Sarwar, and Hussain, were the three to make trips to Pakistan.[103]

Soon after Ali's return in late June 2006, the probe became "red hot" according to then-serving senior British police officials.[104] MI5 agents and police began round-the-clock surveillance of Ali's activities. Investigators believe, but cannot say with certainty, that Ali had recruited most of the cell members not already committed in participating in an attack in the months before departing for Pakistan in late May because when he returned, his movements, which they tracked, did not appear to correspond with a recruitment drive.[105] According to a senior U.S. counterterrorism official, Ali's e-mails with Rauf suggested some recruitment efforts continued after he returned to the U.K.[106] Rauf wrote that when the plot was thwarted, the ringleaders had still to reach out to brief two men who had previously indicated they would be prepared to be suicide bombers.[107] Ali claimed in court that he told Tanvir Hussain about his YouTube bomb plan in April, but waited until July to approach others.[108]

Most of the dozen men eventually charged in relation to the plot were either school friends of Ali or people he got to know at the London and Pakistani offices of the IMA charity.[109] Ali's charismatic appeal appears to have helped him persuade them to sign up for the operation. His school friend Arafat Khan, for example, was "born again" into Islam after Ali persuaded him to abandon his partying lifestyle. Khan, whose defense team claimed he came to view Ali with something like hero worship, had gone off the rails as a teenager—using drugs, drinking heavily, and sleeping around.[110]

It was striking how short a time (likely several months in most cases, but in some cases possibly only several weeks) it took for some of the foot soldiers to move from radicalization to volunteering for a suicide-bombing operation against their countrymen. By the time of their arrests, Ali and five of his recruits had recorded martyrdom tapes. The anger in the Muslim community over Israel's initiation of a month-long bombing campaign in Lebanon in mid-July may have helped Ali persuade some of his circle to take the final plunge.

PURCHASE OF BOMB-MAKING SUPPLIES

The cell started laying some of the groundwork for the plot in late June 2006. In late June and early July several of the plotters applied for the first of several loans they presumably did not intend to pay back—a ploy used in other terrorist plots—successfully raising more than $40,000 before the plot was broken up.[111] New information that has come to light since the trials indicates these loan applications were not made to finance the attack but because the men expected to die and wanted to provide funds for their families.[112]

At some point during this period, al-Qaeda conducted a successful test run with the bomb components minus the explosives on a flight, according to Rauf's account. "The purpose of the exercise was to test that none of the components would be checked manually," Rauf wrote.[113] In early July, Ali and Tanvir Hussain began shopping around for some of the equipment they would need in order to manufacture the bombs. Despite the return of Sarwar, the bomb chemist, from Pakistan on July 8, the cell's preparations did not yet have the mark of urgency.[114]

That would change after the arrival of Mohammed Gulzar, a British man of Pakistani descent, to the U.K. from South Africa on July 18.[115] Authorities say that Gulzar, who flew in to the U.K. with a false South African passport, was a senior figure within the al-Qaeda organization, tasked with supervising the last stages of the airline plot. A senior British counterterrorism source speculates that Gulzar was sent to tell the U.K. plotters "to get a move on."[116] In court, Gulzar denied any terrorist ties and was acquitted of all charges. Possibly, the outbreak of hostilities between Israel and Hezbollah on July 12 led al-Qaeda to accelerate their plans. A successful strike against the United States in such a heated atmosphere would no doubt have been a huge propaganda coup for the terrorist organization.[117]

THE TWO BEST FRIENDS

Gulzar, whose identity British police only ascertained after his arrest, was no stranger to Rashid Rauf; they were best friends. Both sons of Pakistani immigrants, they had grown up together in Birmingham.[118] Rauf was just ten months old when his father, Abdul Rauf, a religious judge, brought his family to the U.K. from Mirpur in Pakistani Kashmir and set up a bakery delivery business in the Bordesley Green area of Birmingham.[119] Although Rauf appears to have been brought up a strict Muslim and regularly attended his local mosque, a family friend said he was more into sports than religion when he was young and did not care much for politics.[120]

In 1999, Gulzar and Rauf both started courses at Portsmouth University on the south coast of England. In late 2000, Gulzar started attending sessions of Tablighi Jamaat in the city.[121] Rauf joined the movement at some point, too, becoming more religious.[122] It is not clear to what degree they had radicalized by this stage, but their lives would forever change after the death of Rauf's uncle, Muhammed Saaed, who was stabbed to death in Birmingham in April 2002, after what detectives believe was a family dispute over an arranged marriage.[123] West Midlands Police wanted to question both Rauf and Gulzar in connection with the murder, but they fled to Pakistan before they could be found.[124]

Rauf headed for Bawhalapur in southern Punjab, where he knew an imam who was a family friend, and while living there he married a relative of the founder of the Kashmiri militant group Jaish-e-Mohammed, a match that likely brought him into al-Qaeda's orbit.[125] The Pakistani terrorist group had a significant presence in the town, operating a number of madrassas. Gulzar, for his part, also eventually based himself in the Punjab, living in his mother's hometown of Chohakhalsa.[126]

THE SOUTH AFRICA CONNECTION

Gulzar, for reasons unknown to investigators, moved to South Africa in the summer of 2004, where he lived at an address in the Johannesburg area. At least once a week during his time there, he met with Mohammed Patel, the founder of the IMA charity that Ali and Sarwar were volunteering for, who had temporarily moved there.[127] By 2004, South Africa had emerged as a logistical base for al-Qaeda.

Investigators have noted that Haroon Rashid Aswat, an alleged British operative with suspected links to the July 7, 2005, London bombings, was in South Africa at the same time as Gulzar. According to a senior U.S.

intelligence source made privy to records of Rauf's later interrogation by Pakistani authorities, Aswat, Gulzar, and Rauf spent time together in Pakistan before Aswat and Gulzar traveled to South Africa.[128] U.S. and British security services believe that Aswat was also in contact with Rauf after he traveled to South Africa. The overlap between Aswat and Gulzar in South Africa (Aswat spent significant time there in 2004 and 2005) suggested to Western intelligence agencies they may have worked together there.[129] According to the senior U.S. intelligence source, though Rauf made no specific mention of Aswat's involvement in his interrogation, Aswat is suspected by U.S. intelligence of having played a role in the early stages of the airline plot.[130] Aswat was arrested in Zambia in late July 2005 and deported to the U.K., where he has been fighting extradition to the United States on charges of material support for al-Qaeda in connection with an alleged effort to set up a jihadist training camp in Oregon before 9/11. Aswat has never been charged for any role in the airline plot and has denied he has any connection to terrorism.[131]

According to a senior British counterterrorism source, British al-Qaeda recruits, rather than traveling directly back and forth from Pakistan, have in the past traveled through South Africa to mask their origin. South Africa, the source stated, is a convenient transit hub because it has a well-developed market in false documents and a large South Asian community that can provide natural cover for British Pakistanis.[132]

Gulzar spent one year in South Africa before returning to Pakistan in September 2005. He was therefore in Pakistan when Ali, Sarwar, and Khatib visited in the second half of the year. In April 2006, just as Sarwar was purchasing a first batch of hydrogen peroxide in Wales, Gulzar flew back to South Africa, dispatched there by al-Qaeda—British authorities suggested—to be in position to enter the U.K. without attracting suspicion. Soon after his arrival in Johannesburg, two individuals flew over from the U.K. to meet him. One was Mohammed Patel's seventeen-year-old son, Abdel Manem Patel, and the other was Mohammed al-Ghabra, an alleged al-Qaeda facilitator and a gym buddy of Ali, the U.K. ringleader.[133] The connection was typical of the complex nexus of friendship and family links investigators have grappled with in this plot and other al-Qaeda conspiracies.[134]

During this stay in South Africa, Gulzar organized cover for his planned return to the U.K., fraudulently acquiring a South African passport in the name of Altaf Ravat.[135] Gulzar claimed in court that he took this new identity because British authorities sought him in relation to an incident that made him flee the U.K. in 2002. Although he did not spell it out in court, he was referring to their desire to question him for the 2002 murder in Birmingham.[136] Prosecutors alleged that to further reduce suspicion, he also got married. The woman in question was Zora Saddique, a British-born woman of Pakistani descent, whom he claims to have met in Islamabad airport in March 2006 on his way over to South Africa. Wooing her through phone calls and text messages, Gulzar persuaded her to travel to South Africa to get married, which they did on June 30.[137] Prosecutors, however, maintained the marriage was a sham, designed to minimize scrutiny at Heathrow airport on his return to the U.K.[138] Taking the stand at trial, Gulzar claimed he traveled to the U.K. because his wife had accepted a job offer in London.[139] Saddique was not charged in relation to the plot.

On arriving in the U.K. on July 18, Abdel Manem Patel greeted Gulzar and his wife at Heathrow airport and gave Gulzar SIM cards for him to use in his mobile phone.[140] The next day Gulzar texted and phoned a number in Pakistan.[141] The number, investigators say, likely belonged to his best friend Rashid Rauf, whom he would be in touch with frequently over the next three weeks.[142] Rauf was not identified by name during the trial. Gulzar claimed his communications to Pakistan were to a relative and concerned obtaining a Pakistani identity card as part of his overall plan to invent a new identity.[143] After spending several days with relatives of his wife, Gulzar moved into a small row house in Barking, east London.[144]

COMMUNICATIONS WITH PAKISTAN

According to U.K. authorities, Ali, Sarwar, and Gulzar were all in frequent contact by text, e-mail, and phone with Rashid Rauf during July and August 2006, suggesting that Rauf actively participated in the day-to-day management of the plot.[145] Rauf used multiple cell-phone numbers to communicate with the ringleaders in the U.K. When he was arrested in Pakistan, the cell phones found on him corresponded to the numbers the U.K. ringleaders were in touch with.[146] The communications were mostly short and in code.[147] In court, Sarwar testified that when he met with "Jamil" in Islamabad, Pakistan, in June 2006 he exchanged code books with him so that Rauf could "troubleshoot" if he ran into problems man-ufacturing the HMTD detonators and hydrogen peroxide explosives in the U.K.[148]

To maximize operational security, Rauf set up a system with the U.K. plotters whereby he could frequently change his e-mail address.[149] According to British counterterrorism sources, Rauf exerted "command and control" over the plot by e-mailing the U.K. cell ringleaders at least every other day, sometimes several times a day, with instructions and questions.[150] At times Rauf appeared to be micromanaging the plotters. For example, on July 24, Ali received a coded text message from him ask-ing, "Have you spoken to NB [Sarwar] about the colors," referring to Ali's plan to dye the liquid explosives to make them resemble the colors of sports drinks.[151]

Rauf confirmed his extensive contact with the U.K. plotters through e-mails, text messages, phone calls, and instant messaging. Rauf wrote that he also used Yahoo Messenger. Rauf wrote that he set up a system of cell-phone communications in which the U.K. group would regularly change the SIM cards in their phones and provide details of new numbers through coded messages. Rauf wrote that he had four phones with him at all times in Pakistan—three to communicate with the plotters in the U.K. and one to communicate with his colleagues in Pakistan. His report showed he was paranoid that Western intelligence agencies might be able to track his voice and at one point requested that Sarwar purchase him a "voice changer."[152]

PREPARATIONS ACCELERATE

Gulzar's arrival in east London coincided with an acceleration in the activity of the U.K. plotters, according to prosecutors. On July 20, three days after Gulzar got to the U.K., Ali and Tanvir Hussain took possession of a small row house on Forest Road, Walthamstow, which, under secret observation by MI5, they quickly converted into a bomb factory.[153] The securing of these premises appeared to be fortuitous. The purchase of the residence by Ali's brother, who dabbled in property speculation, had been finalized the day before, and Ali, seizing an opportunity, had offered to renovate it. On July 21, Ali called Rauf in Pakistan to inform him that he had moved into the house.[154]

In the days after acquiring the bomb factory, the plotters went on a veritable shopping spree to buy items for the devices. In London, the plotters bought glass jars, syringes, conical flasks, and sports drinks, and Sarwar traveled back to Wales to buy another twenty liters of hydrogen peroxide.[155] On July 25, Ali became the first of several plotters to make a fast-track application for a replacement passport. He did not want Pakistani visa stamps to be present in his passport when he boarded the planes.[156]

On July 29, Sarwar called Gulzar for the first time in order to arrange a meeting between them that afternoon. The call was placed from a phone kiosk using a calling card.[157] At trial Gulzar claimed he got in touch with Sarwar seeking help in obtaining a new British passport as part of his attempt to create a new identity and denied it was in furtherance of a terrorist plot.[158] "I have no involvement in this plot that the other defendants were in. I was not in contact with them for anything to do with that and my contact with Sarwar was for passports and later on for money and that's it," he stated.[159]

When communicating with one another in the U.K. the alleged plotters used layers of defense to make their calls more difficult to trace. When Ali, Sarwar, or Gulzar received a call from another alleged member of the conspiracy on his cell phone, the call nearly always originated from a phone kiosk. The individual making the call—in this case Sarwar—would nearly always also use a calling card to try to mask the call. The alleged plotters also each had several different cell-phone numbers.[160] After meeting Gulzar in a public park, Sarwar drove to Walthamstow to meet with Ali, in all likelihood, British authorities suggested, to pass on Gulzar's instructions from al-Qaeda's top command.[161]

During this period, Gulzar also met several times in east London with Mohammed al-Ghabra, the alleged al-Qaeda facilitator whom he had recently seen in South Africa. Gulzar and al-Ghabra also spoke several times on the phone. On at least two occasions Gulzar phoned al-Ghabra immediately after speaking to Sarwar, raising suspicions among some investigators that al-Ghabra was in on the plot.[162] Ghabra also had connections to other members of the conspiracy, hanging out occasionally with Umar Islam in London.[163] Gulzar claimed the meetings were for business reasons.[164] Al-Ghabra has not been charged in relation to the plot, and there is no suggestion from this author that he was involved.

SUICIDE TAPES

During the last few days of July, five of the plotters recorded martyrdom tapes in front of a black banner in the bomb factory, most of them reading from prepared scripts, which one of the plotters scrolled down a laptop monitor in front of them. According to courtroom testimony, much of the scripting was done by Ali, who was present at all the tapings.[165] A sixth plotter, Umar Islam, would record a tape on August 9.[166] Rauf, in his subsequent account of the plot, revealed that Ali had been instructed to record martyrdom tapes for those taking part in the attack.[167]

Assad Sarwar, the bomb chemist, appears to have been tasked with disseminating the tapes after the attack. The tapes were found in his house and car by police on August 9.[168] At trial, Sarwar admitted he was in charge of disseminating them for propaganda purposes but denied they were suicide tapes.[169] British authorities suggested al-Qaeda had specific requirements about which tape format the cell used. On August 6, a police officer who was shadowing Gulzar heard him say on a phone call to Sarwar, "I definitely need it to be 8 millimetres."[170] Under cross-examination at trial, Gulzar, who would be acquitted, denied he ever made the remark.[171] The cell appeared to expect the tapes would be edited and cut to produce maximum effect. One of the plotters recorded instructions for unnamed "media brothers" on how his words should be edited.[172]

The suicide videotapes made clear the plotters' resolve to launch the strikes. Their language and the calm manner in which they expressed their grievances appeared to be modeled on the suicide tape recorded by Mohammed Siddique Khan, the July 7 ringleader, clips of which several of the airline plotters were found to have had in their possession.[173] Ali, dressed in black robes with a checkered black and white Palestinian scarf wrapped around his head, spoke for sixteen minutes. Looking straight into the camera and continually wagging his index finger, Ali made it clear that the attack was being carried out in al-Qaeda's name: "Enough is enough. We've warned you so many times to get out of our lands, leave us alone, but you have persisted in trying to humiliate us, kill us, destroy us and Sheikh Osama warned you many times to leave our lands or you will be destroyed and now the time has come for you to be destroyed and you have nothing to expect but floods of martyr operations."[174] No reference was made to bombing airplanes in the tapes, presumably because they knew their audience would not need reminding.

An analysis of the tapes reveals five messages the plotters were trying to get across. The first was an articulation of the foreign policy grievances behind the attacks. The plotters singled out the United States, Britain, and Israel for their oppression of Muslims and their occupation of Muslim land and made specific reference to Iraq, Afghanistan, and Palestine. "This is revenge for the actions of the USA in Muslim lands and their accomplices such as the British and the Jews," stated Umar Islam. In a familiar al-Qaeda refrain, the plotters also called on the United States and its allies to cease supporting secular Arab dictatorships. "Stop supporting the puppets and helping our enemies," exclaimed Tanvir Hussain, "If you don't, you're going to feel the wrath of the Mujahedeen."[175]

The plotters asserted that they had clear-eyed political reasons for launching the attacks. Waheed Zaman, a graduate of London's Metropolitan University, insisted, "I have not been brainwashed, I have been educated to a high standard. I am old enough to make my own decisions." Zaman was equally disdainful of socioeconomic explanations for his actions, stating, "I could have lived a life of ease but instead chose to fight for the sake of Allah's Deen."[176]

A second message in the tapes—one perhaps designed to inspire al-Qaeda sympathizers—was that the attacks, as well as being politically motivated, were an act of holy war, for which the plotters joyously expected heavenly reward. "I'm doing this because the rewards, the big rewards that Allah has promised those who step on his path and Inshallah become a martyr," claimed Ali. He continued, "And the best of those to me is the guarantee of Jannah [paradise] for myself and my family and those that are close to me."[177]

A third message running through the tapes was directed at Muslims, admonishing them for compromises made with a rapacious and degenerate West. "All Muslims take heed," instructed Ibrahim Savant, a convert to Islam, "remove yourself from the grasp of the Kuffar before you are counted as one of them. Do not be content with your council houses and businesses and Western lifestyle." Arafat Waheed Khan, for his part, had particularly harsh words for Muslim critics of al-Qaeda's terrorism, referring to them as "bootlickers who stand shoulder to shoulder with the Kuffar in condemning these beautiful operations and the Mujahedeen."[178]

Fourth, the plotters sought to respond preemptively to the charge that they were killing innocent civilians. "I do not consider anyone innocent who . . . sits back and pay taxes which is funding this army to do what it is doing," stated Umar Islam. He continued:

> Even if you disagree that you've done nothing, you're just sitting there and you're still funding the army. You haven't put down your leader. You haven't pressured them enough. Most of you are too busy, you know, watching Home and Away and Eastenders, complaining about the World Cup, drinking your alcohol, to even care anything. That's all you seem to care about, and I know because I've come from that.[179]

Finally, the plotters clearly wanted their tapes, which they hoped would be disseminated after the killing of thousands, to amplify the terror felt by the British, American, and Canadian populations and to weaken their resolve. Arafat Khan promised, "We will rain upon you such a terror and destruction that you will never feel peace and security."[180]

PREPARATORY WORK ON BOMB COMPONENTS

By the end of July, Ali and Tanvir Hussain had started preparatory work on bomb components in the bomb factory on Forest Road, some of it experimental.[181] Tanvir Hussain, Ali's assistant, was not always radical. The eldest son of Pakistani immigrants to the U.K., he stated in court that he was brought up in family that "weren't really practicing that much" and said that much of his time at school in east London and at Middlesex University was spent chasing girls, clubbing, drinking, and smoking dope. Although he developed friendships with Ali, Khan, and Savant during these years, he was at the time more conscious of fashion than religion or politics. His first brush with hydrogen peroxide came in 1997, when he used it to dye his hair. In the years after 9/11, Hussain became born again into Islam after being persuaded by Ali to do voluntary work for the IMA charity. He also became more politicized. In 2003 he joined a large demonstration against the Iraq war in London, a conflict that appears to have turned his views more militant. Increasingly devout, Hussain married in 2005. In February 2006, he traveled to Pakistan for two months, during which time he appears to have received training.[182] By the summer of 2006 his views had turned extreme. An acquaintance was shocked when he overheard him talking about the necessity of killing "Kuffar" during a football match.[183]

The design of the cell's improvised explosive devices was straightforward and based around substances that were easy to attain legally. A disposable camera was planned as the trigger for the device. The exposed filament of a modified miniature light bulb would be connected to the power supply in the camera. The filament in turn would be connected to a detonator made out of the chemical compound HMTD. The bombers planned to insert the HMTD paste inside hollowed-out batteries.[184]

The flash on the camera would send a small current through the filament into the HMTD-filled batteries. The resulting explosion would then provide enough energy to detonate the main charge inside sports drinks bottles. The liquid explosives inside the sports drinks bottles would be a mixture of concentrated hydrogen peroxide and Tang, a sugar-based powdered drink that would act as a fuel in the explosion. Dye would then be added to make the contents look like sports drinks. The bombers intended to boil down the hydrogen peroxide they purchased, which they knew would explode to devastating effect at the right concentration. At trial the jury was shown a British government test which showed that the hydrogen peroxide, at a high enough concentration, could be successfully detonated.[185]

Rauf later followed news reports of the prosecution case against the cell members in the U.K. "They understood the basic idea of the plot but were unaware of some of the minor details," he wrote in his report.[186]

Ali had brought some of the bomb-making materials back from Pakistan, including AA batteries acquired during his 2006 trip and packets of Tang bought during an earlier visit. Ali claimed that Toshiba batteries sold in Pakistan were easier to modify than other brands, but he may just have wanted to use the same batteries that he had been trained to modify in Pakistan.[187]

Sarwar purchased the chemicals necessary to manufacture HMTD from a variety of outlets. He purchased citric acid at a pharmacy in High Wycombe at the beginning of August and 500g of hexamine, a fuel used in gas camping stoves, by mail order. By the time of his arrest, he had stored enough chemicals to manufacture 100g of HTMD, enough for twenty detonators, the prosecution claimed.[188]

Sarwar also purchased more than forty liters of hydrogen peroxide from a variety of outlets. By the time of his arrest, he had stored enough hydrogen peroxide to boil it down to fourteen liters of 93 percent by volume, enough to make twenty-eight half-liter bottles. The jury was told that their bomb design had striking similarities to explosives used in previous U.K. terrorist plots. Hydrogen peroxide was the main ingredient in the explosives used in both the July 7 and July 21 plots, and HMTD was also used as the detonator in the July 7 attack. In the failed July 21 attack, al-Qaeda operatives had built detonators using a different substance—TATP—but it had failed to explode the main charge. Prosecutors claimed that this was the reason the airline plotters reverted to HMTD.[189]

In their preparatory work in the bomb factory, Ali and Tanvir Hussain drilled holes in the sports drink bottles to drain them; the plan was to refill them with the explosive mixture and reseal the bottles with superglue.[190] Ali also figured out how to remove the AA battery contents in order to insert the HMTD.[191] Beyond that, they were working on modifying disposable cameras to act as triggers and modifying subminiature light bulbs to carry the current to the detonator. By the time of their arrest, they had modified and tested eighteen light bulbs.[192]

As the plotters geared up to launch their attacks, they also had some downtime. Ali, Tanvir Hussain, Ibrahim Savant, and Waheed Arafat Khan met for several games of tennis in late July and early August on courts in Walthamstow.[193] Ali continued to be in touch with Rauf during this period. At trial Ali claimed he did not need detailed help: "Regarding the electronics, I've got a degree in computer systems engineering and in that we did about three or four modules in electronics or digital electronics so I was familiar with the electronics so I didn't need his help as of yet, but if I would have got stuck I would have probably asked him."[194]

The plotters were unaware that on July 31, MI5 broke into the apartment and installed an audio probe. By August 3, agents had also installed a video probe to record their every move.[195] The jury heard how that day investigators watched as Ali and Tanvir Hussain made an apparent breakthrough in their bomb design. "That's the boom," one said, followed later by the phrase, "We've got our virgins."[196] Prosecutors said the comment referred to the rewards the men hoped to receive in the afterlife for carrying out their impending suicide mission.[197] During the same session Ali and Tanvir Hussain appeared to count the number of recruits they had for the suicide mission. Hussain appeared to count eighteen individuals in total.[198] Later that day Ali wrote an e-mail to Rauf: "By the way, I've set up my mobile shop now. Now I only need to sort out an opening time." Rauf replied from Pakistan: "Do your opening timetable. Give your girlies a big up from me."[199] By this time, Ali had become increasingly concerned that British security services were following him, Rauf later revealed. "I told him not to panic," Rauf wrote.[200]

On August 3, Tanvir and Ali were still waiting for Sarwar to deliver the concentrated hydrogen peroxide. They were overheard saying they were "waiting for HP" and that "he's got to boil it down."[201] Ali and Tanvir were also waiting for Sarwar to deliver the HMTD for the hollowed-out batteries. One of them was overheard saying, "It ain't a hydrogen bomb 'till the batteries." The deliveries never came. When he was arrested six days later, Sarwar had not yet started concentrating hydrogen peroxide or making HMTD.[202] His slow pace frustrated Rauf. On August 6, Sarwar sent Ali an e-mail claiming that "Joseph" (another codename for Rauf) "had a go at me because I haven't sorted my things."[203]

On the morning of August 6, 2006, authorities grew increasingly concerned when they observed Ali, the cell leader, looking up timetables for transatlantic flights departing between August and October 2006.[204] That same morning Sarwar searched for additional hydrogen peroxide suppliers on the Internet before making calls to Ali and Gulzar. Minutes later, according to British authorities, Gulzar phoned Rauf in Pakistan to tell him the latest developments.[205] That night Ali, Sarwar, and Gulzar met in east London. Prosecutors described the meeting as a key "summit" among the ringleaders as it was the only time the three of them met in person.[206] British agents were secretly watching them.[207] Gulzar, at trial, denied the meeting had anything to do with a terrorist plot. He stated Sarwar set up the meeting with Ali so Ali could provide him merchandise for him to sell.[208]

AUTHORITIES MOVE IN

On August 8, 2006, at his ranch in Crawford, Texas, President George W. Bush was briefed on the case. Secretary Chertoff of Homeland Security would not disclose the president's specific comments but told NBC, "Generally, the president's concerns were, first and foremost, 'Let's make sure no lives get lost.'" Counterterrorism sources told NBC News that by that time, U.S. intelligence services were tracking the movements of Rashid Rauf, the suspected al-Qaeda point man in Pakistan, and officials saw indications that Rauf might try to travel the tribal areas of Pakistan, where they feared he could evade capture. Counterterrorism investigators indicated to NBC that the situation created some friction between international allies. U.S. officials did not want to risk losing Rauf and pressed the Pakistani authorities to arrest him immediately. British officials preferred to wait a few more days to gather more intelligence and evidence. The Pakistanis found themselves in the middle, according to a former senior Pakistani official with knowledge of the investigation. The former official described the pressure from the United States as "enormous."[209]

On August 9, the case reached critical mass: bugs planted in the terrorist safe house picked up audio of one of the men, Umar Islam, recording a suicide video, the first time investigators were aware of a suicide video being produced.[210] In conversation with Ali, Umar Islam asked, "What's the time-frame? . . . how long we got to go?" Ali replied "a couple of weeks." Chillingly, the duo also discussed the possibility of their wives participating in the mission. "If I was to say to her that this one was a significant operation she might even find herself to do that," Islam said of his pregnant wife. Islam also remarked, "This mission is a great mission. It's not easy man."[211]

Rauf was in frequent contact with the alleged U.K. ringleaders on August 9, underlining his micromanagement of the plot's developments. In the early afternoon, British authorities allege that Gulzar called Rauf in Pakistan to ask him to call Sarwar, whom he could not reach. Rauf obliged but could not get through because Sarwar was busy buying ten more liters of hydrogen peroxide at a supplier in London. According to prosecutors, Gulzar, in frustration, then tried to call Sarwar, the only time he made a direct call to him from his own cell phone.[212] In the late afternoon, aware of the planned purchases, Rauf sent Ali a text asking him, "How much stock has CMG [Sarwar] bought? Better to get as much as possible."[213] A few minutes later, with Gulzar still unable to get through to Sarwar, Rauf again intervened, sending Sarwar a text saying, "Yaq [prosecutors stated this was Gulzar, which Gulzar denied] says switch your phone on. I have left you email. I don't know about the leather belts."[214] At seven p.m. U.K. time (eleven p.m. Pakistani time), Rauf sent one more text to Ali stating, "I will text you to let you know when we can chat."[215]

That was Rauf's last communication. Less than two hours later, Pakistani authorities arrested him near Bahawalpur in southern Punjab. The U.S. intelligence agencies who had been tracking his communications electronically had informed their Pakistani counterparts of his location.[216]

In his report on the plot, Rauf recounted his arrest in detail. He wrote that Pakistani security services arrested him on a bus after it was pulled over by elite Pakistani police wielding Kalashnikovs. He realized he had mistakenly left his phone turned on, which he believed was how the United States had tracked him. As he struggled to turn it off, he was taken into police custody, a hood was placed over his head, and he was transferred to an army camp.[217] British officials were informed shortly after he was arrested. They immediately ordered the cell rounded up. British police feared that if the plotters found out about Rauf's arrest, it could serve as a "go signal" to trigger an attack. Andy Hayman later told NBC: "Given how high the stakes were, you couldn't second guess."[218]

British and U.S. authorities were satisfied that they had neutralized the threat from all the main players in the airline plot in the U.K.[219] MI5 believes that several individuals recruited as suicide bombers may still be at large.[220] "We don't stop thinking about those individuals, it's a real worry," said one British counterterrorism source.[221] Rauf, in his report on the plot, wrote that two of those he had been informed were ready to carry out martyrdom operations were not arrested by police because the plotters in the U.K. had not yet reached out to them to brief them on the plan at the time of their arrest.[222]

In June 2007 a British Indian extremist from the north of England, then eighteen or nineteen years old, who can only be identified as "AM" was placed under a Control Order for suspected ties to the airline plotters.

British security services asserted that AM had traveled to Pakistan for terrorist training in 2004–2005, had contact with, and may have met with Rauf and senior the al-Qaeda operative Abu Ubaydah al-Masri. They also asserted that just before British police moved in to make arrests in August 2006, one of the plot's ringleaders established contact with AM to brief him on his role in the overall plot.[223]

According to a senior U.S. intelligence source made privy to the report of his interrogation by Pakistani authorities, Rauf admitted to the "airline dimension" of the plot.[224] Rauf wrote that Pakistani authorities were initially "very happy at pleasing their U.S. masters," but when they found out that Rauf had trained in Kashmir, they feared the United States would blame them and blocked the British and Americans from accessing him for questioning.[225]

Astonishingly Rauf managed to escape from Pakistani custody in December 2007. It took almost a year to track him down, during which he was able to follow the progress of the trial of the airline plot cell in the U.K. In November 2008, Rauf was reported killed in a U.S. Predator drone strike in North Waziristan in Pakistan's tribal areas.[226]

CONTINUED SECURITY CONCERNS

The airline plot case highlighted severe vulnerabilities at the time in airline security. John Reid, who oversaw the investigation as U.K. home secretary in 2006, told NBC that he had no doubt that the bomb could have worked. "They had the components. And they had them cunningly, very sophisticated, but very simply made as everyday commodities that you might take onto a plane with you."[227] Liquid explosives were used precisely because they would not be picked up by metal detectors.

In 2008, *Dateline NBC*, in conjunction with the British broadcaster ITN, commissioned a demonstration of the planned bombs by an explosives expert. It showed that a device similar to the one described in the court case—a half-liter hydrogen peroxide explosive with an HMTD detonator—could blow a hole in the side of an airplane.[228] After the airline plot was broken up, new security regulations were introduced limiting the volume of liquids passenger could take on airplanes to minimize the risk that terrorists could bring sufficient quantities of liquid explosive on board to inflict structural damage to an aircraft.

––––––––––

Of all the terrorist plots since 9/11, the airline plot was "exhibit A" in demonstrating the danger posed by al-Qaeda's organized structures in Pakistan. The plot was no less ambitious in its scope and complexity than the 9/11 attack itself and had many similarities. In both cases, key plotters radicalized in Europe and operationalized in al-Qaeda's training camps. There is no evidence Abdulla Ahmed Ali nor Mohammed Atta was seeking to launch attacks against the United States when they first traveled to South Asia, but al-Qaeda persuaded them to lead suicide-attack plots. The airline plotters had no less potential for destruction than the men who carried out the 9/11 attacks. "If the plotters had not been stopped," Andy Hayman told NBC, "I believe they would have been successful."[229]

Although the airline plotters did not meet bin Laden like the 9/11 hijackers or attend the sorts of large camps that al-Qaeda maintained in Afghanistan, al-Qaeda, through Rauf, arguably exerted as much command and control over the planes operation as they did over the 9/11 attacks. Rauf—in many ways the Ramzi Binalshibh of the airlines plot—appears to have contacted Ali, the acquitted Gulzar, and Sarwar in the U.K. more frequently than Binalshibh contacted Atta in the United States.[230] As with the 9/11 attacks, the airline plot saw al-Qaeda draw on assets across the globe from its South Asian hub, as evidenced by the dispatching of Mohammed Gulzar, the alleged plot supervisor, to the U.K. from South Africa in July 2006 to oversee final preparations for the attack. Gulzar's alleged supervisory role, though not proven beyond a reasonable doubt in front of a jury, demonstrated—if true—the continued importance of hierarchical structures within the al-Qaeda organization. Moreover, Rauf's account revealed that al-Masri was the driving force behind the plot and received briefings on progress from Rauf. Furthermore, in Ali, the U.K. cell had a clearly designated "emir."

The airline plot demonstrated al-Qaeda's continued ability to recruit and train Western-based operatives. Rauf's account revealed that Ali was recruited into al-Qaeda after he put him in touch with al-Masri. The plot illustrated in particular the potential threat posed by British-born radicals and the potential for Britain to serve as a staging ground for attacks against the United States, something policy makers need to consider. That radicalization levels are probably higher in Britain than any other Western country, many British militants have close family ties back to Pakistan, and trained British operatives can theoretically board planes to the United States without needing to obtain visas mean that British radicals trained by al-Qaeda in Pakistan have emerged as a primary national security threat to the United States.[231]

The plot also underlined the threat posed by al-Qaeda's safe haven in FATA as several members of the U.K. cell received explosives training there. After a failed Pakistani military offensive in South Waziristan in March 2004, al-Qaeda was able to strengthen its position in the FATA.[232] In 2007, a U.S. National Intelligence Estimate found that al-Qaeda had regenerated its capabilities to attack the United States from these areas.[233]

The airline plot made clear that greater monitoring was needed of Western militants traveling to Pakistan. For several years afterward, the numbers traveling to FATA continued to rise.[234] Dozens of Western recruits trained with al-Qaeda or its affiliates in the tribal areas in the years since the airline plot was broken up. Those sent back to the West to launch attacks included four Germans convicted of plotting to target U.S. troops in Germany in 2007; an al-Qaeda terrorist cell (also recruited by Rauf) led by Najibullah Zazi, an Afghan who grew up in Queens, New York, who pleaded guilty to plotting to blow up targets in New York City in 2009; a German resident who plotted to attack Dusseldorf in April 2011; and several members of an alleged Birmingham terrorist cell in arrested in September 2011.[235] In several of the terrorist conspiracies linked to FATA, like in the Airline plot, plotters had started preparing components for Hydrogen Peroxide bombs, which had increasingly become al-Qaeda's weapon of choice for attacks in the West.[236]

Despite increased military pressure from Pakistan on militants in the North West Frontier Province and some parts of the tribal areas and an intensification of the number of drone strikes, counterterrorism officials believe that significant swaths of the tribal areas remained a safe haven for al-Qaeda and its allies in the years after the airline plot.[237] The interrogation of several of the Western recruits who trained with al-Qaeda in the tribal areas from 2008 through 2011 illustrated that al-Qaeda continued to be able to offer recruits bomb-making training, including instruction in high explosives. The recruits revealed that al-Qaeda had adapted to drone strikes by decentralizing their operations and conducting training inside mountain shacks rather than out in the open. However, by 2014 al-Qaeda's capability to orchestrate international terrorist attacks from the Afghanistan-Pakistan border region had diminished because of attrition caused by drone strikes and the "brain drain" created by operatives returning to the Arab world to take advantage of the political turmoil of the Arab Spring and the civil war in Syria. Anecdotal evidence from Western recruits suggested a significant deterioration in the quantity and quality of terrorist training on offer. But the recent strengthening of a broad network of al-Qaeda-affiliated and -linked groups in the Arab world has created a new set of national security challenges for Western countries. Despite losing control of territory, al-Qaeda's affiliate in Yemen remains a potent threat. It is sobering that though responsible for three failed plots against U.S. aviation, the group has to date dedicated only a fraction of its resources to international terrorist operations because of its focus on Yemen. No jihadist front has created more concern than Syria. By early 2014 almost 2,000 Europeans had traveled to fight there, with many joining al-Qaeda-affiliated groups. If al-Qaeda's affiliates in Syria, currently focused on fighting the "near enemy," prioritize hitting the West in the future they will be well positioned to offer these recruits the same type of bomb-making training that the airline plotters received, and send them back to launch attacks.[238]

While more plots may have been hatched in the West by homegrown cells acting autonomously from al-Qaeda than by al-Qaeda itself in recent years, many of the most dangerous plots, such as the airline plot, the July 7 bombings in London, and the 2009 "underwear" bombing have had deep connections to the organized structures of al-Qaeda. According to a study by this author for the New America Foundation, al-Qaeda or its allies in Pakistan had direct operational ties to 44 percent of "serious" terrorist plots against the West between January 2004 and July 2011. Plotters received training in Pakistan from these groups in 53 percent of these serious plots.[239] Arguably, these findings reflect the fact that homegrown cells tend not to have the sort of terrorist tradecraft or bomb-making expertise that al-Qaeda operatives develop during training in terrorist camps. Al-Qaeda has inculcated a heightened sense of mission and Islamic obligation in its recruits in the mountains of northwestern Pakistan.

Testimony in the airline plot trial confirmed that it is much more difficult than is generally realized to make a bomb from commercially available chemicals by downloading instructions from the Internet. According to a Western explosives expert, making HMTD detonators is a particularly tricky enterprise because of how unstable it is as a compound.[240] While Sarwar spent a significant amount of time conducting Internet research in preparation for the attacks, it is revealing that he felt it necessary to travel to Pakistan to receive instruction on how to make the high explosive HMTD. Ali testified in court that he conducted research on the Web about how to make explosive devices but found online sites to be "a bit wishy washy, and not very detailed." Ali added, "The whole point of us learning how to do it from someone who's done it before or someone would know about the thing is obviously it's quite dangerous dealing with these materials. We don't want to injure ourselves or anything."[241]

As Rauf himself indicated, the airline plotters' connections with the top echelons of al-Qaeda appeared to give them a sense of purpose and drive that has sometimes been lacking among "homegrown wannabes." "This mission is a great mission," Umar Islam said to Ali just before they were arrested, underlining the plotters' appreciation that they were part of a leader-led jihad. "Sheikh Osama warned you many times to leave our lands or you will be destroyed and now the time has come for you to be destroyed," said Ali in his suicide tape, apparently relishing being under al-Qaeda senior leadership's direct orders. While the airline plotters were being directed from overseas, they still had to show significant self-initiative in preparing the attacks. There is no evidence that al-Qaeda leaders provided the cell with direct financing as they did for the 9/11 plotters.[242]

If successful, the plot would have killed thousands and would have had repercussions for the global economy. It would also have been a huge propaganda victory for an al-Qaeda organization approaching the height of its power and reach. In Iraq, al-Qaeda suicide bombers had plunged the country into a virtual civil war, and al-Qaeda fighters were increasingly gaining control of territory. In Pakistan, al-Qaeda was regenerating its operational capabilities in the northwestern tribal areas. Israel's military operation in southern Lebanon had also led to a spike in anti-American sentiment in the Muslim world. There could hardly have been a better time than the summer of 2006 for al-Qaeda to strike a blow against the far enemy. When the plot was broken up the silence from al-Qaeda's leaders was deafening, clearly showing their disappointment.

NOTES

1. Richard Greenberg, Paul Cruickshank, and Chris Hansen, "Inside the Terror Plot That 'Rivaled 9/11,'" *Dateline NBC*, September 14, 2009.

2. Author's notes from opening day of airline plot retrial, Woolwich Crown Court, London, February 17, 2009.

3. Greenberg, Cruickshank, and Hansen, "Inside the Terror Plot That 'Rivaled 9/11'"; "Trio Guilty of Suicide Bomb Plot," *BBC*, July 8, 2010; Sean O'Neill, "Bomb Plot Leader's Friends Convicted of Terror Offences," *Times* (London), December 10, 2009.

4. Regina v. Abdulla Ahmed Ali [a.k.a. Ahmed Ali Khan], Assad Sarwar, Tanvir Hussain, Ibrahim Savant, Arafat Waheed Khan, Waheed Zaman and Umar Islam [a.k.a. Brian Young], Woolwich Crown Court, Official Transcript of Court Proceedings, April 3, 2008, 1–29. The author attended portions of the trial and obtained and reviewed more than 5,000 pages of official transcripts of the proceedings.

5. Regina v. Ali et al., April 3, 2008, 3, 16–29, 31–32; Greenberg, Cruickshank, and Hansen, "Inside the Terror Plot That 'Rivaled 9/11.'"

6. Regina v. Ali et al., April 3, 2008, 41, 8, 25.

7. Interview by telephone with Metropolitan Police Investigator, London, March 2009.

8. See Nic Robertson, Paul Cruickshank, and Tim Lister, "Document Shows Origins of 2006 Plot for Liquid Bombs on Planes," CNN, April 30, 2012. The Al-Qaeda point person, Rashid Rauf, wrote in an internal al-Qaeda report on the plot that nine suicide bombers had been recruited in the U.K. The document was discovered on an al-Qaeda recruit in Berlin by German authorities in the spring of 2011.

9. Greenberg, Cruickshank and Hansen, "Inside the Terror Plot That 'Rivaled 9/11.'"

10. Regina v. Ali et al., April 3, 2008, 15, 21, 21–29, 29.

11. Greenberg, Cruickshank and Hansen, "Inside the Terror Plot That 'Rivaled 9/11.'"

12. Ibid.

13. The plotters had stored enough hydrogen peroxide to concentrate 14 liters at 93 percent weight per volume, enough for 28 half-liter bottle bombs, and had the chemicals necessary to make 100g of HMTD, enough for 20 detonators. They had also already adapted and tested 18 subminiature light bulbs, which they intended to use as a trigger for the device. Regina v. Ali et al., June 4, 2008, 133–34.

14. British and American counterterrorism officials stated that the plot was only weeks from being put into operation. However, it does not appear that the plotters

had settled on an exact date to launch the operation. Their aim seemed to be to purchase air tickets only a few days before. An entry in a diary seized from Ali, the U.K. ringleader, in which he had sketched out plans for the attack, read "Select Date. Five days B4" (Regina v. Ali et al.).

15. Regina v. Ali et al.

16. Lieutenant General Michael D. Maples, "Current and Projected National Security Threats to the United Stats," Senate Select Committee on Intelligence, January 11, 2007.

17. Zawahiri videotape, al-Jazeera, March 4, 2006.

18. Regina v. Ali et al. Ali denied plotting to bring down planes, instead arguing that the final plan he settled on was to set off devices at terminal buildings in Heathrow to cause panic. The aim was not to kill, Ali claimed, but to gain publicity for a YouTube documentary he wanted to put together on U.S. and British "oppression" of Muslims overseas. In the context of his claimed plan, Ali admitted to researching when flights left Heathrow for Canada so that Canadians would be in the terminals when the devices went off.

19. Thomas H. Kean et al., *The 9/11 Commission Report: Final Report of the National Commission on Terrorist Attacks Upon the United States* (New York: Norton, 2004), 147. Demonstrating the ease with which liquid explosives could be smuggled through security, Youssef even successfully tested a small version of the device on a Philippines airliner in late 1994, which killed a Japanese businessman who was sitting above the bomb.

20. Kean et al., *The 9/11 Commission Report*, 148.

21. Robertson, Cruickshank, and Lister, "Document Shows Origins of 2006 Plot for Liquid Bombs on Planes."

22. Greenberg, Cruickshank, and Hansen, "Inside the Terror Plot That 'Rivaled 9/11'"; Kim Barker, "In Pakistani Village Disbelief at Allegations of Terror Plot," *Chicago Tribune*, August 20, 2006.

23. The ties between JeM and al-Qaeda date back to the 1980s Afghan Jihad.

24. Nic Robertson, Paul Cruickshank, and Tim Lister, "Documents Give New Details on al Qaeda's London Bombings," CNN, April 30, 2012.

25. In an interview with *Dateline NBC*, the senior British Metropolitan Police investigator Andy Hayman refused to comment directly on that possibility. "Until you absolutely know for sure through evidence, intelligence what happened when they went to Pakistan, you could never reliably answer that question. But," adds Hayman, "on the balance of probability, do you not find it rather strange that the country that they visited, and whatever went on there precipitated them coming back to the UK and committing acts of terrorism? I leave that open for others to draw their own conclusions" (Greenberg, Cruickshank, and Hansen, "Inside the Terror Plot That 'Rivaled 9/11'").

26. Greenberg, Cruickshank, and Hansen, "Inside the Terror Plot That 'Rivaled 9/11.'"

27. Greenberg, Cruickshank, and Hansen, "Inside the Terror Plot That 'Rivaled 9/11.'"

28. Interview with U.S. counterterrorism source, March 2009.

29. Bruce Hoffman, "Who Is Abu Ubaidah al-Masri and Why Should We Care? An Obituary", *InSITE: The Official Newsletter of the SITE Intelligence Group*, 1, no. 2 (May 7, 2008): 3–6; Laura Marie Sørensen, "Al-Qaeda-leder trænede dansk terrorist," *Politiken*, October 11, 2009.

30. Bruce Hoffman, "Who is Abu Ubaidah al-Masri and Why Should We Care?"

31. Ali traveled to Pakistan in 2003, 2004, 2005, and 2006 (Regina v. Ali et al.). It is conceivable that Ali, the U.K. ringleader, met with al-Libi on one of his trips to Pakistan. The two had a mutual acquaintance: Mohammed al-Ghabra, a gym buddy of Ali in east London who stayed with al-Libi in Pakistan in 2002 (interview with Hanif Qadir, London, August 2008). Before Ali's arrest, Qadir often observed Ali and al-Ghabra training together at the Walthamstow gym he owns. Al-Ghabra, a naturalized British citizen born in Damascus in 1980, was designated an al-Qaeda facilitator by U.S. authorities several months after the airline plot was thwarted (US Department of the Treasury, "Treasury Designates Individual Supporting Al Qaida, Other Terrorist Organizations," December 19, 2006).

32. Personal Communication with Western counterterrorism source, 2012.

33. Osama bin Laden audiotape, first aired on al-Jazeera, January 19, 2006.

34. Greenberg, Cruickshank, and Hansen, "Inside the Terror Plot That 'Rivaled 9/11.'"

35. Personal interview with senior U.S. counterterrorism official, April 2012.

36. Interview by telephone with Metropolitan Police investigator, London, March 2009. Assad Sarwar, the "bomb chemist" of the airline plot testified at trial that he received bomb-making instruction from a certain "Jamil" in Pakistan and had established a code so that further instructions could be transmitted by e-mail and text message. The investigator said that they had established that Jamil was almost certainly an alias for Rashid Rauf.

37. Interview by telephone with Metropolitan Police investigator, London, March 2009.

38. Interview with Peter Clarke, London, June 2009.

39. Robertson, Cruickshank, and Lister, "Document Shows Origins of 2006 Plot for Liquid Bombs on Planes."

40. Interview by telephone with Metropolitan Police investigator, London, March 2009.

41. Biographical data on the twelve men charged was drawn from the trial of eight of their number and interviews the author conducted with British investigators.

42. Greenberg, Cruickshank, and Hansen, "Inside the Terror Plot That 'Rivaled 9/11.'"

43. Interview by telephone with Metropolitan Police investigator, London, March 2009. Additionally, Mohammed Usman Saddique, from east London, was charged

when he was twenty-four with "engaging in conduct in preparation for an act of terrorism with intent to carry out such an act," but a judge dismissed the case against him in 2010.

44. Interview by telephone with Metropolitan Police Investigator, London, March 2009.

45. Greenberg, Cruickshank, and Hansen "Inside the Terror Plot That 'Rivaled 9/11.'"

46. Regina v. Ali et al., June 4, 2008, 35–37, 58.

47. Regina v. Ali et al., June 2, 2008, 10, and June 18, 2008, 21–22.

48. Interview by telephone with Metropolitan Police investigator, London, June 2009.

49. Regina v. Ali et al., April 4 (morning session), 1–24.

50. Interview with Hanif and Imtiaz Qadir, London, August 2008; Greenberg, Cruickshank, and Hansen, "Inside the Terror Plot That 'Rivaled 9/11.'"

51. Regina v. Ali et al., June 2, 2008, 1–14.

52. David Harrison and Adam Lusher, "Abdulla Ahmed Ali: A Terrorist in the Making at the Age of Fourteen," *Daily Telegraph* (London), September 13, 2008.

53. Regina v. Ali et al., June 2, 2008, 3–6.

54. Harrison and Lusher, "Abdulla Ahmed Ali."

55. Regina v. Ali et al., June 2, 2008, 10. Several of those implicated in terrorist plots in recent years, such as 7/7 ringleader Mohammed Siddique Khan and several members of other plots in Europe, were once members of Tablighi Jamaat. The criticism may be somewhat unfair. Tablighi supporters point out that with hundreds of thousands of members around the world, and tens of thousands in the U.K., it is not statistically surprising that some have involved themselves with terrorism. Additionally, they point out that Tablighi is largely apolitical, focusing on preaching a pure Islamic lifestyle. Nevertheless, Tablighi does appear to some extent to have become a recruiting ground for violent extremists. A relatively low emphasis on Islamic jurisprudence combined with the zealousness of many of its members may make them vulnerable to terrorist recruiters.

56. Regina v. Ali et al., June 2, 2008, 11, 13–14.

57. Harrison and Lusher, "Abdulla Ahmed Ali."

58. Regina v. Ali et al., April 4, 2008, 16–17.

59. Regina v. Ali et al., June 2, 2008, 16.

60. Interview with Imtiaz Qadir, London, August 2008.

61. Regina v. Ali et al., June 2, 2008, 22–25.

62. Greenberg, Cruickshank, and Hansen, "Inside the Terror Plot That 'Rivaled 9/11.'"

63. Regina v. Ali et al., June 2, 2008, 25.

64. Regina v. Ali et al., June 4, 2008, 139. British authorities have not, however, accused the IMA of any wrongdoing. The head of the charity, Mohammed Patel, was placed under investigation in 2006 for his ties to several members of the plot, but authorities were not able to collect sufficient evidence to press charges against him.

65. Regina v. Ali et al., June 2, 2008, 17–26.

66. Greenberg, Cruickshank, and Hansen, "Inside the Terror Plot That 'Rivaled 9/11.'"

67. Regina v. Ali et al., June 2, 2008, 27.

68. Regina v. Ali et al., June 9, 2008, 116.

69. Regina v. Ali et al., June 9, 2008, 1–123, 137–38, 124.

70. Regina v. Ali et al., June 2, 2008, 34, 77.

71. Regina v. Ali et al., June 3, 2008, 112.

72. Regina v. Ali et al., June 2, 2008, 40.

73. Duncan Gardham, "Young Mother Denies Failing to Inform on Her Husband," *Daily Telegraph* (London), August 23, 2006; "Airline Bomb Plotter's Wife Cleared of Terror Charge, BBC, March 5, 2010.

74. Regina v. Ali et al., June 2, 2008, 40–50.

75. Regina v. Ali et al., June 2, 2008, 53.

76. Robertson, Cruickshank, and Lister, "Document Shows Origins of 2006 Plot for Liquid Bombs on Planes."

77. Regina v. Ali et al., June 2, 2008, 54.

78. Interview with an acquaintance of Ali living in Walthamstow, London, August 2008.

79. Regina v. Ali et al., June 2, 2008, 60.

80. Interview by telephone with Metropolitan Police investigator, London, June 2009.

81. Robertson, Cruickshank, and Lister, "Document Shows Origins of 2006 Plot for Liquid Bombs on Planes."

82. Regina v. Ali et al., June 9, 2009, 151.

83. Interview with Metropolitan Police investigator, London, February 2009.

84. Interview by phone with Metropolitan Police investigator, London, June 2009.

85. Robertson, Cruickshank, and Lister, "Document Shows Origins of 2006 Plot for Liquid Bombs on Planes."

86. Regina v. Ali et al., June 2, 2008, 86–100, 98; June 5, 49.

87. Greenberg, Cruickshank, and Hansen, "Inside the Terror Plot That 'Rivaled 9/11.'"

88. Regina v. Ali et al. The Bacton document retrieved from Sarwar's memory stick was created on February 22, 2006; last written on March 12, 2006; and last accessed on March 16, 2006.

89. Regina v. Ali et al.

90. Robertson, Cruickshank, and Lister, "Document Shows Origins of 2006 Plot for Liquid Bombs on Planes."

91. Regina v. Ali et al., June 10, 2008, 22.

92. Robertson, Cruickshank, and Lister, "Document Shows Origins of 2006 Plot for Liquid Bombs on Planes."

93. Ibid.

94. Duncan Gardham, "Airliner Bomb Trial: How MI5 Uncovered the Terror Plot," *Daily Telegraph* (London), September 9, 2008.

95. Greenberg, Cruickshank, and Hansen, "Inside the Terror Plot That 'Rivaled 9/11.'"

96. Interview by telephone with Metropolitan Police investigator, London, March 2009.

97. Regina v. Ali et al., June 11, 2008, 21.

98. Robertson, Cruickshank, and Lister, "Document Shows Origins of 2006 Plot for Liquid Bombs on Planes."

99. Greenberg, Cruickshank, and Hansen, "Inside the Terror Plot That 'Rivaled 9/11.'"

100. Interview by telephone with Metropolitan Police investigator, London, March 2009.

101. Regina v. Ali et al., June 19, 2008, 142.

102. Robertson, Cruickshank, and Lister, "Document Shows Origins of 2006 Plot for Liquid Bombs on Planes."

103. In 2006 Tanvir Hussain went to Pakistan between February and April, Ali between May and June, and Sarwar between June and July (Regina v. Ali et al.).

104. Greenberg, Cruickshank, and Hansen, "Inside the Terror Plot That 'Rivaled 9/11.'"

105. While Ali did meet with some of the conspirators, many of whom were his friends, when he returned, these meetings were not of a length or frequency to suggest he was "cold-recruiting" them. It is possible he was checking to see whether they were still committed to carrying out an attack (interview by telephone with Metropolitan Police investigator, London, March 2009).

106. Personal Interview with senior U.S. counterterrorisim official, October 2009.

107. Robertson, Cruickshank, and Lister, "Document Shows Origins of 2006 Plot for Liquid Bombs on Planes."

108. Regina v. Ali et al.

109. Seven of the plotters were from Ali's east London circle of friends. Ali went to school with Khan and Savant, two of the "foot soldiers" in the plot. Ali knew Zaman through Savant and Tanvir Hussain through Khan. Osman Adam Khatib was the younger brother of his best friend. Nabeel Hussain and Mohammed Usman Siddique were part of Ali's Walthamstow circle. Ali got to know Sarwar and Umar Islam through the IMA charity. Don Stewart-Whyte was introduced to him by Sarwar (interview by telephone with Metropolitan Police investigator, London, March 2009; testimony in Regina v. Ali et al.).

110. Regina v. Ali et al., June 4, 2008, 57–58, June 26, 2008, 143.

111. Before the arrests Tanvir Hussain successfully applied for loans totalling £8,000, Savant £10,000, and Khan £8,000. Applications by the alleged plotters for a further £51,000 ($83,000) in financing were either still pending (£8,000), about to be submitted (£8,000), or denied (£35,000) when they were arrested (Regina v. Ali et al.,

May 13, 2008, 105–106). An al-Qaeda cell plotting to blow up targets around London with a fertilizer bombs in 2004, which was thwarted by Operation Crevice, also fraudulently applied for loans. See "Profile: Omar Khyam," BBC, April 30, 2007.

112. Personal interview with Western counterterrorism source, 2012.

113. Robertson, Cruickshank, and Lister, "Document Shows Origins of 2006 Plot for Liquid Bombs on Planes."

114. Regina v. Ali et al., April 4, 2008, 34; interview with senior British counterterrorism source, London, February 2009.

115. Regina v. Ali et al., April 4,2008, 23.

116. Interview with senior British counter-terrorism source, London, February 2009.

117. Israel's bombing campaign, which was initiated on July 12 after Hezbollah abducted several Israeli soldiers in the border region of the two countries, created intense anger in the Muslim world not only against Israel but also against Britain and the United States because of their refusal to demand an immediate cease-fire. By the time hostilities ended in mid-August more than a thousand Lebanese had been killed. There was further anger at the United States because of its weapons supplies to the Israeli military. One of the plotters, Waheed Zaman, alluded to this in his suicide tape, "America and England have no cause for complaint for they are the ones . . . who supply weapons to the enemies of Islam, including the accursed Israelis." British police sources say it was a war that may have accelerated Gulzar's plans to travel to London as he bought his airline ticket two days after the outbreak of hostilities. In court Ali testified that the situation in Lebanon did affect the cell's timing. "We said we should try and speed things up a bit. This would be the best opportunity to do anything while the Lebanon situation was going on," Ali recalled Sarwar and him agreeing when he met Sarwar in east London on July 15, a week after Sarwar's return from Pakistan.

118. Interview by telephone with Metropolitan Police investigator, London, June 2009.

119. Barker, "In Pakistani Village Disbelief at Allegations of Terror Plot."

120. Cahal Milmo et al., "From Birmingham Bakery to Pakistani Prison, the Mystery of Rashid Rauf," Independent (London), August 19, 2006.

121. Regina v. Ali et al., June 18, 200 21–22.

122. Jason Burke, "Top British Terror Suspect Killed in US Missile Strike," Observer (London), November 23, 2008.

123. Milmo et al., "From Birmingham Bakery to Pakistani Prison."

124. Greenberg, Cruickshank, and Hansen, "Inside the Terror Plot That 'Rivaled 9/11.'"

125. JeM and al-Qaeda are believed to be closely affiliated (Ian Cobain and Matthew Weaver, "Rashid Rauf: The Mysterious Life of a Birmingham Baker's Boy Turned Alleged Al-Qaida Terrorist," Guardian, November 22, 2008).

126. Regina v. Ali et al., June 18, 2008, 31.

127. Ibid., 45–48.

128. Interview with senior U.S. counterterrorism source, 2009.

129. Ibid; "South African Police Said Investigating Presence of Al Qa'ida cells," *Radio 702* (South Africa), August 4, 2005. Duncan Gardham, "Rashid Rauf's Connections to Terror," *Daily Telegraph* (London), September 8, 2009. In the weeks after the 2005 London bombings, several news reports stated that the 7/7 plotters phoned a number linked to Aswat in South Africa before the attacks, but British authorities did not charge him with any involvement. See Richard Woods, David Leppard, and Mick Smith, "Tangled Web That Leaves Worrying Loose Ends," *Sunday Times* (London), July 31, 2005.

130. Interview with senior U.S. counterterrorism source, 2009

131. United States v. Aswat et al., superseding indictment, February 6, 2006 (S.D.-N.Y.); "Al Qaeda Suspect Denies Terror Links," *Daily Telegraph* (London), August 8, 2005

132. Interview with senior British counterterrorism source, London, February 2009.

133. Regina v. Ali et al., June 18, 2008, 63–64; interview with Hanif Qadir, London, August 2008. In South Africa, Ghabra allegedly dropped off a laptop which he had obtained in the U.K. from Assad Sarwar, the bomb chemist. Gulzar would take the computer with him to the U.K.

134. Ghabra, a naturalized British citizen born in Damascus in 1980, was designated an al-Qaeda facilitator by U.S. authorities several months after the airline plot was thwarted (U.S. Department of the Treasury, "Treasury Designates Individual Supporting Al Qaida, Other Terrorist Organizations," December 19, 2006). Mohammed Patel, Abdel Manem Patel, and Mohammed al-Ghabra were investigated by police in connection with the airline plot. Police, however, failed to find sufficient evidence to charge them in relation to the conspiracy (personal interview with Metropolitan Police investigator, London, February 2009). The younger Patel was convicted in 2007 for possession of a bomb-making manual. See "Explosives Manual Teenager Jailed," BBC, October 26, 2007.

135. Regina v. Ali et al., June 18, 2008, 67–68.

136. Regina v. Ali et al., June 18, 2009, 1–154.

137. Regina v. Ali et al., June 18, 2008, 6–154.

138. Ibid., 154.

139. Regina v. Ali et al., June 23, 2008, 1–2.

140. Regina v. Ali et al., June 24, 2008, 24–25.

141. Regina v. Ali et al., June 5, 2008, 102.

142. Interview by telephone with Metropolitan Police investigator, London, March 2009.

143. Regina v. Ali et al., June 19, 2008, 35, 75.

144. Regina v. Ali et al., June 24, 2008, 29.

145. Interview by telephone with Metropolitan Police investigator, London, March 2009.

146. When confronted with evidence of communication with phone numbers in Pakistan, Ali testified that he had been in contact with an individual called "Yusuf"; Sarwar said he knew his contact as "Jamil"; and Gulzar had a Pakistani number listed in his phone simply as "B." In reality all these individuals were almost certainly Rauf. According to investigators, the numbers these plotters were in contact with in Pakistan corresponded to cell phones that were seized from Rauf when he was arrested by Pakistani police on August 9 (interview by telephone with Metropolitan Police investigator, London, March 2009).

147. According to a British counterterrorism source who was privy to communications that were intercepted between England and Pakistan and within England, their contents would not have provided any "smoking gun" if they had been admissible in court. Intercept evidence is generally inadmissible in British criminal cases. (interview with senior British counterterrorism source, London, February 2009).

148. Regina v. Ali et al., June 12, 2008, 68.

149. At trial Sarwar explained that "Jamil" (Rauf) would send him a message with a new email address and that he would then have to decode it by removing the letters L, R and K to get his actual address. Regina v. Ali et al., June 12, 2008, 77–80.

150. Interview by telephone with Metropolitan Police investigator, London, March 2009.

151. Regina v. Ali et al., May 6, 2008, 29; British Press Association, "Timeline of the Airline Plot."

152. Robertson, Cruickshank, and Lister, "Document Shows Origins of 2006 Plot for Liquid Bombs on Planes."

153. Regina v. Ali et al., June 3, 2008, 40.

154. Regina v. Ali et al.; interview by telephone with Metropolitan Police investigator, London, March 2009.

155. Regina v. Ali et al., April 4, 2008, 38, April 7, 2008, 4.

156. Regina v. Ali et al., April 4, 2008, 29.

157. Regina v. Ali et al., April 7, 2008, 46.

158. Regina v. Ali et al., June 19, 32.

159. Regina v. Ali et al., June 23, 2008, 47

160. Interview by telephone with Metropolitan Police investigator, London, March 2009.

161. Regina v. Ali et al., April 7, 2008, 48.

162. Regina v. Ali et al., June 19, 2008, 22–104; interview with U.K. counterterrorism investigator, London, June 2008.

163. Ghabra and Islam were filmed chatting together in east London in a video viewed by the author.

164. Regina v. Ali et al., June 18, 2008, 22.

165. Regina v. Ali et al.

166. The extracts quoted by the author were read out in court (ibid.).

167. Robertson, Cruickshank, and Lister, "Document Shows Origins of 2006 Plot for Liquid Bombs on Planes."

168. Regina v. Ali et al., April 4, 2008, 14.

169. Regina v. Ali et al., June 10, 2008, 1–60.

170. Regina v. Ali et al., July 14, 94.

171. Regina v. Ali et al., June 23, 2008, 59–60.

172. Regina v. Ali et al., April 4, 2008, 22.

173. Phone interview with Metropolitan Police investigator, London, July 2008.

174. Regina v. Ali et al., April 4, 2008, 21.

175. Ibid., 7, 23.

176. Ibid., 20.

177. Ibid., 21.

178. Ibid., 18, 24.

179. Ibid., 10.

180. Ibid., 23.

181. Greenberg, Cruickshank, and Hansen, "Inside the Terror Plot That 'Rivaled 9/11.'"

182. Regina v. Ali et al., June 16, 2008, 7, 25, 8, 13.

183. See "Inside the Cell," Dateline NBC, NBC, September 15, 2008.

184. Ibid.

185. Greenberg, Cruickshank, and Hansen, "Inside the Terror Plot That 'Rivaled 9/11.'"

186. Robertson, Cruickshank, and Lister, "Document Shows Origins of 2006 Plot for Liquid Bombs on Planes."

187. Regina v. Ali et al.

188. Regina v. Ali et al., June 12, 2008, 23, 26.

189. Regina v. Ali et al., June 4, 2008, 133–34, 142–143; Duncan Gardham, "We've Never Seen a Bomb Like 21/7 Devices," Daily Telegraph (London), July 11, 2007.

190. Regina v. Ali et al., June 3, 2008, 20.

191. Greenberg, Cruickshank, and Hansen, "Inside the Terror Plot That 'Rivaled 9/11.'"

192. Regina v. Ali et al., June 4, 2008, 133–34.

193. Regina v. Ali et al., June 16, 2008, 110.

194. Regina v. Ali et al., June 3, 2008, 39. Ali testified he was in touch by phone with "Yusuf" during this period, the Pakistan-based trainer who had instructed Sarwar in making HMTD and hydrogen peroxide bomb manufacture in June 2006. According to British counterterrorism sources, this individual was almost certainly Rauf.

195. Greenberg, Cruickshank, and Hansen, "Inside the Terror Plot That 'Rivaled 9/11.'"

196. Regina v. Ali et al., June 3, 208, 127.

197. Regina v. Ali et al., June 5, 2008, 91.

198. Regina v. Ali et al., April 4, 2008 (afternoon session), 15.

199. Duncan Gardham, "Airline Bomb Plot: Investigation One of Biggest Since World War II," *Daily Telegraph* (London), September 8, 2009.

200. Robertson, Cruickshank, and Lister, "Document Shows Origins of 2006 Plot for Liquid Bombs on Planes."

201. Regina v. Ali et al., June 3, 2008, 145.

202. Regina v. Ali et al., April 4, 2008 (morning session), 46.

203. Regina v. Ali et al., July 10, 2008, 59. While Sarwar came across as very well versed in the chemical formulae necessary to make the bombs when he spoke in court, he did not come across as having a great deal of practical intelligence. During the trial it emerged that he had struggled to quickly accomplish some of the more menial tasks assigned to him in the conspiracy.

204. Regina v. Ali et al., April 21, 19.

205. Regina v. Ali et al., July 14, 2008, 90–93.

206. Regina v. Ali et al., April 7, 55–56.

207. Greenberg, Cruickshank, and Hansen, "Inside the Terror Plot That 'Rivaled 9/11.'"

208. Regina v. Ali et al., June 19, 2008, 36.

209. Ibid.

210. Ibid.

211. Regina v. Ali et al., April 4, 2008 (afternoon session), 13, 26.

212. Regina v. Ali et al.; British Press Association, "Timeline for Airline Plot."

213. Regina v. Ali et al., July 14, 2008, 100.

214. Regina v. Ali et al., June 23, 2008, 96–103.

215. Regina v. Ali et al.; British Press Association, "Timeline for Airline Plot."

216. Duncan Gardham, "Airliner Bomb Trial: George W. Bush Took Decision That Triggered Arrests," *Daily Telegraph* (London), September 8, 2008.

217. Robertson, Cruickshank, and Lister, "Document Shows Origins of 2006 Plot for Liquid Bombs on Planes."

218. Greenberg, Cruickshank, and Hansen, "Inside the Terror Plot That 'Rivaled 9/11.'"

219. Mohammed Gulzar, despite being acquitted, was placed under a "Control Order," on his release from prison, a legal mechanism significantly restricting his movement and communications. See Greenberg, Cruickshank, and Hansen, "Inside the Terror Plot That 'Rivaled 9/11.'"

220. Duncan Gardham and Gordon Rayner, "Airline Bomb Trial: Five Potential Suicide Bombers Still at Large," *Daily Telegraph* (London), September 8, 2008.

221. Interview with British counterterrorism source, London, February 2009.

222. Robertson, Cruickshank, and Lister, "Document Shows Origins of 2006 Plot for Liquid Bombs on Planes."

223. Robin Simcox, "Control Orders: Strengthening National Security," the Centre for Social Cohesion (2010); England and Wales High Court (Administrative Court)

Decisions, Secretary of State for the Home Department AM [2009] EWHC 3053 (Admin) (21 December 2009).

224. Interview with senior U.S. intelligence source, 2009

225. Robertson, Cruickshank, and Lister, "Document Shows Origins of 2006 Plot for Liquid Bombs on Planes."

226. "Reports: Airstrike Kills Suspect in Jet Bomb Plot," *MSNBC.com*, November 22, 2008.

227. Greeenberg, Cruickshank and Hansen, "Inside the Terror Plot That 'Rivaled 9/11.'"

228. Ibid.

229. Ibid.

230. Binalshibh communicated with Atta through coded phone calls, e-mails, and instant messaging (Kean et al., *The 9/11 Commission Report*, 249). While the 9/11 Report makes clear that Binalshibh was in frequent contact with Atta, Rauf was in near constant contact with the U.K. plotters, according to British investigators.

231. Peter Bergen and Paul Cruickshank, "Kashmir on Thames," *The New Republic*, September 4, 2006.

232. Valentinas Mite, "Offensive Against Suspected Militants in South Waziristan Ends," Radio Free Europe, March 30, 2004. The Pakistani government signed a peace deal with militants in South Waziristan in February 2005 (Ismail Khan, "Waziristan Draft Accord Approved, *Dawn* (Karachi), February 1, 2005). The Pakistani government signed a peace deal with militants in North Waziristan in September 2006.

233. "The Terrorist Threat to the US Homeland," *National Intelligence Estimate*, July 2007.

234. Paul Cruickshank, "The 2008 Belgian Cell and FATA's Terrorist Pipeline," *CTC Sentinel*, April 2009; Paul Cruickshank, "The Militant Pipeline Between the Afghanistan-Pakistan Border Region and the West," New America Foundation, February 2010.

235. See Paul Cruickshank, "The Militant Pipeline Between the Afghanistan-Pakistan Border Region and the West," New America Foundation, July 2011; Paul Cruickshank, "Alleged UK Cell Charged with Terror Training in Pakistan," CNN, September 26, 2011.

236. These cases include the Zazi "New York" plot and an alleged al-Qaeda plot broken up in Norway in 2010. See Paul Cruickshank, "The Militant Pipeline," July 2011.

237. Interviews with U.S. and European counterterrorism officials, 2009–11

238. Nic Robertson and Paul Cruickshank, "Recruits Reveal Al Qaeda's Sprawling Web," CNN, July 31, 2009; Paul Cruickshank, "The Militant Pipeline," July 2011; Paul Cruickshank, "Resurgent Al Qaeda: New Concern About U.S. Homeland," CNN, December 2, 2013; Aaron Zelin, "Up to 11,000 Foreign Fighters in Syria; Steep Rise Among Western Europeans," ICSR Insight, Washington Institute for Near East Policy, December 17, 2013.

239. Serious plots were classified as those plots that had the capacity to kill at least ten people in which plotters obtained weapons or bomb-making components without the help of undercover law-enforcement agents. See Paul Cruickshank, "The Militant Pipeline," July 2011.

240. Interview with Western explosives expert, July 2008.

241. Regina v. Ali et al., June 3, 2008, 29.

242. Kean et al., *The 9/11 Commission Report*, 172.

The Foiled Attacks in Italy in 2006

JAVIER JORDÁN

Toward the end of March 2006, the Italian police carried out an antiterrorist operation in Milan that ended with the arrest of seven Moroccans and Tunisians.[1] A few days later, on March 24, Moroccan police arrested a group of nine other individuals connected to the group in Italy. According to Moroccan police,[2] the head of the cell broken up in Morocco was a Tunisian by the name of Mohamed Benhadi Msahel. Based on information provided by Italian and Moroccan authorities, both groups were preparing a terrorist attack on the metro in Milan and against the Basilica of San Petronio in Bologna.[3] The Salafist Group for Preaching and Combat (GSPC in French) had ordered the attack.[4] In Milan, the terrorists were to commit the attack just before the general elections on April 9 and 10 in order to prevent the reelection of President Silvio Berlusconi after he sent Italian troops to Iraq. Based on the testimony of those arrested, the terrorist attack on the metro in Milan was inspired by the attacks in Madrid in March 2004.[5]

After his arrest, Msahel confessed that he was the central link in a much wider chain.[6] Both the idea of attacks in Italy and the strategic coordination for the terrorist operation originated at higher levels: from the GSPC and from the principal leaders of al-Qaeda in Central Asia.

Despite the fact that police operations intercepted the attacks at an early phase, the case is of special interest because it reveals the direct involvement of the GSPC and al-Qaeda in the preparation of attacks in Europe. The Italy plots also reveal a relatively detailed picture of the command, control, and coordination exercised by both of these organizations when carrying out terrorist actions. Examining the principal protagonists in this plot and the details of the terrorist plan reveals the role played by the GSPC and al-Qaeda in the attacks and elucidates recommendations for antiterrorist policies based on the lessons learned from this case study.

ANALYSIS OF THE PROTAGONISTS IN THE TERRORIST PLOT

On March 24, 2006, Moroccan police arrested and accused nine individuals of terrorism. They were identified as: Mohamed Benhadi Msahel, Lahcen Mhater, Faris Said, Ghrar Said, Abdelghani Aouiouch, Abdelhaq Touri, Adil Kaoutari, Mohamed Hermouch, and Abdelfettah Hidaoui. At the time of their arrest, no weapons or explosives were seized by the police.[7] The names of those arrested by Italian police during the same month connected to the cell broken up in Morocco were not publicly released. Having little proof to convict the group (they had no weapons nor had they begun to manufacture explosives), Italian authorities decided to expel almost all of them and not initiate criminal proceedings against them.[8]

In the terror plot, five individuals stand out: the Tunisian Msahel; the Moroccans Anouar Majrar and Abdelghani Aouiouch; the Algerian Amer Laaraj; and the mysterious Abu Hamza.[9] The characteristics of each and the nature of the relationships they maintained among themselves provide valuable insights into the workings of the GSPC and AQ.

Mohamed Benhadi Msahel: The Recruiter and the Tactical Coordinator in Italy

The radicalization process of Mohamed Msahel was similar to other cases that occurred in Italy. At the time of his arrest, Msahel was thirty-seven years old and unmarried. Of Tunisian origin, Msahel immigrated to Italy and led a relatively impious life. Msahel returned to devout Islamic practice in 1999. In 2001, he began to regularly attend the Islamic center Segrate, close to the mosque on Via Padova in Milan. There, he met Ali Addahaoui, who spoke with him about the necessity of jihad.[10]

Little by little, Msahel was introduced into the radical circles of Milan by Addahaoui. In the mosque in Segrate, he attended classes on jihadist subjects. There he had access to radical videos, including those of Abu Qatada (Omar Mahmoud Othman). In 2002, at the mosque on Via Padova he met an individual who a few years later would be key in the participation of Msahel in the terrorist plot: the Moroccan Abdelghani Aouiouch.[11]

In May of 2005, Msahel was in Paris at a family party of the Moroccan Anouar Majrar at the same time as Aouiouch. It seems that this meeting was crucial to involving Msahel in the terrorist plot in Italy. Msahel had been invited to the party by a friend from Tunisia who introduced him there to another person who would become central to the terrorist plot: the Algerian Amer Laaraj.[12] Laaraj was a midlevel leader within the GSPC in France. After the party, Msahel began to develop a closer relationship with the GSPC and decided to join the ranks of al-Qaeda in Iraq with the aim of fighting the jihad against the United States and its allies.

In June 2005, Msahel went to Syria and established himself in Damascus with the idea of entering Iraq, but he never managed to cross the border. During his stay in Syria, he met with supporters of al-Qaeda in Iraq who coordinated the entry of volunteers into the country.[13] Msahel left Syria fully committed to the jihadist cause and began to recruit volunteers in Italy and Morocco to travel to Iraq via Syria.[14] Msahel showed himself to be a good recruiter and committed to the jihadist cause. He seemed to have gained the confidence of some members of the GSPC at this time, and they invited him to participate in the terrorist plot in Italy. His network of contacts with radicals in Italy from recruiting suicide terrorists for Iraq had made him a valuable asset who could locate operatives and coordinate the same type of actions in Italian territory. Initially, Anouar Majrar proposed that Msahel join the plot, but Majrar was arrested in Greece at the end of 2005, sent to France, and from there extradited to Morocco.[15] Consequently, other members of the GSPC reached out to Msahel again about his possible participation. In February 2006, Msahel entered Algeria from Morocco to receive more precise instructions about the terrorist plan.[16]

Anouar Majrar: The Primary Tactical Coordinator in Italy

Anouar Majrar operated in Italy and France but was of Moroccan descent. He had been radicalized during his stay in a French prison in 2001.[17] In

March 2005, when he met Msahel, Majrar was already well connected to and enjoyed the trust of some members of the GSPC in France.

In June of 2005, Majrar joined Msahel in Damascus with the intention of entering Iraq. During his stay in Syria he received instructions by telephone to travel to Algeria. There, Majrar met with various leaders of the GSPC, among them Amer Laaraj. They proposed he participate in a terrorist plan in Italy, a project that he would have to coordinate with a cell in Spain. Majrar accepted, and when he returned to Syria, he invited Msahel to join in the terrorist project.[18]

Majrar tried to return to Italy from Syria through Greece. He was detained there, sent to France, and from there extradited to Morocco.[19] Majrar confessed the details of the terrorists' plot to Moroccan authorities and alerted them to the intentions of the GSPC and the role that Msahel was playing in the plot.[20]

Abdelghani Aouiouch: Tactical Coordinator of the Attacks in France

The Moroccan Abdelghani Aouiouch first introduced Msahel to the GSPC in Europe. Aouiouch was a member of a logistical cell of the GSPC in France that financed the organization through criminal activities, principally through the robberies of businesses and shops. His relationship to jihadism predates 9/11. Aouiouch specialized in acting as an intermediary among the social networks of radical individuals.[21] Aouiouch introduced Msahel to Majrar and Amer Laaraj and later also acted as intermediary among Laaraj, Msahel, and the Moroccan Abdelfettah Hidaoui.[22]

Additional proof of the role Aouiouch played as an intermediary is that Laaraj entrusted him with the coordination of Moroccan and Algerian jihadists in France to orchestrate attacks there.[23] At Laaraj's request, Aouiouch was also going to support Msahel's group in carrying out the attacks in Italy.[24]

Amer Laaraj: The Intermediary with the GSPC and Operational Coordinator

Amer Laaraj was a versatile GSPC operative who functioned as both a logistical coordinator and specialized technician, indicative of the expertise available to the GSPC. Laaraj (a.k.a. Salim el-Ouahrani) led a logistical cell of the GSPC in France for many years and later returned to Algeria to receive training in a GSPC camp. Laaraj was not arrested in the antiterrorist operations in Italy and Morocco when Msahel was detained. Rather, Laaraj was based in Algeria but traveled with ease to other countries to coordinate GSPC activities. He attended the family party in Paris where he met Msahel and, later, went to Rabat-Salé to meet in person with Msahel and Aouiouch. During that meeting, he passed on instructions to them from high-level commanders of the GSPC. He was also in regular contact with both Msahel and Aouiouch through e-mail, sent from cybercafes in Algeria.[25]

In addition to acting as an intermediary between the tactical coordinators and strategic commanders, Laaraj appears to have been tasked with manufacturing the homemade explosives that were going to be used in Italy and in GSPC attacks in France and Denmark.[26] Laaraj had been trained as an explosives technician at a training camp in Algeria, and helped other groups plan terrorist attacks.

Abu Hamza

The testimony of the arrested cell members identified Abu Hamza (real name unknown) as the Algerian coordinator between the GSPC and al-Qaeda. However, as a security measure, none the cell members had met him in person or seen his photograph. Majrar and Msahel both received instructions from Hamza by telephone, through the mail, or through intermediaries. Hamza called Msahel by phone in September of 2005 after Msahel displayed interest in participating in the terrorist plan. The object of the call was to confirm Msahel's commitment to the jihadist cause and his willingness to participate in the plan. Subsequently, Msahel received a letter from Hamza that set out the plan to commit various terrorist actions in Europe, including in Italy. Hamza told Msahel that the terrorist plan corresponded to directives set by Osama Bin Laden.[27]

From this, it can be assumed that Abu Hamza was going to supervise the preparations for the attacks and that he was probably going to provide support for them by acting as coordinator with other cells. It is unknown whether Abu Hamza maintained direct communication with bin Laden

or if the directives were deduced from bin Laden's public communications. From the degree of detail involved in the attacks, it seems some
type of communication between al-Qaeda and the GSPC existed. This link
is also reflected in one of the orders Msahel received in Algeria. Msahel's
GSPC contacts asked him to recruit someone of European nationality in
Italy to travel to Pakistan and receive more concrete instructions from
Ayman al-Zawahiri.[28]

During his brief stay in Algeria, Amer Laaraj opened an e-mail account
for Msahel and gave him the instructions for communicating.[29]

PARTICIPATION OF JIHADIST ORGANIZATIONS
IN THE TERRORIST PLAN IN ITALY

Degree of Involvement of the GSPC

The GSPC was the principal driving author and force of the terrorist
plan. The leaders of the GSPC initially proposed the attacks to Majrar,
and they solicited his trip to Algeria before raising this possibility with
him. Subsequently, when Majrar was detained, the leaders of the GSPC
contacted him to confirm his commitment and readiness to participate
in the terrorist project. When his willingness was confirmed, Msahel was
summoned to a meeting in Algeria by the GSPC for the detailed instructions on the plan and to discuss the operation with the leaders of the
organization.

Once Msahel agreed to participate in the plan, the GSPC gave him
the liberty to recruit radicalized individuals as he thought necessary for
implementing it. Msahel and the GSPC counted on the support of members already on the ground in Italy for the attack on the Milan metro: those
others who were arrested by the Italian police shortly before Msahel's
group in Morocco was detained.[30] Thus, the GSPC used formally unaffiliated individuals to carry out the terrorist acts planned and coordinated
by the group. These operations were planned and executed at the tactical
level by homegrown networks that were conceived and supported on the
operational and strategic level by the GSPC. These tactical cells should
therefore be considered part of the organization in functional and ad
hoc terms, given that to commit the terrorist actions planned, they were

subordinated to the GSPC and benefited from coordination with other cells controlled by the organization.

This organizational structure has the advantage of providing the GSPC the flexibility and capacity for the next generation of networks across Europe. The organization, in the Italy plot, demonstrated the ability to create ad hoc teams of individuals who had previously demonstrated a certain degree of commitment to terrorism. At the same time, this practice offers operative advantages to the networks of individuals trying to contribute to the global jihad. In this case study, groups that were preparing attacks in Italy counted on the support of Amer Laaraj for his explosives expertise. The formulas for manufacturing explosives available on the Internet are of little use—and even dangerous—if one does not use an authentic specialist in the area.[31] For this reason, the support of the GSPC through Laaraj was crucial for successfully executing the attacks. The same support linkages, such as financial backing, refuge, and communications infrastructure, also benefited the local group. In this way, the subordination of homegrown radicals to a higher organization multiplies their capacities and reduces one of the principal vulnerabilities that grassroots jihadist networks have: their lack of professionalism.

The Degree of Involvement of al-Qaeda

According to Msahel, Abu Hamza's letter indicated that the terrorist operations in Europe, particularly in Italy, had been recommended by the "lion of Islam" and leader of al-Qaeda, Osama bin Laden. The fact that the mysterious Abu Hamza was named in the testimony of those under arrest as the coordinator between the GSPC and al-Qaeda leads us to assume that the instructions of bin Laden were sent directly to the Algerian organization through secret communication. In other words, this was not a simple interpretation by the leaders of the GSPC deduced from public statements of al-Qaeda.

Additionally, on March 5, 2006, the television network al-Jazeera broadcast a communiqué from Ayman al-Zawahiri threatening European countries for the caricatures of Mohammed released in Denmark and congratulating Hamas for its electoral victory in the Palestinian territories. What was most interesting about this communiqué, however, was that in it Zawahiri also explicitly threatened President Berlusconi for the presence of Italian troops in Iraq and demanded that they be withdrawn from that country. By refusing to do so, threatened al-Zawahiri, "Italy would dig its own grave in Iraq." Additionally, al-Zawahiri referred to the Madrid and London attacks as the template for any terrorist assault on Italy.[32]

Another local cell linked to the GSPC and dismantled in Morocco in November 2005 shed further light on the connections between al-Qaeda and the Italian plot. Khaled Azig and Mohammed Reha, two young Moroccan men who operated in Syria and Morocco under the coordination of the GSPC, led this group. Azig and Reha were coordinated by Abu Bashir, who, according to the confession of both individuals, was the coordinator of al-Qaeda in Europe and North Africa and was the go-between for the organization with the GSPC. Abu Bashir coordinated different cells in Syria, Morocco, and Europe and maintained communication with them by telephone and over the Internet. None of those arrested saw him in person or in a photograph. This information was confirmed by at least two Spanish antiterrorist operations when Abu Bashir's name once again emerged as a high-level al-Qaeda coordinator.[33]

Over the course of the interrogations of the Moroccan terrorists, details emerged on the communication links between the GSPC, al-Qaeda in Iraq, and al-Qaeda in Afghanistan/Pakistan. Azig, Reha, and Bashir spoke, for example, about the plans to create a division of al-Qaeda in the Maghreb and about an oath of loyalty that Abdelmalek Droukdel, the leader of the GSPC, intended to make to bin Laden.[34] In September of 2006, it appears these plans came to fruition when the GSPC leader formally rendered loyalty to Osama bin Laden. The testimony of Azig and Reha confirmed that the leaders of both organizations, before their merger, communicated through human couriers who carried letters by hand between Iraq and Afghanistan.[35] This pattern also corresponds with the testimony of Msahel, who confessed GSPC's practice of sending couriers from Europe to Pakistan with the details of the terrorist operation they were planning in Italy.

The Msahel and Abu Hamza case and the Azig, Reha, and Abu Bashir case demonstrate that there was and likely is a direct communication between the GSPC and al-Qaeda. However, because of security concerns, the communication appears to have been excessively slow and consequently dealt only with strategic questions. The channels of communication would have made close collaboration between the leaders of both organizations in the coordination of operations at the tactical level difficult.

Therefore, in the case of the terrorist plot in Italy in 2006, al-Qaeda likely intervened by designating the objectives and the dates for committing the attacks. However, they seem to have delegated the concrete details about the terrorist attacks and, particularly, all of the ground preparation to the GSPC. The GSPC had a larger support network of radical Islamists of Maghrebi origin, which makes them a valuable allied organization capable of attacking European countries with a high number of immigrants from Northern Africa.

THE TERRORIST PLAN IN ITALY

The action in Italy was part of a wider campaign of attacks instigated by al-Qaeda in Europe. Based on the testimony of the arrested suspects, it can be deduced that the terrorist plan in Italy had two primary objectives: an attack against the metro in Milan and an attack on the Basilica de San Petronio in Bologna.

Attack Against the Metro in Milan

The metro portion of the plan was to be executed by a group of five suicide attackers, who planned to explode themselves in the interior of the trains, thereby inflicting massive civilian casualties. According to the testimony of the suspects, the choice of Milan as the target was because it was the city where President Berlusconi was born.[36]

It can be also assumed that the existence of a large community of Muslim immigrants in Milan, which made it easier for the terrorists to pass unnoticed, also contributed to the target choice. However, Milan has also been a primary focus of antiterrorist operations against jihadist cells, some tied to the Islamic Cultural Center at Viale Jenner.[37] Between 2002 and 2005, Italian security forces carried out at least four operations against cells composed primarily of Algerians, Moroccans, and Tunisians, who in at least one case were trying to acquire arms and explosives.[38] The presence of radical Islamists in Milan goes back to the middle of the 1990s. It was already a hotbed of terrorist and antiterrorist activity before 2006, and a likely location for a plot to emerge.

The choice of the metro as a target was also in keeping with the preference of jihadist terrorism. Subway-like transportation systems are very difficult to protect because tens of thousands of people use the system simultaneously each day. The metro was a jihadist target in Europe on July 7, 2005, in London and during the campaign of attacks by the GIA in Paris in July of 1995.[39]

In addition, the choice of the metro was consistent with previous attempts to attack the same objective. In 2004, the Italian press revealed that the Milan metro had been chosen as a target for multiple suicide attacks before 9/11, based on information from an informer with the Italian security services who had infiltrated a jihadist cell.[40] In 2002, Domenico Quaranta, an Italian convert to Islam caused a small fire in the Milan metro with a canister of gas that failed to explode.[41] According to Italian authorities, in 2004, a cell made up of Moroccans and Tunisians that operated in the city of Cremona also tried to attack a church in Cremona and the metro in Milan in a station below the cathedral.[42] Therefore, the attacks in Milan were not planned in isolation but likely built on the efforts of previous groups operating in the area.

The motivation of the attack against the metro in Milan was clearly political. In 2003, the Berlusconi government supported the U.S. invasion of Iraq and sent troops that were still there in April 2006. Msahel added in his statement that the attack on the metro in Milan was inspired by the attack on the trains in Madrid in March 2004, which, in the opinion of the terrorists, led to the defeat of the party of Jose María Aznar in the elections held in Spain three days later.[43]

The Milan plan, therefore, demonstrated once again the desire of the jihadists to affect, through terrorism, the foreign policy of Western governments toward the Muslim world. This idea reoccurs in the messages of responsibility for attacks by al-Qaeda and in the statements of Osama bin Laden and Ayman al-Zawahiri aimed at Western societies. In both the Madrid case and the failed plot in Milan, the terrorists intended to affect policy through direct intervention on the eve of elections, in this way magnifying their importance as actors in the internal politics of Western democracies.

The climate of alarm around an election also benefits the terrorists from a propagandistic perspective as it generates headlines in the media and public statements from politicians. For example, in the Italian case of 2006, President Bush warned Italian authorities about the possibility of an attack similar to Madrid, even before the arrest of Msahel and his group. The vice president of the European Commission, Franco Frattini, also warned about the need for maximum security measures on the eve of Italian elections.[44] Italy was also on alert because of the diffusion of the video from Ayman al-Zawahiri condemning the caricatures against Mohammed and proposing attacks in Europe.[45]

The Attack on the Basilica de San Petronio in Bologna

The second objective of the terrorists was a Catholic church in the Italian city of Bologna. In the San Petronio basilica, there is a fresco from 1415 AD painted by Giovanni da Modena in which Mohammed appears naked and in hell as Dante described in the *Divine Comedy*. The principal objective was to destroy the basilica and the fresco because it is seen as an insult to Islam. The information currently available on this plot offers little detail about how the cell planned to carry out this terrorist attack. It was scheduled after the attacks in Milan, and the concrete date depended on the calendar established by Ayman al-Zawahiri.[46] It is unknown if the cell intended to use suicide bombers or how many people were going to participate in the attack. It is unknown if the terrorists intended to create a large number of casualties by attacking when a religious ceremony was in progress or if the symbolism of destroying the fresco was the only goal.

Regarding the choice of objective, it is interesting to note how the leaders of al-Qaeda and the GSPC knew of the existence of the fresco. They most likely learned of it because of a Vatican controversy in 2001 and 2002 that attracted the attention of the global media. In June 2001, the Union of Muslims of Italy sent a letter to Pope John Paul II asking for the "disappearance" of the fresco, considered offensive to Islam. Shortly afterward, Abdel Aziz el-Mataani, a professor at the Egyptian University of Al-Azhar, joined the controversy by declaring to the Italian news agency ANSA, "Whoever tries to destroy this image will be blessed by Allah, because he will do it to change an attitude that is harmful and rejected by Islam."[47] Consequently, the Italian police enforced security at the basilica for a month to avoid acts of vandalism against the fresco. One year later, in the middle of 2002, the story again attracted media attention when the news was disseminated (unconfirmed by Italian security agencies) that the church had been designated a target of al-Qaeda.[48]

The plan to attack the Basilica of San Petronio also had a religious context. Through this attack, the jihadists attempted to present themselves as the authentic defenders of Islam, taking advantage of the controversy raised in Italy around the fifteenth-century fresco. In this sense, the motivation for this terrorist plan resembles more that raised by the murder in November 2004 of the Dutch film director Theo Van Gogh, who was accused of insulting Islam with his movie *Submission*.[49]

The targeting of a Christian church was consistent with prior attack plans, too. As was already mentioned, in 2004 the Italian police arrested a group of Moroccans who were allegedly intending to attack near the cathedral of Milan and more specifically against a church in Cremona. In Iraq, attacks by al-Qaeda against Christian churches have been common, and the same pattern has occurred in Algeria, Pakistan, Indonesia, and the Philippines with other jihadist groups. On Christmas day in 2000, Jemaah Islamiyah in Indonesia carried out simultaneous attacks against several churches during midnight mass, which caused dozens of deaths.[50] Al-Qaeda has also planned and carried out attacks against Jewish houses worship, such as the terrorist suicide attack against the synagogue in Djerba in April 2002.[51] The attacks against Christian and Jewish religious buildings is consistent with the jihadist vision of carrying out a religious war. According to radical Islamists, Christianity and Judaism have conspired against Muslims since the birth of Islam. According to this vision, Christians and Jews are guilty of not having recognized the message of the Prophet Mohammed, which was the culmination of the revelations of the God of Abraham. For these reasons, the plan to attack the basilica in Bologna combined a defense of Islam and the Prophet with the jihadist viewpoint of a world war among religions.

This case study shows how al-Qaeda delegated the Italian attacks to the GSPC and how the GSPC further delegated the logistics to a homegrown network with minimal means. The local network enjoyed a multiplier effect to its small size by counting on the technical support and the strategic leadership of higher organizations. This symbiotic relationship among groups allows large organizations like al-Qaeda to project their strength from Central Asia and the Maghreb into the center of Europe, in a manner analogous to Western countries' military interventions at a distance of thousands of kilometers. In addition, homegrown networks composed of radicals who aspire to emulate the heroic deeds of al-Qaeda stand to benefit from similar arrangements in terms of material, technical, and cognitive resources through their subordination to the higher organization. Through this relationship, the local groups' profile rises suddenly, converting it into a useful part of the jihadist mechanism in the fight against the infidels.

In facing this system of delegation and cooperation among global organizations (al-Qaeda), regional organizations (GSPC), and homegrown networks of radicalized individuals, the principal policy recommendation for counterterrorism leaders is to recognize the urgent need for international cooperation on antiterrorist efforts. This case study confirms the need for fluid channels of communication at the police, judicial, and intelligence levels among the states engaged in combating Islamic extremists. At the same time, it is essential that state agencies that receive information from allies be empowered to share that information with local agencies that specialize in investigating terrorism at the law-enforcement level. In this case study, the terrorists plotting an attack in Italy traveled to and cooperated (or planned to cooperate) with networks established in Italy, France, Spain, Syria, Morocco, Algeria, Pakistan, and Greece. If the analysis was limited a single state, this small group of radicals could, at first sight, appear to be harmless. However, as this case demonstrates, local terrorist groups can and do engage in contact with more established terrorist networks, empowering them with the means to carry out lethal terrorist attacks. In the majority of cases, the only way to discover the connections among jihadist networks and to thwart their efforts is through international cooperation.

NOTES

The content of this chapter is part of the research project CSO2010–17849 "International Terrorism's Organizational Structure: Analysis of its Evolution and Implications for the European Security" funded by the Spanish Ministry of Science and Innovation.

1. Three others managed to flee.

2. "Une cellule terroriste voulait détruire l'ambassade des Etats-Unis à Rabat," *Maroc Hebdo International* (Casablanca), no 693 (April 2006).

3. Biagio Marsiglia and Guido Olimpio, "Volevano colpire il metro: Presi 5 terroristi a Milano," *Corriere della Sera* (Milan), January 5, 2009.

4. Biagio Marsiglia, "Preparavano attentati a Milano e Bologna," *Corriere della Sera* (Milan), March 21, 2006.

5. Rabat Court of Appeal, Chamber No 5, Summary 5/2006, Resolution No 38, June 22, 2006, 22.

6. Youssef Chmirou, "Les Marocains aux trousses des terroristes d'Al Qaida: Le Maroc sauve l'Italie," *La Gazette du Maroc* (Casablanca), April 10, 2006.

7. "Une cellule terroriste voulait détruire l'ambassade des Etats-Unis à Rabat," *Maroc Hebdo International* (Casablanca), no 693, April 2006.

8. Ruotolo Guido, "Italia a rischio facevano parte di un gruppo di sette marocchini," *La Stampa* (Turin), April 6, 2006.

9. These last two were not arrested.

10. Rabat Court of Appeal, Chamber No 5, Summary 5/2006, Resolution No 38, June 22, 2006, 10.

11. Ibid., 10.

12. Ibid., 11.

13. Youssef Chmirou, "Mohamed Benhedi Msahel, l'émir tunisien: Le mollah tunisien qui voulait bombarder Milan," *La Gazette du Maroc* (Casablanca), May 15, 2006.

14. Daniel Lav, "The Al-Qaeda Organization in the Islamic Maghreb: The Evolving Terrorist Presence in North Africa," *MEMRI: Inquiry and Analysis*, no. 332, March 7, 2007.

15. Chmirou, "Mohamed Benhedi Msahel."

16. Youssef Chmirou, "Les Marocains aux trousses des terroristes d'Al Qaida: Le Maroc sauve l'Italie," *La Gazette du Maroc* (Casablanca), April 10, 2006.

17. Mohamed Boudarham, "Le groupe Messahel tombe au Maroc," *Aujourd'hui le Maroc* (Casablanca), April 6, 2006.

18. Rabat Court of Appeal, Chamber No 5, Summary 5/2006, Resolution No 38, June 22, 2006, 13–14.

19. Boudarham, "Le groupe Messahel tombe au Maroc."

20. Chmirou, "Mohamed Benhedi Msahel."

21. Rabat Court of Appeal, Chamber No 5, Summary 5/2006, Resolution No 38, June 22, 2006, 25–26.

22. This last individual was a leader of the Moroccan Islamic Combatant Group that was preparing an attack against the U.S. embassy in Rabat. According to the testimony of those arrested, this plan consisted in exploding a charge beneath the foundation of the building for the purpose of creating a tunnel.

23. The terrorists' objectives selected in France were a restaurant where civil servants from French intelligence services had lunch, the Paris metro, Orly Airport, and a shopping mall in La Defense ("Des attentats étaient prévus à Bologne et dans le métro de Milan," Aujourd'hui le Maroc [Casablanca], April 6, 2006; Craig S. Smith, "Eight Sentenced in Morocco for Plotting Terror Attacks," New York Times, March 3, 2007).

24. Rabat Court of Appeal, Chamber No 5, Summary 5/2006, Resolution No 38, June 22, 2006, 36.

25. Ibid., 11, 20, 24.

26. Ibid., 35.

27. Ibid., 21, 23.

28. Ibid., 22.

29. Ibid., 24.

30. Marsiglia, "Preparavano attentati a Milano e Bologna." The arrests carried out by the Italian police in the second half of March were the result of an investigation of at least six months that had been initiated by the judges Armando Spataro and Nicola Piacente. The Italian press on March 21, 2006, reported on the arrests (a few days before the arrest of Msahel in Morocco) and the plans to attack the metro in Milan and the Basilica of San Petronio in Bologna. According to what later came to be known, some of the names of the seven arrested in Italy coincided with the information that the Moroccan authorities would subsequently pass to the Italian police. See Guido, "Italia a rischio facevano parte di un gruppo di sette marocchini."

31. Fred Burton, "Beware of 'Kramer': Tradecraft and the New Jihadists," Stratfor, January 18, 2006.

32. Mahan Abedin and Federico Bordonaro, "The Terrorist Threat to the Italian Elections," Terrorism Monitor 4, no. 6 (March 23, 2006).

33. Juzgado Central de Instrucción No 5, Auto de Procesamiento del Sumario 21/2006 L, October 23, 2007, 11; Juzgado Central de Instrucción No 5, Auto de Procesamiento, June 13, 2008, 2.

34. Lav, "The Al-Qaeda Organization in the Islamic Maghreb."

35. Reuven Paz, "Qa'idat al-Jihad: Moving Forward or Backward? The Algerian GSPC Joins Al-Qaeda," PRISM Occasional Papers 4, no. 5 (September 2006): 9.

36. Rabat Court of Appeal, Chamber No 5, Summary 5/2006, Resolution No 38, June 22, 2006, 22.

37. Maria Do Céu Pinto, *Islamist and Middle Eastern Terrorism: A Threat to Europe?* (Soveria Mannelli: Rubbettino, 2004), 60.

38. Kathryn Haahr, "GSPC in Italy: The Forward Base of Jihad in Europe," *Terrorism Monitor* 4, no. 3 (February 9, 2006).

39. Petter Nesser, "Chronology of Jihadism in Western Europe 1994–2007: Planned, Prepared, and Executed Terrorist Attacks," *Studies in Conflict and Terrorism* 31 (2008): 924–46.

40. John Hooper, "Al-Qaida Man Planned Italy Bomb," *Guardian*, March 26, 2004.

41. Guastella Giuseppe, "Attentati islamici, caccia ai fiancheggiatori" *Corriere della Sera* (Milan), July 19, 2002.

42. "Terror Suspects Arrested in Italy," *BBC News*, February 25, 2004.

43. Rabat Court of Appeal, Chamber No 5, Summary 5/2006, Resolution No 38, June 22, 2006, 22.

44. Abedin and Bordonaro, "The Terrorist Threat to the Italian Elections."

45. "Bin Laden's No. 2 Condemns Mohammed Cartoons," CNN, March 5, 2006.

46. Rabat Court of Appeal, Chamber No 5, Summary 5/2006, Resolution No 38, June 22, 2006, 22.

47. Marta Lobato, "Mahoma clama desde el infierno," *El Mundo* (Madrid), July 30, 2002.

48. "Italy Arrests Men Over 'Church Plot,'" *BBC News*, August 20, 2002.

49. "Life of Slain Dutch Film-Maker," *BBC News*, November 2, 2004.

50. "Arrests Follow Church Bombings," *BBC News*, December 26, 2000.

51. "Al-Qaeda Claims Tunisia Attack," *BBC News*, June 23, 2002.

[11]

The German "Sauerland" Plot,
Central Asia, and Turkey

GUIDO STEINBERG

On September 4, 2007, German police arrested three young jihadis in the small town of Oberschledorn, in the Sauerland region of the state of North-Rhine Westphalia. Two of them, Fritz Gelowicz (born in 1979), the ringleader of the cell, and Daniel Schneider (born in 1985) were German converts to Islam, and the third member, Adem Yilmaz (born in 1978), is a Turk who had grown up in Germany from 1986. The three had assembled bomb-making materials, including highly concentrated hydrogen peroxide, in order to produce an explosive mixture using flour.[1] However, the police had clandestinely substituted the highly concentrated hydrogen peroxide with a less concentrated solution, which looked the same but could not be used to manufacture explosives.[2]

In the most important terrorist plot in Germany after 9/11, the three had planned to attack American targets using truck bombs loaded with the explosives. They did not want to perpetrate suicide attacks but rather return to Pakistan after the attack. Although American targets seem to have been their top priority, the perpetrators were still discussing different alternatives shortly before their arrests. They seem to have planned to attack nightclubs frequented by American military personnel in western Germany and possibly the American air base in Ramstein in the German state of Rhineland-Palatinate, the largest U.S. base in Germany.[3]

It is unknown when exactly the three young men embarked on their terrorist careers. They were members of a larger group of young

Islamists radicalized in the southern German twin cities of Ulm (in the state of Baden-Württemberg) and Neu-Ulm (in Bavaria). Gelowicz and several other people close to the Sauerland group were frequent visitors at the Multikulturhaus in Neu-Ulm, a Salafist cultural center that after 2001 had become a popular meeting place for young Turks, Kurds, Arabs, and German converts.[4] The physician and Salafist preacher Yahia Yusuf headed it. An Egyptian born in Alexandria in 1958, Yusuf was a member of the Islamic Group (al-Gama'a al-Islamiya) in his home country and was imprisoned for a few months after the murder of President Sadat in October 1981. In 1988, he enrolled at the University of Freiburg in southwestern Germany. There, Yusuf joined a group of Arab Islamists based in the Ibad al-Rahman mosque who supported the jihad in Bosnia during the early 1990s. In 2000, he moved to Neu-Ulm where Yusuf became the head of the Multikulturhaus and—in the following years—the most prominent jihadi spiritual guide and ideologue in Germany. He served as an inspiration and mentor to several young visitors to the Multikulturhaus who went on to join other jihadi movements. The first young man to have traveled to South or Central Asia to receive additional training seems to have been Yusuf's son, Umar Yusuf (born in 1983). He reportedly trained in a Lashkar-e-Taiba (LeT) camp in Pakistan in 2001.[5] In 2002 and 2003, several young visitors of the Multikulturhaus joined the Chechen mujaheddin and were subsequently killed by Russian forces.[6] By 2004, Gelowicz and Selek were known as ardent supporters of Yusuf.[7]

Before pursing jihad, however, the future terrorists traveled to the Middle East in order to study Arabic. Gelowicz, Yilmaz, and Atilla Selek, a German of Turkish origin and close associate of the two who later provided the cell with explosive detonators, chose Syria for their studies. They arrived in August 2005 and remained, respectively, until April 2006, December 2005, and October 2005. Schneider also visited a language school in Cairo, Egypt, in the spring of 2006. It seems the Syrian group had planned to look for a way to join the jihad in Chechnya or—if that did not work out—in Iraq. They were recruited by a group of jihadists from Azerbaijan, who promised to send them to Chechnya once they had sufficiently trained. The Azerbaijanis stood in contact with the Uzbek Islamic Jihad Union (IJU) and brought two of the young Germans, Gelowicz and Yilmaz, and, later, the rest of the group to Waziristan via Turkey and Iran.[8]

From spring 2006, the future Sauerland plotters traveled to Pakistan via Turkey and Iran and trained in an Islamic Jihad Union camp in Mir Ali, North Waziristan. They received instruction in the manufacture of explosives and use of small arms. It is no coincidence that the Azerbaijani recruiters sent the young men to an Uzbek group's training camp. The most important reason might have been language. Although Gelowicz, Schneider, and Yilmaz had studied Arabic in the Middle East, they were far from fluent in the language, which meant that they could not go to al-Qaeda and Taliban camps where Arabic and Pashtu were spoken. Gelowicz, Yilmaz, and Selek all spoke Turkish, however.[9] Since Turks and Uzbeks (and Azerbaijanis) are related Turkic peoples who speak mutually intelligible languages, ease of communication could have been the motive. Furthermore, the future plotters belonged to a larger network of young jihadis who went to train in Pakistan from 2006, a majority of whom were of Turkish origin. The Uzbek camps were the most suitable to host Turkish speakers and their friends.

In the fall of 2006, the IJU sent the new recruits back to Germany. In their home country, they started preparations for the attack. The plotters lacked detailed orders about targets, although American installations were a priority. Furthermore, the IJU leadership asked the plotters to attack official Uzbekistani targets if possible.[10] Within this limit, the group enjoyed a certain freedom to maneuver. Until summer 2007, the cell remained in close contact with its superiors in Iran and Waziristan: One of them was Gofir Salimov, a logistics officer mainly based in the Iranian city of Zahedan. The second was Suhail Buranov, a person known under his pseudonym, Sulaiman, the IJU leader's right hand in Mir Ali. In early September 2007, the IJU leadership demanded action within the coming two weeks.[11] The IJU wanted the attacks to take place during the German debate over the extension of the Afghanistan mandates for participation in the International Security Assistance Force (ISAF) and Operation Enduring Freedom. The IJU leaders evidently calculated that attacks just before the Bundestag votes in October and November 2007 could prevent an extension and force the withdrawal of German troops.[12]

The main logistical problem before constructing the bombs was procuring functioning detonators. During the summer of 2006, Atilla Selek sent detonators from Istanbul to the cell. After he had studied with the group in Syria and taken part in the training in Waziristan in 2006, Selek settled in Turkey. He was tasked with the procurement of the detonators and the facilitation of the group's escape after the attack. In Istanbul, Selek was in contact with other Turkish jihadis, who helped him procure the detonators.[13]

The German authorities first gained knowledge of the group in October 2006. Then the U.S. government informed German authorities about e-mail contacts between Pakistan and Germany that the NSA monitored. After following the initial information, the German services and police started a huge counterterrorism operation, code-named "Operation Alberich," and followed the group throughout the coming months.[14] This was the largest German counterterrorism operation to date. The plotters were arrested before they realized that the police had exchanged the hydrogen peroxide.

THE CONTEXT: JIHADISM IN GERMANY AFTER 2001

The Sauerland plot was the result of a growing trend toward radicalization among young Muslims in Germany. Most notably, however, this was the first major plot that had been designed by a network in which Turks and Germans of Turkish origin were well represented. For six years after the attacks of 9/11, Arabs dominated both hardcore jihadi circles and their sympathizers and supporters in Germany. Although there were suggestions pointing to the increasing radicalization of young Turks, Turkish jihadis were clearly underrepresented in a country where the overwhelming majority of Muslims (4.3 million) are of Turkish descent (around 2.6 million).[15]

In the first years after 9/11, jihadis of Arab origin affiliated with foreign organizations such as al-Qaeda, al-Qaeda in Iraq, and the Kurdish Iraqi Ansar al-Islam dominated the terrorist scene in Germany. These groups or cells were regionally homogenous and consisted of North Africans, Palestinians, and Iraqi Kurds—most of them with closer ties to their home countries than to Germany.[16] These activists tended to regard Germany primarily as a refuge, a financing hub, and a support base for operations elsewhere. Some of the legal loopholes that existed until 2001 were closed. For instance, until August 2002 it was not punishable to be a member of a foreign (as opposed to domestic) terrorist organization.

Nevertheless, Germany remained an attractive haven for those organizations that had a social base in Germany because it remained relatively liberal. For instance, until 2009, it was not punishable by law to train in a terrorist training camp.[17]

Between 2002 and 2007, a number of cells and their supporters were arrested and brought to trial. Some of them were on the verge of perpetrating attacks, hinting at the potential threat emanating from groups within Germany. Perhaps the most dangerous cell was the "Abu Ali" or "Tawhid" group. It was named after its leader, the Palestinian Muhammad Abu Dhess, or Abu Ali, and operated in the Ruhr region in the western part of the country. The group of close to a dozen mainly Palestinians and Jordanians were part of the larger Tawhid ("Monotheism") organization, which was founded and led by the Jordanian Abu Musab al-Zarqawi (1966–2006) and was later renamed al-Qaeda in Mesopotamia. In Germany, Abu Ali and his friends mainly forged travel documents, collected money, and facilitated travel for the wider organization. However, its members were arrested in April 2002, shortly after Zarqawi had personally ordered an attack that most likely would have targeted a discotheque in Düsseldorf and an undisclosed Jewish institution in Berlin.[18]

From 2005 through 2006, a trend toward more independent terrorist action became evident in Germany. Just like their jihadi forbears, who belonged to larger networks, these new groups were nationally or regionally homogeneous. In some cases, the terrorists were Germans or had lived in Germany from birth or childhood, and in others, they came from the Middle East but relocated to Germany. In one especially disturbing case, three young Turks between fifteen and eighteen years of age set up an ambush for two policemen in a quarter of Cologne heavily populated by Turkish immigrants. When the police fired into the air, they fled. Radicalized through jihadi videos on the Internet, the boys wanted to kill the policemen, take their weapons, and start a jihad against American installations in Germany.[19] In another, more well-known case, two Lebanese university students who had only arrived to Germany a year and a year and a half before the attacks, planted homemade bombs in two regional trains in North Rhine-Westphalia. Because of a technical mistake, however, the bombs did not detonate. In this case, the so-called suitcase bombers were motivated by reprints of the Danish cartoons of the prophet Muhammad in German newspapers.[20]

Because of the lack of organizational affiliation, it is considerably harder for the security services to track these small groups of individuals than their more organized colleagues. The cells affiliated with the larger movement tend to communicate intensively with their superiors in the Middle East and South Asia, but the independents do so only among themselves. On the other hand, however, the independent jihadis lack training, so their plots fail in most cases. It was the third group of German jihadis, however, who combined the strengths of both the organized and the independents, forming what might be called the "Ulm-Sauerland network." First, this group acquired qualified explosives training in the camp of an established terrorist organization in the Pakistani tribal areas. Further, the plotters acted in relative independence from an organization that primarily provided training and some vague targeting suggestions. Therefore, the Sauerland plotters were able to pursue their plan with a high degree of flexibility.

The term "Ulm-Sauerland network" refers to the fact that the Sauerland cell was part of a larger network that originated in the Multikulturhaus in Ulm and revolved around Yahia Yusuf and his companions. Besides planning the attacks, the Sauerland plotters were active in helping several of their comrades make the trip to Pakistan in order to obtain terrorist training. Beginning in early 2007, a handful of young recruits—most of them Turks from Langen in the Frankfurt region where Yilmaz lived—traveled to Pakistan via Turkey and Iran and joined the IJU. In early March 2008, one of the recruits, Cüneyt Çiftçi, a Turk born and raised in Germany, carried out a suicide attack on American and Afghan troops in the Afghan province of Khost.[21] Since then, at least several dozen young German Muslims have traveled to Pakistan in order to join the IJU and other organizations.[22] Most of them seem to have joined the IJU, but some young Germans appeared on videos produced by al-Qaeda and the Islamic Movement of Uzbekistan.[23] Others decided to leave Germany without joining their brethren in Pakistan. Many suspects with direct and indirect connections to the Ulm-Sauerland plotters traveled to Egypt, Syria, and Yemen in order to study Arabic at different language schools. There are reports about Yahia Yusuf and his son Umar—both of whom lived in Saudi Arabia—maintaining relations with followers in Egypt.[24] Most important, however, the Ulm-Sauerland network seems to have become the nucleus for the emergence of a larger jihadi scene among German Muslims.

The main difference between the members of this network and their organized and independent predecessors is that they were truly international. For the first time in Germany (and perhaps worldwide), Turks, Arabs, Kurds, and German converts were cooperating in a truly internationalist network—mirroring the broader trends toward an internationalization of jihadist ideology, strategy, and practice after 9/11. In Germany, this trend began in the Multikulturhaus in Neu-Ulm after Yahia Yusuf arrived from Freiburg in 2000. By 2002, Turkish-Arab cooperation was already a prominent feature of Salafist activities in the center.[25]

THE ORGANIZATION: THE ISLAMIC JIHAD UNION (IJU)

A Splinter Group of the Islamic Movement of Uzbekistan

The IJU was founded in 2002 as a small and at first insignificant splinter group of the Islamic Movement of Uzbekistan (IMU). The IMU had emerged in the 1990s in Uzbekistan but only announced its existence in 1998 in Kabul.[26] Its leaders were two Uzbeks from the Fergana Valley, Tahir Yoldashev (1968–2009), the emir of the organization, and Juma Namangani (1968/1969–2001), its military head. While Yoldashev was responsible for organizational matters and ideological guidance, Namagani developed a reputation as a charismatic military leader. After Namangani was killed by an American airstrike in Afghanistan in November 2001, Yoldashev and the remaining fighters fled to Pakistan. Both leaders of the IMU had to leave their home country in the early 1990s after the government cracked down on the increasingly assertive Islamist opposition. Namangani moved to Tajikistan, where he participated in the civil war on the side of the Islamist Islamic Renaissance Party. Yoldashev spent most of this time in Peshawar, where he built relations with a number of local Pakistani and Afghan organizations, including the Taliban. Although Namangani retained a base in Tavildara, Tajikistan, whence the IMU would later stage its attacks on the Fergana Valley, in 1998 the organization moved to Afghanistan, where it could count on the protection of the Taliban.[27]

Like other, more nationalist-inclined jihadi organizations, such as the Libyan Islamic Fighting Group (LIFG) and the Algerian Salafist Group for Preaching and Combat (GSPC), the IMU in its early years exclusively focused on toppling the local regime of President Islam Karimov of Uzbekistan—with the goal of replacing his postcommunist regime with an Islamic state governed by sharia law. However, because of peculiarities of the territorial situation in Central Asia, the IMU's activities gained a transnational element over time. The overwhelming majority of the organization's members were recruited from the Fergana Valley. In the 1920s, the valley was divided between the three Soviet republics—Uzbekistan, Tajikistan, and Kyrgyzstan—with Uzbekistan taking the main share of the mainly Uzbek-populated region. The division brought about a complex mixture of territories and ethnic groups, which was one of the reasons the IMU targeted Tajikistan and Kyrgyzstan. Consequently, the IMU has always been more of a Fergana Valley liberation movement, fighting the three ruling regimes there, rather than a purely Uzbek organization. This became most obvious in 1999 and 2000, when the IMU went on the offensive in Uzbekistan and the Fergana Valley.

In February 1999, the IMU perpetrated a string of attacks in Tashkent, Uzbekistan. Six car bombs detonated during an attempt to assassinate President Karimov. Thirteen people died, and more than one hundred were wounded.[28] During the following two summers, IMU guerrillas entered the Fergana Valley from Tajikistan and tried to destabilize Uzbekistan by attacking security forces stationed in the border regions. The IMU raids provoked an intensification of already existing conflicts among the governments of Uzbekistan, Tajikistan, and Kyrgyzstan. Each regime made its neighbor responsible for the escalation of violence.[29]

While support from some Tajik Islamist politicians for the IMU was running out at this time, the organization benefited from the protection afforded to its fighters by the Taliban government in Afghanistan. It established its headquarters in Mazar-e Sharif and Kunduz in the north of the country. Between 1998 and 2001, it commanded between 2,000 and 3,000 fighters, many of whom fought with the Taliban against the Northern Alliance.[30] Most of its personnel were Uzbeks, but there were Kyrgyzs, Tajiks, Chechens, and even some Uighurs from the Chinese Central Asian province of Xinjiang among them. The Taliban seem to have sent Chechen and Uighur volunteers north to join the IMU. This way, they were able to deny hosting these groups whenever Russian and Chinese officials protested the presence of their militant opposition on Afghan soil.[31]

Because of the alliance with the Taliban and the integration of other Central Asian fighters, the IMU in its Afghan years developed into an increasingly transnational, Central Asian rather than an exclusively Uzbek organization without, however, adjusting its leadership structure or redefining its goals and strategy. The IMU's leaders repeatedly declared that they aimed exclusively for the downfall of the Uzbek government and not those of the other Central Asian states.[32] However, the organization's activities in Tajikistan and especially Kyrgyzstan suggested otherwise. Within the organization, there were serious debates about a possible internationalization, in which the more conservative nationalist forces seem to have gained the upper hand. Therefore, in 2001, the IMU leadership denied reports that the organization had changed its name to Islamic Party of Turkestan and that it now aimed at an Islamic revolution in the whole of Central Asia.[33] Nevertheless, there was a noticeable trend toward internationalization among Uzbek jihadists, and the news about the foundation of a more internationalist structure revealed internal debates over ideology and future strategies within the IMU.

The Emergence of the Islamic Jihad Union

The IJU formed in 2002, after a small group of more internationalist-minded activists left the IMU.[34] There is no concrete evidence of the reasons for this split, but circumstantial evidence points to conflicts over ideology and strategy. Most important, the split came shortly after news about conflicts over internationalization within the IMU, at a time when other jihadi organizations such as al-Qaeda went through a period of intense debate over future strategy after the loss of their bases in Afghanistan.

In 2002, the IMU was not yet willing to change its focus from Uzbekistan and Central Asia. During the American invasion of Afghanistan, beginning in October 2001, the IMU suffered massive losses. Most important, its charismatic military leader, Namagani, other leaders, and hundreds of fighters were killed.[35] Under the leadership of Tahir Yoldashev, its remaining members retreated from northern and central Afghanistan to the Pakistani side of the border zone, to Wana in South Waziristan.[36] Yoldashev responded to the trend toward internationalization by devoting more of his speeches to conflicts outside Central and Southern Asia, declaring that the IMU supported the struggle against the West in Chechnya, Iraq, and Palestine. But this change in rhetoric seems to have been mainly propaganda, for elsewhere in his messages, Yoldashev repeatedly emphasized that the IMU's primary aim remained overthrowing the regimes in the Central Asian states of Uzbekistan, Kyrgyzstan, and Tajikistan and that it had not renounced its original goals in Central Asia.[37] Even more important, the IMU did not take part in the Taliban insurgency in Afghanistan, preferring to stay on the Pakistan side of the border and support the Pakistani Taliban, who later began targeting the Pakistani government. Therefore, the foundation of the IJU was likely a consequence of the IMU's refusal to be more responsive to demands of the internationalists within its ranks.

The loss of Namangani as the military leader of the IMU might have played a role in the split as well.[38] Namangani had been an experienced and charismatic commander of probably the best-trained jihadi guerrilla forces east of Chechnya and as such prominent throughout the region. Yoldashev, however, seems to have had problems asserting his control over parts of the organization. Although he led the organization with an iron fist, he was not able to replace Namangani as a military commander, nor could he match his personal charisma among the Uzbek jihadists. Lacking these qualities was even more serious because many IMU fighters were dispersed in Afghanistan and Pakistan and needed directions. It is possible that the emerging IJU leadership simply refused to submit to the command of someone who they thought lacked essential qualities for a jihadist leader. There is evidence that the IJU leader Najmiddin Jalolov had personals problems with Yoldashev.[39] Even so, however, the IJU would have claimed ideological motives. In any case, the rupture does not seem to have caused major conflicts. In fact, it seems that the relations between IMU and IJU personnel remained quite strong. The national bond among Uzbeks proved to be more important than organizational affiliations, which likely do not concern many simple recruits.

The IJU was most likely founded in North Waziristan, where the organization is based to this day. Until his death in September 2009, its leader was Najmiddin Jalolov (born in 1972, a.k.a. Abu Yahia), an Uzbek from Andijan in the Fergana Valley who had been sentenced to death in absentia by an Uzbek court in 2000 but was never caught.[40] Jalolov was identical with a person frequently posing as the emir of the IJU on the Internet called Abu Yahia Muhammad Fatih.[41] His second-in-command was Suhail Buranov (a.k.a. Mansur Suhail or Abu Huzaifa), a native of Tashkent (born in 1983) and an ethnic Uzbek as well.[42] The military leader was a certain Abdallah Fatih (a.k.a. Raushan), who—after Jalolov's death—took the overall lead of the IJU.[43] Not much is known about the rest of the organization, only that it remains relatively small, with not more than 200 members and at times perhaps fewer than 100. Since the fall of 2007, several IJU fighters have been killed in American airstrikes, and, as a result, others might have decided to move around in North Waziristan. Most members are still from Uzbekistan, but the organization also includes Tajiks, Kyrgyz, and Kazakhs, and it also cooperates with Chechen and Uighur militants, in keeping with its IMU roots.

Whatever the exact nature of the disagreements between IJU and IMU, the IJU—although considerably smaller than the IMU—has been far more active in international terrorism since 2001. It first focused on Uzbekistan, where it perpetrated attacks on Uzbek, American, and Israeli targets in 2004 and in 2006 carried its jihad to Pakistan as well. The planned attacks in Germany were the first culmination point of a trend toward the internationalization of its strategy that began in 2002. Because of its new fame in jihadist circles, the number of recruits from Germany seems to have risen ever since.[44]

The IJU is identical with the Islamic Jihad Group (IJG), the organization that claimed responsibility for suicide attacks in Uzbekistan in late March, April, and July 2004—the first suicide attacks in Central Asia. In late March and early April 2004, some of its members engaged in suicide attacks and firing raids targeting the Uzbek police in Bukhara and Tashkent. Forty-seven people died in the attacks, most of them militants.[45] In July 2004, members of the IJG staged suicide attacks on the Israeli and U.S. embassies in Uzbekistan and on the office of the attorney general in the Uzbek capital, Tashkent.[46] These were the first attacks on Western targets in Central Asia, hinting at the group's growing internationalist character. The strikes coincided with the trials of members of the IJG who had organized the attacks in spring 2004. In both cases, claims of responsibility by a "Jama'at al-Jihad al-Islami" or Islamic Jihad Group were posted on Arabic Jihadist websites.[47]

Subsequent investigations established that the IJG was indeed a Central Asian and not a uniquely Uzbekistani organization. In November 2004, Kazakh authorities confirmed earlier reports of contacts between the perpetrators of the attacks in Bukhara and Tashkent and Kazakhstan. They reportedly discovered a terrorist grouping called the "Mujahedin of Central Asia Group," which seems to have been the name used for the IJG or one of its cells operating in Kazakhstan. According to the reports, it formed in 2002 and consisted of fifty Uzbek and twenty Kazakh citizens. The group in Kazakhstan was lead by a Kyrgyz, its branch in Uzbekistan by an Uzbek, both former members of the IMU. Some of the perpetrators of the bombings in Tashkent in spring 2004 trained in the southern Kazakh city of Shimkent, close to the Uzbek border. Although the exact relationship between the local cells and the leadership in Pakistan remains unclear, it seems as if Jalalov had some hand in the planning process.[48]

Most important, however, the attacks could hardly be considered successful for the IJU. Primarily, the number of terrorists killed was far higher than the number of Uzbek victims. The perpetrators did not manage to kill any foreign nationals. While the attacks gained some international attention, information about the group behind it was so scarce that when the IJU later became active in Pakistan and Germany, most commentators did not know whether there was any relation between the IJG in 2004 and the IJU. Indeed, the organization seems to have changed its name to IJU in early 2005.[49]

The IJU as an Internationalist Organization

In 2006, scattered media reports emerged about the IJU, heralding its emergence as a threat in South Asia. The first target was Pakistan. Subsequent events must be seen within the context of the rise of the Pakistani Taliban, i.e., Pashtun militants from the Pakistan side of the border region who increasingly targeted the Pakistani state and its institutions. Foreigners living under the protection of Taliban leaders in the tribal areas were likely to support their activities in Pakistan proper. The Uzbeks were no exception, and although the IMU seems to have been more active in this regard, the IJU followed suit.

In November 2006, a cell of Pakistani IJU members was arrested for planning rocket attacks on government targets in Islamabad. The IJU leadership in North Waziristan is said to have trained those who were to carry out the attacks, supplied them with weapons, and issued them with orders. Their motive was allegedly opposition to the Pakistani government's support for the United States. While there is no independent way to verify this version of the events, the mode of action closely resembled that of the Sauerland plot. The attackers—non–Central Asians, like the "Sauerland three"—trained in IJU camps in North Waziristan, where the IJU leadership and its allies planned the attacks.[50] They then returned to their home countries, Pakistan and Germany, to organize and perpetrate the attacks. The Central Asian IJU members themselves took part in the guerrilla campaign in Afghanistan on the side of the Taliban.

In fact, the rank-and-file members of the IJU concentrated on the fight against coalition forces in Afghanistan in 2006. The IJU is closely allied with the Haqqani network and has built its headquarters in Mir Ali, a city in North Waziristan. In order to build a presence there, it needed the protection of the Haqqani family and its followers, who constitute the most important local Taliban grouping. The network is named after Jalaladdin Haqqani (born probably between 1930 and 1938), an almost legendary commander of the Afghan mujaheddin already during the 1980s, when he developed close ties to Osama bin Laden. The Haqqani network constitutes an almost separate wing within the Taliban movement, although it nominally operates under the authority of Mullah Omar. From its headquarters in Miranshah, the capital of North Waziristan, it is responsible for most Taliban operations in the central part of Eastern Afghanistan, namely in the provinces of Khost, Paktia, and Paktika. Although the elder Haqqani is still alive, his eldest son, Sirajaddin, seems to have taken over the command over the Haqqani forces. Sirajaddin Haqqani has proved to be an even more ruthless and brutal commander than his father. Besides having adopted al-Qaeda in Iraq–style tactics, Haqqani and his followers increasingly operate in Kabul and its surroundings. For instance, coalition forces have claimed Haqqani is responsible for the attack on the Kabul Serena Hotel in January 2008.[51]

The Haqqani network has increasingly sent foreign fighters to the battlefields of Afghanistan, among them Pakistanis, Arabs, and Central Asian members of the IJU. How close the relations were between the IJU and Haqqani was documented in a video that was passed on to the *Spiegel* reporter Matthias Gebauer in Afghanistan in late March 2008. On the video, Haqqani praised "military operations" in an Afghan border district and claimed that he had been present during the events. The comments referred to the suicide attack of Cüneyt Çiftçi in the province of Khost in early March 2008. The video contained video footage of the attack and Çiftçi's preparations.[52]

Behind the Scenes: Al-Qaeda and the Sauerland Plot

Al-Qaeda and its supporters developed a new interest in Germany beginning in 2006. Because of the success of the Taliban in invigorating the insurgency in Afghanistan, al-Qaeda refocused its own strategy. While the war in Iraq had dominated the organization's strategic thinking after 2003, Afghanistan regained its importance because of the newfound strength of the Taliban and the weakness of its adversaries in Afghanistan. Therefore, Germany became a more prominent target for possible terrorist attacks. After 2003, al-Qaeda and its allies invested considerable efforts to perpetrate attacks primarily against those countries that had sent troops to Iraq in an effort to undermine U.S. alliances. The attacks in Madrid 2004 and London 2005 were consistent with this strategy. Consequently, Germany—having refused to support the United States in Iraq—was not a top priority for the jihadi movement. After al-Qaeda returned its focus to Afghanistan, however, Germany became a much more important potential target. The country provides the third-largest contingent of foreign troops after the United States and the United Kingdom, but subsequent German governments have shown an obvious lack of enthusiasm for the Afghanistan operation—mainly because of widespread public resistance to the presence of German troops at the Hindu Kush. Therefore, al-Qaeda likely regards Germany as the weak link in the chain of major troop providers and hoped that attacks on German targets might trigger a withdrawal of German troops.

From 2005–2006, al-Qaeda's operations were led by a new generation of field commanders who rebuilt the alliance with the Taliban after its defeat in Afghanistan in 2001. The Egyptian Mustafa Abu l-Yazid served as the most important liaison to the Taliban and was named its commander for Afghanistan. Others, such as the Egyptian Abu Ubaydah al-Masri concentrated on planning attacks in Europe. He seems to have been the mastermind of the London bombings on July 7, 2005, and the transatlantic airliner plot thwarted in London in August 2006.[53] Another important field commander, the Libyan Abu Laith al-Libi (a.k.a. 'Ali 'Ammar al-Ruqay'i, 1972–2008), served as al-Qaeda's liaison to the IJU and a kind of Central Asia representative for the organization. He is the chief suspect as the true mastermind of the Sauerland plot.[54]

Al-Libi cultivated particularly close ties with the Taliban and the Uzbeks but long retained a certain distance from al-Qaeda. Already before the fall of the Taliban, the relationship between the Uzbek IMU and al-Qaeda was strained. The reason seems to have been al-Qaeda's efforts to recruit Central Asians. While in at least one case Mullah Omar himself seems to have prevented the outbreak of hostilities between Arabs and Uzbeks, relations remained strained after the Taliban's escape to Pakistan. Early on, the Uzbeks rejected any contacts with al-Qaeda and other Arabs, with al-Libi the only exception.[55] Some of the resentment seems to have stemmed from al-Qaeda's responsibility for the fall of the Islamic emirate after 9/11. Al-Libi belonged to a not-small group of jihadis critical of bin Laden and his organization. These Arab leaders, like the aforementioned Mustafa Abu l-Yazid and the Syrian ideologist Abu Musab al-Suri, were ardent supporters of the Taliban and Mullah Omar and therefore critical of al-Qaeda's attack on the United States, which provoked the downfall of the Islamic emirate.

Although al-Libi's position is not exactly known, he is reported to have fallen out with al-Qaeda, at least temporarily, because of the domination of Egyptians in the upper ranks of the organization.[56] By 2007 at the latest, however, al-Qaeda managed to bring al-Libi back to the fold and convinced him to declare the merger of the Libyan Islamic Fighting Group with al-Qaeda in November of that year.[57] By integrating commanders like al-Libi into the organization, al-Qaeda broadened its appeal not only among those Arabs who had been critical of the group's strategies in the past but also among the Uzbeks for whom the Libyan seems to have been a prominent leader.

Soon after the arrests of the Sauerland cell in September 2007, news emerged about al-Libi's possible role as a mastermind of the plot. However, the German authorities did not present any conclusive evidence.

The depth of his involvement with the IJU became obvious, however, after he was killed in an American drone attack on his hideout near Mir Ali in January 2008.[58] Soon afterward, the IJU confirmed that al-Libi was killed during the attack. Most important, however, six Central Asian members of the organization are reported to have died with al-Libi.[59] In a declaration, the IJU authors called the field commander "our Sheikh," a designation hinting at al-Libi's leading function within or for the organization. In certain contexts, the title "Sheikh" can indicate a religious function as well. As al-Libi was a man of action, a field commander as opposed to a preacher or strategist, he must have been seen as a military leader by the IJU.[60]

A Public Relations Campaign

From 2007, the IJU embarked on efforts to raise its profile in jihadist circles by starting a vigorous public-relations campaign. In June 2007, the IJU published an interview with its leader, "Ebu Yahya Muhammed Fatih," in which he outlined the goals and the ideology of the IJU.[61] However, it was the IJU's public-relations efforts after the arrest of the Sauerland cell in September 2007 that have allowed deeper insights into the nature of the organization. The campaign seems to have been an effort to exploit the sudden attention of the international media and was made possible only by the integration of Turks from Germany or Turkey into the organization, as most of the propaganda material was published in the Turkish language on a website hosted in Turkey. Some of the texts were written in faulty Turkish, possibly hinting at the involvement of diaspora Turks who had spent most of their lives in Germany.[62]

The website the IJU used until June 2008 was www.sehadetvakti.com, but it later moved to www.sehadetzamani.com.[63] Right after the German arrests were made public in early September, a "press declaration" signed by the "political leadership" of the IJU appeared on the site, commenting on the arrest of the Sauerland cell some days earlier. It stated that the three "brothers" had planned attacks on the U.S. airbase in Ramstein, Germany, and on the U.S. and Uzbek consulates. Their aim had been to protest against U.S. and Uzbek policy and to prompt Germany to give up its base in Termez, Uzbekistan.[64]

In the following months, the IJU tried to develop a corporate identity under its Turkish name, "İslami Cihad İttehadi."[65] The videos on its website frequently feature black banners with its Arabic name, "Ittihad al-Jihad al-Islami" or its (abbreviated) English translation "Islamic Jihad."[66] The videos were produced by the organization's media wing, "Badr at-Tawhid" (literally "the full moon of monotheism"), and mostly contain a short lead text in Arabic, hinting at the desire to impress Arabic-speaking sympathizers and possibly financiers. The videos show training camps in the Pakistani tribal areas and give an insight into the arenas of conflict where the IJU claims to be active, namely, Afghanistan and the Swat valley in the North-West Frontier Province of Pakistan.

Beginning in March 2008, the IJU produced a number of videos featuring both German and Turkish recruits who had been recruited by members of the Sauerland cell in 2007. Most important, in early March 2008, the website announced the death of Cüneyt Çiftçi in a suicide attack on American and Afghan troops in the Afghan province of Paktika.[67] The website showed pictures of Çiftçi while training for and preparing the attack. In April 2008, Çiftçi's video was followed by one of a German convert training in an IJU camp in Pakistan, Eric Breininger, who called for Muslims living in Germany to join the "jihad" against the West.[68] Breininger and several other German recruits appeared in a number of IJU videos until 2009.

On the Internet, the IJU tries to present itself as a transnational organization with supporters in Pakistan, Afghanistan, Central Asia, and Europe fighting the Karimov regime, the Pakistani government, the coalition troops in Afghanistan, and their local allies. It is noteworthy that the development of the IJU's own media wing mirrored a similar trend among the Taliban and other groups after 2005, who followed al-Qaeda's model in disseminating its message worldwide using the Internet as a key distribution platform.

The Turkish Dimension

From the 1990s, Turkey had been an important logistics hub for al-Qaeda and a way station for jihadis traveling to Pakistan and Afghanistan. One important jihadi transit route led Europeans, North Africans, and Middle

Easterners to Turkey, in most cases to Istanbul first, and from there overland to Iran and Pakistan. The most important operative based there seems to have been Muhammad Bahaiah (Abu Khalid al-Suri), a Syrian.[69] To what extent Turkish operatives are implicated in these activities has not yet been established. However, it seems as if the Turkish dimension seems to have been more significant than previously known. To an extent, the IJU and other jihadi groups may have benefited from the Turkish authorities' preoccupation with the threat posed by the Kurdistan Workers Party, or PKK, by far the strongest terrorist organization in the country.

The Sauerland cell heavily relied on an infrastructure already in place in Turkey. Most members of the group and the young men they recruited in 2007 traveled to Pakistan via Turkey and Iran. From February 2007, Atilla Selek remained in Istanbul in order to build a logistics hub for the group and facilitate the travels of other personnel to Iran and Pakistan. Most important, in July and August 2007, Selek sent the detonators needed for the Sauerland plot from Istanbul to Germany.[70]

Selek, however, seems to have entertained relations to a bigger terrorist structure in Istanbul. First, the IJU website was hosted in Turkey in 2007 and 2008, so other members of the organization must have lived in the country. Second, the detonators were provided by a contact from Istanbul, the German Turk Mevlüt Kar, a shadowy figure and seemingly an important jihadi logistics officer channeling recruits to Chechnya and the Caucasus. Kar (born in 1979) had been living in the industrial city of Ludwigshafen, in southwestern Germany. He left Germany in August 2002 after the police had identified him as the head of a German terror cell allegedly in contact with Abu Musab al-Zarqawi. After spending several months in a Turkish jail, he seems to have been based in Istanbul and reappeared on the jihadist scene in summer 2007.[71] It would not come as a surprise if Kar played a key role in jihadist networks after 2003.

Perhaps the most important open question with regard to the Ulm-Sauerland network is whether it is part of a wider trend toward the integration of Turks into international jihadist networks. This would be a significant success for the jihadi movement, which still suffers from important national and regional divisions. Relations among Punjabis and Kashmiris, Arabs and Uzbeks, Libyans and Egyptians, Palestinians and Saudis, Turks and Kurds are often fraught with conflicts over aims, ideologies, strategies, and leadership, and in most cases these groups are united only tactically by the existence of common enemies. Contrary to their claim of solidarity among members of the same supranational community of believers (*umma*), national and ethnic dividing lines have to this day hindered the emergence of a truly global movement. Nevertheless, there are many indications of a trend toward abolishing many of these differences. For instance, in the Pakistani tribal areas, the jihadi organizations seem to have started a process of integration that has rendered national and ethnic and organizational borders weaker than some years ago. Pakistanis and Pakistani-origin Europeans seem to have fewer qualms about cooperating with Arab organizations than they had in 2001. And Turkish jihadis seem to have given up some of their focus on their home country and their prejudice concerning Arabs. The Ulm-Sauerland network is a first strong indication that the Turkish jihadis are going through an internationalization process. If that is the case, Turkey and those European countries with strong Turkish minorities—first and foremost Germany—will have increasing problems with Turkish jihadis in the future.

NOTES

1. Various explosive devices using hydrogen peroxide have become popular with jihadi groups especially after 2001 and have featured in a number of attacks. Most important, TATP (triacetone triperoxide), the most popular hydrogen-peroxide-based explosive, has been used, for instance, in the attacks in Djerba in 2002, Casablanca in 2003, and London in 2005.

2. "Der Hass des Abdullah," *Der Spiegel*, September 1, 2008.

3. "Ein Urteil für die Zukunft," *Der Spiegel*, April 11, 2009.

4. "Rekrutierung von Islamisten in Deutschland," *Süddeutsche Zeitung* (Munich), October 31, 2007.

5. On his biography and the history of the Multikulturhaus, see "Islamisten aus der schwäbischen Provinz," *Neue Zürcher Zeitung* (Zurich), June 21, 2006.

6. The Multikulturhaus was closed by the Bavarian authorities in December 2005. Many visitors moved to the Islamic Information Center (Islamisches Informationszentrum, IIZ) in Ulm, which was closed in 2007.

7. "Der innerste Ring," *Der Spiegel*, November 12, 2007.

8. Adem Yilmaz described the recruitment and the travels in the presence of the author in his confession in court in September 2009.

9. Turkish is the native tongue for Selek and Yilmaz. According to his confessions in the Düsseldorf court, Gelowicz improved his spoken Turkish during his travels and his stay in Waziristan.

10. "Yassin Musharbash: Phantom IJU wird greifbar," *Der Spiegel*, September 2, 2009, available at http://www.spiegel.de/politik/ausland/0,1518,646268,00.html (accessed September 20, 2009).

11. "Aladins Erzählungen," *Der Spiegel*, October 8, 2007; "Operation Alberich," *Der Spiegel*, September 10, 2007.

12. "Sauerland-Gruppe wollte mit Anschlag ISAF-Mandat torpedieren," *Der Spiegel*, August 30, 2008, available at http://www.spiegel.de/panorama/justiz/0,1518,575384,00.html (accessed June 1 2009).

13. "Der fünfte Mann," *Der Spiegel*, April 20, 2009.

14. On the details, see "Operation Alberich," *Der Spiegel*, September 10, 2007.

15. "Gläubig und integriert," *Süddeutsche Zeitung* (Munich), June 23, 2009.

16. For a journalistic overview of the plots in Germany so far, see Annette Ramelsberger, *Der Deutsche Jihad. Islamisten planen den Anschlag* (Berlin: Econ, 2008).

17. See "Vorbereitung einer schweren staatsgefährdenden Gewalttat," Strafgesetzbuch (criminal law code), available at http://dejure.org/gesetze/StGB/89a.html (accessed October 15, 2009).

18. On the Abu Ali case, see "Ziele in Deutschland," *Der Spiegel*, April 29, 2004, 94.

19. On this case in detail, see "Gotteskrieger verurteilt," *Kölner Stadt-Anzeiger* (Cologne), April 3, 2009.

20. "'Lebenslänglich' für Kölner 'Kofferbomber,'" *Neue Zürcher Zeitung* (Zurich), December 10, 2008.

21. "Islami Cihad İttehadi Basın Açıklaması," available at http://www.sehadetvakti.com/haber_detay.php?haber_id=1889 (accessed March 7, 2008).

22. In most cases, German police and intelligence officials speak about 200 volunteers who have trained in "terror camps" after 2001.

23. See, for instance, the video entitled "Islamische Bewegung Usbekistan: 'Die Vorzüge des Jihads,'" September 2009.

24. Several members of the network in Ulm went to the Cordoba language school in Yahia Yusuf's hometown, Alexandria. The school is reported to have been closed to students from Germany in 2008.

25. Personal communication by Ahmet Senyurt, a television journalist specializing in the Islamist scene in Germany, November 8, 2002.

26. On the history of the IMU, see Vitaly V. Naumkin, *Radical Islam in Central Asia: Between Pen and Rifle* (Lanham, Md..: Rowman & Littlefield, 2005), 51–126.

27. 'Umar 'Abd al-Hakim (Abu Musab al-Suri), *Da'wat al-Muqawama al-Islamiya al-'Alamiya*, (n.p.: n.d. [2004]), 783–85.

28. For an account of the events that depends heavily on Uzbekistani official information, see Oleg Yakubov, *The Pack of Wolves: The Blood Trail of Terror* (Moscow: Veche, 2000).

29. Vitaly V. Naumkin, "Militant Islam in Central Asia: The Case of the Islamic Movement of Uzbekistan," Berkeley Program in Soviet and Post-Soviet Studies, University of California, 2003, http://iseees.berkeley.edu/bps/publications/2003_06-naum.pdf, 39.

30. 'Abd al-Hakim, Da'wat al-Muqawama al-Islamiya, 785; Ahmed Rashid, Jihad: The Rise of Militant Islam in Central Asia (New Haven, Conn.: Yale University Place, 2002), 174.

31. Rashid, Jihad, 176.

32. "Uzbek Islamist Denies Plans for Regional Hegemony," Radio Free Europe/Radio Liberty, Uzbek Service, June 2, 2001

33. Rashid, Jihad, 176, 180.

34. On the IJU, see Guido Steinberg, "A Turkish Al Qaeda: The Islamic Jihad Union and the Internationalization of Uzbek Jihadism," Strategic Insights 7, no. 3 (July 2008), available at http://www.ccc.nps.navy.mil/si/2008/Jul/steinbergJul08.asp; Ronald Sandee, "The Islamic Jihad Union," NEFA Foundation, October 14, 2008, available at http://www.nefafoundation.org/miscellaneous/FeaturedDocs/nefaijuoct08.pdf (accessed June 3, 2009); Einar Wigen, "Islamic Jihad Union: Al-Qaida's Key to the Turkic World," Norwegian Defence Research Establishment, February 23, 2009, available at http://www.mil.no/multimedia/archive/00122/00687_122609a.pdf (accessed June 16, 2009).

35. 'Abd al-Hakim, Da'wat al-Muqawama al-Islamiya, 785.

36. Zahid Hussain, Frontline Pakistan: The Struggle with Militant Islam (New York: Columbia University Press, 2007), 144.

37. See, for instance, his audio message on the occasion of the fifth anniversary of 9/11, "Islamist Leader Threatens Central Asian Presidents," BBC Monitoring: Former Soviet Union, September 17, 2006.

38. Didier Chaudet interprets the foundation of the IJU as a result of a leadership struggle: Didier Chaudet, "Islamist Terrorism in Greater Central Asia: The 'Al-Qaedaization' of Uzbek Jihadism," Russie.Nei.Visions, no. 35 (December 2008), available at http://www.ifri.org/files/Russie/ifri_uzbek_jihadism_chaudet_ENG_december2008.pdf (accessed January 10, 2009).

39. During his interrogation in court (and in the presence of the author), Fritz Gelowicz elaborated on the bad relations between the two leaders. He had his information from Suhail Buranov.

40. On Jalolov, see U.S. Department of the Treasury, "Treasury Designates Leadership of the IJU Terrorist Group," June 18, 2008, available at http://www.treasury.gov/press-center/press-releases/Pages/hp1035.aspx (accessed January 9, 2012).

41. "Fatih" is the Turkish and Arabic word for "conqueror" and the famous sobriquet for the Ottoman Sultan Mehmet (Muhammad) Fatih (1432–1481), the conqueror of Constantinople. "Muhammad Fatih" is a name familiar to most Turkish speakers and was obviously chosen to attract young Turks.

42. U.S. Department of the Treasury, "Treasury Designates Leadership of the IJU Terrorist Group"; Dawn (Karachi), Internet Edition, November 4, 2006, quoted in

"Pakistani Al-Qa'idah Link to Failed Islamabad Rocket Attacks," *BBC Monitoring South Asia*, November 4, 2006.

43. See the press declaration "İslami Cihad İttihadi Basın Açıklaması," available at http://www.sehadetzamani.com/haber_detay.php?haber_id=2246 (accessed October 16, 2009).

44. "Deutsche Kolonie," *Der Spiegel*, September 21, 2009, 27.

45. Centrasia Website, Moscow, quoted in "Unknown Group Pledges to Fight to 'The Last Drop of Blood' in Uzbekistan," BBC Monitoring Newsfile, April 3, 2004.

46. On the IJG's claim of responsibility, see MIPT Terrorism Knowledge Base, "Islamic Jihad Group (Uzbekistan)," available at http://www.tkb.org/Group.jsp ?groupID=4582 (accessed March 7, 2008).

47. It seems to have been first posted on the prominent "Islamic Minbar" website in Switzerland, which has been closed in the meantime, at http://www.islamicminbar .com/forum/viewtopic.php?t=338 (accessed September 7, 2004).

48. Daniel Kimmage, "Kazakh Breakthrough on Uzbek Terror Case," *RFE/RL*, November 15, 2004, at http://www.rferl.org/featuresarticle/2004/11/f85202a7-d2ce -4c73-b3be-c280401be768.html; "Suspect in Uzbek Terror Trial Says Group Leader Was Follower of Taliban Fugitive Mullah Omar," *The America's Intelligence Wire*, July 27, 2004.

49. The State Department hinted at a change in name or a parallel usage of "Group" and "Union" in *Country Reports on Terrorism 2005*, US Department of State, Office of the Coordinator for Counterterrorism, Washington, April 2006, 107.

50. "Pakistani Al-Qa'idah Link to Failed Islamabad Rocket Attacks." The Pakistanis were said to have belonged to Pakistani militant organizations.

51. Imtiaz Ali, "The Haqqani Network and Cross-Border Terrorism in Afghanistan," *Terrorism Monitor*, March 24, 2008.

52. See Matthias Gebauer, "Top-Taliban kommandieren Deutsche Gotteskrieger," *Der Spiegel*, April 5, 2009, available at http://www.spiegel.de/politik/ausland/0,1518 ,545562,00.html (accessed May 26, 2009).

53. On the new strategy, see Guido Steinberg, *The Return of al-Qaida: Current Developments in International Terrorism and Their Consequences for Europe* (Berlin: Stiftung Wissenschaft und Politik: 2007).

54. Shortly after the attacks were thwarted, German officials hinted at al-Libi as the possible mastermind, without, however, providing any conclusive evidence.

55. Interview with Noman Benotman, a former member of the Libyan Islamic Fighting Group leadership, London, July 21, 2008.

56. "Regional Fissures Within al-Qaida," *Al-Hayat* (London), April 5, 2006 (in Arabic).

57. "Al-Qaida Extends Its Influence: Direction Maghreb," *Al-Hayat* (London), November 4, 2007 (in Arabic).

58. The attack targeted a house in the village of Khushali Torikhel, twelve kilometers south of Mir Ali. See "Abu l-Laith al-Libi and al-Darnawi Were Killed on Their Way

to a Meeting with the Prime Suspect in the Bhuttto Assassination," *Al-Hayat* (London), February 2, 2008 (in Arabic).

59. "Abu Laith al-Libi's Death Together with Eleven Others in Pakistan," *Al-Hayat* (London), February 1, 2008.

60. In this declaration, the IJU sent the first report about the suicide attack perpetrated by Cüneyt Çiftçi: "Our operation was in retaliation for our Sheikh, the Mujahid Abu Laith al-Libi, who was killed a short while ago in retaliation for our killed mujaheddin" (my translation from the Turkish original). See "İslami Cihad İttehadi Basın Açıklaması," available at http://www.sehadetvakti.com/haber_detay.php?haber _id=1889 (accessed March 7, 2008).

61. The interview was posted in Turkish: "İslami Cihad İttehadi Emiri Ebu Yahya Muhammed Fatih ile Röportaj," available at http://www.cihaderi.net/haber .php?item_id=770.html, (accessed February 23, 2008). An English translation was available at the IJU website: http://sehadetvakti.com/haber_detay.php?haber_id =1203 (accessed May 14, 2008).

62. While most migrants from Turkey stick to their mother tongue, Turkish is hardly ever taught at German schools. This leaves most Turkish speakers in Germany with limited Turkish-language capabilities.

63. The translation of both titles is "Time for Martyrdom." The older texts quoted in this article can still be found at http://sehadetzamani.com/.

64. "İslami Cihad İttehadi Basın Açıklaması," September 11, 2007, available at http://sehadetvakti.com/haber_detay.php?haber_id=1587 (accessed September 17, 2007).

65. In fact, even this Turkish translation for Islamic Jihad Union, is old-fashioned at best. The modern Turkish name is "İslami Cihad Birliği," and even if one uses Ottoman vocabulary, the correct spelling would be "İttihadi."

66. See the IJU video collection on the "Time for Martyrdom" website, http:// www.sehadetzamani.com/kategori_haber.php?&kat_id=55 (accessed October 16, 2009).

67. "İslami Cihad İttehadi Basın Açıklaması," http://www.sehadetvakti.com /haber_detay.php?haber_id=1889 (accessed March 7, 2008).

68. On Eric Breininger, see "Der Weg ins Paradies," *Der Spiegel*, September 29, 2008. On the video, see Matthias Gebauer and Yassin Musharbash, "Deutscher Islamist meldet sich mit Dschihad-Aufruf-Behörden alarmiert," *Der Spiegel*, April 29, 2008, available at http://www.spiegel.de/politik/ausland/0,1518,550507,00.html (accessed May 28, 2005).

69. On this person, see Brynjar Lia, *Architect of Global Jihad. The Life of Al-Qaida Strategist Abu Musab al-Suri* (London: Hurst 2007), 189–93.

70. "Der fünfte Mann."

71. Ibid.

[12]

The Danish Glasvej Case

MICHAEL TAARNBY

A t two a.m. on September 4, 2007, the Danish Security Intelligence Service (PET) carried out a large police operation at eleven locations in the Copenhagen area. The operation, the result of an investigation into the activities of individuals suspected of terrorist activity, successfully apprehended eight alleged terrorists. According to PET, the operation went peacefully and according to plan. In PET's assessment, the suspects in the case were militant Islamists with international connections to al-Qaeda.[1]

This news startled Denmark on the morning of September 4. A large number of terrorist suspects had been apprehended in multiple raids, and the head of PET made it abundantly clear that the intelligence service had uncovered links between Danish terrorists and al-Qaeda. In the following weeks, one sensational headline after another led local news programs, and media commentators, politicians, and terrorism experts had the dubious task of guessing what was really behind the dramatic arrests by PET. PET itself refused to comment on the case, citing the need for discretion in the ongoing investigation.

The two previous cases of domestic jihadi cells in Denmark, known as the Glostrup and Vollsmose cells, also had ties to radical Islamists outside Demark, but not on this scale. If Danish domestic jihadis have evolved from relative amateurs to professional terrorists capable of linking up with the al-Qaeda core, it would have significant repercussions for Danish counterterrorism. This third case of domestic terrorism appeared to have extensive external links, and for this reason may indicate a change in the Danish jihadi milieu.

This chapter examines the Glasvej plot and inserts it into a European and global context, using the previous Danish plots as a baseline for comparison. Although these links are difficult to trace with certainty, sufficient information has been released about the perpetrators, their ideological motivation, and their actions. This information seems to corroborate the claim by PET that there was a connection between Danish terrorists and foreign jihadi groups. Of particular interest is the link between jihadis in Denmark and in Pakistan and their contact during the planning stage of the alleged attack. Finally, this chapter provides an assessment of the incident in the context of the debate between leader-led jihad and the growth of independent, localized terrorist networks and the implications for future counterterrorism efforts in Europe.

THE EVOLUTION OF ISLAMIST TERRORISM IN DENMARK

Unlike other European nations, Denmark remained almost unaffected by international terrorism from the 1960s to the end of the 1990s. Relative to countries like Germany, France, Italy, the United Kingdom and Spain, few incidents occurred, and they had little impact on Danish society. Nationalistic and right-wing terrorism are still unknown phenomena in Denmark, and left-wing terrorism found limited support during the 1970s and 1980s. As a country, Denmark remained relatively unaccustomed to dealing with international terrorism, including Islamist movements and organizations. However, the first generation of militant Islamist activists appeared in the late 1980s, partly because of the jihad in Afghanistan.

This first generation of internationally oriented jihadis in Denmark is notable for several reasons. They were primarily if not exclusively preoccupied with national causes, especially in Egypt, Morocco, and Algeria. The concept of a global jihad attracted little following among the few dozen activists during the 1990s. This small group of dedicated individuals was largely free to disseminate their ideas and propaganda, yet they managed to draw few recruits to their causes. Their influence remained quite limited.

Nonetheless, a closer look at the first generation reveals a surprisingly intricate web of international contacts. While the domestic jihadis were, quantitatively speaking, of a modest nature, the quality of their associates deserves mentioning. The verified contacts include the following prominent jihadis or jihadi scholars Ayman al-Zawahiri, Abu Zubaydah, Abu Qatada, Omar Abdul Rahman, Abu Dahdah, Abu Talal, Shamil Basayev, and Hassan Khattab. This list is not complete, but it illustrates how well connected the Denmark-based activists were since the people they corresponded with or knew personally form a veritable "who's who" of the jihadi scene in the 1990s.[2]

The second generation of Danish jihadis appeared in the aftermath of 9/11 and was predominantly homegrown. Unlike the first generation, they had no affiliation with established terrorist groups in the Middle East or North Africa. They lacked experience, training and organizational skills and were largely more interested in global jihad, although they took an interest in the conflicts in Palestine, Iraq, Afghanistan, and elsewhere.

Their lack of skill and experience was not a hindrance. Even though the second generation at times acted amateurishly, their dedication should not be underestimated. From this homegrown jihadi environment, two terrorist cells emerged, popularly known by their place of residence: the Glostrup cell and the Vollsmose cell. While the former cell maintained relations to affiliated individuals in Sweden, Bosnia, and the U.K., the latter can largely be described as a local phenomenon. The absence of links to established jihadi terrorist groups, especially the al-Qaeda core, is noteworthy. The groups' global interests and outlook did not come about through direct experience or interaction with known terrorists organizations. Danish Islamist militants underwent an evolutionary change between the 1990s and the present in terms of their external ties to the broader jihadi community. It is in this changed terrorist environment that the Glasvej case emerged in 2007.

THE GLASVEJ PLOT

On May 30 2007, PET received information from a foreign intelligence service that Hammad Khürshid, who would later be arrested in September along with the other suspects, was present at a terrorist training facility in Pakistan. According to the U.S. media, the tip was based on electronic intercepts by an American intelligence agency.[3] It is not known whether PET had been aware of Khürshid's activities before his latest trip to Pakistan as this information has not been disclosed to the public. Acting on this information, PET began a massive surveillance operation that would run for three months. A significant portion of the information gathered during the surveillance operation was later used in court and was instrumental in securing the conviction of two jihadi terrorists, Hammad Khürshid and Abdoulghani Tokhi. Although the suspects were apprehended before any violent incident took place the surveillance provided a glimpse into an otherwise inaccessible radical milieu.[4]

THE SURVEILLANCE OPERATION IN DENMARK

When Khürshid returned to Denmark from Pakistan his luggage was secretly searched at the Copenhagen airport. A couple of unusual tourist items were discovered: his suitcase contained both electrical wires and a small three-volt light bulb. During the summer of 2007, cameras were secretly installed in all rooms of his apartment, which he shared with his older brother, in order to monitor the activities and intentions of the suspect. This surveillance operation revealed interesting details about the daily life of Tokhi and Khürshid, especially with regard to their jihadi interests.[5]

For instance, tracking their Internet searches revealed that they had an interest in keywords such as "Muslim soldier," "direct attack," "Taliban footage," "al-Qaeda in Iraq," "global jihad," and "suicide attack." Together, the two men also watched movies produced by al-Qaeda about martyrs in Iraq. These searches in isolation may indicate a benign interest in the topic of jihad. The terrorists' subsequent actions, as well as Khürshid's previous travel, put this Internet activity in a different light. A surveillance tape showed Khürshid and his older brother watching a farewell ceremony for a suicide bomber about to embark on his last mission. During the video Khürshid's brother breaks down in tears. It is difficult not to interpret this outburst as related to concern about Khürshid's intentions. The older brother refused to testify against Khürshid in court.[6]

In another video recording, Khürshid is busy in the living room preparing TATP explosives while singing a jihadi tune. He is later joined by Tokhi, who is proudly invited to admire Khürshid's handiwork. Their conversations focused on how much explosive was needed to kill a certain number of people, but this takes place after the trial detonation. At one point, they discussed the purchase of a remote-controlled car to deliver the explosive charge but stated that it must be able to carry twenty kilos.[7] The apartment was secretly searched several times to keep track of developments concerning the manufacture of explosives. Tokhi and Khürshid were in frequent contact about the purchase of bomb components, including light bulbs, acetone, and hydrogen peroxide, as well as a pair of night-vision goggles.[8]

A small amount of TATP was tested in the staircase of the apartment building on September 1.[9] Later, the surveillance microphones caught Khürshid and Tokhi saying that they must get hold of something more powerful as their current substance would kill only two or three people. They planned to post a video of the explosion on YouTube, but they did not manage to edit it before their arrest. Khürshid did manage to produce ten grams of TATP, and after testing a sample, both of them talked enthusiastically about making a twenty-kilo bomb. He later explained to Tokhi how these explosives could be mounted inside a vest supplemented by ball bearings. The effect of this device would be several hundred people killed, according to Khürshid.[10]

ARRESTS AND SEARCHES

By September 2007, PET was concerned about the presence of highly unstable explosives hidden in a residential area and decided to move on the suspects. In all, eleven addresses were searched, and eight people were arrested on September 4, six of whom had Danish citizenship. They were a diverse group with origins in Turkey, Somalia, Pakistan, and Afghanistan. They frequented the Heimdalsgade mosque before their arrest and ranged from nineteen to twenty-nine years of age; however, six of the suspects were released without charges on the same day. From then on the PET investigation focused on two personalities: Adoulghani Tokhi, a twenty-one-year-old of Afghani background, and Hammad Khürshid, a twenty-one-year-old Danish national of Pakistani background who was suspected of being the inspirational leader of the group.[11]

Obviously, PET decided it had acquired sufficient evidence to success-fully prosecute these two, but little has been reported about the larger group and their presumed role. Interestingly, as late as April 2008 the prosecutor insisted that the court hearing be held behind closed doors. The justification was that the investigation had not yet been closed and that PET was still looking for what it euphemistically called "known per-sons."[12] Little is known about these individuals and their role, if indeed they had any involvement in the cell; the media has shown little interest in this aspect of the Glasvej case.

In the apartment on Glasvej the police found seven mobile phones containing video recordings of Tokhi and Khürshid shouting: "Death to America—jihad, jihad!" Further, there were video clips of the World Trade Center attacks in 2001 and martyr profiles of the nineteen hijackers.[13] A bomb manual written in Urdu was also found hidden inside a pillow. The investigation also revealed that an excerpt of a manual had been copied at the Red Mosque in Islamabad. A thorough search of Khürshid's hard disk revealed a homemade video of the mock execution of an American soldier or collaborator. This recording was made on October 31, 2005, and featured two other people besides Khürshid, his brother and one other person, known as SÜ, playing the role of the victim. He would later be tried separately. Khürshid announced on the clip that the captive is kill-ing his Muslim brothers and sisters in Iraq and then proceeds to decapi-tate the prisoner while shouting "Allah Akbar" to the camera.[14]

At Tokhi's residence, another bomb manual was retrieved, as well as footage of the 2005 London bombings. This document was part of the original manual copied by Khürshid in Pakistan; Tokhi was translating it into Danish, instructed by Khürshid. An envelope was discovered at Khürshid's residence, where a drawing on the back may have been a bus or a regional train. In the middle of the vehicle, something had been drawn that, according to the prosecution, could have been a backpack.[15] This discovery would later become quite significant as the prosecution claimed the drawing represented a likely target of the conspirators.

A further development in the case occurred on November 11, 2007, when a twenty-two-year old man of Turkish origin, known as SÜ, was arrested on suspicion of encouraging the abduction of Danish citizens abroad. The purpose of the abductions was ostensibly to secure the release of Khürshid and Tokhi from prison. He would later be tried separately, although there was a clear link to the original Glasvej case. Legal procedures in Denmark might involve a prohibition on using the suspect's name in the public domain, as in the case of SÜ, which explains why he can only be mentioned by his initials.[16]

The surveillance operation clearly revealed a profound interest in the global jihad on the part of the terrorists, supplemented by foreign travel and the manufacture of explosives. However, in terms of planning an actual terrorist attack, the conspirators were at an early stage. The amount of explosives produced was insufficient for a large-scale attack, yet they were highly unstable and completely unsuitable for storage in a residential area. As for possible targets, several theories circulated in the Danish press, yet no credible plan of action has been revealed. While speculation still exists in terms of a likely target, it is worth noting that official or military targets were not mentioned at all in public reports. If the intended target was indeed some sort of public transportation, then the plot would be reminiscent of the terrorist bombings in Madrid and London.

BACKGROUND OF THE CONSPIRATORS

Hammad Khürshid and his older brother were both born in Denmark but spent most of their childhood in Pakistan. Their childhood, according to their father, was not a happy time. He insisted that the youngest son, Khürshid, was psychologically ill, and explained that because they grew up in Pakistan without their father, who worked as a welder in Denmark after the family relocated to Pakistan, they were considered orphans and often ridiculed and beaten.[17]

Khürshid and his brother, who was also arrested in September, had only recently moved to Denmark. Khürshid worked as a painter's assistant at the time of his arrest; he had previously worked as a painter's apprentice but dropped out because of the better pay as an assistant. His previous employer had discussed plans with Khürshid about starting their own company. Besides working quite hard on his several painting jobs, he contemplated acquiring a special driver license that would allow him work for a taxi company.

Although Khürshid grew up in Pakistan, he never attended a madrassa and was not particularly religious. In Denmark, however, he started to frequent several different mosques in Copenhagen in 2005 and began to pray five times a day. Both brothers frequented the mosque in Heimdalsgade in Copenhagen, which at the time had a reputation for attracting young, rootless, and disenfranchised Muslims. According to their father, this was not because they were particularly religious but because they felt lonely in Denmark.[18] In the months before his arrest, Khürshid had attended meetings organized by the radical Islamist organization Hizb-ut-Tahrir, but there is no evidence to suggest that he became involved in organizational activities.[19] While the Hizb-ut-Tahrir propagates an Islamist ideology, it does not advocate the violent overthrow of governments. This important doctrinal issue has alienated the Salafi jihadi community, which has argued that the meetings, protests, and rallies carried out by the Hizb-ut-Tahrir are essentially useless. This division has also been evident over the last decade in Denmark, where there has been little or no collaboration between Hizb-ut-Tahrir and the globally oriented jihadi groups.

Khürshid visited Pakistan three times between 2004 and 2007, and during his last visit, when he attended his sister's wedding, he actually contemplated leaving Denmark for good and settling in Pakistan. He was not happy with Danish culture, complaining that it was difficult to be a good Muslim in Denmark because there were inappropriately dressed women everywhere.[20]

Khürshid planned to marry a Danish Romanian girl living in Aalborg in northern Denmark, known only as G to the public. They held long and difficult conversations over the phone. He really wanted to get married but also told the girl that there was a 70 percent chance of her being alone later on, although he did not specify the reason behind the anticipated separation. He was stressed and had sleepless nights because of worries about the girl and his marriage. In court, he explained that his concerns were because he was on his way back to the Red Mosque in Islamabad. In another conversation, he told G that he was convinced that he was on the right path, even though he did not have a beard and wore Western clothes, and that his time had come.[21] Once again, while these statements may indicate Khürshid's anticipation of his own premature and violent death, they do not constitute singular evidence of his true intentions or plans.

It is difficult to map in precise detail Khürshid's increasing interest in jihad from the evidence available. However, certain events help place his eventual arrest and conviction in perspective. In 2006, he planned to go to Lebanon together with a friend, Abu Ali, whom he had met in Pakistan, to fight against the Israeli army, but nothing happened because his friend kept making up excuses and Khürshid did not want to leave on his own. This lack of commitment is interesting because, to some extent, it confirms his gradually deepening involvement in jihad. Abu Ali (Muhammad Ilias Subhan Ali) would emerge as an al-Qaeda facilitator according to an expert witness during the trial.

Khürshid intellectually rationalized his jihadi interests as similar to those of Danish young men who surfed the Internet for pornographic material; it was just another harmless pastime. When he was confronted in court about his involvement in the manufacturing of explosives, his reply was that he was simply interested in firearms and bombs. In a surveillance tape dated August 31, Khürshid was mixing explosives while singing a known martyrdom song popular in the terrorist community. When the prosecutor later confronted him about the song, he stated that it meant nothing in particular; he just happened to like the song and sang it while cooking or in the bathroom.[22]

Khürshid's journey to Pakistan in the spring of 2007, which PET believed to have lasted for about two and a half months, seems to mark his real entry into the world of global jihad. In court, he would later explain that while in Pakistan, he actively sought to fight alongside his Muslim brothers, no matter where. His first primary contact appears to be a man known as Osman whom he met at the notorious Red Mosque in Islamabad. This well-known radical stronghold would provide an entry into Waziristan, although the details of these developments are sparse. The bomb manuals seized in September were copied from Osman's possessions. Khürshid and Osman would remain in contact after he had returned to Denmark as Osman became a key figure in Khürshid's life.

In late May 2007, Khürshid was present in the village of Mir Ali in Waziristan. According to information revealed during the trial, he was in Mir Ali between April 27 and May 23, 2007, visiting a friend, although U.S. intelligence intercepts place him in a terrorist training camp at that time. A friend he had met at the Red Mosque, Hamza, accompanied him on the trip from Islamabad to Waziristan on what was termed a visit to see some friends.[23] However, a video recording discovered on Khürshid's mobile phone revealed a sequence where a person in Waziristan dressed in traditional robes states: "I have spoken to them, and if you have come to fight that is all right." In the background, Khürshid's voice is audible as he replies: "My lord, I have come to fight."[24] This recording testifies to his intent to join some insurgent or terrorist group and to fight on their behalf. Khürshid was an avid user of his mobile phone, but during the period he spent in Mir Ali, there were no calls or messages registered to or from his cell phone. Upon his return to Denmark, he did not tell his parents or his older brother about his trip to Waziristan.[25]

Khürshid's fascination with martyrdom and his disgust with Western culture are apparent in his writings in a notebook discovered in his apartment. Several statements were quite explicit: "martyrdom is truth" and another saying that "the dirty Western culture should be soiled." He explained in court that he had copied the text while at the Red Mosque simply because he liked the phrases and it had nothing to do with terrorism whatsoever. But another comment taken together with his stated intention to fight in Waziristan indicates another purpose: "I don't care when I give my life to Allah to which side I will fall when I will be killed while being a believing Muslim, and this my sacrifice is only for the sake of Allah, and if He wants He can bless the larger and the smaller pieces of my body."[26]

During his trial, Khürshid stated in court that he rejected the morality of the terrorist attacks in New York and London, based on the killing innocent people. When asked specifically abut Osama bin Laden, he admitted to ascribing to some of the ideas of al-Qaeda but not all. He elaborated, stating that he had become religious a few years ago and would support a Taliban-controlled Pakistan. Even though he had participated in several meetings organized by Hizb-ut-Tahrir and had strong opinions about life in Denmark, he had decided that Denmark should not be ruled according to sharia law.

The second conspirator arrested and later convicted on terrorism charges was Abdoulghani Tokhi, a twenty-one-year-old Afghan, who worked at the subway in Copenhagen as a guard before his arrest. Two years before his arrest, there was little in Tokhi's views or behavior to suggest that he would later receive a long prison sentence for his involvement in a terrorist plot. In 2005, Tokhi was a high school student in Copenhagen and seemed well integrated and easy-going. However, it was during this year that he started to change his appearance and his beliefs, to the astonishment of his friends. He let his beard grow, began to wear traditional robes, and got in trouble at his high school for distributing leaflets advising Muslim students not to wish the Christians a merry Christmas and not to celebrate Christian holidays. This intolerant behavior resulted in a week's suspension. Tokhi's father was concerned about the changes in his son and went to see the principal of the high school. At the meeting, he said that Tokhi was under the influence of an older Muslim who was teaching Quran classes and that he was obviously concerned about the increasing radicalization of his son.

Eventually, Tokhi dropped out of high school and began to take classes elsewhere. He also frequented the mosque in Heimdalsgade in Copenhagen but did not seem to have any interest in the Hizb-ut-Tahrir. The mosque has been the meeting place of hard-line Islamist and jihadis, among them Abderrahmane Slimane, who spent several years at Guantánamo Bay; Omar Marouff, a Moroccan who has received the death penalty in Morocco for his jihadi activities; and several of the convicted terrorists from the Glostrup case. The spiritual leader at the Heimdalsgade mosque was Abu Ahmed, who is known for his low profile and uncompromising views on Islam. He would later be asked to leave by the board of the mosque because of his radical views. Hammad Khürshid would refer to Abu Ahmed as his spiritual guide.[27]

Though Khürshid was the more active and action-oriented of the two, he was obviously awed and inspired by Tokhi's religiosity, which was in part based in the religious instruction he had received from childhood. In court, Tokhi claimed that he had no knowledge of or interest in weapons or explosives. However, this is contradicted by the fact that Tokhi copied parts of the bomb manual that Khürshid brought back from the Red Mosque. While Khürshid probably introduced him to the world of improvised explosives, Tokhi followed Khürshid's example and went shopping for the chemical components they needed.[28]

The third and final person tried in court was SÜ, a Turk. SÜ was arrested on November 11, 2007, in a slightly bizarre turn of events. He had first met Tokhi at the mosque and then later became acquainted with Khürshid and his older brother. According to the prosecutor, SÜ had been in contact with a person abroad and encouraged him to kidnap

Danish citizens. The abductions would be part of a plan to have the two suspected terrorists released.[29] SÜ's separate trial is a reflection of the fact that his alleged crime was different from the terrorist plot planned by Khürshid and Tokhi.

On November 1, 2007, he encouraged an unknown person via e-mail to kidnap Danes abroad to secure the release of Khürshid and Tokhi, but PET was monitoring his computer. Unknown to him, PET was able to intercept a message to a Sihad Aslan in Turkey, who was known to the Turkish authorities. At 5:12 p.m. SÜ wrote: "My Brother, I want to tell you something . . . two Brothers has been caught here by us. They are connected to the AL group. . . . If they are convicted it's Guantanamo for one and 30–40 years in prison for the other." The reply: "May Allah help them. Is it necessary to do something about it?" SÜ answered: "Life for life, blood for blood. Punish an infidel for a Muslim. Retribution through exchange. . . . Give me back my Brother or an infidel dies." Finally, to explain the identity of the detained he wrote: "One of the two persons was in the AL group; the other one didn't know anything."[30]

PET actually tried to recruit SÜ as an informer five days after his e-mail exchange with Aslan. During a two-hour session at a hotel in Copenhagen, two PET agents did their best to persuade SÜ to assist them in obtaining information. Unknown to the agents, SÜ's mobile was turned on, and the entire conversation was recorded. Parts of this recorded meeting would later appear on the homepage of a Danish tabloid, thus providing academics, aspiring jihadis, and the public a unique window into a normally closed world. Eventually, SÜ declined the offer and was arrested. He was tried separately and charged with conspiracy to kidnap but was acquitted of the charges on November 18, 2008.[31]

DOMESTIC AND FOREIGN JIHADI LINKS

Though it has not been verified, it can be assumed that the mosque at Heimdalsgade played an important role in establishing relationships among like-minded militant Islamists in the Copenhagen area. It is no coincidence that this particular mosque had been singled out by members of the Danish Muslim community as the gathering place where young hotheads who craved action would go for worship.[32] It should be remembered that while both Khürshid and Tokhi were regulars at the mosque, so were the other suspects who were initially arrested and subsequently released.

At the domestic jihadi level, contact between Tokhi and Abdulkadir Cesur has been verified. Cesur was part of the Glostrup cell and was apprehended by the police in Sarajevo in 2005, where he is currently serving a seven-year sentence for his role in planning a terrorist attack. Khürshid had talked to Cesur over the phone along with several other people associated with the Glostrup case.[33] These contacts are of exceptional importance because they allow analysts to map the militant Islamist milieu in overview if not in detail. In establishing a connection among several cells active in the Copenhagen area, the linkages support the assumption that the jihadis moved within the same quite small circles.

Of special interest are the links between the individual cell members and the larger global Jihadi community, especially the al-Qaeda core. In this respect, the Glasvej cell represents an interesting set-up because there has been no indication that Tokhi was in any way connected to anyone of interest abroad. Khürshid, on the other hand, made some interesting acquaintances during his trip to Pakistan. His known contacts will be elaborated slightly in the following section. However, details are sparse, and there are significant gaps in our knowledge on these linkages.

The Pakistani known as Osman likely functioned as a gatekeeper or someone who could screen new volunteers and send them on if they were considered ready and trustworthy. Being Pakistani, and having spent most of his childhood there, Khürshid was familiar with the reputation of the Red Mosque and the people who operated from it. For someone without prior terrorist connections but able to converse in the local language, this would be an ideal first stop. Osman allowed Khürshid to copy the available bomb manuals and appears to be the person that sent him to the militants in Mir Ali. While in Islamabad, he copied a manual that contained information on several types of explosives, the use of poisons, and the manufacture of suicide-bomber vests. This was the manual later discovered during the searches of his apartment, disguised as a marriage contract.[34] Their relationship developed into a mutual trust, evidenced by their subsequent e-mail correspondence after Khürshid returned to Denmark

Osman also showed a keen interest in the Danish embassy in Islamabad and wanted to know where Danish tourists in Karachi would be located, indicating a continued obsession with Danish targets. At one time Osman asked Khürshid about security precautions at the Danish embassy in Islamabad, but Khürshid did not reply to this particular e-mail for unknown reasons.[35] The Danish embassy was attacked with a car bomb on June 2, 2008, which I will deal with separately.

When the head of PET mentioned a link to al-Qaeda on the day of the arrests, he could have had one of several people in mind. It may have been Abu Nasser al-Qahtani who was in charge of operations in eastern Afghanistan. A Saudi Arabian national, al-Qahtani had a fearsome reputation for his involvement in strikes against U.S. military posts in Afghanistan and has been described as a senior al-Qaeda leader there. Khürshid denied in court that he had ever met al-Qahtani but stated that the younger brother of a friend knew him personally. The PET surveillance operation disclosed a video recording where Khürshid and Tokhi are seated in front of the computer watching footage of a prisoner escape from Bagram in 2005. At some point during the video Khürshid indicates that al-Qahtani was one of his associates through a mutual friend. This expression does not indicate a close personal relationship, yet it indicates the circles Khürshid was moving in.[36]

According to the testimony of a prosecutor from the U.S. Department of Justice, Muhammad Ilias Subhan Ali (also known as Abu Ali), was a mid-level al-Qaeda leader who functioned as a controller for young recruits before they were dispatched on terror missions.[37] It should be recalled that Khürshid and Abu Ali had planned to join the fight in Lebanon in 2006, although nothing materialized at the time. There was intensive contact between Ali and Khürshid through e-mails and over the phone. In their conversations, they spoke consistently about an assignment that Khürshid had been tasked to undertake by the "Firm." Khürshid was referred to as the "sheikh of sheikhs" by certain people in Pakistan, and it was said that he had a promising future in the Firm, according to Ali.

Just a few weeks before his arrest, Lebanon was still on Khürshid's mind. If Abu Ali could introduce him to the right people in Saudi Arabia, where he was located, he would keep all options open concerning future travel. Khürshid's difficulty in choosing between jihadi groups in Lebanon and Pakistan is evident in an intercepted conversation with his Pakistani contacts. Khürshid enquired politely if he could also start planning with others about the Lebanese angle but was brushed off by his contact, who told him directly, "You cannot be disloyal and move to another firm. There are expectations of you that you will deliver a good product and do a good job." When asked directly about this term, Khürshid's testified that the "Firm" referred to holy warriors.[38]

The expert witness described Ali and people like him as the real link between the al-Qaeda leadership and the foot soldiers. They arranged travel, acquired forged identity documents, moved the recruits, and located them near their area of operations.[39] In an interesting conversation, Khürshid complained that he and other likeminded individuals would be on their own when they started their business. His foreign contact told him not to worry; God would be there with them.

Khürshid's interest in various locations in Pakistan, particularly the Danish embassy, is of interest in this context. His contact at the Red Mosque, Osman, asked him to provide specific information on Karachi, yet there is no documentation indicating that Khürshid delivered anything related to Islamabad. In response to Osman's request, Khürshid copied and inserted addresses of several consulates, hotels, and so on, but he was told clearly that this feedback was highly unsatisfactory.

Though it is not known if he played a role in the subsequent suicide bombing of the Danish embassy in Islamabad on June 2, 2008, this incident deserves mentioning. The day after the attack, Mustafa Abu'l Yazid (Said al-Masri) issued a communiqué wherein al-Qaeda claimed responsibility for the bombing. His statement made clear that the attack was retaliation for the anti-Muslim cartoons in the Danish media and Denmark's refusal to apologize for this perceived blasphemy. Moreover, Yazid explicitly pointed out the operational assistance provided by Pakistani jihadis: "This operation also provides the major role being played by Pakistani Mujahideen, who participated in preparing this operation."[40]

The suicide bombing by al-Qaeda and its Pakistani allies does not directly entail a link between the al-Qaeda core and Danish jihadis. However, this chain of events indicates an ideological relationship and perhaps explains the usefulness of Khürshid to more senior members. As a dedicated individual who had traveled to Pakistan to enlist in the cause and had a Danish passport, someone like Khürshid would likely have been perceived as much too valuable to be sent to the frontline in Afghanistan.

THE ROLE OF THE INTERNET: CONNECTING JIHADIS

The role of the Internet in this particular terrorist incident is worth analyzing for two distinct reasons. First, the Internet played an important part in the development of the plot, and, second, examing its role allows for a comparison between this and other terrorist networks.

It is unclear if in the early stages of the radicalization process the main characters were influenced by jihadi propaganda. What is beyond doubt, however, is the evidence obtained through the surveillance operation that detailed the specific interest in propaganda by Khürshid, in particular, and Tokhi as a seemingly curious observer. The classic materials of aspiring jihadis, such as bomb manuals, details on explosives, martyrdom videos, combat footage, and information on Iraq and Afghanistan were clearly sought out.

The intention to upload the TATP testing exercise to YouTube is interesting. This act does not appear as professional conduct befitting hardcore terrorists as it would certainly invite unwanted attention from the authorities. The explanation for this behavior may be that they simply thought this would be a cool thing to do. However, it is also possible that this video clip would later be supplemented by other homemade productions of an unknown character.

It is interesting to note that after Khürshid's return from Waziristan, the correspondence between him and Muhammad Ilias Subhan Ali and Osman continued. This relatively frequent contact served two purposes: first, the exchange of operational information and ideological support and, second, in a move reminiscent of classic terrorist techniques, to set up a free e-mail account and then write draft messages that are saved but never sent. Providing that several people have access to the account and the associated password, sensitive information can be exchanged without leaving tell-tale electronic signs. This method was also practiced by Khürshid, who falsely believed that his communications would be safe from intrusion.

These brief examples illustrate the significant role of the Internet in the case, specifically in terms of the exchange of operational details and moral support. These two elements appear to be interrelated as Khürshid became the prime operative of the cell after his return from Waziristan with little supervision except online encouragement. However, there is no evidence of the Internet's being used to recruit other militant Islamists either in Europe or beyond, nor was there any attempt at fund raising or issuing political statements.

ASSESSMENT OF THE GLASVEJ CASE

The Glasvej plot is an excellent case subject for the current debate around the question of whether new terrorists are operating independently or if a group of senior terrorist leaders, most often referred to as the al-Qaeda core, manages them. Upon close investigation of the Glasvej cell, it appears that this was not an instance of a small group of Danish Muslims acting on their own but rather a local group tapped into the global jihad network that became part of a potentially centrally organized plot. It should be recalled that Khürshid traveled to Pakistan on his own initiative to establish contact with jihadi groups; he had not been recruited in Denmark and dispatched for training or operational assignments in Waziristan. This chain of events is singularly important when discussing radicalization and recruitment patterns in Europe and elsewhere.

First, PET stressed at the time of the arrests that the suspects had direct relations with al-Qaeda. A closer look at the evidence presented during the trial and referred to here makes this claim subject to some modification. The single sequence where Khürshid identifies Abu Nasser al-Qahtani in a movie clip on YouTube does not constitute a firm relationship. However, his frequent correspondence with Abu Ali indicates a much closer relationship and trust, and Abu Ali has been described as someone with the right connections. Friendships and frequent communications with identified jihadis should not lead to the conclusion that Khürshid was a full-fledged member of al-Qaeda or another militant Islamist group, however. Instead, it can be said that Khürshid's voluntary and active association with these individuals constitutes the moving parts of the current form of the global jihad.

In terms of radicalization, the investigation and the information available has not revealed any outside interference or scheme. From what is known, it seems clear that the radicalization process took place within Denmark, starting several years before the arrests. As for actual recruitment, it seems that this connection is only relevant concerning

Khürshid's involvement, but perhaps "volunteering" is more accurate. After all, Khürshid and his friend Abu Ali were ready to fight Israel and volunteer their services to an unknown organization in Lebanon in 2006. When this did not happen, he apparently set his sights set on Pakistan instead.

There is no indication that Khürshid knew whom to contact at the Red Mosque before his departure, and it therefore seems highly unlikely that he was acting under orders at this stage. His subsequent visit to Waziristan again confirmed his intention to fight. A question remains: having volunteered to fight and being accepted by an insurgent group, why did he not stay in Pakistan to complete his mission? Upon his return to Denmark he was even more dedicated in his jihadi activities and progressed to making explosives. His sincerity at this stage seems beyond doubt, and his frequent contacts via e-mail and telephone with militant Islamists may indicate at least some sort of operational guidance or, at the very least, spiritual and ideological encouragement to pursue his endeavors.

Without any evidence concerning what occurred in Waziristan, there is no way of confirming or rejecting the possibility of al-Qaeda's outsourcing a plot to Khürshid. Moreover, it cannot be ruled out that a Pakistani jihadi group was involved instead of al-Qaeda. It is entirely possible that Khürshid was considered too valuable to the militants he met in Pakistan to become yet another battlefield casualty in Pakistan or Afghanistan. Khürshid did not attempt to hide his intention to fight with a jihadi group in either Lebanon or Pakistan. Yet this did not happen, even though he appeared to have been in the right place at the right time.

Even if the details of his adventure in Waziristan remain unknown, his actions upon his return to Denmark indicate a continued dedication to the jihadi cause. Concerning the question of whether the Glasvej plot should be categorized as leader-led or leaderless, the continued communication with contacts in Pakistan clearly indicates some sort of organizational affiliation. Khürshid is reminded that he is part of the "Firm" and cannot switch his allegiance to another group without being disloyal. This form of control over terrorist operatives has to be practiced through long-distance communication that connects loosely affiliated jihadi individuals. This globally dispersed terrorist network hinges on the ability of jihadi volunteers to operate independently and largely unsupervised with little or no direct control, and the Glasvej plot seems to fit this pattern. While leadership matters, the continued success of terrorist networks of this character is dependent on a number of recruits who volunteer and commit themselves to the task.

The small militant Islamist milieu in Denmark has evolved over the past twenty years. The first active individuals were foreigners who arrived in Denmark dedicated to continuing their jihadi activities. Most if not all came with previous experience and established organizational links. The Glasvej case represents a break from previously known patterns of radicalization, recruitment, and association with known jihadi groups. A homegrown cell that radicalized within Denmark and later made contact with senior jihadi individuals connected to al-Qaeda's core had not been seen in Denmark before the emergence of the Glasvej cell. Khürshid's willingness to return to Denmark from Pakistan and to acquire the materials for an improvised explosive device clearly demonstrates the seriousness of the cell members involved. Whether the explosives were to be used in a suicide bombing within Denmark will probably never be known with certainty; however, this possibility cannot be easily discarded.

The trial started on August 11, 2008, at the court in Glostrup, and the verdict came on October 21, 2008.[41] Both were found guilty of manufacturing explosives with the intent to cause damage. The court determined that Khürshid was the leading conspirator and that Tokhi had sufficient knowledge about the manufacture of the TATP and was ready and willing to participate in a terrorist act. Khürshid was sentenced to twelve years in prison, and Tokhi received a seven-year sentence and is scheduled to be deported from Denmark after he serves his sentence. Both Khürshid and Tokhi appealed their cases and were tried again in June 2009. Khürshid received an identical sentence, but a year was added to Tokhi's sentence.[42]

This overview of the Glasvej plot does not answer all questions. Indeed, there are significant gaps in our knowledge of events in Waziristan, the personal relationships involved, and the intended target, to mention a few. These may never be fully disclosed, but there is sufficient information to acquire a general overview of this incident. Denmark's having experienced three incidents of homegrown jihadis clearly indicates a necessity for continued vigilance. Experience has shown that in the case of Denmark, recruitment patterns change over time and the younger generation of jihadis is more attracted to the global jihad than the first generation. Current radicalization patterns clearly indicate a profound interest in the ideology and achievements of al-Qaeda, which has gained mythical proportions. Perceptions clearly matter, irrespective of the recent setbacks for al-Qaeda, especially in Iraq. Aspiring jihadis are likely to be attracted by the lore of al-Qaeda, and some of them will actively attempt to become part of this global movement.

This raises important questions and concerns for the future even though the actual number of volunteers is expected to be low. The strength of a globally dispersed clandestine terrorist network is dependent on the ability of operatives to plan, communicate, and function in secrecy. Looser affiliations have replaced the more formal training and membership acquired through extended stays in Afghanistan in the 1990s, and this has made counterterrorism efforts in Denmark, as in the rest of Europe, much more challenging. Current networks are difficult to detect precisely because of the relatively weak links with established terrorist groups and their leadership.

However, these weak organizational links also makes the terrorist networks vulnerable, and in this regard, the Glasvej case provides an important reminder. Khürshid's ability to establish a personal link to Islamist militants in Pakistan was indeed personal. Since no dedicated recruitment effort is known to have been carried out after his return to Denmark, the link to Pakistan must be considered to have been severed after his arrest because there was no one in line to take over from Khürshid in the event he became inactive, regardless of the circumstances.

NOTES

1. Danish Security and Intelligence Service, statement concerning terror-related arrests, September 4, 2007, available at http://www.pet.dk/Nyheder/Pressconf.aspx.

2. Michael Taarnby, "Jihad in Denmark. An Overview and Analysis of Jihadi Activity in Denmark, 1990–2006," Danish Institute for International Studies, Working Paper, November 2006, available at http://www.diis.dk/sw30537.asp.

3. Nicholas Kulish, "New Terrorism Case Confirms That Denmark Is a Target," *New York Times*, September 17, 2007.

4. Elisabeth A. Haslund, "Skyldige i Terror?," *Berlingske Tidende* (Copenhagen), October 18, 2008.

5. Ibid.

6. Elisabeth A. Haslund, "Terrortiltalts Bror Nægter at Vidne," *Berlingske Tidende* (Copenhagen), September 19, 2008.

7. Rikke Fauerfelt, "PET: Fjernstyret Bil Skulle Være Bombe," *Politiken* (Copenhagen), August 11, 2008.

8. Carsten Ellegaard, "Glasvej-Sagen del III: PET på Sporet," *Jyllandsposten* (Viby). September 1, 2008.

9. Martin Justesen, "PET Leder Efter Flere i Terrorsag," *Politiken* (Copenhagen), April 4, 2008.

10. Frederiksberg court, press release on the Glasvej terror case, October 21, 2008,http://www.domstol.dk/frederiksberg/nyheder/Pressemeddelelser/Pages/TerrorsagenfraGlasvej.aspx.

11. "To er Fængslet og ses Løsladt i Dansk Terrorsag", September 5, 2007, Danish Broadcasting Corporation.

12. Martin Justesen, "PET Leder Efter Flere i Terrorsag," *Politiken* (Copenhagen), April 4, 2008.

13. "Terrorsigtede Filmet Med Bombe," TV2 News, January 10, 2008, available at http://nyhederne.tv2.dk/krimi/article.php/id-9975184.html.

14. Rikke Fauerfelt, "Terrortiltalt Lavede Fingereret Henrettelse," *Politiken* (Copenhagen), August 11, 2008.

15. Fauerfelt, "PET: Fjernstyret Bil Skulle Være Bombe."

16. Bo Soendergaard and Bo Maltesen, "Anklager: Sigtet Ville Kidnappe Danske Soldater," *Politiken* (Copenhagen), November 11, 2008.

17. "Far Til Terrorsigtet: Han er Syg," TV2 News, September 8, 2008, available at http://nyhederne.tv2.dk/article.php/id-8202112:far-til-terrorsigtet-han-er-syg.html.

18. Ibid.

19. Carsten Ellegaard, "Venner Paa Afvejde. Glasvej Sagen del I," *Jyllandsposten* (Viby), September 1, 2008.

20. "Tiltalt Nægter Bombeplaner," *Politiken* (Copenhagen), August 14, 2008.

21. "Terrorsigtet Opgavsit Livs Kærlighed," *Avisen.dk*, August 30, 2008, available at http://avisen.dk/terrorsigtet-opgav-sit-livs-kaerlighed_97650.aspx.

22. Morten Skjoldager, "Terrortiltalt Sang Martyrvise," *Politiken* (Copenhagen), September 5, 2008.

23. Carsten Ellegaard, "Turen til Pakistan. Glasvej Sagen del II," *Jyllandsposten* (Viby), August 1, 2008.

24. "Terrortiltalt: Kommet for at Kæmpe," TV2 News, September 3, 2008, available at http://nyhederne.tv2.dk/article.php/id-15086990.html?nidk.

25. Ellegaard, "Turen til Pakistan. Glasvej Sagen del II."

26. Morten Skjoldager, "Terrortiltalt Hyldede Martyrdøden," *Politiken* (Copenhagen), August 26, 2008.

27. Ellegaard, "Venner paa Afveje. Glasvej Sagen del I."

28. "Bombemanden og den Religiøse," *Berlingske Tidende* (Copenhagen), August 15, 2008.

29. Claus Blok Thomsen, "PET ville Hverve Terrorsigtet," *Politiken* (Copenhagen), November 12, 2007.

30. "Terrortiltalt: Liv for Liv, Blod for Blod," TV2 News, September 24, 2008, available at http://nyhederne.tv2.dk/article.php/id-15950622.html.

31. "Retten Frifandt Terror-Sigtet," *Information* (Copenhagen), November 19, 2008.

32. Morten Skjoldager and Claus Blok Thomsen, "Fængslede Kom i Samme Moske," *Politiken* (Copenhagen), September 5, 2007.

33. "TV: Danske Terrorsager Hænger Sammen," *Jyllandsposten* (Viby), September 5, 2007.

34. Frederiksberg court, press release on the Glasvej terror case.

35. "Terrorsigtet Videregav Oplysninger," TV2 News, August 15, 2008, available at http://tvtid-dyn.tv2.dk/nytomtv/article.php/id-14291071.html.

36. Soeren Astrup and Morten Skjoldager, "Anklager: 22-årig Kendte Al-Qaeda-leder," *Politiken* (Copenhagen), September 4, 2008.

37. Soeren Astrup and Morten Skjoldager, "Amerikansk Terrorchef Vidnede i Glasvej-retssag," *Politiken* (Copenhagen), September 26, 2008.

38. Elisabeth A. Haslund, "Terrortiltalt Kunne Ikke Vælge Mellem Pakistan og Libanon," *Berlingske Tidende*, August 29, 2008.

39. Astrup and Skjoldager, "Amerikansk Terrorchef Vidnede I Glasvej Retssag."

40. "Al-Qaida Claims Suicide Attack on Danish Embassy in Islamabad, Pakistan," NEFA Foundation, June 3, 2008, available at http://www.nefafoundation.org/miscellaneous /FeaturedDocs/nefadenmarkpakistan0608.pdf.

41. Frederiksberg court, press release on the Glasvej terror case.

42. Eastern District Court, press release on the terror case from Glasvej, June 26, 2009, at http://www.domstol.dk/oestrelandsret/nyheder/Pressemeddelelser/Pages /Pressemeddelelse(TerrorsagenfraGlasvej).aspx.

[13]

The January 2008 Suicide Bomb Plot in Barcelona

FERNANDO REINARES

On January 19, 2008, between the hours of 12:40 and 5:00 a.m., fourteen individuals were arrested in Barcelona, Spain's second-largest city, because of a counterterrorism operation initiated two days before and intended to thwart what was evaluated by the state security agencies to be a suicide-bombing plot against the local subway system. Eleven of the arrests took place inside two Islamic places of worship, and three others were conducted in two private homes, all located in and around a quarter of Barcelona's old town popularly known as the Raval. The operation had been initiated in these surroundings by the Centro Nacional de Inteligencia (CNI, National Intelligence Center) on January 17. Nevertheless, it was not for the Spanish intelligence services but for the Guardia Civil (GC, Civil Guard), one of the two police agencies endowed with nationwide antiterrorism responsibilities in Spain, to subsequently apprehend the suspects.[1] As is mandatory, these arrests received prior approval from one of the six central investigative judges at the Audiencia Nacional (AN, National Court), the special criminal jurisdiction that deals with terrorist offenses throughout the country, based in Madrid.

Among those arrested were twelve people of Pakistani origin—all but one foreigners in Spain, the other a naturalized Spaniard—and two Indian nationals. They were all subjected to incommunicado detention for five days beginning January 19—the maximum period allowed by Spanish law—and transferred to Madrid for interrogation at the GC headquarters. Two of them, a Pakistani and an Indian, were released on January 22 by the GC, and two others, both of them Pakistanis, were freed without charges by the overseeing investigative judge on January 23. Yet the magistrate, at the same time, decided to indict the remaining ten individuals and ordered their provisional imprisonment.[2] Some weeks later, on March 14, an additional suspect, another Pakistani national who was also in Barcelona with the rest of the group but left the city hours before the police intervened, was detained in Breda, the Netherlands.[3] He was then handed over by the Dutch to Spanish authorities on August 13 and was prosecuted as well. Thus, eleven individuals were formally accused in connection with the plot to carry out suicide-bombing attacks in the Barcelona metro, a train system that runs underground throughout the city.[4]

Nearly two years later, on December 11, 2009, all eleven defendants were convicted. The sentence established as proven facts that seven of these individuals radicalized ideologically and that this "led them to take the decision to carry out a violent action, using explosives against the Barcelona metro, to cause a large number of victims." Judges at the Audiencia Nacional also asserted that the convicts had connections outside Spain, mentioning in particular a Pakistani group linked to al-Qaeda and headed by the Pakistani Taliban leader Baitullah Mehsud—who was killed by a U.S. drone strike in South Waziristan in August 2009. The sentence also noted that the existence of such contacts "allowed other people to be sent to Barcelona from different countries, members of the same organization, for them to take part in the action, even as suicide terrorists, if necessary," referring to at least four other individuals. Maroof Ahmed Mirza, the terrorist-cell ringleader, was sentenced to ten and a half years in jail. Mohammad Ayub Elahi Bibi, Hafeez Ahmed, Mohamed Tarik, Roshan Jamal Khan, Imram Cheema, Mohammed Shoaib, Mehmooh Khalid, and Aqueel Ur Rahmnan Abassi were all convicted and sentenced to eight and a half years for belonging to a terrorist organization. Two others, Qadeer Malik and Shaib Iqbal were also found guilty of possessing explosives, receiving fourteen years and six months each.[5]

What happened, or what was being planned, in Barcelona in January 2008? Moreover, how can we asses both the characteristics and scope of the foiled terrorist plot? Who are the individuals actually convicted in this case, and how did they come to constitute a terrorist cell in the city?

What kind of connections did these individuals or the cell as a whole have with terrorist actors abroad or, as stated in the court sentence, in Pakistan? A proper answer to these four questions, which can also illuminate issues of leadership and strategy behind the thwarted suicide attacks, based on information in the official judicial documents of this case at the National Court in Spain, should provide us with substantive knowledge on an important incident related to jihadist terrorism. Further, this sound evidence allows reflection on the dynamics of the global terrorism threat in Western Europe as it was evolving more than six years after the 9/11 attacks in New York and Washington, nearly four years after the 2004 Madrid commuter-train blasts, and two and a half years after the July 2005 series of suicide bombings in London.

A THWARTED SUICIDE BOMB ATTACK

On January 17, 2008, the CNI received an urgent communication from its French counterpart. According to information provided by what was presented as a credible source, suicide attacks targeting Barcelona's mass-transit system were in their final stages of preparation and could even be the first of a series of similar incidents in other Western European countries. The highly sensitive and trusted source was a Pakistani national who used to reside in Paris and had moved to Barcelona on January 16 with concrete instructions to contact someone referred to as Maulana Ashraf, whose real name was Maroof Ahmed Mirza. He expected to join other members of Mirza's group to perpetrate the bombings. He also happened to be a collaborator of the French intelligence services and acted as their informant on this occasion, alerting them to what was being prepared in Barcelona, its timing, and his own expected role in the planned attacks.[6]

After the communiqué, measures were immediately adopted to identify and locate the suspects in order to neutralize the threat. Soon afterward, CNI agents placed some of the presumed members of the cell under close surveillance. On January 17 at ten p.m., a CNI agent recovered from a street garbage container a trash bag left there minutes before by one of the suspects, Qadeer Malik, who resided nearby with other members of the cell. An initial examination of the bag's contents yielded a number of elements used in the manufacture of explosive devices, including manipulated clock mechanisms, batteries, electric cables, eight laptop connectors, latex gloves, a variety of hand tools, and pasteboard cylinders with residues of a powdery substance.[7] This seemed to validate the warning transmitted by French intelligence. On January 18 at around six p.m., eight of the suspected terrorists, carrying backpacks and handbags, were spotted moving guardedly from Tarek ben Ziyad Mosque—where the protected witness said they had previously gathered to "pray with jihad and martyrdom songs"[8]—to another location in Barcelona's old town. Security agencies quickly confirmed that the suspects were heading toward an address where two other individuals had also arrived carrying similar bundles.

Because of these developments, and based on all the background information provided by the French security services, the CNI assessed the threat of a suicide attack or a series of suicide attacks on Barcelona's public transport system as critical. The CNI decided to coordinate with the Guardia Civil and intervene as soon as special operations personnel from the latter police agency could deploy to the scene and they could obtain formal judicial authorization. As it reads in the judges' formal decision to approve the police operation, the terrorist cell "was apparently very close to achieving full technical capability in terms of explosive devices," in order "to carry out several suicide terrorist attacks between January 18 and 20 against means of public transport in Barcelona."[9]

The CNI urgently briefed the central unit of the GC charged with preventing and fighting international terrorism around one p.m. that same day, January 18, with the information provided by the French intelligence and with their own findings from field surveillance in Barcelona. The GC finally initiated its own enter-and-search intervention on January 18, focusing on six premises located in and around the Raval, including three used as private homes, two Islamic places of worship or local mosques, and a small bakery.[10] As already indicated, the operation concluded with the arrest of fourteen individuals in four neighboring locations. The Pakistani informant who alerted the French security services of the ongoing plot was apprehended and became a protected witness under specific provisions of Spanish law.[11] From that moment on, his identity has remained secret and the Audiencia Nacional's criminal proceedings of the case refer to him simply as F-1. The protected witness benefited from immunity in this case because, in accordance with domestic legal requirements, he voluntary helped to disrupt the bombing plot.[12]

At an Islamic worship place on Maçanet Street, where most of the arrests took place, officials discovered another cache of materials likely to be used in the manufacture of explosive devices, complementing the items found in the garbage container on January 17.[13] One of the bags contained steel balls and nearly 800 grams of gun pellets, both probably intended as shrapnel. In what became another key piece of criminal evidence for the case, they discovered eighteen grams of "a mixture of nitrocellulose and potassium perchlorate," commonly employed to manufacture industrial explosives.[14] The amount found in the bag was not sufficient for a major attack but was adequate for experimental and training purposes. Spanish security officials believe that the hidden explosives were found only because the counterterrorism operation was brought forward and prompted by information from the protected witness. Another cell member, Shaib Iqbal, informed the protected witness that a call he made to his wife on January 17 was to be his last to her and that he understood, contrary to his initial expectations, that the suicide attacks were to happen immediately.[15] However, the cell might have been waiting to receive enough material to prepare the explosive devices.[16] Corroborating this position is the fact that when F-1 received instructions to travel to Barcelona, he was told that he should expect to remain in the city for two or three months.[17]

The protected witness declared that he was informed on that same day, January 17, of the specifics of the terrorist action being planned in Barcelona. He noted, too, that Imran Cheema was to be his companion in executing a suicide attack on the metro, both of them carrying the explosives in bags or backpacks, and that Mohammed Shoaib, Mehmooh Khalid, and an unidentified pair were designated to commit a coordinated series of suicide bombings in the underground.[18] It is unclear from the existing judicial documents if other members of the cell were to trigger the explosive devices or if timers or a combination of both were to serve as triggers. F-1 explained that the metro was the preferred target in Barcelona since, as a prominent member of the group told him personally, "if an explosion takes place in the metro, the emergency services cannot come."[19] The ringleader, Maroof Ahmed Mizra, chose different subway stations as the locations for the blasts. He also declared that the terrorist plan included a suicide mission followed by at least two other attacks in that same city, with similar attacks planned for Germany and France and subsequently perhaps in Belgium, Portugal, or even the United Kingdom. In fact, the protected witness stated in his declaration before the GC that "Abassi was to act in Germany."[20]

According to the Audiencia Nacional tribunal, however, the facts did not imply that the terrorists had "a sufficiently concrete and determined plan." The judges affirmed that "the plan comprised an action with explosives in the metro of the city of Barcelona," but at the time of the arrests on January 19, 2008, the defendants "had no more than a small amount of explosive, and of other elements to prepare the devices." Buttressing this claim, they noted, "Neither the day nor place had been specified with precision, . . . only the decision to place it in the metro." This is why the panel ruled out convictions for a crime of conspiracy under Spanish law as distinct from "the resolution to commit a crime as understood by the offence of belonging to a terrorist association," clearly acknowledged by the court in the Barcelona bombing-plot case.[21] This particular decision was firmly contested by both the public prosecutor and the attorneys who were acting on behalf of the Asociación Catalana de Víctimas de Organizaciones Terroristas (ACVOT, Catalonian Association of Victims of Terrorist Organizations), all of whom protested the sentence precisely in this respect, even if they agreed with the rest of the judicial verdict.

Little is known regarding the financing of the terrorist cell, including travel and equipment, such as a portable computer—which, as F-1 said during the trial, was to be equipped with a webcam—purchased in the morning of January 18 by order of the ringleader. Only the limited facts unveiled through the GC investigation are known.[22] This includes the fact that the bank account of Sahib Iqbal, one of the two convicted bomb makers, registered on July 12, 2007, an incoming international money transfer of more than 9,000 euros.[23] Moreover, at the time of their arrest, he and other two cell members were each carrying more than 500 euros in cash, with Qadeer Malik carrying around 1,160 euros, something unusual and unjustified considering their circumstances. Asked about this by a prosecutor during the first session of the trial on November 12, 2009, the latter replied that money "sometimes accumulated in the pocket" from tips from his job delivering butane gas cylinders but refused to explain why he had around sixteen fifty-euro bills. F-1 who had previously been implicated in moving and delivering funds across Europe to support jihadist terrorism elsewhere, spoke about an individual, not included among the arrested members of the cell, who allegedly was in charge of money transactions and said his ticket to Barcelona was paid with money provided by those who sent him from France.[24]

THE TERRORIST CELL AND ITS MEMBERS

As already indicated, seven of the eleven men convicted in the Barcelona metro bomb plot were residents in the city, and five others arrived from abroad to take part in the attacks, including the individual who subsequently became protected witness F-1. Regardless of whether the cell's composition was limited to them, its internal articulation was relatively clear, with a recognized leadership and the specialized assignment of tasks among its integrants.[25] The ringleader—Maroof Ahmed Mirza—frequently acted as imam of Barcelona's Tariq ben Ziyad Mosque, where he was known for his hate-filled sermons and calls for the faithful to join the fighting in Iraq.[26] From all indications, he was closely assisted by Mohammad Ayub Elahi Bibi and helped by other cell members such as Roshan Jamal Khan and Mohamed Tarik. At least two individuals, Qadeer Malik and Shaib Iqbal, functioned as bomb makers. It seems Hafeez Ahmed, another notorious cell member, also had expertise in manufacturing explosive devices. Imram Cheema, Mohammed Shoaib, Mehmooh Khalid, and Aqueel Ur Rahmnan Abassi were all designated suicide bombers, as was F-1.[27]

All eleven convicted individuals were from South Asia, ten of them originally from Pakistan and one from India. All the plotters, save one of the Pakistanis, Mohammad Ayub Elahi Bibi, were nationals of their native countries; Bibi obtained Spanish citizenship in 2001. Bibi had lived in Barcelona for approximately thirty-three years when arrested, an unusual length of time compared to the other cell members. It should be noted that during his testimony in his trial, he seemed to have serious difficulties expressing himself in Spanish and required assistance by an Urdu translator. Five other convicted members were also living in or around the city as legal immigrants at the time of their arrest, and most, if not all of them, arrived in Spain between 1996 and 2007.[28] These included

Maroof Ahmed Mirza, Mohamed Tarik, Qadeer Malik, Shaib Iqbal, and Hafeez Ahmed. Therefore, a total of six out the eleven individuals convicted in this terrorism case were already legal residents in Spain by January 2008. More than half of the 43,000 natives of Pakistan registered as living in Spain in 2007 were residents of Barcelona and its metropolitan area—nearly all foreign immigrants and 87 percent of them male—and some 5,000 inhabited the old Raval quarter, where the terrorist cell was constituted.[29]

In September 2004, there was already an antiterrorist operation underway in Barcelona conducted by the Mossos d'Esquadra—the Catalan autonomous police force—in which ten Pakistani immigrants of Punjabi origin who had arrived in Spain during the 1990s were arrested and prosecuted, although only five of them received final condemnatory sentences in May 2007, at the Audiencia Nacional.[30] It was proven in the court verdict that those convicted sent money, partly acquired from illicit drug trafficking, through the *hawala* system between the spring and summer months of 2004. The individuals receiving the funds were linked to jihadist organizations and networks that included prominent al-Qaeda members in Pakistan such as Mohammed Naeem Noor Khan, Ahmed Khalfan Ghailani, and Amjad Farooqui, as well as to the man known as Mohamed the Egyptian, Rabei Osman el-Sayed Ahmed, then residing in Italy, who was involved in the Madrid train bombings of March 11, 2004. However, none of those arrested in January 2008 Barcelona plot had been among the arrested in the September 2004 counterterrorism operation in that city. It is important to note that the most prominent detainees from the 2004 case attended the Tarek ben Ziyad mosque, the same worship place in the Raval where the 2008 group gathered.

Of the remaining five convicted for the January 2008 plot, four were designated suicide bombers who arrived in Barcelona at some point within the four months before their arrests.[31] Roshan Jamal Khan arrived in Spain in September 2007 on a direct flight from Pakistan; Mehmooh Khalid, in October of the same year from Pakistan via Sweden; Mohammed Shoaib, in November from Pakistan via Germany; Imram Cheema, in December 2007 from, Portugal; and Aqueel Ur Rahmnan Abassi, as late as January 9, 2008, from the Netherlands, where he had been granted a student visa the previous year, even if he was not really engaged in his presumed scholarly activities at the Avans Hogeschool in Breda.[32]

Authorities interpreted these arrivals from Pakistan as suspicious, especially because Hafeez Ahmed returned to Barcelona from a five-month stay in Pakistan between March and August 2007, weeks before the others began arriving.[33] Perhaps it is not that irrelevant that Ahmed reacted fiercely to his arrest and openly threatened the agent who arrested him, loudly saying, "In my country I have killed many policemen like you."[34] The two men who made the arrangements to prepare the explosive devices, Qadeer Malik and Shaib Iqbal, were both in Pakistan in the fall of 2007.[35] Previously, the cell's ringleader, Maroof Ahmed Mirza, had also spent three to four months in Pakistan, between November 2006 and February 2007.[36]

All of the plotters were men aged 25 to 63 at the time of their arrest in January 2008. Although their average age was almost 36, five of them were between 25 and 29—including the four individuals designated as suicide bombers. A total of nine were between 25 and 40. Only two of the plotters were older, age 50 and 63.[37] Six of the eleven men convicted in this case were single, including the four individuals preparing to act as suicide bombers. Four others were married at the time of their arrest. Among the latter, three had children. Mohammad Ayub Elahi Bibi, the outlying older member of the Barcelona terrorist cell who had lived in the city for more than three decades, is a widower with descendants, including several grandsons.[38]

The plotters varied widely in their educational backgrounds. One of them was illiterate, three had attended primary school in Pakistan, and two more had some secondary schooling—which is not compulsory in their country. Another of the eleven convicted underwent madrassa and formal Islamic religious instruction; Maroof Ahmed Mirza referred to others in the cell as "maulana." Most significantly, the remaining four had some level of university-level educations, including the man from India.[39] Incidentally, this latter presented himself as an occasional tradesman, although this claim was not properly substantiated during the judicial process. Mirza worked as an imam and taught the Quran to children of Muslim immigrants in Barcelona. Bibi, the oldest among them, owned a small bakery after laboring as an assistant cook for many years, but a majority of those convicted held unskilled jobs as construction workers or delivered and cleaned butane cylinders. Unfortunately, little is known of the actual occupations of the four individuals who intended to become suicidal terrorists, except for Aqueel Ur Rahmnan Abassi, then registered as an international business management student in the Netherlands.[40]

Interestingly, eight of the eleven plotters were born in major cities of the Punjab province of Pakistan, such as Gujranwala, Rawalpindi, Jhelum, Multan, and Islamabad.[41] More than half of Pakistan's population of approximately 150 million is in this restive province, where the radical deobandi view of Islam proliferates. Shaped by these cultural preconditions and stimulated by certain sectors of the national armed forces and intelligence establishment, a number of jihadist terrorist outfits formed since the 1990s in this area.[42] Some of these radical groups associated with al-Qaeda are currently active not only on the other side of the border in Kashmiri territories and the rest of India but also on Pakistani soil. The native localities of the two other convicted individuals of Pakistani origin are not too distant: Kohat, in Khyber Pakhtunkhwa, formerly known as the North Western Frontier Province (NWFP), and the major southern harbor metropolis of Karachi. The Indian citizen is a native of Mumbai.

The cell constituted an ideologically coherent collective based on its members' rigid Islamic beliefs. During the trial, ten of the eleven defendants exhibited rather thick and long beards, an external sign of such ideas. Indeed, all of those indicted consider themselves Sunni Muslims and, according to what they declared to the police and judges, are either members of—or were closely related to—the Muslim missionary fundamentalist movement Tablighi Jamaat.[43] However, this particular description should be taken with some caution since the protected witness, in his own testimony, indicated that in Paris he received instructions to travel to Barcelona and say, if asked, that he was traveling only for the Tablighi movement, a religious sect that has spread considerably across Western Europe.[44] Nonetheless, at least two of the convicted plotters were known for active Tablighi practices or frequented Barcelona's Tarek ben Ziyad Mosque. This mosque—named after a historical figure who led the Arab and Berber warriors that in 711 crossed what is now called the Strait of Gibraltar and initiated more than seven centuries of Muslim dominion over most of the Iberian Peninsula—is known for hosting Tablighi.[45] Additionally, copies of a book authored by Muhammad Zakariya, considered a main ideologue of the Tablighi movement, were found in one of the homes searched during the counterterrorism operation by the

GC, next to a commentary of the Quran by Abul Ala Maududi, a radical Islamist of Pakistani origin whose writings became a constitutive element of the violent global jihadi doctrine promoted by al-Qaeda. Inside the Tarek ben Ziyad Mosque, the GC also found taped political sermons by Abd al-Hamid Kishk,[46] an Egyptian preacher who has been praised more than once by Ayman al-Zawahiri, who in those days was al-Qaeda's second in command to Osama bin Laden.

LINKS TO SOUTH WAZIRISTAN

F-1 explained during his testimony that he became involved in a jihdist organization that led him to France three years before the January 2008 events in Barcelona. Between early 2005 and the middle of 2006, the organization often tasked him and his companions with collecting and moving money among Brussels, Amsterdam, and Brescia. In northern Italy, F-1 would meet with an individual born in the tribal areas of Pakistan, presumably linked to al-Qaeda, and his Moroccan assistant, usually in a mosque. Allegedly, both of them were transferring funds to final destinations in Pakistan, Iraq, and even Algeria to the terrorist organization Lashkar-e-Taiba (LeT), allied with al-Qaeda, among others.[47]

F-1 also consistently reiterated, in different formal statements before police and judicial authorities in Spain, that over the year and a half preceding January 2008, the same organization ordered him to attend training on the use of weapons and bomb making in different facilities in the Waziristan region of northwestern Pakistan and in Afghanistan.[48] While at a training center there, F-1 met the former operational commander of the Pakistani Taliban, Baitullah Mehsud, among other prominent militant figures. Furthermore, he indicated in his oral testimony during the trial that the plotters were "working under the instructions of Baitullah Mehsud." During his first statement before the GC on January 22, 2008, the protected witness described the Barcelona terrorist cell members as related to both Mehsud and al-Qaeda. In a subsequent statement before an investigative judge at the Audiencia Nacional, F-1 indirectly alluded to his own organization as al-Qaeda.[49] However, it was during the trial that when explicitly asked by the public prosecutor about the name of the organization he consistently spoke about, he clearly and concisely replied, "Al-Qaeda."

Baitullah Mehsud took charge as operational commander of the Taliban militants in the South Waziristan territories dominated by the Mehsud tribes around the middle of 2004.[50] He became particularly prominent earlier in the year by organizing his fellow tribesmen àgainst the Pakistani government. Troops launched their first full-scale military operation in the areas populated by the Wazir tribes, targeting mainly al-Qaeda members and foreigners belonging to its affiliated groups who had taken refuge there to escape the post-9/11 U.S.-led military intervention in Afghanistan. Al-Qaeda militants then found shelter in the Mehsud areas.[51] Shortly after the government signed an agreement with the Mehsud tribes in February 2005, Baitullah Mehsud violated the terms by supporting Talibanization process and enforcing an extremist version of Islamic law, before establishing a parallel administration in May.[52] Al-Qaeda trained in facilities there, either directly or through associated groups, such as the local Pakistani Taliban, as well as in other areas of the Federally Administered Tribal Areas (FATA) and Khyber Pakhtunkhwa.

Baitullah Mehsud became the overall leader of Tehreek-e-Taliban-e-Pakistan (TTP) when this entity formed in December 2007, aligning under one leader nearly forty previously existing local militant groups and factions operating in the seven agencies of Pakistan's FATA and in several districts of the former NWFP. TTP, a force of between 30,000 and 40,000 men, was organizationally distinct from the Afghan Taliban, but its leaders pledged allegiance to Mullah Omar. It emerged as the most dominant al-Qaeda partner in these territories, and Baitullah Mehsud expressed "utmost love and respect" for both Osama bin Laden and Ayman al-Zawahiri.[53] It was precisely at that time, the end of 2007, that the protected witness, F-1, was ordered back from Waziristan to France, where he had to await further instructions from his organization. These proved to be the order to travel from Paris to Barcelona and join others in carrying out attacks in early January 2008. F-1, despite his acknowledged membership in al-Qaeda, was acting under the command of Baitullah Mehsud.

Based on F-1's testimony, the Barcelona plot was connected to Baitullah Mehsud, TTP, and al-Qaeda. The connections with Mehsud and TTP were corroborated in the months following the arrests. In a video interview recorded on August 1, 2008, by a associate of the NEFA Foundation, the TTP's top official spokesman and a member of its central *shura* or council, Maulvi Omar, claimed that the organization was responsible for the foiled suicide bombing plot in Barcelona. When asked whether TTP could ever carry out an attack against the West, Omar replied, "The one in Barcelona was conducted by twelve of our men. They were under pledge to Baitullah Mehsud, and TTP has already claimed responsibility, because of Spain's war involvement with its military presence in Afghanistan."[54] When he said that TTP had claimed responsibility for the plot, he probably meant that, in February 2008, during a difficult conversation by satellite phone with a journalist, he had acknowledged that "we sent them, and we will do de same with other countries of the Alliance"—meaning in Afghanistan. He added that TTP had provided training in Pakistan's tribal areas to individuals involved in the thwarted attacks in Barcelona, but as he pointed, "they had their own plans" with respect to target selection and the execution of the attacks.[55]

These statements by Maulvi Omar—who was later captured by Pakistani security forces in August 2009 in Mohmand—are consistent with a reference made by F-1 during his January 22, 2008, declaration before the GC. According to him, based on what he heard from a prominent member of the Barcelona cell following the first attack in Spain, "Al-Qaeda would make some demands through the emir Baitullah Mehsud."[56] A second and even a third explosion were scheduled to follow in Spain if these demands were not met, followed by further attacks in other European countries.[57] F-1 also stated during the trial, "After the explosion, Baitullah Mehsud was going to announce al-Qaeda's demands and if they were not met there was to be a second explosion and afterwards more in Germany, Portugal and France." All the European countries mentioned in F-1's testimony contribute troops to the International Security Assistance Force (ISAF) in support of the government of the Islamic Republic of Afghanistan. It is worth remembering that at this point, on November 29, 2007, the Islamist website al-Ekhlaas posted an audio message from Osama bin Laden, produced by al-Qaeda's media branch, al-Sahab, in which he called upon Europeans to withdraw their forces from Afghanistan and threatened to continue taking revenge and defeat them.[58] Interestingly, when thinking about the strategy behind the Barcelona bomb plot, the counterterrorism operation in this city took place less than two months before national elections in Spain, scheduled for March 9, 2008.

Therefore, F-1 and perhaps other members of the Barcelona bombing plot, if not the terrorist cell as a whole, might have belonged to al-Qaeda, but his recruitment took place outside of South Asia, in France. At the same time, the plotters had strong links to al-Qaeda-associated jihadist groups in South Waziristan and explicitly to TTP by December 2007. Under the operational command of Baitullah Mehsud, some of the members of the Barcelona cell, including F-1, likely underwent training at camps in the FATA and across the border in Afghanistan as well. Moreover, the overall direction for the attacks planned in Spain was provided by the same leader following strategic guidelines set forth by Osama bin Laden as the emir of al-Qaeda, most of whose senior members and activists were then based in Pakistani tribal territories under the protection of Mehsud militant groups and commanders.

The fact that eight of the eleven Pakistanis convicted in the Barcelona plot come from Punjab and not from these tribal areas should not come as a surprise. On the one hand, it is known that by 2007, in FATA and in the administrative unit known until recently as the North West Frontier Province, local jihadist organizations, including the local militant groups and al-Qaeda, were mobilizing Punjabis. On the other hand, the Pakistani Taliban have allies across Pakistan and particularly from the Punjab province, where various militant al-Qaeda-related jihadist groups, such as Lashkar e Jangvi (LeJ) and Jaish-e-Mohammed (JeM), established deep roots during the past three decades. Interestingly, al-Sahab, al-Qaeda's propaganda wing, commonly features Pakistani Taliban leaders, including a eulogy for Baitullah Mehsud by Ayman al-Zawahiri—al-Qaeda's second in command—from September 28, 2009.

The individual and collective actors behind the January 2008 Barcelona bomb plot form an intriguing combination. The protected witness, F-1, one of the suicide bombers designated by the terrorist cell ringleader, made it clear to both police and judges in Spain that the organization he belonged to, as well as those who sent him from France, was al-Qaeda. Further, according to his declarations before these authorities, as transcribed in the official criminal proceedings of the case reviewed throughout this chapter, he received training in the Waziristan region of Pakistan under the instructions of the now-deceased Pakistani Taliban commander Baitullah Mehsud. Moreover, Tehreek-e-Taliban-Pakistan, which Mehsud headed since its inception in late 2007, claimed responsibility for the planned attacks in Barcelona. However, TTP is a jihadist alliance composed of ethnic Pashtu militant groups based in the tribal areas and nearby lands in the northwest of Pakistan, but most of those convicted for belonging to the terrorist cell formed in the Raval quarter of are from the heartland province of Punjab.

This combination may be indicative of relevant developments other than al-Qaeda or TTP recruiting of Punjabis and other Pakistanis living in their own country or abroad. On the one hand, it may be considered an expression of the increasing operational limitations faced by al-Qaeda after 2002 and its reliance, often because of mutually beneficial arrangements, on allies such as the Pakistani Taliban, that is, on the same militant groups from which al-Qaeda receives protection and support in the tribal areas along the porous border with Afghanistan. These alliances allow training activities in the area and give al-Qaeda assistance in conducting acts of terrorism abroad, aimed at Western societies in general and European nations in particular, as the Barcelona case shows. On the other hand, the same combination can be seen as an early manifestation of multiple overlapping linkages among the Pakistani Taliban, the Afghan Taliban, and other militant groups based in northwest Pakistan, including former and current elements of one or more banned jihadist organizations traditionally established in the Punjab, including al-Qaeda associates. This agglomeration later, from the spring of 2009, became widely referred to as the Punjabi Taliban and, more appropriately, the Punjabi Taliban network.[59] As a whole, the January 2008 suicide-bomb plot in Barcelona reflects a composite terrorist threat from Pakistan.

Thus, the foiled January 2008 plot against the metro in Barcelona evidenced both the polymorphous character of post-9/11 global terrorism and the composite nature of the main threat it seems to pose in the West. The thwarted attacks were the product of a mixture of foreign extremists coming from Pakistan and radicalized first-generation immigrants to the West. This second factor, distinctive with respect to other successful and foiled attacks involving second- and third-generation descendents of immigrants, as in the United Kingdom, is consistent with the relatively recent settling of Muslim communities in Spain. Moreover, the fact that all but one of those convicted are Pakistanis and that TTP, a Pakistani entity affiliated with al-Qaeda, claimed responsibility, is best understood with respect to the unusually heavy concentration of people from Pakistan in Barcelona, a circumstance unparalleled in the country or in any other major Western European city outside England. The case of Barcelona also draws attention to the disturbing role played by the Tablighi Jamaat missionary movement in allowing the violent radicalization of adherents and the use of its meetings and sponsored travel for recruitment and training purposes by terrorist organizations and the cross-border circulation of jihadist terrorists.

The Barcelona plot was intended to use suicide bombers to detonate explosive devices against soft targets, such as the mass transit system, likely to ensure high lethality among civilians. Its underlying goal was to force a withdrawal of European troops in general and Spanish soldiers in particular from Afghanistan. Thus, once again, jihadist terrorists aimed at distancing national governments from their publics and creating divisions among Western countries, NATO member nations, and the ISAF. Had the metro attacks in Barcelona not been thwarted on time, thanks to a domestic counterterrorism operation prompted by bilateral intelligence exchanges, a message from Osama bin Laden would have been expected to follow, through the Pakistani Taliban commander Baitullah Meshud. A hierarchy of leadership can therefore be observed in this foiled episode of global terrorism, from the local cell formed in Barcelona to execute the bombings up to Tehreek-e-Taliban-e-Pakistan as an articulated entity affiliated to al-Qaeda.

NOTES

1. Dirección General de la Policía y de la Guardia Civil, Jefatura de Información U.C.E. 2 / G.I.E., Sección de Investigación 7ª Zona de Cataluña, Servicio de Información, *Atestado 01/2008*, 1–9, 112–173; Audiencia Nacional, Juzgado Central de Instrucción no. 2, *Sumario 26/2008*, Tome 2, 333–41.

2. *Sumario 26/2008*, Tome 1, 81.

3. He took a flight to Germany on the morning of the counterterrorism operation. It is believed that this individual ended up in the Netherlands when the attacks in Barcelona did not take place.

4. As is required by the legal system in Spain, the formal indictment of all the suspects was confirmed on October 9, 2008, by a tribunal dealing with serious criminal offenses and formed by three judges of the Audiencia Nacional unrelated to the proceedings of this case.

5. Audiencia Nacional, Sala de lo Penal, Sección Primera, *Sentencia 78/2009*, 7–8, 32–34.

6. *Atestado 01/08*, 1–9; *Sumario 26/2008*, Tome 2, 334.

7. *Atestado 01/2008*, 2–3, 691–93; *Sumario 26/2008*, Tome 2, 334; *Sentencia 78/2009*, 9.

8. *Atestado 01/2008*, 730.

9. *Atestado 01/2008*, 6–8; *Sumario 26/2008*, Tome 1, 4, 7, 32, 47 and 107.

10. *Atestado 01/2008*, 1, 60–106; *Sumario 26/2008*, Tome 1, 4, 7, 32, 47 and 107; Tome 2, 392–439.

11. In particular, article 2 of Ley Orgánica 19/1994.

12. This was in application of article 16.2 of the Código Penal (Spain's criminal code). See *Sentencia 78/2009*, 15.

13. *Atestado 01/2008*, 710–16; *Sumario 26/2008*, Tome 1, 60–102, Tome 2, 394, Tome 3, 1051–52; *Sentencia 78/2009*, 22–23.

14. *Atestado 01/2008*, 8–9; *Sumario 26/2008*, Tome 3, 1051–52.

15. *Atestado 01/2008*, 728; *Sumario 26/2008*, Tome 3, 1057, 1150, and Tome 4, 1470; *Sentencia 78/2009*, 9.

16. *El Periódico* (Barcelona), January 27, 2008, 19.

17. *Sumario 26/2008*, Tome 3, 1057, 1150, Tome 4, 1470.

18. *Sentencia 78/2009*, 9.

19. *Atestado 01/2008*, 725; *Sumario 26/2008*, Tome 3, 1065.

20. *Atestado 01/2008*, 1, 726; *Sumario 26/2008*, Tome 3, 1065.

21. *Sentencia 78/2009*, 30.

22. In this as in all other facets of the case, the Pakistani security authorities were markedly uncooperative, as I deduced from personal interviews, first, with a liaison officer acquainted with the Pakistani police, held in Madrid on November 30, 2009, and, then, with two senior officials from the GC in charge of investigating the Barcelona bomb plot, also in Madrid on May 28, 2010.

23. *Atestado 01/2008*, 774; *Sumario 26/2008*, Tome 3, 1115.

24. *Atestado 01/2008*, 764, 726.

25. *Sentencia 78/2009*, 7.

26. "Terror Threat From Pakistan Said to Expand," *New York Times*, February 10, 2008, available at http://www.nytimes.com/2008/02/10/world/europe/10spain.html.

27. *Sentencia 78/2009*, 8; *Sumario 26/2008*, Tome 3, 1065.

28. *Atestado 01/2008*, 210–689; *Sumario 26/2008*, Tome 2, 545–855, Tome 3, 858–1031.

29. These data refer to individuals registered in municipalities according to the *Revisión del Padrón Municipal de 2007* and can be consulted at the website of the Instituto Nacional de Estadística at www.ine.es. On Pakistanis living in Barcelona, see Montserrat Solé y Josep Rodríguez, "Paqustaníes en España: Un estudio basado en el colectivo de la Ciudad de Barcelona," *Revista CIDOB d'Afers Internacionals*, no. 68 (2005): 97–118; Jordi Moreras, "¿Ravalistán? Islam y configuración comunitaria entre los paquistaníes en Barcelona," *Revista CIDOB d'Afers Internacionals*, no. 68 (2005): 97–118;

Mònica Tolsanas, "Las calles de Barcelona, las casas de Paquistán. Transnacionalismo y generación posmigratoria," *Revista CIDOB d'Afers Internacionals*, no. 78 (2007): 33–56.

30. Aundiencia Nacional, Sala de lo Penal, Sección Primera, *Sentencia 39/2007*.

31. *Sumario 26/2008*, 1112–14.

32. "Aqueel Ur Rahmnan Abassi Aqeel Abassi" allegedly started his studies in international business management in September 2007 and dropped out in February 2008. I am grateful to Dr. Edwin Bakker, from the Netherlands Institute for International Relations, Cligendael, for providing me access to this information on April 7, 2010.

33. *Sumario 26/2008*, 1112–14.

34. *Atestado 01/2008*, 162, 759; *Sumario 26/2008*, Tome 2, 496.

35. *Sumario 26/2008*, 1113; *Sentencia 78/2009*, 8.

36. *Sumario 26/2008*, 1112.

37. *Atestado 01/2008*, 112 and 210–689; *Sumario 26/2008*, Tome 2, 545–855, Tome 3, 858–1031.

38. *Atestado 01/2008*, 383–421; *Sumario 26/2008*, Tome 2, 738.

39. *Atestado 01/2008*, 224–690.

40. *Atestado 01/2008*, 224–690.

41. *Atestado 01/2008*, 210–689; *Sumario 26/2008*, Tome 2, 545–855, Tome 3, 858–1031.

42. See, for instance, Bruce Riedel, "Pakistan and Terror: The Eye of the Storm," *Annals of the American Academy of Political and Social Sciences*, no. 618 (2008): 31–45.

43. *Atestado 01/2008*, 210–689; *Sumario 26/2008*, Tome 2, 545–855, Tome 3, 858–1031.

44. *Sentencia 78/2009*, 27–28.

45. "Los amigos de un terrorista del Raval reviven su fanatización," *El Periódico* (Barcelona), February 12, 2008, 22.

46. *Atestado 01/2008*, 752–55; *Sumario 26/2008*, Tome 3, 1092–93.

47. *Sumario 26/2008*, Tome 3, 1057–59, Tome 4, 1472.

48. *Atestado 01/2008*, 725. Also see *Sumario 26/2008*, Tome 4, 1470; *Sentencia 78/2009*, 19.

49. *Sentencia 78/2009*, 25; *Sumario 26/2008*, Tome 4, 1472.

50. Muhammad Amir Rana, "Evolution of Militant Groups in FATA and Adjacent Areas," in Muhammad Amir Rana, Safdar Sial and Abdul Basit, *Dynamics of Taliban Insurgency in FATA* (Islamabad: Pak Institute for Peace Studies, 2010), 50–51.

51. Muhammad Amir Rana, "Post-9/11 Developments and Emergence of Local Taliban Groups," in Muhammad Amir Rana, Safdar Sial and Abdul Basit, *Dynamics of Taliban Insurgency in FATA* (Islamabad: Pak Institute for Peace Studies, 2010), 83.

52. Ibid., 90–91.

53. MEMRI, Special Dispatch no. 1830, 30 January 2008. On September 28, 2009, shortly after Baitullah Mehsud died, Ayman al-Zawahiri eulogized him as both as an organizer of jihadist uprising in Afghanistan and Pakistan as well as a role model for youth. The transcript of the original Arabic-language audio recording is available at www.nefafoundation.org/miscellaneous/FeaturedDocs/nefazawahiri0909.pdf.

54. The video interview with top Maulvi Omar is available at http://www1 .nefafoundation.org/multimedia-intvu.html (accessed August 1, 2010).

55. *El Periódico* (Barcelona), February 11, 2008, 2. On February 10, 2008, the U.S. secretary of defense, Robert Gates, during a visit to Europe, linked the Barcelona plot to Baitullah Mehsud and the Pakistani Taliban.

56. *Atestado 01/2008*, 726; also *Sumario 26/2008*, Tome 3, 1065.

57. *Atestado 01/2008*, 726–27.

58. MEMRI, Special Dispatch no. 1776, November 30, 2007, available at www .memri.org/bin/opener_latest.cgi?ID=SD177607.

59. Hassan Abbas, "Defining the Punjabi Taliban Network," *CTC Sentinel* 2, no. 4 (2009): 1–4; Katjia Riikonen, "'Punjabi Taliban' and the Sectarian Groups in Pakistan," University of Bradford, Department of Peace Studies: Pakistan Security Research Unit, brief no. 55, 2010.

[14]

Ansar al-Fatah and "Iraqi"
Networks in France

JEAN-PIERRE FILIU

I n July 2005, Ayman al-Zawahari described the U.S. invasion of Iraq as a "blessing" since it paved the way for "jihad in the heart of the Islamic world."[1] This candid admission was not uttered for public consumption but was part of an internal al-Qaeda document, a letter sent by bin Laden's deputy to Abu Musab al-Zarqawi, field commander of the Iraqi branch of the global organization. The American offensive on Iraq, launched in March 2003, was indeed crucial for al-Qaeda to arrest the downward spiral it had been caught in since the collapse of the Taliban emirate in fall 2001. The "blessed" jihad against the Western "Crusaders" on an Arab land offered al-Qaeda a strategic foothold in the Middle East. It also gave the global jihad privileged access to a new militant generation in Europe, as well as in North Africa.

The European continent had long been a fertile ground for innovative and polymorphous jihadi organizations. The antagonism between local (or national) jihad, on the one hand, and global (or al-Qaeda-inspired) jihad, on the other hand, is valid all over the Muslim world. This distinction, however, loses relevance in Europe, where dozens of young Muslims left to join the jihad in Iraq after the U.S. invasion. While most of these networks began as grassroots initiatives, the very process of channeling human and financial resources led the local groups to blend into the transnational networks of global jihad. This process indoctrinated local groups with a global ideology that in turn transformed the focus of their targeting from "infidels" in Iraq to objectives closer to home.

There is a precedent for this in the 1980s, when activists left Europe to join the anti-Soviet jihad in Afghanistan. Differences between the "Afghan" and the "Iraqi" generations of jihadi volunteers are manifold however. The absence of an equivalent to the Peshawar-based "Services Bureau" made the outreach process more difficult and more risky. On the other hand, the Iraqi struggle struck a much deeper chord among radical Muslim youth in Europe. Additionally, the "veterans" from Iraq are more battle-hardened than their "Afghan" predecessors, and their military expertise could prove far more devastating.

This mixture of characteristics gives the Iraq generation a more defiant nature, with a renewed underground discipline and evolving agenda, from local jihad in Iraq, to global jihad in Europe. Al-Qaeda understood as early as 2004 the benefits it could reap from this European angle. One month after the Madrid bombings, Osama bin Laden proposed a "truce" to Europe on the condition that it shun the U.S. alliance. Since European governments and opinion did not even consider this position, al-Qaeda's propaganda increasingly focused on threatening Europe.

In the case of France, the transition from the Afghan to the Iraqi generation occurred on the historical background of the terror campaign waged on French soil by the Algerian Islamic Armed Group (Groupe Islamique Armé; GIA) in 1995–96. Most of the networks dismantled on the eve or in the aftermath of 9/11 in France had strong connections with the GIA or its more "global" offshoot, the Salafist Group for Preaching and Combat (Groupe Salafiste pour la Prédication et le Combat; GSPC). The French security apparatus proved successful in handling the Algerian jihadi threat that it fought for years. The American invasion of Iraq changed the whole picture, however, and radicalized a new generation of activists in Europe and in North Africa. A fateful triangle emerged among Europe, North Africa, and the Middle East, with al-Qaeda-in-Iraq as a magnet for jihadi recruitment and mobilization on both sides of the Western Mediterranean. It is through these Iraqi dynamics that the GSPC became, in 2007, al-Qaeda in the Islamic Maghrib (AQIM).

The group Ansar al-Fatah is a fascinating example of this Iraq-induced change of terrorist guards: Safe Bourada, an Algerian-born French citizen, received a ten-year sentence for his involvement in the GIA attacks in the 1990s, but when released from prison in 2003, he established a new group, Ansar al-Fatah, to support jihad in Iraq. By switching the group's focus, Bourada reached out to a new generation of militants attracted by the Iraqi horizon. Interestingly enough, this international network never operated in Iraq. France and Algeria served as places for recruiting volunteers and raising funds, and the military training took place in Lebanon. Eventually, the targeting planning evolved from the Middle East to French territory, but Ansar al-Fatah was fortunately dismantled before going into action.

This case study highlights how the Iraqi theme helped to globalize local militant networks in Europe through their modus operandi, their international connections, their political agenda, and their potential strategies. Two other, less-documented outfits also focused on Iraq complement this experience: one based in Northern Paris, the other one stemming from the Southern city of Montpellier. To understand how those "Iraqi" networks could (or could not) develop, it is necessary to briefly review France's troubled record with Middle Eastern terrorism that started long before al-Qaeda launched its "global jihad" in 1988. This historical wrap-up is essential for assessing how the U.S. invasion of Iraq opened a new phase, even though French territory has been protected from jihad-fueled violence since 1996.

THE FRENCH WAVES

France has been the target of Middle Eastern–inspired terror since the beginning of the 1980s. This early exposure forced the French security apparatus to develop new expertise and techniques. Antiterrorist legislation was adopted, empowering both the judiciary and the police to face this specific threat. During the two decades preceding the 2003 invasion of Iraq, France faced three waves of terror attacks, each one with its own rationale and dynamics.

The first terror wave hit France from 1982 to 1986. Paris was struck twice in 1982. On April 22, a car bomb exploded near the Champs-Elysées, targeting the offices of a pro-Iraqi Arabic newspaper, killing one person. Then, on August 9, a drive-by shooting in a historically Jewish neighborhood (rue des Rosiers) left six dead. Those attacks echoed anti-French violence in Beirut, including the bombing of the French embassy on May 24 that killed eleven people. It was French support to Iraq during its war against Iran that triggered the worst terror attacks of this period, first in Beirut, where 58 French paratroopers were killed on October 23, 1983 (a simultaneous suicide bombing killed 241 Americans), and several French citizens were abducted (some of them were detained for more than three years). Then in Paris, between 1985 and 1986, a series of bombings rippled through the city, culminating on September 17, 1986, with the killing of seven people in the popular rue de Rennes, near Montparnasse train station. The network responsible for this bloodshed was eventually dismantled; led by the Tunisian Fuad Ali Saleh, it proved to be Iranian-inspired and Shia-oriented.[2] The whole crisis caused the parallel blockades of the French embassy in Teheran and the Iranian embassy in Paris during the summer of 1987. The end of the Iran-Iraq conflict in 1988 effectively closed this chapter of the French experience with state-sponsored terror as a means of proxy war.

The second terror wave hit France between 1995 and 1996 and was intimately bound to the escalating Algerian civil war. In late 1994, Jamal Zaytouni took over the Islamic Armed Group (GIA) and embarked on an all-out conflict against the Algerian security forces and the rival Islamic Salvation Front (Front Islamique du Salut; FIS). His extremist propaganda associated his Algerian enemies with the former French colonial power in an ominous alliance of "infidel" France with "apostate" Algerians. In a spectacularly innovative plot, he ordered four of his GIA followers to hijack an Air France airplane in Algiers on December 24, 1994, to crash it in Paris, possibly against the Eiffel tower. Fortunately, the hijackers were duped into believing that the plane had to refuel before reaching Paris, and the flight was diverted to Marseilles, where French security stormed it and killed the four terrorists. As U.S. counterterrorism expert Bruce Riedel aptly commented, "Save for the French commandos and their counterterrorism expertise, 9/11 would have happened on Christmas 1994."[3]

After this raid failed, Zaytouni refocused his networks on a more classical bombing campaign on French soil. The worst attacks occurred against the Paris central subway stations on July 25, 1995, and December 3, 1996, which killed twelve people. Several other attempts were foiled, including one on a high-speed railway track and others against marketplaces in Paris and Lille. Most of the media attention focused on the twenty-four-year old French Algerian Khaled Kelkal, whom the police killed in a shoot-out near Lyon in September 1995. The GIA terror attacks went on after his death until the dismantling of the Zaytouni-inspired networks. This second wave was again a war by proxy as the Algerian jihadi guerrillas tried to import to France their conflict with their "apostate" enemies. The eventual collapse of the GIA in 1997, engulfed in the mass slaughters of civilians in Algeria, closed this cycle of terror against France.

The third wave of terror attacks was more global but was fortunately thwarted before and after 9/11. The GIA had a complex and defiant relationship with al-Qaeda, and Zaytouni intentionally kept his full independence from bin Laden's international movement.[4] On the other hand, his fellow Algerian Rashid Boukhalfa, better known as Abu Doha (nicknamed "Doctor Haidar"), chose to join the archipelago of jihadi camps in Taliban-run Afghanistan. He opened his own training facility there in 1998 in close cooperation with al-Qaeda. This Abu Doha network, involved in the 1999 "Millennium plot" in North America, also spread its own cells in Europe. A planned attack in 2000 in Strasbourg, France, against the city's cathedral and the Christmas market, was foiled mainly by the joint action of the French and German police. International cooperation was also crucial in the detention of Djamel Beghal (Abu Hamza), an al-Qaeda-trained Algerian militant. His arrest in Dubai in July 2001 and his transfer to France helped prevent a major attack against the U.S. embassy in Paris in the wake of 9/11.[5]

The success in preventing the potentially devastating "third wave" of anti-French terror plots stemmed from active cooperation among European, Arab, and U.S. security apparatuses. It also built upon the experience acquired during the first and second waves of terror attacks, when state and nonstate actors imported their terror onto French soil as a sideshow to their main confrontation. The French intelligence community became quite efficient at detecting and neutralizing imported terror cells, which was one of the main reasons for the successful dismantlement of the jihadi networks in the fall of 2001. The security situation changed dramatically with the 2003 invasion of Iraq, which created a magnet for jihadi activism in the Middle East and fueled homegrown radicalization.

SAFE BOURADA AND ANSAR AL-FATAH

Safe Bourada, born in 1970 in Algeria, fled the country at the beginning of the 1990s, when the civil war between the army and the Islamist guerrillas was escalating. Instead of siding with the more political Islamic Salvation Front (FIS), Bourada enlisted in the extremist GIA, which pledged to topple the Algerian "apostate" regime ("no dialogue, no reconciliation, no truce" with the government was the GIA battle cry).[6] The GIA established its propaganda division in London, nicknamed "Londonistan" because of the facilities enjoyed by the various jihadi factions in the United Kingdom. The GIA newsletter, *al-Ansar* (The partisans), was launched in London in July 1993 with the support of two prominent figures of the global jihadi community, the Jordanian Abu Qatada (Omar Mahmoud Othman) and the Syrian Abu Musab al-Suri (Mustafa Setmarian Nasar).[7] The title of the newsletter was a direct reference to the Prophet Muhammad's Partisans, who joined him in his emigration (Hejira) from Mecca to Medina in 622 and helped him achieve the conquest (Fatah) of his native city eight years later. The whole jihadi emigration to Europe was therefore ideologically packaged as a necessary step before the ultimate triumph over the "apostates" ruling the Muslim lands.

Bourada became more involved in the GIA European outfit during the 1990s. He was only twenty-four when Jamal Zaytouni took over the GIA and declared jihad against "infidel" France in December 1994. Bourada then acted as a GIA liaison officer, shuttling between Brussels and Lyon. After the terror campaign that struck France during the summer of 1995, Bourada was among the dozens of GIA activists rounded up by the police. During his trial, he denied any direct participation in the bombing attacks. His responsibility in the propaganda and logistical dimensions of the GIA campaign was well established, though, and he was sentenced to ten years in prison. Bourada was eventually released in 2003, before the end of his term.

It appeared that those years in jail, far from watering down Bourada's jihadi inclinations, only hardened them. Bourada acted as a veteran figure among his fellow inmates, and he grew infatuated with his own importance.[8] Shortly after his release, he wrote the founding charter of "Ansar al-Fatah" (Partisans of the Conquest), a clandestine group whose name echoed a theme seen prominently in the GIA literature of the early

1990s. Bourada was also influenced by the transition from the GIA to the Salafist Group for Preaching and Combat (GSPC), since he pledged his own Ansar al-Fatah to "bind preaching and combat together."[9] Bourada organized a close-knit cell of followers who acknowledged him as their emir or commander. He felt confident enough to stage in October 2004 his own "emigration" (Hejira) from "infidel" France to Egypt, where he planned to study classical Arabic, in order to bolster his credentials as a self-styled emir.

Bourada also designated a younger deputy, Kaci Ouarab, born in 1977, who enhanced Ansar al-Fatah's Middle Eastern credentials. Ouarab traveled to Syria in January 2005 and met a Tunisian militant active in the smuggling of foreign fighters into Iraq.[10] Instead of crossing over into Iraq, Ouarab moved west and joined a jihadi training camp in Northern Lebanon.[11] This was likely in response to the increasing pressure on Iraq-focused networks from Syrian security, which prompted many groups to move their training facilities to the friendlier environment of the Tripoli province, where there was a deep-rooted tradition of jihadi militancy. Ouarab paved the way for the operational training of other members of Ansar al-Fatah. However, since no direct steps were made to join the anti-U.S. jihad in Iraq, the group was accused of planning to use their training in Europe in general and in France in particular.[12]

While Ouarab was organizing future operations, Kais Melliti, born in 1972, was left in charge of the financial dimension of Ansar al-Fatah, specifically the racketeering of "un-Islamic" activities. Since the emir Bourada had deemed this legal, Melliti felt entitled to extort money from prostitutes to fund operations. Aggression against an Algerian transsexual hooker in Paris in July 2005 led to the arrest of Melliti and two of his aides. During the arrest, the French police found the charter of Ansar al-Fatah and other internal documents. A few weeks later, Algerian security detained another member of the group, Mohammed Benyamina, at the Oran airport. After his interrogation, Algerian sources warned that members of Ansar al-Fatah attended a jihadi meeting in Damascus in April 2005 and were planning bombings in either the Paris subway or the Orly airport. Algerian officials also confidentially shared information with French intelligence.[13]

In September 2005, Bourada returned from Egypt to France, stopping in Turkey on his way. It was not long before the French police arrested him along with his devoted followers. In October 2008, Bourada was sentenced to fifteen years in jail, Ouarab to nine, and Melliti to eight. Djamel Badaoui, who assisted Melliti in the extortion business, was sentenced to five years in jail, and his partner, Samir Bouhalli, to four. Two French converts who joined Ansar al-Fatah, Stéphane Hadoux and Emmanuel Nieto, received three-year sentences. Benyamina, whose arrest in Oran had triggered the dismantlement of the whole group, had previously been condemned to three years in jail by an Algerian court and therefore could not stand trial in France. This meant accusations that would have elevated the charges against the network could not be used in the French trial. French reporters stated that Benyamina's absence "cast a shadow" over the Ansar al-Fatah trial, leaving open the question of how far advanced the terror planning had become.[14]

THE NINETEENTH ARRONDISSEMENT

The key figure in the "Nineteenth Arrondissement Iraqi networks" is Farid Benyettou, born in Paris in 1981 to a French family of Algerian origin. The third of four children, he grew up in a mixed neighborhood around the famous Buttes-Chaumont Park, the largest in the French capital city. He was exposed early to jihadi militancy when the Algerian Youssef Zemmouri married Asmahou Benyettou, Farid's elder sister, and moved into the five-room family flat in 1997. Zemmouri was already active in the GIA-inspired networks; he received his radical friends at his new home, which likely left a lasting impression on sixteen-year old Farid Benyettou.[15] In May 1998, the French police arrested Zemmouri and fifteen other militants for allegedly planning a major attack during the World Cup soccer championship a few weeks later.

After finishing high school, Benyettou worked like his father in the cleaning business. He spent most of his free time and his wages buying and studying Salafi literature. He was self-taught and spent time on the Internet browsing jihadi websites, which influenced his rhetoric. At twenty-two, Benyettou was displaying evidence of his radicalization. He started wearing attire traditionally reserved for confirmed preachers, confronted well-established imams in his neighborhood mosques, and was expelled from the Pré Saint-Gervais mosque, joining the Daawa mosque, in Paris's Nineteenth Arrondissement.[16] Up to 3,000 people can come and pray at the Daawa mosque every Friday, yet Benyettou operated in the margins of the religious community, defying the older imams and scorning their speeches. He started gathering a close-knit group of followers that respectfully called him "Abu Abdallah" and eventually began meeting them outside of the mosque.

In the five-million-strong Muslim community in France, Salafi believers represent only a tiny minority of a few thousands, and most of them adhere to the quietist version of Salafism, associated with the Medina-based Sheikh Rabi al-Madkhali. These mainstream Salafi abstain from any political activity or public demonstration, and their emphasis on nonviolent preaching and indoctrination has led to them being described as "anti-jihadi."[17] Benyettou, however, built up his own brand of Salafi-esque preaching, far from any established guidance, with a strong emphasis on jihad. On February 14, 2004, he joined the street protests against the law banning the veil at government schools, and he staged defiant prayers with his hardcore followers. This public display of self-righteousness tends to confirm the hypothesis that radical preaching often precedes jihadi organizing.

Crucially, Benyettou focused his anger on America because of the invasion of Iraq while keeping France psychologically distinct. Benyettou reasoned: "France is an unbeliever country. I do not like this country. It does not respect the Muslims, through discrimination and Islamophobia. We have to fight in France, but through legal means. We have to turn democracy against France. But we should not fight with weapons nor throw bombs. France has not declared war on us."[18] Therefore, the anti-U.S. jihad in Iraq was the ultimate goal, with no plan to bring its violence home to France.

Benyettou's charisma and his very personal interpretation of Islam bound together a group of people who already shared the same neighborhood experience. They all studied in the same schools, grew up in the same streets, and played on the same football fields. Among this tight-knit group, Iraq and the self-imposed duty to fight the American occupation became a new rallying cause.

To enhance the group's jihadi credentials, Benyettou relied on the "veteran" figure of twenty-year old Boubaker al-Hakim, who volunteered with thousands of other militants as a "human shield" in Iraq before the

U.S. invasion. Boubaker al-Hakim traveled to Syria in March 2003 and contacted the Iraqi embassy to volunteer his services. He enrolled in the Baath-sponsored "Arab legion" and was used in the propaganda operations staged by Saddam Hussein's regime. He boasted to French reporters that he was going to "kill Americans," and he called his "buddies from the Nineteenth Arrondissement" to join him.[19] Rather than effecting a sweeping victory over the Americans, the Iraqi officers disbanded during the U.S. offensive, and Boubaker al-Hakim was left alone as a foreign volunteer. After the invasion, he drifted back to Syria and then to France. After his return to the Nineteenth Arrondissement in May 2003, Benyettou praised him as a role model.

For a full year, Boubaker al-Hakim served as the jihadi star in Benyettou's group and traveled again to Damascus, this time as a vanguard to organize the transfer of his "buddies" to Iraq. No assistance could now be expected from Iraqi diplomats in Syria, which had turned friendly to the United States. Instead, Boubaker al-Hakim had to pay two hundred dollars to be smuggled into Iraq. He made his way to the insurgent-controlled city of Falluja, where he became part of a six-man unit, in a jihadi sequel to his short-lived experience in the "Arab legion." He was barely involved in active fighting, but Sheikh Abdallah al-Janabi, the militant imam of Falluja, received him and complimented his efforts.[20] During his five months in Falluja, Boubaker al-Hakim urged Benyettou's followers to join him and formally extended the call for jihad to the Nineteenth Arrondissement.

The Paris-born militants answered the call, using Damascus as their gateway into Iraq. Despite their limited knowledge of Arabic, Benyettou's followers were sent to the Iraqi battlefield, mostly to Falluja. Their military preparedness, however, was minimal, and the death rate of the newcomers was impressive: Redouane al-Hakim, Boubaker's brother, was killed during a U.S. bombing on July 17, 2004; Tarek Ouinis was killed by a U.S. patrol on September 20; and Abdelhalim Badjouj died in a failed suicide attack on October 20. These three "martyrs" were nineteen years old. Two other volunteers of the same network, Peter Cherif, age twenty-two, and Chekou Diakabi, age nineteen, were detained by the U.S. forces in the wake of the fall of Falluja in November 2004. Additionally, Mohamed al-Ayouni, age twenty-two, lost an eye and an arm during the fighting and, after a painful recovery that lasted several months, was transferred to passive missions in the city of Hit, Iraq.[21]

Significant losses, however, did not deter Benyettou from pushing his remaining followers to join the Iraqi jihad. Two older activists assisted him, the Moroccan Saïd Abdellah, who delivered military guidance, and the Algerian Nacer Eddine Mettaï, who forged false documents. Both of these recruits were in their thirties, with more life experience than Benyettou's other followers. One of them, Thameur Bouchnak, age twenty-two, had already traveled to Syria in July 2004 but did not cross into Iraq. He devoted most of his time to studying Arabic at the Abi Nur mosque, a private institution run by the pro-government Sheikh Kaftaru, but he found the experience quite frustrating. He came back to France then performed the pilgrimage to Mecca before Benyettou eventually convinced him to try again in Syria. He was to travel along with Cherif Kouaci, aged twenty-two, and they were supposed to meet a fourteen-year old contact at the Damascus airport to buy their weapons before being smuggled into Iraq (the support network in Syria had been dismantled after Boubaker al-Hakim was arrested by local security in August 2004).[22]

In January 2005, just before the planned trip to Damascus, Benyettou, Bouchnak, and Kouaci were arrested in Paris, marking the end of the Nineteenth Arrondissement Iraqi networks. No explosives or weapons were found on the group at the time, but more than 8,000 euros (roughly 12,000 dollars) were seized, money supposedly earmarked to buy weapons in Syria (one of the main differences between the "Afghan" generation and the "Iraqi" one is that the fighters seem to provide their own weapons in Iraq).[23] Mohammed al-Ayouni and Boubaker al-Hakim were later arrested in Syria before being deported to France. On March 2008, Farid Benyettou was sentenced to six years in jail, and Boubaker al-Hakim, because of his operational responsibility in Damascus, and Saïd Abdellah, the self-styled recruiting agent, received a slightly higher sentence of seven years. Bouchnak, Kouaici, and al-Ayouni were condemned to three years in jail and Mettai to four. After their release, both Abdellah and Mettai will be forbidden to return to French territory.

Interestingly, the fate of Benyettou's network received far more media attention than Ansar al-Fatah's. The tragic saga of those youngsters lost in the Iraqi war played an essential part in this exposure and even inspired a major TV drama, entitled *Jihad*. The cable channel Canal Plus assigned a $6 million budget to this two-part drama. The actor Said Taghmaoui played one of the "buddies" from a poor French neighborhood who goes all the way to Iraq but escapes death and goes back home to preach Islam as a religion of peace (in 1999, Taghmaoui had played an Iraqi officer, confronting George Clooney in *Three Kings*). The American writer Richard Schlesinger recycled the key elements from the story of Benyettou's followers, but when *Jihad* aired in late fall 2006, Canal Plus insisted on the "fictitious" nature of his movie.[24]

THE MONTPELLIER NETWORK

Benyettou recruited his followers on the margins of the mainstream Daawa mosque in Paris, but a parallel exists with another jihadi network established in the southern French city of Montpellier. This network also developed around radicalized individuals frustrated by the preaching at the main mosque in the popular La Paillade neighborhood. Two Moroccan activists involved in the group, Hamid Bach and Hamza Safi, became increasingly involved with jihadi Salafism and even traveled to London to listen to Abu Hamza, the extremist imam at the Finsbury Park mosque.[25] Safi went to Iraq in 2003, and after his return to Montpellier, he acquired jihadi prestige comparable to Boubaker al-Hakim's.

Safi maintained contact with the Iraqi insurgency and later traveled with Bach on a trip to Syria in June 2004. They headed for the northern city of Aleppo, which had become a hotbed for jihadi militants, especially under the influence of the charismatic preacher Abu al-Qaqa.[26] Bach eventually backed down from crossing to Iraq to join the insurgency. Safi, however, had no hesitations and died in combat near Falluja. Bach, now deeply involved with the jihadi underground, planned to travel back to France but pledged to wait for a call to action from the "brothers in Italy."[27] Bach expanded his network, working out of La Paillade to target fellow Moroccans studying at the university of Montpellier. Bach, now aged thirty-five, exerted quite an influence over Reda Barazzouk and Youssef Bousag, both in their early twenties. Barazzouk studied electronics, and Bousag, computers.

Bach was unaware that French authorities had been monitoring him since his return from Syria. When he was arrested in June 2005, electronic circuits and diagrams were found at his place, along with nineteen containers of oxygenated water. While the evidence was not enough to substantiate an accusation of terrorist plotting, his arrest led to the dismantling of a wider network with connections in Morocco and Algeria to the Salafist Group for Preaching and Combat (GSPC). The Kabylia-based GSPC developed an active coöperation with al-Qaeda in Iraq, then headed by Abu Musab al-Zarqawi, and established training camps for volunteers preparing to fight the anti-U.S. jihad. Through these Iraqi connections, the GSPC avoided the downward spiral that had led to the GIA's demise and plugged itself into the global propaganda network of the online jihad community, enhancing its militant profile and reaching out to new recruits.

Contrary to the French and Iraqi focus of Benyettou's network, the Montpellier cell was part of a more complex triangle among France, North Africa, and the Middle East, more reminiscent of Ansar al-Fatah's dynamics. Barazzouk's and Bousag's arrests in January 2006 coincided with other GSPC-related detentions in Morocco and Algeria. In November 2008, the French judiciary condemned Bach to six years in jail, Barazzouk to four years, and Bousag to three years. After their release, Bach will be banned from French territory for ten years, and Barazzouk will be restricted from entering for five years.

THE FATEFUL TRIANGLE

Out of the three networks presented in this study, Ansar al-Fatah seemed to be the most dangerous one because of its wide international connections. While the anti-U.S. jihad in Iraq was the main driving force behind Benyettou's and Bach's groups, it appeared more a pretext than an actual objective for Bourada's followers. The training acquired under the mentorship of jihadi partners in Syria and Lebanon was likely aimed at French targets rather than in preparation for assisting the Iraqi insurgency. In the same vein, Hamid Bach traded his withdrawal from the Iraqi jihad for a commitment to follow operational orders back in Europe. This pattern supports the Algerian counterterrorist conclusion that global jihadi leaders were reaching far beyond Iraq and the Middle East to decide the targeting and the timing of pending terrorist attacks. Iraq served as a well-known channel for building solidarity networks and sleeper cells for al-Qaeda-inspired outfits.

Benyettou's group, on the other hand, grew dedicated to the Iraqi cause and provided "cannon fodder" to the local insurgency but lacked the global connections to develop a post-Iraq agenda.

In 2004, the insurgent-controlled city of Falluja served as a magnet for militant energies and as a beacon for anti-American activism. After the fall of this Iraqi stronghold, Syria remained an anteroom for deeper jihadi involvement, but Damascus had to compete in that regard with the northern city of Aleppo and with the neighboring Lebanese town of Tripoli. In addition to jihadi opportunities, Syria offered easy access to a crucial resource for France-based militants: Arabic studies and training in classical Arabic through a variety of private schools. The Fateh al-Islami institute was popular among French activists in Damascus not only as a means of acquiring student status during their stay in Syria but also for the exposure it provided to the "noble" Arabic much more revered than the Maghribi colloquial language. The extent of the linguistic alienation of Islamist radicals of North African origin or background is often underestimated, as is their desire to compensate for it. Even the "emir" Bourada felt he had to become more fluent in classical Arabic to match his jihadi ambitions.

This process of radicalization also entailed a return to French society before the recruits fully turned against it. The British concentration of jihadi preachers and activists in the "Londonistan," just across the Channel, was a strong incentive, and the post-2005 repression of this extraordinary European safe haven after the 7 July London bombings definitely helped lessen the attractiveness of jihadi radicalization in France and its neighbors. At odds with their French environment, the Iraq-focused networks were not familiar with the North African countries of origin of most of the militants' families. Algeria, Morocco, and Tunisia were merely considered potential sources of jihadi fighters for Iraq. This vision matched the GSPC bet on recruitment for the Iraqi jihad to give new blood and perspective to its own outfit.

The years 2005 and 2006 were the turning point for the GSPC, whose cooperation with al-Zarqawi's faction in Iraq eventually led to the GSPC's merging with al-Qaeda as its North African branch (Drukdal, GSPC's emir, pledged allegiance to bin Laden in September 2006, and his organization was renamed al-Qaeda in the Islamic Maghrib in January 2007). While Benyettou's network was focused on the French-Iraqi equation, Ansar al-Fatah and Bach's followers were more integrated in a global jihadi triangle, incorporating the North African dimension and GSPC input. Those connections likely contributed to their transnational agenda and readiness to engage in violence on French soil. Their networks were fortunately disrupted and dismantled before becoming operational.

The comparative strength of Ansar al-Fatah also emerged out of the dual legitimacy of its leader, who displayed both the charisma of a politician and the credentials of an experienced militant. Safe Bourada used his time in jail to cultivate his prestige both as a pious detainee and as a GIA-hardened activist. This gave him the ability to establish his own group with an ambitious title and to fully delegate operational and financial responsibilities. Farid Benyettou, in contrast, was undoubtedly the charismatic leader of the Nineteenth Arrondissement network, but even his self-proclaimed imam credentials paled in front of Boubaker al-Hakim's jihadi record. In Montpellier, militant legitimacy was embodied in Hamza Safi and was partially transferred to Hamid Bach after his death, but Bach had to enhance his own charisma and served as a replacement figurehead rather than emerging as a leader based on his established credentials.

Those "Iraqi" networks were built upon the individual and collective rage fueled by the U.S. invasion and its various excesses (the images of Arab prisoners tortured by American personnel at the Abu Ghraib jail in April 2004 are often mentioned by the French militants).[28] The religious dimension was either very weak or rudimentary, and Benyettou is the ultimate illustration of self-proclaimed "guru," despite all his Islamic pretences. After years of studying this brand of militancy, Farhad Khosrokhavar concluded, "Most people who join jihadist movements in Europe are culturally uprooted" and "in the European context, the radicalization of young Muslims precedes jihadism. These youngsters have no history of being pious Muslims and most of them know very little or nothing about Islam."[29]

The Internet plays a significant role in the collection and dissemination of selected jihadi references and fatwas. For instance, Sheikh Hamud al-Shu'aybi's fatwa legitimizing 9/11 is easily accessible on French-speaking jihadi websites, most of them based in the United States.[30] The Internet is not only the privileged medium of self-fueled jihadi radicalization: it serves to spread militant propaganda and to popularize potential terrorist techniques. Phone calls were traced between Benyettou's (or Bach's) followers and jihadi activists in Syria (or Iraq), but the Internet quickly emerged as the safest and quickest way to communicate. A more recent case proved how the Internet had become a key element in structuring European-based networks. During his trial in Paris in December 2008, Kamel Bouchentouf admitted to communicating via e-mail with Salah Gasmi, the information leader of the GSPC/AQIM.[31] The prosecution presented him as a potential jihadi "lone wolf," based in the French city of Nancy, but monitored through the Internet by the global networks. He was sentenced to six years in jail.

The number of jihadi militants who went from France to Iraq was quite limited, with only around twenty volunteers through 2006, compared with seventy U.K.-based activists involved in Iraq between 2003 and 2005.[32] Those global connections, along with the military techniques acquired in Iraq, pose potentially serious threats in Europe. Contrary to the "Afghan" returnees in the 1980s and 1990s, counterterrorism officials in Europe closely monitor the "Iraqi" veterans because the global nature of al-Qaeda makes the transfer of jihad from Iraq to Europe all the more seamless. The anticipation of any Iraqi blowback in France was crucial in the successful neutralization of Ansar al-Fatah, Benyettou and Bach's networks. Cooperation with various security services in the region also helped to detect, deter, or defuse this new threat.

From 2003 to 2007, the anti-U.S. jihad in Iraq fueled triangular dynamics of transnational radicalization and mobilization. In the Middle East, al-Zarqawi's networks grew, notably through their access to foreign volunteers, and merged formally into al-Qaeda as its Iraqi branch in the fall of 2004. In North Africa, the Algerian GSPC became the regional hub for training and recruiting for the Iraqi jihad, which paved the way for its transformation into al-Qaeda in the Islamic Maghrib. In Europe, the Iraqi cause drew new militants and networks to jihadi activism, building connections between the western and eastern ends of the Mediterranean. These triangular dynamics ran out of steam after 2007, when al-Qaeda in Iraq engaged in open conflict with its former allies of the Sunni insurgency, thus losing most of its appeal to militant outsiders. The threat has not faded away since the new al-Qaeda franchise for North Africa inherited and incorporated part of the subversive energy of the Iraqi jihad.

Seen from that angle, the U.S. invasion of Iraq certainly made France, along with the rest of Europe, a more dangerous place to live. It will take years to assess the long-term impact of this deterioration of the security environment, triggered by the radicalization of homegrown cells and their manipulation by global outfits. The isolation of al-Qaeda's leadership gives more leverage to the regional branches, even in targeting decisions. Just as al-Zarqawi forced al-Qaeda central to endorse his anti-Shia strategy, GSPC has significantly enhanced the anti-French dimension of al-Qaeda's propaganda, and al-Qaeda in the Islamic Maghrib has embarked on a systematic search for French targets, killing four French tourists in Mauritania in December 2007 and one French engineer in Algeria in June 2008 (there was also a foiled suicide attack against the French embassy in Mauritania in August 2009). Iraq has not brought jihad back home in France, fortunately, but it has drawn it closer and increased the danger through the ominous triangle among the Middle East, North Africa, and Europe.

NOTES

1. Ayman al-Zawahiri's letter to Abu Musab al-Zarqawi, July 9, 2005, *CTC Harmony Database*, available at http://ctc.usma.edu/harmony/pdf/CTC-Zawahiri-Letter-10-05.pdf

2. To conceal the direct Iranian involvement, most of the attacks were claimed by a "Committee for Solidarity with the Arab and Middle Eastern Political Prisoners" (CSPPA), which proved to be only a front.

3. Bruce Riedel, *The Search for Al Qaeda* (Washington: Brookings, 2008), 4.

4. Jean-Pierre Filiu, "The Local and Global Jihad of Al-Qa'ida in the Islamic Maghrib," *The Middle East Journal* 63, no. 2 (Spring 2009): 217–20.

5. Christophe Dubois, "Procès des lieutenants de Ben Laden à Paris," *Le Parisien*, January 3, 2005.

6. This GIA slogan echoes Abdullah Azzam's motto, and its author is most probably Qari Sa'id, a veteran from the Afghan jihad with close ties to Ayman al-Zawahiri. See Luis Martinez, *The Algerian Civil War* (New York: Columbia University Press, 2000), 209.

7. Brynjar Lia, *Architect of Global Jihad* (London: Hurst, 2007), 121, 153.

8. A fascinating study about jihadism in French jails is Farhad Khosrokhavar, *Quand al-Qaïda parle* (Paris: Grasset, 2006).

9. "France: Les méthodes de l'islamisme radical," Reuters, September 30, 2008.

10. Abu Mohammed al-Tunsi ("the Tunisian"), whose real identity has not been confirmed.

11. Eric Pelletier and Jean-Marie Pontaut, "Ansar al-Fatah: Les pèlerins du djihad," *L'Express*, October 23, 2008. The Lebanese militant in charge of the training facility in Tripoli was known as Abu Hafs, a very popular moniker in the jihadi underground. Al-Qaeda's military commander from 1996 to 2001, Mohammed Atef, was nicknamed Abu Hafs al-Masri, and al-Qaeda claimed several terror attacks on behalf of the "Abu Hafs al-Masri Brigades."

12. "Quinze ans de prison pour avoir créé un groupe terroriste," *Le Figaro* (Paris), October 23, 2008.

13. Christophe Cornevin, "Les islamistes s'entraînent au Liban et en Algérie," *Le Figaro* (Paris), October 2, 2008.

14. Pelletier and Pontaut, "Ansar al-Fatah."

15. Jean Chicizola, "Un chef spirituel de 23 ans à la tête du groupe des Buttes-Chaumont," *Le Figaro* (Paris), February 4, 2005.

16. Patricia Tourancheau, "Un ticket pour le jihad," *Libération* (Paris), February 21, 2005.

17. Jean-Pierre Filiu, "Algeria and France: The Quiet Salafists," *Jane's Islamic Affairs Analyst*, no. 5 (May 2009).

18. Farid Benyettou, interview with Samir Amghar, April 6, 2004, quoted in Bernard Rougier, ed., *Qu'est-ce que le Salafisme?* (Paris: PUF, 2008), 253. During the same spring of 2004, while Benyettou was stressing his focus on Iraq, a debate went on at the French-speaking jihadi website al-Mourabitoune, and most of the participants favored jihad in Iraq against activism in Europe. See Thomas Hegghammer, "Global Jihadism After the Iraq War," *The Middle East Journal* 60, no.1 (Winter 2006): 25.

19. Boubaker al-Hakim, interview LCI (French TV), March 17, 2003 (the U.S. invasion started three days later); the popular expression "potes du 19ème" was used in an interview broadcast by Radio-Télé-Luxembourg (RTL), March 13, 2003.

20. Christophe Dubois, "Des français racontent leur guerre en Irak," *Le Parisien*, October 2, 2006.

21. Ibid.

22. Tourancheau, "Un ticket pour le jihad."

23. Christophe Dubois, "Filières irakiennes, un troisième français mis en examen," *Le Parisien*, January 30, 2005.

24. The DVD version of *Jihad*, directed by Félix Olivier, has been available since January 2007. While this movie attracted a sizeable audience, it is worth noting that the vibrant French hip-hop scene never adapted jihadi stories. There was no French equivalent to Steve Earle's "John Walker's Blues," singing the story of John Walker Lindh, nicknamed the "American Taliban."

25. Peter Taylor, "A Reason to Hate," *Guardian*, September 1, 2006.

26. Abu al-Qaqa (Mahmud al-Aghasi's moniker) was an Aleppo cleric of Kurdish origin who rose to fame for preaching anti-U.S. jihad in Iraq. But he also accused the CIA of manipulating al-Qaeda, and his complex relationship with the Syrian regime

has been questioned. Abu al-Qaqa was gunned down on September 28, 2007, as he was leaving an Aleppo mosque after the Friday prayers. Al-Qaeda, among others, has been accused of the murder. See, for instance, Sami Moubayed, "An Anti-US, Anti-al-Qaeda Voice Is Silenced," *Asia Times*, October 2, 2007.

27. Sebastian Rotella, "Bringing Jihad Home to Europe," *Los Angeles Times*, September 23, 2005.

28. For instance, Thameur Bouchnak, one of Benyettou's followers. See Tourancheau, "Un ticket pour le jihad."

29. Washington Institute for Near East Policy (WINEP), *Al Qaeda Today*, Policywatch 1477, February 13, 2009.

30. The Saudi Sheikh Hamud al-Shu'aybi was the only scholar from the Islamist opposition to endorse the attacks against New York and Washington. On September 17, 2001, he published a fatwa justifying al-Qaeda's indiscriminate killing of civilians. One month later, his call for armed support to the Taliban regime was also isolated, even in the radical circles in Saudi Arabia. He died in January 2002, but his fatwas remain popular on jihadi websites, including the French-speaking al-Mourabitoune or "La voix des opprimés," based for a long time in Florida.

31. Isabelle Mandraud, "Frère Abou Zhara, apprenti jihadiste ou infiltré de la DST," *Le Monde* (Paris), December 19, 2008.

32. Christophe Chaboud, France's antiterrorism coordinator, quoted in Taylor, "A Reason to Hate"; the estimate on U.K. numbers was published in the *Times*, June 26, 2005.

[II]

Outside the West

15

Al-Qaeda Terrorism in Afghanistan

SETH G. JONES

In August 2011, the al-Qaeda leader Ayman al-Zawahiri released a statement about the death of Osama bin Laden, imploring his supporters to be hopeful in the face of adversity. The Arab Spring, he argued, provided an opportunity to increase the group's support base and expand its influence across North Africa and the Arabian Peninsula. Perhaps more important, Zawahiri argued that one of al-Qaeda's most striking successes was in Afghanistan, where the United States and its allies agreed to withdraw combat forces by 2014. "Today," he remarked, the United States "is being defeated in Afghanistan and thus will withdraw, and all of that is grace from Allah on the hands of the Mujahideen who are weak in their equipment, but strong in their faith."[1] Over the next several months, he repeated a common theme: overthrowing the Kabul regime and winning the war in Afghanistan were critical objectives for al-Qaeda.

Before bin Laden's death, al-Qaeda leaders had apparently engaged in a vigorous debate about targeting the U.S. homeland. While most wanted to conduct attacks in the United States and other Western countries, some suggested focusing on Afghanistan and other local wars. In a May 2010 letter to bin Laden, al-Zawahiri indicated that the struggle with the United States and the West would be settled on the battlefields of Iraq and Afghanistan rather than "in [America's] backyard." A few months before, Sheikh Said al-Masri (Mustafa Abu'l Yazid) had written to bin Laden and argued that al-Qaeda could not expand operations in the United States for the moment because of financial constraints, limited operatives, and improved U.S. security procedures. In a January 2010 letter to bin Laden, Said al-Masri and Atiyah abd al-Rahman had warned bin Laden that attempts to attack the United States might "not succeed."[2]

In many ways, these discussions were not new. Al-Qaeda leaders made similar statements two decades earlier during the anti-Soviet jihad, when the organization formed. What changed from those years, however, was al-Qaeda's modus operandi. In the 1980s, the contributions of Osama bin Laden, Ayman al-Zawahari, and other Arabs were extremely limited during the anti-Soviet wars. Mohammad Yousaf, who was in charge of the Afghan campaign for Pakistan's Directorate for Inter-Services Intelligence (ISI), does not even discuss the Arabs in his account of the Soviet defeat because their role was so insignificant.[3] As Lawrence Wright explained in *The Looming Tower*, "The presence of several thousand Arabs—and rarely more than a few hundred of them actually on the field of battle—made no real difference in the tide of affairs."[4] The Afghan mujaheddin would have won with or without their help, thanks in large part to the significant amount of arms, money, and other assistance provided by the governments of Pakistan, the United States, and Saudi Arabia.[5] After the overthrow of the Taliban regime in 2001, however, al-Qaeda reemerged to play a different—and more fundamental—role in Afghanistan.

Consequently, this chapter asks two questions. First, what is al-Qaeda's role in Afghanistan? Second, what do its operations indicate about the issue of leader-led jihad? To answer these questions, I adopted two methodological approaches. The first was to review a range of primary-source statements from al-Qaeda officials, jihadist websites, and secondary sources. The second was to conduct interviews with government officials from Afghanistan, Pakistan, the United Kingdom, the United States, and other NATO countries on several trips to Afghanistan and Pakistan from 2008 to 2013.

The evidence suggests that al-Qaeda has played an important role in Afghanistan's insurgency as a force multiplier. Unlike al-Qaeda's role in some parts of the world, where it plans and organizes specific terrorist attacks, al-Qaeda has embedded itself into a much broader insurgency in Afghanistan. It has helped to reinforce the radical religious views of local groups, shaped their propaganda campaigns, provided financial assistance to the war effort, and improved guerrilla tactics and techniques.

This finding has important implications for al-Qaeda's modus operandi. It indicates that the al-Qaeda threat is not a bottom-up effort among homegrown radicals who, as one assessment argued, "are autonomous and unknown to al-Qaeda central," causing them to "finance their own operations."[6] Rather, al-Qaeda's resurgence comes from a carefully maintained direct relationship between al-Qaeda central and key allies, such as Mullah Mohammad Omar's Taliban and the Haqqani network.

This chapter is divided into five sections. The first outlines the broad nature of Afghanistan's insurgency and al-Qaeda's role. The second provides an overview of al-Qaeda's aims and motivations in Afghanistan, which have a history dating back to the anti-Soviet jihad. The third section provides an analysis of al-Qaeda's organizational structure. The fourth outlines al-Qaeda's involvement in improvised explosive devices, financing, propaganda, and training. And the fifth offers some brief policy conclusions.

A COMPLEX ADAPTIVE SYSTEM IN AFGHANISTAN

Al-Qaeda has directly embedded itself in a much broader insurgency in Afghanistan, which might be termed a "complex adaptive system."[7] The term refers to systems that are diverse (comprising multiple networks) and adaptive (possessing the capacity to evolve and learn from experience). One key element of complex adaptive systems is that they include a series of networks. These networks are often dispersed and small, but different nodes can communicate and conduct their campaigns with some coordination. Individual groups may be hierarchically structured, but there is little or no single command across groups. This structure is different from the nearly anarchic structure supported by the U.S. white supremacist Louis Beam, who advocated an organizational structure called "leaderless resistance" to target the United States government. "Utilizing the Leaderless Resistance concept," Beam argued, "all individuals and groups operate independently of each other, and never report to a central headquarters or single leader for direction or instruction, as would those who belong to a typical pyramid organization."[8] Groups in a complex adaptive system often can—and do—communicate with one another and provide assistance.

A range of transnational terrorist, criminal, and insurgent groups have adopted networked strategies. In the United States, for example, some urban gangs, rural militias, and militant single-issue groups have developed networked attributes. A range of left-wing revolutionaries, radicals, and anarchists have adopted more decentralized organizational structures. As John Arquilla and David Ronfeldt argued:

> The organizational structure is quite flat. There is no single central leader or commander; the network as a whole (but not necessarily each node) has little to no hierarchy. There may be multiple leaders. Decision-making and operations are decentralized and depend on consultative consensus-building that allows for local initiative and autonomy. The design is both acephalous (headless) and polycephalous (Hydra-headed)—it has no precise heart or head, although not all nodes may be "created equal."[9]

There are several categories of groups in Afghanistan that al-Qaeda has embedded itself within. The first are insurgent groups, who are motivated to overthrow the Afghan government and coerce the withdrawal of international forces. Virtually all have their command-and-control nodes on the Pakistan side of the border. They range from Mullah Mohammad Omar's Afghan Taliban to smaller groups such as the Haqqani network and Gulbuddin Hekmatyar's Hezb-i-Islami.

Several have developed a relationship with al-Qaeda. Perhaps the most significant is Mullah Omar's Taliban, headquartered in Baluchistan Province, Pakistan, whose primary area of operations is in southern Afghanistan. The al-Qaeda-Taliban relationship has deep historical roots going back to the close personal links that Mullah Omar developed with Osama bin Laden in the 1990s. Bin Laden arrived in Afghanistan in 1996 and installed many of the senior Arab fighters in residential complexes near Kandahar and Jalalabad. The leaders came almost entirely from the first generation of militants that had come to Afghanistan to fight the Soviets.[10] In 1998, the Clinton administration launched a series of cruise missile strikes against al-Qaeda bases in eastern Afghanistan after al-Qaeda targeted the U.S. embassies in Tanzania and Kenya in 1998. U.S. intelligence assessments suggested that the attacks brought al-Qaeda and the Taliban closer together.[11] One State Department cable reported,

"Taliban leader Mullah Omar lashed out at the U.S., asserting that the Taliban will continue to provide a safe haven to bin Laden." After all, bin Laden sometimes stayed at Mullah Omar's residence in Kandahar. The Taliban's military structure also included al-Qaeda members such as the elite Brigade 055, which consisted of foreign fighters.[12]

The al-Qaeda-Taliban relationship strengthened after the 2001 overthrow of the Taliban regime. Senior al-Qaeda and Taliban officials communicated and coordinated efforts to overthrow the Karzai government in Afghanistan. Indeed, the Taliban evolved into a strikingly different organization from what existed in the 1990s when they controlled most of Afghanistan, thanks in part to al-Qaeda. Though the Taliban's goal remained establishing an Afghan state under their Deobandi interpretation of sharia (Islamic law), the group's tactics evolved. The Taliban increasingly adopted suicide attacks, more sophisticated improvised explosive devices, and media-savvy practices such as conducting television interviews, establishing Internet websites and chat rooms, and making video recordings. The Taliban began to post statements on al-Qaeda and other jihadi websites and publish magazines such as *al-Sumud* that expressed support for al-Qaeda's broader global aims.[13] In addition, senior al-Qaeda leaders regularly referred to Mullah Omar, the head of the Taliban, as "Amir al-Mu'minin [Commander of the Faithful]."[14] Even bin Laden swore allegiance while he was alive, stating that the Taliban "are fighting America and its agents under the leadership of the Commander of the Believers, Mullah Omar, may Allah protect him."[15] By 2014, operatives like Faruq al-Qatari, al-Qaeda's paramilitary commander and emir for northeastern Afghanistan, were able to retain a sanctuary in Afghanistan because of their relationship with local Taliban commanders.

Another group that developed close ties with al-Qaeda was the Haqqani network. It was based in North Waziristan, Pakistan, including such locations as the Darpakhel madrassa on the outskirts of Miramshah.[16] Jalaluddin Haqqani, the organization's founder and a mujaheddin fighter during the anti-Soviet war, established a close relationship with al-Qaeda senior leadership and adopted a similar message in characterizing the United States as a crusader force. "The financial expenses that the United States spends in Afghanistan as well as the killing of dozens of the U.S. forces at the hands of the mujahidin every day reflect the victory of the mujahidin and the defeat of the aggressive Crusader forces," he wrote in one jihadist magazine.[17] Jalaluddin even married an Arab woman, a symbol of his support. Jalaluddin's son Sirajuddin (or "Siraj"), who was given the title "khalifa" as the leader of the Haqqani network, also developed a close relationship with al-Qaeda leaders in Pakistan, who helped him orchestrate a range of audacious terrorist attacks in Afghanistan.[18]

A second category of al-Qaeda affiliates includes criminal groups involved in drug trafficking and illicit timber and gem smuggling. Timber smuggling is common in northeastern Afghan provinces such as Konar and Nuristan, where al-Qaeda regional commanders developed links among some traffickers.[19] Drug-trafficking organizations are most active in southern Afghanistan, where they are involved in the cultivation, production, and trafficking of poppy. Laboratories in Afghanistan convert opium into morphine base, white heroin, or one of several grades of brown heroin. Traffickers move through Pakistan, Iran, Central Asia, and other areas into markets in Western and Eastern Europe.

A third category includes tribes, subtribes, and clans—most of which are Pashtun. Several Pashtun tribes developed close links with al-Qaeda after the overthrow of the Taliban regime. In December 2001, for example, Wazir tribes helped Osama bin Laden move from Afghanistan into Pakistan through Tora Bora. Mariam Abou Zahab noted that "after the American intervention, foreign militants, Taliban, and others who fled Afghanistan entered the tribal areas and a sizeable number of foreigners settled in Waziristan where they developed deep links with Ahmedzai Wazirs." She continued that "almost every tribe supported Al Qaeda, actively or passively, as guests."[20] Over the next several years, al-Qaeda leaders effectively established a foothold with several tribes and subtribes in the region, such as some Ahmadzai Wazirs, Mehsuds, Utmanzai Wazirs, Mohmands, Salarzais, and Zadrans. The secret to al-Qaeda's staying power was its success in cultivating supportive networks in an area generally inhospitable to outsiders. Some al-Qaeda operatives and other foreign fighters also established a relationship with Baitullah Mehsud, a Pashtun from the Shabikhel subtribe of the Mehsuds based in South Waziristan. He was killed in August 2009 in South Waziristan by a U.S. unmanned aerial vehicle and replaced by Hakimullah Mehsud, who continued to develop a relationship with al-Qaeda leaders until his death in November 2013 by a U.S. strike. One al-Qaeda leader offered a eulogy after Baitullah Mehsud's death, reinforcing Mehsud's cooperation with al-Qaeda. "I myself," Said al-Masri noted, "witnessed him saying, 'My desire is to advance at America's heart and strike it, and to destroy Americans' pride and self conceit.' "[21]

What is striking about this complex adaptive system is that it has allowed al-Qaeda to embed itself in multiple networks, giving it greater redundancy. Al-Qaeda has not limited itself to a central location in Pakistan to execute operations in Afghanistan, nor has it limited itself to coordinating its efforts with one group. In addition, this networked approach also means that al-Qaeda has not regularly become involved in combat operations in Afghanistan, which are largely run by local groups. U.S. military reports indicate small numbers of al-Qaeda operatives in Afghanistan. In July 2008, for example, an Arab was involved—and ultimately killed—in the insurgent attack on a U.S. vehicle patrol base in Wanat Village, Konar Province. A U.S. Army After Action Report on the attack described the Arab fighter as wearing "traditional Afghan clothing over a set of woodland camouflage military fatigues."[22]

At the same time, the practical reality of a complex adaptive system means that groups often do not share the same goals. Most Afghan insurgent groups have limited and parochial interests in Afghanistan and broader Pashtun areas of Pakistan. Members of the Afghan Taliban's inner *shura*, for example, have pushed for the creation of an Islamic emirate in—and only in—Afghanistan, where they could implement their radical version of sharia law. Nonetheless, they still invoke Muslim oppression in Palestinian territories, Chechnya, and other areas as noted in one online publication: "In the end, the Islamic Emirate of Afghanistan brings to the oppressed Muslims of Gaza good tidings of killing tens of U.S. soldiers. They consider this attack an attempt to avenge their martyrs against the Zionist usurping killers who shed the pure blood of Palestinians and are still insolently protected by the Americans."[23]

AL-QAEDA'S AIMS

Al-Qaeda's goals have long been to overthrow key regimes in the Muslim world (the near enemy, or *al-adou al-qareeb*) to establish a pan-Islamic caliphate, and fighting the United States and its allies (the far enemy, or *al-adou al-baeed*) who support them. In Afghanistan, al-Qaeda's aims include establishing a sanctuary that would allow its leadership to plan and execute attacks elsewhere. The deployment of U.S. and other Western forces to Afghanistan in 2001 also allowed al-Qaeda the opportunity to attack the "far enemy" so close to its sanctuary. The desire to use Afghanistan as a sanctuary had historical roots for al-Qaeda.

In the late 1980s, elite foreign fighters began to congregate in a camp near Khowst, Afghanistan, called al-Maasada (the lion's den). Osama bin Laden was the leader of this group and said he had been inspired to call it al-Maasada by the lines of one of the Prophet's favorite poets, Hassan Ibn Thabit, who wrote: "Whoever wishes to hear the clash of swords, let him come to Maasada, where he will find courageous men ready to die for the sake of God."[24] The Soviets attacked al-Maasada in 1987, and bin Laden fought back, along with a group including Hassan Abdel Rab al-Saray, a Saudi who later carried out the November 1995 attack in Riyadh; Abu Zubayr Madani, who was killed in Bosnia in 1992; Ibn al-Khattab, who emerged later in Chechnya; and Sheikh Tamim Adnani, who lost a son when Abdullah Azzam was killed in November 1989. Al-Qaeda emerged shortly thereafter. In August 1988, a group gathered in bin Laden's house in Peshawar to form a new organization, which they referred to as al-Qaeda al-Askariya (the military base). They created an advisory council and membership requirements. According to notes taken during the meeting by one of the participants, "al-Qaeda is basically an organized Islamic faction, its goal is to live the word of God, to make His religion victorious."[25] After the overthrow of the Taliban regime in 2001, al-Qaeda leaders based out of Pakistan developed two main objectives in Afghanistan.

First, they want to overthrow the "apostate" Afghan regime, which, in their view, is doubly guilty of failing to establish a "true" Islamic state and of cooperating with Western governments. In its place, they want to replace the Afghan government with one that followed a radical version of sharia law envisioned by Sayyid Qutb and others. Qutb argued in his book *Milestones* that anything non-Islamic was evil. Only the strict following of sharia as a complete system of morality, justice, and governance would bring significant benefits to humanity.[26] Modern-day Islam, according to Qutb, had also become corrupt. Qutb stigmatized the recent history of Muslim states with an Arab word from the Qur'an: *jahiliyya*. The term captured the state of ignorance or barbarism in which Arabs were supposed to have lived before the revelation of Islam to the Prophet Mohammed at the beginning of the seventh century AD. In two of his key works, *In the Shadow of the Qur'an* and *Signposts on the Road*, Qutb called for a new Quranic generation to build a contemporary Islamic community, just as the Prophet and his generation had built a community of the faithful on the ruins of Arab paganism.[27]

Al-Qaeda leaders thus condemned Afghan government officials as guilty of apostasy for failing to impose sharia on the country and collaborating with Western governments such as the United States. Mustafa Abu'l Yazid (Said al-Masri) bluntly noted that President Karzai's future "will not be different to that of other puppet governments in Afghanistan. He conspired with the Americans against the Muslims whom he tortured and helped send to Guantanamo Bay." The Prophet Mohammad argued that the blood of Muslims cannot be shed except in three instances: as punishment for murder, for marital infidelity, or for turning away from Islam. Al-Zawahiri adopted this line of argument, noting that regimes that departed from Islam and failed to establish sharia law were not true Muslims. Muslims could indeed be punished if they did not adequately follow Islam. Abdel Aziz bin Adel Salam (also know as al-Sayyid Imam), an Egyptian militant who was one of al-Zawahiri's oldest associates, argued that Muslims who did not join the fight against apostate rulers were themselves impious and must be fought.[28]

For al-Qaeda, an Islamic state in Afghanistan is part of a broader goal of establishing a pan-Islamic caliphate across the Muslim world. As al-Zahawiri noted, the "establishment of a Muslim state in the heart of the Islamic world is not an easy or close target. However, it is the hope of the Muslim nation to restore its fallen caliphate and regain its lost glory." Al-Zawahiri continued that it "is also a battle over to whom authority and power should belong—to God's course and shari'ah, to man-made laws and material principles, or to those who claim to be intermediaries between the Creator and mankind." Al-Zawahiri also followed the Salafist teachings of Ibn Tamiyyah, the thirteenth-century reformer who had sought to impose a literal interpretation of the Quran.[29]

Second, al-Qaeda leaders want to weaken the United States and other Western governments and push them out of Muslim lands, including Afghanistan. The United States is the most significant far enemy. "The white man" in America is the primary enemy, Qutb wrote. "The white man crushes us underfoot while we teach our children about his civilization, his universal principles and noble objectives. . . . We are endowing our children with amazement and respect for the master who tramples our honor and enslaves us." The response to this enslavement, Qutb argued, had to be anger and violence. "Let us instead plant the seeds of hatred, disgust, and revenge in the souls of these children. Let us teach these children from the time their nails are soft that the white man is the enemy of humanity, and that they should destroy him at the first opportunity."[30]

Consequently, al-Qaeda leaders have couched their aims in Afghanistan as an effort to remove U.S. and other Western forces intent on destroying Islam. As Shaykh Sa'id al-Masri noted, "The United States is a non-Muslim state bent on the destruction of Muslims . . . The Americans empower their government and army to annihilate Muslims." In their propaganda campaign, al-Qaeda leaders repeated the theme that American objectives included killing innocent Muslims and destroying Islam. "O Muslims in Afghanistan," Zawahiri remarked in one video, "if the Crusader occupation of Afghanistan continues, it will corrupt your sons and daughters, and they will turn their backs on the values of Islam, honor, chastity and piety. So who among you is happy with that," he continued, "other than one who has lost his religion, jealousy and honor?"[31] In addition, al-Qaeda leaders frequently pointed to U.S. airstrikes that killed civilians as evidence of its malign intentions.[32]

Al-Qaeda also directed its Afghan propaganda campaign toward Europe since the United Kingdom, the Netherlands, Germany, Italy, and other countries deployed forces to Afghanistan. In an audio message, bin Laden rhetorically asked the people of Europe: "So what is the sin of the Afghans due to which you are continuing this unjust war against them? Their only sin is that they are Muslims, and this illustrates the extent of the Crusaders' hatred of Islam and its people." Westerners also brought with them democracy, which Islamists considered *nizam al-kufr* (a deviant system). Al-Qaeda leaders view democracy as supplanting the rule of God with that of a popular majority. Al-Qaeda leaders are also quick to draw parallels between the United States and the Soviet Union in Afghanistan. The Afghan jihad against the United States, al-Zawahiri argued, was an extension of the struggle fought against the Soviets, making it "of the utmost importance to prepare the Muslim mujahideen to wage their awaited battle against the superpower that now has sole dominance over the globe, namely, the United States."[33]

Al-Qaeda's current goals are similar to the aims al-Qaeda leaders had forged during the Afghan jihad against the Soviet Union, except that the United States has replaced the Soviet Union as the main enemy. They want to unite Muslims to fight the United States and its allies (the far enemy) and overthrow Western-friendly regimes in the Middle East (the near enemy) to establish a pan-Islamic caliphate. Ultimately, al-Qaeda leaders envisioned the establishment of an "Islamic belt" that connected Afghanistan to South and Central Asia, and then moved into the Middle East and North Africa.[34]

ORGANIZATIONAL STRUCTURE

Al-Qaeda developed a fairly hierarchical organizational structure for the Afghan front, even though it embedded itself within a broader complex adaptive system. Al-Qaeda's hierarchy includes an inner *shura*, as well as a range of *shura*s for key functions based in Pakistan: a media *shura* responsible for propaganda using the Internet, television, print, and other forms of communication; a military *shura* that organizes operations in Afghanistan (and other areas around the globe) and trains operatives; a finance committee responsible for acquiring funds, financing operations, and managing money; and a religious committee in charge of issuing fatwas (religious decrees). This arrangement was largely replicated by the organizational structure of Mullah Omar's Taliban, which also included an inner *shura* and a series of functional committees.[35]

In addition, al-Qaeda deployed a number of regional front commanders who operated in the Afghan theater. Al-Qaeda's main focus was on eastern Afghanistan, though there were small numbers of operatives in southern Afghan provinces such as Helmand.[36] While al-Qaeda did not play a major role in ground operations in Afghanistan, its front commanders were helpful in coordinating operations among the panoply of militant groups and providing some logistical assistance. Like any business operation, there is plenty of friction within al-Qaeda, including from managers who want to account for finances and evaluate the effectiveness of lower-level operatives. As with al-Qaeda in Iraq, al-Qaeda's

Afghan organizational structure attempts to exercise control over its operatives by creating spreadsheets, tracking expense reports, and using policy memoranda.[37] Security concerns prohibited many of al-Qaeda's operational commanders from gaining daily access to al-Zawahari.

To remedy these concerns, al-Qaeda adopted a four-tiered courier system for communications. There was an administrative courier network for communication pertaining to the movement of members' families and other administrative activities. Another courier network dealt with operational instructions. Where possible, unwitting couriers were substituted for knowledgeable people to minimize detection. A media-support courier network was used for propaganda. Messages were sent in the form of CDs, videos, and leaflets to television networks such as al-Jazeera. Finally, a separate courier network was used only by al-Qaeda's top leadership, who usually did not pass written messages to one another. Their most trusted couriers often memorized messages and conveyed them orally.[38]

At least two factors began to affect al-Qaeda's Afghanistan operations beginning around 2008. One was the U.S. MQ-1 Predator and MQ-9 Reaper strikes, which killed a range of key al-Qaeda figures. Better U.S. and Pakistani intelligence collection and cooperation against al-Qaeda targets contributed to a deadly campaign from the air.[39] Drones targeted al-Qaeda's operatives in Pakistan's tribal areas, especially North and South Waziristan. U.S. intelligence indicated that al-Qaeda operatives became increasingly concerned about their operational security, and some considered transiting to other areas such as Somalia, Yemen, and even the Swat District in Pakistan's North West Frontier Province to relieve the pressure.[40] Al-Qaeda operatives involved in Afghan issues who were killed by drone strikes include general manager Sheikh Said al-Masri in May 2010, senior operations officer Abu 'Abd al-Rahman al-Najdi in September 2010, and head of external operations Ilyas Kashmiri in June 2011. U.S. strikes also killed operatives from groups that cooperated with al-Qaeda, such as Tehreek-e-Taliban leader Hakimullah Mehsud in November 2013 and Haqqani senior official Maulvi Ahmad Jan in November 2013.

A second factor that may have affected al-Qaeda's Afghan operations was the effectiveness of local militant groups. As Mia Bloom argued, terrorism is akin to a two-level game: it is a rational strategy to coerce states into adopting specific political objectives, as well as to outbid rival groups and win support and resources from local constituencies.[41] Competition among terrorist groups for limited resources is common, including among such Palestinian groups as Hamas, Palestinian Islamic Jihad, and al-Aqsa Martyrs Brigades. Mullah Omar's Taliban, the Haqqani network, and other groups became increasingly proficient in conducting military operations. The Taliban developed an effective strategy in southern and western Afghanistan, and set up shadow governments to adjudicate disputes. The Haqqani network conducted several high-profile attacks, targeting the Indian embassy in July 2008, the U.S. embassy in September 2011, and U.S. Forward Operating Base Salerno in June 2012.[42]

These factors appeared to affect al-Qaeda's funding and logistical operations. Some Pakistani and Western intelligence analyses indicated that a growing number of al-Qaeda operatives complained that they were running into financial problems, their training camps faced money shortfalls, and the drone attacks were negatively affecting their ability to plan operations and move freely in Pakistan.[43] In 2009, Said al-Masri pleaded for increased financial assistance from al-Qaeda sympathizers and supporters, noting that the "Jihad needs a lot of money, and the Jihad battlefields need much money. . . . If there wasn't money with which the mujahid can buy his weapons, food, drink, and jihad machines, then he cannot carry out Jihad."[44] His argument is illuminating not just because it illustrates al-Qaeda's apparent funding constraints but also because it highlights a long-established position that jihad was a *duty* of Muslims. Al-Qaeda leaders increasingly raised the status of militant jihad by rhetorically placing it on par with the five pillars of Islam. For instance, bin Laden argued that "fighting is part of our religion and our sharia. Those who love God and the prophet and this religion many not deny a part of that religion. This is a very serious matter." Bin Laden considers jihad an individual duty (*fard 'ayn*) and a critical pillar of Islam.[45]

Despite the loss of several key leaders, however, al-Qaeda remains capable of conducting—or, more frequently, assisting in conducting—lethal attacks in Afghanistan. According to a CIA assessment of al-Qaeda, "The group's cadre of seasoned, committed leaders has allowed it to remain fairly cohesive and stay focused on its strategic objectives."[46] In fact, al-Qaeda began opening new channels of communication by issuing propaganda directed at American audiences, either in translation or given directly by English-speaking al-Qaeda members based in Pakistan.

One of the most visible spokesmen to the West was Adam Gadahn, an American raised in southern California who converted to Islam at the age of seventeen and moved to Pakistan in 1998. With his head wrapped in a black turban and sporting a jet-black beard, his video exposés on YouTube expressed profound rage. "We love nothing better than the heat of battle, the echo of explosions, and slitting the throats of the infidels," he thundered in one video. In another he callously quipped, "It's hard to imagine that any compassionate person could see pictures, just pictures, of what the Crusaders did to those children, and not want to go on a shooting spree at the Marines' housing facilities at Camp Pendleton."[47]

Indeed, Afghanistan is one of the most important strategic areas for al-Qaeda. According to a U.S. Defense Intelligence Agency analysis, "Al-Qaeda remains committed to reestablishing a fundamentalist Islamic government in Afghanistan and has become increasingly successful in defining Afghanistan as a critical battleground against the West and its regional allies." Al-Qaeda was also able to leverage its resources through its "increasingly cooperative relationship with insurgent networks."[48]

AIDING AND ABETTING

Al-Qaeda plays a critical role in supporting the insurgency in several ways: providing financial aid, assisting with propaganda efforts, and improving military tactics through training and education.

One important area is funding. Al-Qaeda's international contacts enable Afghan insurgent groups to access a key source of funds, including from the Persian Gulf. Al-Qaeda personnel have met with wealthy Arab businessmen during the Tablighi Jamaat annual meeting in Pakistan, which attracts one of the largest concentrations of Muslims after the Hajj.[49] Appealing to the international jihadi network is consistent with historical patterns of funding for both al-Qaeda and the Taliban. During the rise of the Taliban in the 1990s, an important source of funding was the "Golden Chain," an informal financial network of prominent Saudi and Gulf individuals established to support Afghan fighters. This network collected funds through Islamic charities and other nongovernmental organizations for jihad. Bin Laden has also drawn on a network of Islamic charities, nongovernmental organizations, and educational institutions to recruit volunteers. Al-Qaeda's fund-raising efforts are helpful to Afghan groups, and Iran and Gulf-based al-Qaeda facilitators raise money on behalf of groups such as the Taliban.[50]

In addition, al-Qaeda has been instrumental in improving the communications capabilities of Afghan groups. These groups leverage al-Sahab, al-Qaeda's media enterprise, to distribute video propaganda and recruit supporters. "Al-Qaeda spreads its propaganda through taped statements," a CIA assessment reported, "sometimes featuring relatively sophisticated production values."[51] A UN report similarly found that there was an "increasing level of professionalism achieved by Al-Sahab, the main Al-Qaida media production unit." It continued by noting that Osama bin Laden's September 2007 video, like many others, was "expertly produced and, like previous videos, was subtitled in English and uploaded almost simultaneously onto hundreds of servers by what must be a large group of volunteers."[52]

In addition, al-Qaeda helped transform the Taliban's propaganda efforts. In the 1990s, the Taliban was generally averse to modern technology, including video cameras, CDs, and the Internet. They closed cinemas and banned music. As one Taliban decree ordered, "In shops, hotels, vehicles and rickshaws cassettes and music are prohibited." If music or a cassette was found in a shop, "the shopkeeper should be imprisoned and the shop locked." The same was true if a cassette was found in a vehicle.[53] The Taliban also banned almost every conceivable kind of entertainment, such as television, videos, cards, kite flying, and most sports. They punished theft by amputating a hand and often punished murder by public execution. Married adulterers were stoned to death. In Kabul, punishments were carried out in front of crowds in the city's former soccer stadium.[54]

With al-Qaeda's assistance, however, the Taliban fundamentally transformed itself after 2001 to take advantage of modern technology for propaganda purposes. Senior Taliban leaders began to appear in videos produced with the help of al-Qaeda, reciting passages from the Quran and outlining their ideology. Taliban leaders such as Mullah Omar also increasingly adopted al-Qaeda's global rhetoric. In a statement in December 2007, for example, Omar turned to Muslims across the globe: "We appeal to Muslims to help their Mujahideen brothers against the international invader economically. . . . Now you know both religion and country are in danger, you follow the way of good and religious leaders and leave the way of bad and dishonest and do Jihad." Additionally, jihadi websites with links to al-Qaeda, such as those run by Azzam Publications (including www.azzam.com and www.qoqaz.net, which were eventually shut down), helped raise funds for the Taliban. Some websites solicit military items for the Taliban, including gas masks and night-vision goggles.[55]

Insurgent groups also use al-Qaeda support to construct increasingly sophisticated improvised explosive devices (IEDs), including remote-control detonators.[56] When asked in 2006 by an al-Jazeera reporter whether the Taliban coordinated with al-Qaeda, Taliban military commander Mullah Dadullah answered, "Yes, when we need them, we ask for their help. For example, the bombings we carry out—we learned it from them. We learn other types of operations from them as well. We have 'give and take' relations with the mujaheddin of Iraq. We cooperate and help each other."[57] A few al-Qaeda commanders occasionally traveled into Afghanistan from Pakistan to train Taliban and other insurgents on tactics and techniques through face-to-face meetings and DVDs. Al-Qaeda ran a handful of manufacturing sites in Pakistan's Federally Administered Tribal Areas, especially in North and South Waziristan. They ranged from small IED-building facilities hidden within compounds to much larger "IED factories," which doubled as training centers and labs where recruits experimented with IED technology.[58]

Some of this IED expertise came from groups in Iraq and other locations, including Syria, who provided information on making and using various kinds of radio-controlled and dual-tone multifrequency devices.[59] There is some evidence of cooperation between Afghan insurgents and jihadists fighting in such countries as Iraq and Syria. Islamic militants in Iraq—sometimes with al-Qaeda facilitation—provided information via the Internet and face-to-face visits with Taliban, Gulbuddin Hekmatyar's Hezb-i-Islami forces, the Haqqani network, and other militants. In addition, there is some evidence that a small number of Pakistani and Afghan militants received military training in Iraq and Iraqi fighters met with Afghan and Pakistani extremists in Pakistan.[60]

Perhaps most troubling, however, is that insurgents have increasingly adopted suicide tactics, especially in such major cities as Kandahar and Kabul.[61] The number of suicide attacks increased from 1 in both 2001 and 2002 to 2 in 2003, 6 in 2004, 21 in 2005, 139 in 2006, 140 in 2007, and 150 in 2008. They rose over the next several years to 461 in 2011 and 328 in 2012.[62] Afghan National Police are a common target of suicide bombers. Al-Qaeda leaders in Pakistan encouraged the use of suicide attacks. In his book *Knights Under the Prophet's Banner*, Ayman al-Zawahiri outlined the "need to concentrate on the method of martyrdom operations as the most successful way of inflicting damage against the opponent and the least costly to the Mujahedin in terms of casualties."[63] Al-Qaeda's involvement is particularly important because Afghan insurgent groups have sometimes been inept at suicide attacks without outside assistance.[64]

Despite its initial reluctance, the Taliban began to use suicide attacks as a tool of the insurgency for a variety of reasons.[65] First, al-Qaeda and the Taliban saw the success of such groups as Hamas in the Palestinian territories, Hezbollah in Lebanon, the Tamil Tigers in Sri Lanka, and Iraqi groups, and concluded this was an effective method to disrupt coalition actions.[66] Suicide attacks allow insurgents to achieve maximum impact with minimal resources, and the chance of killing people and instilling fear increases several-fold with suicide attacks.[67] Second, suicide attacks provide media visibility for the Taliban, al-Qaeda, and other groups, which previous guerrilla attacks have not generated. Because many attacks were spectacular and usually lethal, suicide bombings tend be reported in the national and international media.

Of particular note were suicide attacks during high-profile periods, such as the August 2009 presidential elections in Afghanistan.[68] In general, most of the suicide-bomb recruits have been Afghans or Pakistanis, though some foreigners have been involved.[69] Many are recruited from Afghan refugee camps and madrassas in Pakistan, where they are radicalized and immersed in extremist ideologies. Taliban-affiliated Deobandi madrassas in Pakistan afford access to bombers, and the Taliban and other groups seek assistance from some teachers and administrators to help recruit.[70]

———————————

Al-Qaeda's role in Afghanistan might be summarized by the advertising slogan used by the German-based chemical giant BASF: "We don't make a lot of the products you buy. We make a lot of the products you buy better." Al-Qaeda played an important role in Afghanistan as a force multiplier by embedding itself in a network of Sunni militant groups. Its leaders improved the tactical and operational competence of Afghan groups, who were able to manufacture a better array of products from improvised explosive devices to videos. Al-Qaeda also shied away from direct involvement in ground operations in Afghanistan, leaving much of the operational work to local Afghan groups. This practice was deliberate since Arabs and other foreign fighters are often viewed as illegitimate among Afghans. Despite being targeted by Predator and Reaper strikes, however, al-Qaeda has continued to play an important force-multiplier role in Afghanistan. In an online interview, a Taliban spokesman indicated that al-Qaeda "is effective and constructive in fighting the occupiers."[71] This assessment leads to several policy conclusions.

First, the primary terrorist threat to the United States and other Western countries is not from a "bottom-up mechanism of group formation" but from a range of top-down organized groups that receive direct support from senior al-Qaeda operatives based in Pakistan. Al-Qaeda coordinates with a range of Afghan insurgent groups such as the Taliban and the Haqqani network. In addition, terrorism in Afghanistan is not homegrown, or characterized by informal networks that could "no longer establish any physical link to al-Qaeda Central."[72] Rather, it has been the result of a long and carefully crafted relationship between al-Qaeda central and well-organized insurgent groups. Al-Qaeda's modus operandi of embedding in a broader insurgency marks a stark shift from its operations in a range of other countries, where it became *directly involved* in conducting high-profile terrorist attacks. Yet it still plays a key role in Afghanistan.

Second, al-Qaeda's role in the insurgency highlights an important vulnerability: foreign fighters, including Arab fighters, tend to have little support in the country. A public opinion poll conducted by the University of Maryland, for instance, found an overwhelming majority of Afghans opposed al-Qaeda. Eighty-one percent of Afghans said they thought that al-Qaeda was having a negative influence, and only 6 percent said that it was having a positive influence. An even higher percentage—90 percent—said they had an unfavorable view of Osama bin Laden, and 75 percent said they have a very unfavorable view.[73] This suggests that al-Qaeda's involvement in the insurgency—including in suicide attacks that kill civilians—could potentially be exploited by the Afghan government and coalition forces. Indeed, United Nations data indicates that insurgent groups kill significantly more civilians (74 percent) than Afghan government and coalition forces do (9 percent), partly because of al-Qaeda's encouragement of tactics such as suicide attacks.[74]

Third, al-Qaeda's relationship with Afghan insurgent groups suggests that the success of the Taliban and other groups could significantly undermine the security of the United States and other Western countries, especially after the formal end of U.S. combat operations in December 2014. Taliban leaders permitted al-Qaeda and other militant groups to establish training camps in Afghanistan in the 1990s, and Taliban and Haqqani commanders cooperated with al-Qaeda operatives in Afghanistan through 2014. This should cause policy makers to think twice about listening to the chorus of people questioning the wisdom of fighting a war in Afghanistan. As Steve Simon argues, for example, "Washington should concentrate on its already effective policy of eliminating al-Qaeda's leadership with drone strikes" rather than targeting the Taliban since "the moment to rescue the mission . . . has passed."[75] In addition, as Vice President Joseph Biden explained to General Dan K. McNeill, the former U.S. military commander in Afghanistan, the best strategy in Afghanistan is "to keep a small footprint, have an offshore strategy as the sole approach to seeking better security and stability in Afghanistan and focus on counterterrorism and the hard-core ideologues who won't change."[76]

As this chapter has demonstrated, however, there is a direct link between al-Qaeda and several Afghan insurgent groups. A policy focused on targeting al-Qaeda—and not the Taliban, Haqqani network, or other groups—would ignore one of the most egregious lessons from September 11, 2001: areas controlled by insurgent groups that have ties to al-Qaeda can be used as a sanctuary for al-Qaeda and other violent jihadist groups targeting the United States and its key allies. These groups and al-Qaeda have developed a close link, and there is little evidence that senior Taliban or other leaders would break those links if they succeeded in controlling more territory in Afghanistan—and perhaps eventually Kabul itself. Instead, United States and other NATO forces need to help the Afghan government more effectively counter these al-Qaeda-linked insurgent groups through a lean but lethal combination of military, political, and economic assistance.[77]

NOTES

1. Ayman al-Zawahiri, "And Be Neither Weakened Nor Saddened," August 15, 2011, reproduced by the NEFA Foundation at http://nefafoundation.org//file /zawahiri_81511.pdf.

2. White House official, interview with author, December 3, 2011.

3. Mohammad Yousaf and Mark Adkin, *Afghanistan—the Bear Trap: The Defeat of a Superpower* (Havertown, Pa.: Casemate, 1992).

4. Lawrence Wright, *The Looming Tower: Al-Qaeda and the Road to 9/11* (New York: Knopf, 2006), 110. Gilles Kepel also argues that "the Arabs seem to have played only a minor part in fighting the Red Army. Their feats of arms were largely perpetrated after the Soviet withdrawal of in February 1989 and were highly controversial." See Gilles Kepel, *Jihad: The Trail of Political Islam* (Cambridge, Mass.: Harvard University Press, 2002), 147. Fawaz Gerges notes that "there exists no evidence pointing to any vital role played by foreign veterans in the Afghan victory over the Russians." See Fawaz A. Gerges, *The Far Enemy: Why Jihad Went Global* (New York: Cambridge University Press, 2005), 83–84.

5. See, for example, ABC reporter John Miller's interview with bin Laden in May 1998, a little over two months before the U.S. embassy bombings in Tanzania and Kenya. Part of the transcript was played at the trial of Zacarias Moussaoui, who was arrested in August 2001, shortly before the September 11, 2001, attacks in the United States (U.S. v. Zacarias Moussaoui, Cr. No. 01-455-A [E.D. Va.], March 6, 2006).

6. Mark Sagemen, *Leaderless Jihad: Terror Networks in the Twenty-First Century* (Philadelphia: University of Pennsylvania Press, 2008), 140.

7. See, for example, Murray Gell-Mann, *The Quark and the Jaguar* (New York: Henry Holt, 1994); John Holland, *Hidden Order* (Reading, Mass.: Addison-Wesley, 1995); Kevin Dooley, "A Complex Adaptive Systems Model of Organization Change," *Nonlinear Dynamics, Psychology, and Life Science* 1, no. 1 (1997): 69–97.

8. Louis Beam, "Leaderless Resistance," *Seditionist*, no. 12 (February 1992): 5.

9. John Arquilla and David Ronfeldt, "The Advent of Netwar," in *In Athena's Camp: Preparing for Conflict in the Information Age*, ed. John Arquilla and David Ronfeldt (Santa Monica, Calif.: RAND, 1997), 280.

10. Mariam Abou Zahab and Olivier Roy, *Islamist Networks: The Afghan-Pakistan Connection*, trans. John King (New York: Columbia University Press, 2004), 51–52. On the conflict between the Taliban and al-Qaeda, see U.S. Embassy (Islamabad), "TFX01: SITREP 5: Pakistan/Afghanistan Reaction to U.S. Air Strikes," Cable, August 24, 1998, released by the National Security Archive.

11. See, for example, Dr. Gary W. Richter, "Osama bin Laden: A Case Study," Sandia National Laboratories, U.S. Department of Energy, December 6, 1999, released by the National Security Archives.

12. U.S. Embassy (Islamabad), "TFXX01: Afghanistan: Reaction to U.S. Strikes Follows Predicable Lines: Taliban Angry, Their Opponents Support U.S.," Cable, August

21, 1998; U.S. Embassy (Islamabad), "Afghanistan: Reported Activities of Extremist Arabs and Pakistanis Since August 20 U.S. Strike on Khost Terrorist Camps," Cable, September 9, 1998, released by the National Security Archives; Ahmed Rashid, *Taliban: Militant Islam, Oil, and Fundamentalism in Central Asia* (New Haven, Conn.: Yale University Press, 2000), 98–100.

13. See, for example, *al-Samud*, no. 30 (December 2008). The fifty-six-page magazine contained articles on the Islamic Emirate's stance toward the presence and "failing" strategies of U.S. and other coalition forces in Afghanistan. The magazine was published on the Hanin Net website at www.hanein.info/vb.

14. See, for example, *Sheikh Mustafa Abu'l Yazid's Words of Condolences on the Martyrdom of Emir Baitullah Mehsud*, al-Sahab Foundation, September 30, 2009; Ayman al-Zawahiri, *Knights Under the Prophet's Banner*, trans. Laura Mansfield (Old Tappan, N.J.: TLG, 2002), 130; Ayman al-Zawahiri, "Supporting the Palestinians," statement released in June 2006.

15. Osama bin Laden, "Message to the Peoples of Europe," released in November 2007. An interview with Taliban officials also indicates that al-Qaeda leaders recognize Mullah Omar as "Commander of the Faithful" ("On-line Question and Answer with Ahmad Mukhtar," spokesman from the Afghan Taliban Media Wing, May 2009, www.nefafoundation.org).

16. Interview with NATO officials, Afghanistan, September 2013.

17. "Haqqani Says No Use of Negotiations; Vows to Defeat 'Crusaders' in Afghanistan," *al-Samud*, no. 30 (December 2008).

18. Interview with NATO officials, Afghanistan, September 2013.

19. Interview with U.S. government officials, Afghanistan, September 2013.

20. Mariam Abou Zahab, "Changing Patterns of Social and Political Life Among the Tribal Pashtuns in Pakistan," paper presented at the U.S. Naval Postgraduate School, Monterey, Calif., September 2006.

21. Rohan Gunaratna, "Al Qaeda in the Tribal Areas of Pakistan and Beyond," *Studies in Conflict and Terrorism* 31 (2008): 775–807; interview with NATO government officials, Afghanistan, September 2013; *Sheikh Mustafa Abu'l Yazid's Words of Condolences*.

22. U.S. Army Memorandum for Commander, Combined Joint Task Force—101, Bagram Airfield, August 13, 2008, Subject: AR 15-6 Investigation Findings and Recommendations—Vehicle Patrol Base (VPB) Wanat Complex Attack and Casualties, July 13, 2008.

23. The statement was published on the Sawt al-Jihad website on January 21, 2009. It was attributed to Qari Muhammad Yusuf (Ahmadi) and Dhabihallah (Mujahid), the official spokesmen of the Islamic Emirate of Afghanistan-Taliban, and to the Media Commission of the Islamic Emirate of Afghanistan-Taliban.

24. Basil Mohammed, *Al-Ansar al-Arab fi Afghanistan* (Jeddah: House of Learning, 1991), 241.

25. Gerges, *The Far Enemy*, 38–40; Zahab and Roy, *Islamist Networks*, 48–52; Peter Bergen, *The Osama bin Laden I Know: An Oral History of Al Qaeda's Leader* (New York:

Free Press, 2006); Wright, *The Looming Tower*, 133. The quotes are from the exhibit "Tareekh Osama" (Osama's history), document presented in United States of America v. Enaam M. Arnaout, United States District Court, Northern District of Illinois, Eastern Division.

26. Sayyid Qutb, *Ma'alim fi-l-Tariq* (Karachi: International Islamic Publishers, 1981).

27. On Qutb's work, see Gilles Kepel, *The Prophet and Pharaoh: Muslim Extremism in Egypt* (Berkeley: University of California Press, 1985); Olivier Carré, *Mystique et politique* (Paris: Presses de la FNSP et Cerf, 1984); Ibrahim M. Abu Rabi, *Intellectual Origins of Islamic Resurgence in the Muslim Arab World* (Albany: SUNY Press, 1996).

28. Interview of Sheikh Mustafa Abu'l Yazid (Said al-Masri), Geo TV; al-Zawahiri, *Knights Under the Prophet's Banner*, 61; Osama Rushdi, "How Did the Ideology of the 'Jihad Group' Evolve?," *Al-Hayat*, January 30, 2002; Gerges, *The Far Enemy*, 97.

29. Al-Zawahiri, *Knights Under the Prophet's Banner*, 201, 47. Al-Zawahiri's references to Ibn Tamiyyah come out in multiple places in his writings, including *Knights Under the Prophet's Banner*.

30. Sayyid Qutb, letter to Tewfig al-Hakeem, in Salah Abdel Fatah al-Khaledi, *Amerika min al-dahkhil bi minzar Sayyid Qutb* [*America from the Inside Through the Eyes of Sayyid Qutb*], 2nd ed., trans. Nidal Daraiseh (Damascus: Dar al-Qalam, 1986), 39.

31. Ayman al-Zawahiri, "From Kabul to Mogadishu," video released in February 2009.

32. On civilian casualties, see United Nations Assistance Mission in Afghanistan, *Afghanistan: Mid-Year Report 2013, Protection of Civilians in Armed Conflict* (Kabul: United Nations Assistance Mission in Afghanistan, 2013).

33. Osama bin Laden, "Message to the Peoples of Europe"; Gerges, *The Far Enemy*, 49. Al-Zahawari's reference to the Afghan jihad in this context means the anti-Soviet war in the 1980s. He argued that it provided a critical opportunity for training Arabs against the forthcoming war with the United States. See al-Zawahiri, *Knights Under the Prophet's Banner*, 38.

34. Zawahiri, *Knights under the Prophet's Banner*, 132. On the establishment of a caliphate see, for example, Abu Bakr Naji, "The Management of Savagery: The Most Critical Stage Through Which the Umma Will Pass," trans. and ed. John M. Olin Institute for Strategic Studies at Harvard University, May 23, 2006.

35. Interview with British and Pakistani government officials, Islamabad, May 2009; Seth G. Jones, *In the Graveyard of Empires: America's War in Afghanistan* (New York: Norton, 2009).

36. Interview with NATO officials, Afghanistan, September 2013.

37. See, for example, Harmony Documents NMEC-2007-657921, NMEC-2007-657945, NMEC-2007-658021, continued in NMEC-2007-657988. Also see Brian Fishman, ed., *Bombers, Bank Accounts, and Bleedout: Al Qaeda's Role In and Out of Iraq* (West Point, N.Y.: Combating Terrorism Center at West Point, 2008), 66–80.

38. Interview with Pakistan government officials, Pakistan, May 2009. Also see Pervez Musharraf, *In the Line of Fire: A Memoir* (New York: Free Press, 2006), 221.

39. Interview with NATO officials, Afghanistan, September 2013.

40. Eric Schmitt and David E. Sanger, "Some in Qaeda Leave Pakistan for Somalia and Yemen," *New York Times*, June 11, 2009.

41. Mia Bloom, *Dying to Kill: The Allure of Suicide Terror* (New York: Columbia University Press, 2005). On two-level games, see Robert D. Putnam, "Diplomacy and Domestic Politics: The Logic of Two-Level Games," *International Organization* 42, no. 3 (Summer 1988): 427–60.

42. Interview with NATO officials, Afghanistan, September 2013.

43. Interview with Pakistan and British government officials, Pakistan, May 2009.

44. Statement from Sheikh Mustafa Abu'l Yazid (Said al-Masri), June 9, 2009.

45. "Terror Suspect: An Interview with Osama bin Laden," *ABC Television News*, December 22, 1998 (conducted in Afghanistan by ABC News producer Rahimullah Yousafsai). See, for example, Wright, *The Looming Tower*, 48; Gerges, *The Far Enemy*, 3–4.

46. Michael V. Hayden, "The Current Situation in Iraq and Afghanistan," Central Intelligence Agency, November 15, 2006.

47. Both quotes are from Raffi Khatchadourian, "Azzam the American: The Making of an Al Qaeda Homegrown," *New Yorker*, January 22, 2007.

48. Lieutenant General Michael D. Maples, *The Current Situation in Iraq and Afghanistan* (Washington, DC: Defense Intelligence Agency, 2006), 6.

49. Alex Alexiev, "Tablighi Jamaat: Jihad's Stealthy Legions," *Middle East Quarterly* 12, no. 1 (Winter 2005). On *zakat* and jihad, also see Marc Sageman, *Understanding Terror Networks* (Philadelphia: University of Pennyslvania Press, 2004).

50. See, for example, Alfred B. Prados and Christopher M. Blanchard, *Saudi Arabia: Terrorist Financing Issues* (Washington, D.C.: Congressional Research Service, 2004); Thomas H. Kean, et al., *The 9/11 Commission Report: Final Report of the National Commission on Terrorist Attacks Upon the United States,* (New York: Norton, 2004), 55; interview with NATO officials, Afghanistan, September 2013.

51. Hayden, *The Current Situation in Iraq and Afghanistan*, 2.

52. United Nations Security Council, letter Dated November 15, 2007 from the Chairman of the Security Council Committee Established Pursuant to Resolution 1267 (1999) Concerning Al-Qaida and the Taliban and Associated Individuals and Entities Addressed to the President of the Security Council, November 29, 2007, S/2007/677, 8.

53. Decree Announced by General Presidency of Amr Bil Maruf, Religious Police, Kabul, December 1996.

54. See, for example, Rashid, *Taliban*, 82–94.

55. Statement from Mullah Omar, leader of the Taliban, released December 17, 2007; United States of America v. Babar Ahmad, United States District Court, District of Connecticut, No. 3:04-CR-301-MRK, Indictment, filed October 6, 2004; United States of America v. Syed Talha Ahsan, United States District Court, District of Connecticut, No. 3:06-CR-194-JCH, Indictment. Also see United States of America. v. Hassan Abujihaad, a/k/a Paul R. Hall, Abu-Jihaad, United States District Court, District of Connecticut, No. 3:07-CR-57, Indictment.

56. Interview with NATO and Afghan government officials, Afghanistan, September 2013. Also see Ali Jalali, "The Future of Afghanistan," *Parameters* 36, no. 1 (Spring 2006): 8.

57. Interview with Taliban military commander Mullah Dadallah, *Al Jazeera TV*, aired on May 31, 2006.

58. Interview with NATO officials, Afghanistan, September 2013.

59. Interview with NATO officials, Afghanistan, September 2013.

60. Interview with U.S. government officials, Afghanistan, September 2013.

61. On the rationale for suicide bombers, see al-Jazeera interview with Mullah Dadullah, February 2006.

62. U.S. Department of Defense data; United Nations Assistance Mission in Afghanistan, *Afghanistan: Annual Report 2012, Protection of Civilians in Armed Conflict* (Kabul: United Nations Assistance Mission in Afghanistan, 2012).

63. Zawahiri, *Knights Under the Prophet's Banner*.

64. Christine Fair et al., *Suicide Attacks in Afghanistan, 2001-2007* (Kabul: United Nations Assistance Mission in Afghanistan, 2007), 10.

65. Hekmat Karzai, *Afghanistan and the Logic of Suicide Terrorism* (Singapore: Institute of Defence and Strategic Studies, 2006); "Taliban Claim Responsibility for Suicide Bomb Attack in Afghan Kandahar Province," *Peshawar Afghan Islamic Press*, October 9, 2005; "Pajhwok News Describes Video of Afghan Beheading by 'Masked Arabs,'" Taliban," *Kabul Pajhwok Afghan News*, October 9, 2005; "Canadian Soldier Dies in Suicide Attack in Kandahar," *Afghan Islamic Press*, March 3, 2006; "Taliban Claim Attack on Police in Jalalabad, Nangarhar Province," Kabul National TV, January 7, 2006.

66. See, for example, Robert Pape, *Dying to Win: The Strategic Logic of Suicide Terrorism* (New York: Random House, 2005); Bloom, *Dying to Kill*; Christoph Reuter, *My Life Is a Weapon: A Modern History of Suicide Bombing* (Princeton, N.J.: Princeton University Press, 2004); Bruce Hoffman, *Inside Terrorism*, 2nd ed. (New York: Columbia University Press, 2006).

67. Hekmat Karzai and Seth G. Jones, "How to Curb Rising Suicide Terrorism in Afghanistan," *Christian Science Monitor*, July 18, 2006.

68. Interview with NATO officials, Afghanistan, September 2013.

69. In its public rhetoric, the Taliban tended to identify the suicide bombers as Afghans since it suggested there was a significant indigenous component of the insurgency.

70. Fair et al., *Suicide Attacks in Afghanistan*, 28.

71. "On-line Question and Answer with Ahmad Mukhtar," spokesman from the Afghan Taliban Media Wing, May 2009, at www.nefafoundation.org.

72. Sagemen, *Leaderless Jihad*, 143, 133.

73. Program on International Policy Attitudes, *World Public Opinion Poll: Afghan Public Overwhelmingly Rejects al-Qaeda, Taliban* (Washington, DC: Program on International Policy Attitudes, University of Maryland, 2006).

74. United Nations Assistance Mission in Afghanistan, *Afghanistan: Mid-Year Report 2013, Protection of Civilians in Armed Conflict, 2013.*

75. Steven Simon, "Can the Right War Be Won? Defining American Interests in Afghanistan," *Foreign Affairs* 88, no. 4 (July/August 2009): 134. Also see, for example, Rory Stewart, "How to Save Afghanistan," *Time*, July 17, 2008.

76. Peter Baker, "Biden No Longer a Lone Voice on Afghanistan," *New York Times*, October 13, 2009.

77. On key strategies to defeat the Taliban see, for example, Michael Semple, *Reconciliation in Afghanistan* (Washington, D.C.: United States Institute of Peace, 2009); Jones, *In the Graveyard of Empires*, 313–25. Also see, for example, memo from Stanley A. McChrystal to Secretary of Defense Robert M. Gates, Subject: COMISAF's Initial Assessment, August 30, 2009.

16

Attacks of al-Jemaah al-Islamiyah in Southeast Asia

ROHAN GUNARATNA

The most violent terrorist group in Southeast Asia is al-Jemaah al-Islamiyah (The Islamic community), commonly known as Jemaah Islamiyah (JI). Influenced and supported by al-Qaeda, JI spearheaded most of the significant terrorist attacks in the region, especially since 2001. Although the stated aim of the group is to establish an Islamic state (*daulah Islamiyah*), JI was directly influenced and supported by al-Qaeda's strategy of targeting Americans and others whom they consider to be enemies of Islam.

The existence of an al-Qaeda-linked JI in Southeast Asia came to the attention of Southeast Asian governments after Singapore's Internal Security Department (ISD) detected and disrupted a JI plot aimed at U.S., British, Australian, and Israeli diplomatic targets in early 2002. JI's operational leader Riduan Isamuddin (alias Hambali), a close associate of Khalid Sheikh Mohammed, the 9/11 mastermind, provided al-Qaeda funding to JI to attack Bali in October 2002. Although the Indonesian authorities attempted to dismantle JI, the group survived and continued to conduct intermittent attacks in Indonesia. Despite the arrest of key leaders and raids on their safe houses, JI's most violent faction—led by Noordin Mohomed Top, a Malaysian—attacked the Marriott hotel in Jakarta in August 2003. Then in September 2004, JI attacked the Australian embassy in Jakarta and Bali in October 2005. Most recently, in July 2009, JI attacked the Marriott and Ritz Carlton hotels. JI's original goal to transform Indonesia into an Islamic state has now expanded into a more collective vision: an Islamic state, Daulah Islamiya Nusantara, consisting of other Southeast Asian regions. Despite US efforts to dismantle al-Qaeda, JI continues to pursue al-Qaeda's agenda of a global jihad and poses a serious threat to Southeast Asia.

The multinational Afghan mujaheddin campaign against the Soviets (1979–1989) galvanized Muslim groups and Muslims worldwide to participate in the jihad. As in other regions, Muslim youth from Southeast Asia participated in the fight. Eventually, the Afghan veterans became the leaders and influential members of existing and emerging groups throughout Southeast Asia. After the Soviets withdrew, al-Qaeda, the core of Arabs that remained in Afghanistan, continued to provide training, weapons, finance, and ideology to groups waging multiple struggles in Southeast Asia.

Although the interest of the local groups was to wage their local jihads, their interaction with al-Qaeda enabled them to craft joint projects to attack U.S. and other Western targets. The mutually beneficial al-Qaeda-JI business model enabled al-Qaeda to expand its reach into Southeast Asia. Through training and instruction, the high-end capabilities for mounting operations were transferred by highly trained and motivated al-Qaeda operatives to JI and other groups in the region.

Throughout the 1990s, al-Qaeda ideologues, financiers, and operational leaders relocated or visited the region. With the increased pace of activity, some joint al-Qaeda-JI operations were detected, such as the Singapore plot, but others, such as the Bali attack, succeeded. If not for the multinational investigations that followed these successful, failed, and aborted operations, the links between al-Qaeda and other groups, notably JI, would not have surfaced. If not for the al-Qaeda-JI nexus, JI would have remained very much a provincial group with an Indonesia-centric ideology. The link with al-Qaeda also influenced and empowered JI to think regionally and stage global attacks that mirrored classic al-Qaeda attacks against predominately Western targets. To generate high fatalities and injuries, JI adopted the suicide tactic and staged coordinated and simultaneous attacks against high-profile targets.

JI originated as Darul Islam (DI) in the 1940s. DI fought to establish an Islamic state in Indonesia. DI was joined by Abdullah Sungkar and his assistant Abu Bakar Ba'asyir, the founders of Islamic boarding school Pondok al-Mukmin in the village of Ngruki in Solo, Central Java, in 1971.[1] In 1976, the Indonesian government claimed that Sungkar and Ba'asyir swore an oath of loyalty to Darul Islam and proceeded to prosecute them. In 1978, both were sentenced to nine years in prison for subversion. Their sentences were reduced on appeal, and they were released. In 1985, Ba'asyir and Sungkar fled to Malaysia to escape another jail term.

While in Malaysia, they dispatched their followers to Pakistan to train and fight in Afghanistan. The two men gathered like-minded Indonesians, Malaysians, Filipinos, and Singaporeans, inculcating their vision for a regional pan-Islamic state. Many of the Southeast Asians that trained in Afghanistan later held central positions in JI and other terrorist organizations upon their return. The process of sending recruits to Afghanistan began at least seven years before JI formally came into being. The first batch was sent to Afghanistan in early 1985. This event marked the formal institutionalization of the network.[2]

In May 1996, influenced by al-Gama'a al-Islamiya (Islamic Group of Egypt), Sungkar and some veterans of the Afghan war consolidated the structure of Jemaah Islamiyah and documented it in a book titled *Pedoman Umum Perjuangan al-Jamaah al-Islamiyah* (General guidelines for the Jemaah Islamiyah struggle), or PUPJI.[3] In fact, all of JI's top leaders and many of the men involved in the JI bombings between 2002 and 2009 trained in Afghanistan between 1985 and 1995. As a result of al-Qaeda's influence on JI, the individual and institutional ties between Abdullah Sungkar and Osama bin Laden began. The jihad in Afghanistan shaped their worldview, reinforced their commitment to jihad, and provided them with terrorist and guerrilla training. Most JI leaders went back to Indonesia after the end of Suharto government in 1998, during the Reformasi transition.[4] Around the same time, JI's leadership also changed: Sungkar passed away in 1999 shortly after returning to Indonesia, and Ba'asyir became the leader of JI.

Furthermore, at the request of Khalid Sheikh Mohammed, a high-ranking member of al-Qaeda, Hambali, the former leader of JI, provided significant assistance to al-Qaeda. Hambali arranged for a U.S.-trained biochemist Yazid Sufaat to head the al-Qaeda anthrax program. Sufaat's apartment in Kuala Lumpur in January 2000 housed four figures involved in the 9/11 attacks in the United States, including the first two 9/11 hijackers to enter the United States, Khalid al-Midhar and Nawaz al-Hazmi.[5] Furthermore, Zacarias Moussaoui, a hijacker who was subsequently detained in the United States, was a guest of JI in Malaysia.

Although the key link between al-Qaeda and JI was disrupted with the arrest of Khalid Sheikh Mohammed and his JI counterpart, Hambali, JI built an alliance with threat groups in Asia, Africa, and the Middle East. JI also built Rabitatul Mujahidin (RM), a platform linking the key Southeast Asian threat groups. Influenced by the World Islamic Front for Jihad Against the Jews and the Crusaders created by al-Qaeda in 1998, Rabitatul Mujahidin held three meetings to discuss strategy, share resources, and forge a common direction. As the regional vanguard, JI worked with Darul Islam, Action Committee for Crisis Response (KOMPAK), Moro Islamic Liberation Front (MILF), Anti-Apostasy Movement Forum (FAKTA), Jamaah Anshorut Tauhid (JAT), Tauhid wal Jihad, Gerakan Pemuda Islam (GPI), Laskar Mujahidin, Laskar Jundullah, Malaysian Mujahidin Group (KMM), Gerakan Mujahidin Islam Patani (GMIP), Mujahidin KOMPAK, Republic of United Islam of Indonesia (Republic Persatuan Islam Indonesia), and Abu Bakar Battalion.[6]

THE ATTACKS IN SOUTH EAST ASIA

Beginning in August 2000, JI mounted terrorist operations in Indonesia and throughout the region. First, the residence of the Philippines ambassador in Jakarta, Leonides Caday, was bombed by JI on August 1, 2000, injuring the ambassador severely and killing two others. The attack was staged in retaliation for Philippine military operations against the Moro Islamic Liberation Front, an associate group of JI and al-Qaeda.

A classic al-Qaeda-style coordinated simultaneous attack followed on Christmas Eve, 2000, when bombs exploded in thirty-eight places, mostly churches, in Jakarta, Bandung, Mojokerto, Medan, Batam, Pekanbaru, Sukabumi, Mataram, and Pematangsiantar.[7] This series of bombings was masterminded by Hambali. Furthermore, the HKBP Church and Santa Ana Church in Jakarta were bombed on July 22, 2001. More than forty people were reported injured in the first blast at Santa Ana Church. The second explosion, minutes later at the HKPB church caused no injuries as the morning service had already finished.[8] JI also bombed the Atrium Mall in Jakarta on August 1, 2001. The bomb exploded prematurely, injuring six.

As a result, JI attacks inspired other Southeast Asian groups linked to JI through a common ideology.

For instance, Petra Church was bombed in North Jakarta on November 9, 2001. The bombing was carried out by Wahyu Handoko and Ujang Haris, members of Mujahidin KOMPAK, a radical group working with JI active in Christian-Muslim conflicts in Maluku.[9] JI's early attacks were not confined solely to Indonesia but also to the Philippines and Malaysia. Another al-Qaeda-esque simultaneous attack in Manila on December 30, 2000, killed twenty-two people. Called the Rizal Day bombings, these were once again directed by Hambali and conducted by Fathur Rahman al-Ghozi, Muklis Yunos, and Faiz Abu Bakar Bafana of JI.[10] Although it was difficult for JI to mount attacks in Malaysia, it operated in Kuala Lumpur, Negri Sembilan, Selangor, Johor, Kelantan, Sabah, and Sarawak.[11] After JI robbed the Southern Bank in Kuala Lumpur, the Malaysian authorities arrested Zainuri of JI on May 18, 2001, implicating both JI and its Malaysian associate, KMM. The investigation by the Malaysian Special Branch revealed that Ba'asyir and Sungkar had established *usroh* (religious discussion group) cells all over Malaysia.

In addition, while operating with al-Qaeda, JI planned another spectacular attack in Singapore in 2001. In December 2001, Singapore's Internal Security Department arrested thirteen JI members, eight of whom had trained in al-Qaeda camps in Afghanistan.[12] Simultaneous arrests of JI members in Singapore and Malaysia led to arrests of JI members in the Philippines and Thailand and surveillance of JI's network in Australia. Based on Singaporean intelligence, Fathur Rahman al-Ghozi in the Philippines was arrested on January 15, 2002.[13] Further investigations led Singapore to arrest eighteen other JI operatives in August 2002. All thirty-one were accused of plotting to carry out attacks on both domestic and foreign targets.

Following the U.S. intervention in Afghanistan, the threat against Western targets increased, especially in Indonesia. JI conducted its worst bomb attack to date in Bali on October 12, 2002. Considered one of the worst terrorist attacks after September 11, 2001, this was the first suicide attack in East Asia. Two bombs detonated around 11:17 p.m., first in Paddy's Bar and then in an L-300 minivan in front of the Sari Club. The death toll was 202.

Nevertheless, further investigations revealed that Mohomed Mansour Jarabah, a Canadian al-Qaeda operative, met with Hambali in February

2002 in Thailand to discuss the bombing of night clubs, bars, and restaurants.[14] A Ph.D. candidate in statistical modeling from the UK, Azahari Husein, the key bomb maker, and Noordin Top, Ali Imron, and other JI members also met in Thailand before the attack.[15] In addition to al-Qaeda funding from Hambali, Wan Min Wan Mat, detained in Malaysia, said that during the meeting, he gave Ali Ghufron, indicted in the Bali bombings, US $35,000.[16] However, Abu Bakar Ba'asyir, the leader of JI, was arrested on October 20, 2002. His trial began in April 2003.

Furthermore, Mukhlas was arrested for his involvement in the Bali bombings on December 3, 2002. On September 2, 2003, Ba'asyir was sentenced to four years in jail. An Indonesian court acquitted him of charges that he ordered a series of terrorist attacks in Indonesia and plotted the assassination of the Indonesian president. He was, however, found guilty of aiding and abetting treason, apparently based on his support of the organization's goal to establish an Islamic state. As a result, the U.S. State Department added Jemaah Islamiyah to the Foreign Terrorist List on October 23, 2002. Furthermore, the UN Security Council 1267 Committee added JI to its consolidated list of al-Qaeda-related entities on October 25, 2002.[17] The UN listed the names of ten JI leaders as terrorists on September 5, 2003.

In addition, a plan by the JI cell in Bangkok to hit Western diplomatic targets and the Singapore embassy was disrupted on May 16, 2003. Thai authorities arrested and extradited alleged JI member Arifin Ali, a trainer in JI's military and security unit, to Singapore. In 1999, he allegedly underwent training in the handling of weapons and explosives at the Moro Islamic Liberation Front's Camp Abu Bakar in Mindanao. On July 8, 2003, Samarn Wakaji, the fourth suspect in a JI bomb plot against embassies and tourist spots in Thailand, surrendered to authorities in the Muslim-majority south.

TARGETING OF JI OPERATION CELLS IN SOUTHEAST ASIA

Detachment 88, Indonesia's elite counterterrorism unit, created with Australian and U.S. support, began targeting JI operational cells in 2003. The Semarang arrests led to the discovery of a JI base camp, where police recovered enough explosives to make ten Bali-size bombs. The Marriott bombing was followed by the news of the arrest of Hambali, the most wanted man in Southeast Asia. His arrest in Thailand by its Special Branch II on August 11, 2003, allowed Thai authorities to confiscate explosive devices and weapons, which Hambali confessed were being prepared for use in a terrorist attack during the APEC summit.

Although JI remained most active in Indonesia, it also functioned in the Philippines, Malaysia, and Pakistan. Under pressure in Southeast Asia, JI began secretly grooming its next generation of leaders in Pakistan. Taufik Rifki, an Indonesian JI member, was arrested in Cotabato City, southern Mindanao on October 2, 2003. Taufik was JI's number-two man in the Philippines. Authorities recovered a JI chemical and biological weapons manual in his home. In addition, the Philippines became the principal training ground for Malaysian and Indonesian members of JI. On June 1, 2005, Detachment 88 arrested twenty-four people suspected of membership in JI in a raid in Semarang.

Even these arrests were not sufficient to disrupt JI's operational activity. For instance, three coordinated simultaneous suicide attacks took place in Bali on October 1, 2005. Two explosions occurred at 7:50 p.m. at two crowded beachside restaurants at Jimbaran. Ten minutes later, another blast took place at Kuta in Raja restaurant at the Matahari Square shopping center. Detachment 88 raided the hideout of Azahari Husin in the town of Batu, near Malang city in East Java on November 9, 2005. Azahari was killed in the ensuing shoot-out, which lasted for over an hour. Nevertheless, four suspected terrorist with close links to Noordin Top were arrested in Central Java on January 13, 2006, in connection to the Bali bombing. They were identified as Joko, Wahyu, Ardi Wibowo, and Aditya. Subur Sugiarto was also arrested in Boyolali, Central Java, on January 18, 2006.

While JI was recovering from the arrests, Noordin Top, declared himself the leader of a new regional terrorist group called Tandzim Qaedatul Jihad on February 1, 2006. A month later Detachment 88 raided a safe house at Binangun village in Central Java belonging to Noordin Top and his followers. Two of Top's aides were killed, and two others were captured during the ensuing gun battle. The two militants killed were identified by police as Abdul Hadi, alias Bambang, and Jabir; the captured men were named Solahuddin and Mustagfirin. Abdul Hadi and Jabir were bomb-making experts and the successors of Azahari Husin.

Hence, with information that Abu Dujana had assumed the operational leadership of JI, Detachment 88 mounted a series of raids against JI in March and April 2007. On June 9, 2007, Abu Dujana was arrested along with seven other members of JI in Banyumas, Central Java. On June 15, 2007, Abu Dujana admitted in an interview, aired on Indonesian television, that he had sent funds to Mindanao and was the head of Jemaah Islamiyah. Zarkasih, arrested on June 9, 2007, by Detachment 88, admitted in a videotaped interview shown to reporters, to becoming the emergency head of JI in 2005.[18] On April 21, 2008, Abu Dujana and Zarkasih were both sentenced to fifteen years imprisonment. Additionally, for the first time in Indonesia, the South Jakarta State Court decreed JI an illegal organization and guilty of terrorism.[19] This permitted the release of suspects who were guilty of no crime other than membership in JI.

Despite arrests and convictions, JI continued to regenerate its infrastructure by reaching out to other radical networks in the Middle East. For instance, two individuals tasked by the JI leadership were Abu Husna, the head of the Education Division of JI's Central Board, and Agus Purwantoro, the leader of JI Poso, responsible for organizing training during brutal Muslim-Christian clashes in the restive Poso region of Sulawesi Island. Husna was integral to recruiting fighters for JI. A former teacher at the Ngruki Islamic School in Central Java, a school founded by Abu Bakar, Husna sent many students for training in Afghanistan in the late 1980s and early 1990s. Husna was sentenced to nine years in jail, and Purwantoro was given an eight-year sentence. These sentences were lighter than the fourteen years sought by prosecutors.[20] Furthermore, the investigation into Purwantoro and Husna revealed that the two used fake passports stolen from Indonesian travelers at London's Heathrow Airport in 2003 and purchased tickets to Syria in Thailand to facilitate their activities. The journey was arranged by an Algerian called "Jaffar," who gave them air tickets, militant contacts in Syria, and fake passports.[21]

Despite significant gains made against JI in 2009, the hunt for Noordin Top by Detachment 88 continued. In the meantime, Parmin (alias Faiz Fauzan) one of Top's aides, was sentenced. The judge revealed that Parmin sheltered Top, translated his lectures on holy war into Arabic, and sent them to the Qatar-based news channel al-Jazeera. Parmin also helped to conceal attack plans hatched by another top JI leader, Azahari Husin. Parmin was given an eight-year sentence, lighter than the thirteen years recommended by prosecutors.

On July 17, 2009, JI executed the first successful terrorist attack in Indonesia in almost four years, bombing the J.W. Marriott and the Ritz-Carlton in Jakarta, injuring fifty-five and killing nine, including the two suicide bombers. The police believed that the mastermind was Noordin Top. In the aftermath of the attacks, police conducted a massive manhunt for the perpetrators. On August 8, 2009, Detachment 88 launched simultaneous raids in Bekasi (West Java) and Temenggung (Central Java). They found half a ton of explosives.[22] On September 17, 2009, Noordin Top, who had been on the police's most-wanted list for more than six years, was killed in a police raid.[23] His death was a critical transitional point for JI because no other radical Islamic militant leader in Indonesia was able to spread extremist ideology by creating splinter groups throughout the region. Nonetheless, this demonstrates that with the influence of al-Qaeda, splinter groups such as JI have evolved into an amorphous movement—leaderless jihad.

IDEOLOGICAL AND OPERATIONAL TRAINING OF JI

JI heavily emphasizes the ideological and operational training of its leaders and members. More than 200 members trained in Afghanistan from 1985 to 1995 at Camp Saddah, run by the Saudi-funded Afghan mujaheddin leader Abdul Rasul Sayyaf. Saddah was located in Khurram Agency, near Parachinar on the Pakistan-Afghanistan border.[24] In 1993, DI members who refused to recognize Sungkar as the emir were told to return to Indonesia. Thereafter, all the Indonesian mujaheddin in Afghanistan became JI members.

For example, in the Singapore case, at least eleven JI members detained there had received training in al-Qaeda camps in Afghanistan. The Academy of Military Education and Training (DikLat AKMIL) was created as part of the long-term strategy to produce highly capable fighters for JI in Southeast Asia. The first two batches of recruits sent to Afghanistan had problems with the training as the instructors used English or Arabic. However, the graduates from these two classes later became the instructors for the subsequent batches and facilitated training, creating a generation of JI members trained in Afghanistan.

Graduates from each batch were then selected for advanced study while the rest were sent home to Indonesia. Among the advanced courses at AKMIL were lessons in rifle marksmanship, shooting with a pistol or revolver, chemical explosives, ammunition and weapons, electronic circuits, tankers (e.g., T-60, T-59, T-72), infantry combat, and skirmishing. In addition, advanced students received intense training as preachers at the camp or at schools owned by Arabs at Peshawar, such as Maahad Salman and Dakwah al-Jihad University. Alumni later set up training facilities in Southeast Asia, which demonstrates how Islamic radicalization takes place within an integrated global culture where shared experience training in Afghanistan has linked JI members in Indonesia.

The series of arrests in March and April 2007 revealed that JI held armed training on Mount Sumbing in Central Java.[25] Training camps in Indonesia were makeshift mobile camps located within private house compounds. JI had also been conducting training camps in Malaysia since 1990. Up to 1994, the training was focused mainly on maintaining physical fitness. From 1995, however, the training camps in Gunung Pulai and Kulai began to also teach "military" skills (except firearms training). In 1997, additional modules like guerrilla warfare, infiltration, and ambush were included. Around 2000, reconnaissance and observation courses were conducted in Kota Tinggi; these classes were dubbed "urban warfare." The JI even conducted recall and operation exercises to ensure that members were operationally ready.

After a decade of receiving training, funding, and ideology from al-Qaeda, JI came to model itself on the Arab organization. Under the guidance and influence of al-Qaeda, JI evolved from a domestic terrorist group in Indonesia into a regional terrorist group starting in 1993. The adoption of suicide attacks, a classic al-Qaeda strategy , made JI a lethal group. Because of JI's links with al-Qaeda, many regional militant Islamic groups became more radical and lethal in their ideologies. As a result of al-Qaeda's continuous search for new training bases in Southeast Asia, local leaders were co-opted into the organization while maintaining their indigenous organizations. Nevertheless, JI created al-Qaeda's pan-Asian outfit where several key operatives such as Omar al-Faruq received expert knowledge from al-Qaeda regarding sophisticated terrorist tradecrafts.[26]

Furthermore, while Hambali and the operational branch of JI pursued the militant agenda, Ba'asyir actively pursued a *syariah* agenda and established the Majelis Mujahidin Indonesia (Mujahidin Council of Indonesia). He was reelected as the emir of the MMI for a second term (2003–2008), a term he served even while in prison for his role in the Bali bombing and other activities. When Ba'asyir formed MMI, JI splintered into factions: the mainstream and Noordin Top's. To participate in the political process was seen by the hardliners as modifying the system in a way that contradicted *syariah* and an Islamic state. After Ba'asyir's arrest, the senior JI leader Abu Rushdan, alias Thoriqudin, replaced Ba'asyir as the leader of JI in 2002. Abu Rushdan was jailed for three and a half years starting in 2004 for helping to hide one of the suspects of the 2002 Bali bombings. However, in January 2006, he was given an early release for good behavior. Abu Rushdan was succeeded by Adung in 2003, and when he was arrested in 2004, Zarkashi succeeded him. After Zarkashi was arrested in 2007, JI once again came under the influence of Ba'asyir. On June 14, 2006, Ba'asyir was released from Cipinang prison in Jakarta after serving twenty-six months.

His release was greeted by a large group of his supporters, mainly from the MMI. In the absence of a robust counterterrorism law, Indonesia's legal system failed to deliver justice. On December 21, 2006, Indonesia's Supreme Court overturned a lower court's conviction of militant cleric Abu Bakar Bashir, clearing him of any involvement in the first Bali bombings in October 2002. The five-judge court ruled that the cleric, who was jailed for more than two years and had completed his term in June, was not guilty.[27] Ba'asyir announced his new mission: merging JI and MMI into one openly operating political movement. Nonetheless, Ba'asyir continued to hail those who died in suicide attacks or those terrorists killed by the police as martyrs. He invested most of his time politicizing and radicalizing the next generation of youth in Indonesia.

Finally, it is critical not to underestimate the perseverance of the regional JI network in Indonesia. Despite arrests and convictions, JI continued to regenerate its infrastructure. Lessons from JI cases in Southeast Asia can help counter current terrorist threats. First, enhancing security measures on a regional basis is be essential, for instance, tightening border controls, observing money-laundering operations, researching new threats such as bioterrorism, and increased security at central locations. It is important to recognize the need to act together with transnational intelligence and security agencies.

Second, it is critical to create a broader strategic approach to the problem by cooperating with the greater Muslim community in Indonesia. For instance, in order to detect extremist teachings, the government could create a comprehensive system to monitor religious instruction in the Muslim community without disrupting legitimate practices. Also, it is important to further educate the public on how to report any suspicious activity and to exercise vigilance against extremist teachings in their communities. This may assist in understanding JI's distinctive characteristics, such as its recruitment methods, clandestine religious practices, and distorted teaching methods. Therefore, countermeasures should be implemented with the support of the local Muslim community.

Third, it is critical to improve interethnic peace and religious harmony in the area affected by terrorism. This may facilitate strengthening social cohesion among Muslims and non-Muslims. Collective approaches to unequivocally condemning JI attacks and creating trust between Muslims and non-Muslims should be strengthened. Interreligious and interracial understanding creates a platform for a cohesive and a tolerant society. As a result, it will be difficult for JI to establish a foothold to spread terrorist and extremist ideology in Indonesia.

NOTES

1. Maria Ressa, *Seeds of Terror: An Eyewitness Account of Al-Qaeda's Newest Center of Operations in Southeast Asia* (New York: Free Press, 2002), 48.

2. "Jemaah Islamiyah in South East Asia: Damaged but Still Dangerous," International Crisis Group, Asia Report, no. 63, August 26, 2003.

3. Ibid., 2.

4. According to the Singapore Ministry of Home Affairs.

5. The Malaysian government released six JI members, including Yazid Sufaat, in November 2008. They had been detained under the country's Internal Security Act (ISA) for over six years. See "Surprised but Not Alarmed," *Straits Times* (Singapore), December 11, 2008, available at http://www.straitstimes.com/Breaking+News /SE+Asia/Story/STIStory_313007.html (accessed February 18, 2009); "Malaysian Home

Minister Defends Release of ISA Detainees," *Channelnewsasia.com*, December 2008, http://www.channelnewsasia.com/stories/southeastasia/view/395379/1/.html (accessed February 18, 2009); "Malaysia Frees Alleged Militant Tied to 9/11 Attackers," *Channelnewsasia.com*, December 10, 2008, available at http://www.channelnewsasia.com/stories/afp_asiapacific/view/395344/1/.html (accessed February 18, 2009).

6. Global Pathfinder Database, International Center for Political Violence and Terrorism Research, October 2009.

7. The police came to know the perpetrators, but as individuals not as a group. The bomb materials were from the same source, and the explosives were all composed of carbon, potassium, and sulphur, with a small amount of trinitrotoluene (TNT). The use of objects such as pellets, pieces of iron plates, and sharp nails also indicated that the bombs had most likely come from one producer.

Bombs exploded in Jakarta (Koinonia Church in Jatinegara, Santo Yosef Church in Matraman, Oikumene Church, the Cathedral, Istana Restaurant in Menteng; : 4 dead; losses: 24 vehicles damaged, four stalls destroyed; perpetrators: Edi Setiyono, alias Abbas, now serving life sentence; bomb type: mixture of black powder, pellets, and TNT); Pemantangsiantar (house of Rev. El Imanson Sumbayak, Kasuari Street; perpetrator: Edy Sugiharto, 11 years in jail; bomb type: mixture of sulphur and pellets); Bandung (house of Aceng Suhari, Jalan Terusan Street, Jakarta; victims: 4 dead, 7 badly injured; perpetrators: Hambali, arrested; Iqbaluzzaman, alias Enceng Didin, 15 years in jail; Aceng Suheri, 8 years in jail; Roni Miliar Iqbal, alias Ade Syamsuddin, 9 years; and other accomplices; bomb type: mixture of sulphur, ammonium, and TNT); Sukabumi (Sidang Kristus Church, Huria Kristen Batak Protestan Church; victims: 3 dead, 13 badly injured; losses: Windowpanes of churches and PGRI building damaged, 1 car destroyed; perpetrators: involvement of Hambali suspected; bomb type: mixture of sulphur and TNT); Mojokerto (Eben Haezer Church, Pantekosta Allah Baik Church, Santo Yosef Church; victims: 2 dead, 5 badly injured, losses: Eben Haezer and Pantekosta churches severely damaged; perpetrators: unknown, involvement of Hambali suspected); Batam (Pentecostal Church, Simalungun Christian Protestant Church, Bethany Church; victims: 29 badly injured; losses: churches severely damaged; perpetrator: Imam Samudra; bomb type: mixture containing black powder and TNT); Pekanbaru (HKBP Church; victims: 5 dead, 21 injured; losses: church destroyed, 10 nearby houses damaged; perpetrators: Basuki, serving jail term; Imam Samudra; bomb type: mixture containing black powder and TNT); Mataram (Christian Cemetery, Imanuel GPIB Church, Central Bethlehem Pentecostal Church Surabaya; victims: none; perpetrator: unknown; bomb type: TNT).

8. "Explosions Shake Indonesian Capital," BBC, available at http://news.bbc.co.uk/2/hi/asia-pacific/1450799.stm, July 22, 2001 (accessed November 18 2008).

9. "Bom Meledak di Gereja Petra Jakarta Utara," *Liputan 6*, November 11 2001, available at http://berita.liputan6.com/read/23441/bom_meledak_di_gereja_petra_jakarta_utara (accessed January 14, 2012).

10. "Understanding the Human Security Act of 2007 (R.A. No. 9372)," *Manila Times*, July 11, 2007

11. "Some Still Roam Free," *Tempo*, October 14–20, 2003.

12. The orders of detention against the thirteen JI members were extended by the government for a two-year term as of January 2004. The ISA Advisory Board chaired by Justice Chao Hick Tin reviewed their cases and heard representations by detainees directly or through their legal counsels or both.

13. On July 15, 2003, al-Ghozi and two Abu Sayaf members escaped from a high-security prison, Camp Crame, in Manila. They walked out with the help of Abu Ali, al-Ghozi's explosives supplier, who had been allowed to work as a janitor in the detention facility.

14. Shawn W. Crispin, "Falling in Step," *Far Eastern Economic Review*, June 26, 2003.

15. "Dr. Death from Johor," *Tempo*, October 14–20, 2003.

16. "Bin Laden and Bali Bombings Linked to Thailand," *Thaipro.com*, July 13, 2003.

17. The Foreign Terrorist Organization designation permitted the United States to freeze the organization's assets in U.S. financial institutions, criminalized the knowing provision of material support or resources to the organization, and allowed members of the terrorist group to be excluded from the United States. The United States joined Australia, Brunei, Burma, Cambodia, Indonesia, Japan, Malaysia, the Philippines, Singapore, South Korea, Thailand, Timor Leste, and other partners around the world to ask the relevant United Nations sanctions committee to include JI on its consolidated list of individuals and entities whose assets all member states are required to freeze in accordance with UN Security Council Resolutions 1267 and 1390. UN member states were obliged to take measures against JI, including freezing its assets; banning the sale or transfer of arms, military equipment, and technical advice or training; and preventing the entry and transit of individual members of JI.

18. "Head of JI Captured: Police Say," http://www.news.com.au/breaking-news /head-of-ji-captured-police-say/story-e6frfkp9-1111113757505 (accessed January 12, 2012).

19. "15 Tahun Buat Abu Dujana," *Republika Online*, April 21, 2008.

20. "Three Convicts from Poso Receive Prison Sentences for Terrorism," *Tempo Interactive*, February 10, 2009, available at http://www.tempointeractive.com/hg /nasional/2009/02/10/brk,20090210-159307,uk.html, (accessed February 19, 2009); "Indonesian Court Jails Islamist Militants on Terror Charges," *Antara*, February 10, 2009.

21. "Two Indon Terror Leaders in Iraq to Get Al Qaeda Funds," *Straits Times* (Singapore), July 30, 2008.

22. "Noordin's Identity: Children Undergo DNA Testing," *Jakarta Post*, October 8, 2009.

23. "Spot Report on Police Raid in Solo, 16–17 September 2009," International Center for Political Violence and Terrorism Research, available at http://pvtr.org/pdf /GlobalAnalysis/SpotReportOnPoliceRaidInSolo.pdf.

24. "The General of Suicide Bombers" TEMPO, Bali Bombing: One Year On, 14–20 Oct. 2003

25. "JI Militants Held Armed Exercises at Volcano on Java, Says Report," *Straits Times* (Singapore), April 3, 2007.

26. "The Jemaah Islamiyah Arrests and the Threat of Terrorism," January 7, 2003, available at http://www.channelnewsasia.com/cna/arrests/whitepaper.pdf.

27. " Bashir's Terror Conviction Overturned," *Straits Times* (Singapore), December 22, 2006.

[17]

The Mombassa Attacks
of November 28, 2002

JONATHAN FIGHEL

On the morning of November 28, 2002, al-Qaeda launched coordinated attacks in Mombassa, Kenya, against the Israeli-owned Paradise Hotel and an Israeli passenger jet.[1] The nearly simultaneous attacks involved al-Qaeda operatives supported by a local infrastructure. In the first attack, the terrorists fired two SA-7 surface-to-air missiles at a departing Israeli Arkia charter Boeing 757 carrying 261 passengers and crew. Both missiles missed. The second occurred twenty minutes later, when an explosives-laden vehicle driven by two suicide attackers blew up in front of the Paradise Hotel. The attack was timed just as the hotel's Israeli guests arrived—having traveled aboard the same Arkia plane that had just left on its return flight to Israel. In the Paradise Hotel attack, fifteen people were killed (twelve Kenyan nationals and three Israeli tourists), and approximately eighty other people were injured.[2]

THE ISRAELI REACTION

This was the first al-Qaeda attack specifically directed against overseas Israeli targets. In reaction to the attack, Prime Minister Ariel Sharon stated, "Our long arm will get those who carried out the terror attacks. No one will be forgiven." Benjamin Netanyahu, the Israeli foreign minister at the time, said, "It's just a question of time before they'll (terrorists) down civilian aircraft. And may I say, it always begins with Israel, it never ends with Israel. So this is not just our battle, it's a common battle against this global terror network." The Israeli Defense minister, Shaul Mofaz declared on December 2, 2002, that he suspected al-Qaeda was behind the attack, although there was no tangible evidence at that point.[3]

In response to the attacks, the Israeli prime minister reportedly ordered the Israeli Institute for Intelligence and Special Operations, known as the "Mossad," to be the leading agency within the Israeli intelligence community for collecting information, analyzing intelligence, and performing special covert operations beyond its borders. The Mossad was assigned with thwarting global jihad overseas activities against Israel and tracking down those responsible for the Mombassa attacks.[4] Ephraim Halevy, then the head of the Israeli Mossad and later head of the National Security Council for Prime Minister Sharon, stated, "The plane attack should be viewed as if it actually happened. If this attack had ended as was planned, it would not have been (just) another terror event against Israel. And as such, it would change the rules of the game and it would open options, which, up to now, have not been opened."[5]

Before the Mombassa attack, Israel and the international intelligence community were unaware of al-Qaeda's strategic decision to attack Israeli/Jewish targets, which was made in early 2001 and before the 9/11 attacks.[6] In 2002, Israel received vague information that al-Qaeda was conducting reconnaissance missions in Kenya in order to carry out terrorist attacks, with no specific details regarding the target, location, or timing. This was not enough to define any concrete threat to Israeli targets and did not meet the criteria of the Israeli intelligence community for issuing an alert. A former head of the Mossad, Danny Yatom, has noted that Israel received so many terror warnings in the past that most of them were proven to not be serious. Yatom added that: "It's very, very hard . . . to relate to specific information unless it's very clear and defined and the source is reliable."[7]

Intelligence and the reliability of sources were and still are vital factors in countering terrorism and major components for operational measures. Stella Rimington, a former head of MI-5, described intelligence work as comparable to "the unraveling of a knotted skein of wool. You get hold of an end and you have to follow it through until you are near enough to the heart of the knot to see what it consists of."[8]

Until the Mombassa attack, there was no clear internal Israeli definition about which intelligence agency was responsible for the evolving threat of al-Qaeda attacks on Israeli targets outside of its borders. The main Israeli focus was the protective measures of the Israeli Internal Security Agency (Shabak), responsible for securing Israeli and Jewish interests overseas. It is worth mentioning that from September 2000 (the outbreak of the second Palestinian intifada) until the Mombassa attack, Israeli intelligence efforts were focused mainly on the Israeli-Palestinian conflict and suicide attacks in Israeli cities. Security on the home front was a major factor in dictating the priorities of Israeli intelligence and security policy.

The Mombassa attacks, which came as surprise to Israel, represented a watershed moment that obliged the Israeli government to adjust its existing agencies and capacities to address the emerging threat. The Israeli intelligence community had to reallocate money and personnel; redefine its human intelligence, (HUMINT), signal intelligence (SIGINT), and open-sources intelligence (OSINT, mainly jihad-affiliated websites and media); broaden international intelligence cooperation; set up new priorities and methodologies; and embrace adaptive structural changes and synchronization within the chain of command. The Mombassa attack shifted Israeli counterterrorism policies regarding al-Qaeda from passive protective measures toward a more active and preemptive approach designed to dismantle al-Qaeda cells and threats on Israeli targets overseas.

Since the Mombassa attack, the Mossad "has improved dramatically its intelligence penetration into global jihad networks conspiring to attack Israeli targets overseas and has carried out successful covert special operations in thwarting planed attacks. These activities were highly classified and never took place in public view."[9] Intelligence and operational capabilities needed to evolve and meet new global jihadi threats with a broader focus, from the "near enemy" (the Israeli-Palestinian conflict and cross-border terrorism threats), to the "far enemy" (al-Qaeda and its affiliated global jihad groups).

CHARACTERISTICS OF AL-QAEDA'S POST-9/11 ATTACKS

Al-Qaeda officially claimed responsibility for the Mombassa attack six days after the fact in a statement broadcast by the Qatar-based al-Jazeera television channel.[10] The attacks conformed to the pattern of many post-9/11 al-Qaeda operations against soft targets ranging from tourist resorts, nightclubs, and synagogues to hotels and public transportation. In this manner, al-Qaeda seemed to demonstrate its ability to strike wherever and whenever it wished—preferably against less-protected and more accessible targets. The group was also intent on combining the searing psychological impact of mass-casualty suicide attacks with targets that would have a particularly high potential for economic disruption.[11]

This strategy was defined in al-Qaeda's "Economic Jihad" doctrine as published by Salem al-Maki on al-Qaeda-affiliated websites several days after the strike on the *Limburg* oil tanker in October 2002. The author, apparently with access to al-Qaeda's inner circles, stated that one of the objectives of jihad was to inflict strategic economic damage. It emphasized and confirmed that the attack against the World Trade Center and the French oil tanker and other strikes were part of the economic jihad concept.[12]

AL-QAEDA'S MASTERMIND

Fazul Abdullah Mohammad (alias Abdul Karim), orchestrated the attack and was the Mombassa network leader. Fazul was not unknown. He had been indicted by a U.S. court in connection to the 1998 al-Qaeda bombings of the U.S. embassies in Nairobi and Tanzania and was on the international watch list. Fazul comes from the Comoros Islands off East Africa, where he attended a Wahhabi madrassa and, at the age of sixteen, received a scholarship to study at a Wahhabi madrassa in Pakistan, where "Islamic militancy and military training were emphasized far more than religious scholarship." From Pakistan, he went to Afghanistan to join al-Qaeda and later to become the leader of al-Qaeda's network in East Africa. During the early 1990s, he moved to Nairobi, Kenya, and in 1994 became the secretary of Wadih el-Hage, a top bin Laden lieutenant who worked under the cover of a Muslim charity organization. In late 2001, Fazul traveled to Monrovia, Liberia, with another suspect in the embassy bombings, Ahmed Khalfan Ghailani. In 2002 it was reported that the "two men allegedly ran a lucrative al-Qaeda financing operation, trading illegal diamonds for cash." On July 12, 2002, four and a half months before the Mombassa attack, Fazul (already designated as wanted international terrorist) was arrested in Nairobi with Saleh Ali Nabhan for using forged credit cards. Fazul managed to fool the police and to escape shortly after his arrest.[13]

In August 2002, Fazul sneaked back into Kenya and began to organize the Paradise Hotel attack. Using the alias Abdul Karim, he spent much of the time before the attack at the farmhouse of some al-Qaeda collaborators, which served as the base of operation. A few days before the attack, after completing necessary operational preparations, Fazul fled back to Somalia.[14]

A 2003 draft report by the United Nations established that the terrorists involved in the Mombassa attack had received training and weapons in Somalia and that the perpetrators had fled back into Somalia after the attack.[15] In August 2003, Fazul barely escaped arrest when his Kenyan host blew himself up with a hand grenade in the old city of Mombassa, preventing the Kenyan police from catching Fazul. Again, in October 2003 he evaded arrest, arriving two hours late to a meeting with a former colleague who had cut a deal with the Kenyan authorities and become a police informant. In May of 2004, the FBI and the Department of Homeland Security included Fazul on its alert list, but by then he had temporarily disappeared.[16] On January 7, 2007, after the Ethiopian-Somali war ended, the United States carried out an airstrike in Somalia to kill Fazul, but he again managed to escape unharmed.[17]

PLANNING THE OPERATION

The Mombassa attacks were planned as two independent synchronized operations. The plotters were innovative in their use of sea routes to smuggle the weapons and explosives into Kenya and to facilitate their own infiltration and escape. The al-Qaeda attack team had actually first gathered in Mogadishu some two years earlier to plan the attacks. In December 2001, reconnaissance of potential targets in Kenya began, and by April 2002, a short list had been drawn up. Meanwhile, beginning that same month and lasting until August 2002, al-Qaeda team members held meetings in Mogadishu for continued indoctrination and specific weapons training in the use of pistols, AK-47 rifles, and hand grenades. Upon completion of these preparations, the team relocated to Mombassa in late August 2002, to safe houses provided by Fazul's local Kenyan collaborators. The preparations also included the smuggling shoulder-launched SA-7B missiles (shipped from Yemen to Somalia and then smuggled into Kenya in August 2002), and explosives bought in Somalia and smuggled into Kenya.[18]

Between August 2002 and October 2002, Omar Said Omar, a local Kenyan al-Qaeda collaborator, met several times with the cell members (Issa Osman Issa and Fazul) at the Mombassa Polytechnic Mosque to discuss preparations. During the meetings, Fazul instructed Omar Said Omar to go to Lamu Island harbor and purchase a boat. During those meetings, Fazul mentioned the fact that they were committed to carrying out a terrorist operation that would occur soon in the beach region.[19]

On November 20, 2002, Omar Said Omar received 20,000 Kenyan shillings from Issa Osman Issa to purchase the boat from Lamu Island and to rent a safe house for use immediately after the attack. One day before the attack, Omar called Issa on his cell phone to report that all of the preparations for the escape had been completed.[20]

Funds for the operation were funneled through Tariq Abdullah (a.k.a. Abu Talha al-Sudani), a Sudanese national and al-Qaeda member who operated between Somalia and the UAE. Abu Talha al-Sudani has been a senior al-Qaeda figure in East Africa since early 1990s and was implicated in the 1998 bombings of the U.S. embassies in Dar es Salaam, Tanzania, and Nairobi, Kenya.[21]

THE ATTACK

The attack in Mombassa was clearly intended to cause mass casualties. It was also innovative, entailing a multidimensional synchronized operation that comprised three types of operational aspects: a land-based suicide operation, an aviation attack employing surface-to-air missiles, and the use of the sea-borne dhows for infiltration and escape. Five perpetrators carried out the attacks, divided into two groups by Fazul.[22] The first group, charged with executing the suicide attack on the Paradise Hotel, included Fumo Muhammad Fumo and Harun Abdisheikh Bamusa, two local Kenyan al-Qaeda recruits who had taken part in the 1998 bombing of the American embassy in Nairobi.[23]

The second group, the aircraft assault group, comprised Issa Osman Issa, Saleh Ali Nabhan and Abdul Malik. Issa and Nabhan were both senior al-Qaeda operatives in East Africa who had been indicted in U.S. federal court in connection with the 1998 Nairobi embassy bombing. Abdul Malik was also a senior al-Qaeda operative based in East Africa. On the morning of November 28, just after a group of Israeli tourists had arrived to the lobby of Paradise hotel in the town of Kikambala, Fumo Mohamad Fumo and Harun Abdisheikh Bamusa launched the suicide attack. One of them blew himself up at the hotel's entrance. The second bomber crashed a Mitsubishi Pajero loaded with 200 kg of explosives and enhanced by gas canisters and containers of fuel into a wall of the hotel. The blast killed fifteen people and destroyed the hotel.[24]

The secondhand sport utility vehicle used in the attack had been purchased by Saleh Ali Nabhan. The explosive device was assembled in a farmhouse on the outskirts of Mombassa, under the direct supervision of Fazul Abdullah Mohammad. Two days before the attack, Fazul visited and briefed the suicide bombers. The ensuing Kenyan police investigation established that the suicide attackers had in their possession a 7.62 mm MpiKM assault rifle (an East German version of the AK-47 assault rifle), and a 7.62 mm Tokarev pistol S/No. CC33238 manufactured in the former Soviet Union.[25] This broke an established pattern because suicide bombers had never before been armed when sent on their missions. The suicide attackers may have prepared a contingency plan in case of a malfunction in the explosives. Or it is possible that terrorists that might have needed guns for their own protection or in an escape from security forces. The weapons were regularly stored in the car during the preparation stages and the attack.

Almost simultaneously, the second team, positioned at the end of the Mombassa International Airport runway, fired two shoulder-mounted anti-aircraft missiles toward the Arkia airliner carrying 261 passengers as it took off. Although the planning and the surveillance work of the airport in Mombassa were performed personally by Fazul, the missile attack was a complete failure.[26] MANPADS (man-portable air-defense system) is a cheap, widely proliferated weapon among terror organizations and state sponsors of terrorism. MANPADS is easy to use and conceal and poses a potentially lethal threat to all classes of aircraft.[27] Al-Qaeda demonstrated for the first time its operational strategy and ability to target a vulnerable civilian plane from a distant point on the ground. During the investigation, one on the key concerns within the international intelligence community was to trace the source of the MANPADS.

The MANPADS used in the attack were Strela-2/2M (SAM 7) missiles, serial number (9M32M, 04-78,041033,04-78) from a batch of weapons manufactured in 1973. The investigation established that the missiles' source was the same as that of missile remains that were found at Prince Sultan Air Base in Saudi Arabia in May 2002, probably intended to be fired at an American military plane.[28]

It remains unclear why the two missiles failed to hit their target, although investigators cite several possibilities. One is that the angle of attack or the plane's low altitude kept the explosives from charging. Another possibility is that the infrared seeker was faulty and failed to acquire the target. A third is that the target acquisition system could also have been outdated, or there was a fault in the missile's propulsion system. Of course the attack could also have failed because of operator ineptitude or inexperience. It's worth noting that this attack was the first time that al-Qaeda employed MANPADS and that it represents a turning point regarding future al-Qaeda operational threats.[29]

THE ESCAPE

During the investigation of Omar Said Omar, it was confirmed that after the attacks, the terrorists regrouped in Lamu Island harbor, returning to Somalia by boat.[30] According to Omar, Fazul's choice of Lamu Island was not accidental; from this isolated, largely Muslim coastal region, the perpetrators could slip away easily by boat toward the Persian Gulf or across the border into Somalia.[31] Omar Said Omar recounted that right after the morning attack, at approximately 10 a.m. Issa Osman Issa called him to inform him that the operation was over. Later that afternoon, Fazul contacted Omar to check if Issa Osman Issa, Saleh Ali Nabhan, and Abdul Malik (the missile attack team) had arrived safely to Lamu Island. On November 29 the group successfully escaped back to Somalia.[32]

Saleh Ali Nabhan joined al-Shabaab al-Mujahideen in Somalia and was added to the wanted list of the FBI in connection with the attacks in

Mombassa.[33] In March 2008, Nabhan was targeted by U.S. Navy Tomahawk missiles at a village in southern Somalia; this followed similar strikes in 2007 from which he managed to escape.[34] In 2008, Nabhan released a recorded message inciting jihad from Somalia, proving his escape from the attack and his continued active involvement in terrorism.[35] After a long international pursuit and almost seven years after the Mombassa attack, Saleh Ali Nabhan was killed in an American special operation on September 14, 2009.[36] Airborne U.S. Special Operations forces attacked a convoy carrying suspected al-Qaeda targets near the southern coastal town Barawe, Somalia. Nabhan was directly involved in the killing of 238 and wounding hundreds more in the 1998 bombings of the U.S. embassies in Kenya and Tanzania and the 2002 Mombassa attack.[37]

Issa Osman Issa also maintained contact with the radical group al-Shabaab al-Mujahideen and commanded a Council of Islamic Courts militia near the interim Somali capital of Baidoa.[38] Abdul Malik was finally apprehended on February 17, 2007, by Kenyan Anti-Terrorism Police Unit (ATPU) in Mombassa, and on March 27, 2007, he was handed over to American investigators, who transferred him to Guantánamo Bay, Cuba.[39] Fazul Abdullah—al-Qaeda's mastermind—is still at large.

THE NETWORK'S MEANS OF COMMUNICATIONS

The terrorist network involved in the two attacks used the Internet, satellite phones, cellular communications, and e-mail for communicating among themselves for reconnaissance and surveillance operations in Kenya.[40] These means of communications, known to be less monitored or supervised, were presumably considered by the network to be relatively safe. The network members used generic or widely available, publicly accessible e-mail accounts to communicate with one another, allowing the Internet to replace face-to-face contact.[41] The Kenyan cellular forensic investigation, aided by the Israeli Mossad's advanced tactical technologies, enabled the reconstruction of the operational stages and timeline of the attack, identifying cell members and collaborators. This operational intelligence enabled the engagement and pursuit of the perpetrators, who were at that time still at large.[42]

Cellular Phones Communications Forensic Analysis

During the preparation phase and the attacks, the perpetrators used cellular phones as the primary method of communication. The attackers implemented code words during their phone communications in case their conversations were monitored. Code words included "rain," for all is well; "dry," indicating a lot of police operations or tight security; "njuluku," for money; "wedding," as attack on targets; and "guest," for visitors. It is worth mentioning that in past events, Palestinian terror organizations have also used the code word "wedding" for terror attacks. The group also used primitive codes to hide real phone numbers.[43]

After the November 28 attack, Kenyan police used forensic cellular analysis, which established that Omar Said Omar was the subscriber and user of mobile telephone number 0722-610837 from early 2002, when planning of the terrorist attacks began. In January 2002, during the preparatory stages of the attack, Omar Said Omar purchased a prepaid cellular card at the local post office in the Kwale district in Mombassa. After the arrest of Omar Said Omar on August 1, 2003, his residence was searched, and two additional mobile phones were recovered. Further analysis of Omar Said Omar's cellular communications established that during November 2002, he conducted eight phone conversations with someone on a Somali landline in Mogadishu. Kenyan experts determined that this Somali landline was used as a central link of communication for the rest of the terror cell operatives who escaped after the attack and remained at large.[44]

Before the attack in Mombassa, the mobile phone used by Omar Said Omar placed calls to Sudan nine times and to Ethiopia once during November 2002. Omar Said Omar revealed during his interrogation that he used his mobile to contact the other mobiles used by all other perpetrators in the weeks before the attack (the Kenyan forensic investigation corroborated this). On November 28, the day of the operation, Omar coordinated the separate assaults from his mobile phone. At 5:15 a.m., Omar was called by Saleh Ali Nabhan, a member of the airliner attack cell, and at 5:27 a.m., he called Saleh Ali Nabhan after Fumo Mohammad Fumo, one of the suicide bombers, had also called Nabhan. At 10:25 a.m., immediately after the bomb blast, Omar called Nabhan again. Omar confessed that he left Mombassa for Lamu Island two days before the attack, arranging accommodation and means of escape back to Somalia for the others. On November 29, Omar switched off his mobile phone at approximately 11:51 p.m. when the escape back to Somalia had started.[45]

Fazul Abdullah's Cellular Communications

Kenyan police established that between November 4, 2002, and January 4, 2003, a mobile number held by Fazul Abdullah was used for communications with the cell members as well with local Kenyan al-Qaeda collaborators. During the police interrogation of Saleh Kubwa, another local collaborator, it was revealed that Fazul Abdullah resided in Kubwa's home in Kenya for almost two years and handed over his mobile phone to him.[46]

Through his cellular phone, Fazul Abdullah also communicated with a local Kenyan female, Fatuma Said Saggar, known to be the daughter of Said Saggar, another al-Qaeda collaborator. Fatuma is married to Mustafa Mohammad Fadhil, an Egyptian national and an al-Qaeda terrorist wanted for the 1998 bombing of the U.S. embassy in Nairobi. Further analysis of the landline belonging to Said Saggar revealed communications with other cell members involved in the bombing, including Issa Osman Issa, Saleh Ali Nabhan, and Fumo Mohammad Fumo.[47]

AL-QAEDA OPERATIONAL FINGERPRINTS

The Mombassa attack was the operational implementation of a strategic decision taken by al-Qaeda's leadership during 2001 and before September 11, 2001, to attack Jewish and Israeli targets. Based on transcripts of the hearing released by the Pentagon and the 9/11 commission report, Khalid Sheikh Mohammed (KSM) was "the operational director of Sheikh bin Laden and Al Qaeda's military operational commander for all foreign operations around the world under the direction of Sheikh Osama bin Laden and Dr. Ayman Al-Zawahiri." KSM claimed that according to bin Laden's directive given to him in early 2001, he sent an al-Qaeda operative Dhiren Barot (Issa al-Britani) to the United States to locate potential economic and "Jewish" targets in New York City. Later that year, in July,

KSM approached bin Laden with the idea of recruiting a Saudi Arabian air force pilot to seize a Saudi fighter jet and crash into buildings in the Israeli southern city of Eilat. Bin Laden reportedly liked KSM's proposal but instructed him to concentrate on the 9/11 operation first. Khalid Sheikh Muhammad described his position in al-Qaeda central leadership and has admitted responsibility for the bombing of the hotel in Mombassa and the launching of the SA-7 missiles.[48]

The Mombassa attack was planned and executed as a top-down al-Qaeda-led operation developed by a core of senior professionals and experienced operatives who had been involved in past terror attacks. To oversee the implementation of the attack, a top al-Qaeda regional leader directed the planning and maintained direct connections to al-Qaeda leadership. The investigation of the attacks established that Fazul Abdullah and at least seven of the network members were al-Qaeda operatives involved in the 1998 bombing of the U.S. embassy in Nairobi. Al-Qaeda's return to Kenya, a country where the organization had already carried out a terrorist attack, stemmed from its assessment of the weakness of the local security forces, who failed to apprehend the members of the network in Kenya in 1998.[49]

The investigation established the fact that the network comprised thirteen people (five attackers and eight local collaborators) who operated under the direction of Fazul Abdullah, a top al-Qaeda operative in East Africa. The attackers, mostly local Kenyan collaborators, were already involved in the 1998 U.S. embassy bombing in Nairobi, motivated by al-Qaeda ideology, and had professional terrorist operational experience.

The network in Kenya was based on local Muslim supporters of al-Qaeda, bound by personal, family, and matrimonial ties. These individuals formed a "knowledge hub" of al-Qaeda's accumulated ideological and operational knowledge, acting as authorized influence agents, facilitating critical information, operational knowledge, and worldwide personal connections and channels of financing.

The al-Qaeda attackers were recruited and aided by individuals from the wider Muslim community in Mombassa. They were married to daughters of local collaborators and maintained active lives within a small community linked by marriage, emotional commitment, and the obligation to fulfill the organization's goals. On June 23, 2003, Kenyan authorities officially accused a group of eight local Kenyan suspects of assisting in the Mombassa attack.[50]

Three of the attackers, the MANPADS, and the explosives used in the attack were smuggled into Kenya from Somalia aboard a commercial fishing boat. The maritime smuggling phase was led by local al-Qaeda collaborators using local dhow owners, who were acquainted with the naval routine and navigation in the region north of Lamu, one of Kenya's offshore islands. Local dhow owners are familiar with sea routes and naval commercial traffic and can blend into local maritime activity (which was probably already being monitored by international Task Force 150, which had deployed vessels in the Gulf of Aden after the 9/11 attacks).

The advanced coordination and motivational meetings took place in a Mombassa mosque and in residential houses. Fazul Abdullah's personal involvement leader was essential in the two critical phases. First was the preparation, in which personal commitment and bonds were established as motivational factors. The second phase came just before the attack, in which Fazul's airport surveillance data and operational instructions were presumably given to the missile group, along with the leader's ability to inspire as a representative of al-Qaeda.

SELECTION OF TARGETS: THE ECONOMIC JIHAD AND THE SHIFT TO SOFT TARGETS

Al-Qaeda identified the targets in Kenya as suitable because they were soft and unprotected. Al-Qaeda also exploited the fact that Kenya, given its lax security, was unable to efficiently enforce its own laws. Kenya was also convenient as a staging point for the operation because of the presence of a local, supportive, radical Islamic infrastructure. Additionally, Kenya's costal area is inhabited by a large Muslim community.

Osama bin Laden's "Declaration of War Against the Americans Occupying the Land of the Two Holy Places" as published in the London based Arabic newspaper *al-Quds al-Arabi* in 1996, and his sequel declaration from February 23, 1998, establishing the "World Islamic Front for Jihad Against Jews and Crusaders" legitimized attacks against Americans and Zionists.[51] But at the same time, the Mombassa attack reflected a change of emphasis, a shifting and evolving strategy adopted by al-Qaeda after 9/11, which focused primarily on attacking soft targets with high potential for economic disruption, creating economic instability while maintaining emphasis on suicide strikes inflicting mass casualties.

During the years after the Mombassa attack, both bin Laden and Ayman al-Zawahiri emphasized in their statements the need to cause economic damages to Western interests. In a 2004 statement, bin Laden said that Muslims were called "to attack reinforcement lines and oil (pipe) lines, to sow powerful mines . . . and to assassinate the owners of companies aiding the needs of the enemy, whether in Riyadh, Kuwait, Jordan, Turkey, or other (countries)."[52]

In 2006, as a reaction to cartoons of the prophet Muhammad published in Denmark, al-Zawahiri called on Muslims to "cause damages to the Western Crusades through bleeding attacks . . . prevent the West from stealing Muslim oil—the big theft in history . . . conduct popular economic boycott against: Denmark, Norway, France, Germany and countries attacked and humiliated Islam and Muslims."[53]

The Mombassa attack was the first direct attack by al-Qaeda specifically against an Israeli-owned tourist resort and an Israeli airliner, which were both regarded by al-Qaeda as soft targets. Up until then, al-Qaeda had attacked only Jewish tourist or worship places that were not identified as Israeli. The first successful al-Qaeda attack on a Jewish target occurred after 9/11 when the ancient synagogue in Djerba, Tunisia, was attacked on April 11, 2002. The Mombassa attack followed this pattern, adding a new dimension: direct confrontation with Israel.[54]

AL-QAEDA CLAIMS RESPONSIBILITY

The day after the attacks, a false statement was issued by an unknown organization, "Jaish Falastin" (the Army of Palestine), claiming responsibility for the attack in a printed leaflet in Arabic that appeared on Islamic websites and was distributed to Western news agencies in Beirut.[55] On December 2, 2002, the authentic al-Qaeda claim of responsibility was published on a number of websites associated with the group under the name "Tanzim Qaedat al-Jihad—the Political Office."[56] Al-Qaeda's audio and written statement was posted on several websites that had carried al-Qaeda statements in the past and was then broadcast by the Qatar-based al-Jazeera television channel.[57]

Suleiman Abu Ghaith, al-Qaeda's formal spokesman, issued a statement of responsibility posted on an Islamic website affiliated with al-Qaeda on the occasion of the Muslim holiday 'Eid al-Fiter. According to the statement, "The Jewish Crusader coalition will not be safe anywhere from the fighters' attacks." Abu Ghaith warned of more attacks on American and Israeli targets by land, air, and sea: "We will hit the most vital centers and we will strike against strategic operations with all possible means."[58] In addition, the message indicated that the attack was intended to smash the dreams of the Jewish-Crusader alliance, safeguard Muslim interests in the region, and demonstrate to Muslims around the world the steadfastness of the mujaheddin to the Palestinian cause, and protest against Israel's occupation of the holy places.[59] Al-Qaeda's statement reiterated that its operatives were acting as agents of the Muslim *umma* against the "Jews and Crusaders" while blurring the missile attack fiasco orchestrated by al-Qaeda's top leader in East Africa, Fazul. The statement "was providing the Mombassa operation justification that was all the more necessary because the attack had fallen so far short of its original goals."[60]

STRATEGIC INSIGHTS AND IMPLICATIONS

Terrorist Safe Havens

The safe havens in Somalia and Kenya, the availability of electronic communication, and maritime lawlessness were three key factors that contributed to al-Qaeda's operational success. Somalia and Kenya serve as safe havens and are exploited by terrorists to indoctrinate, recruit, train, and regroup followers, as well as to prepare and support their operations. Al-Qaeda's return to a country where the organization had already carried out a terrorist attack stemmed from its assessment of the weakness of the local security forces. According to a high-ranking Kenyan police official, al-Qaeda based its selection of Kenya as a convenient target on the presence of a local network, which functioned freely among the large Muslim community in Mombassa and along the Kenyan shore.[61]

Maritime Safe Havens

The attack also emphasized the lack of maritime security in the Horn of Africa, exploited by al-Qaeda for smuggling, infiltration, and escape, using the routes between Somalia and Kenya. The region in general and Kenya in particular has insufficiently integrated command and control centers, poor early warning and intelligence capabilities, and no maritime air surveillance and reconnaissance capability to monitor, deter, or engage infiltrations and cross-border terrorism.[62] Within Kenya, the lack of a credible well trained maritime force with sufficient mobility, flexibility, and firepower for sustainable operations and deterrence allows terrorists to operate with ease.[63]

The international Combined Task Force 150, established in 2001 for policing the lawless maritime routes in the Horn of Africa, was ineffective against the Mombassa plot.[64] In retrospect, the CTF 150 tried to track possible al-Qaeda boat traffic among Kenya, Somalia, and Pakistan but was unable to stop the suspected crucial traffic between Somalia and Kenya before the November 28 attack.[65]

The Mombassa attack highlighted the continuation of al-Qaeda's soft-target strategy and introduced innovative operational trends in its top-down strategy after 9/11. These were the attempt to down a civilian airliner from the ground, the cross-border sea infiltration of terror operatives and weapons, and the first deliberate attack on Israeli targets.

Three of the Mombassa attackers, already notorious as al-Qaeda members who were directly were involved in the 1998 embassies attacks, were operating undisrupted, free to carry out the Mombassa attack. Although their identity was known and some of them were indicted in U.S. court, local East African and international law enforcement and intelligence agencies were unresponsive to the evolving threat posed by these individuals. According to the 9/11 commission, after the 1998 embassy bombings, "although disruption efforts around the world had achieved some successes, the core of bin Laden's organization remained intact."[66]

Al-Qaeda has reintroduced the MANPADS as a threat to aviation. Although terror organizations had used MANPADS in two failed attempts to gun down Israeli airliners in Rome and Nairobi in the mid-1970s,[67] the

Mombassa attack was the first time since then that the system was used by a terror organization against an Israeli plane.

The assaults bore many of al-Qaeda's trademarks: simultaneous, well-organized, and coordinated attacks that were based on good intelligence and precision timing, in a part of East Africa where al-Qaeda previously operated. The attack was carried out by the same al-Qaeda network involved in the 1998 attacks on U.S. embassies in Kenya and Tanzania and was one of the most sophisticated terror attacks attempted to date by al-Qaeda, despite the failed missile launch.

NOTES

1. "Israeli Report Links Kenya Terrorist to Al Qaeda," CNN, November 29, 2002. See also Foreign Minister Benjamin Netanyahu, press conference, Jerusalem, November 28, 2002, at http://www.mfa.gov.il/MFA/Government/Speeches+by+Israeli+lead ers/2002/Press+Conference+by+FM+Netanyahu-+Terror+attacks+i.htm.

2. U.S. Department of State, "Patterns of Global Terrorism," April 30, 2003, available at http://www.state.gov/s/ct/rls/crt/2002/html/19981.htm.

3. "Simultaneous Attacks on Israeli Tourists in Kenya," Fox News, November 28, 2002, available at http://www.foxnews.com/story/0,2933,71672,00.html; *Ha'aretz*, December 2, 2002.

4. "Simultaneous Attacks on Israeli Tourists in Kenya".

5. CNN Transcripts, December 2, 2002, available at http://transcripts.cnn.com /TRANSCRIPTS/0212/02/asb.00.html.

6. "Summary of Evidence for Combatant Status Review Tribunal—Khalid Sheikh Muhammad," Department of Defense, Office for the Administrative Review of the Detention of Enemy Combatants at US Naval Base, Guantanamo Base, Cuba, February 8, 2007, 17, available at http://projects.nytimes.com/guantanamo/detainees/10024 -khalid-shaikh-mohammed/documents/5/pages/828#20. Also see Thomas H. Kean et al., *The 9/11 Commission Report: Final Report of the National Commission on Terrorist Attacks Upon the United States* (New York: Norton, 2004), 150, available at http://www.9 -11commission.gov/report/911Report.pdf.

7. "Israel knew Kenya Was Target," BBC, December 3, 2002, http://news.bbc .co.uk/2/hi/africa/2538997.stm.

8. Stella Rimington, "Humint Begins at Home," *Wall Street Journal*, January 3, 2005.

9. Interview with a former top Mossad official, Tel Aviv, September 14, 2009.

10. "Al Qaeda Claims Responsibility for Kenya Attack," *Financial Times*, December 8, 2002.

11. Yoni Fighel and Yoram Kehati, "Mending the Hearts of the Believers—Analysis of Recent Al-Qaida Documents, Part 1," *Institute for Counter-Terrorism*, November 28,

2002, available at http://212.150.54.123/articles/articledet.cfm?articleid=453. Also see Abd al-Aziz 'Anzi, "Ruling on Targeting the Oil Facilities and the Basis for Economic Jihad," 2004, Supplement of the declaration of al-Qaeda in Arabia on the attack in the oil field of al-Buqayq, February 2006, available at http://www.e-prism.org/images/Al-Anazi_-_Hukm_Istihdaf_al-Masaleh_al-Naftiyyah.pdf.

12. Abd al-Aziz 'Anzi, "Rulling Ruling on Targeting the Oil Facilities."

13. Steve Coll, Ghost Wars: *The Secret History of the CIA, Afghanistan, and bin Laden, from the Soviet Invasion to September 10, 2001* (New York: Penguin, 2005), 403–4; Federal Bureau of Investigation, FBI Most Wanted Terrorists, Fazul Abdullah Mohammad, available at http://www.fbi.gov/wanted/terrorists/termohammed.htm; "The Journey of Harun Fazul," *Frontline*, PBS. http://www.pbs.org/wgbh/pages/frontline/shows/saudi/fazul/; "U.N.: Al Qaeda Terrorists Trained, Bought Weapons in Somalia," *USA Today*, November 4, 2003; "Profile: Ahmed Khalfan Ghailani," BBC, May 21, 2009, available at http://news.bbc.co.uk/2/hi/africa/3938267.stm; Omri Asenhaim, *Ma'ariv* (Tel Aviv), October 3, 2005, 18. See also Fazul Abdullah Mohammed, "Global Jihad," available at http://www.globaljihad.net/view_page.asp?id=235.

14. Asenhaim, *Ma'ariv* (Tel Aviv), October 3, 2005, 18.

15. "U.N.: Al Qaeda Terrorists Trained, Bought Weapons in Somalia."

16. "Ashcroft, Mueller News Conference," CNN, May 26, 2004, at http://www.cnn.com/2004/US/05/26/terror.threat.transcript/. See also "News About Fazul Abdullah Mohammed," *New York Times*, June 13, 2011, http://topics.nytimes.com/topics/reference/timestopics/people/m/fazul_abdullah_mohammed/index.html.

17. "Profile: Fazul Abdullah Mohammed," *Global Security*, http://www.globalsecurity.org/security/profiles/fazul_abdullah_mohammed.htm. See also "Raid Killed Somali Allies of Al Qaeda," *New York Times*, January 12, 2007.

18. Office of OIC Prosecutions, High Court Nairobi, Kenya, Superintendent John Muthusi Mulaulu, Anti-Terrorism Police Unit, Nairobi, statement.

19. Office of OIC Prosecutions, High Court Nairobi, Kenya, "Anti Terrorist Police Witness Statements—Suicide of Al Qaeda Suspect—Mombassa," in NO. 219209, Superintendent John Muthusi Mulaulu.

20. Office of OIC Prosecutions, High Court, Nairobi, Kenya, Omar Said Omar police statement.

21. U.S. Department of State, "Eliminating the Terrorist Threat—al-Qaida Operatives in Somalia," January 25, 2007 http://web.archive.org/web/20070214092116/http://www.state.gov/p/af/rls/fs/2007/79383.htm

22. Three of the attackers are known to be involved in the 1998 bombing of the U.S embassy in Nairobi.

23. Office of OIC Prosecutions High Court Nairobi, Kenya, "Government Chemist Department Analysis," report Reference No.: L.4/02, KIJIPWA INQ.12/2002.

24. Ibid.; Kenyan Police sketch of the Paradise Hotel scene, exhibit memo form, general view of the scene, December 2, 2002.

25. Office of OIC Prosecutions, "Government Chemist Department Analysis"; Kenya Police Report of Examining Officer CID/F'ARMS LAB/635/2002 and LAB 239/2003.

26. Omar Said Omar police statement; Office of OIC Prosecutions, High Court Nairobi, Kenya, Paradise Hotel Bombing Trial, documentary/exhibit evidence bundle, C/O BOX 84996.

27. Arms Control Association, "Countering the MANPADS Threat Strategies for Success," September 2007, available at http://www.armscontrol.org/ (accessed September 25, 2008).

28. Shaul Shay, *The Shahids: Islam and Suicide Attack* (Herziya: Interdisciplinary Center of Herziya, 2004), 134.

29. H. D. Kuhn, "Mombassa Attack Highlights Increasing MANPAS Threat," *Jane's Intelligence Review* 15, no. 2 (February 2003): 29.

30. Office of OIC Prosecutions, Superintendent John Muthusi Mulaulu, statement.

31. U.S. Department of State, "Country Reports on Terrorism—Terrorist Safe Havens," Office of the Coordinator for Counterterrorism, April 28, 2006, http://www.state.gov/s/ct/rls/crt/2005/64333.htm.

32. Office of OIC Prosecutions, Superintendent John Muthusi Mulaulu, statement.

33. Shabaab al-Mujahideen was designated by the United States as a foreign terrorist organization on February 29, 2008.

34. "Notorious Al Qaeda Operative the Target in U.S. Strike in Somalia," Fox News, March 3, 2008, available at http://www.foxnews.com/story/0,2933,334531,00.html. Also see "Top Militant Saleh Ali Saleh Nabhan 'Killed' in Helicopter Raid on Somali Village," *Times* (London), September 15, 2009, available at http://www.timesonline.co.uk/tol/news/world/africa/article6834451.ece.

35. "Shabaab al-Mujahideen Media Wing—Video Statement from the Commander Sheikh Saleh Nabhan," NEFA Foundation, October 10, 2008, available at http://www.nefafoundation.org/miscellaneous/somaliashebab0908.pdf.

36. "Kenyan Behind 2002 Attacks on Israelis Said Killed in Somalia," *Ha'aretz* (Tel Aviv), September 14, 2009, available at http://www.haaretz.com/hasen/spages/1114493.html.

37. "Elite U.S. Forces Kill Top Al Qaeda Fighter," *Wall Street Journal*, September 15, 2009. Also see "Terrorist Wanted Over 2002 Attacks in Kenya Killed in Somalia Raid," *Jerusalem Post*, September 14, 2009.

38. U.S. Department of State, "Saleh Ali Saleh Nabhan: Senior al-Qaida Operative in East Africa; Wanted for Questioning in Connection with the 2002 Attacks Against a Hotel and an Israeli Airliner in Mombasa, Kenya," http://web.archive.org/web/20070214092116/http://www.state.gov/p/af/rls/fs/2007/79383.htm

39. "Profile: Kenyan Terror Suspect," BBC News, March 27, 2007, available at http://news.bbc.co.uk/1/hi/world/africa/6500333.stm; "Kenya Suspect Moved to Guantanamo," al-Jazeera TV, March 27, 2007, available at http://english.aljazeera.net/news/americas/2007/03/200852512583876870.html.

40. Office of OIC Prosecutions, Superintendent John Muthusi Mulaulu, statement.

41. Office of OIC Prosecutions, "Anti Terrorist Police Witness statements—Suicide of Al Qaeda suspect—Mombassa."

42. Interview with former top ranking Mossad official, Tel Aviv, September 14, 2009.

43. Office of OIC Prosecutions, "Anti Terrorist Police Witness Statements—Suicide of Al Qaeda Suspect—Mombassa."

44. Ibid.

45. Office of OIC Prosecutions, High Court, Nairobi, Kenya, "Further Statement of Inspector Paul Mumo," September 3, 2003.

46. Fazul Abdullah's cellular communications revealed that he communicated with Mohammad Kubwa, a local Kenyan member of the network, and with two other local collaborators, Aboud Rogo, and Hania Rogo. Another mobile phone used by Fazul Abdullah was used to communicate with mobile number 0722-669566, held by a local Kenyan collaborator named Kubwa Mohammad Seif. Office of OIC Prosecutions, High Court, Nairobi, Kenya, police inspector Paul Mumo statutory declaration, April 3, 2003, CID. HQRS.

47. Ibid.

48. "Summary of Evidence for Combatant Status Review Tribunal—Khalid Sheikh Muhammad"; Kean et al., *The 9/11 Commission Report.*

49. "Same Suspects Tied to Mombassa and '98 Embassy Attacks," *New York Times*, February 22, 2003.

50. According to statutory declaration given by inspector Paul Mumo, criminal investigation department, 312/318/02 (3.4.03 CID.HQRS), Kenyan national Fatuma Said Saggar married Mustafa Mohammad Fadhil, an Egyptian national, and a wanted al-Qaeda terrorist for the 1998 bombing of the U.S. embassy in Nairobi. Fatuma Ahmad, a local Kenyan female married Saleh Ali Nabhan. Amina Badroudine Fazul, born in October 1976, a Comoro national, married Fazul as his first wife on April 4, 1994. See "Deposition of Harun Fazul's Wife," *Frontline*, PBS; Court of Appeal of Moroni, September 18, 1998, available at http://www.pbs.org/wgbh/pages/frontline/shows/saudi/fazul/depo.html. Amina Kubwa, a Kenyan national, is the daughter of local Kenyan al-Qaeda collaborator Kubwa Mohammed and married Fazul Abdullah Mohammed in late December 2002. Office of OIC Prosecutions, High Court, Nairobi, Paradise Hotel Bombing Trial, Copy of Judge's File, "Witness Evidence Bundle," 92.

51. See http://www.pbs.org/newshour/terrorism/international/fatwa_1996.html; "Nass Bayan al-Jabhah al-Islamiyah al-Alamiyah li-Jihad al-Yahud wa-al-Salibiyin" (Declaration of the World Islamic Front for Jihad against Jews and Crusaders), *al-Quds al-Arabi*, February 23, 1998, 3.

52. Osama bin Laden, "To the Muslims in Iraq in Particular and the (Islamic) Nation in General," videocassette, December 27, 2004, available at http://www.dazzled.com/soiraq/Index.htm.

53. "Zawahiri Audio Tape," al-Jazeera Television, March 4, 2006. Also see "Al Zawahiri Video Reference," Intel Center, August 2, 2006, 10, available at http://www .intelcenter.com/ZVR-V1-7.pdf.

54. "The New Realities of Terror," *Time*, December 1, 2002, available at http:// www.time.com/time/magazine/article/0,9171,1101021209-395237,00.html.

55. "Jaish Falastin Yatabana Hugumei Kenya" (Palestine Army claims responsibility on Kenya attacks), Islamonline.net, November 29, 2002.

56. Published on websites linked to al-Qaeda: www.asfalrasas.com and www.arabforum.net. Also see "Statement on Al-Qaida Website Claims Kenya Attacks," Institute for Counter-Terrorism, December 2, 2002, available at http://212.150.54.123/spotlight /det.cfm?id=851.

57. See http://www.jehad.net/index.htm (accessed December 8, 2002); also see "Al Qaeda Claims Responsibility for Kenya Attack."

58. See http://www.jehad.net/index.htm (accessed December 8, 2002).

59. "Qaeda Claims Link to Kenya Attacks," *Ha'aretz* (Tel Aviv), December 3, 2002.

60. Gilles Kepel, *The War for Muslim Minds: Islam and the West* (Cambridge, Mass.: Harvard University Press, 2004), 126–28.

61. Interview with police provincial commissioner of the Nairobi area, June 2009.

62. Thean Potgieter, "The Maritime Security Quandary in the Horn of Africa," discussion paper, Stellenbosch University, January 2008, 5, available at http://www.hss .or.ke/documents/MaritimeSecurity.pdf.

63. Ibid., 4; interview with a group of police commissioners, Nairobi, June 2009.

64. The International Maritime Force adjunct of "Operation Enduring Freedom" was launched by the United States in response to the 9/11 attacks. Also see U.S. Fifth Fleet Combined Maritime Forces, "Combined Task Force 150," available at http:// www.cusnc.navy.mil/cmf/150/index.html; "Coalition Naval Force Secures Energy Assets," *Gulf Times* (Doha), December 13, 2007.

65. "U.S. Suspects Qaeda Link to Bombing in Mombassa," *New York Times*, November 30, 2002.

66. Kean et al., *The 9/11 Commission Report*, 174.

67. In January 1973, the Palestinian "Black September" terror organization smuggled fourteen SA-7 missiles into Italy, planning to attack the airplane of Prime Minister Golda Meir of Israel. On January 25, 1976, Baader Meinhof group members (with PLO associate Wadia Hadad) were arrested during an unsuccessful attempt to gun down an Israeli El Al airliner at the Nairobi airport with Soviet-made Strella ground-to-air missiles.

[18]

The Origins of Sectarian Terrorism in Iraq

MOHAMMED M. HAFEZ

On February 22, 2006, as night turned to dawn, an explosion rocked the Iraqi city of Samarra. The powerful blast destroyed the awe-inspiring golden dome of the al-Askari shrine, one of the four major Shiite shrines of Iraq, and among its holiest. It is the burial place of Ali al-Hadi (d. 868) and his son, Hassan al-Askari (d. 874), the revered tenth and eleventh imams, respectively. According to the Twelver tradition, the largest branch of Shiism and the second largest in Islam after Sunnism, the shrine is the place near which the twelfth imam, Muhammad al-Mahdi, son of Hassan al-Askari, is believed to have entered into occultation in the ninth century. The Shiite faithful await his return to redeem humanity and usher in justice and peace on earth before Judgment Day; his reappearance is central to Shiite eschatology.[1]

The bombing of the al-Askari shrine struck at the heart of Shiite symbolism and identity. Its intent was to insult, enrage, and, above all, provoke Iraq's Shiites into random acts of violence toward their Sunni countrymen. The bombing did indeed open the gates of hell in Iraq as sectarian bloodletting reached new heights. Iraqis turned on one another as never before—Shiites killing Sunnis, Sunnis killing Shiites. In interviews with Iraqis in Amman, Jordan, I was introduced to the Arabic expression "qatl 'ala al-hawiyah [killing based on one's identity]."[2] It was repeated often, each time with gory details about sectarian abductions, intimidation letters, bullets to the head, holes drilled in skulls, and savage beheadings.

Iraqis turned to sectarian militias for security and retribution because it appeared to them that the Iraqi government was incapable of offering its citizens basic protection from insurgents and death squads.[3] Muqtada al-Sadr's Mahdi Army, in particular, benefited tremendously from the rage fueled by the Samarra bombing as his militias went on a rampage to clear Sunnis from mixed neighborhoods in Baghdad, seize their property, and offer Shiites fleeing predominantly Sunni areas shelter and services.[4]

The actual death toll of sectarian violence is hard to measure. Data collected by the Brookings Institution show that Iraqi civilian fatalities surged after February 2006 to more than 3,500 per month. Civilian death rates did not drop below 2,000 per month until September 2007, a month after al-Sadr's Mahdi Army declared a unilateral cessation of militant activities and three months after U.S. forces completed their troop surge in Baghdad.[5] In 2006 and 2007, it was common to turn the pages of a newspaper and find images of dead Iraqis with bound hands and mutilated faces dumped in the side of a street or next to scattered garbage.

In addition to the rise of the death toll, the sectarian conflict produced mass migration and the internal displacement of both Sunnis and Shiites. According to the United Nations Assistance Mission for Iraq, more than 700,000 Iraqis fled their homes to escape sectarian killing and intimidation following the shrine attack. Many sought ethnically homogenous areas inside the country, and others fled to neighboring states.[6]

Just as damaging as these casualty and migration rates is the deep and lingering mistrust between the various communities of Baghdad. What began as spontaneous acts of violence born out of rage quickly turned into a systematic campaign to cleanse sect-mixed neighborhoods. Criminal gangs and kidnapping syndicates connected to militias, police, and death squads linked to the interior ministry were implicated in this violence.[7] Local militias set up checkpoints to control access to the newly redefined sectarian boundaries, as well as to mete out revenge against the opposite sect. In a tragicomic turn of events, Sunnis had to learn the names of the twelve Shiite imams in case they were quizzed by militiamen at the many checkpoints that sprouted in Baghdad, even before the Samarra bombing.[8]

According to Muwaffak al-Rubaie, the national security adviser to the Iraqi government, the principle culprit behind the Samarra bombing is an Iraqi named Haitham Sabah Shaker Mohammed al-Badri, an al-Qaeda in Iraq (AQI) military commander in the Salahuddin province and previously a government official under Saddam Hussein. Al-Badri led a team of seven men—two Iraqis, four Saudis, and a Tunisian with the nom de guerre Abu Qudamah al-Tunisi (his real name is Yosri ben Fakher Trigui).[9] Dressed in Iraqi Special Forces attire, the men entered the shrine the night of February 21 and proceeded to detain five interior ministry Facilities Protection Service guards in a small room. Over the next few hours, the terrorists carefully rigged explosives to the interior of the shrine to ensure the destruction of its stunning golden dome. At 6:55 a.m. they detonated their bombs as they fled the scene.

Al-Badri, who was killed in an airstrike by U.S. forces east of Samarra on August 2, 2007, had been under the command of another Iraqi named Hamid Juma Faris Jouri al-Saeedi (also known as Abu Humam and Abu Rana). Al-Saeedi was captured in August 2006 and is believed to be a high-ranking commander in AQI, which was led by Abu Musab al-Zarqawi before he was killed by a U.S. airstrike north of Baqubah on June 7, 2006.[10]

Although these claims cannot be verified independently, they seem credible in light of the sectarian war that AQI has been waging against the Shiites of Iraq since 2003. The Samarra bombing was not the first catastrophic strike against the symbols of Shiism in Iraq, nor would it be the last. The first major attack took place on August 29, 2003, when a car bomb detonated by a suicide bomber exploded outside the Imam Ali shrine in Najaf, killing Grand Ayatollah Mohammed Baqr al-Hakim along with several dozen worshippers. The perpetrator is believed to be Yassin Jarad, the father of al-Zarqawi's second wife.[11]

Seven months later, on March 2, 2004, insurgents carried out several explosions in Baghdad and Karbala during the Shiite Ashura processions, killing 181 people. Six months after that, on December 19, a suicide bomber killed at least forty-seven people in a funeral procession near the Imam Ali Shrine in Najaf. On that same day, a suicide car bomb in Karbala killed at least twelve people near the twin shrines of Hussein and Abbas and near the home of Grand Ayatollah Ali al-Sistani. Eight days later, a suicide bomber detonated his vehicle outside the home of Abdul Aziz al-Hakim, the son of Muhammad Baqr al-Hakim and the head of the Islamic Supreme Council of Iraq (ISCI, previously known as Supreme Council of the Islamic Revolution in Iraq, SCIRI) until he died of lung cancer in 2009.[12]

In addition to attacks on Shiite shrines, processions, and religious and political representatives, AQI targeted ordinary Shiites in markets and neighborhoods, wantonly killing men, women, and children. One of the most devastating attacks was carried out by Raed Mansour al-Banna, a Jordanian suicide bomber deployed by AQI, on February 28, 2005, in Hilla, south of Baghdad, killing 125 people.[13] Overall, Iraq witnessed 1,178 suicide bombings between March 2003 and December 2008, 250 of which targeted civilians in markets, buses, mosques, and processions. Most suicide bombings targeted Iraqi security forces, which are largely populated by Shiites.[14]

These facts and figures raise a number of important questions. First, why would AQI engage in a ferocious campaign of violence against Iraq's Shiite population? What lay behind this campaign against the Shiites—strategic calculus or religious fanaticism? Second, who inspired this strategy of sectarian warfare? Was it Iraqi leaders driven by local grievances or external leaders affiliated with the al-Qaeda global terror network? What role, if any, did Osama bin Laden, the leader of al-Qaeda before his violent demise in 2011, and Ayman al-Zawahiri, previously his deputy and now the leader of al-Qaeda, play in shaping the strategic orientation of AQI? An examination of the Samarra bombing and AQI's sectarian terrorism reveals the nature and limits of al-Qaeda's transnational terrorist network.

An analysis of AQI's campaign against Iraq's Shiite population between 2003 and 2008 offers three conclusions. First, AQI's anti-Shiite strategy was concocted inside Iraq by al-Zarqawi with minimal consultation with external al-Qaeda leaders. It is a product of Iraq's sectarian makeup, the realignment of power relations following the precipitous collapse of the old regime, and the ambition of one man to earn a place in the pantheon of jihad heroes. Second, al-Qaeda leaders saw AQI's strategy as a liability and tried to convince Zarqawi to refocus his violence on the occupation forces and the new Iraqi government. In other words, rather than drive the strategy, al-Qaeda leaders in Pakistan sought to redirect it after the fact. Ultimately, but grudgingly, they accepted the reality of sectarian warfare imposed by AQI because they valued having an insurgent movement bear their brand in Iraq over the prospect of being marginalized completely from a central front in the war against the United States. The third and final conclusion is that the case of AQI strongly suggests that al-Qaeda's transnational jihadist movement, at least in Iraq at the time, is fragmented and operationally decentralized. This is not to argue that the movement is one of leaderless jihad, but it does call into question the extent to which al-Qaeda leaders have been able to set the agenda of Islamist insurgent movements, much less call the shots when it comes to strategies, tactics, and targets in insurgent theaters. Al Qaeda's leaders in Pakistan are undoubtedly planning intricate conspiracies to attack Western states and secular governments in the Muslim world, but their influence over active insurgent movements such as AQI is more apparent than real. Nonetheless, sectarian violence in Iraq is orchestrated and perpetrated by a hierarchical terrorist organization with a clear strategy to undermine the emerging Iraqi state and produce a situation conducive to the survival of an otherwise marginal and ideologically unappealing insurgent group in Iraq.

ABU MUSAB AL-ZARQAWI AND THE ORIGINS OF AQI

The rapid demise of one of the most oppressive regimes in the world created new political grievances and opportunities in Iraq. The U.S. invasion of Iraq in 2003 and the subsequent occupation by coalition forces threatened Iraq's Sunnis, who were blamed for the sins of Saddam Hussein, and empowered Shiites and Kurds, who had been marginalized and oppressed by his regime. As expected, foreign occupations engender resistance and insurgency, and Iraq was no exception to the rule. An insurgency began in August 2003, led by local and highly decentralized groups of nationalists, disenfranchised Baathists, disgruntled former soldiers, Saddam loyalists, local Islamists, and foreign jihadists.[15] It is the latter, in particular, who seem to have been the unlikely beneficiaries of insurgency in Iraq.

Foreign fighters in Iraq exhibited multiple motivations that can be divided into two broad but overlapping categories. The first consists of individuals seeking to fight against the invaders of a Muslim Arab country under false pretenses. They believe that the United States and its allies are self-interested powers seeking oil, greater security for Israel, and compliant regimes that do not challenge American hegemony. Their aim is to fight U.S. forces and local collaborators that welcome occupation forces in Iraq. Some of these volunteers are martyrdom seekers, hoping to fight and die for God.[16]

The second category of foreign jihadists sees the war in Iraq in broader strategic terms: as an opportunity not only to expel U.S. forces but also to establish a genuine Islamic state based on the model of the Prophet Muhammad and his companions. This emirate would be the launching pad for regional jihads to topple secular regimes and build a pan-Islamic union akin to the caliphates that reigned over Muslims for so many centuries before the advent of the modern nation-state. Such an objective requires the establishment of a strategic base for the global jihadist movement in the heart of the Arab world, the birthplace of Islam. A base in Iraq would give global jihadists new strategic depth because it would operate in a country with a substantial geographic area that borders on Saudi Arabia, Jordan, Turkey, Syria, Kuwait, and Iran. Four of these countries are close allies of the United States and, thus, possible targets for the jihadists. The other two (Iran and Syria) are detested by radical Salafists because they are ruled by Shiites. A base in Iraq would be a major achievement for the global jihadist movement.

A monograph linked to the al-Qaeda movement, entitled "Jihad in Iraq: Hopes and Dangers," affirms the importance of Iraq for the global jihad: "If the United States is defeated this time—and this is what we pray will happen—the doors will open wide to the Islamic tide. For the first time in modern history, we will have an advanced foundation for Islamic awakening and jihad close to the land of the two mosques [Saudi Arabia] and Al-Aqsa mosque [Jerusalem]."[17]

Abu Musab al-Zarqawi, the founder of AQI, is emblematic of the second category. He was born on October 30, 1966, as Ahmad Fadil al-Khalayilah of the Bani-Hasan clan in the dilapidated city of Al-Zarqa in Jordan. In 1989, as a wayward young man, al-Zarqawi traveled to Pakistan and Afghanistan, apparently to take part in the fighting between Afghan factions and the communist regime that was left to fend for itself after the departure of Soviet forces. In 1993, he returned to Jordan and was arrested a year later for plotting terrorism with others against the Jordanian monarchy. In 1999, he was released from prison under a general amnesty issued by the newly enthroned King Abdullah II. Al-Zarqawi returned to Afghanistan, this time with plans to train fellow militants from the Levant region.[18] He set up a camp in Herat, Afghanistan, near the Iranian border, for the purpose of training like-minded militants in guerrilla warfare.

The invasion of Afghanistan following 9/11 and the demise of the Taliban regime left al-Zarqawi and his network in a lurch. The rapid collapse of the Taliban resistance meant that fighting was futile. Al-Zarqawi and his men were never part of the Taliban regime, but instead used Afghanistan as a haven to build their capabilities to attack their own government. Fleeing was the best choice, but going back to Jordan was not a viable option given that he was a wanted man in that country.

In late 2001, al-Zarqawi made plans to move his cadres to northern Iraq under the protection of Mullah Krekar, the head of the Kurdish Islamist faction Ansar al-Islam. The latter competed with other Kurdish groups, especially the Democratic Party of Kurdistan under Massoud Barzani, and the Patriotic Union of Kurdistan led by Jalal Talabani.[19] Ansar al-Islam took in escapees from Afghanistan via Iran. When the war in Iraq broke out, U.S. forces and their Kurdish allies struck at Ansar al-Islam camps with air and ground attacks, nearly eliminating the group. Al-Zarqawi once again had to flee with his men, this time to Fallujah in the Anbar province in Western Iraq. It was there that the Iraqi nationalist insurgency began.

Al-Zarqawi may have been a rebel without a cause after his abrupt departure from Afghanistan, but the invasion of Iraq in 2003 gave him his ultimate raison d'être: defeating the United States and establishing a genuine Islamic state (or, at least, a safe haven) in the heart of the Arab world. Underlying al-Zarqawi's motivation to fight a jihad against the United States was perhaps a personal ambition to redeem a career on the margins of the radical Islamist movement and to become a heroic figure in the Muslim world, harking back to Saladin, the liberator of Jerusalem from the Crusaders in the twelfth century. Iraq borders on al-Zarqawi's home country, Jordan, and the land where Islam was born more than 1,400 years ago, Saudi Arabia. Establishing his presence in Iraq could elevate his status in the jihadist movement and open up opportunities to strike at targets that he had envisioned attacking in the past, which is indeed what happened in the November 2005 suicide bombings of three western hotels in Amman, Jordan, killing sixty people. Paradoxically, the U.S. government, which erroneously linked al-Zarqawi with Saddam Hussein to justify hostilities against the Baathist regime, gave al-Zarqawi the opportunity to rise above his relative obscurity in the jihadist movement by invading Iraq.

To achieve his grandiose objectives, al-Zarqawi had to overcome the rather mundane problems of small group size, a dearth of resources, and relative obscurity in the country. Foreign jihadists constitute a tiny percentage of Iraq's insurgents. In September 2004, only 130 to 140, around 2 percent, of the 5,500 suspected insurgents detained by the authorities were foreigners. In March 2006, of the estimated 15,000 to 20,000 insurgents, only 700 to 2,000 (no more than 10–14 percent) were said to be non-Iraqis.[20]

Many of the initial local and foreign fighters connected to al-Zarqawi formed the group al-Tawhid wal-Jihad in Iraq, which changed its name in October 2004 to al-Qaeda in the Land of the Two Rivers (or Mesopotamia).[21] They came from a variety of Islamist networks in Jordan, Syria, Lebanon, Saudi Arabia, Yemen, North Africa, and Europe, usually through Syria or Turkey.[22] The Israeli analyst Reuven Paz estimates that the majority (61 percent) of these volunteers were Saudi nationals.[23] However, others show the membership distribution was relatively similar across countries, with Algerians at 20 percent, Syrians at 18 percent, Yemenis at 17 percent, Sudanese at 15 percent, Egyptians at 13 percent, and Saudis at 12 percent.[24] A subsequent study by the U.S. military puts the number of North Africans, especially Libyans, at a much higher level than previously thought and confirmed Saudis as the main foreign volunteers in absolute terms.[25]

At its apex in 2007, AQI was one of the most notorious insurgent groups in Iraq. It was a hierarchical, even bureaucratic organization flush with money, munitions, and experienced Iraqi cadres.[26] It used all forms of violence, from conventional guerrilla tactics to mass-casualty suicide bombings. It even experimented with chlorine bombs in 2006 and 2007. Despite the major blow it received at the hands of its former allies in the Sunni tribal areas, the organization still commands several hundred fighters and can wage devastating bombings in Iraq's major cities. In 2011, as U.S. forces departed Iraq, Leon Panetta, the former CIA chief, and Maj. Gen. Jeffrey Buchanan, the U.S. military's top spokesman in Iraq, estimated AQI's network at about 800–1,000 people and its operations at about thirty attacks a week.[27]

Thus, before al-Zarqawi became one of the deadliest insurgent leaders in the world, his cadres were few, alien, and overmatched by coalition

forces. He had to devise a grand strategy to win over parts of the population and attract internal and external support. Declaring allegiance to
Osama bin Laden and al-Qaeda more generally by adopting the name of
AQI was useful to this effort, but attacking the Shiites and sparking sectarian warfare became the centerpiece of his grand strategy.

AQI'S STRATEGY OF SECTARIAN WARFARE

Al-Zarqawi's plans in Afghanistan before 9/11 were not in sync with the
al-Qaeda leadership. Consequently, he did not consider himself part of the
organization and did not pledge fealty to bin Laden. Al-Zarqawi's camp in
Herat, Afghanistan, was set up separately from those of al-Qaeda and with
the purpose of training militants from the Levant region. Al-Zarqawi's
focus at the time was on fighting the near enemy, which encompassed
the Jordanian regime and Israel.[28] This orientation conflicted with bin
Laden and al-Zawahiri's strategy of attacking the far enemy represented
by the United States and its Western allies.[29]

Furthermore, although al-Zarqawi is an adherent of Salafism, a puri-
tanical form of Sunni Islam deeply perturbed by Shiism and other "heretical innovations" to Sunni orthodoxy, there is no evidence to suggest that
he harbored a particular animus toward the Shiites before setting foot
in Iraq. Nor is there evidence that al-Zarqawi ever planned attacks on
Shiites while he was in Afghanistan, despite the animosity between the
ruling Taliban regime and the Hazara Shiites.

Between 2003 and 2004, al-Zarqawi altered his earlier orientation.
Despite his fundamentally different strategy from the one envisioned
by bin Laden and Zawahiri, al-Zarqawi declared allegiance to the original leaders of al-Qaeda in 2004, something he did not do during his
stay in Afghanistan from 1999 to 2001.[30] It is reasonable to conclude
that this move was calculated to give al-Zarqawi organizational brand-
ing and recognition, which could attract financing, recruits, and media
coverage. Given that many Saudis were making their way to Iraq, associating himself with bin Laden, a Saudi, would be a great boon for
al-Zarqawi.

Al-Zarqawi's anti-Shiite strategy, at first glance, seems linked to
the ascendancy of Shiite elites in Iraq's new order. Al-Zarqawi and

like-minded Salafists view Shiism as a heretical creed. The Shiites, they argue, reject the legitimacy of the first three caliphs who succeeded the Prophet Muhammad after his death: Abu Bakr al-Siddiq, Omar Ibn al-Khattab, and Uthman bin Afan. However, these three caliphs, along with Ali bin Abi Talib, the fourth, constitute the core of the pious ancestors (*as-salaf as-salih*) for Sunnis.[31] Rejecting their legitimacy casts doubt on the seminal authorities of Sunni Islam. Furthermore, the Twelver Shiites believe in an awaited imam in occultation, which Sunnis reject as an extra-Quranic innovation on the majority's view of Islamic eschatology.[32] Another complaint against the Shiites is that they engage in unacceptable rituals and excessive veneration of fallible mortals, not the one God and his Prophet.[33] Thus, it appears that Shiite dominance in Iraq is anathema to the Salafis that make up al-Qaeda and AQI, and serves as an added motivation to attack them.

Despite these appearances, however, sectarian terrorism in Iraq does not center on a theological dispute. It is more accurate to describe attacks on the Shiite communities as part of a calculated strategy to win over Sunnis in order to create an environment suitable for the survival of a foreign organization. This would also prevent Sunni-Shiite reconciliation under a new order that would be hostile to the idea of Iraq as a safe haven for Islamist militants.

Al-Zarqawi was explicit about the need to attack the Shiites to galvanize Sunni support for the insurgency. In January 2004, coalition forces intercepted a courier for al-Zarqawi with a seventeen-page document sent to al-Qaeda leaders in Afghanistan or Pakistan.[34] It was an internal report in which he outlined his strategy for fighting in Iraq. Some have raised doubts about the authenticity of the document, but al-Zarqawi's persistent anti-Shiite rhetoric, as well as bombing attacks against Shiites before and after the report's appearance, lends it credence.[35] It is one of only a few captured strategic documents and thus provides valuable insight into al-Zarqawi's decision making.

Al-Zarqawi based his report on the argument that the ordinary Sunnis in Iraq "have little expertise or experience" in fighting. "For this reason," he wrote, "most of the groups are working in isolation, with no political horizon, farsightedness, or preparation to inherit the land. . . . With God's praise we are trying to ripen them quickly." Al-Zarqawi was dissatisfied with the insurgency's "safe" tactics:

Jihad here unfortunately [takes the form of] planting mines, launching rockets, and mortar shelling from afar. The Iraqi brothers still prefer safety and returning to the arms of their wives, where nothing frightens them. Sometimes the groups have boasted among themselves that not one of them has been killed or captured. We have told them in our many sessions with them that safety and victory are incompatible, the tree of triumph and empowerment cannot grow tall and lofty without blood and defiance of death. . . . People cannot awaken from their stupor unless talk of martyrdom and martyrs fills their days and nights.[36]

In this passage, it becomes apparent that the foreign jihadists are trying to convince their Iraqi brothers to adopt the tactics of martyrdom. Thus, rather than being an organic development of occupation, suicide attacks seem to have been imported into Iraq by foreign jihadists. Al-Zarqawi confirmed this in the report: "We have been the keys to all of the martyrdom operations that have taken place except those in the north. Praise be to God, I have completed 25 [operations] up to now, including among the Shia and their symbolic figures, the Americans and their soldiers, the [Iraqi] police and soldiers, and Coalition Forces."[37]

Al-Zarqawi proceeds to reflect on the vulnerabilities of the foreign jihadists: "[The number of immigrant holy warriors] continues to be negligible as compared to the enormity of the expected battle. . . . There is no doubt that the space in which we can move has begun to shrink and that the grip around the throats of the holy warriors has begun to tighten. With the deployment of [Iraqi] soldiers and police, the future has become frightening." He goes on to identify four target sets that could be attacked and the logic behind attacking or avoiding them. First, the Americans: al-Zarqawi writes that they "are the biggest cowards that God has created and the easiest target." He believes, however, that they are not the only or most important target of his group because they are determined to stay safe in their bases while they build up local "agents" (i.e. police, intelligence, and army). Second are Kurds in the north, who are a "lump [in the throat] and a thorn whose time to be clipped has yet to come." Al-Zarqawi sees them as the "last on the list," but he does not say why. Mentioned third are the Iraqi security forces, who al-Zarqawi identifies as "the eyes, ears and hand of the occupier." These forces are an immediate target because they are the principal means by which the U.S. and the Iraqi government will counter the insurgency.[38]

Finally, al-Zarqawi views Shiites as the key to getting the neutral Sunnis to join the insurgency, embrace martyrdom, and create a base of support for the foreign jihadists. He writes:

> [The Shiites] in our opinion are the key to change. I mean that targeting them and hitting them in [their] religious, political, and military depth will provoke them to show the Sunnis . . . the hidden rancor working in their breasts. If we succeed in dragging them into the arena of sectarian war, it will become possible to awaken the inattentive Sunnis as they feel imminent danger and annihilating death. . . . Despite their weakness and fragmentation, the Sunnis are the sharpest blades, the most determined, and the most loyal when they meet those [Shiites], who are a people of treachery and cowardice.

To strengthen his case for this anti-Shiite strategy, al-Zarqawi reflects on what it would mean to fail: "We pack our bags and search for another land, as is the sad, recurrent story in the arenas of jihad, because our enemy is growing stronger and his intelligence data are increasing day by day." The only chance the jihadists have for victory is to drag the Shiites into an overt war with Sunnis:

> If we are able to strike them with one painful blow after another until they enter the battle, we will be able to reshuffle the cards. . . . This is what we want, and, whether they like it or not, many Sunni areas will stand with the holy warriors. Then the holy warriors will have assured themselves land from which to set forth in striking the Shiites in their heartland, along with a clear media orientation and the creation of strategic depth and reach among the brothers outside [Iraq] and the holy warriors within.[39]

Three factors help explain why al-Zarqawi strategically targeted the Shiites. First, the discourse that accompanied the American invasion and occupation of Iraq was rooted in a sectarian narrative. The United States framed the Baathist regime as minority Sunni dominance over a majority Shiite population. This framing amounted to the collective blaming of Sunnis for the sins of Saddam Hussein. Many Sunnis saw themselves as equal victims of this tyrannical dictatorship because they, too, bore the heavy costs of Iraq's wars with Iran and the United States during the 1980s and 1990s, respectively. The sanctions that were imposed on all Iraqis by the international community in the decade before the invasion had no sectarian limitations, and Saddam's ruinous economic policies and torturous security apparatus affected both groups. Additionally, Saddam's reigning elite consisted of a narrow clique based on kinship and tribal ties, not one based on a sectarian identity of Sunnis versus Shiites. Yet the Sunnis were portrayed as Saddam's willing torturers and executioners who should be put back in their proper minority position in relation to the majority Shiites. This rationale was applied despite the fact that many Sunnis attempted coups during the Saddam era to overthrow his government and, consequently, bore the brunt of Saddam's brutal purges in the officer corps. As one insurgent leader of the Islamic Army in Iraq put it:

> It is known by all Iraqis that not all ex-Iraqi army leaders or security officers of the ex-regime are Baathists. There was a group of them who opposed the bad policies adopted by the ex-regime; some of them were arrested and jailed because of their honorable positions, and moreover, some of them were killed [executed] because of their courageous positions.[40]

Purges took place within the Sunni tribes, military, police, party, and state bureaucracies. Some of the major Sunni tribes in Al Anbar province, such as the Jubburis, Ubaydis, and Dulaymis, tried to assassinate Saddam and other Baathists during the mid-1990s and led a revolt in al-Ramadi.[41] Thus, al-Zarqawi's strategy sought to take advantage of a collective sense of humiliation many Sunnis felt toward the occupation authorities as well as those Shiite organizations that went along with this narrative.

The second factor, related to the first, was the rise of sectarian Shiite parties and militias (particularly the Badr Corps of the late Abdel Aziz al-Hakim of SCIRI/ISCI), which were bent on excluding all former Baathists, including those who were nominally loyal to the former regime, from government positions and the security services. Instead, the new Shiite elite wanted to replace former Baathists with personnel loyal to political parties largely based on a Shiite sectarian identity. It is widely recognized that the bulk of active support for the insurgency comes from displaced Iraqi officers, soldiers, and security-services personnel dismissed from their jobs without compensation or a pension or as a result of the "de-Baathification" measures of the Coalition Provision Government (CPA, April 2003–June 2004).[42] Many of those dismissed were members of the Baath party out of expediency or necessity, not ideological commitment. It is widely known in Iraq that membership in the Baath party was often necessary to gain entry or promotion in public-sector employment, including positions in the military, security services, public administration, universities, professional associations, or industry. Membership in the Baath party also was part of the survival strategy of ordinary Iraqis seeking to evade the omnipresent eye of the state *mukhabarat* (secret police). Joining was a way of feigning loyalty to the regime and gaining access to networks of intermediaries (*wasta*) in case one's family or relatives needed a job or an "insider" who could bail them out of trouble should they ever be suspected of activities against the regime.

Al-Zarqawi's sectarian strategy sought to win over those who resented the new power brokers in Iraq. Instead of being called upon to help restore order and security in Iraq, nominal Baathists with expertise were dismissed en masse as bungling, incompetent, and oppressive. These Sunnis feared the new security services dominated by Shiites and Kurds because they, understandably, harbored animosity toward the old regime and have sought to settle scores through the interior ministry and the other branches of the security forces.[43] Al-Zarqawi often justified his indiscriminate violence against the Shiites by referring to the transgressions of the Badr Corps. He even formed a distinct militia, known as the Umar Brigades, which specialized in hunting down members of the Badr Corps.

The third facilitating factor behind al-Zarqawi's sectarian strategy was the fact that Shiites and Kurds, collectively, seemed to benefit the most from the invasion and post-occupation sociopolitical developments. Shiites, with the exception of Muqtada al-Sadr, did not join the insurgency because they had little stake in the old regime. Their political parties were well positioned to take advantage of a pluralistic political system based on democratic elections that naturally favors the majority sect. Sunnis, on the other hand, were ethnically divided between Arabs and Kurds.

Moreover, while the old regime did not empower the Sunnis as a sect per se, it did rely on selective patronage to Sunni tribes in central Iraq and Anbar Province to shore up its base of support. This was particularly the case during the 1990s, when the state's legitimacy came under stress following the military debacles with Iran (1980–1988) and Kuwait (1990–1991). The old regime gave privileges to Sunni tribes through land reform, contracts, military bases, and employment in Baathist institutions and security services. The latter, in particular, were paid generously compared to ordinary Iraqis and received a number of fringe benefits that supplemented their relatively high salaries. The tribes loyal to Saddam received financial and developmental support; their members were recruited into Saddam's elite forces and personal guards; and they were permitted to control the lucrative smuggling trade that flourished during the years of sanctions.[44] These tribes did not care for democracy or major social change, but they did not mind it as long as they retained some of the privileges bestowed on them by the former regime. Talk of federalism and regional autonomy promoted by some Shiite and Kurdish parties invariably implied depriving Sunni Arabs of the oil-rich regions of Iraq and control over the patronage that characterizes many developing economies in the Middle East.

These three factors heightened Sunni uncertainty about the future and generated feelings of humiliation and insecurity, all of which made al-Zarqawi's strategy of sectarian targeting possible and, indeed, desirable from his vantage point. Shiite-Kurdish ascendancy, de-Baathification, and physical insecurity combined with political instability, inadequate security forces, and an abundance of experienced local military cadres were the objective conditions that made the AQI sectarian strategy feasible in Iraq.

AL-QAEDA LEADERS REJECT AQI'S STRATEGY

Al-Zarqawi's broad strategy of establishing an Islamic state in the heart of the Arab world was not too different from what Ayman al-Zawahiri, deputy commander to bin Laden, advocated following the 9/11 attacks.

However, the two disagreed on the tactic of attacking the Shiites of Iraq and its long-term implications. In his book *Knights Under the Prophet's Banner*, serialized by the London-based *Asharq al-Awsat* newspaper in November and December 2001, al-Zawahiri wrote: "Victory by armies cannot be achieved unless the infantry occupies territory. Likewise, victory for Islamic movements against the world [Zionist-crusader] alliance cannot be attained unless these movements possess an Islamic base in the heart of the Arab region."[45]

He goes on to say that the jihadist movement must seek to "control a piece of land in the heart of the Islamic world on which it could establish and protect the state of Islam and launch its battle to restore the caliphate based on the traditions of the Prophet." He concludes:

> If the successful operations against Islam's enemies and the severe damage inflicted on them do not serve the ultimate goal of establishing the Muslim nation in the heart of the Islamic world, they will be nothing more than mere nuisance, regardless of their magnitude, that could be absorbed and endured, even if after some time and with some losses.[46]

The Zarqawi-Zawahiri synthesis appeared to be taking hold in Iraq, but it ultimately had its limits because of its strategy of targeting Shiites. Al-Zawahiri and other al-Qaeda leaders saw this as detrimental to their overall plans—attacking the far enemy and building a movement behind their extremist cause. Bin Laden, true to his strategy of attacking the far enemy, avoided anti-Shiite rhetoric despite the popularity of such discourse among radical Salafists. One is hard pressed to find a speech or a single tract by the founder of al-Qaeda in which he criticizes the Shiites. Thus, it is no surprise that al-Qaeda leaders reacted negatively to al-Zarqawi's sectarian strategy.

Al-Zarqawi's persistent attacks on Shiite civilians unleashed a torrent of criticism from al-Zawahiri and other al-Qaeda leaders. These critiques, collectively, made two arguments against AQI's actions in Iraq. First, these attacks, even if permissible from a religious viewpoint, alienate broader Muslim support, which is essential for the long war against the United States and local regimes. Second, these attacks unnecessarily opened too many fronts when the priority should be given to expelling invading forces from Muslim lands.

In 2005, U.S. forces in Iraq captured a letter by al-Zawahiri addressed to al-Zarqawi. The letter is dated July 9, 2005, and its contents were released by the U.S. Office of the Director of National Intelligence three months later. Zawahiri begins his letter by acknowledging the valuable leadership of al-Zarqawi and his efforts in Iraq, but he proceeds to remind him that the short-term objectives of the jihad in Iraq require the support of its people and mass publics in neighboring countries. He writes, "Therefore, our planning must strive to involve the Muslim masses in the battle, and to bring the [jihadi] movement to the masses and not conduct the struggle far from them." Moreover, the movement "must avoid any action that the masses do not understand or approve."[47]

Al-Zawahiri argues that while confronting the Shiites is a historical inevitability, now is not the time for sectarian attacks. He writes:

> The majority of Muslims don't comprehend this [confrontation] and possibly could not even imagine it. For that reason, many of your Muslim admirers amongst the common folk are wondering about your attacks on the Shia. . . . My opinion is that this matter won't be acceptable to the Muslim populace however much you have tried to explain it, and aversion to this will continue.

Zawahiri was particularly concerned with the ability of adversaries to exploit these operations and other excesses, such as the beheading of hostages to tarnish the image of the jihadists in the media, portraying them as bloodthirsty killers of innocent people:

> I say to you: that we are in a battle, and that more than half of this battle is taking place in the battlefield of the media. And that we are in a . . . race for the hearts and minds of our [Muslim nation]. And that however far our capabilities reach, they will never be equal to one thousandth of the capabilities of the kingdom of Satan that is waging war on us.[48]

Another al-Qaeda leader named Atiyah echoed al-Zawahiri's admonition of AQI's actions in a separate letter to al-Zarqawi. He writes, "True victory is the triumph of principles and values, the triumph of the call to Islam. True conquest is the conquest of the hearts of people." Drawing on the earlier lessons of failed jihad in Algeria, Atiyah explains how Islamists in that country snatched defeat from the jaws of victory by their excessive violence toward the general population:

> Ask me whatever you like about Algeria between 1994 and 1995, when [the movement] was at the height of its power and capabilities, and was on the verge of taking over the government . . . I lived through that myself, and I saw first hand; no one told me about it. However, they [the insurgent Islamists] destroyed themselves with their own hands, with their lack of reason, delusions, their ignoring of people, their alienation of them through oppression, deviance, and severity, coupled with a lack of kindness, sympathy, and friendliness. Their enemy did not defeat them, but rather they defeated themselves.[49]

Al-Zawahiri also asked al-Zarqawi a series of rhetorical questions to illustrate the danger of sectarianism:

> Is the opening of another front now in addition to the front against the Americans and the government a wise decision? Or, does this conflict with the Shia lift the burden from the Americans by diverting the mujahedeen to the Shia, while the Americans continue to control matters from afar? . . . And what loss will befall us if we did not attack the Shia?[50]

Atiyah's words of warning proved prescient in light of the conflict that developed between AQI and the Sunnis of Iraq in 2006: "If you [are] hostile to and [argue] and [push] away everyone who [does not] please you, then most people would shun you, be hostile towards you, argue with you and try to make war on you as well, and they would turn towards your enemy."[51]

These critiques appear to have fallen on deaf ears. AQI intensified its attacks against Iraq's Shiites in 2006 and produced sectarian strife that consumed the lives of thousands of innocent Iraqis—Shiites and Sunnis alike. AQI's war extended to attacking Sunni tribes and insurgents who turned against it after the United States reached out to these forces in an effort to win them over with jobs, monetary subsidies, and prospects of greater inclusion in Iraq's political process and security forces.[52] The words of the critics proved prophetic in foretelling the misfortunes of AQI.

Despite these criticisms, al-Qaeda leaders in Pakistan continued to provide verbal support for AQI, al-Zarqawi, and his successor, Abu Hamza al-Muhajir (killed in April 2010). Bin Laden sided with the group against Sunni tribes and insurgents who waged war on AQI.[53] As the Sunni-Shiite civil war intensified in Iraq, al-Qaeda leaders were left with a fait accompli. Withdrawing their support from AQI would have exposed the ideological incoherence of the jihadist movement and revealed the limits of bin Laden's and al-Zawahiri's leadership. Moreover, it would have meant that al-Qaeda had no representative organization on one of the most important fronts in the war with the United States. Such a prospect was hardly appealing to an organization that claims to be the leader of global jihad. Finally, given that many Iraqi insurgent groups had reconsidered their struggle against coalition forces in response to monetary incentives and jobs protecting their neighborhoods and cities from criminals, terrorists, and insurgents, AQI appeared to be one of the few remaining fighting groups in Iraq. Its ongoing guerrilla and terrorist attacks helped keep U.S. forces bogged down in Iraq, preventing their complete and rapid redeployment to Afghanistan, where the Taliban are waging their own struggle against the United States and its local allies.

AQI's strategy of sectarian terrorism was concocted in Iraq by Abu Musab al-Zarqawi, independently of the judgments of the original al-Qaeda leadership in Pakistan. Seeking to build a base of support among Iraq's Sunni population, al-Zarqawi calculated that a sustained campaign of violence against Iraq's Shiite communities, their political leaders, and their symbols of identity would provoke them to undertake indiscriminate retaliatory violence against Sunnis. Sectarian polarization would enable outsiders with an extreme Salafist worldview to survive, grow, and set up a safe haven for their transnational jihad on the ashes of a failed Iraqi state. This strategy and its inner logic were exemplified best by the February 2006 plot to destroy the al-Askari shrine in Samarra. As a consequence of that diabolical act, the sectarian civil war in Iraq escalated to an unprecedented level and tore the country apart.

Al-Qaeda leaders in Pakistan, who were focused on radicalizing Muslim masses worldwide for mobilization against the United States and its Western allies, raised objections to AQI's sectarian bloodletting because they correctly assessed that this strategy would alienate Muslim publics and delegitimize the insurgents. In the end, however, they were not able to influence AQI and redirect its activities according to their wishes. Worst still, Iraq's Sunni population—especially the tribes and insurgents—began to view sectarian violence as a greater threat to their existence than the occupying coalition forces led by the United States. This shift in perspective made possible an alliance between Sunni tribes and insurgents, on the one hand, and U.S. counterinsurgency forces and the Iraqi government, on the other.

The case of AQI does not support the theory of leaderless jihad, which is predicated on the assumption that Islamist violent extremism is increasingly inspired, not organized, by al-Qaeda operatives or its affiliates. Sectarian violence in Iraq was systematically planned and executed by a jihadist organization with local, regional, and transnational networks of supporters and recruiters, as well as leaders with jihadist credentials linked to Afghanistan's training camps—even if those camps were outside of the direct purview of bin Laden. The anti-Shiite violence in Iraq was not born out of a reactive impulse of an autonomous group of disgruntled Sunnis but was rather a planned campaign by professional terrorists intent on fomenting civil war in order to create the conditions necessary for their survival and growth in a new theater of operations.

The case of AQI, however, does highlight the limits of the global jihadist movement and calls into question the view that al-Qaeda is a well-coordinated organization operating on multiple fronts. This is an ideologically incoherent and, at least so far as Iraq was concerned, operationally decentralized movement that is capable of plotting terrorist attacks but seems incapable of exerting significant command and control over extant insurgent movements. The limitation in coordinating strategy between al-Qaeda leaders in Pakistan and their affiliate in Iraq was not attributable to the leaderless nature of contemporary violent extremism but rather to a number of factors, not the least of which was the security environment imposed by the presence of significant numbers of coalition forces in Iraq and Afghanistan. Such a presence hindered direct travel and ongoing contact and coordination between al-Qaeda leaders and AQI.

Moreover, al-Zarqawi's independence from al-Qaeda before pledging fealty to bin Laden in 2004 is a critical factor that enabled him to exercise strategic autonomy. Had he been more closely integrated in bin Laden's leadership structure before the invasion of Iraq in 2003, he may well have been more receptive to al-Qaeda's far-enemy strategy. Al-Zarqawi instead chose to respond to the structure of opportunities and constraints offered by the Iraqi arena, including growing Sunni grievances toward a Shiite-dominated government and the threat posed to insurgents by a Shiite-controlled security establishment. Tragically, the sectarian terrorism that claimed thousands of lives and destroyed countless others was the outcome of this calculated opportunism by an ambitious leader and his extremist organization.

NOTES

1. Moojan Momen, *Introduction to Shi'i Islam: The History and Doctrines of Twelver Shi'ism* (New Haven, Conn.: Yale University Press, 1985), 161–62; Jane Idleman Smith and Yvonne Yazbeck Haddad, *The Islamic Understanding of Death and Resurrection* (New York: Oxford University Press, 2002).

2. Interviews with Iraqi immigrants in Amman, Jordan, February and March, 2007.

3. Megan K. Stack, "Neighborhood Militias Add Another Armed Layer," *Los Angeles Times*, April 1, 2006; Dan Murphy and Awadh al-Taiee, "Seeking Safety, Iraqis Turn to Militias," *Christian Science Monitor*, July 24, 2006; Edward Wong, "Fearful Iraqis Avoid Mosques as Attacks Rise," *New York Times*, August 19, 2006.

4. Joshua Partlow, "Mahdi Army, Not Al Qaeda, Is Enemy No. 1 in Western Baghdad," *Washington Post*, July 16, 2007; Alissa J. Rubin, "Cleric Switches Tactics to Meet Changes in Iraq," *New York Times*, July 19, 2007.

5. Brookings Institution, "Iraq Index," July 17, 2008, available at http://www .brookings.edu/iraqindex (accessed August 2, 2008), 4.

6. "More Than 700,000 Iraqis Fled Homes Since Shrine Bombing," Agence France-Presse, April 25, 2007; Sudarsan Raghavan, "War in Iraq Propelling a Massive Migration," *Washington Post*, February 4, 2007.

7. Sudarsan Raghayan, "Distrust Breaks the Bonds of a Baghdad Neighborhood: In Mixed Area, Violence Defies Peace Efforts," *Washington Post*, September 27, 2006; Sabrina Tavernise, "Sectarian Toll Includes Scars to Iraq Psyche," *New York Times*, September 17, 2007.

8. Sudarsan Raghavan, "At Checkpoints in Baghdad, Disguise Is a Lifesaving Ritual," *Washington Post*, September 29, 2006.

9. Edward Wong, "Prisoner Links Iraqi to Attack on Shiite Shrine, Official Says," *New York Times*, June 29, 2006. Al-Badri was killed by U.S. Special Forces in an airstrike east of Samarra in August 2007. Trigui was arrested by U.S. forces in May 2006. He was sentenced to death by the Central Criminal Court of Iraq in October 2006 and was executed by the Iraqi government on November 16, 2011.

10. Richard A. Oppel Jr., "Iraqi Official Reports Capture of Top Insurgent Leader Linked to Shrine Bombing," *New York Times*, September 4, 2006.

11. Hazem al-Amin, "Jordan's Zarqawists Visit Their Sheikhs in Prison and Await the Opportunity to Join Abu Musab in Iraq" (Arabic), *Al-Hayat* (London), December 14, 2004.

12. Robert F. Worth, "Bombings Across Iraq Kill Five Iraqis and Four Marines," *New York Times*, February 8, 2006; John F. Burns, "At Least Sixty-Four Dead as Rebels Strike in Three Iraqi Cities," *New York Times*, December 20, 2004; Erik Eckholm, "Attacks on Iraqi Shiite Leaders Raise Fears of Civil Strife," *New York Times*, December 28, 2004.

13. Caryle Murphy, "Iraq-Jordan Dispute Deepens," *Washington Post*, March 21, 2005.

14. Data on Iraq's suicide bombings are collected by the author and are available upon written request. For analysis of earlier waves of suicide attacks, see Mohammed M. Hafez, *Suicide Bombers in Iraq: The Strategy and Ideology of Martyrdom* (Washington, D.C.: United States Institute of Peace, 2007).

15. Habib Jaber, "Who Resists in Iraq? What Is Not Said About the Truth of the Iraqi Resistance" (Arabic), *Asharq al-Awsat* (London), August 12, 2004; Hiwa Osman, "What Do the Insurgents Want? Different Visions, Same Bloody Tactics," *Washington Post*, May 8, 2005; Zaki Chehab, *Inside the Resistance: The Iraqi Insurgency and the Future of the Middle East* (New York: Nation Books, 2005).

16. Al-Jazeera estimated the number of Arab volunteers in Iraq before the invasion from 5,000 to 8,000. See Open Source Center, "Al-Jazirah Program Examines Issue of Arab Volunteers in Iraq," April 24, 2003. For an analysis of the first wave of volunteers to Iraq, see Muhammad Sulieman, "An Invitation to Reflect on and Discuss 'The Phenomenon of Arab Volunteers'" (Arabic), *Al-Asr* (Amman, Jordan), October 4–5, 2003 (three-part series).

17. Open Source Center, "Jihad in Iraq: Hopes and Dangers," July 29, 2004. The document does not have an author or date, but it is dedicated to Yusuf al-Ayiri, the al-Qaeda leader in Saudi Arabia killed in 2003. It was issued by the Media Commission for the Victory of the Iraqi People (Mujahidin Services Center) sometime in 2003.

18. Fuad Husayn, "Al-Zarqawi: The Second Generation of Al Qaeda" (Arabic), *Al-Quds al-Arabi* (London), parts 1–15, May 13–30, 2005,.

19. Fatih Krekar, "The Zarqawian Vision and its Heavy Load" (Arabic), al-Jazeera, June 15, 2006, available at www.aljazeera.net (accessed June 16, 2006).

20. Ahmed S. Hashim, *Insurgency and Counter-Insurgency in Iraq* (Ithaca, N.Y.: Cornell University Press, 2006), 27–28; Faris Bin Hazam, "The Outsiders Are Not the Majority of al-Qaeda's Cadre in Iraq" (Arabic), *Al-Hayat*, February 10, 2006.

21. Mashari al-Zaydi, "Jordanian Papers Concerning Fundamentalism and Politics" (Arabic), *Asharq al-Awsat* (London), part 4 of 5, October 13, 2005; Krekar, "The Zarqawian Vision."

22. Hazem al-Amin, "Lebanese 'Jihadists' in Iraq: 'Salafis' from Peripheral Regions and Cities" (Arabic), *Al-Hayat* (London), August 11, 2004; Hazem al-Amin, "Strangers Come during 'al-Qaeda Season' to Recruit Suicide Bombers to Iraq" (Arabic), *Al-Hayat* (London), parts 1 and 2, January 26–27, 2006; Jean Chichizola, "Four Recruiters for Jihad in Iraq Arrested" (French), *Le Figaro* (Paris), January 26, 2005; Muhammad al-Ashhab, "European Networks for Smuggling Jihadists" (Arabic), *Al-Hayat* (London), February 11, 2005; Saud al-Sarhan, "Al-Qaeda in Saudi Arabia" (Arabic), *Asharq al-Awsat* (London), May 20, 2005; Peter Beaumont, "Insurgents Trawl Europe for Recruits," *Observer* (London), June 19, 2005; Ahmed al-Arqam, "The Moroccan Judiciary Sentences to Prison Deportees from Syria on Their Way to Fight in Iraq" (Arabic), *Asharq al-Awsat* (London), July 2, 2005; Nir Rosen, "Iraq's Jordanian Jihadis," *New York Times*, February 19, 2006.

23. Reuven Paz, "Arab Volunteers Killed in Iraq: An Analysis," Global Research in International Affairs Center, Occasional Papers 3, 1 (March 2005), 2.

24. Nawaf Obagid and Anthony Cordesman, *Saudi Militants in Iraq: Assessment and Kingdom's Response* (Washington, D.C.: Center for Strategic and International Studies, September 19, 2005), 6.

25. Joseph Felter and Brian Fishman, *Al-Qa'ida's Foreign Fighters in Iraq: A First Look at the Sinjar Records* (West Point, N.Y.: Combating Terrorism Center, 2007), 8–9.

26. Brian Fishman, ed., *Bombers, Bank Accounts, and Bleedout: Al-Qa'ida's Road in and Out of Iraq* (West Point, N.Y.: Combating Terrorism Center, 2008); Benjamin Bahney et al., *An Economic Analysis of the Financial Records of al-Qa'ida in Iraq* (Santa Monica, Calif.: RAND Corporation, 2010).

27. "Some 1,000 al Qaeda Still in Iraq—CIA Chief Says," Reuters, June 9, 2011; Michael S. Schmidt and Eric Schmitt, "Leaving Iraq, U.S. Fears New Surge of Qaeda Terror," *New York Times*, November 5, 2011.

28. Peter L. Bergen, *The Osama bin Laden I Know* (New York: Free Press, 2006), 357–58.

29. Fawaz A. Gerges, *The Far Enemy: Why Jihad Went Global* (New York: Cambridge University Press, 2005).

30. Bergen, *The Osama bin Laden I Know*.

31. Vali Nasr, *The Shia Revival: How Conflicts Within Islam Will Shape the Future* (New York: Norton, 2006).

32. Smith and Haddad, *The Islamic Understanding*.

33. Interview with Sunni Iraqis in Amman, Jordan, February 2007. Interviewees were particularly critical of Ashura processions in the Islamic month of Muharram.

34. The report was not dated and it is not clear to whom it was sent in al-Qaeda. Excerpts from the report can be found in "Letter May Detail Iraqi Insurgency's Concerns," CNN, February 10, 2004, available at http://edition.cnn.com/2004/WORLD /meast/02/10/sprj.nirq.zarqawi/ (accessed March 10, 2009). Excerpts can also be found in Bergen, *The Osama bin Laden I Know*, 362–63.

35. Al-Zarqawi's anti-Shiite rhetoric can also be found in his video montages and audio recordings. See, for instance, the transcript of an hour-long recording his supporters entitled "The Descendents of Ibn al-Alqami Are Back" (Open Source Center, "Al-Zarqawi Justifies Killing of Innocent Muslims, Condemns Shi'a 'Betrayal' of Sunnis," May 18, 2005) and the transcript of an audio recording to his supporters entitled "Here Is a Message for Mankind, Let Them Take Warning Therefrom" (Open Source Center, "Al-Zarqawi Calls for 'All-Out War' Against Shi'a," September 14, 2005).

36. "Letter May Detail Iraqi Insurgency's Concerns."

37. Ibid.

38. Ibid. It is important to note that the majority of the Kurds are Sunnis, but Zarqawi views them negatively anyway, which suggests that his strategy is not based mainly on sectarian grounds.

39. Ibid.

40. Interview, , *Al-Fursan* (Islamic Army in Iraq's online magazine), no. 9 (August 2006). Also see Open Source Center, "Al-Fursan Magazine Interview with Amir of Islamic Army in Iraq Discusses Strategy, Targets, Cooperation," August 30, 2006.

41. Samir al-Khalil, *Republic of Fear: The Politics of Modern Iraq* (Berkeley: University of California Press, 1989); Amatzia Baram, "Neo-Tribalism in Iraq: Saddam Hussein's Tribal Policies 1991–1996," *International Journal of Middle East Studies* 29, no. 1 (February 1997): 1–31.

42. Thomas E. Ricks, *Fiasco: The American Military Adventure in Iraq* (New York: Penguin, 2006).

43. Michael Slackman, "Fearing Revenge: Hussein's Militia Forces Lie Low and Deny Hurtful Role," *Los Angeles Times*, April 16, 2003; Huda Jasim and Niaman al-Haimas, "Iraqi Air Force Officers and Military Doctors Are Suddenly Killed in Their Homes" (Arabic), *Asharq al-Awsat* (London), July 7, 2005; Anthony Shadid and Steve Fainaru, "Militias on the Rise Across Iraq: Shiite and Kurdish Groups Seizing Control, Instilling Fear in North and South," *Washington Post*, August 21, 2005; International Crisis Group, "The Next Iraqi War? Sectarianism and Civil Conflict," *ICG Middle East Report* 52, February 27, 2006.

44. Baram, "Neo-Tribalism in Iraq"; Amatzia Baram, "Who Are the Insurgents: Sunni Arab Rebels in Iraq," United States Institute of Peace Special Report 134 (Washington, D.C.: United States Institute of Peace, April 2005); Hashim, *Insurgency and Counter-Insurgency in Iraq*, 25–26.

45. Ayman al-Zawahiri, "Knights Under the Prophet's Banner" (Arabic), *Asharq al-Awsat* (London), December 12, 2001, part 11.

46. Ibid.

47. The original Arabic text and the English translation are available in Open Source Center, "Report: Complete Text of Al-Zawahiri 9 July 2005 Letter to Al-Zarqawi," October 11, 2005. There is little public information regarding the circumstances under which this letter was discovered, leading some to cast doubt on its authenticity. Its content, however, appears consistent with statements subsequently made by al-Zawahiri in answers he gave in reply to online questions posed by participants in the al-Ikhlas Islamic Network about the permissibility of attacking neutral Shiites in Iraq (http://ek-ls.org/forum, accessed April 2, 2008).

48. Open Source Center, "Report: Complete Text of Al-Zawahiri 9 July 2005 Letter."

49. The identity of the author is not known for certain, but it is most likely Atiyah Abdel Rahman, a high-ranking member of al-Qaeda's general command and a person who communicated regularly with bin Laden before he (Atiyah) was killed by a CIA drone strike in August 2011. His letter was discovered shortly after U.S. forces killed al-Zarqawi in an airstrike on a safe-house near Baquba, Iraq, in June 2006. An English translation of the letter can be found in a report by the West Point Combating Terrorism Center (CTC) Harmony Document Database available at http://ctc.usma.edu /harmony/pdf/CTC-AtiyahLetter.pdf. See "Letter Exposes New Leader in Al-Qa'ida High Command," CTC, September 25, 2006.

50. Open Source Center, "Report: Complete Text of Al-Zawahiri 9 July 2005 Letter."

51. CTC, "Letter Exposes New Leader."

52. Mohammed M. Hafez, "Al-Qa'ida in Iraq Losing Ground," *CTC Sentinel* 1 (December 2007): 6–8.

53. Bin Laden, after initially expressing some implied criticism of AQI in a speech released on October 22, 2007, in which he called for reconciliation between Iraq's Sunni insurgents and the Islamic State of Iraq (AQI's front organization in Iraq since October 2006), unambiguously affirmed his support for AQI in a speech dated December 27, 2007.

19

The November 2003 Istanbul Bombings

GUIDO STEINBERG AND PHILIPP HOLTMANN

I n November 2003, suicide bombers attacked Jewish and British targets in Istanbul, Turkey. Overall, 61 people (including the four attackers) were killed and more than 700 wounded. The first wave of attacks took place on November 15, when two suicide attackers detonated car bombs close to the Neveh Shalom and Beit Yisrael synagogues in the Galata and Sisli quarters, respectively, in Central Istanbul. They killed 27 and wounded more than 300 people. Five days later, on November 20, another two bombers targeted the local branch of the British HSBC bank in the Levant and the British consulate in the Beyoğlu quarters. They killed 30, among them the British consul, and injured almost 400 people. Most of the victims, though, were Turkish Muslims. The bombings were the most devastating terrorist attacks in Turkish history and were subsequently dubbed Turkey's "September 11."[1] In a country where the authorities were and are preoccupied with the ethnonationalist terrorism of the Kurdistan Workers Party (PKK), the events made clear that Turkey would have to concentrate on the threat of jihadist terrorism more than hitherto.

The Istanbul bombings are a rare example of a leader-led plot in which two organizations played a leading role: al-Qaeda and the al-Zarqawi network. While al-Qaeda trained some of the perpetrators before 9/11 and chose Turkey as a theater of operations and made suggestions in regards to possible targets, the al-Zarqawi network in 2003 played a leading role in organizing and financing the plot. This dual leadership was embodied by the Syrian jihadist Luayy Sakka, who in 2007 was convicted as the financier and mastermind behind the Istanbul bombings. Sakka first joined al-Qaeda in Afghanistan in the mid-1990s and built structures for the organization in Turkey. In 1999 and 2000, though, he joined Abu Musab al-Zarqawi (1966–2006) and his organization and became one of the Jordanian's most important lieutenants. In 2003, Sakka formed the link between the two organizations responsible for the Istanbul bombings.

THE TARGETS

The consulate, the bank, and the synagogues had not been the plotters' original targets. The suicide attackers and other members of the group that perpetrated the bombings had completed courses in al-Qaeda training camps in Afghanistan before September 11, 2001. During the investigations following the Istanbul attacks, the suspects stated that shortly before the attacks in New York and Washington, the Turkish cell had met with Osama bin Laden and the organization's number three, its military commander, the Egyptian Mohammed Atef (Abu Hafs al-Masri, died 2001).[2] The al-Qaeda leadership wanted the Turks to attack Western or Israeli targets. The discussion had centered on attacking Israeli ships at the southern port city of Mersin and an attack against Incirlik Airbase. Situated near the city of Adana in southern Turkey, the base is used by the American and Turkish air forces. Incirlik is the most important American installation in Turkey. The U.S. military has used it since the early 1950s, and in jihadist circles in Turkey and beyond, it has become a symbol for the close alliance between Ankara and Washington.[3]

In May 2003, after returning to Turkey from Afghanistan, the plotters decided they would have to look for softer targets because of tight security around the airport. They opened a store for cell phones in Istanbul, which enabled them to switch their communications equipment frequently and inconspicuously.[4] In addition, they rented a small workshop where they would prepare the explosives and assemble the home-made bombs based on hydrogen peroxide, which they had been trained to use in an al-Qaeda camp in Afghanistan.[5]

The final decision to attack Jewish and British targets seems to have been made by the attackers after the invasion of Iraq by U.S. and British forces in the spring of 2003. Britain's role during the war was a powerful motive for the group's plot. British forces took part in the invasion of Iraq in early 2003 and played a prominent role as an occupation power in the southern part of Iraq. Although Britain has always been a prominent target for jihadist groups because of its strong alliance with the United States, the Iraq war strengthened al-Qaeda's resolve to hit British installations. Osama bin Laden made this clear when in October 2003 he issued an audiotape in which he called upon his followers to perpetrate attacks on countries that had provided troops to help the United States stabilize Iraq, most prominently the United Kingdom, Spain, and Italy.[6] By that time, however, the Istanbul plot was already in its final stages of preparation.

It is equally of no surprise that al-Qaeda would try to hit Jewish targets. However, the organization had not shown any interest in the Israeli-Palestinian conflict before late 2001. This changed when al-Qaeda came under pressure by the invasion of Afghanistan in October 2001. Coinciding with the beginning of the American attacks, al-Qaeda published a video in which Osama bin Laden concentrated on the Palestinian issue in an attempt to gain support from a wider Muslim public.[7] Ever since, the organization modified its strategy and increasingly attacked Jewish and Israeli targets. The most striking example of this trend were the attacks in Mombassa, Kenya, on November 28, 2002, when a suicide bomber crashed his bomb-laden vehicle into the lobby of an Israeli-owned hotel and a second team fired surface-to-air missiles at an Israeli charter plane.[8] Attacks on Jewish targets in Turkey were also intended by al-Qaeda to affect the close alliance between Israel and Turkey.[9]

Turkey was also targeted not only because it was the native land of the attackers but also because of its strategic importance to al-Qaeda. Turkey has been an important NATO member since 1952 and is the closest U.S. ally in the Muslim world. Islamists in general and the jihadist movement in particular hold special scorn for the Turkish state and its political elites because of its secular and largely democratic political system based on the state ideology of Kemalism. Its founder, Kemal Atatürk (1881–1938), has always been an important enemy for the Islamists because he abolished the caliphate in 1924 and enacted the secular reforms that bear his name.[10]

It is not known to what extent the plotters and al-Qaeda aimed at the destabilization of the conservative Muslim government of the Justice and

Development Party (Adalet ve Kalkınma Partisi or AKP) and Prime Min ister Recep Tayyip Erdogan. In March 2003, the Turkish parliament had voted against giving the United States permission to attack Iraq from Turkish soil, seriously hampering the American war effort. Turkey was also late in granting the U.S. Air Force the permission to over-fly Turkish territory in order to attack targets in Iraq. More importantly, the AKP, which came to power in December 2002, had splintered from the Islamist Refah/Fazilet Party in 2001. By taking part in elections and aiming at the moderation of the Islamist movement in order to gain power, Erdogan and his colleagues became targets for the jihadists. One of the cell mem bers said that the ultimate goal of the attacks, irrespective of the targets, was to destabilize the democratic system in Turkey.[11]

CLAIMS OF RESPONSIBILITY

There were two competing claims to responsibility for the Istanbul bomb ings, one in Arabic from a rather obscure group of internet jihadists, the Abu Hafs al-Masri Brigades (Kata'ib Abu Hafs al-Masri), and a second one from the Turkish Great East Islamic Raiders' Front (İslami Büyükdoğu Akıncılar Cephesi, IBDA-C). Both were published shortly after the attacks, but only the IBDA-C claim might have some basis in reality.[12]

The Abu Hafs al-Masri Brigades are named after al-Qaeda's Egyptian military chief who died from an American airstrike in Afghanistan in November 2001. However, the Brigades were sympathizers active on the jihadist Internet and did not have any connection to a real terrorist orga nization. While they were active online between July 2003 and August 2005, they took responsibility for actual terrorist attacks as well as for events that were not connected to terrorism at all, for example, the elec tricity blackout in the Northeast of the United States in November 2003.[13] The factual involvement of al-Qaeda's military chief al-Masri in the early planning of the attacks and the claim of responsibility by the virtual jihadist media group that adopted his name should not be confused.[14]

The IBDA-C's claim appears more authentic because some of the plot ters had connections to this relatively small militant organization, which had been active in Turkey since the mid-1980s. A former jihadist insider and a usually reliable source, the Libyan Noman Benotman, stated in

November 2003, that there was a clear operational connection between IBDA-C and al-Qaeda. Moreover, he took IBDA-C's claim of responsibility more seriously on the grounds that it was placed via telephone, not the Internet. According to Benotman, al-Qaeda's Internet statements were viewed with suspicion in Islamist circles in late 2003. In November 2003, U.S. intelligence services had shut down "al-Nida" (the Call), which was regarded as the quasi-official website of al-Qaeda. Afterward, numerous jihadist websites issued conflicting claims of responsibility on behalf of al-Qaeda for the Riyadh and Istanbul attacks in the same month. Activists who frequented these sites said that these statements differed in tone and style from al-Qaeda's "originals."[15] Although the IBDA-C's claim of responsibility looks more authentic under these circumstances than the statement of the Abu Hafs al-Masri Brigades, no concrete evidence for an involvement of the organization was found.

THE PLOTTERS

The plotters seem to have been a rather loose group of people with former connections to Turkish terrorist groups—namely the Turkish Hizbullah and IBDA-C—who had grown out of their local contexts. Together they built their own network, externally guided by al-Qaeda central and the al-Zarqawi network and led by Turks at the local level. While al-Qaeda chose Turkey as a theater of operations and the al-Zarqawi network took an active leadership role through financing, the locals remained relatively independent and seem to have chosen the final targets themselves. Attacking the military base in Incirlik and Israeli ships in Mersin was too challenging, so they opted for softer targets in Istanbul.

The Istanbul cell consisted of a broad range of different jihadist profiles. Its members were about a dozen young Turks, a majority of them ethnic Kurds. The ethnic Kurds mainly hailed from southeastern Turkey, where several of them had formerly maintained connections to the Turkish Hizbullah, a Kurdish organization. The dire economic situation in their hometowns might have played a role for their radicalization. There were some other members of the group, though, who were from different social backgrounds living in the big cities of the Turkish west. They seem to have been mainly ethnic Turks. It seems as if the initial cell around the ringleader, Habib Akdaş, started recruiting in southeastern Turkey among friends and ethnic Kurds who belonged to the network of Hizbullah members, supporters, or sympathizers. Yet not all of the Kurdish cell members appeared to sympathize with Hizbullah. The family of Gökhan Elaltuntaş, for example, who attacked one of the synagogues on November 16, had trouble with extortionists from Hizbullah.[16] When the cell grew and shifted its activity to western Turkey in preparation for the Istanbul attacks, it also integrated ethnic Turks.

Habib Akdaş and Azad Ekinci were the ringleaders of the actual cell, with Akdaş serving as the head of operations but also as a propagandist and recruiter.[17] In the 1990s, Akdaş (born in the early 1970s), a native of Mardin, had been to Bosnia and Chechnya, destinations popular among Turkish jihadists. He then joined al-Qaeda in Afghanistan and met Osama bin Laden and Abu Hafs al-Masri in 2001. While in the Khalden camp in Afghanistan, Akdaş was the emir of a close-knit Turkish group, in which Baki Yiğit and Adnan Ersöz, whom he met in a training camp in Pakistan in the late 1990s, served as lieutenants. Ersöz also seems to have played an important role as contact-man to al-Qaeda central organization in the run up to the attacks.[18] In Turkey, Akdaş expanded the group and integrated Gürcan Baç and Harun Ilhan as council members, as well as Ekinci as senior lieutenant.

The idea to perpetrate attacks in Turkey was proposed by al-Qaeda in 2001, when Akdaş, together with Yiğit and Ersöz, was in Afghanistan to discuss the future training of Turkish jihadists with al-Masri. On this occasion, al-Masri asked him if he would be able to execute double attacks on two Israeli ships in Mersin. Akdaş confirmed this, but asked for support. Al-Masri and the three Turks then met with bin Laden, and all agreed upon an assault.[19] It seems that al-Masri pushed for Israeli targets in Mersin, though bin Laden preferred an attack against the U.S. air base in Incirlik. According to Ersöz's testimony, the Turks demanded US$150,000 dollars from al-Qaeda for the attacks, which were set for the end of 2002, but delayed because of the U.S. invasion of Afghanistan.[20]

The number two of the cell, Azad Ekinci (b. 1978), is said to have been a member of the Turkish Hizbullah who also fought in Chechnya and trained with al-Qaeda in Afghanistan.[21] Ekinci's radicalization in Bingöl in the early 1990s was strongly influenced by Mesut Çabuk, one of the suicide bombers, who was connected to Hizbullah as well. Natives from

Bingöl described the two as inseparable, quiet, and introverted friends. Together, they went to fight and train in the northern Caucasus.[22]

Most members of the cell were Turkish citizens from the southeastern part of the country, many of them ethnic Kurds. The largest single group (Azad Ekinci, Gökhan Elaltuntaş, and Mesut Çabuk) were Kurds from Bingöl, a remote, predominantly Kurdish town in eastern Anatolia, where unemployment rates are high and the devastating repercussions of the civil war of the 1980s and 1990s are all too prominent.[23] Others came from Malatya, Mardin, Batman, and Van, all towns and cities in similarly miserable conditions to Bingöl and centers of Kurdish opposition to the Turkish state for decades.

Of the fifteen men accused of being directly involved in the plot, i.e., having planned, prepared, and executed the attacks, at least ten came from southeastern Turkey. Three of the four suicide bombers, Elaltuntaş, Çabuk and Feridun Uğurlu were southeasterners. Five of the eight defendants who were tried in 2007, namely Adnan Ersöz, Harun Ilhan, Fevzi Yitiz, Yusuf Polat, and Baki Yiğit, also stem from that region. The other three defendants were Osmak Eken, Seyit Ertal, and Luayy Sakka. Although living in Aleppo, Sakka's family originally came from Diyarbakir, in the southeast. The two senior leaders, Akdaş and Ekinci, also hailed from southeastern Turkey.

Despite the similarities in their background, the ethnic structure of the cell was mixed, consisting of both Turks and Kurds. Therefore, the Istanbul attacks cannot be misconstrued as a genuinely Kurdish plot. The initial circle around Akdaş that started recruiting in southeastern Turkey possibly coalesced among friends and ethnic Kurds who belonged to the network of Hizbullah members, supporters, or sympathizers. When the cell grew and shifted its activity to western Turkey in preparation for the Istanbul attacks, it also integrated ethnic Turks. This might explain why, for example, İlyas Kuncak, the fourth suicide bomber who attacked the HSBC Bank, participated in the plot. Kuncak, forty-seven, was an ethnic Turk and successful middle-class business owner.[24] There is another possible explanation for the integration of ethnic Turks. It may have been suggested by outsiders, either al-Qaeda central or al-Zarqawi's group, who pushed for integrating operatives from their own Turkish networks.

Kuncak, in particular, does not fit into the Turkish cell's profile, if solely examined through the lens of socioeconomic deprivation and the political struggle in the predominantly Kurdish southeast. Yet he became an important operative in the plot. There were several other plotters who were relatively well educated. Ersöz was a graduate in political science from Istanbul University in 1996 and had climbed the social ladder successfully. The year 1996, however, was also a turning point for Ersöz, when he decided to join the jihadists. It is not known, however, why exactly he radicalized. Elaltuntaş, Uğurlu, and most other group members were also high school graduates.[25] In at least two cases, it is possible that personal trauma played a role in the radicalization of cell members. Ekinci's father, a secular Kurdish activist, was shot by Turkish police when Ekinci was only two, and Mesut Çabuk's mother died when he was just a small boy. The Kurdish element seems to have played a major role in the early phase of the cell's formation and the radicalization of many of the cell's members. Yet the cell's final structure was much more diverse, crossing social classes and ethnic divisions, with contacts that spanned Afghanistan, Syria, and Iraq.

THE MASTERMIND

Shortly before and after the bombings, the surviving senior group members fled. Akdaş, Ekinci, and Gürcan Baç, the explosives expert of the group, made their way to Syria, where they found refuge in the Aleppo home of Luayy Sakka. This was the moment when the importance of Sakka for the Istanbul bombings became clear. He was the link between the local Turkish group, al-Qaeda, and the al-Zarqawi network in the financing, planning, and organization of the plot.

Sakka (born 1974) grew up in a culture of nationalist Islamist struggle in Syria and in his early twenties began to partake in jihadist activity. Sakka's family—which is probably of Kurdish descent—had lived in eastern Turkey until 1960 but then emigrated to Aleppo, the most important Islamist stronghold in Syria. He first joined al-Qaeda in Afghanistan in the mid-1990s and built up a close relationship with the Palestinian Abu Zubaydah, an important logistics official based in Pakistan and a close associate of Osama bin Laden. In 1997, Abu Zubaydah sent him to the Khalden training camp in Afghanistan and later to Turkey in order to build structures for the organization there. When he returned to Afghanistan in 1999, he moved to Herat with the Jordanian terrorist Abu Musab al-Zarqawi and joined his organization.[26]

In a letter describing al-Zarqawi's career, the former military chief of al-Qaeda, the Egyptian Saif al-Adel, mentioned that among the five followers who joined al-Zarqawi in his Herat training camp was a Syrian with a Turkish and German connection.[27] This was Sakka, whose two sisters were married to two converts to Islam in southern Germany. From 2000, Sakka seems to have become an important personality in al-Zarqawi's network. He undertook several dozen journeys to Syria, Turkey, and Jordan and spent time in Afghanistan and Germany.[28] In all these countries, Sakka seems to have built an extensive network of jihadists linking groups and individuals primarily in Turkey, Syria, and Germany. Later, Sakka joined al-Zarqawi in Iraq but kept up his network in Syria and, especially, Turkey. After his arrest in 2005, he claimed to have fought for al-Zarqawi in Iraq and that he had taken part in kidnappings and executions.[29] Most importantly, however, Sakka is said to have provided the perpetrators of the Istanbul bombings with the necessary finances, providing up to US$160,000.[30] The Turkish authorities probably correctly named (and later convicted) Sakka as the mastermind of the Istanbul bombings. In contrast to Akdaş, the actual ringleader of the cell, Sakka acted behind the scenes as a financier and a liaison to al-Zarqawi and al-Qaeda.

The role of Sakka in the Istanbul plot can best be categorized as "cell builder" (in Arabic, *bani al-saraya*). In al-Qaeda's global strategy, as articulated by the strategist Abu Musab al-Suri (Mustafa Setmarian Nasar), a cell builder is inconspicuous, well educated, and able to provide a cell with start-up money—in short, a jihadist professional with ties to al-Qaeda. Ideally, he will assist in the formation of a local network and commit a suicide attack afterward to wipe away his traces.[31] This description fits Sakka's role in the Istanbul plot, including the exit from the jihadist scene: Sakka prepared his own suicide attack on Israeli cruise ships in the southern Turkish port city and tourist center of Antalya in August 2005 but was arrested in the plot's early stages, when parts of the explosives caught fire in an apartment in Antalya. Sakka was subsequently caught in Diyarbakır, carrying US$120,000 in cash.[32]

Sakka served not only as financial support but also as a liaison between the Turkish cell, al-Qaeda, and the al-Zarqawi network. Sakka testified that in addition to the Istanbul bombings, he also assisted the 9/11 attackers.³³ At the same time, Sakka provided the authorities' best chance to thwart the attacks in advance. Numerous traces led to him, and intelligence agencies in Turkey, the United States, and Germany knew about some of his activities. During the run-up to the Istanbul attacks and in their wake, Turkish intelligence allegedly held back important information and did not share it with national law-enforcement agencies.³⁴ Moreover, the CIA seems to have been in contact with Sakka in 2000 to persuade him to become a double agent. Yet it lost him and turned to the Turkish MIT for help.³⁵ Shortly afterward, Sakka applied for asylum in southern Germany, where he stayed with his wife until summer 2001. His stay was interrupted by frequent travels to numerous countries in the Middle East and Asia to foster his terrorist network.

THE LOCAL DIMENSION: THE PLOTTERS AND JIHADIST ORGANIZATIONS IN TURKEY

Turkey has the most diverse and one of the most dangerous terrorist scenes in Europe and the Middle East. The Turkish government since the 1980s has concentrated on the fight against the Kurdistan Workers Party (PKK). Since the early 1980s, it fought an insurgency in southeastern Turkey that escalated into a civil war and involved brutality on both sides. The PKK's aim was to gain independence for the Kurdish people in Turkey. Although it has never come close to achieving its goals, it has been able to hinder the stabilization of Turkish rule in the eastern provinces— mainly from its bases in Iraqi Kurdistan—and it remains a threat today.

The Turkish government's preoccupation with the threat emanating from the activities of the PKK led it to take the jihadist threat less seriously than it should have. This might have been partly because the Turkish jihadists always showed a keen interest in the situation of Muslims in Bosnia and Chechnya and were therefore somewhat in line with the nationalist elites of the country. Both saw the plight of the Muslims in the Balkans and the Caucasus through historical lenses: both regions had at least partly been ruled by the Ottoman Empire, and there were strong relations between Islamists there and their Turkish brethren. For the Islamists, the idea of supranational solidarity among Muslims played an additional role. Therefore, an unknown but substantial number of Turks took part in the wars in Bosnia and Chechnya. The majority of foreign fighters who were killed in Chechnya from the mid-1990s until 2005 were Turks. This indicates that they were one of the biggest contingents of nonnative fighters in Chechnya.[36] Others went to fight in Afghanistan, but Chechnya remained the most popular destination. It is no coincidence that several of the Istanbul plotters are reported to have fought or trained in the Caucasus republic. There are indications that the Turkish government ignored the activities of jihadist recruiters as long as they channeled recruits to Chechnya and not to al-Qaeda.[37]

Turkey has also been home to two important militant Islamist organizations since the 1980s. These are the Turkish Hizbullah (which is not in any way affiliated to the Lebanese Hezbollah) and the Great East Islamic Raiders' Front (IBDA-C), whose common aim has been to establish an Islamic state in Turkey. The original group that formed around ringleader Habib Akdaş in southeastern Turkey had a predominantly Kurdish ethnic background. This initial cell had close connections to the Turkish Hizbullah. Both Hizbullah and the IBDA-C were connected to the Kurdish struggle and Hizbullah (in its formative period) because of the influence of the Iranian revolution. Several of the Istanbul plotters were connected to these organizations before their stay in Afghanistan. Nevertheless, the perpetrators of the attacks seem to have grown out of the local milieu of these organizations when they trained in al-Qaeda camps in Afghanistan. In Afghanistan, the Turkish fighters seem to have formed a cohesive group. Relatively small in numbers, they worked secretively and focused exclusively on training. Their stay in Afghanistan facilitated the building of intra-Turkish contacts and the development of the Istanbul network.[38]

THE TURKISH HIZBULLAH (PARTY OF GOD)

The Turkish Hizbullah is a primarily Kurdish organization that has its social base in the predominantly Kurdish eastern part of the country and among the Kurdish populations of the major cities in the west such as Istanbul and Izmir. It emerged in Diyarbakır, the largest city in the Kurdish southeast, in the early 1980s under the leadership of Hüseyin Velioğlu (1952–2000) but soon split into two factions called "Ilim" (lit.

knowledge, science) and "Menzil" (lit. way station).[39] The Ilim branch was led by Velioğlu and was responsible for most of the organization's terrorist activity. Ilim demanded immediate violent action, but Menzil argued for a gradual, propaganda-based strategy of winning over supporters before embarking on holy war.[40] The groups finally split in 1987 and fought each other bitterly in the early 1990s. From 1994, the Ilim faction gained ground and became the dominant branch. In the 1990s it concentrated its attacks primarily on pro-PKK intellectuals and politicians, whom it regarded as the vanguard of secular Kurdish nationalism. In the late 1990s it turned to kidnapping rich businessman and often murdered them instead of releasing them for ransom. It has been proven that the organization gruesomely murdered almost 500 people, but the real number of victims is estimated three times as high.[41]

From 1987, Hizbullah posed as a competitor to the PKK among Turkish Kurds in Eastern Anatolia and tried to win the loyalty of those Kurds who opposed the PKK's Marxist ideology on religious grounds. A violent struggle between the two groups developed, which escalated in the early 1990s. The clash between Hizbullah and the PKK prompted many observers to suspect the involvement of the Turkish security forces. They claimed that the Hizbullah was created in order to fight the PKK on behalf of the Turkish government and armed forces. In fact, on a local level, the security forces and Hizbullah cadres cooperated closely in their fight against the PKK. Here, the Turkish state committed a mistake similar to that of other Middle Eastern governments in the 1970s and 1980s, who cooperated with Islamists in order to weaken their secular and nationalist adversaries. However, it is rather unlikely that the Turkish army founded Hizbullah in order to use it as an instrument in the civil war. Nevertheless, the Hizbullah's role in the struggle against the PKK might explain the leniency with which the Turkish government dealt with Islamist militancy until 2000 and in some later cases.

After the arrest of the PKK leader Abdallah Öcalan, the Turkish government decided to crack down on Hizbullah, too, and successfully fought the organization in 1999. In the meantime, the Hizbullah had expanded its activities in the big cities in western Turkey, where it tried to attract Kurds who had migrated in large numbers from Eastern Anatolia. Shifting activities westward was reinforced by the weakened role of the PKK in the southeastern provinces, which led to heightened government presence and the closing of Hizbullah's shelters. Hizbullah's leader, Velioğlu, then prematurely called for the implementation of the second phase of Hizbullah's strategy, aiming to create a mass movement in western Turkey.[42] However, the majority of Turks did not identify with the organization since it was a predominantly Kurdish phenomenon and associated with horrible crimes rather than political goals.

In January 2000, Turkish police raided a house in Istanbul and killed Velioğlu. When Hizbullah tried to retaliate by assassinating the chief of police in Diyarbakır, the government cracked down on the organization. Many of the top leaders were arrested, and others fled the country for Europe.[43] Between 1998 and 2001, Turkish police found data on more than 1,000 members in safe houses and arrested more than 7,000 suspects, which led to the dismantling of Hizbullah's cells. Despite these developments, many members, supporters, and sympathizers in Turkey remained undetected. This was partly because of the highly secretive, cultlike structure of the organization. In addition, a large network of followers was not affected by the wave of arrests in 2000 and 2001. This was the case especially with the Bingöl Kurds among the Istanbul plotters, who are said to have had strong connections to Hizbullah.[44]

THE GREAT EAST ISLAMIC RAIDERS' FRONT (IBDA-C)

The Great East Islamic Raiders' Front or IBDA-C was founded in 1984 by Salih Mirzabeyoğlu (Salih Izzet Erdiş, born 1950). As with Hizbullah, IBDA-C members are mainly Kurds, and its leader stems from a Kurdish family. Mirzabeyoğlu had first joined the Islamist National Salvation Party (Millî Selamet Partisi, MSP) of former prime minister Erbakan but left in order to build a more radical, militant group. He was deeply influenced by the writings and personality of the Islamo-nationalist poet Necip Fazil Kısakürek (1904–1983), who—in a book entitled *Büyük Doğu İdeolocya Örgüsü* (The ideological network of the great east)—had propagated the idea of a supranational Islamic state. This state, called "Great East," would comprise the territory of several Middle Eastern states and be ruled by a caliph from Istanbul. In fact, Kısakürek followed quite a peculiar mix of Islamism, Ottomanism, and Turkish nationalism, which is still typical for many jihadists in Turkey.

Mirzabcyoğlu set out to fulfill Kısakürek's vision by fighting the Turk-ish state and Turkish secularism as the main obstacles to an Islamic state. The IBDA-C is strongly anti-Shiite, anti-Alevite, anti-Christian, and anti-Jewish, making the organization a suspect in the bombings of the synagogues. During the 1990s, the group perpetrated numerous attacks on prominent secularists, but also Jews, Alevites, and Christians. It frequently attacked banks and governmental installations as well as churches, bars, brothels, and nightclubs. The IBDA-C was, and remains, a relatively small organization, with no more than a few hundred support-ers. Its resources are so limited that its activities have never been very effective. Furthermore, it is highly fragmented. The group has always fol-lowed a strategy that now is termed "leaderless jihad."[45] The IBDA-C cells normally consist of no more than three to five members, and the organi-zation relies on cells' forming independently after having been attracted by the IBDA-C's propaganda activities.[46] Therefore, arrests of individual members and cells did not damage the organization as much as in cases of more centralized structures. Therefore, the IBDA-C relied heavily on the dissemination of its ideas. Mirzabeyoğlu wrote more than fifty books in which he expounded the ideology of his group. Even after he was arrested in late 1998, Mirzabeyoğlu continued his propaganda efforts in Turkish jails. His followers continued these activities. From 2001, they published a journal called *Beklenen Yeni Nizam* (The awaited new order). In 2005, the IBDA-C published a journal called *Kaide* (Al-Qaeda) in which the authors openly supported Osama bin Laden's organization.[47] IBDA-C activists increasingly began to publish their materials on the Internet.

DUAL LEADERSHIP: AL-QAEDA'S ROLE IN THE ISTANBUL BOMBINGS

Al-Qaeda and the al-Zarqawi network played different roles in different stages of the plot: In 2001, al-Qaeda trained the future ringleader and some of the perpetrators in Afghanistan. At the same time, bin Laden and Abu Hafs al-Masri (Mohammed Atef) dominated the planning process by defining Turkey as a theater of operations for al-Qaeda, recruiting the Turkish group for the attack, and giving some rough target guidance. After the loss of its rear base in Afghanistan, however, the organization seems to have lost at least some of its influence on the Turkish group. At this point, the al-Zarqawi network represented by Luayy Sakka stepped in, securing the necessary finances and possibly interfering in the organization of the attacks as well.

The Istanbul bombings give an insight into the uneasy relation between al-Qaeda and the al-Zarqawi network. Although the latter pledged allegiance to bin Laden in October 2004, cooperation and competition simultaneously informed their relationship. This was especially true in the years before 2004, when al-Zarqawi repeatedly told followers not to cooperate with al-Qaeda and tried to develop his own profile as a terrorist leader equal to bin Laden.[48] There may even have been an organizational conflict between al-Qaeda central and the al-Zarqawi network over influence in the Istanbul plot. If the two organizations competed in the case of the Istanbul bombings, it seems that al-Zarqawi usurped the earlier planners in Afghanistan and gained the upper hand in November 2003.

Osama bin Laden and Mohammed Atef asked the group to target Israeli ships at Mersin and the American airbase at Incirlik. However, the plotters took their own operational decisions when it turned out that they would not be able to successfully attack those hard targets. Al-Qaeda, for its part, seems to have been satisfied with the opportunity to influence the planning of an attack in Turkey. Consequently, after the recruits left Afghanistan, there are no indications that al-Qaeda had any operational control over the Istanbul cell. This was probably because of the problems al-Qaeda experienced after the loss of its base in Afghanistan. Nevertheless, it is striking that the attack took place shortly after bin Laden, in October 2003, called upon his followers to perpetrate attacks on countries that had provided troops to help the United States stabilize Iraq. As Turkey was expressly named here, it is highly likely that the al-Qaeda leadership was informed about the activities of its Turkish followers.

The recruitment of the young Turks and Kurds was an important new development for al-Qaeda. From its inception, al-Qaeda has been an Arab organization, dominated by the Egyptians and Saudi Arabians around its two leaders, Ayman al-Zawahiri and Osama bin Laden. Until 2001, the organization was not able to integrate fully other national or regional groups into its hierarchy. North Africans, Syrians, and Palestinians still tended to organize in nationally or regionally homogenous groups independent of al-Qaeda. Furthermore, non-Arab jihadists saw al-Qaeda as an Arab organization, which therefore had problems recruiting them. Not surprisingly, Turkish nationals seem to have been a small minority among the volunteers trained in the Afghan camps.

The Istanbul plot is noteworthy because of its task sharing. Besides the connection to al-Qaeda, the al-Zarqawi network played an important role in it by financing at least parts of the operation. Until 2003, Abu Musab al-Zarqawi, who would later declare his allegiance to Osama bin Laden, led a group of Palestinians, Jordanians, and Syrians who did not want to join al-Qaeda. After his release from jail in Jordan in early 1999, al-Zarqawi returned to Afghanistan, where he stayed in the late 1980s. Al-Qaeda and the Taliban granted him permission to establish his own training camp in Herat close to the Iranian border and far from al-Qaeda's headquarters in Kandahar. It was a camp established exclusively for Jordanians, Palestinians, Syrians, and Lebanese, who formed the core of Zarqawi's Tawhid organization.[49]

Al-Zarqawi stuck to his original goal, namely, fighting the Jordanian regime and for the "liberation" of Palestine, rather than joining al-Qaeda's more internationalist jihad.[50] In late 2001, al-Zarqawi fled to northern Iraq via Iran. When it became clear that the United States would attack Iraq, al-Zarqawi took the chance to reorganize his network and redirect it for the fight against U.S. forces and, increasingly, against the new Iraqi government. He relied on a growing number of Iraqi personnel in his network and cooperated with former regime loyalists.[51] Subsequently, he changed the name of his organization to al-Tawhid wal-Jihad (Monotheism and holy war) and, in October 2004, after he had pledged allegiance to Osama bin Laden, to al-Qaeda in Mesopotamia.

However, al-Zarqawi was unable to continue implementing his former agenda, focusing exclusively on Jordanian and Israeli targets. In order to rebuild his organization and fight U.S. forces in Iraq, he had to rely heavily on new Iraqi recruits. According to one of his followers, al-Zarqawi adjusted his strategy to the new situation: first, the militants would have to expel the Americans from Iraq, where they would install an Islamist regime, and then they would extend their Jihad to the neighboring countries, with the final aim of "liberating" Jerusalem.[52] The Istanbul attacks fitted al-Zarqawi's new scheme to destabilize Iraq's neighbors, and his lieutenant, Luayy Sakka, seems to have been tasked with executing this strategy in Turkey.

The role of the two major jihadist organizations in the Istanbul bombings were embodied by Sakka: a Syrian from Aleppo with strong connections to Turkey who joined al-Qaeda in Afghanistan first but then joined al-Zarqawi when he established his training camp in Herat. This was noteworthy because al-Zarqawi refused to pledge allegiance to al-Qaeda in order to pursue his own agenda. For Sakka, the al-Zarqawi group likely fit his own background and outlook better than al-Qaeda proper. Syrians—like Palestinians, Jordanians, and Lebanese—were grossly underrepresented in the organization because of al-Qaeda's lack of interest in the Palestinian cause and the future of the surrounding countries. When al-Zarqawi appeared on the scene in Afghanistan, Sakka quickly joined the Jordanian and subsequently became one of his most important lieutenants. Furthermore, Sakka was not the only person in the al-Zarqawi organization with close relations to Turkey. The German Turk Mevlüt Kar seems to have been an important logistics officer for the Zarqawi organization in Germany and Turkey from the late 1990s.[53]

TURKISH JIHADISM ON THE RISE?

The Istanbul bombings were the result of al-Qaeda's 2001 decision to attack Western and Israeli targets in Turkey, the al-Zarqawi network's goal of destabilizing Iraq's neighbors, and a violent reaction by Turkish jihadists to events in Iraq 2003. The American invasion of the country and the subsequent emergence of an Iraqi insurgency fostered Turkish anti-Americanism and drew nationalist-inclined Islamists to target the United States and its allies.[54]

The attacks should have come as no surprise since Turkey had already witnessed several smaller jihadist bombings in 2003. After the Istanbul bombings, however, no major terrorist attacks were perpetrated by jihadists in Turkey. One important exception was a shoot-out near the American consulate in Istanbul on July 9, 2008, in which three policemen and three of the four attackers were killed. Regular news of smaller bombings (sometimes with no identifiable perpetrator) and arrests of terrorist suspects were evidence that the jihadist scene in Turkey continued to be active and remained an important threat to the country.

Most noteworthy, a growing number of members of the Turkish diaspora in Germany joined the jihadist movement from 2005.[55]

It remains an open question to what extent Turkish jihadism is a predominantly Kurdish phenomenon. If that were the case, it would pose a serious problem to the Turkish state. The Kurds in Turkey still suffer from cultural, socioeconomic, and political discrimination and populate the least-developed parts of the country and the poorest quarters of the big cities. A further spread of jihadist thought among Kurds might lead to the emergence of an explosive alliance with a national struggle. However, Turkish jihadism does not seem to have developed along these lines after 2003. Rather, the Turkish, like other groups, seem to have gone through a process of internationalization. The Istanbul cell already hinted at that development insofar as it was not as exclusively Kurdish as, for instance, the Turkish Hizbullah has been. This trend—which has been most obvious on the jihadist Internet, where Turks in recent years have developed a profound interest in conflicts in Iraq, Afghanistan, and further afield—has allowed for greater cooperation with Uzbek, Afghan, Pakistani, and Arab jihadists. Turks are likely to play a prominent role in jihadist terrorism in the years to come.

NOTES

1. *Cumhuriyet* (Istanbul), November 17, 2003, 8.

2. Karl Vick, "Al Qaeda's Hand in Istanbul Plot," *Washington Post*, February 13, 2007.

3. In the 1990s, Incirlik was used by U.S. planes to patrol the northern no-flight zone in Iraq. In the first phase of the war in Afghanistan and in the aftermath of Operation Iraqi Freedom in 2003, Incirlik was used as an important logistics hub by U.S. forces. See "Anatolischer Alptraum," *Der Spiegel*, March 24, 2003; Frank Hyland, "U.S. Air Base at Incirlik Faces Political and Security Threats," *Jamestown Terrorism Focus* 4, no. 42 (2007), available at http://www.jamestown.org /single/?no_cache=1&tx_ttnews[tt_news]=4619.

4. "Eşler, El Kaide'nin Bomba Kuryesi çıktı" (The wives acted as bomb couriers for al-Qaeda), February 28, 2004, *Milliyet.com.tr* (accessed February 10, 2010).

5. Vick, "Al Qaeda's Hand in Istanbul Plot."

6. "We reserve the right to retaliate . . . against all countries that take part in this unjust [Iraq] war, namely Britain, Spain, Australia, Poland, Japan and Italy" (bin Laden, October 18, 2003, quoted in "Timeline: Messages from bin Laden," al-Jazeera, available

at http://english.aljazeera.net/news/middleeast/2010/01/2010124123232335456.html [accessed February 11, 2010]).

7. Guido Steinberg, *Der nahe und der ferne Feind* (Munich: C. H. Beck, 2005) 84–85. Since the U.S. invasion of Afghanistan in 2001, bin Laden has stressed the Palestinian issue in his audio and video speeches to legitimize attacks against Jewish and Israeli targets.

8. "The Mombassa Attacks: Al Qaeda's New Weapon," *New York Times*, November 30, 2002.

9. "The Softest Target," *Observer* (London), November 23, 2003.

10. See, for example, an early jihadist propaganda text against modern Turkey and Kemalism by Abdallah Azzam, *al-Manara al-Mafquda* (The lost light tower) (Peshawar: Markaz Shahid Azzam al-I'lami, 1987).

11. "El Kaide Davası'nın Gerekçeli Kararı" (Judgment in Al Qaeda trial), *Hürriyet* (Istanbul), April 24, 2007, available at http://hurarsiv.hurriyet.com.tr/goster/haber .aspx?id=6396475 (accessed February 4, 2010)

12. "Turkey Expects to Identify Synagogue Bombers Soon," *New York Times*, November 18, 2003.

13. See Y. Karmon, "Assessing the Credibility of the 'Abu Hafs Al-Masri Brigades' Threats," The Middle East Media Research Institute, Inquiry and Analysis Series, Report no.185, August 10, 2004, available at http://www.memri.org/report /en/0/0/0/0/0/0/1190.htm#_edn6 (accessed February 11, 2010).

14. Yassin Musharbash, "Al-Masri-Brigaden. Die Aasgeier des Terrorismus," *Der Spiegel*, August 10, 2004, available at http://www.spiegel.de/politik/ausland /0,1518,312712,00.html.

15. "Usuliyu London: Khasirat Al Qaeda Mu'ayyidiha Ba'd Tafjirai Riadh Wa Istanbul" (Fundamentalists in London: al-Qaeda has lost its supporters after the two attacks of Riyadh and Istanbul), *Asharq al-Awsat* (London), November 19, 2003, available at http://www.aawsat.com/details.asp?section=4&article=203846&issueno=9122 (accessed February 11, 2010).

16. "Codename Abu Nidal," *Der Spiegel*, December 8, 2003.

17. Vick, "Al Qaeda's Hand in Istanbul Plot."

18. In 1990, Akdaş graduated from high school in Mardin and afterward went to Pakistan for the first time to attend "religious studies." In 1996 and 1997, Ersöz also went to Islamabad in Pakistan for "religious studies," and in 1998, he met Akdaş there. In July of that same year, both returned to Istanbul. From that time on, they spent a lot of time together, including a "business trip" to Iraq in 1999. See Fuat Akyol, "Milli İstihbarat Teskilatı'nın, bombalama eylemlerinden beş ay önce İstanbul'daki grubun liderlerinden Adnan Ersöz'e ulaştığı, ancak saldırıları önleyemediği ortaya çıktı (Although the MIT, five months prior to the attacks, was close to one of the leaders of the Istanbul group, the attacks could not be prevented)," *Aksiyon* (Istanbul), April 3, 2004.

19. "Eşler, El Kaide'nin Bomba Kuryesi çıktı." On the discussions, see "Sakka'dan çarpıcı itiraflar" (Spectacular confession by Sakka), *Hürriyet* (Istanbul), February 21, 2006, available at http://arama.hurriyet.com.tr/arsivnews.aspx?id=3965926 (accessed January 28, 2010).

20. Fuat Akyol, "Milli İstihbarat." Ersöz stated that the arrest of his al-Qaeda contact in Afghanistan caused considerable trouble and delayed the attacks.

21. After the attacks, he is reported to have fled to Dubai or Syria. See "Codename Abu Nidal." He was later on suspected to have gone to Iraq. As of 2010, his whereabouts were unknown.

22. "Suicide Bombers Are Buried in Turkey's Breeding Ground of Extremism," *Guardian*, November 27, 2003.

23. "Turkish Town's Despair Breeds Terrorists, Residents Fear," *New York Times*, November 27, 2003.

24. "Codename Abu Nidal."

25. Fuat Akyol, "Milli İstihbarat." During his political science studies at Istanbul University, Ersöz became increasingly interested in religious and language studies. He wanted to study Arabic in Syria but was turned down. After his graduation in 1996, he decided to go to Pakistan.

26. "Wein, Whisky und Waffen," *Der Spiegel*, August 22, 2005, 114–15.

27. "After two years of work and setting things up in Herat, Abu Mus'ab started to think about sending his good companions whom he trusted to regions outside of Afghanistan. There, they should recruit and finance. It started, as far as I remember, with Turkey and Germany because the Syrian brothers who had joined him had a good outreach to these two regions" (Saif al-Adel, *Al-Sira al-jihadiyya li-l-qa'id al-dhabbah Abi Mus'ab al-Zarqawi* (The jihad career of the slaughterous leader Abu Mus'ab al-Zarqawi), available at http://alboraq.info/showthread.php?t=97685 [accessed June 21, 2010]).

28. Sakka had met one of his future brothers-in-law, Christian K., in Khalden, in 1997. From September 2000 to July 2001, he was based in the southwestern German town of Schramberg. See "Wein, Whisky und Waffen," 114–15.

29. "Sakka'dan çarpıcı Itiraflar (Spectacular confession by Sakka)."

30. "A Bomb-Builder, 'Out of the Shadows'" *Washington Post*, February 20, 2006.

31. See Philipp Holtmann, *The Jihad Concept of Abu Mus'ab al-Suri* (Tel Aviv: Moshe Dayan Center, 2009), 106. For the original text, see 'Umar 'Abd al-Hakim (Abu Musab al-Suri), *Da'wat al-muqawama al-'alamiya al-islamiya* (Global Islamic resistance call) (n.p.: n.d. [2004]), 1402.

32. "Aladin aus dem Schwarzwald," *Der Spiegel*, August 15, 2005, 108–9.

33. "Al Qaeda Kingpin: I Trained 9/11 Hijackers," *Sunday Times* (London), November 25, 2007.

34. "Fırat Yaldız, 11 Eylül, El Kaide ve İstanbul" (9/11, al-Qaeda, and Istanbul), available at http://www.egm.gov.tr/temuh/terorizm10_makale3.htm (accessed February 4, 2010).

35. "Wein, Whisky und Waffen," 115.

36. Brian Glyn Williams, "Turkish Volunteers in Chechnya," *Terrorism Monitor* (Jamestown Foundation) 3, no. 7 (May 5, 2005). Chechnya remains an important interest of Turkish Internet activists, and the leaders of the Chechen jihad, such as Khattab and Shamil Bassajev, have cult status among Turkish jihadists

37. In 2007, for instance, this seems to have been the case with Mevlüt Kar, a German Turk living in Istanbul and a recruiter for the jihad in Chechnya. On Kar, see this volume, chapter 11.

38. "Nash'at Tanzim Al Qaeda" (The emergence of al-Qaeda organization), available at http://www.muslm.net/vb/showthread.php?s=ec894489f2c5aea4dd19085a60 00e1a5&t=232749 (accessed February 11, 2010). Members of the outlawed Caliphate State organization, also known as Union of Islamic Communities and Societies (ICCB) or Kaplan organization, a militant Turkish group based in Germany probably trained in Afghanistan. There has been a lot of speculation about a possible involvement of the group in the Istanbul plot and contact with the plotters. However, there is no hard evidence to substantiate this claim. See Ben Lombardi, "Jihadist Bombings in Istanbul," Department of National Defense Canada, Directorate of Strategic Analysis, Research Note, 2004, 11.

39. Both were named after bookshops that the leaders of the group had opened in Diyarbakır in the early 1980s, which were the locations where the group had formed. Fidan Güngör opened the Menzil bookshop in 1981. The Ilim bookshop was opened by Hüseyin Velioğlu in 1982.

40. Rusen Cakir, "The Reemergence of Hizballah in Turkey," The Washington Institute for Near East Policy, September 2007, 8.

41. "Der fromme Weltkrieg," *Der Spiegel*, November 24, 2003.

42. The first goal of Hizbullah's strategy was to fight rival secular and religious groups in the southeast of Turkey, and the final goal was to overthrow the Turkish government. See John T. Nugent, "The Defeat of Turkish Hizballah as a Model for Counter-Terrorism Strategy," *Middle East Review of International Affairs* 8, no. 1 (March, 2004); Asli Aydintasbas, "Murder on the Bosphorus," *Middle East Quarterly* 7, no. 2 (June 2000).

43. Cakir, "The Reemergence of Hizballah in Turkey," 13.

44. "Suicide Bombers Are Buried in Turkey's Breeding Ground for Terrorism."

45. Marc Sageman, *Leaderless Jihad: Terror Networks in the Twenty-First Century* (Philadelphia: University of Pennsylvania Press, 2008).

46. Lawrence E. Cline: "From Ocalan to Al Qaida: The Continuing Terrorist Threat in Turkey," *Studies in Conflict and Terrorism* 27 (2004): 325; Gareth Jenkins: "Turkey's Islamic Raiders of the Greater East Seeking Ties with Al Qaeda?," *Jamestown Terrorism Focus* 4, no. 40 (December 5, 2007): 6.

47. "Kaide (Al Qaeda) Magazine Published Openly in Turkey," Memri Special Dispatch Series No. 951, available at http://www.memri.org/report/en/0/0/0/0/0/0/1432.htm, accessed January 11, 2012.

48. "Zarqawi and Bin Laden: Brothers in Arms?," BBC, October 18, 2004, available at http://news.bbc.co.uk/2/hi/3754618.stm (accessed February 12, 2010)

49. See Guido Steinberg, "From Local to Global Jihad and Back: Islamist Terrorists and Their Impact on U.S. Gulf Policy," in *Great Powers and Regional Orders*, ed. Markus Kaim (Farnham: Ashgate, 2008), 155.

50. "How Terror Groups Vied for a Player," *Christian Science Monitor*, May 11, 2004

51. " 'The Arab Mujahidin' in Iraq are 2000" (Arabic), *Al-Hayat* (London), November 8, 2004.

52. "Al-Zarqawi: An Islamic Government in Iraq" (Arabic), *Al-Hayat* (London), September 10, 2004.

53. "Der fünfte Mann," *Der Spiegel*, April 20, 2009.

54. Jenkins, "Turkey's Islamic Raiders of the Greater East Seeking Ties with Al Qaeda?"

55. This volume, chapter 11.

20

The Sinai Terrorist Attacks

HOLLY L. MCCARTHY AND AMI PEDAHZUR

Between 2004 and 2006, a series of attacks in the Sinai Peninsula killed more than 120 people and threatened key interests of al-Qaeda's main enemies. The perpetrators belonged to a group that was well organized, well trained, and well financed and held Salafist ideology. The attacks were the first of their kind in Sinai and threatened the security of both Egypt and Israel—two of Washington's main allies in the Middle East. In addition to presenting a challenging (but straightforward) set of security interests, these events also threatened the foundations of the historic Egyptian-Israeli peace treaty and cast a shadow over Egypt's efforts to promote a comprehensive peace deal in the Middle East. The perpetrators were primarily from Bedouin tribes, which held peaceful relations with both Egypt and Israel; that they were behind such destabilizing events took many in the region by surprise.

THE ATTACKS

The first of the attacks took place on October 7, 2004, when a group of four men carried out a series of three bombings targeting the Taba Hilton Hotel and two small retreats south of the Israeli-Egyptian border in Sinai. The truck bomb at the Hilton exploded with 600 kg of TNT, taking down ten floors of the hotel and killing thirty-four people. The two subsequent bombs targeted two lodges south of Taba using vehicles but did not result in any casualties.[1] These attacks occurred during the Israeli holiday week of Sukkoth, when many Israelis celebrated in Sinai. Egyptians were celebrating the anniversary of the October War (also known as the Yom Kippur War) between Egypt and Israel. About nine months later, on July 23—the anniversary of Egypt's 1952 bloodless coup d'état in which Egyptians gained independence from the British—three much larger and more devastating bombs exploded at the southern-most tip of Sinai in the resort area of Sharm el-Sheikh.

Sharm el-Sheik is a summer tourist destination that sits at the southern tip of the Sinai Peninsula. It has more than one hundred luxury hotels, a dynamic nightlife, shopping, water sports, and restaurants, and its airport makes it only a few hours away for European and Middle Eastern vacationers. In the early hours of that July morning in 2005, two pickup trucks loaded with 1,100 kg of TNT cleared security checkpoints, entered the city, and split up. One driver stashed a suitcase loaded with explosives near a taxi station then fled the scene and headed toward the Ghazala Gardens Hotel. He plowed through a security gate and into the hotel lobby as his truck exploded, killing more than forty people. The other truck stopped a few kilometers away in traffic awaiting clearance through a checkpoint near the Old Market—an area popular with local Egyptians. Minutes after the first explosion, the suitcase bomb detonated in the parking lot, and the truck bomb in the Old Market exploded, killing seventeen, mostly Egyptian citizens. Egyptian government reports list the death toll from all three attacks at sixty-four foreigners and Egyptians.[2]

Sinai Liberation Day celebrates the end of the Israeli occupation of the peninsula in 1982.[3] In 2006, the holiday fell on the weekend of the Pharaonic festivities of Shams an-Nisseem, which coincide with the Coptic Christian Easter holiday. Egyptians of all religions take the chance to travel or spend leisure time outside in celebration. Only nine months after the attacks in Sharm el-Sheikh, on April 24, three smaller bombs exploded in Dahab, a small city located between the sites of the two previous attacks that caters to budget travelers and backpackers, including scuba divers and windsurfers. Two of the bombers detonated their explosives in rapid succession on opposite sides of a pedestrian bridge that links the restaurant and shopping districts of Dahab. Moments later, in an alley lined with glass-front shops, about one hundred meters from the pedestrian bridge, the third bomb detonated. All three attackers, who died in the explosions, used about 2 kg of TNT. Some reports state the men wore suicide vests, but most eyewitness accounts report they were carrying bags with them.[4] Twenty-three people died in the Dahab bombings.

The Multinational Force and Observers is an independent peacekeeping mission created because of the 1978 Camp David Accords and the 1979 peace treaty between Egypt and Israel. They maintain bases in Sinai to monitor the Egyptian-Israeli border. On April 26, two more bombers blew themselves up at their base close to the al-Gorah Airport but did not succeed in claiming any victims. Each of the bombs consisted of two to four kilograms of the same type of TNT used in the previous attacks.[5]

THE OFFICIAL ASSESSMENT

In direct response to Osama bin Laden's foundational premise for global jihad in 1996, al-Qaeda has built target sets that include "the alliance of Jews, Christians, and their agents."[6] Less than a decade later in Sinai, the target, type, planning, scope, and simultaneous attacks in a number of places all displayed hallmarks of al-Qaeda operations—as Egyptian officials initially observed.[7] As the investigation progressed, however, the Egyptian government denied al-Qaeda's involvement as anything more than inspiration, instead placing responsibility on a previously unknown group of self-radicalized men who—Egyptian officials asserted—acted alone.[8]

To arrive at this conclusion, the Egyptian government followed a line of logic also put forth by Marc Sageman in *Leaderless Jihad*. In his 2008 book, Sageman says that "homegrown" terrorists perpetrate the current wave of terrorist events and belong to a social movement inspired by al-Qaeda.[9] These terrorists belong to a phenomenon of "global Islamist terrorism" and make up cells that receive little or no help from their predecessors, and in cases where all indicators point to al-Qaeda involvement, in fact, nothing more than ideology can be attributed to Osama bin Laden and his cohorts.

From the evidence, Egyptian officials determined the Sinai attacks were perpetrated by an informal group of men who, while possibly sympathizing with Salafist ideology, executed their operations independently and for different reasons. Officials from the Egyptian Interior Ministry believe the leaders of this group "targeted the stability of the state first of all, under the pretext that its institutions are heretical and that its leaders ally themselves with the enemies of Islam." They also believe the leadership aimed to use the ongoing events in the region to encourage the implementation of this plan. Allegedly, the group of men grew unhappy with the secular character of the Egyptian regime and wanted to undermine its foundations by targeting foreign tourists. Reports allude repeatedly to the impoverished nature of the Bedouin community in Sinai and—some media suggest—understandable resentment on the part of these Bedouin men. After the attacks in Sharm el-Sheikh, alleged members of the group issued a statement: "We, Tawhid wa al-Jihad in Egypt, are continuing our war to expel the Jews and Christians from the land of Islam. Our war has begun by targeting the axis of Zionist evil and immorality in Sinai, where Moses spoke to God, in Taba, Ras Shaytan, and Nuweiba. May God accept our martyrs who fell in this blessed raid."[10] Therefore, the attacks were all attributed to this elusive group, *Tawhid wa al-Jihad* (Monotheism and Jihad), with no known ties to the Iraqi variant led by the late Abu Musab al-Zarqawi.

Under Sageman's theory, all of this makes clear sense but only if key issues and facts are ignored. An objective observer would question several aspects of the group behind the Sinai attacks as put forth by Egyptian officials. Specifically, evidence contrary to Sageman's theory includes the way the group financed itself, the means by which the group acquired explosives, connections between group members and foreign elements, and claims issued by other groups for the attacks. The willingness of governments to look critically at the facts surrounding the attacks and to address objective discrepancies lies at the heart of counterterrorism efforts to combat al-Qaeda's operations. Therefore, examining whether the group self-radicalized and operated independently or was part of a cell that received instruction and material assistance from al-Qaeda is paramount to taking action against a terrorist network's capabilities. Considering this, one must ask if a different theory could be applied to explain these facts.

AN ALTERNATIVE APPROACH

Sageman's theory states that an al-Qaeda-inspired social movement influences "homegrown cells" to act independently of al-Qaeda but with similar ideologies. Specifically, he explains, "each small terrorist network pursues its own activity for its own local reasons, and in doing so promotes far more effectively the overall goals and strategy of the al-Qaeda terrorist social movement than al-Qaeda Central could." As Bruce Hoffman points out, Sageman's analysis of terrorism dismisses "much of the existing academic literature on terrorism in general and terrorist networks in particular."[11] Likewise, in this case, such a premise necessitates excluding any evidence indicating assistance from or connection to al-Qaeda. This overlooks a well-known history of al-Qaeda's relationship to Egypt and the desire of both bin Laden and Ayman al-Zawahiri to establish a presence in the area. Al-Zawahiri is one of al-Qaeda's key ideological influences, and his radical form of jihad derives from Egypt. His group, Egyptian Islamic Jihad, is responsible for the assassination of Egyptian president Anwar Sadat in 1981, an assassination attempt against the former Egyptian president Hosni Mubarrak in 1995, and two failed assassination attempts against two other Egyptian officials. So it is possible al-Qaeda operatives could have provided assistance. Therefore, would a theory allowing the possibility of al-Qaeda's involvement in the Sinai attacks explain the evidence ignored thus far by Egyptian officials?

Based on the description of the group offered by the Egyptian Interior Ministry, this was a remarkably resourceful and capable group of Bedouin peasants. They offer further evidence of this by explaining how the group self-radicalized and provisioned itself through theft and petty crimes, acknowledging that some financial assistance—though no more than $1,500—came from "extremist elements" in Gaza.[12] All five automobiles that exploded in the attacks were simply stolen, eliminating one of the most significant expenses. In addition, the more than 1,700 kg of explosives were not purchased but recovered from old land mines by a handful of what must have been the group's most highly skilled members

One of the toughest challenges in understanding the Sinai attacks is the fact that a majority of the suspects were killed without being questioned. Added to that, almost all of the information available about these attackers derives from the very establishment that has based its case on a faulty premise. If one is to believe these men were sitting in the desert growing increasingly unhappy about their situation until they decided to assemble into a network of dozens of men, hide out in the mountains, and proceed to orchestrate the most deadly attacks on Egyptian soil, one must also believe there was no chance these men had any assistance from outsiders.

Using the premise that follows Mark Sageman's theory, Egyptian authorities explain that this group of men radicalized and waged their attacks because of the poverty and deprivation they experienced as Sinai Bedouin. Egyptian officials describe the group as Muslim men who predominantly originate from the area of al-Arish in northern Sinai. Five of the eleven attackers lived in Sheikh Zuwayid, a settlement of a few hundred Bedouin on the outskirts of al-Arish that sits just across the border from the Gaza Strip and Israel. A majority of the houses in Sheikh Zuwayid and the villages surrounding al-Arish are little more than mud-brick huts and have electricity for just six hours each day. The mastermind of all of the attacks, Nasr al-Mallahi, was "observant but not fanatical" and was from this area. He took over the group from the original leader, Mosaed, who went missing just before the Taba attacks.[13] When al-Mallahi took over leadership of the group, his intent was to continue the original mission to target the stability of the state "under the pretext that its institutions are heretical and that its leaders ally themselves with the enemies of Islam." He also aimed to use the ongoing events in the region to encourage the implementation of plan. While hunting him, the Egyptian Interior Ministry reported finding a hideout containing machine guns, ammunition, and notebooks detailing some of the attacks in Sinai.[14] Aside from this description, Egyptian officials offer little in the way of an explanation as to how or why the group became radicalized.

Rising tensions between the Bedouin population in Sinai and the Egyptian government about land, water, and development do contribute to a general dissatisfaction among the Sinai population.[15] Despite obviously difficult living conditions, however, it is unlikely that simple issues of poverty contributed to the radicalization of the perpetrators. As a number of studies have shown, the connections between poverty and terrorism are tenuous at best.[16] Bedouins are a traditionally nomadic population who, in many cases, prefer to live in the open desert in tents without electricity and other modern comforts. There is nothing to indicate that difficult living conditions contributed in any significant way to the radicalization of these men. Aside from this minor detail, Egyptian officials offer—then dismiss—several key pieces of evidence indicating the likelihood that someone from outside could have been involved in the process of radicalization for the group.

The attacks on Taba, Sharm el-Sheikh, and Dahab all display characteristics of a network that held ties to extremist groups in both Egypt and Gaza. Two Bedouin brothers and a Palestinian carried out the attacks in Taba. The brothers, Mohammed and Suleiman Flayfil, tried to travel to Libya, Jordan, and Saudi Arabia "on several occasions," and went missing from their family altogether after 1996.[17] Three other brothers in the group, Ayman, Yusri, and Munir Muharib, established connections to Palestinian fundamentalist elements that frequented the area of al-Arish. Ayman and Yousri traveled to Gaza at some point for training in weapons and explosives. Abu-Sulayman was a Palestinian who reportedly provided Yusri with US$1,000 and a cell phone connected via the Israeli telecommunications network to maintain contact. The third brother, Mounir, received US$500 from Palestinian activists and was found with the Israeli cell phone chip when police killed him. Ayman and Yousri also received congratulations from the Palestinians after carrying out the Dahab bombings.[18]

Twenty-two-year-old Moussa Badran, who drove the truck into the Ghazala Gardens Hotel in Sharm al-Sheikh, also held ties to fundamentalist groups in Egypt. Atillah al-Qarm was one of the Dahab attackers and in charge of the ground planning for his cell. He was an uneducated twenty-four-year-old who worked at a fruit and vegetable stand in Dahab for several years before the attacks. He and the other two Dahab attackers, Mohammad Yaqub, a primary school teacher, and Mohammad al-Karimi, a student from al-Arish, were sent by al-Mallahi along with a number of others to the Gaza Strip to receive training in weapons and explosives.[19] These connections are clear evidence the group received assistance from outside this specific network. Yet under the premise of the "homegrown" network, Egyptian authorities are forced to dismiss this in constructing their assessment of the group. This is important because of al-Qaeda's connection to Egypt and the fact bin Laden used the Palestinian cause as part of his main recruitment strategy as the group has long held an interest in gaining a foothold there. One obvious way for a terrorist group to establish itself among strangers would be to help with financial matters

Financing is a primary concern for any group that has to feed, house, educate, and transport its members and ultimately provide the means for them to carry out their assigned duties. According to Egyptian officials, several men assisted in the operations. Nasr al-Mallahi, the mastermind of the group, apparently recruited some forty new elements and established an elaborate support structure to disperse and maintain the recruits in various locations throughout the Sinai Peninsula.[20] He is said to have appointed the brothers Salim al-Zayud and Salman al-Zayud, farmers from al-Arish, to recruit members and disseminate the group's ideology.[21] Al-Mallahi also seems to have appointed intermediaries for communication with the suicide attackers. This group of middlemen was allegedly responsible for provisioning the outposts where fugitives and recruits were dispersed.[22]

Mohammed Riba'a, a forty-two-year-old metalworker, was charged with building steel casings and fitting the bombs onto the vehicles. Mohammad Sobh, an appliance dealer, was identified as "the engineer" who prepared the electrical devices used as timers for the bombs in the first attacks. Osama al-Nakhlawi and another man, Ihab Rabia, were charged with fashioning the explosives and training the others in how to use them. In order to finance the operations, Mohammad Elian, a.k.a. Abu Grair, reportedly committed a number of robberies. Abu Grair, Salah al-Tarawi, a student at al-Azhar University, and Salim al-Zayud apparently also gathered landmines from minefields dating back to previous wars in the Sinai. Then they removed the TNT from the landmines and put it into gas canisters, which al-Tarawi later prepared with electrical connections. Salim al-Shenoub, a forty-seven-year-old Bedouin known for drug smuggling and arms trafficking, was identified as the protector of the Taba and Sharm suspects, sheltering them at his homes in the Jabal al-Hallal mountains. Al-Tarawi also ostensibly stole the vehicles used in the Sharm el-Sheikh attacks.[23]

With this description, the Egyptian officials neglect to consider realistic operational capabilities by claiming the group could pull off the attacks through enterprising members, some good fortune, and what amounts to petty crimes. Egyptian reports claim the group used a variety of resources to finance themselves. These included stealing the cars for both the Taba and Sharm el-Sheikh attacks, gathering money for charity pledged to Palestinians, and the sale of other stolen property, including gold pieces.[24] If one takes into account at least forty group members and the costs of their most basic essentials for the minimum time in question of eighteen months, the financing does not seem to suffice. Added to this, one must consider the weapons found, the weapons used in various shoot-outs with police forces, and transportation to provision members at the hideouts, which makes the notion that the group was self-funded seem even less feasible.

Two of the group's members reportedly stole the vehicles used in the Taba and Sharm el-Sheikh attacks, but a more likely scenario is that they paid for them.[25] Vehicles are expensive in Egypt, and they usually represent the life savings and sole source of income for the owner. It would be difficult to hide a stolen vehicle among the Sinai Bedouin and more difficult still to prevent the police from detecting it with the ubiquitous checkpoints set up throughout the Sinai Peninsula. It is unlikely that, on two separate occasions, two to three stolen vehicles would have passed through these checkpoints without police forces discovering any of them.

The vehicles used in the Taba attacks did not have the serial numbers removed, but those used in the Sharm el-Sheikh attacks did. Skilled car thieves know that clearing the vehicle of serial numbers is the first thing one does with a stolen car. It would appear the thieves for the Taba attacks were inexperienced, but those involved in the attacks in Sharm el-Sheikh were not. However, because Egyptian police used the serial numbers from the vehicles at the Taba bombings to arrest and interrogate the relatives of anyone connected in any way to the attacks, the change in tactics in Sharm el-Sheikh indicates their motives were to prevent such interrogations again. This casts further doubt on the notion that the group stole the cars. Otherwise, if the group is responsible for stealing the cars but did not know to remove the serial numbers in the Taba attacks, one must question the theory that these were criminals with the skill to provide for a network of more than forty members almost entirely through crime. Therefore, either the group had money to buy the vehicles or someone wealthy donated them. None of the members of the group was identified as wealthy, and given that the International Monetary Fund ranked Egypt number 101 out of 181 countries with $5,897 GDP per capita (in 2008), the financial situation for Bedouin men with their qualifications does not suggest they funded the purchase of the vehicles on their own. Had Egyptian officials considered the possibility that someone outside of the network was assisting the group, they may have noticed how difficult it would be to carry out attacks on such a scale with the apparent resources among the group's members.

Another main issue for the attackers was acquiring and using the explosives. Egyptian officials report the perpetrators used TNT from landmines left over in Sinai from previous wars. Landmines vary in size, but a large one might contain 20 kg of TNT. This means three of the Bedouin group members detected, uncovered, deactivated, removed, and repackaged approximately one hundred landmines. While this is not impossible, one must question how likely it is that this group did not simply purchase some of the vast quantities of explosives moving through the Sinai Desert on a regular basis en route to Gaza.

One of the most significant aspects in the case of the Sinai attacks remains the Egyptian government's dismissal of claims issued by other groups. On the day of the Sharm el-Sheikh attacks, three groups claimed responsibility. One was the previously mentioned al-Tawhid wal-Jihad, to which the Egyptian authorities attributed the attacks. On the same day, another group calling itself the "Holy Warriors of Egypt" also claimed responsibility but seems to have incorrect information about the number of attacks and attackers, which casts considerable doubt on their claim.[26] A third group, known as "Abdullah al-Azzam Brigades of al-Qaeda in the Levant and Egypt," also claimed responsibility for the attacks. This group previously claimed a suicide bombing and another shooting in Cairo in April 2005. The statement issued says that the attacks were a "response against the global evil powers which are spilling the blood of Muslims in Iraq, Afghanistan, Palestine, and Chechnya." It added, "Your brothers, the holy warriors of the martyr Abdullah Azzam Brigades succeeded in launching a smashing attack on the Crusaders, Zionists and the renegade Egyptian regime in Sharm el-Sheikh." The statement went on to say, "We declare it loud and clear we will not be frightened by the whips of the Egyptian torturers and we will not tolerate violation of our brothers' land of Sinai." The al-Qaeda-affiliated group has also claimed responsibility for the Taba attacks and for the failed rocket attacks on August 19, 2005, against U.S. Navy ships in the Jordanian Gulf of Aqaba.[27]

Immediately following the attacks in Taba, Egyptian officials acknowledged the possibility that al-Qaeda might be involved.[28] Then just months after the attacks in Sharm el-Sheikh, when the three known claims were issued, General Ahmad Omar, spokesman for the Egyptian Interior Ministry, clarified the official position: "The training was in Sinai, the vehicles used were stolen in Sinai, and the technology used is available in Sinai mines. We have not found any foreign involvement."[29] The fact that Egyptian authorities dismissed the single claim coming from a previously known group is another example of how they were forced to dismiss any evidence indicating outside involvement once they decided the group was operating alone.

Following the attacks in Dahab, further evidence surfaced that the groups could have been working with al-Qaeda when Egyptian security services found more than 720 kg of TNT near the town of al-Arish. Two gas canisters and twelve bags packed with TNT and detonators were reported to have been hidden by people connected to the Taba attacks and who pledge allegiance to al-Qaeda.[30] More recently, Egyptian authorities arrested a group of men who were not Bedouin but were identified as al-Qaeda affiliates and reportedly trained in Gaza with the plan to carry out attacks in Egypt.[31]

Taking all this into consideration, the notion the perpetrators acted without any assistance from outside groups or from al-Qaeda itself is indeed questionable. The demonstrated need for finances, substantial quantities of explosives, known connections between the Badran brothers and Egyptian fundamentalist groups, and evidence the Muahrib brothers and others traveled to Gaza for assistance suggest they were meeting with someone outside of their operating group. Two of the prominent groups in the region, the Egyptian Muslim Brotherhood and Hamas, were quick to condemn the attacks and denied any involvement. Aside from that, no specifics were offered as to which extremist groups in Egypt and Gaza these men held connections with. This is further indication that Egyptian authorities dismissed the notion the Sinai attackers may have been working with the al-Qaeda agents who were in the area trying to establish a presence.

The fact these attacks threatened the interests of three of al-Qaeda's main enemies and focused attention on one of the foundations of al-Qaeda's causes—the Palestinians—prompts the question whether the group was behind them. It should be noted that neither bin Laden nor al-Zawahiri ever took public responsibility for the attacks in Sinai, but bin Laden never accepted responsibility for other strikes attributed to him, including the 1998 bombings of the U.S. embassies in Kenya and Tanzania or the USS *Cole* in Yemen in 2000.[32] In each of the Sinai attacks, prominent members were known to hold ties to extremist groups in Egypt and Gaza and to have traversed borders to gain training and support. Furthermore, the nature of the attacks indicates far more sophistication and financing than the members seem to have reported receiving. While this in itself does not directly implicate al-Qaeda, it does cast doubt on the notion that these Bedouin men were a self-radicalized, self-trained, and self-financed "bunch of guys."

With so much evidence challenging the notion that this group of men could have carried out the Sinai attacks in 2004, 2005, and 2006, it is unlikely they did not have help from an outside source. The likely suspects from groups in the region denounced the attacks, and among those that claimed them, only one existed before, during, and after the time period in question. Likewise, attacks claimed by this group apart from those in Sinai demonstrate it very well could provide the type of financial assistance and training the Sinai attackers seem to have acquired. Coupled with the demonstrated desire of al-Qaeda to maintain a foothold in the specific area in question and the most credible group claiming the attacks identifies itself as an al-Qaeda affiliate, it is much more plausible that these attacks were part of a leader-led jihad than it is that they sprung up as a leaderless group.

The Egyptian government has a long history with handling challenges to both its domestic and regional security. With each subsequent attack in Sinai, Egyptian authorities made clear their determination to eliminate such threats and to protect Egyptian citizens and the economy from elements aimed at destabilizing the region. In doing so, they set down a path that limited their field of vision by using a premise that the nature of the threat they faced was an issue of a self-radicalized group in Sinai. This premise addresses what Marc Sageman explains as the current wave of terrorist threat, which "comes from inside." To defend against it, he proposes that policy makers try to "understand the process of radicalization and devise strategies to prevent its reaching the point of violence." The danger in this theory is that by subscribing to such an approach, Egypt is making policy and trying to stamp out self-radicalized groups to the exclusion of threats that, as Bruce Hoffman and a good deal of evidence in this case point out, could very likely be coming from outside of Egypt's borders.[33]

NOTES

1. "Toll Climbs in Egyptian Attacks," *BBC News,* July 23, 2005, available at http://news.bbc.co.uk/go/pr/fr/-/2/hi/middle_east/4709491.stm (accessed September 12, 2006); Israel Ministry of Foreign Affairs, "Terror Bombings Hit Taba and Ras a-Satan in Sinai," October 10, 2004, available at http://www.mfa.gov.il/MFA/MFAArchive/2000_2009/2004/10/Sinai%20terror%20bombings%207-Oct-2004 (accessed January 4, 2005).

2. Salah Nasrawi, "Egypt Announces Arrest of Terror Plotters, Says Mastermind Killed in Attack," *Associated Press Worldstream,* October 26, 2004; Mark Landler and Greg Myre, "Attackers Tried to Hit Tourists, Egypt Says," *International Herald Tribune,* July 26, 2005. Information about the events of the attacks was retrieved through interviews by Holly L. McCarthy, August 2006.

3. Israel annexed and held possession of the Sinai Peninsula after the Arab-Israeli War of 1967.

4. Ihab Daoud (Dahab resident), interview Dahab, August 2006; "Egyptian Interior Ministry Statement Details Dahab, Al-Jura Bombings," MENA, May 23, 2006; Jailan Halawi, "Operation Mastermind," *Al-Ahram Weekly,* no. 794, May 11–17, 2006.

5. "Egyptian Interior Ministry Statement Details Dahab, Al-Jura Bombings."

6. "Declaration of Jihad Against the Americans Occupying the Land of the Two Holy Mosques," *Al Islah* (London), September 2, 1996.

7. Jailan Halawi, "Blast Puzzle Incomplete," *Al-Ahram Weekly,* no. 754, August 4–10, 2005. Egyptian officials also expressed concern that the attackers had ties to Ayman al-Zawahiri, the leader of Egypt's Islamic Jihad network that merged with al-Qaeda when al-Zawahiri became Osama bin Laden's top advisor. See Sarah El-Deeb, "Egypt Detains Bedouin Tribesmen in Sinai Terror Attacks That Killed at Least Thirty-Three," Associated Press, October 9, 2004 (accessed January 4, 2005).

8. Scott Wilson and Molly Moore, "Egypt Inquiry Slowed by Lack of Evidence," *Washington Post,* October 23, 2004.

9. Marc Sageman, *Leaderless Jihad: Terror Networks in the Twenty-First Century,* (Philadelphia: University of Pennsylvania Press, 2008), 133–36.

10. "Egyptian Interior Ministry Statement Details Dahab, Al-Jura Bombings"; Jailan Halawi, "Sinai Terror Suspects Get the Gallows," *Al-Ahram Weekly,* no. 812 September

14–20, 2006; Mohammed Al Shafey, "Dahab Bombers Inspired by Al Qaeda," *Asharq al-Awsat* (London), April 29, 2006, available at http://www.aawsat.com/english/news .asp?section=1&id=4749 (accessed September 12, 2006).

11. Sageman, *Leaderless Jihad*, 145; Bruce Hoffman, "The Myth of Grassroots Terrorism: Why Osama bin Laden Still Matters," *Foreign Affairs* 87, no. 3 (May/June 2008): 133–38."

12. "Egyptian Interior Ministry Statement Details Dahab, Al-Jura Bombings."

13. Michael Slackman and Abeer Allam, "Out of Desert Poverty, a Cauldron of Rage," *New York Times*, May 7, 2006. Little is known about Mosaed, and reports conflict as to his level of involvement. Initial reports claim that he was killed before the Taba attacks, leading Al-Mallahi to take over the group. See Halawi, "Operation Mastermind." Subsequent reports list him as a suspect in the Sharm attacks and say he was later arrested in Al-Arish. See "Egypt: Most Sinai Suspects Behind Bars," *Mail and Guardian Online* (Johannesburg) , August 23, 2005, available at http://www.mg.co.za /article/2005-08-23-egypt-most-sinai-bomb-suspects-behind-bars; "Deaths of Leading Terrorists," American Jewish Committee, *Counterterrorism Watch*, November 16, 2008, available at www.ajc.org/site/apps/nlnet/content3.aspx?b=1717409&c=ijITI2P HKoG&ct=2513299. None of the reports indicates how he became the original leader or what, specifically, motivated him.

14. "Egyptian Interior Ministry Statement Details Dahab, Al-Jura Bombings."

15. For land and water issues in Sinai, see "Egypt's Sinai Question," International Crisis Group, *Middle East/North Africa Report*, no. 61, January 30, 2007; Scott Anderson, "Under Egypt's Volcano," *Vanity Fair*, no. 554 (October 2006).

16. Alberto Abadie, "Poverty, Political Freedom, and the Roots of Terrorism," *The American Economic Review* 96, no.2 (2006): 50–56; Alan B Krueger and David D. Laiti, "Kto Kogo? A Cross-Country Study of the Origins and Targets of Terrorism," in *Terrorism, Economic Development, and Political Openness*, ed. Philip Keefer and Norman Loayza (New York: Cambridge University Press, 2008), 148–73; Alan B Krueger and Jitka Maleckova, "Education, Poverty, and Terrorism: Is There a Casual Connection?," *Journal of Economic Perspectives* 17, no.4 (2003): 119–44; James A Piazza, "Rooted in Poverty? Terrorism, Poor Economic Development, and Social Cleavages," *Terrorism and Political Violence* 18, no.1 (2006): 159–77.

17. Amira Howeidy, "Explosive Reactions," *Al-Ahram Weekly*, no. 714, (October-November 2004).

18. "Egyptian Interior Ministry Statement Details Dahab, Al-Jura Bombings."

19. "Egypt Identifies Sharm Attackers," *Tour Egypt*, August 5, 2004, available at http://touregypt.net/teblog/sharmnews/?p=89 (accessed September 20, 2006); "Egyptian Interior Ministry Statement Details Dahab, Al-Jura Bombings"; Mohamed El-Sayed, "Palestinians Aided Dahab Attack," *Al-Ahram Weekly*, no. 796, May 25–31, 2006.

20. Halawi, "Blast Puzzle Incomplete."

21. "Egyptian Interior Ministry Statement Details Dahab, Al-Jura Bombings." The two were also charged with preparing additional terrorist attacks. See Halawi, "Blast Puzzle Incomplete."

22. "Egyptian Interior Ministry Statement Details Dahab, Al-Jura Bombings."

23. Halawi, "Sinai Terror Suspects Get the Gallows"; Jailan Halawi, "Give Up," *Al-Ahram Weekly*, June 8–14, 2006; Halawi, "Operation Mastermind"; "Egyptian Interior Ministry Statement Details Dahab, Al-Jura Bombings"; Daniel Williams, "Egypt Gets Tough in Sinai In Wake of Resort Attacks," *Washington Post Foreign Service*, October 2, 2005. Al-Tarawi was killed later in a shoot-out with police. See Halawi, "Operation Mastermind."

24. Al Shafey, "Dahab Bombers Inspired by Al Qaeda."

25. "Egypt: Perpetrators of Sinai Bombings Arrested; Mastermind Palestinian," Doha Al-Jazeera Satellite Channel Television in Arabic, October 25, 2004.

26. Al Shafey, "Dahab Bombers Inspired by Al Qaeda."

27. "Egypt Sharm el-Sheikh Bombings (ESSB) v1.1," IntelCenter/Tempest Publishing, July 23, 2005; "Attack in Jordan: A New Jihadist Theater in the Levant," *Stratfor*, August 19, 2005.

28. Halawi, "Blast Puzzle Incomplete." Egyptian officials also expressed concern that the attackers had ties to Ayman al-Zawahiri, the leader of Egypt's Islamic Jihad network, which merged with al-Qaeda when al-Zawahiri became Osama bin Laden's top advisor. See El-Deeb, "Egypt Detains Bedouin Tribesmen."

29. Williams, "Egypt Gets Tough in Sinai In Wake of Resort Attacks."

30. "700 Kilos of Explosives Found in Egypt's Sinai," *Kahleej Times* (Dubai), January 15, 2007 (accessed October 6, 2009).

31. Avi Issacharoff, "Al-Qaida Suspected of Plotting Attack on Israel-Egypt Gas Lines," Xinhua, July 6, 2009 (accessed October 15, 2009).

32. "Text of Fatwa Urging Jihad Against Americans," *Al-Quds al-Arabi* (London), February 23, 1998.

33. Hoffman, "The Myth of Grassroots Terrorism."

[21]

Comparing the 2003 and 2007
Incidents in Casablanca

JACK KALPAKIAN

Unexpectedly, a group of terrorists attacked four targets on the night of May 16, 2003, in Casablanca, Morocco. They were motivated by religious-political ideology and were only partially successful in their tactical goals. The attacks were relatively minor compared to attacks in nearby Algeria, but Morocco dramatically changed everything. At the societal level, the attacks marked the end of Moroccan exceptionalism—the belief that the country was immune to the political trends of the Arab Middle East because of its Sufi heritage and open approach to Islam. A series of incidents involving several groups followed the May 16, 2003, attacks. The same group organized some, and other groups launched autonomous attempts at violence as well.[1] The focus in this chapter is groups linked clearly to al-Qaeda by inspiration, coordination, or "franchising." To the extent that other organizations are discussed, they are included only for the purposes of comparison. The al-Qaeda affiliate in Morocco has a bevy of names, including al-Salafiya al-Jihadiya (Jihadi Precedent), the Moroccan Islamic Combat Group (MICG), Sirat al-Mustaqim (the Straight Path), and al-Qaeda in the Maghreb, but these terms essentially refer to the same entity. In addition, the Moroccan Islamic Combat Group and the Salafist Group for Preaching and Combat (Groupe Salafiste pour la Prédication et le Combat; GSPC) have declared their al-Qaeda affiliation, so the issue of international links is now significantly less controversial than it has been in the past.[2] Furthermore, the names appear to be chosen operationally rather than set in stone. I will examine two sets of operations involving cells belonging to the Moroccan al-Qaeda affiliate. The May 16, 2003, attacks will be compared to the incidents of March–April 2007. The first part of the chapter will provide a sequential description of the events. The second part addresses the identities and demographics of the perpetrators and suspects and examines patterns associated with the group's leadership dynamics. The third section addresses the aims and motivations of the organization, including its strategy.

In contrast to the 2003 attacks, the government had the initiative against al-Qaeda's affiliates in 2007. This chapter's fourth section addresses the outcome of the incidents. Both sets of incidents led to change in the Moroccan context, including enhanced security measures and proposals to toughen antiterrorism laws. The fifth section outlines the international links of the Moroccan al-Qaeda affiliates. It is has never been a question that these operations are linked to the global al-Qaeda network. By comparing the two sets of incidents in a manner informed by patterns we see in other organizations, we can draw a clearer picture of the global al-Qaeda's involvement in its Moroccan franchise. The final section revisits some earlier policy recommendations and concludes with some thoughts on the Moroccan counterterrorism effort, including the closure of Islamist Dor al-Quraniya, "Quranic Houses," which are the Moroccan equivalent of the madrassa. These establishments appear to be involved in the recruiting process despite their earlier endorsement by the regime. This comparative study argues that the 2007 incidents were a direct result of the government's improved security policies because the 2007 events were not initiated by the terrorists. Chief among these policies is Law 03.03, which enables prosecutors to issue wiretap warrants rapidly to the police, authorizes twelve days of detention without charge, and defines verbal support for terrorism as a crime.[3]

Overall, Morocco has suffered a great deal from the small-scale intermittent violence brought on by the violent minority within the Islamist movement. The cost to the country in terms of lost foreign investment, tourism, and even remittance money cannot be underestimated; ironically, inflicting economic damage does not appear to have been a motivating factor at all. The population backs the government's response, but it faces dissent based on human rights.[4] The camp emphasizing a human rights perspective tends to be drawn heavily from the Moroccan left, which continues to entertain scenarios of a common front against the regime with the Islamists—which it has began to interpret along "sputnik" or fellow-revolutionary lines. This tendency has seen the former communists (the Party of Progress and Socialism) openly declaring that they "have no objections" to an alliance with the Islamist Party of Justice and Development, an alliance that materialized in the Benkirane PJD government.[5] Associated with the human rights discourse is some disbelief among some Moroccans leftists that terrorism is a threat at all, with some even suggesting that it is a government conspiracy to seize more power. Among the majority that believes terrorism is a problem, leftists and liberals tend to emphasize "root-causes" discourse rather than event- and actor-based analysis.[6] A minority within the intellectual establishment remains firmly opposed even to the use of the term and attempts to use it in an obfuscating way—alleging "terrorism" by the United States or Israel, for example.[7] Fortunately, these perspectives cannot be said to be representative of the general public, and there is a great deal of good work conducted by Abdullah Saaf, Mohammed Darif, Mohamed Taouzi, and others. Unlike these journalists, a large minority of Morocco's intellectual elites is detached from both the state and the population, not only on terrorism. This detachment in turn creates wide lacunae to be filled in the literature about the country and its problems. The importance of this development lies in the problem associated with the relative decline of al-Qaeda in Morocco—it gained political sympathy even as its operational power withered away.

MAY 16, 2003 AND MARCH–APRIL 2007

Many Moroccan intellectuals do not view these events as "real" in the sense that we can make out what they entail at all. Yet it is possible to construct a picture of these events using media resources, transcribed court testimony, and survivors' statements. A group of terrorists, formed only six months earlier, attacked four targets in Casablanca on the night of May 16, 2003. The targets included the Farah Hotel (now Tulip Farah Casablanca), the Jewish Community Center, the Bouzianto Restaurant (a Jewish owned establishment), and Casa España. One of the bombs was used at the Jewish cemetery, but this appears to have been a secondary target, after the attacker failed to detonate his bomb at one of the primary targets. The attackers were in four units of about three to five people each. Table 21.1 discusses each group's target, leader, and effect. Aside from the four principal targets, the Jewish cemetery appears to have been a backup target, and the attackers there are not yet clearly identified.

The group conducting the attacks was a nascent organization with minimal training. They formed out of a Quranic study group that met in a shop in the Karian Toma (also known as Sidi Moumin) neighborhood. They were first trained ideologically and afterward given paramilitary training in a nearby nature reserve. They also produced their own explosives from precursors. They used facilities owned by their relatives as production sites for the explosives, which were tested in an abandoned cemetery. The attacks were mounted with the jurisprudential blessing of clerics such as Mohamed Fizazi, who was in touch with the Hamburg cell of al-Qaeda. The attackers did not intend to survive the attacks, and the main source of this information is a pair of attackers, one who changed his mind in the last moment and another whose bomb failed to explode properly. The group intended to attack on May 14, which is Royal Armed Forces Day in Morocco, but they were delayed. They spent their last days together and ate a ritual meal of dates and milk before the attacks. They appear to have vowed to meet one another in heaven, and the field commander died in the attack. The reported cash cost of the attacks was about 18,000 Moroccan dirhams, which amounted to about US$2,000 at 2003 exchange rates. Other expenses were assumed either directly by the attackers or by their supporters. The total cost of the operation probably did not exceed US$5,000.[8] While the operational aspects of the attacks were certainly local, many people connected to the attacks were linked to the global al-Qaeda networks. The most significant local contact appears to have been Sa'ad al-Husayni, whose story united May 16, 2003, with the events of March–April 2007. Others included Abdelatif Mourafik (Malek el-Andalusi; Malek al-Maghrebi), a Moroccan associate of Abu Musab al-Zarqawi, arrested in Turkey for involvement with the May 16 attacks.[9] Mourafik was involved in the 2004 Madrid train bombings. From an operational point of view, the attacks were a local affair, but they appear to fit into a strategic design coordinated abroad through the al-Zarqawi network.

TABLE 21.1

Al-Husayni al-Qaeda cell members and their fates

Name	Date Arrested or Killed	Circumstances of Arrest or Death	Remarks
Sa'ad al-Husayni	After February 2007 and before March 11, 2007	Arrested at a cybercafé	Traveled extensively in Europe and the Islamic World
Abd al-Aziz Benzain	On or shortly before March 11, 2007	Acted as a communication conduit for al-Husayni	Arrest set off subsequent events
Abd al-Fatah al-Raidi	Self-destructed on March 11, 2007	At a cybercafé in Sidi Moumin (Karian Toma)	Cybercafé owner had called the police over his suspicious behavior
Youssef al-Khadouri	Fled the same cybercafé where al-Raidi committed a suicide attack, March 11, 2007	Caught by the police and provided information and evidence	Mint, rabbit, and squab raiser, 14 years old at the time of his arrest
Abd al-Aziz al-Rakesh	Surrendered on March 23, 2007	Was holed up in a residential building	Had threatened to set off his explosive belt
Mohammed Mantala*	Shot dead by police on April 10, 2007, in the Farah district of Casablanca	Left a besieged house, sword in hand to attack the police	Did not follow the standard method used for suicide
Mohammed al-Rashdi*	Detonated his explosive belt on April 10, 2007	Climbed to the roof to set off his explosive belt in the Farah neighborhood	Sent out his wife and children to surrender to the police
Ayoob al-Raidi*	Detonated his explosive belt on April 10, 2007	Took place during the siege of the al-Qaeda house in the Farah neighborhood	Murdered Moroccan police Inspector Mohammed Zenbaiba in the course of his suicide
Sa'id Belwad*	Detonated his explosive belt on April 10, 2007	Part of the events that took place in Casablanca on April 10, 2007	Attack failed to harm anyone else
Samir al-Shami*	Caught on April 12, 2007	Hid under a coach in a nearby apartment	Apprehended by civilians
Omar Moha and Mohammed Moha	Detonated their explosive belts on April 14, 2007	Tried to attack the U.S. consulate general in Casablanca	No one else was harmed
Hicham al-Moumni	Arrested on March 29, 2009	Caught in al-Dakhla attempting to travel to Mali and Mauritania	Admitted connections to the al-Raidi brothers
About twenty others	Arrested in March and April 2007	From Meknes, Tétouan, and Casablanca	Including one more minor, but all others between the ages of 18 and 27

* Part of the April 10, 2007, siege in the Farah neighborhood.
Source: Idriss Benani et al., "Resurrection Day: How Did We Get to This?" *Nichane*, no. 98, April 21–27, 2007, 26–37; Anneli Botha, *Terrorism in the Maghreb: The Transnationalisation of Domestic Terrorism*, ISS Monograph (Pretoria: ISS, 2008), 102–3.

The attacks caught the country by total surprise. They were minor in terms of the physical damage, and the number of dead was not as large as it might have been had the security guards failed to delay the attackers. The consequences for the country were immense in terms of law, policy, and approach to Islam, however. The attackers' main achievement was the awakening of the Moroccan state and society to the threat violent Islamism posed not only to the royal establishment but also to the livelihoods of millions of Moroccans dependent on tourism, the motion picture industry, and related support industries. Nevertheless, there appears to have been no intentional economic logic in the ideology of the attackers. They viewed society as mired in *jahiliya*, so their feelings toward it were not warm. But there was no deliberate targeting of the Moroccan economy. To the extent that the attacks damaged the livelihood of other Moroccans, the news would have been welcome to the attackers, but it was not an essential aspect of their thinking or targeting. The consequences were not what the attackers expected because society and the political and intellectual establishment turned against them. The surviving perpetrators were almost immediately apprehended, but their support networks appear to have been extensive and were not immediately dismantled. The overall leader, Bentasser, died in police custody some weeks after the attacks.[10] Other people wanted in connection with the attacks of May 16, 2003, later died in the confrontations with the government in March and April 2007. The most prominent character among these was Sa'ad al-Husayni—a chemist wanted in connection to the 2003 Casablanca attacks and the 2004 Madrid attack. He was arrested at an Internet café some time in early 2007. Using information extracted from his interrogation, the security forces were able to begin dismantling the network operating beneath him. Al-Husayni was apprehended thanks to information provided by men arrested in February 2007 in Tétouan and Meknes. Al-Husayni relied on a courier to communicate to the rest of the network. Abd al-Aziz Benzain was arrested shortly after al-Husayni. This led one member of the cell to get nervous at a cybercafé when Internet communication did not arrive from Benzain on March 11, 2007; Abd al-Fatah al-Raidi, accompanied by a junior cell member, panicked and set off an explosive belt when the cybercafé owner called the police because of his erratic behavior. His accomplice, Youssef al-Khadouri, first fled but later turned informant after his arrest.

Using information provided by al-Khadouri, the security forces identified about forty-three members of the cell, and located about 200 kilograms of explosives. Between late March and mid-April 2007, Morocco endured nerve-wrecking times as the cell and the security forces fought a cat-and-mouse game that ended lethally for many on both sides. One known cell member attempted to flee to Mauritania, and while some were arrested, others fought back with suicidal tenacity using explosive suicide belts and, in one case, a sword. In the case of the Moha brothers, their suicide was intended as a political statement against the United States, whose consulate they targeted in a failed bombing attempt that left no fatalities except for themselves.[11] The battle between the security forces and the al-Husayni cell shows that the Moroccan security forces have captured the initiative in the conflict with terrorists. The terrorists have been forced to fight back at times that are not of their choosing and in places that are not necessarily their preference. It is also clear that their ability to melt into the population has significantly lessened, which as the final encounters show, has begun to express its support for the police and the state in general.

After April 2007, the threat posed by terrorism to the lives and livelihoods of ordinary people was increasingly clear to the population. The attacks showed that the law-enforcement-oriented responses to the events of May 16, 2003, were broadly appropriate. The state's tools were strengthened with Law 03.03, which allowed it intercept phone calls and communications quickly. A comparison of the attacks of May 16, 2003, with the events of March and April 2007 shows that the initiative for action had indeed shifted from the terrorists to the security forces. In 2003, the terrorists were on the attack, selecting targets, training in relative safety from the security forces, and enjoying the element of surprise. By March 2007, the game had changed dramatically. The government moved to arrest people, besiege safe houses, and secure the help of people wanting to switch sides and inform on their former partners after their arrest. The ultimate sign of the government's success lies in the behavior of the residents of the Farah neighborhood, who apprehended a terrorist two days after the siege's end and, in one case, provided the security forces with traditional pastries during the siege. Commenting and reporting on these events, Ahmed Ben Shemsi, an opposition journalist, argues the people had a choice between the security forces and the terrorists, and in the Farah neighborhood, they demonstrated that they side with the security forces.[12]

WHO WERE THE ATTACKERS?

In both cases, the al-Qaeda affiliate in Morocco followed a "lords and serfs" model of demographic recruitment. At the apex of the organization, the seat of power is usually occupied by a well-traveled, self-made, or well-educated man with international connections. In short, the leader at the lord level enjoys a level of sophistication that his recruits do not. Unlike their leaders, the men who carry out the attacks tend to be less central in Moroccan society overall, not necessarily in terms of wealth or education but in terms of their location within the distribution of power in the larger society. Of the ninety-four people immediately arrested in connection with the May 16, 2003, attacks, forty-seven were street peddlers and herbalists, and the remaining half were unemployed or fishmongers, tailors, and other traditional craftsmen. Among the attackers, there was one martial arts instructor, one English teacher, and various traditional craftsmen and peddlers. While these professions lack stigmatization in the Moroccan context, they represent deeply threatened modes of production and distribution. Further, they typically belong in the informal economy of Morocco.[13]

The same pattern repeated itself with the cell involved in the March–April 2007 attacks. Using a more concentrated sample that focuses on the dead terrorists, a familiar picture emerges. Of the seven deceased terrorists who took part in the March–April 2007 attacks, three were street peddlers, one was a fruit-juice vender, another was an electrician, and two (the Moha brothers) were small businessmen who worked with their father, who seems to have developed many micro-businesses—all of which were legal in a Moroccan context. In contrast to the deceased attackers, the surviving leader of the cell, Sa'ad al-Husayni had degrees in physics and chemistry and came from a respected family of Meknes merchants.[14] These al-Qaeda cells stand in sharp contrast to the nearly all-elite nature of the Belliraj organization—a non-al-Qaeda movement. Of the thirty-two suspects initially arrested, only one was unemployed, and only two were employed in the informal sector, one as a waiter and

another as a parking attendant. The remaining members were politi-
cians, computer technicians, university professors, and schoolteachers.
In short, those accused of being in the Belliraj organization represented
Morocco's elites.[15]

Comparing al-Qaeda's Moroccan affiliates to other Moroccan terrorist organization illustrates distinct recruitment methods, internal discipline, and class dynamics within the organization. The "lord and serf"
distinction within al-Qaeda seems to replicate closely the divisions that
exist between commissioned officers and enlisted men in regular militaries. While the field leader of the May 16 attacks, Bouqaidan, emerged
"naturally from the ranks," the intellectual and strategic leadership is
definitely not representative of the membership.[16] The Ansar al-Mahdi
organization, an independent violent Islamist outfit linked with a charismatic leader, displayed a greater mixture of members than the simple demographic structure displayed by the al-Qaeda affiliates.[17] Like
the al-Qaeda affiliates, it had connections overseas. In contrast to both
other organizations, the Belliraj organization's international links were
primarily with the relatively wealthy Moroccan overseas community. In
the case of Belliraj himself, the most appropriate description may have
been political exile. The Moroccan al-Qaeda affiliate, in contrast to other
Moroccan terrorist organizations, is more dependent on young, impressionable, and marginalized men in the informal sector. Unlike the Belliraj organization, it is more reliant on ideological training, team-building
exercises, and other training devises reminiscent of regular military
organizations. In contrast, the other two organizations were either composed of elite cadres or were under the influence of a charismatic leader.
This suggests that it is possible to disrupt the process of recruitment,
ideological team building, training, and full induction into the Moroccan
al-Qaeda.

AIMS AND MOTIVATIONS

These Moroccan al-Qaeda affiliate shares the general overall aims of its
global parent. In their public pronouncements, the movement's imprisoned ideologists have clearly stated its goals, discussed below. In its
Moroccan context, a profound level of hostility toward Jewish people

exists. The targets of the May 16, 2003, attacks included the Jewish Community Center, a Jewish restaurant, and the Jewish cemetery in Casablanca. In some of his public pronouncements, Omar Hadoushi, one of the leaders behind the May 16 attacks, condemns the official religious establishment of Morocco as "Zionist."[18] However, this animosity toward Jews is not unique to al-Qaeda among Moroccan terrorist organizations. One of the defining features of the violent segment of the Moroccan Islamist movement is its constant demonization the Jewish community in Morocco and the Jewish community more broadly. A cell associated with al-Salafiya al-Jihadiya, dubbed "the New Morabatin," in southern Morocco included eight people planning to attack Jewish "interests" in Morocco. Some of these eight were recruited in "Quranic Houses."[19] While much has been made of al-Qaeda's not fighting Israel, such an argument misses an important point: al-Qaeda and its affiliates are profoundly anti-Jewish, with an intensity rarely seen worldwide and almost never experienced in traditional Muslim history. In the words of Issam al-Barqawi (a.k.a. Abu Mohammed al-Maqdisi, the spiritual advisor to Abu Musab al-Zarqawi), "The hostility of Jews, Christians and other polytheists against us is an undeniable fact. They are against our religion and God told us this fact in the Holy Quran."[20]

Aside from basic anti-Semitism, the main motivation of al-Qaeda in Morocco lies in ideology—the idea that Muslim states must enforce the harshest form of the sharia, the one deriving from the prescriptions of Ibn Tammiya.[21] In their analysis of Moroccan life, the ideologists behind the May 16 attack rejected any interaction with the Moroccan state and society except through violence.[22] They offered a standard laundry list of alleged sins by the Moroccan state, including the availability of alcohol, the existence of Marxist Moroccans, the presence of tourists, the existence of a gaming industry including a lottery, extra-Quranic taxation, the freedom granted women concerning attire, women working outside the home, and the legal equality between men and women in marriage.[23] Far from violence being a political option, the violent segment of the Islamist movement in Morocco sees it as a divine enjoinment.[24] In their conceptualization of Islam, it is not possible to be a Muslim unless one is a Salafi (a follower of the correct precedent, today understood as the Islam advocated by Wahhabis), and it is not possible to be a Salafi without jihad—itself understood in the unorthodox definition of violence against all who do not accept the Salafi interpretation of Islam (*takfir*).[25] There are of course nonviolent Salafis, and not all jihadis are *takfiris*, but under the system advocated by the Moroccan al-Qaeda affiliates, to be a Muslim means to be a Salafi, a jihadi, and a *takfiri*.[26] In a lecture before their arrest for inciting the May 16, 2003, attack, Abd el-Wahab "Abi Hafz" Rafiki and his clerical colleagues clearly state that they have no quarrel with anyone except secularists and leftists and openly challenged the Moroccan state to hold inquisition trials to execute "heretics" "if it were Muslim."[27] In other words, they do not regard the Moroccan state as Islamic or Muslim and act accordingly to undermine what they see as an illegitimate government.

In a more recent declaration, the same group of imprisoned clerics argues, "It is the duty of every Muslim to do justice to us and support us"; the group went on a hunger strike in May 2009, protesting their designation as *kharijites* by the state—a step before apostasy in Sunni Islam.[28] They plead that they are victims of the state's campaign against them. In their repeated public pronouncements, the prisoners have openly denied that they did anything wrong without ever refuting the charges ascribed to them. They simply rejected the legitimacy of the state that holds them accountable for inspiring violence. According to Abd al-Rahim Mouhtad, of the Naseer Association to Support Islamist Prisoners, dialogue has proven difficult because of the diversity of the state and the prisoners themselves, "many of whom believe that they have done nothing wrong."[29] In a direct response to a demand by the minister of information that they repent and renounce violence, Rafiki and his colleagues came out with a declaration that they have done nothing to demand repentance.[30] Since then, the state did manage to pursue dialogue with some of these imprisoned clerics, trading pardons for renouncing extremism. Among those pardoned are Rafiki and Hadoushi. The pardons came in return for renouncing violence, supporting the monarchy, and cutting ties with foreign jihadists.[31]

While the state has managed to induce some of the pro-al-Qaeda clerics to recant, there are still more cells. Put simply, the aim of the Moroccan al-Qaeda affiliate is to wage war against both the Moroccan state and the society it represents because it views both as pagan. The aim of this war is not a political or a military victory but rather to enforce obedience to a divine injunction to fight paganism and apostasy by violent force wherever and whenever possible. As Mohammed Damir, one of the suspects arrested in connection with the events of May 16, 2003, told the judge: "I would like to surround you with the knowledge that I committed the actions of which I am accused; I committed them and did them upon the knowledge of the book of God and the *sunna* of his prophet. . . . I am happy . . . because I being tried for commanding the good and prohibiting that which is forbidden."[32] As al-Kahal argues, for the Moroccan al-Qaeda affiliates, violence is its own aim, and attempts to "explain" its activities with reference to competing sets of socioeconomic and political variables are simply exercises in futility. Nevertheless, in a rather distressing example of the negative influence of al-Qaeda in Moroccan politics, its weakness appears to attract sympathy. During "question time" for ministers in parliament in May 2009, the interior minister, Choukaib Benmoussa, was criticized by a member of the Islamist Party of Justice and Development, Mustapha al-Ramid, about the conditions that the state had imposed on the prisoners including renouncing their interpretations of Islam, repentance, and formal requests for a royal pardon. For al-Ramid, dialogue must take place before pardons are granted—duplicating the experience of other Arab countries.[33] The prospect of the PJD beginning to act politically to bring pressure on the state on behalf of the prisoners, both pardoned and current, was not encouraging. The party is also associated with promoting the notion that "hundreds are innocent and unfairly imprisoned." The party initially condemned the attacks because doing otherwise would have been electoral suicide. A mere two years later, its official newspaper began to suggest that the events were a "mystery." Some of its supporters were already blaming Western intelligence services for the attacks in private. It has now begun trying to cast doubt about the state's efforts against terrorism. The party is now in power, holding the presidency of the government after winning Morocco's first post–Arab Spring elections. It remains to be seen how its discourse would pan out in the aftermath of an attack. Al-Ramid is currently serving as the minister of justice and liberties (attorney general). His tenure saw the pardons he advocated as an opposition leader. While the case of the imprisoned Islamists made for good politics for the PJD, the party found itself having to argue for counterterrorism and rule of law in addition to human rights protection in the wake of the 2011 Argana attacks in Marrakech.

CONSEQUENCES

Aside from the single victim of the events of March–April 2007, Police Inspector Mohammed Zenbaiba, the attackers failed to inflict any serious damage on their targets. Seven members of al-Salafiya al-Jihadiya died without achieving any of their original ends. As with May 16, 2003, the operations also clearly cost the terrorists public support. Moroccan Law 03.03 was a direct result of the earlier attacks; it was passed a mere thirteen days later. Like the Racketeer Influenced and Corrupt Organizations Act (RICO) in the United States, it allows for the summary seizure of all assets used in the commission of the crimes listed therein.[34]

The state also initiated a series of religious reforms in response to the violence of 2003. Becoming an imam in Morocco today requires training, including instruction in social psychology and foreign languages, and a bachelor's degree earned with a "mention"—the equivalent of a B average in the U.S. system. Women were given access to leadership roles in the religious field through the appointment of female counselors (*murshidates*) to advise women and youth in religious affairs. The selection criteria for women include a bachelor's degree and memorization of the Quran.[35] Inviting women into the religious establishment was viewed as a step short of revolutionary in most of the Islamic world. The king also launched the National Initiative for Human Development (INDH), which funds development projects in the poorest 360 urban and 250 rural districts in the country.[36]

According to Selim Hemimat, a researcher on Islamist movements in Morocco, the state's response to the events of March and April 2007 took a longer period to take shape. The response focused on the state's decision to limit the role played by both Salafism and Wahhabism in Moroccan life. The policy appears to have developed in stages after May 2007. It became clear after a Saudi-trained Salafi cleric, Mohammed Abd al-Rahman al-Maghraoui, issued his now well-known fatwa No. 371 on his website in August 2008. In that particular fatwa, al-Maghroui enjoined the marriage of nine-year old girls, claiming there was prophetic precedence for child marriage for girls. After a flurry of anger on the part on women's and children's rights activists as well as widespread protest by secularists and freethinkers, the state felt that it was time for a major shift in policy with regard to people like al-Maghraoui. On September 21,

2008, the High Religious Council of Morocco issued a decree condemning him and his fatwa. Shortly thereafter, the Ministry of Interior shut down access to his website in Morocco, his association, and dozens of "Quranic Houses" controlled by it. By the end of 2008, the government had shut down about sixty-seven "Quranic Houses," including thirty-three linked personally to al-Maghraoui. The government argued that the closures target a form of Islamic education that is alien to Morocco and that aims to replace the particularities of Moroccan Islam. Speaking from Saudi Arabia, al-Maghroui first attempted to justify his fatwa and then began to back off and began arguing that his opinion is being used to shut down the instruction of "correct" forms of Islam in Morocco.[37] He returned to Morocco after the reforms of 2011 but has since recanted his fatwa. Through their newspaper, *Al-Sabil*, the Salafi movement used the occasion to attack the minister of religious affairs, Dr. Ahmed Tawfik, for his Sufism and claimed to be suffering from an American plan to suppress Salafism by supporting Sufism, which they equated with secularism.

That the Salafi tendency, in its nonviolent guise, had been tolerated for several years after the events of May 16, 2003, suggests that something did indeed change after the events of March and April 2007. The movement is no longer seen as an ally of the Moroccan government against the opposition. It is now seen as a threat to the Moroccan state and is being treated accordingly. The involvement of several students of the Salafist "Quranic Houses" in disbanded terrorist cells, such as the New Morabatin, strongly suggests that the government's decision to go after them and to order their closure was a warranted decision from a security standpoint. Of course, this does raise some serious questions about the Salafi movement and its links with the PJD, which has defended it against the state on more than one occasion. It also raises some serious questions about the nature of Salafism.

EXTERNAL LINKS

In many ways, the relationship between the Moroccan al-Qaeda affiliates and their franchisers in the global al-Qaeda network are straightforward. In the case of May 16, 2003, attacks, Mohamed Fizazi, one of the ideologists who provided a jurisprudential enjoinment for the attack, had links with the Hamburg cell of al-Qaeda. This relationship became public through the support expressed for al-Qaeda by Fizazi and Abd al-Karim Shadali, an individual formerly imprisoned for activities related to the 9/11 attacks and al-Qaeda in general.[38] In the case of al-Husayni and the cell dismantled during the confrontation in March and April 2007, the international links to al-Qaeda are even clearer. Sa'ad al-Husayni lived and fought in Chechnya, Bosnia, Pakistan, Afghanistan, and France. He openly endorsed al-Qaeda and was deeply involved in recruiting Moroccan youths for the battlefields of Afghanistan and Iraq, according to the Moroccan Ministry of Interior. The issue of al-Qaeda affiliation is now moot in North Africa because the Algerian Islamic Group for Preaching and Combat, as well as its Moroccan counterpart, have openly declared their al-Qaeda ties. Moroccan and Algerian al-Qaeda affiliates appear to be conducting joint operations and using each country's nationals against the other. In June 2009, Algeria held a trial of five Moroccan terror suspects who crossed the border illegally to conduct jihad. Al-Qaeda and its local branches are crossing the borders to attack Algeria and all of its neighbors, including Morocco.[39] Should there be any doubt left about the existence of a link between al-Qaeda and the Moroccan jihadists, it was laid to rest by the statements of Omar Hadoushi in an open letter to Osama bin Laden:

> And at last, I would say to Shaykh Osama, take it easy on yourself, be firm in the rights of your nation, you would be a valuable slave of God, in your society an upright citizen. You should know that everything has its price; the price of dignity is some oppression, the price of safety some damage, the price of leadership, heroism and manliness is all the nuisances, the price of gravitas is some enmity. . . . Our God, please return the military initiative against your enemies to us, make us live up to requirements of your victory, grant us your calm, supply us with your aid and support, make us more reactive . . . Our God, firm up your anger against America and whoever aligned themselves with it from humanity and genies. Our God, freeze the blood in their necks, send upon them birds, send your unknowable hosts upon them, and your sword of vengeance. Our God, please make them, their soldiers, money, equipment, and planes war booty for Taliban. Our God, grant glory to Islam and victory to Taliban, and humiliation to pagans and Americans.[40]

As al-Kahal argues, it is now irrelevant whether these movements began internally in Morocco or not; they are now linked with and are a integral part of the al-Qaeda network, regardless of the absence of a military-style command-and-control relationship. Anneli Botha shares the same perspective in her monograph, *Terrorism in the Maghreb: The Transnationalisation of Domestic Terrorism*. At this stage, the Moroccan al-Qaeda affiliates are linked with and act in unison with the regional and global manifestations of al-Qaeda and associated Salafi-jihadi-*takfiri* movements within Islam—which are first and foremost at war with all the other expressions of the Islamic faith, including, ironically enough personal and apolitical versions of Salafism.

Since the 2003 attacks, the Moroccan state has used an arsenal of legal, political, and social strategies to cope with the threat posed by the al-Qaeda affiliates in Morocco, which have used various names and identities but essentially reflect a coherent and clear segment within the larger violent Islamist movement in Morocco. There are clearly two levels of leadership within the Moroccan al-Qaeda, with underlings sometimes unaware of the name of the organization they represent. Contacts with the global al-Qaeda take place at the level of leading current and former members like Fizazi and al-Husayni. Along with the grape-cluster structure, leadership is distributed, duplicated, and networked. To conduct a security campaign against such an organization meant that the Moroccan government needed more than its own internal resources. To the extent that al-Qaeda made enemies with both Western and Islamic governments, the Moroccan state was able to find allies overseas as well as at home.

As one critical journalist cited earlier noted, the population appears to have decisively rejected the Salafi jihadi suicide bombers and sided with the security forces. Consequently, the government is left with less of a need to appease the overall Islamist movement as a means of preventing further attacks. Combined with a social program targeting some of the weaker classes in Moroccan society and a religious reform program, the Moroccan state's security-oriented response appears to be yielding results. It is safe to say that over the four years that separate May 2003 and April 2007, the Moroccan al-Qaeda affiliate lost the initiative, finding itself on the run and fighting a defensive war against a state that has been reassured by the population of its support. The Salafist attacks against Sufism are also helping damage the ideology's overall appeal in Morocco because of the persistence of the orders as well as Sufi beliefs and perspectives. The movement's attacks against folk and popular expressions of Islam have also helped limit its appeal, dooming the possibility of significant popular support for the Moroccan al-Qaeda. That being said, the aim of this particular movement remains to carry out God's will as it sees it, and so it does not follow the state's political calculus. It will try to kill as many people, whether foreign or Moroccan, for the sake of killing. Consequently, it would be a mistake to assume that a "victory" is possible in a political, military, or law-enforcement sense of the word. The conflict is bound to continue for years and perhaps decades, so it is important to point out some thoughts on some policies that could help Morocco and the region reduce the extent of the threat posed by these movements.

First, the relationship between Morocco and Algeria needs to be altered into one where cooperation is the rule of the day in order to prevent al-Qaeda from using the disputes between the two states as means of securing space in which to operate against both. Security is not an issue that is given to fragmentation; continued hostilities between Algeria and Morocco in matters related to the Polisario Front (which seeks to end Moroccan control in the Western Sahara) will weaken ties between the two countries. The two states cannot cooperate against one set of threats and continue the dispute over the Sahara, particularly when the level of threat faced by each from al-Qaeda is different. Algeria still faces a threat from its own Islamist insurgency, and it needs to focus its energies on truly neutralizing it. Maintaining its current policies concerning Morocco is counterproductive. In short, it needs to be encouraged to think realistically about a solution to its disputes with Morocco that ends in a win-win outcome rather than a zero-sum game.

Second, Moroccan security guards and police continue to be underequipped and undertrained. Their salaries are also too low given the threats they face. At the very least, flak jackets and body armor should be made available for private security guards and police to prevent tragedies such as that faced by Zenabaiba's family. At present, Moroccan security guards continue to lack this equipment. To conclude, victory in the conflict will be achieved at the level of the minds of the terrorists themselves; revisions and renunciations such those carried out by Rafiki and Hadoushi offer a glimmer of hope. Allowing the demonologies they espouse to continue to influence youth will ensure new attacks. This is a responsibility that clearly belongs to the Moroccan state and the society it represents. Through its religious reforms, the government has clearly moved to ensure that Islamic tradition works with the modern condition. Achieving an amalgam that works in a Moroccan context will take time, but it is clear that the state is pursuing this aim—and, to that end, it is possible to say that the first step, and perhaps most important step, toward defeating terrorism has already been taken.

NOTES

1. For more on the attacks and incidents that followed, see Jack Kalpakian, "Against Both Bin Laden and Belliraj: Lessons from Moroccan Counterterrorism," *Contemporary Security Policy* 3, no. 3 (December 2008): 453–76. All Moroccan and Arab sources are in the Arabic language.

2. The affiliation has been openly declared on at least two occasions. In 2005, Mohamed al-Fizazi endorsed al-Qaeda in an interview by Anas Mansour: "I corresponded with the King, and there is no role for the intelligence services in my arrest" (*Al-Ayam* [Manama, Bahrain], no. 207, December 17, 2005, 6). Also see Said al-Raihani et al., "Bin Laden Searching for a Foothold in the Maghreb," *Al-Ousbaya,* no. 114 (April 14–20, 2007), 7.

3. Kingdom of Morocco, "Law 03.03 Concerning Combating Terrorism," *Al-Jarida al-Rasmiya: Al-Nashra al-A'ma* [The official journal: general publication], May 29, 2003, 1,755.

4. For criticism of the Moroccan approach to terrorism from a human rights perspective, see Hind Aroub, "Criticizing the Security Approach Against the Salafi Jihadists in Morocco," in *Mouajahat bain al-Islamiyin wa al-Ilmaniyin bi-al-Maghrib* [Confrontations between Islamists and secularists in Morocco], ed. Mounjib Maati, Wajhat Nazr Booklets no. 15 (Rabat: Wajhat Nazr, 2008), 150–56. For evidence of the population's preferences, consult Ahmed Ben Shemsi, "Love in the Neighborhood of Happiness," *Nichane,* no. 98, April 21–27, 2007, 4.

5. Abd al-Wahid Souhail, a member of the Political Committee of the Party of Progress and Socialism, as quoted by Yassine Qutaib, "Souhail: The Party of Progress and Socialism Has No Objections to Alliance With the PJD," *Al-Ahdath al Maghribiya,* no. 3739, May 24, 2009, 4.

6. See Aroub, "Criticizing the Security Approach Against the Salafi Jihadists in Morocco," as an example of root-causes discourse. Mustafa al-Mu'tasim, "The Left and the Islamists: Is Agreement and Coexistence Possible?," in *Mouajahat bain al-Islamiyin wa al-Ilmaniyin bi-al-Maghrib* [Confrontations between Islamists and secularists in Morocco], ed. Mounjib Maati, Wajhat Nazr Booklets no. 15 (Rabat: Wajhat Nazr, 2008), 21–28. Al-Mu'tasim was the secretary-general of the dissolved Civilizational Alternative Party, which was accused of being a front for the Belliraj Organization. He and his party have since been exonerated.

7. One example is Mohamed Adib al-Salaoui, *Al-Irhab Yaridou Halan* [Terrorism demands a solution] (Kenitra: al-Boukeili Printing, 2004). Al-Salaoui essentially equates al-Qaeda with the United States: "If you follow the history of the terrorist operations of the 'American State,' during the last two centuries, you would see that state terror is akin to an article of faith in American political thought" (59).

8. For the details of the May 16, 2003, attacks, summarized here, see Jack Kalpakian, "Building the Human Bomb: The Case of the 16 May 2003 Attacks in Casablanca," *Studies in Conflict and Terrorism* 28, no. 2 (March–April 2005): 113–27.

9. Matthew Levitt, "USA Ties Terrorist Attacks in Iraq to Extensive Zarqawi Network," *Jane's Intelligence Review*, April 1, 2004, available at http://thewashingtoninstitute.com/pdf.php?template=C06&CID=471 (accessed November 2, 2009).

10. United States Department of State, *Morocco: Country Report on Human Rights Practices*, February 25, 2003, available at http://www.state.gov/g/drl/rls/hrrpt/2003/27934.htm (accessed November 2, 2009).

11. Idriss Benani et al., "Resurrection Day: How Did We Get to This?," *Nichane*, no. 98, April 21–27, 2007, 26–37.

12. Ahmed Ben Shemsi, "Love in the Neighborhood of Happiness," *Nichane*, no. 98, April 2007, 21–27, 4.

13. Abd al-Aziz Bouradwan al-Idrissi, "Religious Extremism in Morocco, Its Social Origins and Theoretical Underpinnings," *Wajhat Nazr*, no. 21 (Winter 2003): 51.

14. Idriss Benani et al., "Who Are the Terrorists?," *Nichane*, no. 98, April 21–27, 2007, 30–31; Idriss Benani et al., "Chemical Sa'ad," *Nichane*, no. 98, April 21–27, 2007, 34.

15. Mohammed Abou Yahda, "Rich and Poor and Telecommunications Specialists in Belliraj's Organization," *Al-Ahdath al-Maghribiya* (Casablanca), February 21, 2008, 3.

16. For the emergence of Bouqaidan to field leadership, see Khalid Attaoui, "How the Terrorists Prepared to Attack the Peaceful City Six Months Before Last May," *Al-Ahdath al-Maghribiya* (Casablanca), Special Edition, no. 1689 (September 2003), 5.

17. For the composition of the Ansar al-Mahdi cell and organization, see "Fourth Woman Arrested. Part of Investigation into Ansar al-Mahdi Terror Cell, Minister," *Maghreb Arabe Press*, August 31, 2006, available at http://www.map.ma/eng/sections/imp_general/fourth_woman_arreste/view (accessed May 15, 2007). See also Mathew Chebatoris, "Islamist Infiltration of the Moroccan Armed Forces," *Terrorism Monitor* 15, no. 3 (February 15, 2007): 9; Craig Smith "Moroccan Terror Plot Foiled with Fifty-Six

Arrests, Officials Say," *New York Times*, September 2, 2006, available at http://www
.nytimes.com/2006/09/02/world/africa/02morocco.html (accessed November 2, 2009).

18. As quoted by al-Idrissi, "Religious Extremism in Morocco," 53.

19. "The New Morabatin Target Jewish and Security Interests," *Al-Ahdath al-Maghribiya* (Casablanca), May 24, 2009, 4.

20. As cited by Mark E. Stout et al., *The Terrorist Perspectives Project* (Annapolis, Md.: Naval Institute Press, 2008), 85–86.

21. El-Mailoudi Zakaria, Mohammed Fizazi, and Omar Hadoushi as quoted by El-Idrissi, "Religious Extremism in Morocco," 47–48.

22. Sa'id al-Kahal, "The Exaggerated 'Innocence' of the Leaders of Extremism," *Al-Ahdath al-Maghribiya* (Casablanca), May 27, 2009, 19. The author is a leftist scholar and a critic of the Islamist movement.

23. Jamal Hashim, "Al-Salafi ya al-Jihadiya and the Legitimation of Jihad," in *Mouajahat bain al-Islamiyin wa al-Ilmaniyin bi-al-Maghrib* [Confrontations between Islamists and secularists in Morocco], ed. Mounjib Maati, Wajhat Nazr Booklets no. 15 (Rabat: Wajhat Nazr, 2008), 185.

24. Al-Idrissi, "Religious Extremism in Morocco," 48–51.

25. Abd al-Latif Hasani, "Jihad in the Conceptualization of al-Salafi ya al-Jihadiya in Morocco," in *Mouajahat bain al-Islamiyin wa al-Ilmaniyin bi-al-Maghrib* [Confrontations between Islamists and secularists in Morocco], ed. Mounjib Maati, Wajhat Nazr Booklets no. 15 (Rabat: Wajhat Nazr, 2008), 144–49.

26. For more on the term Salafi, see Ahamd Moussalli, "Wahhabism, Salafism, Islamism: Who Is the Enemy?," Conflicts Forum Monograph (January 2009).

27. As quoted by Sa'id al-Kahal, "The Exaggerated 'Innocence' of the Leaders of Extremism."

28. "Morocco Dissolves 'a Nascent Terrorist Cell' and Sends Its Members to the Judiciary System," *Asharq al-Awsat* (London), May 21, 2009, 4.

29. As quoted in "Morocco: Confirming Kettani's Sentence and Reducing Abi Hafs' in the Casablanca Case," *Asharq al-Awsat* (London), May 24, 2009, 4.

30. The request was made on May 14, 2009. The response came shortly thereafter. See Mohammed Darif, a Moroccan researcher on Islamist movements, as interviewed by Sa'id Jadali, "Benmoussa's Conditions Are Not About Dialogue, but to Allow Salafists to Get Pardons," and "*Salafiya* File: Dialogue or Repentance," *Al-Ahdath al-Maghribiya* (Casablanca), May 25, 2009, 2.

31. Mohamed Saadouni, "Morocco pursues salafist reconciliation," *Magharebia*, May 18, 2012, http://magharebia.com/en_GB/articles/awi/reportage/2012/05/18/reportage-01 (accessed 17 July 2013).

32. As quoted by Sa'id al-Kahal, "Political Use of Religion Leads to Violence," in *Mouajahat bain al-Islamiyin wa al-Ilmaniyin bi-al-Maghrib* [Confrontations between Islamists and secularists in Morocco], ed. Mounjib Maati, Wajhat Nazr Booklets no. 15 (Rabat: Wajhat Nazr, 2008), 271.

33. The exchange took place on May 20, 2009, in the Moroccan parliament. Benmoussa outlined the state's position that discussions between the state and the prisoners focused on the issue of admission and the possibility of requesting royal pardons. "Morocco Dissolves 'A Nascent Terrorist Cell'"; "Salafiya File: Dialogue or Repentance," 2.

34. Kingdom of Morocco, "Law 03.03," 1,755–59.

35. Ministry of Religious Foundations and Islamic Affairs (Habous), Kingdom of Morocco, "A Training Session for Imams and *Murshidates*" (in Arabic), May 3, 2006. Ministry handbill issued for the graduation of the first cohort of imams and *murshidates*.

36. For more detail see Kalpakian, "Against Both bin Laden and Belliraj," 458–60.

37. Salim Hemimat, "A Chronology of the Islamist Scene in Morocco in 2008," *Halat al-Maghreb: 2008-2009* [The state of Morocco: 2008–2009], Strategic Portfolios No. 5, (Rabat: Wajhat Nazr, 2009), 103–11.

38. "The Advocates of Extremism and the Shaykhs of the al-Salafiya al-Jihadiya Laid Fertile Ground for the Growth of Terrorism," *Al-Ahdath al-Maghribiya* (Casablanca), Special Edition no. 1689 (September 2003), 3.

39. Idriss Benani et al., "Chemical Sa'ad"; Al-Raihani et al., "Bin Laden Searching for a Foothold in the Maghreb"; Al-Raihani et al., "Bin Laden Searching for a Foothold in the Maghreb"; "The Algerian Judiciary System Prepares to Try Five Moroccans for the Charges of Terrorism," *Asharq al-Awsat* (London), May 25, 2009, 5; "Profile: Al Qaeda in North Africa," BBC, June 3, 2009, available at http://news.bbc.co.uk/2/hi/africa/6545855.stm (accessed November 3, 2009).

40. Omar Hadoushi, one of the ideologists behind the May 16, 2003 attacks, in an open letter on December 1, 2001 (15 Ramadan 1422 Hijri), as quoted by Sa'id al-Kahal, "The Jihadi Movements and al-Qaeda—What Is Their Relationship?" in in *Mouajahat bain al-Islamiyin wa al-Ilmaniyin bi-al-Maghrib* [Confrontations between Islamists and secularists in Morocco], ed. Mounjib Maati, Wajhat Nazr Booklets no. 15 (Rabat: Wajhat Nazr, 2008), 178–79.

The 2007 Suicide Attacks in Algiers

ANNELI BOTHA

S hortly after the Salafist Group for Preaching and Combat (GSPC) changed its name and metamorphosed into al-Qaeda in the Islamic Maghreb (AQIM), it carried out its first suicide terrorist attack on April 11, 2007. With this attack, Algeria experienced the second suicide terrorist attack in its seventeen-year history with terrorism. The emergence of AQIM raised questions about the influence of al-Qaeda in Algeria before and during the attack and the consequences of the alliance on the organization.

Although the primary focus of this analysis is the attack itself, an analysis starting with the name change will fall short in assessing al-Qaeda's involvement in the attack. In contrast to other incidents in the aftermath of 9/11, terrorism in Algeria was an established occurrence, with an established network responsible for the planning and execution of acts of terrorism. Suicide attacks in Algeria had significant consequences, which are dealt with in this chapter's last section.

INFLUENCE OF AL-QAEDA IN ALGERIA: HISTORIC REVIEW

On January 23, 2007, the Salafist Group for Preaching and Combat (GSPC), headed by Abdelmalek Droukdel, also known as Abu Musab Abdul Wadud officially announced that it had changed its name to AQIM. Months earlier, Ayman al-Zawahiri had announced on September 11, 2006, that the

GSPC was welcomed into the ranks of al-Qaeda. This development did not come as a complete surprise considering that the GSPC openly supported al-Qaeda for a number of years. One might even go as far as to argue that al-Qaeda leadership influenced the split of the GSPC from the Groupe Islamique Armé (GIA) in 1998. Tracing al-Qaeda's influence in Algeria is essential for analyzing al-Qaeda's influence in the planning and execution of the first suicide attack in AQIM's existence.

Afghan Mujaheddin

The Afghan mujaheddin played an important role in the development and ideological direction of Algerian terrorist groups. According to Rédha Malek (the former chief of government and president of the Republican National Alliance) at the end of the 1980s, between 3,000 and 4,000 Algerian nationals went through training camps in Pakistan and Afghanistan.[1] According to General Ali Tounsi, the director general of the Algerian police, approximately 1,000 of the trainees returned to Algeria, and another 1,000 Algerian nationals left for Bosnia.

Upon their return, the Algerian mujaheddin adopted Afghan-style clothing and became known as *les afghanis*. It was also not surprising that one of the first attacks, in November 1991—before a first round of elections—was executed by Emir Abderrahmane Abu Siham, alias Tayeb al-Afghani, an Afghan veteran. The Afghan mujaheddin, including individuals such as Qari Said, Tayeb al-Afghani, Djafar al-Afghani (former emir of the GIA), and Cherif Gouasmi, were later instrumental in the GIA's violent campaign against the Algerian people.[2]

Salafist Group for Preaching and Combat (GSPC)

Hassan Hattab, head of the GIA network in Europe, split away from the GIA and established the GSPC in 1998. According to the testimony of Mohamed Berrached, a former GSPC member, Osama bin Laden encouraged Hassan Hattab to break away from the GIA in an attempt to portray a better image of the jihadist movement after the GIA initiated a campaign of massacres against the Algerian public. Because of its tactics (particularly throat slitting, referred to as a "Kabyle smile") in which not even women and children were spared, al-Qaeda withdrew its support for the GIA in 1996.[3] Recognizing that any domestic insurgent movement needs some form of domestic support, the GSPC exclusively targeted government officials and security personnel, trying to limit civilian casualties.

After the Algerian Afghan mujaheddin initiated an ideological link with Osama bin Laden, al-Qaeda continued to support the training of GSPC members in Afghanistan until 2001. Through training Algerian nationals, al-Qaeda operatives also began to interact with the rank and file of the GSPC. Loyalty to Osama bin Laden (following training in Afghanistan) subsequently led to clashes within the GSPC. As a result of the growing rift, al-Qaeda's leadership sent Emad Abdelwahid Ahmed Alwan (a Yemeni) to meet with Hassan Hattab in an attempt to convince GSPC's leadership to internationalize its operations.[4]

Hattab favored a relationship with al-Qaeda in which the GSPC could retain its Algerian character (remaining independent). Those who supported a closer alliance realized that for this to happen, Hattab had to be replaced. Hattab's first successor as emir of the GSPC, Nabil Sahraoui (alias Abu Ibrahim Mustafa), took over in 2003 and began to openly support al-Qaeda. For example, in an Internet statement on the second anniversary of 9/11, Sahraoui said: "We strongly and fully support Osama bin Laden's *jihad* against the heretic America as well as we support our brothers in Afghanistan, the Philippines, and Chechnya." In a statement published on June 13, 2004, Sahraoui also provided insight to the GSPC's evolving domestic intentions: "The Salafist Group for Preaching and Combat decides . . . to declare war on everything that is foreign and atheistic within Algeria's borders, whether against individuals, interests or installations."[5]

Droukdel continued to strengthen relations with al-Qaeda after Sahraoui's death and contacted Abu Musab al-Zarqawi and Abu 'Abd al-Rahman al-Najdi, a Libyan national and one of Osama bin Laden's deputies in 2004. Al-Rahman was a natural choice to negotiate with the Algerians, having fought as a foreign guerrilla against the Algerian government in the mid-1990s. Droukdel asked if al-Zarqawi could kidnap French citizens to trade for Amari Saifi (alias Abderrazak el-Para) who had been captured by Chadian rebels. Although French forces were not deployed to

Iraq, Droukdel encouraged the kidnapping of French nationals as France was the primary and recognized enemy of Algerian fighters. Although al-Zarqawi indicated his willingness to assist, Saifi was handed over to Algerian authorities on October 27, 2004. Droukdel, however, stayed in contact with al-Zarqawi.[6]

Both al-Qaeda and the GSPC used the U.S. involvement in Iraq to their advantage in justifying not only recruitment inside Algeria but also the use of Algeria as a training ground for fighters bound for Iraq. For al-Qaeda, the GSPC's established networks in Europe provided an added bonus in recruitment, as well as the planning of attacks on European soil. Individuals such as Adil Sakir al-Mukni (alias Yasir Abu Sayyaf, an Algerian national) facilitated this recruitment process and enabled new recruits to travel to Iraq. Abu Sayyaf, who was known to Algerian authorities, was in charge of coordination between the GSPC and al-Zarqawi after he left Algeria in December 2003. He was later arrested in Syria and handed over to Algerian authorities.[7] Several Algerians were involved in terrorist activity in Europe: Italian security forces prosecuted Abderrazak Mahjoub after extradition from Germany for recruiting potential suicide bombers to be sent to Iraq. In Spain, Samir Mahdjoub was accused in May 2004 of helping finance other terrorists' travel to Iraq. Mahdjoub along with Redouane Zenimi and Mohamed Ayat were also accused of being part of a Spanish al-Qaeda cell under the leadership of Abderrazak Mahdjoub (Samir's brother), based in Germany. Abderrazak Mahdjoub was arrested in Germany and later extradited to Italy after an Iraq-recruitment network linked to al-Zarqawi was uncovered in 2004. Another close ally of al-Zarqawi was Said Arif (alias Slimane Chabani or Abderrahmane), a former member of Algeria's security forces who was also trained in Afghanistan. Arif was arrested and later extradited from Syria to France and was implicated as a member of an al-Qaeda cell in France that planned a chemical attack on a U.S. naval base in Spain.[8]

The symbiotic relationship between al-Qaeda in Iraq and the GSPC again came to the forefront in July 21, 2005, when Ali Belaroussi and Azzedine Ben Kadi, two Algerian diplomats, were kidnapped in Iraq. Al-Qaeda claimed responsibility for the attack online two days after the incident. In reply, the message on the GSPC website read: "The GSPC presents its warmest congratulations to its brothers of al-Qaeda . . . the mujahedin in Algeria welcomed with great joy the kidnapping of the Algerian diplomats." Both diplomats later were executed.[9]

Circumstances in Algeria led to a letter written by Khalid Abu Ra'ban, which was published on Islamist websites, formally requesting the assistance of al-Zarqawi in May 2006. The letter referred specifically to "technical and security constraints." However, al-Zarqawi was killed in June 2006 before he could respond. In response, Ayman al-Zawahiri on the fifth anniversary of 9/11 announced the integration of the GSPC into al-Qaeda. Al-Zawahiri explained al-Qaeda's intent with this alliance was to create "a source of chagrin, frustration and sadness for the apostates (of the regime in Algeria), the treacherous sons of France," urging the group to become "a bone in the throat of the American and French crusaders."[10]

In reaction to al-Zawahiri's announcement, Droukdel issued a letter the following day in which he pledged allegiance to al-Qaeda and promised to follow Osama bin Laden "all the way to martyrdom." Above all, Droukdel wrote, "we have full confidence in the faith, the doctrine, the method and the modes of action of [al-Qaeda's] members, as well as their leaders and religious guides."[11] The official alignment of the GSPC with al-Qaeda made practical sense: First, the GSPC simply did not have the operational capacity to overthrow the Algerian government, its initial objective. Second, the public, and also older fighters, had become tired of violence. The Algerian political leadership exploited this vulnerability by offering amnesty. For example, the Charter for Peace and National Reconciliation was put to a national referendum on September 29, 2005. A 97 percent "yes" vote following a turnout of 80 percent reflected the impact the conflict had on the public.[12] As a matter of survival, the GSPC had to adopt a new strategy in reaction to President Bouteflika's reconciliation efforts.

Spelling out the new strategic responsibilities of AQIM, Droukdel issued the following statement on January 9, 2007: "We embrace Jihad to fulfill an ineluctable Divine plan which has been imposed on us since the fall of al-Andalus and the sale of Palestine, and since we were divided by the borders which the invaders invented." In his September 19, 2007, video entitled "The Power of Truth," al-Zawahiri explicitly linked Spain and the mission of AQIM: "Restoring al-Andalus is a trust on the shoulders of the nation in general and on your shoulders in particular, and you will not be able to do that without first cleansing the Muslim Maghreb of the children of France and Spain, who have come back again after your fathers and grandfathers sacrificed their blood cheaply in the path of God to expel them."[13]

At the same time, the Algerian government was so confident of the success of the reconciliation process that it began to refer to the remaining members of the GSPC as thugs who no longer posed a significant threat to its security. Dahou Ould Kabilya, the deputy minister for the interior, during a visit to Tunisia on January 31, 2007, stated: "[The GSPC] has been almost totally eradicated and no longer poses a serious threat." With reference to the threat the new AQIM might pose to foreign interests, the minister added, "They could decide to attack a foreigner, an American or someone they consider their enemy, but it would be an isolated act and we have taken the necessary measures that that won't happen." With reference to links with al-Qaeda central, the minister further stated, "Apart from verbal messages of support, there has never been, to our knowledge, direct aid from al-Qaeda to the Algerians (or the GSPC) neither in terms of logistics and material, nor in the financial sphere."[14] Although AQIM did not present a direct threat to the Algerian government—as GSPC had done in the 1990s—disregarding what the official alignment might imply led to a miscalculation.

In aligning itself with al-Qaeda, the GSPC formally committed itself to al-Qaeda's cause in current hotspots (Iraq and Afghanistan). More important, warning signs, including suicide bombings, should have been recognized. The change in name and tactics implied that AQIM formally changed its focus from a national to a regional perspective that would involve attempts to enhance its influence in the Maghreb and broader Sahel. However, despite interaction and cooperation with both al-Qaeda in Iraq and al-Qaeda central, AQIM still operated independently—controlling of its own recruitment, training, and financing, as well as the planning and execution of attacks.

THE ATTACK ON APRIL 11, 2007

At 10:45 a.m., two suicide bombers simultaneously targeted the Algerian Government Palace and the police station of Bab Ezzouar. Later that same day, members of the Algerian security forces defused a bomb set to detonate remotely in a car parked near the residence of General Ali Tounsi. A day after the attacks Interior Minister Noureddine Zerhouni gave the official casualty rate as 33 killed and more than 220 people injured.[15] The attack came as a surprise not only in terms of the modus operandi but also because it followed four years of relative calm in Algiers.

AQIM claimed responsibility for the attack on the same day, both on the Internet and in a telephone interview with al-Jazeera in Rabat, Morocco. The Internet message that referred to the attack as the "Badr Raid" included pictures of the suicide bombers and referred to three instead of two successful attacks.[16] In the telephone interview, Abu Muhammad Salah, spokesperson for AQIM, provided more information on the targets of the attacks while shedding light on the identity of the three suicide bombers:

> We give the good news to our Muslim brothers that our mujahidin carried out the Badr Raid in the Islamic Maghreb. Three martyrdom seekers . . . hit three targets. The first target was the Algerian prime ministry office in the capital, in which martyr Mu'az Bin-Jabal drove a truck laden with 700 kilograms of explosives and broke into the office, killing about 45 persons, wounding others, and destroying part of the building, according to our own sources. The second target was the headquarters of the Interpol in Al-Dar al-Bayda in Bab-Ezzouar in the capital, in which martyr Al-Zubayr Abu-Sajidah drove a truck laden with about 700 kilograms of explosives, breaking into the den of oppression, infidelity, and fighting jihad. With God's help, he managed to destroy the entire building, killing seven to eight apostates and wounding others. The third target was the headquarters of the police special forces of Al-Dar al-Bayda in Bab-Ezzouar, in which martyr Abu-Dujanah drove a truck laden with about 500 kilograms of explosives and broke into the headquarters, destroying it completely, killing and wounding a number of apostates.[17]

Profile of the Suicide Bombers

Merouane Boudina (alias Mouaad Ibn Djabel), targeted the Government Palace. According to media reports Boudina was in and out of jail for drug trafficking before he disappeared a few months before the attacks. Mouloud Benchiheb Hossine (alias Abu Dujanah or Hocine), who targeted the police station in Bab Ezzouar, was a known drug dealer in the late 1990s. According to officials, Benchiheb Hossine was recruited by the GSPC while serving a prison sentence for drug dealing before joining the insurgency in 1994.[18] Security forces arrested al-Zubair Abu Sajidah in July 2007 when he fled after parking a black Mercedes Benz in front of the Danish embassy. He later revealed that all three suicide bombers came from the al-Jabal suburb in Bourouba, Algiers. Abu Sajidah accompanied and filmed Hafidh Mohamed during the suicide bombing of the military barracks in Lakhdaria on July 11, 2007, before his arrest.[19]

Essentially, only the bomber targeting the Government Palace was successful. Algerian officials speculated on the intention of the second bomber, whose target supposedly was the headquarters of the police special forces of al-Dar al-Bayda in Bab Ezzouar though he actually targeted a police station. One possible explanation was that although the intended target was situated 500 meters from the police station, the bomber saw "police station" on the corner to the Judiciary Police and thought it was the intended target. The Judiciary Police is more involved in counterterrorism, making it a more symbolic target. Al-Zubair Abu Sajidah, the third suicide bomber did not execute his attack and was arrested in July 2007. Abu Muhammad Salah's message identified his intended target as Interpol's headquarters in al-Dar al-Bayda in Bab Ezzouar.[20] Al-Zubair Abu Sajidah might have failed to execute his attack since Interpol did not have an office in Algeria, though security officials revealed to the author that another possible target might have been the African Union's Centre for the Study and Research of Terrorism, which is based in that area. Intelligence failure on the part of the bombers might explain the confusion.

Executing the attack on April 11 signaled to AQIM's followers, al-Qaeda, and the rest of the world that the GSPC now considered itself part of al-Qaeda's global jihad not only in name but also in its modus operandi. While Abu Muhammad Salah's message (claiming responsibility for the attack) had a strong anti-Western sentiment, those killed were Muslim: Algerian and government targets:

> Our jihad aims at defending the religion of Islam and the blood and honour of our Muslim brothers in the entire world, who are oppressed,

detained and tortured in Morocco, Algeria, Mauritania or other countries. It is common that this wretched alliance, which consists of the Crusaders, and their collaborator Arab governments in the region, target our religion, honour, and sanctities. Our strikes are retaliatory, and we will chase them everywhere, God willing. As our master Osama [bin Laden], may God protect him, we swear by God that the United States, and of course its collaborators, will not even dream of enjoying security until we see it a reality in Palestine.[21]

Choosing the eleventh of the month unmistakably reflected AQIM's association with al-Qaeda—reference to al-Qaeda's attacks on September 11, 2001, in the United States as well as the Madrid train bombings on March 11, 2004. The eleventh also held symbolic importance to extremists in the region, in that the eleventh century was the height of the western Islamic empire.[22] Even before the name change, Droukdel referred to Algerians as "the grandsons of Tariq ibn Ziyad" (also the name of an AQIM battalion in the south) and "sons of Yusuf ibn Tashfin." AQIM leadership regularly refers to the glorious era of al-Andalus. During the period between January 2007 and January 2009, reference was made ten times to Yusuf bin Tashfin, Tariq bin Ziyad, and 'Uqba bin Nafi.[23] Reference to these historic heroes serves a number of objectives, most notably justifying their campaign and stirring up sentiments of a glorious past to enhance support and assistance. In explaining the former, Abu Ubayda Yusuf, AQIM sharia committee member, in an audio statement on October 6, 2008, called for the liberation of areas under historic control of the caliphate:

I end my message by saluting the steadfast mujahidin in the lands of the Islamic Maghreb, you the grandsons of Uqba, the conqueror of the Maghreb, and Musa Bin Nasir, the conqueror of Andalusia, and Tariq Ibn Ziyad, the vanquisher of the Romans and the Spanish, and [Yusuf] Tashfin, the hero of Zalaqa, and Abd al-Hamid Bin Badis, the leader of the reforms. Today you are the pride of the umma in a time of exploitation; you are the hope in reclaiming its usurped honor in our broken Islamic Maghreb and the appropriated Andalusia, Cordoba, Sicily, and Zalaqa. We will not rest and we will not be content until we regain every inch of our usurped land including the occupied Sebta and Melilla, and let us meet with our beloved people in the land of Palestine.[24]

An example of the latter can be found in Droukdel's audio statement on September 21, 2008:

> Grandsons of Uqbah and Tariq and Yusuf bin Tashfin and Al-Mu'iz Bin Badis and 'Abd al-Karim al-Khattabi and 'Umar al-Mukhtar, rise from your inertia and put your hands in the hands of your brothers, the mujahidin, in the al-Qaeda Organization in the Land of the Islamic Maghreb who have sacrificed their money, their lives, and their honor for the sake of protecting Islam and the unity and the reverence of the Islamic Maghreb. Gather around the jihad with which Islam started so it becomes the only force and alternative to the regimes of apostasy that are ruling our countries.[25]

The eleventh also has a negative connotation in the Islamic world. For example, on March 11, 1917, the British Army under Lieutenant General Sir Frederick Stanley Maude defeated Ottoman troops in Baghdad.[26] During the same year, on December 11, 1917, British general Edmund Allenby officially entered Jerusalem after the Battle for Gaza, leading to Christian occupation of Jerusalem. For many jihadists this act was an extension of the Crusades.[27] Although AQIM did not specifically refer to this "coincidence," exactly ninety years later on December 11, 2007, AQIM targeted the Algerian Constitutional Council and a United Nations building in a twin suicide attack.

While the date and modus operandi of the April 11 attacks are a reflection of an al-Qaeda-style operation, the target selection mirrored the GSPC's previous operations. In contrast to the GIA, which was responsible for mass-casualty attacks during the 1990s, the GSPC was renowned for limiting its campaign against the state and its security forces. While al-Qaeda in its statement identified civilians as the target, in practice, AQIM targeted the government and police buildings. Although the indiscriminate nature of the suicide attacks involved civilian casualties, the ultimate target of the April 11 attacks was still the Algerian state and its security forces.

Despite the evolution of the GSPC into AQIM, al-Qaeda's senior leadership in south Asia was not directly involved in the planning and execution of the attacks on April 11 or any subsequent attacks. Hassan Hattab, in an interview with *Echourouk el-Youmi* newspaper in Algeria on

July 5, 2009, confirmed that "the affiliation of the Salafi Group for Call and Combat with al-Qaeda is purely formal. Al Qaeda is not linked to the Salafi group in any way, and there is no direct coordination between the two organizations. Nor are there any orders received from the main Al-Qaeda. There used to be contacts with Abu Mus'ab al-Zarqawi in the past but there is not any direct contact between the two organizations."[28] Reconfirming an earlier remark, the GSPC previously and AQIM at the time of the attack on April 11 (and thereafter) operated independently from al-Qaeda central.

Responsibility for the attacks rested first with the national emir, Abdelmalek Droukdel (Abu Musab Abdul Wadud), who officially sanctioned the suicide bombings. AQIM divided Algeria into zones. Zone 2 hosted AQIM's central command and oversaw operations in Algiers, Boumerdes, Tizi Ouzou, and Bouira. At the time of the attack, Emir Zoheir Harkat (alias Sofiane Fassila) ran the zone and was therefore central in planning and executing the attack.[29] Each zone was further subdivided into katibats headed by an emir. Zoheir, Hamzaoui Abdelhamid (alias Abu Tourab, the emir of the El-Farouk katibat), and Osama Abu Ishak (alias Rabah) were killed on October 6, 2007, in Boghni in Tizi Ouzou. All three were linked to the suicide attacks in April 2007.[30] Abou Bekr Seddik katibat was established as a bridge to the El-Feth katibat and the El-Arkam katibat in order to reestablish sleeper cells in Algiers. As a result of stability that returned to Algiers in the early 2000s, AQIM had to rely on structures surrounding the capital to recruit the suicide bombers and execute the attacks.[31] Particularly, Boumerdes played an important role in the execution of the suicide attacks on April 11, highlighted by the discovery and break-up of explosives "laboratories" in the Tijilabine area following the attacks. Although weapons and components used in the manufacturing of explosives were smuggled from other areas, the construction of the car bombs took place in the area. This formed part of a strategy to prevent unnecessary attention from the public or intervention from the security forces. In May 2007, security forces arrested twelve people suspected of being part of a support network behind the April 11 attacks. During the law-enforcement operation, large quantities of chemicals, including acid, and electronic components were discovered.[32] These laboratories, established close to their intended targets for security reasons, were identified as central to the preparations of the April 11 bombing.[33]

In addition to Droukdel and Zoheir the following individuals have also been implicated: Emir Abdelhamid Saadaoui (alias Abou Yahia or Abou Haitem), later killed by Algerian security forces; Fateh Bouder-bala (alias Abdelfattah Abou Bassir), arrested in November 2007; Sehari Makhloufi (alias Abou Meriem or Hodeifa), the suicide bomber that targeted the police station in Tizi Ouzou on August 3, 2008; and Sid Ali Rachid (alias Ali Dix), the second in command in Zone 2 and Drouk-del's military advisor, killed on July 30, 2007, along with Nour Mohamed (alias Haroune el-Esh'ashi).[34] Ali Dix was described as the brains behind the April 11 attack, and Nour Mohamed was an important role-player in the arms-trafficking network from the south of Algeria. Taking charge in liaising between Zone 2 and Zone 9 (southern Algeria) for arms deals into the central area of activity (Zone 2 and eastern Algeria), he was essential in carrying out attacks and also close to Droukdel.[35] Although it is difficult to identify all the players and their responsibilities, the people mentioned here decided that Zone 2 would be where this new tactic would be introduced.

CONSEQUENCES OF THE ATTACK

After the first suicide attack, AQIM had to face a number of challenges, leading to several developments and changes within the organization. The following discussion hopes to provide the reader with a brief overview of some of these trends, most notably in modus operandi, target selection, organization, and AQIM's growing influence in the broader region.

Despite the practical considerations that drove the initial decision to move closer to al-Qaeda, the GSPC membership was torn after the merger between two factions: those who supported and adopted al-Qaeda's vision, strategy, and tactics and saw AQIM's role extending beyond Algeria versus the older generation who supported the GSPC's independence, despite ideological influences from al-Qaeda. Those who originally fought the Algerian state questioned the religious justification of suicide attacks because of their indiscriminate nature and mass-casualty potential. The older generation began to rethink the merger, particularly because of public outrage. In protest against the killing of civilians, this ideological split prompted individuals such as Brahim Boufarik to surrender to authorities after the April 11 attacks. He stated as his justification, "Several *muftis* inside our organization are against using suicide bombings because they hit civilians. It appears that there is no difference between Droukdel's approach and the GIA approach." Religious scholars also questioned GSPC/AQIM's new tactics as unjust.[36] They included Sheikh Abdenasser, a former member of the GSPC's Shura Council; Ahmed Jabri, also a member of the Shura Council; and Abu Abbas, the sharia councilor in Zone 2.[37] In an open letter to President Bouteflika, the GSPC founder, Hassan Hattab, described Droukdel's group as: "a small group that wants to transform Algeria into a second Iraq." To the old guard, including Hattab, "Algeria is composed of three factions: rebels, officials including security forces and the people. The first two groups are the combatants, while the third, or the civilian population, must in no circumstances be targeted. However, Droukdel's group allows one Muslim to declare another Muslim an apostate, or nonbeliever [*takfir*], and then kill him." According to this view, Algeria is divided into just two factions: the rebels and everyone else, justifying discriminate attacks.[38]

Exacerbating the conflict, Droukdel adopted an autocratic style when he took over leadership of GSPC from Sahraoui, and he replaced established GSPC leaders with individuals whom he considered loyal to the new organization. For example, Abdelkader Benmessaoud (alias Mossaab Abou Daoud), the former emir of Zone 9 (the south of the country), upon his surrender revealed that the GSPC's decision to join al-Qaeda was unilaterally taken by Droukdel, indicating resentment within the organization. He also indicated that Mokhtar Belmokhtar was replaced by Yahia Djouadi (alias Abou Amar Abd el-Ber), and Belmokhtar even feared that the new leader would kill him.[39]

These events contributed to friction within the organization and a loss of morale. This became evident in calls for cease fire and surrenders within the organization. Capitalizing on the low morale within AQIM, Algerian security forces allowed Omar Abdelbir, the former head of GSPC's press committee; Abu Zakaria, former head of the medical committee and former emir of Zone 9; and Moussaab Abou Daoud to call on fighters to lay down their arms in a press conference in Algiers in 2009. These calls were echoed by Samir Saayoud, the former head of external relations.[40] Possibly the most damning appeals for surrender, after that of Hassan Hattab, came from Amari Saifi (alias Abderrazak el-Para).[41]

Even its southern command, through Yahia Djouadi and his military commander, Hamid el-Soufi, made a truce offer during negotiations with the Algerian security services in which they would end attacks against foreign workers in Algeria and Mauritania. In exchange, the security forces would not hunt down AQIM members in the areas of the Sahel countries where they were active—specifically in Mali, Mauritania, Algeria, Niger, and up to Burkina Faso.[42]

This decentralization and the independence of substructures are expected to increase especially because of government countermeasures. This depends, however, on the survival of AQIM's central command in eastern Algeria. An increase in audio messages from AQIM leadership might indicate that AQIM is on a similar path as al-Qaeda central: propaganda without significant attacks. Late 2008 and 2009 also showed that AQIM's southern command gradually enhanced its operations and reach compared to the eastern command. Probably as a result of security measures, the Sahara group led by Yahia Abou Ammar and Hamid el-Soufi became almost completely isolated from AQIM's command (in northeast Algeria) when communications became increasingly difficult.[43]

Countering a decrease in experienced fighters in the ranks of AQIM, the organization began to concentrate its recruitment efforts on foreign fighters and younger followers who were inexperienced and easily manipulated. These new recruitment techniques presented a challenge to the security forces because the new recruits were unknown to them. Despite these advantages, younger recruits are less experienced in conventional insurgency-type attacks. Outside the organization, support networks—which provide intelligence and essentials such as food and medicine—are increasingly being broken up following information provided by repentant former members and the public, thus straining the organization's ability to recruit new members within Algeria.

Modus Operandi

Of the nineteen suicide attacks (at the time of writing) executed by AQIM in Algeria, all but three were directed at government officials and security installations. On September 21, 2007, a suicide bomber targeted a convoy of foreign workers employed by Razel, a French company, near

Lakhdaria. Two French citizens, an Italian, an Algerian driver, and five gendarmes were injured in the attack. The bombing came a day after al-Qaeda released an eighty-minute video in which Ayman al-Zawahri, called for attacks against French and Spanish interests in North Africa.[44]

On December 11, 2007, twin suicide truck bombs targeted the Algerian Constitutional Council and the United Nations building housing the UNDP in Algiers, killing nine UN staff members: six Algerians, one Senegalese, one Danish national, and one citizen of the Philippines. In a posting on a militant website, AQIM described the UN offices as "the headquarters of the international infidels' den."[45]

On August 20, 2008, a suicide bomber targeted a bus transporting employees of SNC-Lavalin, a Canadian engineering firm. Although SNC-Lavalin is identified as a Canadian company, the twelve employees killed were all Algerian nationals.[46] Adopting suicide attacks introduced another variable: civilian casualties. While al-Qaeda in its attacks throughout the world hoped for maximum civilian casualties, AQIM's survival in Algeria depends on domestic support. In contrast to 2007 and 2008, AQIM realized that suicide attacks allowed Algerian authorities to capitalize on a decline in support from the broader public and also from within the organization. In other words, the initial "hope" that suicide attacks would sell the GSPC or AQIM as al-Qaeda's representative in the Maghreb and Sahel did tremendous harm to AQIM's image in Algeria. The only suicide attack in Algeria during 2009 was carried out on March 7, in which the barracks of the Tadmait municipal guard, near Tizi Ouzou was targeted. The Tadmait suicide attack, the first since September 28, 2008, killed three—the suicide bomber among them—and wounded eighty-seven civilians and one municipal guard.[47] Instead of using suicide attacks, AQIM returned to its familiar modus operandi, including kidnappings and the use of roadside bombs followed by an ambush against security forces (the number of attacks is still declining).

Instead of attracting media attention with suicide bombings, AQIM resorted to kidnapping Westerners. After the kidnapping of thirty-one European tourists in 2003, the GSPC/AQIM inter alia claimed responsibility for the kidnapping of two Austrians, Andrea Kloiber and Wolfgang Ebner, in February 2008 in Tunisia. This was followed by the kidnapping of Robert Fowler, the United Nations special envoy to Niger, and Louis Guay in December 2008, who both were held on the border between

Algeria and Niger.[48] These were followed by the kidnapping of four European tourists: Edwin Dyer, a British national; Marianne Petzold, a German national; and a Swiss couple, Gabriella Burco Greiner and Werner Greiner, on January 22, 2009—taken hostage near the Algeria-Mali border.

In addition to the familiar ransom demands, AQIM also demanded the release of other extremists and imprisoned members of the group. For example, in exchange for Robert Fowler, Louis Guay, Marianne Petzold, and Gabriella Burco Greiner AQIM demanded and secured the release of four of its members, including Oussama Alboumerdassi from Algeria and Mauritanian members of the group held in Mali.[49] This possibly led to the demand for the release of Omar Mahmoud Othman, better known as Abu Qatada (held in the United Kingdom) in exchange for Edwin Dyer. The release of Abu Qatada would have greatly enhanced the image of AQIM. After AQIM extended the initial deadline, it became apparent that the United Kingdom would not capitulate. Subsequently, AQIM announced in an online statement that Abdelhamid Abou Zeid was responsible for the beheading of Dyer on May 31, 2009.[50] In an attempt to save face, AQIM opted for a beheading (associated with al-Qaeda in Iraq under al-Zarqawi), but what was interesting was the decision not to distribute a video of the execution. AQIM is expected to continue these kidnappings because of the success it has found in attracting media attention and raising funds. Countering this trend, the African Union—encouraged by Algeria—is considering steps to prevent the payment of ransom.[51]

Regional Profile of the Organization

The attacks of April 2007 punctuated the expanded regional ambitions of the GSPC and its official alignment with al-Qaeda. This alignment made the AQIM in Algeria the center of terrorist activity in the region, or at least this is what AQIM hoped. Despite its decreasing success in Algeria, AQIM began expanding its appeal across the Maghreb region to the extent that its survival depends on its ability to spread beyond Algeria. Since extremists in Tunisia and Morocco were unable during the 1990s to establish the same level of activity, the Algerian movement welcomed the incorporation of Moroccan, Libyan, Tunisian, and Mauritanian nationals.

Nabil Sahraoui was the first GSPC emir to pursue a dedicated regional outreach strategy. In October 2003, he started specifically recruiting Libyan and Tunisian Islamists who had returned from al-Qaeda training camps in Afghanistan.[52] The regional appeal of the new GSPC/AQIM created a regional security threat that extended beyond Algeria. Algerian authorities subsequently arrested Libyan, Tunisian, Moroccan, Mauritanian, Nigerian, and Malian nationals involved with the group.[53] The involvement of Libyan nationals in AQIM implied that although Abu Yahya al-Libi aligned the Libyan Islamic Fighting Group (LIFG) with al-Qaeda central, Libyan radicals threw their weight in with the AQIM not only because it was the leading extremist group in the region but also because of the difficulty in organizing and executing acts of terrorism on Libyan soil.[54]

The expanded operational reach of the GSPC/AQIM beyond Algeria was also necessary to present AQIM as al-Qaeda's representative in the Maghreb. The GSPC expanded operations from Algeria into the northern parts of Mali and Niger in February 2003 and 2004, respectively. Early attempts by the GSPC to enhance its regional profile included the ambush of an army patrol in Mauritania in June 2005, in which fifteen soldiers were killed. Mokhtar Belmokhtar (alias Abou el-Abbes Khalid or Belaouar), the former emir of Zone 9, claimed responsibility for the attack. The attackers lost six men, including Abu Mohamed al-Jinki, a Mauritanian national.[55] In other words, the inclusion of foreign fighters in the GSPC did not start with the official alignment with al-Qaeda in 2006. The attackers identified with al-Qaeda and received immediate congratulatory messages on the Internet from other al-Qaeda affiliates, including one from Abu Musab al-Zarqawi. Following the attack on the Mauritanian army, the July 6 issue of Morocco's leading newspaper, the *Liberation*, reported that al-Qaeda had a grand objective to establish terrorist bases in the Sahel similar to those existing in Afghanistan before the Taliban regime was dismantled. The remote nature of the Sahel made it difficult to control and patrol, allowing terrorists to use the terrain to their advantage.[56]

Becoming more decentralized, AQIM in Mauritania separated from the Tariq ibn Ziyad battalion in March 2009.[57] This led to the AQIM announcement in May 2009 that Abderrahmane Abi Anas el-Shanqiti, a commander from Mauritania, was "the judge of the Sahara emirate and member of the consultative council."[58] The Mauritanians refer to themselves as the el-Asmaa battalion. The Nouakchott cell executed the following attacks: On June 22, 2009, gunmen killed Christopher Leggett, an American teacher in Nouakchott. The attack occurred outside a private language and computer school run by Americans in Nouakchott (Leggett also worked for a charity, Noura). The AQIM spokesman, Salah Abu Mohammed, claimed that the group killed Leggett because he was allegedly trying to convert Muslims to Christianity: "Two knights of the Islamic Maghreb succeeded Tuesday morning at 8 a.m. to kill the infidel American Christopher Leggett for his Christianizing activities."[59] On August 8, 2009, three people, two of them French paramilitary gendarmes, were slightly injured in a suicide attack near the French embassy that only killed the suicide bomber.[60]

AQIM's interest in Mauritania, however, is not a new development. After the attack on the military base in 2005, an attack was launched on a French family near Aleg on December 24, 2007; on December 30, 2007, another attack on a military base near Galaouia followed; soon after this incident, on January 31, 2008, gunmen launched an attack on the Israeli embassy in Nouakchott.

In addition to its influence in the Maghreb and Sahel, suspicion that there could be contact between AQIM and extremist organizations in Somalia was confirmed with the arrest of Oussama el-Merdaci in Timbuktu en route to Somalia. El-Merdaci, an Afghan mujaheddin veteran, was also known to GSPC's network in London.[61]

The Internet

The GSPC/AQIM established an information and media committee in 2004, headed at that time by Sheikh Abu Omar Abd al-Birracted. The GSPC then began to distribute information through a website, www.jihadalgeria .com.[62] From 2004 on, the GSPC made documents available, including manuals on how to manufacture explosives and poisons. The website, however, also urged its members and supporters not to introduce these methods before "consulting the *fatwas* of Osama bin Laden."[63] This statement confirmed a closer relationship with al-Qaeda but also indicates a more decentralized network.

Like any other organization, AQIM uses the full range of modern communication in an attempt to sell itself to the jihadi community and the broader public. It uses audio and video messages to justify its actions, influence public opinion, harness support, and recruit new members. The Internet also proved to be a valuable instrument in the recruitment of foreign nationals. Although the Algerian government reacted by closing down a number of websites, the Internet was still used to claim responsibility for attacks in Algeria and beyond (including attacks in Mauritania). AQIM distributed video footage of the attack on U.S.-based Brown & Root-Condor in December 2006—which included footage of how the attack was planned and executed—and other subsequent attacks.[64] As the organization spreads farther south, it is to be expected that its use of and dependence on the Internet will increase.

COUNTERTERRORISM POLICY RECOMMENDATIONS

After the suicide attack on April 11, 2007, Algeria's security forces realized that a primarily military strategy to counter AQIM was insufficient to deal with this new phase of terrorism. Although intelligence-driven operations were used to identify support networks, particularly in urban areas, the focus of Algeria's strategy during the late 1990s had been to keep terrorists away from those areas. The goal of counterterrorism operations during the 1990s was to enable the military to eliminate terrorists by cordoning off suspected areas, followed by aerial bombings and classical search-and-destroy operations. However, the ability of the GSPC/AQIM to execute a successful bombing in the capital city implied not only that the terrorists were able to operate in densely populated areas but also that they received support from people in urban areas. AQIM's comfort with operating in an urban environment reaffirmed the need for better intelligence and cooperation with the public. This new strategy concentrated on increasing intelligence operations to penetrate into strongholds, identifying and eliminating the heads of suicide operations, monitoring cybercafes, and initiatives to introduce a broader CCTV monitoring system. AQIM's loss in stature and support within Algeria only enhanced the intelligence capabilities of Algeria's security forces. Preventing suicide attacks came in the form of arrests and tactical successes. In one example, on July 20, 2009, Algerian security forces successfully prevented a suicide attack directed at the coast guard in Dellys when they shot and killed Omar Toudji (alias Abou Abderrahmane), who was wearing an explosive vest.[65]

The commitment of the international community, particularly neighboring countries, is another essential component in preventing the growing influence of AQIM beyond Algeria's borders. Unfortunately, a regional strategy faces a number of challenges, most notably ungoverned spaces, difficult terrain, and limited human and technological means to enable effective border control, as well as questionable political commitment from neighboring countries. For example, Mali remained neutral as long as AQIM did not carry out attacks against Malian officials; this lasted until AQIM members killed Lieutenant-Colonel Lamana Ould Bou, on June 11, 2009.[66] After this, countries in the Maghreb and Sahel showed a greater resolve to deal with the growing threat of terrorism in the region. Until recently, Algeria drove counterterrorism efforts in the region, and its neighbors considered the threat as predominantly limited to Algeria's security. Despite operational cooperation between a few member states, the Western Sahara and Tuareg situations also prevented closer cooperation. In one example, when Moroccan authorities learned that Algeria planned to include the Polisario Front (based in Tindouf) in operations, Morocco decided to withdraw from the operation. Military assistance from Algeria to Mali and Niger came with the precondition that weapons would not be used against the Tuareg.

These changes form part of a short-term strategy to limit and eventually eliminate the direct threat presented by the execution of attacks, but Algeria and other countries in the region urgently need to implement a long-term strategy to limit the radicalization potential of their citizens. Although the focus of this chapter is not the underlying causes leading to the establishment of the GIA, the GSPC, and, eventually, AQIM, brief reference to the most important issues—as part of an effective and lasting counterterrorism strategy—is essential. Poor economic conditions, particularly unemployment; social challenges because of this poverty, and political frustration (despite democratic developments) require urgent attention. It is also worrying to notice the return of those who benefited from the reconciliation process into the ranks of terrorists, particularly the recruitment of the younger generation.

This development makes it necessary to establish a better deradicalization process in addition to the existing "reconciliation" process. In addition to these domestic challenges, the value of international politics to radicalizing groups is unmistakable. International areas of conflict, most notably Afghanistan, Bosnia, Chechnya, Iraq, Palestine, and Somalia, play an important role in the radicalization process. As mentioned earlier, Iraq was instrumental in keeping the GSPC relevant and enabling its later name change.

CONCLUSION

The GSPC's changing its name to AQIM set a new standard for terrorism in Algeria. It was a visual sign that the GSPC had officially aligned itself with al-Qaeda. This alignment, however, was a reflection of weakness, not strength. The GSPC had to align itself with al-Qaeda to stay relevant since it no longer could fulfill its initial objective of overthrowing the Algerian government. Because of financial and material challenges, the GSPC did not have the manpower to present a real challenge to the Algerian state. Looking for a peaceful solution to years of violence, family members of insurgents began to work with authorities to negotiate the surrender of fighters. The reconciliation process further capitalized on the low morale the organization faced. The only remaining option available to the group was to present the GSPC as al-Qaeda's regional representative in North Africa. Since extremists only managed to establish a foothold in Algeria during the 1990s, repackaging the GSPC as al-Qaeda's representative in North Africa provided guidance to less-structured organizations in the region. The war in Iraq and local dissatisfaction with U.S. foreign policy in the Middle East also served as a lifeline for the organization. Recruitment networks in Algeria and other countries in the region used the U.S. invasion of Afghanistan and Iraq to their advantage. Before sending these foreign fighters to the Middle East and Asia, AQIM training camps were used as a form of "boot-camp."

The AQIM's suicide attacks on April 11, 2007, further confirmed its official alignment with al-Qaeda. Links to al-Qaeda in Iraq and al-Qaeda central was instrumental to the AQIM's transformation from a domestic to a transnational terrorist organization. Al-Qaeda was instrumental in providing the philosophical framework before this attack; however, al-Qaeda had no role to play in the planning and execution.

Despite the alignment and name change, the majority of AQIM's attacks not only in Algeria but also neighboring countries, such as Mali and Mauritania, is still directed against the security apparatus of the state. This status quo depends on the centralized nature of its current structure. The real threat of AQIM lies in the development of more decentralized cell structures beyond its immediate area of control—in other words, those who were trained in AQIM's mobile training camps and returned to their countries of origin, including Nigeria, Chad, Niger, and Mauritania. These individuals are not always known to security forces, and they can initiate attacks against Western targets in the region, with AQIM claiming responsibility.

Keeping these decentralized networks focused will depend on AQIM's ability to capitalize on international developments. As Iraq fades as a rallying point, other attempts to stir emotions are based on events such as France's decision to ban the burqa or unrest in Xinjiang, China. The claim of responsibility for the suicide attack against the French embassy in Nouakchott blamed France for its hostility against Islam and Muslims. These excuses will continue to be the points around which AQIM tried to rally new supporters.

NOTES

1. Rédha Malek, "Islamist Terrorism in Algeria: An Experience to Ponder," in *Voices of Terror: Manifestos, Writings and, Manuals of Al Qaeda, Hamas, and Other Terrorists from Around the World and Throughout the Ages*, ed. Walter Laqueur (Naperville, Ill.: Sourcebooks, 2004), 441.

2. "Algerian Islamist Group Leader Reveals Details of His Life," BBC Monitoring: Middle East, September 14, 2006; Rohan Gunaratna, *Inside Al Qaeda: Global Network of Terror* (New York: Columbia University Press, 2002).

3. "Bin Laden Held to be Behind an Armed Algerian Islamic Movement," Agence France-Presse, February 15, 1999.

4. Dino Mahtani, "Poverty and Graft Breed Extremism in Nigeria," *Financial Times*, July 5, 2007. Alwan was instrumental in helping al-Qaeda fighters from Algeria, Egypt, Libya, Morocco, and Tunisia settle in Yemen after the U.S. invasion of Afghanistan.

5. "Algerian Military: Al-Qaida-Linked Terror Leader Killed," *Dow Jones International News*, June 20, 2004; "Algerian Islamic Rebels Declare War on Foreigners," Reuters, June 13, 2004.

6. Craig Whitlock, "Group in Algeria Turned to Al Qaeda for Assistance," *Washington Post*, May 30, 2007; "Algerian Group Said Contacting Al-Zarqawi to Target French Nationals," BBC Monitoring: Middle East, July 4, 2005. Al-Rahman followed bin Laden to Sudan and from there joined the GIA as a foreign fighter against the Algerian government in the mid-1990s. Al-Rahman followed bin Laden to Afghanistan in 1996, assisting him in establishing terrorist training camps. Al-Rahman and al-Zarqawi met in Afghanistan in 1999, and the former served as another link between al-Zarqawi in Iraq and Algerian fighters.

7. "Algerian Al-Qa'idah-Linked Activist Handed Over by Syria," BBC Middle East, September 13, 2005.

8. "Arrested Algerian Refuses to Testify in Italian Court," Agence France-Presse, March 23, 2004; "Spain Judge Links Qaeda Suspects to Iraq Insurgency," Reuters, May 19, 2004; "Algerian Man Extradited to France for Alleged Terror Ties," *Dow Jones International News*, June 18, 2004.

9. "A List of Some of the Diplomats Attacked in Iraq," Associated Press, October 3, 2007; Michael Georgy, "Qaeda Claims Kidnap of Algerian Envoy in Iraq," Reuters News, July 23, 2005; "Islamist Radicals Praise Al Qaeda for Kidnap of Algerian Diplomats," Agence France-Presse, July 24, 2005; "Al Qaeda in Iraq to Execute Kidnapped Algerian Diplomats," Agence France-Presse, July 26, 2005.

10. "Algerian Salafist Group Seeks Al-Zarqawi's Help," BBC Monitoring: Middle East, May 2, 2006; "Al-Qaida Targets France," Trend News Agency (Azerbaijan), June 16, 2007.

11. Mathieu Guidère, "Import of Jihad and Martyrdom: Algeria's Al-Qaida Franchise," *Le Monde Diplomatique*, November 1, 2006.

12. Manny Thain, "Peace and Reconciliation Charter—Peace in Algeria?" October 17, 2005, http://www.socialistworld.net/eng/2005/10/17algeria.html.

13. Peter J. Pham, "Al Qaeda in the Islamic Maghreb: An Evolving Challenge in the War on Terror," *Family Security Matters*, May 8, 2008, available at http://www.familysecuritymatters.org/publications/id.48,css.print/pub_detail.asp.

14. "Algerian Minister Says Salafist Group 'Not a Threat,'" Agence France-Presse, January 31, 2007.

15. "Al Qaeda-Linked Bombings in Algerian Capital Kill at Least Thirty-Three; Premier's Office, Police Station Hit," *Facts on File World News Digest*, April 12, 2007.

16. Craig Whitlock, "Suicide Attacks Mark Turn in Algeria; Insurgents Seen Taking Cues From Global Al-Qaeda," *Washington Post*, April 13, 2007.

17. "Al-Qa'idah Spokesman Details to Al-Jazeera Algiers Blasts," *BBC News*, April 11, 2007.

18. Aidan Lewis "Al-Qaida's New North Africa Wing Recruiting on Margins of Algerian Society," *Associated Press*, April 17, 2007.

19. "Algerian Authorities Arrest Two Suspects in 11 April Attacks," BBC Monitoring: Middle East, August 18, 2007.

20. Ibid.

21. Al-Jazeera, "Al-Qa'idah in Maghreb Further Detail 11 April Algiers Blasts."

22. The area included modern-day Morocco, Mauritania, Western Sahara, Gibraltar, Tlemcen (Algeria), and parts of Mali and Senegal, as well as al-Andalus across the Mediterranean, consisting of modern-day Portugal and Spain.

23. Lianne Kennedy Boudali, "Leveraging History in AQIM Communications," *CTC Sentinel* 2, no. 4 (April 2009): 16.

24. Ibid.

25. Ibid.

26. "Historic Moments for March 11," Today in History, http://www.todayinhistory .com/s30–3-11-event-results.html.

27. "Primary Documents—Sir Edmund Allenby on the Fall of Jerusalem, 9 December 1917," http://www.firstworldwar.com/source/jerusalem_allenbyprocl.htm.

28. "Algeria: Former Islamist Rebel Emir Views Reconciliation, Salafi Group, AQLIM," BBC Monitoring: Middle East, September 1, 2009.

29. "Background on Killing of Algerian Explosives Expert," BBC Monitoring: Middle East, October 9, 2007.

30. "Algerian Army Engaged in Large-Scale Anti-Terror Operation," BBC Monitoring: Middle East, June 28, 2007.

31. "Algerian Army Kills Three Terror Suspects in Khemis el-Khechna Operation," BBC Monitoring: Middle East, June 25, 2007.

32. "Algerian Authorities Dismantle Cell Linked to Group Behind April Attacks," BBC Monitoring: Middle East, May 20, 2007.

33. "Algerian Investigators Say 11 April Terror Attack Explosives Made in Baraki," BBC Monitoring: Middle East, April 24, 2007.

34. "Al-Qa'idah Commander Killed in Algeria," BBC Monitoring: Middle East, July 3, 2007.

35. "Algerian Troops Kill Terrorist Group's Military Advisor," BBC Monitoring: Middle East, August 2, 2007.

36. "Al-Qa'idah in the Maghreb: A Return to 1990s Violence Feared," BBC Monitoring: Middle East, November 1, 2007.

37. "Opposition Reported Inside Maghreb Al-Qa'idah to Recent Blasts in Algeria," BBC Monitoring: Middle East, May 11, 2007.

38. Lamine Chikhi, "Algeria Police Detect Rebel Rift Over Tactics," Reuters, May 21, 2007.

39. "Algerian Al-Qa'idah Communiqué Attempts to Offset Repentant's Revelations," BBC Monitoring: Middle East, August 22, 2007.

40. "Algeria Deploys Troops in Al-Qa'idah Maghreb Strongholds," *BBC Middle East*, May 10, 2009.

41. "Algerian 'Terrorist' Chief Apologies for Past Actions in Letter from Jail," *BBC Monitoring Middle East*, May 11, 2009.

42. "Paper Says Algerian Security Services Reject Truce Offer by Al-Qa'idah Leader," BBC Monitoring: Middle East, December 23, 2008.

43. Ibid.

44. Pierre-Antoine Souchard, "French Open Probe on Algeria Attack That Injured Two French," Associated Press, September 24, 2007.

45. "Algeria Bombers' Identities Revealed," China Daily, December 14, 2007.

46. Alfred de Montesquiou, "Al-Qaidah Claims to Have Killed 130 in Algeria," Associated Press, August 23, 2008.

47. "Algerian Investigators Suspect Libyan in Tadmait Suicide Bombing," BBC Middle East, March 10, 2009.

48. "Algerian Security Sources Believe Hostages Held by Two Groups," BBC Middle East, February 22, 2009.

49. Stephen Edwards, "Kidnapped Diplomats Were Traded for Terrorists," Canwest News Service, April 26, 2009.

50. Helen Pidd, "Background: The Kidnapping of Edwin Dyer," Guardian, June 3, 2009, available at http://www.guardian.co.uk/world/2009/jun/03/edwin-dyer-hostage -killed-al-qaida.

51. Lamine Chikhi, "African Union Seeks Crackdown on Ransom Payments," Reuters, June 18, 2009, at http://www.reuters.com/article/latestCrisis/idUSLI40628.

52. For example, Zaid Bachir from the Tunisia Islamic Front was transferred back to Tunisia in 2001 after he tried to establish relationships with the GSPC.

53. "Al-Qaeda-Linked Group in Algeria Replaces Founder," Agence France-Presse, October 12, 2003.

54. It should be noted that the LIFG leadership in Libya denied alignment with al-Qaeda. Instead, negotiations with the Libyan government continued.

55. "Algerian Islamist Group Leader Reveals Details of His Life."

56. Jackson Mbuvi, "The Saleh Is Osama's New Playground," All Africa, August 29, 2005.

57. "Algerian Paper Reports Crack in Sahara Militants' Ranks," BBC Monitoring: Middle East, August 28, 2009.

58. "Algerian Paper Says Al-Qa'idah Maghreb Appoints Mauritanian Commander," BBC Middle East, May 31, 2009.

59. "Gunmen Slay American in Mauritanian Capital," Agence France-Presse, June 24, 2009.

60. "France Condemns Mauritania Attack, Blamed on Extremists," Agence France-Presse, August 9, 2009.

61. "Algerian Daily Report Examines Ties Between GSPC/AQLIM, Mali," BBC Monitoring: Middle East, February 10, 2009.

62. Anneli Botha, Terrorism in the Maghreb: The Transnationalisation of Domestic Terrorism (Pretoria: Institute for Security Studies, 2008), 43.

63. "Algeria Salafist Group Web Site Posts Bomb-Making Instructions," BBC Monitoring: Middle East, June 5, 2004.

64. Botha, *Terrorism in the Maghreb*, 44. BRC is an Algerian-registered company created in 1994 and is now owned jointly by the Halliburton subsidiary KBR Inc., formerly known as Kellogg, Brown & Root, and affiliates of the Algerian state-owned oil company, Sonatrach.

65. "Algerian Security Forces Kill Explosive-Belt Bomber," Agence France-Presse, July 22, 2009.

66. "Suspected Al Qaeda Members Kill Malian Army Officer," Agence France-Presse, June 11, 2009.

[23]

The 2003 Riyadh and 2008 Sanaa Bombings

THOMAS HEGGHAMMER

This chapter examines two landmark operations by the Saudi and Yemeni branches of al-Qaeda: the May 12, 2003, bombings of expatriate compounds in Riyadh and the September 17, 2008, bombing of the U.S. embassy in Sanaa. These attacks represented crucial junctures in al-Qaeda's history in its own motherland, the Arabian Peninsula. The Riyadh bombing was the opening shot in a terrorism campaign of unprecedented scale and duration in Saudi history. The Sanaa bombing marked the emergence of a new branch of al-Qaeda in Yemen, which sought to continue the jihad launched by its Saudi predecessors.

In this chapter, I shall take a detailed look at the planning and execution of these operations, paying particular attention to the roles of the attack teams, their local leaders, and "al-Qaeda Central" (AQC), the top leadership presumably based in Pakistan's tribal areas. This chapter relies on publicly available primary and secondary sources, as well as interviews with government officials familiar with the investigation.[1]

This chapter argues that though both operations involved top-down planning and coordination, the role of AQC was much smaller (if at all present) in the Sanaa bombing than the Riyadh bombing. This was probably because operational links had eroded between AQC and the jihadi networks on the Arabian Peninsula between 2003 and 2008. The two case studies also show that the center of gravity of al-Qaeda on the Arabian Peninsula shifted from Saudi Arabia to Yemen in the same period.

I will look first at the Riyadh bombing and then at the Sanaa bombing. Each of the two case studies is divided into five parts: first, I sketch the local political context and history of jihadi networks; second, I describe the plot; third, I identify the perpetrators and their aims; fourth, I look at external links; and, finally, I look at the repercussions of the operation.

THE 2003 RIYADH BOMBING

Background

In the early spring of 2003, the oil-rich Wahhabi kingdom of Saudi Arabia was still marked by a curious paradox: the presence of a large community of militant Islamists and relatively low levels of Islamist violence. There were many terrorist attacks in the kingdom before 2003, and while some were very serious, most were isolated incidents.[2] In November 1979, an apocalyptic sect seized the Great Mosque in Mecca and sparked a bloody siege that left hundreds dead. In the late 1980s, the Shia group Hizbollah of Hijaz attacked oil targets in the Eastern Province. In November 1995, a four-man cell inspired by Osama bin Laden car-bombed the Riyadh office of U.S. instructors for the Saudi National Guard, killing six.[3] In June 1996, Hizbollah of Hijaz, or perhaps al-Qaeda , attacked U.S. Air Force barracks in Khobar with an explosives-filled tanker truck, killing seventeen American servicemen.[4] Still, compared with the experience of other countries, such as Egypt and Algeria, and considering the activities of Saudi militants abroad, terrorism levels inside Saudi Arabia had been remarkably low.

The principal reason was the outward ideological orientation of the Saudi jihadist community. Most Saudi militants were extreme pan-Islamists focused on other Muslims' struggles of national liberation and did not consider the Saudi regime their main enemy or Saudi Arabia a legitimate theater of operations. Al-Qaeda did have the intention to operate in the kingdom from at least 1995 onward but lacked the capability. In 1998, after a series of failed plots followed by crippling police crackdowns, bin Laden decided to suspend operations and cultivate Saudi Arabia as a source for funds and recruits instead.[5] Between 1998 and 2001, Saudi recruitment to al-Qaeda's Afghan camps increased exponentially while little happened on the domestic terrorism front.

In October 2000, a long series of small but lethal attacks on Western expatriates began in the kingdom.[6] Dismissed by authorities as infighting between alcohol smugglers, these operations were probably the work of amateur jihadis. Reports came in mid-2002 of larger foiled attacks, notably against Prince Sultan Air Base and the Ra's Tanura oil facility. In this period jihadi Internet forums boiled with activity, much of it from Saudi-based individuals and radical clerics. Saudi public opinion fumed over international political developments in Afghanistan, Guantánamo Bay, Jenin, and Iraq. In late 2002 and early 2003, shoot-outs between police and suspected militants became increasingly common. In the early spring of 2003, it was clear that unrest brewed in Saudi Arabia. On May 6, police raided a suspected militant hideout in Riyadh and found the handwritten wills of prospective suicide bombers. Authorities immediately published a list of nineteen wanted militants and initiated a frantic search for the attackers.[7] Unfortunately, it was too late; the Riyadh attack was already in motion.

Plot Description

The Riyadh operation consisted of near-simultaneous suicide car bombings at three different Western expatriate residential compounds in Eastern Riyadh late in the evening of Monday, May 12, 2003.[8] At each location, gunmen paved the way through the gate for a bombing vehicle to be detonated at the center of each compound. This succeeded at two of the compounds, killing approximately thirty-five people.

The first target was the Vinnell compound. At 11:15 p.m., a Ford Crown Victoria sedan carrying three attackers rammed the front gate. Gunmen then attacked the guards, entered the gatehouse, and opened the gate. They then returned to the sedan and entered the compound, followed by a Dodge Ram pickup carrying the explosive device. On the way in, the gunmen fired randomly at surrounding buildings. The pickup truck stopped next to a dormitory at the compound's center, where it detonated at 11:18 p.m.

Two minutes later, the Hamra Oasis Village compound was attacked in the same way, but this time the front team, driving a Toyota sedan, was obstructed by another vehicle at the gate. The attackers rammed the car, hoping to push it through the gate. When this failed, the gunmen killed the guards and opened the gate. They then remounted their vehicle and pushed the other car before them, paving the way for a white GMC Suburban carrying another bomb. On the way in, the front team emptied their guns at the surrounding buildings, and a group of residents having a pool party. The Suburban parked next to a building at the center of the compound and detonated at 11:28 p.m.

Meanwhile, the Jadawel compound, which had two layers of security, was stormed by a smaller group of attackers in one Ford sedan, which also carried a bomb. They attacked the gate guards with guns and hand grenades before opening the vehicle barrier manually. This time the other guards closed the inner gate and returned fire. The militants detonated the bomb at the inner gate at 11:24 p.m., killing only themselves. The use of only one vehicle and a smaller attack team at Jadawel was presumably a result of the disruption caused to the plot by the May 6 police raid.

The bombs were made of Rapid Detonation Explosive (RDX), a material frequently used by militants in Saudi Arabia and widely available in Yemen. The devices used at SANG/Vinnell and Hamra contained an estimated 400 to 500 kilograms of explosives, and the device at Jadawel was somewhat smaller. The foot soldiers were armed with AK-47 assault rifles and many hand grenades. They also wore improvised suicide vests made with hand grenades. The serial numbers of the weapons reportedly indicated they had originally come from Saudi National Guard stockpiles. The attackers wore black jumpsuits but did not appear to be impersonating security forces.

Before the attacks, the attackers conducted reconnaissance and Internet research. In early May, guards at the SANG compound observed individuals monitoring and videotaping entry procedures at the gate. Moreover, the house raided on May 6 was only 400 meters from the Jadawel compound. To know what the compounds looked like inside, the planners downloaded information from the compound websites.[9] This enabled the planners to identify the optimal location for the bombs.

The bombs caused extensive damage, especially in the two larger raids. Curiously, for a major attack in the information age, the precise casualty figures remain unclear. The most frequently cited figures are 35 dead and more than 160 wounded.[10] However, the reported number of deaths varied greatly, from 22 to 43.[11] The dead included Saudis, Americans,

Filipinos, Australians, Jordanians, at least one Briton, an Irishman, and a Swiss citizen. The jihadists later claimed that between 250 and 300 people died.[12] It is not known how many attackers were killed as the government initially claimed all attackers died; however, as many as six may have survived and escaped from the scene.[13]

The Perpetrators and Their Aims

The 2003 Riyadh bombing was carried out by a network of recent Saudi returnees from Afghanistan who regrouped in late 2002 and 2003 with the intention of launching a terrorism campaign in the kingdom. This network, which at the time of the bombing called itself the "Mujahidun on the Arabian Peninsula" (MAP), was the precursor to the organization known as "al-Qaeda on the Arabian Peninsula" (AQAP).[14]

During the summer of 2003, MAP ideologues laid out the theological and strategic rationale behind the operation in two long treatises and a video. The first pamphlet, entitled "Criticizing the Reservations Over the Riyadh Bombings," appeared in July 2003 and was intended as a rebuttal of moderate Islamists' criticism of the Riyadh bombing.[15] The second and more substantial work, entitled "The 12 May Raid: The East Riyadh Operation and Our War With America and her Agents" appeared in early September.[16] The anonymous text also included behind-the-scenes operational details. On October 17, 2003, al-Sahab, al-Qaeda's media arm, released a video entitled "Wills of the Heroes: Martyrs of the Two Sanctities."[17] The forty-five-minute film featured recorded statements by four of the suicide bombers (Muhammad al-Shihri, Abd al-Wahhab al-Muqit, Hazim al-Kashmiri, and Ashraf al-Sayyid) and an audio recording of the operation itself.

The choice of targets reflected MAP's declared aim of evicting the "crusaders" from the Arabian Peninsula. The militants viewed the compounds as crusader strongholds and symbols of moral corruption containing "churches and bars, mixed nightclubs and swimming pools, basically all kinds of infidelity and debauchery." Moreover, they argued that "these compounds are subject to an agreement between the [Saudi government] and America by which they are considered part of America."[18] The Jadawel and Vinnell compounds appear to have been chosen because of their association with American defense contractors. The AQAP leader Abd al-Aziz al-Muqrin later pointed out that the building targeted in the 1995 Riyadh bombing also belonged to the Vinnell Corporation, allowing him to boast that "we struck Vinnell in 1995 and we did it again in 2003."[19] The rationale for attacking Hamra Oasis Village is less clear, but the compound seems to have had a reputation as a party den.[20]

We still do not know exactly who participated in the attack. Early in the investigation, Saudi police published a list of twelve names of people identified by DNA tests as having died in the operation: Khalid al-Juhani, Muhammad Uthman al-Shihri, Hani al-Ghamidi, Jubran Khabrani, Khalid al-Baghdadi, Mihmas al-Dawsari, Muhammad Shadhdhaf al-Shihri, Hazim Kashmiri, Majid Uqayl, Bandar al-Mutayri, Abd al-Karim Yaziji, and Abdallah al-Mutayri.[21] MAP/AQAP never specified the total number of attackers, but seven individuals are identified in various jihadi texts as participants, namely Muhammad al-Shihri, Khalid al-Baghdadi, Mihmas al-Dawsari, Hazim al-Kashmiri, Muhammad al-Muqit, Ashraf al-Sayyid, and Hamad al-Shammari.[22] The latter three did not appear on the government list. Michael Knights speaks of fourteen attackers, though he only names the three alleged team leaders: Khalid al-Juhani (SANG/Vinnell compound), Muhammad al-Shihri (Hamra), and Hazim Sa'id (Jadawel). The MAP martyrdom video describes Muhammad al-Shihri as the leader of the whole operation.[23] Other sources indicate that most of these names are Saudi (or Saudi Yemeni) Islamists with experience from al-Qaeda's training camps in Afghanistan.

Identifying the "masterminds" and midlevel coordinators of the attack is difficult both because the jihadi literature does not identify any such figures and because most of the people who might possess such knowledge are either still on the run or were killed before they could be interrogated (as in the case of Yusuf al-Uyayri and Turki al-Dandani). One of the few senior operatives to be captured alive was Ali al-Faq'asi al-Ghamidi, caught in Saudi Arabia in June 2003. Most of what we know about the midlevel organization behind the operation appears to come from the interrogation of al-Ghamidi. According to the Saudi security expert Nawaf Obaid, who had access to al-Ghamidi's testimony, the attack was masterminded by Turki al-Dandani and Ali al-Ghamidi, who in turn reported to Yusuf al-Uyayri, the leader of MAP.[24]

External Links

The Riyadh bombing was carried out primarily by Saudi nationals who procured most of the resources they needed locally. No operatives or trainers were flown in from the outside, and no pre-attack training occurred in Afghanistan, as was the case in the 1998 East Africa bombings and the 9/11 attacks. However, in most other respects, the Riyadh bombing was an externally directed, top-down operation. The exogenous character of the plot is key to understanding why it happened and why it proved a strategic blunder.

First, the very presence of a global jihad network in the kingdom was a product of recruitment and training efforts by al-Qaeda in Afghanistan in the late 1990s. Most of the known Riyadh bombers and a majority of the core members of AQAP had been to Afghanistan before 2002. The rest were mostly relatives and acquaintances of Afghanistan veterans. This shared background initially facilitated rapid mobilization, but it also put the militants out of touch with other Saudi Islamists and made it difficult for AQAP to recruit outside of the veteran community.

Second, several of the Riyadh bombers and their leaders had demonstrably close and long-standing links to the central al-Qaeda organization in Afghanistan. Khalid al-Juhani and Muhammad al-Shihri, for example, had recorded martyrdom wills in Afghanistan in 2001, copies of which were found in the rubble of Mohammed Atef's house in Afghanistan.[25] Yusuf al-Uyayri had known bin Laden personally since the early 1990s, traveled to Afghanistan under the Taliban at least once in 2000, and remained in close and constant contact with the al-Qaeda leader.[26]

Third, there is ample evidence that the mobilization for jihad in Saudi Arabia in 2002 and 2003 was ordered by Osama bin Laden. Several jihadist firsthand accounts of the events in Afghanistan in late 2001 and early 2002 say bin Laden ordered Saudis home to prepare for jihad in the kingdom.[27] In May 2002, the U.S. National Security Agency intercepted messages from bin Laden to al-Uyayri to the same effect.[28] The strategic decision to launch a campaign in Saudi Arabia thus began in Afghanistan over a year before the Riyadh bombing, a consequence of al-Qaeda's eviction from Afghanistan.

Finally, government sources in several countries spoke of signals intelligence proving extensive contacts between Yusuf al-Uyayri and the top al-Qaeda leadership in Afghanistan in the months before the Riyadh bombing.[29] In fact, apparently intense debate took place between the top al-Qaeda leadership and al-Uyayri over the timing of the Riyadh bombing. As Nawaf Obaid explained:

> Even in Afghanistan there were disagreements among the leadership regarding the timing and potential targets of the attack. Al-Ayeri maintained that al Qaeda members were not yet ready and lacked the time, resources and necessary supply routes from Yemen. Furthermore, recruitment proved to be more difficult than expected. Ayman al-Zawahiri . . . dismissed these objections, arguing that the time was right for operations to begin. . . . Abdul Kareem al-Majati, a Moroccan national and main deputy and general strategist of al-Ayeri agreed with his commander's assessment, but was overruled by bin Laden. Soon after, Majati left Saudi Arabia with the belief that attacking prematurely was a huge miscalculation and would compromise the existence and establishment of future al Qaeda cells.[30]

Unfortunately, when these debates took place or when the orders were given to proceed with the operation remains unknown. It is therefore difficult to identify the factors directly influencing the timing of the attack. There are several possible explanations. Al-Qaeda may have wanted to capitalize on the regional surge in anti-Americanism caused by the Iraq invasion. Also, it may have feared that the arrest of senior al-Qaeda operators Khalid Sheikh Mohammed in February 2003 and Walid bin Attash in April compromised existing networks in the kingdom. A third possibility is that they wanted the attack to coincide with the May visit of senior U.S. officials to Saudi Arabia, announced in late April.[31] A fourth theory is that the Riyadh operation was to coincide with the Casablanca operation on May 17, 2003.[32] Of course, the possibility remains that al-Qaeda leaders were simply impatient.

Saudi and U.S. government sources claimed that in the final weeks before the bombing, the attackers received directions from al-Qaeda leaders in Iran.[33] Given Saudi Arabia and America's long-standing enmity with Iran, such accusations should be treated with sound skepticism, but the reports are varied and specific enough to warrant taking them seriously. According to a September 2003 article in the *Washington Post*, Saudi authorities "obtained a trove of evidence—phones, computer hard drives, documents and cash—that pointed back to Iran and [Sayf al] Adel. . . . Ali Faqasi Ghamdi had allegedly also confessed that Adel and his associates were behind the bombings."[34] Other sources said bin Laden's son Sa'd, believed to be based in Iran, placed phone calls to the cell members two days before the May 12 attacks.[35] The Saudis allegedly reacted by dispatching two delegations to Iran, demanding that the Iranians hand over key Saudi al-Qaeda members and that Sayf al-Adl be returned to Egypt. Iran refused the requests but allegedly placed the al-Qaeda group under a form of house arrest.[36]

For logistics, the Riyadh plotters also used a network of Yemenis in Switzerland, Qatar, and Yemen. A Swiss investigation of five Yemenis, a Somali, and an Iraqi based in Switzerland showed that one of the Yemenis had been in close contact with Abdallah al-Raymi, a Qatar-based Yemeni al-Qaeda operative involved in the Riyadh bombing. The Swiss-based Yemeni transferred money to al-Raymi through a Geneva-based *hawaladar* (informal banking clerk) before the operation. In the summer of 2003, the Swiss-based Yemeni attempted to procure a fake Somali passport to facilitate al-Raymi's extraction to Switzerland. Al-Raymi was later arrested and imprisoned in Yemen.[37]

Outcome

The 2003 Riyadh bombing had profound repercussions both for al-Qaeda in Saudi Arabia and for Saudi society as a whole. The operation sparked a crackdown from which al-Qaeda would not recover and led to a change in governmental and popular attitudes toward religious extremism. Although the police had slowly begun hunting al-Qaeda in late 2002, it was not until after the Riyadh bombing that the Saudi government threw its full weight behind the War on Terror. In the summer of 2003 it launched a massive police crackdown on the jihadi community. The capabilities of the Saudi security services increased dramatically as the government poured money into the security establishment and as the United States and Britain offered unprecedented intelligence training and assistance.[38] During the summer of 2003 the police made hundreds of arrests and discovered safe houses and weapons caches across the country. Al-Qaeda's infrastructure in the kingdom was rapidly dismantled. The AQAP campaign was still kept alive for another few years by a small core of committed and Internet-savvy militants with nothing to lose. However, the prospects for a large-scale insurgency were effectively crushed in the summer of 2003.

Widespread popular condemnation of the bombing, including from most of the Saudi Islamist community, facilitated the government crackdown. By late 2003, a broad consensus formed in the kingdom that the militants were terrorists who posed a threat to Saudi society. The attack also triggered public criticism from progressive Islamist intellectuals of the role of religion in Saudi politics and society, leading some observers to speak of a "Riyadh spring" in 2003.[39]

The Riyadh bombing, for the Saudi regime, was "the mother of all wake-up calls," underscoring the dangers of leaving the jihadist community unchecked. The state has since changed its attitude and approach to radical Islamism, making Saudi Arabia a much less hospitable place for militants than it used to be. However, as al-Qaeda weakened in Riyadh, the jihad on the Arabian Peninsula was rekindled across the kingdom's southern border.

THE 2008 SANAA BOMBING

Background

Yemen's experience with political violence could hardly be more different from that of Saudi Arabia. While the kingdom has been among the most stable countries in the region, Yemen has been torn by bitter civil wars, plagued by lawlessness, and flooded with weapons. Yet the history of jihadism in Yemen is not unlike that of its northern neighbor.

As in Saudi Arabia, Yemeni jihadists grew more numerous in the 1980s and the 1990s, but they fought mostly abroad, not inside Yemen, with a few notable exceptions. Between 1992 and 1994, Afghanistan veterans, led by Tariq al-Fadhli and funded by Osama bin Laden, attacked oil installations and Socialist Party officials in South Yemen. In December 1992, two tourists were killed when the same network bombed two hotels in Aden, believed to be hosting American soldiers on their way to a UN peacekeeping mission in Somalia.[40] On December 28, 1998, the "Islamic Army of Aden Abyan," a network with links to the London-based preacher Abu Hamza al-Masri, kidnapped sixteen Westerners, in part to demand the release of fellow militants who had been detained outside Aden five days earlier for planning bombings against Western tourist targets. The situation ended on December 29 with a shoot-out in the desert northeast of Aden, in which four hostages and two militants were killed.[41]

In the late 1990s, Yemen saw a strong increase in recruitment to al-Qaeda's training camps in Afghanistan. The people recruited at this time constituted the first generation of Yemeni al-Qaeda operatives. In 1999, as bin Laden suspended operations in Saudi Arabia, al-Qaeda stepped up activity in Yemen. The al-Qaeda operative Abd al-Rahim al-Nashiri coordinated a failed attempt to bomb the destroyer USS *Sullivan* in January 2000, followed by the successful suicide boat bombing of the USS *Cole* outside Aden in October 2000, which killed seventeen American sailors.[42]

Between 2001 and 2003, jihadists attempted numerous operations against Western targets in Yemen.[43] A few of them succeeded, such as the attack on the French oil tanker *Limburg* in October 2002. However, after 9/11 Yemeni authorities and U.S. intelligence foiled many operations and weakened al-Qaeda in Yemen considerably. The killing of the senior operative Abu Ali al-Harithi and five of his companions by a CIA drone in November 2002 and the capture of his successor, Muhammad al-Ahdal, in November 2003 dealt severe blows to the organization.[44] By late 2003, the first generation al-Qaeda in Yemen had been largely crushed, as a result of which there was minimal Islamist terrorist activity in the country over the next three years. In the meantime, new Yemeni recruits traveled to Iraq by the hundreds.[45]

In February 2006, a jailbreak by twenty-three experienced militants enabled al-Qaeda in Yemen to rebuild.[46] A facilitating factor was the deteriorating security situation in both the north and the south of the country, which diverted the Yemeni government's attention and resources away from al-Qaeda.[47] A "second generation" of al-Qaeda in Yemen emerged: a network consisting of a few senior operatives, Yemeni returnees from Iraq, junior Saudi militants escaping the police at home, and new local recruits. The central figure of the renewed movement was Nasir al-Wahayshi, an Afghanistan veteran and former aide to bin Laden.[48] Briefly in 2007 and 2008 there appeared to be two jihadi organizations operating side by side:

The "al-Qaeda on the Arabian Peninsula—Soldier's Brigade of Yemen" (SBY), which claimed most of the attacks in 2007 and early 2008, and "al-Qaeda in the South of the Arabian Peninsula" (AQSAP), which produced the magazine *Sada al-Malahim* from early 2008 onward. However, in hindsight, the two entities were most likely part of the same network, one that cultivated two separate organizational identities for strategic reasons.[49]

From 2006 to 2008, the frequency and quality of AQAP's attacks gradually increased.[50] In September 2006, four suicide bombers failed spectacularly in their attempt to strike two oil facilities with explosives-packed cars.[51] Then, in July 2007, a suicide car bomb killed eight Spanish tourists and two Yemeni drivers at an archaeological site in Marib.[52] In early 2008, the number of attacks against Western targets increased significantly. In January two Belgian tourists and their Yemeni driver were killed in Hadramawt, and in March the U.S. embassy compound came under mortar attack (which missed and killed a schoolgirl and a policeman instead).[53] There were also a number of small attacks that together prompted the U.S. embassy to order all nonessential staff out of the country in April.[54] Moreover, tensions between militants and police increased over the summer of 2008. On July 25, a suicide bomber struck a military base in Sayyun.[55] On August 11, security forces raided an al-Qaeda cell in Tarim in Hadramout, killing five militants, including the presumed SBY leader, Hamza al-Quyati.[56] Subsequent statements from the attackers promised revenge by attacking Western embassies in the region.[57] Once again, it turned out, AQAP was not issuing empty threats.

Plot Description

In the morning of September 17, 2008, the U.S. embassy in Sanaa was attacked by a group of seven militants riding two bombing vehicles.[58] The tactic used mirrored the Riyadh attacks in the deployment of a "shooter team" charged with paving the way for one or more bombing vehicles to penetrate the security checkpoints. The attackers failed to access the compound, and the bombs detonated at the gate. However, because one of the bombs went off next to a line of visitors and staff waiting to enter the embassy, casualties were high: twenty people died, including all seven attackers.[59]

The U.S. embassy is located in the Dhahar Himyar Zone of the Sheraton Hotel District in Eastern Sanaa. Incidentally, it is next to the Masayk neighborhood, which has a reputation for producing many of the volunteers from the Arabian Peninsula to join the jihad in Iraq.[60] Like other U.S. embassies in the region, it is heavily protected and has a fortress-like appearance. The 250-square-meter compound is protected by a tall blast wall, and at the time of the attack the main perimeter gate was surrounded by an extensive security zone, itself protected by roadblocks and checkpoints manned by the Yemeni Central Security Force (CSF).[61] The CFS is run by the president's nephew Yahya Salih and is considered the most professional and least infiltrated of Yemeni security services. In short, the embassy is among the best protected targets in the country.

At around 9:15 a.m., four gunmen dressed as Yemeni police attacked the checkpoint at the northern end of the security zone. About a minute later, a bomb-carrying vehicle rammed the checkpoint and exploded, killing several of the guards. The shooter team continued engaging other guards with handguns and, according to some reports, rocket-propelled grenades.[62] Shortly afterward, a second bombing vehicle penetrated the security zone and headed toward the compound wall. The vehicle was stopped by CSF gunfire before reaching the wall and detonated alongside a line of civilians waiting to enter the embassy. The gunmen resisted for another hour and a half before being killed.[63]

The attack vehicles were small Suzuki Jeeps fitted with improvised armor covering the windows to protect the drivers from gunfire. Openings had been carved in the car roof to enable gunmen to disembark quickly.[64] The explosive devices were unsophisticated and not very powerful; they included a combination of home-made explosives and gas cylinders.[65]

The planners had conducted reconnaissance of the embassy compound both on the ground and on the Internet. Embassy counter-surveillance experts had noted signs of reconnaissance in the area before the attacks. The operation was most likely timed to coincide with the beginning of the working day, when lines form outside the embassy gate. The militants used Google Maps to obtain satellite pictures of the compound.[66]

Although no American officials or embassy employees were killed or wounded, the human casualties were extensive. Twenty people died, including seven attackers, five CSF guards, one embassy contract guard, and seven civilians.[67] Apart from an American and an Indian woman, all the fatalities were Yemenis. At least a dozen people were injured.

Interestingly, the perpetrators later claimed to have "destroyed" the embassy. An AQSAP statement said the first car had breached the wall and that the gunmen had penetrated the compound and killed the ambassador and his deputy. The second car "moved towards its target without confronting any major obstacles except for the debris of the embassy building."[68] Postincident photographic evidence proved these claims to be wrong.

The Perpetrators and Their Aims

The Sanaa bombing was carried out by "al-Qaeda in the South of the Arabian Peninsula," the organization that emerged in Yemen in 2006 under the leadership of Nasir al-Wahayshi. The group was inspired by bin Laden's call to evict Westerners from the Arabian Peninsula and presumably sought to signal its heightened ambitions and capabilities by attacking the prime symbol of the Western presence in Yemen.[69] AQSAP's responsibility for the bombing is confirmed by the group's own propaganda.[70] The sixth issue of the AQSAP's online magazine Sada al-Malahim, published on November 9, contained a number of articles claiming, justifying, and praising the U.S. embassy attack. The magazine notably contained an AQSAP statement claiming responsibility for the attack on October 30 also provided a number of operational details.[71] On September 13, 2009, the "Malahim Foundation for Media Production" published a video entitled The Furqan Raid: Launching the Attack on the Embassy Den, which showed all the suicide bombers, save one, reading their martyrdom wills.[72] The reasons for the year-long delay in the video's publication are unknown.

The declared rationale for the bombing was resistance to the U.S. "occupation" of the Arabian Peninsula and retaliation for U.S. attacks on Muslims around the world.[73] The attackers drew frequent parallels between their operation and previous jihadist attacks against U.S. embassies and Western targets in the region. The strategic aims behind the Sanaa attack were revealed in an article purporting to describe its six main "outcomes": first, targeting the collaboration between the U.S.

and Yemeni governments; second, signaling the improved capabilities of the mujaheddin in Yemen; third, showing the ability to attack one of the most heavily defended posts in the country; fourth, inspiring people to act; fifth, displaying the fighting spirit among the youth; and, finally, exposing the enemy's intelligence failures.[74] To justify their choice of target, the jihadists argued that the U.S. embassy was the epicenter of the Crusader military presence in Yemen, as well as a den of iniquity and a piece of American territory. They also argued that Muslims who work at or guard a U.S. embassy are collaborators and thus legitimate targets.[75]

AQSAP's statements labeled the attack the "Furqan raid," after the al-Furqan mosque in Hudayda where the seven attackers appear to have met. The spiritual leader of the group was Lutfi Bahr, the imam of the mosque, and the six others were described in the statement as his students. In the video, all the attackers were described as preachers, Quran teachers, or Quran memorizers, presumably to boost the theological credentials of AQSAP. The attack was deliberately timed to occur on the seventeenth day of Ramadan, which is the anniversary of the seventh century Battle of Badr, and a favorite date for major jihadi operations since the 1980s in Afghanistan. This enabled the perpetrators to refer to the attack as the "Badr of Sanaa," echoing the Saudi AQAP's November 2003 bombing of the Muhayya compound in Riyadh, known in jihadi circles as the "Badr of Riyadh."[76]

The seven-man cell called itself the "Abu Ali al-Harithi Brigades," a reference to the al-Qaeda leader killed in a CIA drone strike in Yemen in November 2002. While the forty-year old Lutfi Bahr seems to have been the spiritual leader, the military leader of the operation was Mahmud al-Zukayri, which suggests the latter had more military expertise. The other attackers were Qabus al-Shar'abi, Yahya Fatayni, Rashid al-Wasabi, Walid al-Raymi, and Zayn al-Tuhmas.[77] Several of the attackers had previously been imprisoned in Yemen, and three had allegedly gone through the Yemeni prisoner-rehabilitation program led by judge Hamoud al-Hitar.[78]

We do not know exactly how this seven-man cell was connected to the rest of the AQSAP organization.[79] The seven attackers were clearly not alone. A passage in the biography of Zayn al-Tuhmas suggests that he may have played a coordinating role: "Some years ago he wanted to go to Iraq, but he was imprisoned, [so] he decided to wage jihad on the Arabian Peninsula. Then God led a group [of motivated men] his way, and he proposed his idea to them and they liked it. So he began preparing and training them by sending them to secret training locations."[80] A Yemeni security official also told national media (before the al-Tuhmas account was published) that the attackers had trained at al-Qaeda camps in Hadramawt and Marib provinces.[81] However, Zayn al-Tuhmas's role in AQSAP is still unknown, which leaves open the question of whether the attack was "top-down" or "bottom-up." The attackers' shared background from the Furqan mosque suggests that the cell formed independently first and subsequently sought out AQSAP for operational assistance.

External Links

The 2008 Sanaa bombers, however, were clearly inspired by al-Qaeda, and some of the attackers may have had jihad experience in Iraq. However, the operational links to the top al-Qaeda leadership are less clear than in the 2003 Riyadh bombing.[82] For instance, it is not clear whether any of the seven bombers had jihad experience from abroad. Yemeni security officials told media that three of the bombers had been to Iraq.[83] Another report said al-Wasabi, al-Shar'abi, and Fatayni were "believed to be from the earlier generation of Al-Qa'ida Organization."[84] However, according to the martyrdom biographies published in *Sada al-Malahim*, none of the bombers had fought abroad.[85] The biographies stated that Zayn al-Tuhmas and Yahya Fatayni had tried and failed to go to Iraq and that Rashid al-Wasabi had initially wanted to go but was persuaded by his comrades to fight in Yemen. Martyrdom biographies tend to highlight foreign jihad experience, and it is hard to see why AQSAP would have tried to conceal it if it existed.

If anything, the organization was keen to highlight its links to al-Qaeda central. Their claim of responsibility stated that the operation "came as an answer to the call of the mujahid leader Shaykh Abu-Abdallah, Osama bin Laden, and the call of the wise man of the nation, the mujahid physician, Abu Muhammad, Ayman al-Zawahiri."[86] AQSAP was undoubtedly aspiring to be the Yemeni arm of al-Qaeda. Whether they actually were, in an operational sense, is another matter.

Yet the AQSAP cadre had international connections. Their leader, Nasir al-Wahayshi, had known bin Laden personally, and some other members had been to Afghanistan in the late 1990s. The organization included a few Saudis who had fought with AQAP in the kingdom before seeking refuge in Yemen. There is also anecdotal evidence that Yemeni veterans of the Iraqi jihad have returned to join al-Qaeda.[87] Moreover, in mid-2009, the *New York Times* cited U.S. intelligence sources as saying some top al-Qaeda leaders had relocated from Afghanistan and Pakistan to Yemen.[88] These reports were denied by the Yemeni government but revealed the existence of a certain amount of communication between operatives in Yemen and in Pakistan. However, no open sources have thus far showed evidence of concrete operational links between al-Qaeda central and AQSAP in connection with the embassy attack.

Outcome

The 2008 Sanaa bombing was a landmark operation in the history of jihadism in Yemen. It was the deadliest attack on a U.S. embassy in a decade and the most serious terrorist incident in Yemen since the USS *Cole*. As such, it marked the coming of age of a new, second generation of al-Qaeda in Yemen and placed AQSAP firmly on the map as an al-Qaeda affiliate to be reckoned with.

While the attack embarrassed Yemeni authorities and added tension to the U.S.-Yemeni relationship, it increased AQSAP's status in the international jihadi community.[89] It was probably no coincidence that five months later, in February 2009, AQSAP announce its merger with the remnants of the Saudi al-Qaeda branch.[90] The new organization would keep the latter's name (al-Qaeda on the Arabian Peninsula) but operate under Yemeni leadership. The center of gravity of the jihad on the Arabian Peninsula officially moved southward.

In military terms, the attack neither strengthened nor significantly weakened the organization. AQSAP did not achieve significant operational momentum, nor does it seem to have experienced a massive recruitment boost. At the same time, the postincident crackdown did not crush the organization, despite Yemeni security forces' conducting numerous raids and arresting tens of people. After the bombing, the United States began devoting considerably more attention and resources to hunting al-Qaeda in Yemen.[91] Yet no senior leaders were apprehended, allowing the organization to consolidate with its Saudi neighbor. In a sense, avoiding liquidation following a major attack on a U.S. embassy was a victory for AQAP.

Despite intensified efforts to crush it, al-Qaeda in Yemen grew in size and ambition in the course of 2009. By stepping up its Internet propaganda effort and by cultivating close links with local tribes (especially in Marib), AQAP was able to attract new followers, boosting its membership to somewhere between 100 and 300 individuals.[92] In a significant development, it also began launching high-profile operations outside Yemen. On August 27, 2009, a suicide bomber dispatched by AQAP nearly killed the Saudi deputy interior minister, Prince Muhammad bin Nayif in Jidda, after pretending to surrender to authorities.[93] On Christmas Day 2009, a AQAP-trained and equipped Nigerian came close to blowing up NWA flight 253 from Amsterdam to Detroit in midair; the man had smuggled explosives on board but was overpowered by fellow passengers when he tried to detonate them.[94]

––––––––––

The Riyadh and Sanaa bombings appeared to incorporate different degrees of involvement from the top al-Qaeda leadership in attack planning. In Riyadh, al-Qaeda leaders abroad were heavily involved in the operational planning, but, in Sanaa, they seem to have offered little more than ideological guidance and inspiration. This is consistent with the assessment of many analysts that al-Qaeda central's ability to operationally guide its various local branches decreased over time.

However, absence of involvement from Osama Bin Laden does not mean absence of an overarching organization. The Sanaa bombers may have started as a "bunch of guys" wanting to engage in jihad, but to develop that drive into a serious operation they needed practice, training, and probably other forms of technical assistance. The public-relations side of the operation was clearly handled entirely by AQSAP media professionals who followed established al-Qaeda propaganda templates.

The two cases also illustrate an interesting aspect of the relationship between top-down operational guidance and attack efficiency. Highly organized, top-down initiatives may produce more lethal operations in the short term but not necessarily the best outcomes in the long term. In the case of the Riyadh bombing, al-Qaeda central appears to have overruled local commanders and launched the campaign prematurely. Had Yusuf al-Uyayri's assessment prevailed, the campaign would likely have been launched later, probably with much greater impact. The Sanaa bombing, directed entirely by local commanders, may have been smaller and less sophisticated than the Riyadh bombing, but it proved more sustainable for the organization in the long run.

Another point worth noting is that the Internet was not an indispensable tool for the recruitment of operatives or operational planning of the attacks. The Internet greatly facilitated the postincident propaganda effort, but it was not extensively used in the preparation phase. The main contribution of the Internet in the pre-attack phase was to provide attackers with maps of their targets. Knowing where to place the bombs once they were inside the compounds enabled the Riyadh bombers to inflict more casualties. However, to get into the compounds in the first place, the attackers relied on old-fashioned reconnaissance. While this should not lead us to underestimate the importance of "cyberplanning," it might provide nuance for the widespread view of the Internet as an operational game changer.[95]

Other lessons learned are more intuitive. One is that layered security works; well-designed barriers represent one of the simplest and best protective measures for static high-value targets. Another lesson is that counter-surveillance must be taken seriously. In both Riyadh and Sanaa, terrorist surveillance was observed but not acted upon before the attacks. A third observation is that al-Qaeda in Saudi Arabia and Yemen—like most terrorists—remains relatively conservative in its tactics. The tactic used in Riyadh and Sanaa was essentially the same as that used by al-Qaeda in the 1998 East Africa bombings—or, for that matter, by Lebanese Hezbollah in the 1983 marine barracks bombing.

These two cases also tell us something about the ideology of al-Qaeda on the Arabian Peninsula. For one, they suggest that the West ranked higher than the local regimes in AQAP's enemy hierarchy. The Riyadh and Sanaa operations illustrate a general tendency in the history of al-Qaeda in Saudi Arabia and Yemen toward saving the largest and most resource-intensive operations for Western targets. This challenges the widespread assumption—based on the jihadists' admittedly regime-critical rhetoric and frequent attacks on security forces—that their struggle was "really" about regime change.

Finally, these attacks by two separate networks five years apart under-line the strength and longevity of al-Qaeda's ideology. The Yemen-based AQAP of 2009 and the Saudi AQAP of 2003 have very little in common other than a shared ideological vision. Although they are often described as one and the same organization, there are in fact practically no orga-nizational links between the two groups. The Saudis who joined Yemeni al-Qaeda in 2007 and 2008 were either former Guantánamo detainees or latecomers to the Saudi jihad; as far as we know, none of them had fought with the Saudi AQAP during its heyday. Saudi authorities and Western observers may have breathed a sigh of relief around 2007 when it became clear that the Saudi AQAP had effectively been crushed.[96] The emergence of a new AQAP in Yemen shows that organizations may come and go, but the jihad on the Arabian Peninsula is by no means over.

NOTES

1. All the primary sources cited in this article will be made available on the author's website (www.hegghammer.com) in the "Resources" section.

2. For an overview of political violence in Saudi Arabia since the 1950s, see Thomas Hegghammer, "Jihad, Yes, But Not Revolution: Explaining the Extroversion of Islamist Militancy in Saudi Arabia," *British Journal of Middle Eastern Studies* 35, no. 3 (2009); and John E. Peterson, "Saudi Arabia: Internal Security Incidents Since 1979," *Arabian Peninsula Background Note*, no. 3 (2005).

3. Yaroslav Trofimov, *The Siege of Mecca: The Forgotten Uprising in Islam's Holiest Shrine and the Birth of Al Qaeda* (New York: Doubleday, 2007); John E. Peterson, *Historical Dictionary of Saudi Arabia* (Lanham: Scarecrow Press, 2003), 110; Joshua Teitelbaum, *Holier Than Thou: Saudi Arabia's Islamic Opposition* (Washington, D.C.: Washington Institute for Near East Policy, 2000), 73–82.

4. Experts disagree on who carried out the Khobar bombing. For the Shiite argu-ment, see Thomas Hegghammer, "Deconstructing the Myth about Al-Qa'ida and Kho-bar," *Sentinel* 1, no. 3 (2008); for the al-Qaeda argument, see Gareth Porter's five-part article series from *Inter Press Service*, June, 22–26, 2009, available at www.ips.org.

5. Thomas Hegghammer, *Jihad in Saudi Arabia* (Cambridge: Cambridge University Press, 2010), chap. 5; Thomas Hegghammer, "Islamist Violence and Regime Stability in Saudi Arabia," *International Affairs* 84, no. 4 (2008): 708.

6. Hegghammer, *Jihad in Saudi Arabia*, chap. 4.

7. "Ghazwat al-hadi 'ashar min rabi' al-awwal: 'amaliyat sharq al-riyadh wa-harbuna ma' amrika wa 'umala'iha" [The 12 May raid: the East Riyadh operation and our war with America and her agents], September 3, 2003, available at www.qa3edoon.com,

accessed July 23, 2003, 46; Javid Hassan, "SR300,000 Offered for Capture of Fugitives," *Arab News*, May 9, 2003; "Checkpoints Set Up Near Riyadh to Track Down Terror Suspects," *Arab News*, May 10, 2003; Douglas Jehl, "Saudis Seek Nineteen Suspected of Terrorist Plot," *New York Times*, May 10, 2003.

8. In the following account, I rely heavily on Michael Knights, "The East Riyadh Operation, May 2003," in *Jane's Terrorism and Insurgency Centre Case Study* (London: Jane's Information Group, 2005). Knights's study is not sourced, but he told this author he relied on open-source records and pictures and "a range of [the UK security contractor] Olive Group operators who were in Saudi shortly afterwards to fill in details." He also said that "[the Saudi security analyst] Nawaf Obaid reviewed the text and made a few useful comments" (e-mail correspondence with Michael Knights, June 11, 2009).

9. See, for example, www.alhamra.com.sa.

10. Anthony H. Cordesman and Nawaf E. Obaid, *National Security in Saudi Arabia: Threats, Responses, and Challenges* (Westport, Conn.: Praeger Security International, 2005), 269.

11. Raid Qusti, "Unprecedented Security in Riyadh," *Arab News*, June 3, 2003; Knights, "The East Riyadh Operation"; *Patterns of Global Terrorism, 2003* (Washington, D.C.: U.S. Department of State, 2004), contrast p. 104 and appendix A.

12. "Ghazwat al-hadi 'ashar," 47.

13. According to Michael Knights, only eight of fourteen attackers were killed, and most of the survivors were either captured or killed in subsequent months. A jihadi document stated that "the number declared in the media is not correct. Some of the perpetrators of the Riyadh operation were not martyred" (see "Ghazwat al-hadi 'ashar," 46).

14. The name "*al-mujahidun fi jazirat al-'arab*" first appeared in a June 2, 2003, online statement denouncing the killing of Yusuf al-Uyayri (*Al-Sharq al-Awsat*, June 3, 2003). The name "*tanzim al-qa'ida fi jazirat al-'arab*" first appeared in *Sawt al-Jihad* 5 (November 2003): 6.

15. Abdallah al-Rashid, "Intiqad al-i'tirad 'ala tafjirat al-riyadh" [Criticizing the reservations over the Riyadh bombings], available at www.qa3edoon.com, accessed July 23, 2003. Abdallah al-Rashid was an alias used by the prolific propagandist Abd al-Aziz al-Anzi, who was captured in May 2005.

16. "Ghazwat al-hadi 'ashar."

17. *Al Qaeda's Riyadh Martyrdom Tapes, v. 1.0* (Alexandria, Va.: Intelcenter, 2003), available at http://www.intelcenter.com/QRMT-v1-0.pdf.

18. "Ghazwat al-hadi 'ashar," 46.

19. Abd al-Aziz al-Muqrin, "Dawrat al-tanfidh wa harb al-'isabat" [A course in operational execution and guerrilla warfare], available at www.qa3edoon.com, 2004, 39.

20. Knights, "The East Riyadh Operation."

21. "Interior Ministry Announces Identities of Twelve Perpetrators of Riyadh Blasts," Saudi Press Agency, June 7, 2003.

22. Abd al-Aziz al-Ghamidi, "Min abtal ghazwat sharq al-riyadh [Among the heroes of the East Riyadh raid," *Sawt al-Jihad* 22 (2004): 25–26; Fawwaz al-Nashmi, "Khalid al-Baghdadi (Abu Ayyub al-Najdi)," *Sawt al-Jihad* 18 (2004): 53–54; "Wasaya al-abtal: shuhada' al-haramayn [Wills of the heroes: martyrs of the two sanctities]," al-Sahab Foundation for Media Production, October 18, 2003.

23. "Wasaya al-abtal."

24. Interview with Nawaf Obaid, Riyadh, January 2007.

25. "Authorities Name Fifth 'suicide terrorist,'" *CNN.com*, January 25, 2002.

26. Hegghammer, *Jihad in Saudi Arabia*, chap. 5.

27. See, e.g., Abu Hajir al-Jawfi, "Turki al-Dandani: 'azima wa shuja'a," *Sawt al-Jihad* 7 (2004): 33; and "Ali al-ma'badi al-harbi: batal badr al-riyadh [Ali al-Ma'badi al-Harbi: hero of the Badr of Riyadh]," *Sawt al-Jihad* 24 (2004): 22.

28. Ron Suskind, *The One Percent Doctrine* (New York: Simon and Schuster, 2006), 146.

29. Craig Whitlock, "Al Qaeda Shifts Its Strategy in Saudi Arabia," *Washington Post*, December 19, 2004; interviews with a European intelligence analyst and a U.S. diplomat, 2007.

30. Cordesman and Obaid, *National Security*, 113.

31. "Rumsfeld, Powell, and Spencer to Visit Saudi Arabia," *ArabicNews.com*, April 29, 2003.

32. In June 2003, in a video attributed to al-Qaeda, a figure calling himself Abu Haris Abdul Hakim and claiming to speak on behalf of al-Qaeda, the Taliban, and Gulbuddin Hekmatyar's Hezb-i-Islami claimed responsibility for both the Casablanca and Riyadh bombings. He said, "The recent attacks in Riyadh and Morocco were planned and they were part of our operations. You will see more such attacks in the future" (Kathy Gannon, "Al-Qaeda Claims Riyadh Attacks," Associated Press, June 22, 2003).

33. Dana Priest and Susan Schmidt, "Al Qaeda Figure Tied to Riyadh Blasts," *Washington Post*, May 18, 2003.

34. Peter Finn and Susan Schmidt, "Iran, al Qaeda, and Iraq," *Washington Post*, September 6, 2003.

35. John R. Bradley, "Clues Tie al Qaeda to Saudi Bombings," *Washington Times*, August 18, 2003.

36. Finn and Schmidt, "Iran, al Qaeda, and Iraq."

37. "Switzerland Is to Try Seven Yemenis for Supporting al-Qaeda," *Almotamar.net*, January 21, 2007; "First Swiss al-Qaeda Trial Gets Underway," *Swissinfo.ch*, January 22, 2007; Arrêt du 28 février 2007, Cour des affaires pénales, dossier SK.2006.15, available at http://bstger.weblaw.ch/; interview with Swiss intelligence analyst, July 2009.

38. "Saudi-US Cooperation in War on Terror Sharply Up: Official," *Arab News*, October 25, 2003.

39. Stéphane Lacroix, "Between Islamists and Liberals: Saudi Arabia's Islamo-liberal Reformists," *Middle East Journal* 58, no. 3 (2004): 363.

40. Brian Whitaker, "Yemen and Osama bin Laden," August 1998, available at www
.al-bab.com; Gregory Johnsen, *The Last Refuge: Islam and Insurgency in Yemen* (New
York: Norton, 2012), chap. 1.

41. Brian Whitaker, "Abu Hamza and the Islamic Army," February 1999, available at
www.al-bab.com; Sean O'Neill and Daniel McGrory, *The Suicide Factory* (London: Harper
Collins, 2006), 155–69; Mary Quin, *Kidnapped In Yemen: One Woman's Amazing Escape
from Captivity* (Guilford, Conn.: Lyons, 2005).

42. Thomas H. Kean et al., *The 9/11 Commission Report. Final Report of the National
Commission on Terrorist Attacks Upon the United States* (New York: Norton, 2004), 180,
190–93.

43. For an overview of security incidents in Yemen in this period, see Shaul Shay,
The Red Sea Terror Triangle: Sudan, Somalia, Yemen, and Islamic Terror (Piscataway, N.J.:
Transaction, 2007), 128–38.

44. Gregory Johnsen, "Al-Qaeda in Yemen Reorganizes Under Nasir al-Wahayshi,"
Jamestown Terrorism Focus 5, no. 11 (2008).

45. Joseph Felter and Brian Fishman, *Al-Qa'ida's Foreign Fighters in Iraq* (West Point,
N.Y.: Combating Terrorism Center, 2007), 7.

46. Johnsen, "Al-Qaeda in Yemen Reorganizes Under Nasir al-Wahayshi." One of
the jailbreakers was Abdallah al-Raymi, who was recaptured in May 2006.

47. Brian O'Neill, "Yemen's Three Rebellions," *Jamestown Terrorism Monitor* 6, no.
10 (2008).

48. Johnsen, "Al-Qaeda in Yemen Reorganizes Under Nasir al-Wahayshi."

49. Gregory Johnsen, "Yemen's Two Al-Qaedas," *Jane's Terrorism and Security Monitor*, August 21, 2008.

50. For an overview of attacks between 2006 and 2008, see Michael Knights, "Jihadist Paradise: Yemen's Terrorist Threat Re-emerges," *Jane's Intelligence Review* 20, no. 6
(2008).

51. Hassan M. Fattah, "Suicide Attacks Foiled at Two Oil Sites, Yemen Says," *New
York Times*, September 16, 2006.

52. "Suicide Bomber Attacks Tourists at Yemen Temple, Killing Nine," Associated
Press, July 3, 2007.

53. Robert F. Worth, "Two Belgian Tourists Killed in Yemen Ambush," *New York
Times*, January 19, 2008; Robert F. Worth and Khaled al-Hammadi, "Yemen: Police Officer Killed in Blasts Near U.S. Embassy," *New York Times*, March 19, 2008.

54. "Seven Arrested in Attack on Yemen Compound," Associated Press, April 9,
2008.

55. "Two Killed, Eighteen Injured in Yemen Attack," Reuters, July 25, 2008.

56. Gregory Johnsen, "Assessing the Strength of al-Qa'ida in Yemen," *Sentinel* 1, no.
10 (2010): 10–11.

57. Posted on www.al-ekhlaas.net, August 19, 2008.

58. Unless otherwise specified, most of the following operational details are drawn
from Michael Knights and Richard Evans, "US Embassy Attack, Sanaa, 17 September

2008," Olive Group Post-Incident Analysis (London: Olive Group), 2009. This report relied on a combination of news reports and a on-the-ground research by employees of Olive Group, a U.K. security contractor.

59. Initial reports mentioned sixteen fatalities (four civilians, six guards, and six attackers). But three civilians subsequently died from wounds, and jihadi media later revealed there had been seven attackers, not six; "Yemen: Thirty Are Arrested After Attack on U.S. Embassy," Reuters, September 19, 2008; "Death Toll in Yemen US Embassy Attack Rises to Nineteen," Associated Press, September 21, 2008; Faysal Makram, "Al-Qa'idah in Yemen: Seven Not Six Suicide Bombers Attacked US Embassy," al-Hayat (London), November 10, 2008 (via World News Connection).

60. Author's e-mail correspondence with Gregory Johnsen, September 26, 2009.

61. Knights and Evans, "US Embassy Attack, Sanaa, 17 September 2008."

62. Paul Schemm, "Sixteen Dead in Attack at US Embassy in Yemen," Associated Press, September 17, 2008.

63. Knights and Evans, "US Embassy Attack, Sanaa, 17 September 2008."

64. "Ghazwat al-furqan [The Furqan raid]," Sada al-Malahim 6, November 9, 2008, 15.

65. Knights and Evans, "US Embassy Attack, Sanaa, 17 September 2008."

66. Ibid. The QSAP video The Furqan Raid included a screenshot from Google Maps showing the embassy complex.

67. See note 59.

68. "Ghazwat al-furqan," 15.

69. The various issues of the magazine Sada al-Malahim were replete with passages praising Osama bin Laden and reiterating his call to "expel the polytheists from the Arabian Peninsula."

70. An initial claim of responsibility by an obscure group calling itself the "Islamic Jihad Organization—Yemen Brigades" proved to be inauthentic.

71. "Ghazwat al-furqan," 15–16. An additional four articles—entitled "Damaging Locations," "Ruling on Embassy Employees," "The Truth About Embassies" and "Why the Embassy?"—provided justifications for the attack, using many of the same arguments as the 2003 Riyadh bombers. Three additional articles—"The Significance of the Embassy Operation," "Badr of Riyadh and Badr of Sanaa," and "Jihadi and Official Media"—analyzed the political and strategic impact of the attack.

72. Ghazwat al-furqan: shann al-ghara 'ala wakr al-sifara [The Furqan raid: launching the attack on the embassy den], posted on http://ansaraljihad.tk/, September 13, 2009.

73. Abu Basir, "Al-Iftitahiyya [Opening message]," Sada al-Malahim 6, November 9, 2008, 4.

74. Abu Hurayra al-San'ani, "Dilalat 'amaliyyat al-sifara [Justifications for the embassy attack]," Sada al-Malahim 6, November 9, 2008, 23–24.

75. "Haqiqat al-sifarat [The truth about embassies]," *Sada al-Malahim* 6, November 9, 2008, 14; Thabit al-Adini, "Limadha al-sifara? [Why the embassy?]," *Sada al-Malahim* 6, November 9, 2008, 27; "Risala 'abr al-sifara [Message through the embassy]," *Sada al-Malahim* 6, November 9, 2008, 28; "Hukm al-'amilin fi'l-sifarat [Judgment on those who work in embassies]," *Sada al-Malahim* 6, November 9, 2008, 8–10.

76. Abu Basir, "Al-Ulama al-isthishhadiyyun [The martyrdom-seeking scholars]," *Sada al-Malahim* 6, November 9, 2008, 36; "Badr al-Riyadh wa Badr Sana'a [The Badr of Riyadh and the Badr of Sanaa]," *Sada al-Malahim* 6, November 9, 2008, 25.

77. "Ghazwat al-furqan," 15; Hamil al-Mask, "Abtal ghazwat al-furqan [The heroes of the Furqan Raid]," *Sada al-Malahim* 6, November 9, 2008, 38–40; *Ghazwat al-furqan: shann al-ghara.*

78. Gregory Johnsen and Christopher Boucek, "The Dilemma of the Yemeni Detainees at Guantanamo Bay," *Sentinel* 1, no. 12 (2008): 4.

79. Gregory Johnsen, "Al Qaeda's Grip on Yemen," *Jane's Terrorism and Security Monitor* (online), January 6, 2009.

80. Al-Mask, "Abtal ghazwat al-furqan," 38.

81. "Iraq Link to Attack," *The Age*, November 1, 2008.

82. On November 24, 2008, the *Daily Telegraph* reported the rumor that the bombers had received assistance from Iran; this is highly unlikely.

83. "Iraq Link to Attack."

84. Wahib al-Nassari, "Yemen: Perpetrators of the US Embassy Bombing Are Identified," *Al-Arab Online*, November 5, 2008 (via World News Connection).

85. Al-Mask, "Abtal ghazwat al-furqan," 38–40.

86. "Ghazwat al-furqan," 16.

87. Johnsen, "Al Qaeda's Grip on Yemen."

88. Eric Schmitt and David E. Sanger, "Some with Qaeda Leave Pakistan for New Havens," *New York Times*, June 12, 2009.

89. In a statement released on February 22, 2009, Ayman al-Zawahiri praised the "growing Jihadi awakening on the Arabian Peninsula in general and in the Yemen in particular" (Ayman al-Zawahiri, "From Kabul to Moghadishu," transcript available at http://www.nefafoundation.org/miscellaneous/FeaturedDocs/nefazawahiri0209 -2.pdf.)

90. Thomas Hegghammer, "Saudi and Yemeni Branches of al-Qaida Unite," January 24, 2009, available at www.jihadica.com.

91. "OSC Analysis: Terrorism—Yemen Expresses Public Resolve to Fight Terrorism," World News Connection (online), October 14, 2008; Jeremy M. Sharp, "Yemen: Background and U.S. Relations," CRS Report for Congress, July 7, 2009, 6, 7.

92. Gregory Johnsen, "The Expansion Strategy of al-Qa'ida on the Arabian Peninsula," *Sentinel* 2, no. 9 (2010): 9; Fawaz Gerges, "Al Qaeda Has Bounced Back in Yemen," *CNN.com*, January 7, 2010.

93. Michael Slackman, "Would-Be Killer Linked to Al Qaeda, Saudis Say," *New York Times*, August 29, 2009.

94. Anahad O'Connor and Eric Schmitt, "U.S. Says Plane Passenger Tried to Detonate Device," *New York Times*, December 26, 2009.

95. See for example Timothy L. Thomas, "Al Qaeda and the Internet: The Danger of 'Cyberplanning,'" *Parameters* 33 (2003).

96. Hegghammer, *Jihad in Saudi Arabia*, chap. 10.

The 2008 Mumbai Attack

C. CHRISTINE FAIR

This chapter examines leader-led Islamist militancy (a.k.a. "jihad") in Pakistan. Perhaps unlike the countries featured in some other chapters in this volume, the Pakistani state has long raised and mobilized numerous so-called jihadi groups to secure external as well as internal security objectives.[1] Ashley J. Tellis, a leading expert on South Asian security, wrote on this point that "in fact, of all the Pakistani-sponsored Deobandi [sic] terrorist groups operating against India in Kashmir and elsewhere, only one entity—the Hizbul Mujahedeen—began life as an indigenous Kashmiri insurgent group; the others, including the most violent organizations such as the Lashkar-e-Toiba [sic], the Jaish-e-Muhammad, and the Harkat-ul-Mujahedeen, are all led, manned, and financed by native Pakistanis."[2]

While it is often believed that Pakistan's use of militants dates to the anti-Soviet jihad in Afghanistan, Pakistan in fact began doing so in the founding months of the state.[3] Therefore, Pakistan's Islamist militant groups have been active in and from Pakistan for decades and represent a long-standing facet of national power, whose deployment has been increasingly enabled by Pakistan's nuclear umbrella.

A comprehensive assessment of "leader-led" jihad in Pakistan is beyond the modest length of this chapter. The facts of the Pakistan case reveal state-led jihad as a form of leader-led jihad. Most of the jihadi leaders and groups in Pakistan are—to varying degrees—led, mobilized, or supported by the Pakistani state. Ostensibly, the "leadership" lending strategic guidance and direction to Pakistan's militant groups is Pakistan's intelligence agency, the Interservices Intelligence Directorate (ISI), and the army. These agencies may be more important than any given individual leader who serves at their behest because the agencies provide important resources for arming, recruiting, training, and, ultimately, conducting operations. And of course the most important amenity that the state provides to these groups is the continued use of Pakistani territory for recruitment, raising funds, generating public support for their various "jihads," and training.

This chapter will focus upon one of the most lethal and effective militant groups operating from Pakistan: the Lashkar-e-Taiba or LeT. (LeT regrouped under the name of Jamaat-ul-Dawa when LeT was banned in 2002. For this reason, after 2002, I use the terms JuD and LeT interchangeably.) Because LeT differs substantially from other groups operating in Pakistan, this chapter first briefly lays out the key features of the contemporary militant landscape in Pakistan. Next, it provides key details about the organization and leadership. Third and most important, this chapter provides an account of what is perhaps LeT's most audacious attack to date: the November 26, 2008, coordinated attack on numerous targets throughout Mumbai, which lasted some 60 hours and killed 172 people while receiving full media coverage on Indian and international media. The chapter concludes with a discussion of the policy implications that emerge from this analysis.

PAKISTAN'S CONTEMPORARY MILITANT LANDSCAPE

At present, there are several kinds of militant groups operating in and from Pakistan.[4] The vast descriptive literature of Pakistan's militant groups allows them to be meaningfully disaggregated across several dimensions, beginning with their sectarian background (e.g., Ahl-e-Hadith, Deoband, Jamaat Islami, etc).[5] They can also be distinguished by their theaters of operation (e.g., Afghanistan, India, Pakistan), by the makeup of their cadres (e.g., Arab, Central Asia, Pakistani, and ethnic groups thereof), and by their objectives (e.g., overthrow of the Pakistani government, seizing Kashmir, supporting the Afghan Taliban, etc.), among other characteristics. Employing these characteristics, the following clusters of Islamist militant groups can be discerned (summarized in table 24.1).

Al-Qaeda operatives who are based in Pakistan are largely non-Pakistani. However, they work with and through networks of supportive Pakistani militant groups. The strongest ties are with the Deobandi groups such as the Pakistani Taliban, Jaish-e-Mohammed (JeM), Lashkar-e-Jhangvi (LeJ), etc. From sanctuaries in the tribal areas and from key Pakistani cities, al-Qaeda has facilitated attacks within Pakistan and has planned international attacks.[6]

While the Afghan Taliban operate in Afghanistan, they enjoy sanctuary in Pakistan's Baluchistan province, parts of the Federally Administered Tribal Areas (FATA), the Northwest Frontier Province, and key cities in the Pakistani heartland (e.g., Karachi). The Afghan Taliban emerged from Deobandi madrassas in Pakistan and retain their nearly exclusive ethnic Pasthun and Deobandi sectarian orientation.[7]

Several groups claim to focus upon Kashmir ("Kashmiri groups"). These include the Jamaat-e-Islami-affiliated Hizbul Mujahedeen and related splinter groups; several Deobandi groups (JeM, Harkat-ul-Jihad-Islam, etc.); and the Ahl-e-Hadith group Lashkar-e-Taiba. With the notable exception of Hizbul Mujahedeen, most of these groups claim few ethnic Kashmiris, and most came into being as surrogates of the ISI.

While in the past, notable anti-Sunni Shia groups existed with support from Iran, sectarian groups today are mostly Sunni. Those Sunni groups targeting Shia are almost always Deobandi (Sipah-e-Sahaba-e-Pakistan [SSP], Lashkar-e-Jhangvi). In addition, there is considerable intra-Sunni violence with Ahl-e-Hadith and Deobandi targeting Barelvis (a heterodox Sufi order).[8]

Groups self-nominating as "Pakistani Taliban" appeared in Waziristan as early as 2004 under the leadership of Waziristan-based, Deobandi militants who fought with the Afghan Taliban in Afghanistan. By late 2007, several militant commanders at least nominally organized under the leadership of South Waziristan–based Baitullah Mehsud under the moniker Tehreek-e-Taliban-e-Pakistan (TTP, Pakistani Taliban). There is no serious evidence of coordination among the various leaders operating under this nom de guerre; rather, there are reports of considerable disagreement among local commanders.[9] Indeed, commanders such as Mullah Nazir and Hafiz Gul Bahadur focused upon attacking American and NATO troops in

TABLE 24.1

Summary of Militant Groups Operating in and from Pakistan

Group Name	Sectarian Background	Regional Activities	Overlapping Membership
Al-Qaeda (in Pakistan)	Salafist	Facilitated attacks within and without Pakistan and has planned international attacks from safe havens in Pakistan	TTP, Afghan Taliban, other Deobandi militant groups
Afghan Taliban	Deobandi	Wages insurgency in Afghanistan, enjoys safe havens in Pakistan	TTP and other Deobandi militant groups, al-Qaeda
Jaish-e-Mohamed (Harkat-il-Jihad-Islam [JUJI], Harkat-ul-Ansar/Harkat-ul-Mujahedeen, etc.)	Deobandi	Traditionally focused upon Indian-administered Kashmir, has operated in Afghanistan and continues to do so; factions have targeted the Pakistani state	Al-Qaeda, TTP, Afghan Taliban, Deobandi sectarian militant groups as well as JUI
Sipha-e-Sahaba-Pakistan/ Lashkar-e-Jhangvi	Deobandi	Historically anti-Shia, has operated in Afghanistan for decades; currently targeting the Pakistani state with the TTP and allied groups	TTP, Afghan Taliban, al-Qaeda, other Deobandi militant groups, and JUI
Hizbul Mujahedeen and al-Badr	Jamaat-e-Islami	Indian-administered Kashmir	Jamaat-e-Islami
Tehreek-e-Taliban-e- Pakistan (TTP, Pakistani Taliban)	Deobandi	Targeting the Pakistani state, with some commanders mobilizing fighters in Afghanistan	Afghan Taliban, Deobandi militant groups in Pakistan, and possibly al-Qaeda
Lashkar-e-Taiba	Ahl-e-Hadith	Fights in Indian-administered Kashmir and the Indian hinterland, limited out-of-theater operations	Historical links with al-Qaeda; al-Qaeda members have been detained in LeT safe havens; organizational ties to al-Qaeda remain controversial

Afghanistan and remained locked in disagreement with Baitullah Mehsud, whose forces attacked Pakistani security, intelligence, and civilian targets. Baitullah Mehsud was killed in a U.S. drone strike in August 2009, likely because he could not be reconciled. After considerable speculation about the TTP's fate, it reemerged under the vehemently sectarian Hakimullah Mehsud. After a brief interlude from violence, the TTP has sustained a bloody campaign of suicide bombings, both precipitating Pakistani military activities against their redoubt in South Waziristan and in effort to punish the state for launching the campaign.[10]

There are a number of refinements to this gross disaggregation. First, Deobandi groups often have overlapping membership with one another and with the Deobandi Islamist political party, Jamiat-e-Ulema Islami (JUI). Thus, a member of JeM may also be a member of LeJ or even an office holder at some level with the JUI. Second, Deobandi groups have in recent years begun operating against the Pakistani state following Pakistan's participation in the U.S.-led global war on terrorism. JeM and LeJ, for instance, have collaborated with the TTP by providing suicide bombers and logistical support, allowing the TTP to conduct attacks throughout Pakistan, far beyond the TTP's territorial remit.[11] Both LeT and several Deobandi militant groups have also been operating in Afghanistan against U.S., NATO, and Afghan forces.[12] In contrast, other Kashmiri groups are operating under the influence of the Islamist political party Jamaat-e-Islami, such as al-Badr and Hizbul Mujahedeen, which tend to be composed of ethnic Kashmiris and have retained their operational focus upon Kashmir.

There are several factors that distinguish LeT from the myriad other groups operating in and from Pakistan. First, LeT (along with the Jamaat-Islami based organizations) has *never* targeted the state. The organization's manifesto (*Hum Kyon Kar Rahen Hain*) in fact explicitly forbids violence against Pakistanis.[13] This is further evidence of the tight links between these groups and the Pakistani security establishment. Second, unlike all of the aforementioned groups, LeT has remained organizationally coherent. When the organization has undergone structural changes, it has been because of deliberate and strategic reorganization rather than leadership disputes. In contrast, the ISI has engineered or fomented dissent among the other militant groups to ensure enhanced control over them. LeT is the only group that has been allowed to remain intact without significant divides among top decisions makers. (As with all organizations, some discord has been observed among local commanders.) Finally, whereas the state has taken on several of the Deobandi groups, including the TTP, and al-Qaeda through inept and not always efficacious military operations, it has taken only the most marginal and cosmetic steps in the wake of the Mumbai 2008 attacks. LeT and several other jihadi groups were banned in 2002, but all of them regrouped under other names with their financial assets largely intact.[14] JuD escaped a second round of bans in 2003, which were prompted by complaints lodged by the U.S. ambassador to Pakistan at the time, Nancy Powell, that these militant outfits had reformed without consequence. This enabled JuD to continue to expand its overt as well as covert actions with preferential state treatment. In fact, Pakistan was extremely reluctant to ban JuD after the Mumbai attack and did so only after the UN Security Council proscribed the organization and identified its leadership.[15]

LASHKAR-E-TAIBA: FOUNDATION AND LEADERSHIP STRUCTURE

LeT has focused the attention of U.S. policy makers following the November 2008 terrorist attacks in Mumbai.[16] The attack laid to rest prevailing ambivalence about whether LeT represented a threat mostly to India or whether it also seriously threatened the international community. This insouciance about the LeT threat is somewhat puzzling. Before 2008, LeT had long established a presence in Pakistan and South Asia. Since 2001, it has increasingly expanded well beyond the South Asian region. LeT originally emerged as the military wing of the Markaz Daawat ul Irshad (MDI), headquartered in Muridke near the Punjabi city of Lahore. MDI was founded in 1986 by two Pakistani engineering professors, Hafiz Muhammad Saeed and Zafar Iqbal. Abdullah Azzam, a close of associate of bin Laden who was affiliated with the Islamic University of Islamabad and the Maktab ul Khadamat (Bureau of Services for Arab mujaheddin), also provided assistance. He was killed in Peshawar two years after MDI was founded. MDI, along with numerous other militant groups, was involved in supporting the mujaheddin in Afghanistan from 1986 onward, and it established militant training camps for this purpose.

One camp was known as Muaskar-e-Taiba in Paktia and a second known as Muaskar-e-Aqsa in the Kunar province of Afghanistan.[17] (Kunar is known to be home to numerous Ahl-e-Hadith adherents in Afghanistan, which overall has few followers of that group. For this reason, Kunar has been an attractive safe haven for Arabs in Afghanistan.) Pakistan-based analysts note that MDI/LeT's training camps were always separate from those of the Taliban, which hosted Deobandi militant groups such as HUJI and Harkat-ul-Mujahedeen. This has led some analysts to contend that LeT has not had the sustained and organic connections to al-Qaeda as enjoyed by the Deobandi groups, many of which became "outsourcers" for al-Qaeda in Pakistan.[18]

In 1993, MDI divided its activities into two related but separate organizations: MDI proper continued the mission of proselytizing and education while LeT emerged as the militant wing. The ISI is believed to have funded LeT, and analysts continue to believe that the present-day LeT is a close proxy of Pakistani intelligence agencies.[19] After the Soviets withdrew from Afghanistan, LeT/MDI shifted focus to Indian-administered Kashmir. It staged its first attack (against a jeep carrying Indian air-force personnel) in Kashmir in 1990. The vast majority of LeT operatives are Pakistanis (often Punjabis), and the organization has spawned a vast training infrastructure throughout the country to support its dual mission of training militants and converting Pakistanis to the Ahl-e-Hadith interpretative tradition. For much of the 1990s (with few exceptions), LeT operations were restricted to Indian-administered Kashmir.

LeT's 200-acre headquarters is in Muridke (Punjab), some thirty kilometers from Lahore.[20] However, the organization maintains offices in most of the major cities throughout Pakistan.[21] These offices undertake recruitment as well as funds collection. In addition to overt offices open to the public, JuD/LeT maintains covert training camps throughout Pakistan.[22] Hafez Saeed is the amir (supreme commander) of the organization. LeT has a spokesperson named Yahya Mujahid (with whom the author has met on several occasions) as well as a spokesperson for international media, Abdullah Muntazer, who also edits JuD's website.[23]

JuD has a quasi-military structure with a chief commander, divisional commander, district commander, battalion commander, with substructures organizing cadres along armylike lines. As of 2005 (more current information is not available in the public domain), A. B. Rah-man-Ur-Dakhil was the organization's *naib amir* (deputy supreme commander). In addition, there are commanders and deputy commanders assigned to key operational areas. Notably, Zia-Ur-Rehman Lakhvi is the supreme commander for Kashmir. Lakhvi was the mastermind of the 2008 Mumbai attacks. The apex policy-making body for the JuD is headed by the amir and the *naib amir* among others (e.g., the finance chief).[24] Operations tend to be conducted with a relatively small unit of fewer than a dozen.[25]

JuD's cadres come largely from Pakistan, with smaller numbers from Afghanistan and even fewer from the Middle East and Africa. There is no publicly available—much less accurate—accounting of the organization's strength. But the State Department estimates that it has "several thousand" members in Pakistan-administered Kashmir, Pakistan, the southern Jammu and Kashmir and Doda regions (in India-administered Kashmir), and the Kashmir Valley.[26] In contrast, the Delhi-based South Asia Terrorism Portal estimates that, with some fluctuation, it has more than 750 cadres in Jammu and Kashmir, which constitute the overwhelming bulk of the foreign militants in the Kashmir valley.[27]

A perusal of LeT literature demonstrates a commitment to targeting Indian Hindus, Jews, Americans, and other infidels and apostate Muslims; stoking larger Hindu-Muslim discord in India; and liberating all of India and establishing a caliphate.[28] MDI claims that it has had a leading role in armed struggles across the Muslim world, first in Afghanistan then in Bosnia, Chechnya, Kosovo, the Philippines, and Kashmir, among other venues.[29] There is no independent verification of these claims. However, in recent years, LeT operatives have appeared in small numbers in other theaters. For example, British forces captured two Pakistani LeT operatives in Iraq and rendered them into U.S. custody in February 2004.[30] A number of Australians, including apparent converts to Islam, have been trained in LeT camps, discomfiting Australian authorities.[31] Reports persist that a wide array of American, Canadian, and British nationals have also trained in LeT camps.[32]

LeT has a hallmark modus operandi, which has often been misconstrued as simply "suicide operations." In fact, LeT does not do suicide operations per se, in which the goal of the attacker is to die during the execution of the attack. Rather, LeT's "fidayeen" missions are more akin to high-risk missions in which well-trained commandos engage in fierce combat during which death is preferable to capture. While martyrdom is in some sense the ultimate objective of LeT operatives, LeT selects missions where there is a possibility, however slim, of living to kill more enemy operatives. The goal of LeT commandos therefore is not to merely to commit suicide attacks; rather, they seek to kill as many as possible until they ultimately succumb to enemy operations, barring their ability to survive enemy engagement. Mariam Abou Zahab has described a typical LeT encounter in the following way: "The fighters are well trained and highly motivated and they engage the enemy on its own territory. Small groups of fedayeen ... storm a security force camp and kill as many soldiers as possible before taking defensive positions within the camp and engaging security force personnel till they attain martyrdom. Battles often last 20 hours, if not more."[33]

She further notes that these spectacular and well-planned attacks bring LeT maximum publicity, expand recruiting and donations, and demoralize the enemy—which must resort to heavy fire, destroying their own buildings and causing substantial collateral damage in the process of responding. While LeT claims that it has only assaulted hard targets, their record demonstrates an absolute willingness to kill civilians.

Consonant with the rigor of a typical LeT mission, LeT recruits do not predominantly draw from Pakistan's madrassas. Rather, LeT recruits are generally in their late teens or early twenties and tend to be better educated than Pakistanis on average or even than other militant groups, such as the Deobandi SSP or JeM. A majority of LeT recruits have completed secondary school with good grades, and some have even attended college. This reflects both the background of LeT's founding fathers, who were engineering professors, and MDI's commitment to technical and other education. This stands in sharp contrast to the madrassa-based networks of many of the Deobandi groups, including the Afghan Taliban.[34] In fact, many LeT operatives likely came into contact with LeT through proselytizing programs on college campuses, which in turn lure the potential recruits to the large "*ijtema*" (congregation) held annually in Muridke. The fraction of madrassa-educated LeT operatives is believed to be as low as 10 percent.[35] LeT also actively targets women both to expand its male recruitment base and, reportedly, to recruit women for militant operations.[36]

The early connection between MDI/LeT and Abdullah Azzam, along with the organization's Salafi-jihadi outlook, have fostered beliefs that LeT and al-Qaeda enjoy tight links. These beliefs have been further nurtured by the arrests of al-Qaeda operatives in LeT safe houses. Pakistan-based analysts of LeT tend to discount this rationale and note that al-Qaeda operatives have been arrested in Jamaat Islami safe houses as well and note that LeT infrastructure in Afghanistan, as described above, was separate from that of al-Qaeda and its patrons, the Taliban.[37] Thus, the actual degree to which LeT is allied to al-Qaeda remains an important empirical question for this author despite popular claims advanced by others on this point.

Since the late 1990s, LeT has continued to develop its operational reach into India. While Indian citizens were always required for facilitating LeT and other militant groups' actions within India-administered Kashmir and the Indian hinterland, LeT has successfully cultivated active cadres and figures, especially in founding of the Indian Mujahedeen. In 2002, at least fourteen young men from Hyderabad left for Pakistan for training, reportedly motivated by the massacre of Muslims in Gujarat in 2002. (Praveen Swami reports that even as early as 1992, some Indian Muslims sought training in Pakistan in response to the demolition of the Babri Masjid by Hindu extremists.) The Hyderabad operatives received training in LeT and JeM camps and enjoyed operational assistance from Bangladesh-based Harkat-ul-Jihad-Bangladesh (HUJI-B). This cell was responsible for the May 18, 2007, terrorist attack in Hyderabad's Toli Chowki area.[38] LeT has moved Indian personnel into and out of Pakistan via Bangladesh and other countries through criminal syndicates as well as other Islamist and militant groups, such as the Students Islamist Movement of India (SIMI) and HUJI-B, among others.[39]

Despite the rhetoric surrounding the horrific events in Mumbai on November 26, 2008, there were important antecedents of that attack. In July 2006, LeT, working with local operatives, detonated seven explosions across Mumbai's commuter rail system. That 2006 assault was even more lethal than the 2008 carnage, killing at least 187 people. While that attack focused the public's attention upon LeT's ability to strike deep within India, LeT had reportedly established networks in Mumbai as early as

August 1999. India's intelligence bureau disrupted a pan-India network led by LeT operative Amir Khan, who was tasked with recruiting from India's violence-afflicted communities. In 2000, Indian authorities intercepted three Pakistani LeT cadres who had planned to kill Bal Thackeray, leader of a Hindu nationalist group called the Shiv Sena.[40]

In 2004, another LeT cell was disrupted that aimed to attack the Bombay Stock Exchange. (The Bombay Stock Exchange had been previously hit in 1993 by Pakistan-based terrorists working with an Indian-based mafia syndicate led by Dawood Ibrahim.) In June 2006, the Maharashtra police arrested an eleven-member LeT cell that shipped some forty-three kilograms of explosives, assault rifles, and grenades to India using sea routes. Several of those militants had ties to SIMI. Indian analysts believe that LeT, working with SIMI and smuggling rings, have been able to successfully move large amounts of explosives and weapons by sea along the Gujarat coast.[41] The movement of explosives through the Maharashtra and Gujarat coastlines was reminiscent of logistical routes used to supply explosives for the 1993 Bombay Stock Exchange.[42] Needless to say, these are only illustrative—not exhaustive—examples of LeT's penetration of India and cultivation of Indian networks to conduct terror operations.

THE NOVEMBER 26, 2008, MUMBAI ATTACK

While LeT has conducted dozens—if not hundreds—of attacks throughout India (including Mumbai) since its inception, none has received the attention and coverage of the sixty-hour killing spree perpetrated by ten Pakistani operatives who reached Mumbai by sea in late November 2008. In this attack, LeT targeted significant numbers of international civilians, prompting the United States in particular to reconsider its assessment of the organization's intentions, if not capabilities. (Admittedly, LeT is suspected of targeting international tourists in Kashmir, but these attacks have had few fatalities and have not drawn the attention of the international media.) This section will document the incident and provide a detailed account of the perpetrators, the motivations and goals of the attack, and analysis of the outcome.

The Plot

Ten Pakistani LeT terrorists, who had trained in camps in Muzaffarabad and later in Sindh, departed Karachi on a small boat and transferred to a larger vessel, the *al-Hussaini* where they slept. By some accounts, the militants began training for the operation in mid-2007, with reconnaissance on targets in early 2007, which Indian authorities believed was conducted by two Indian nationals, Faheem Ansari and Sabauddin Ahmed. On November 22 or 23, the terrorists hijacked an Indian fishing trawler and murdered its crew.[43] They arrived in two small inflatable boats at two different points in the southern part of Mumbai. Incredibly, the terrorists navigated the complex mega-city without Indian guides, having studied the city's geography using maps and the Internet. Each terrorist was heavily armed, made all the more incredible given that they came into the city via inflatable boats. Each militant carried an AK-56 assault rifle (a Chinese version of the Russian AK-47) with numerous magazines of ammunition. They also carrieed 9 mm pistols with two clips of ammunition as well as eight to ten grenades per attacker. In addition, the attackers had mobile phones and at least five improvised explosive devices, composed of a military-grade explosive (RDX), ball bearings (for shrapnel), a digital timer, and a nine-volt battery. Once they reached shore, the militants formed four attack teams, one with four men and three with two.[44]

One two-man team comprised the lone survivor, Mohammed Ajmal Amir Kasab (a.k.a. Kasab, alias Abu Mujahid, from Okara),[45] and his partner, Ismail Khan (alias Abu Ismail, from Dera Ismail Khan). (Ajmal was sentenced to death in an Indian court in early May 2010.) Ajmal and Khan took a taxi to the Chhatrapati Shivaji Terminus (CST), Mumbai's main train station. Considerable detail is now known about this attack team because Ajmal was arrested and in late July 2009 made a lengthy confession about the team. According to assembled accounts, once they reached CST station, they began firing on commuters. The police at the train station were ill equipped for such a contingency, and the attackers managed to terrorize commuters for ninety minutes before better-trained and -equipped police arrived, forcing them to leave the station.[46]

The team next fled led to the Cama and Albless Hospital, where they fired on crowds and deployed their grenades. They then escaped in a police car they had ambushed until they were recognized. They next hijacked another vehicle and proceeded to toward the Metro cinema hall, from there to Nariman Point, and, finally, to Chowpatty, where Khan was shot dead and Ajmal was injured and captured.[47] This team accounted for nearly one-third of the civilian casualties. Ajmal, in his confession, claims that they had been instructed to take hostages and escape to nearby buildings, where they were supposed to contact their operational commander, Zaki-ur Rehman Lakhvi. Lakhvi was supposed to provide media contact numbers to place their demands. However, this seems to have been a ploy to garner more media attention as the ultimate objective, according to Ajmal's testimony, was to blow up the target buildings.[48]

A second team (Nasir, alias Abu Umar, from Faisalabad, and Babar Imran, alias Abu Akasha, from Multan) proceeded to Nariman House—a center run by the international Jewish Lubavich movement. (This is often referred to as "Chabad House" in Indian media.) Their team threw grenades at a nearby gas station, opened fire upon the building, and entered the complex firing. They took thirteen hostages as they prepared for the siege. Five hostages were killed in addition to the terrorists after an airdrop of National Security Guard commandos.[49]

A third two-man team (Abdul Rehman, alias Abdul Rehman Chhota, from Multan, and Fahadullah, alias Abu Fahad, from Okara) traveled from the landing site to the Trident-Oberoi Hotel, where they, too, began killing indiscriminately. The siege at this hotel lasted for some seventeen hours before the attackers were killed, by which time they had killed thirty people.[50]

The fourth team was the largest and comprised Hafeez Arshad (alias Bada Abdul Rehman, from Multan), Javed (alias Abu Ali, from Okara), Shoaib (alias Abu Soheb, from Sialkot), Nazeer (alias Abu Umer, from Faisalabad). The team briefly entered the Leopold Café, a popular sidewalk restaurant, where they killed ten people with automatic weapons. The team next moved to the rear entrance of the nearby Taj Hotel. They cut a lethal swath through the ground floor of the hotel to the upper floors, where they set fires and moved constantly to confuse security forces. In part because of the delayed arrival of the National Security Guard commandos, the siege at the Taj ended some sixty hours later, when all of the attackers were at last killed by the commandos.[51]

Several questions about the plot persist, with varying degrees of uncertainty. One of the key questions is whether the attackers intended to lay siege or slaughter. The surviving attacker indicated that they were instructed to take hostages. However, there appears to have been no political objective to this course of action. Rather, it appears to have been a ploy to garner as much media attention as possible while engaging in maximum death and destruction. Indeed, this was the most highly televised terror attack in India. This may explain why this attack has had profound effects upon the Indian citizenry and government even though it is by far not the most deadly attack in the country. Second, it is unclear whether the LeT anticipated that the siege would last as long as it did. The question remains whether inelegant Indian operations, coupled with vibrant (and sensationalist) domestic and international media, delivered an operational and media success that the LeT had not anticipated.

Targets

LeT selected Mumbai as the venue for this audacious attack. Mumbai is a significant arena for LeT—and other militant groups—for a number of reasons. First, Mumbai is target rich as it is India's most populated city, with an estimated 14 million inhabitants, and is likely the world's third-largest city. Second, Mumbai is India's financial hub. Third, it is also home to India's massive film industry and is known for its inhabitants' liberal and westernized lifestyle. Mumbai is the backdrop for the glamorous lifestyles of India's glitterati. Mumbai is also a thoroughly international city populated by foreigners who flock to its opulent hotels. And Mumbai is burgeoning with media coverage as India's private media continue to proliferate.

Mumbai is home to the Hindu-chauvinist/nationalist organization Shiv Sena, which is an ally of the Bharitya Janata Party (BJP, a nationwide Hindu-chauvinist/nationalist party). Mumbai was also the site of anti-Muslim violence between December of 1992 and January of 1993, when as many as 900 people were killed. These anti-Muslim riots came in the wake of the destruction of an ancient mosque in Ayodhya by Hindu zealots, who contended that the mosque was built on the birthplace of Lord Ram, a Hindu deity. The twin disasters are believed to have motivated the Muslim gangster Dawood Ibrahim to support Islamist terrorism. Ibrahim, with help from Pakistan's ISI and militant organizations, facilitated the 1993 attack on Mumbai's stock exchange.

For all of these reasons, Mumbai as a venue for terrorist attacks is endowed with multiple layers of significance. However, there are significant practical aspects that likely guided LeT's selection of Mumbai as a target. First, LeT had operated in Mumbai and environs on several occasions. The sea route had long been used to move men and materiel into the area to stage for attacks. Mumbai's police are riven with corruption and tied to the underworld. Mumbai—like the rest of India—has poor sea-based security and a largely undefended shoreline. Mumbai is home to important mafia organizations, including that of Dawood Ibrahim.

In some ways, the attack's targets resembled those of previous LeT attacks. LeT planned for several primary targets, including the Chhatrapati Shivaji Terminus (CST), the Cama and Albless Hospital, the Leopold Café, the Chabad Center, the Trident-Oberoi Hotel, and the Taj Mahal Palace Hotel. It appears as if the LeT attacked other places along the way as targets of opportunity.[52] All the targets were soft, with little or inadequate security, and were explicitly civilian, with the exception of the security forces killed in the course of engagement. The luxury hotels are owned by Indian firms and represent symbols of Indian wealth and prestige. They are frequented by wealthy Indian and foreign guests. The Leopold Café is a popular sidewalk restaurant frequented by tourists and young Indian customers. The train station, named after Shivaji, is used by largely lower- and middle-class commuters making their way to and from their homes, which are often far away from the city's center.

However, other targeting aspects of this attack were unprecedented. First, while LeT has been operating against U.S., NATO, and Afghan forces in Kunar and Nuristan and LeT operatives went to fight allied forces in Iraq, this was the first significant LeT assault upon American and international *civilians*.[53] Second, in this assault, LeT targeted the Chabad Center, which was distinctive because it was not merely Jewish but also associated with Israelis and international Jewish adherents. Mumbai, like other cities, hosts a historical though shrinking Jewish population and boasts many historical synagogues and Jewish cultural facilities. Despite the decades of Islamist violence perpetrated by a range of groups espousing an anti-Semitic agenda, no Islamist militant group had ever targeted India's Jewish community.[54]

The Perpetrators

As noted above, Zaki-ur Rehman Lakhvi was undoubtedly the mastermind of this operation.[55] Lakhvi's role does not eliminate the possibility that the plot was coordinated at some level with the ISI, given their historical involvement with LeT. Apart from the identity of the lone survivor and his attack partner, little is known about the attackers except for their operational aliases and their Pakistani home towns. In eight of nine cases, the faces of the slain attackers have been published. The body of the tenth was burned beyond recognition.[56] Ajmal knew little about the other militants, likely for operational security reasons. Based upon published accounts of Ajmal's trial proceedings and confession, he had a fourth-grade education and worked for a decorator, suggesting that he is substantially less educated than LeT operatives in general. Dissatisfied with his meager earnings, a coworker named Muzaffar, suggested that they could augment their income through theft and *dacoity* (banditry). While visiting Rawalpindi, they approached LeT activists in Raja market (in the old city of Rawalpindi) and expressed their desire to become "jihadis." After a brief period of vetting, they were given money and told to board a bus to LeT's headquarters in Muridke. At Muridke, Ajmal began studying the Quran and hadith. (LeT also has a proselytizing mission as most of its recruits are not already Ahl-e-Hadith adherents.) He then traveled to an LeT camp in Battal, where he trained in using AK-47s.[57]

He performed so well that he was selected for advanced training, "*duara-e-khaas*," and thus remained in Battal, where he was instructed to engage in mundane affairs of the camp such as cooking. In the advanced training, he continued working with AK-47s, rocket launchers, grenades, pistols, and mortars. He was there for a total of three months, after which he was sent home for one week. Per instructions, he returned to an LeT office, where he stayed for some ten days for evaluation. He was among fifteen boys selected for the operation. After another month, they were taken to Karachi, where they learned to swim, navigate a boat at sea, and use a fishing net. They were again taken back to Muzaffarabad. By this point, the group of fifteen was now seven strong, as apparently six members were sent to Kashmir and two ran away. In a revelation to Indian authorities, he also studied Hindi from an Indian national, Abu Jundal, at Muzaffarabad. (Hindi is grammatically the same as Urdu. However, it uses a Sanskrit-based script rather than the Perso-Arabic Script of Urdu. It also has a somewhat different vocabulary.)[58]

Within a few days, three other "boys" (or "*bacche*" as jihadis are known in Pakistan) arrived to complete their team of ten men. Abu Hamza was one of the principal instructors. He called the boys in pairs of two into his room; Ajmal was already paired with Khan by this point. They were twice shown pictures of CST on Abu Hamza's laptop, after which they returned to the forest for more military training. Upon returning to Muzaffarabad, they obtained identity cards, trousers, and t-shirts (as opposed to Pakistani national dress of *salwar kameez*). They again went to Karachi. Abu Hamza was there and gave them strict orders not to leave the house. As the men set off for their mission, they were accompanied by Abu Jandal, Zaki-ur-Rehman (the mastermind of the operation), Abu Hamza, and Abu Khafa. These four assigned the men into teams and targets—Ajmal's team was assigned to CST—where they were instructed to kill, take hostages to the upper floor, and make contact with Zaki-ur-Rehman. Having completed their training, they then transferred to the *al-Hussaini*, where their bags and weapons had already been placed.[59]

Motivations and Goals

The attack likely advanced several goals. If the LeT remains an extension of the state through the ISI, the attack appears to have served—successfully—several strategic goals. First, it exacerbated tensions between India and Pakistan and disrupted the ongoing peace process. As of July 2009, the Indian political leadership opposed any renewed dialogue with Pakistan because of its dissatisfaction with Pakistan's meager efforts to tackle Pakistan-based terrorism. Second, the attack was likely expected to precipitate some form of calibrated militarized conflict.

(Given that the more egregious December 2001 attack on the Indian parliament nearly precipitated a war and that the 2006 LeT attack on the commuter rail system did not garner even a modest military response, it is doubtful that LeT expected this attack to bring about a war between the two states.) Indeed, India began mobilizing its troops along the eastern border. This provided Pakistan a convenient opportunity to move forces from the west, where it is engaging the TTP, to the east. This suggests a fourth, if ancillary, goal of providing the Pakistan army some respite from the internal enemy and refocusing international and national attention upon the "conventional" Indian threat. Fifth, the attack demonstrates—to the military and intelligence organizations—that attacking India remains an ambition of their organizations. This may have had the effect of invigorating organizations that had grown wary of the "distraction" of conducting internal security operations away from the preferred theater of India. Sixth, the attack may have been intended to politically embarrass Pakistan's civilian leadership. However, this seems unlikely given the planning timelines. (The civilians returned to power in February 2008.) Finally, the attack may have been intended to create space between the United States and the Pakistan army, which bridles under U.S. dictates to target Pakistanis.[60]

While many of the soft targets show continuity with previous LeT actions, the choice of Chabad House is a decisive departure from previous efforts and seems to have served novel strategic goals. While LeT, in its leadership's speeches and its various publications since the late 1980s, has often posited and railed against the "Brahmanic-Talmudic-Crusader" alliance, it had never acted per this agenda until the 2008 Mumbai attack. Possible explanations for targeting the Chabad House include the growing Indo-Israeli military, counterterrorism, and intelligence relationship, which has long irritated Pakistan, and the animated rhetoric of Islamist militants across the region.[61] Moreover, the Israeli lobby apparatus in the United States has nurtured India's own emergent lobbying organizations and is rightly or wrongly associated with helping India achieve the Indo-U.S. nuclear deal.[62] Thus the selection of the Chabad center—rather than any of India's domestic Jewish institutions—may have sought to undermine the important Indo-Israeli relationship. This is supported by transcripts of the phone calls between the militants and their handlers in Pakistan during which the attackers were instructed to kill their Jewish hostages to "spoil relations between India and Israel."[63]

Organizationally, the attack served several goals. First, it demonstrated to cadres disillusioned with Pakistan's "moderate jihad" strategy that both the organization and the anti-India agenda remain relevant.[64] The attack also reminded audiences within and without South Asia that LeT is the preeminent militant group in the region and therefore enhanced LeT recruiting and fund raising. Moreover, since LeT appears to have been cooperating with more proximity with al-Qaeda in Afghanistan, the attack against Israeli and international targets puts LeT more squarely within the operational goals of al-Qaeda, even if the organization remains formally unaligned with al-Qaeda.[65]

Analysis of the Outcomes

LeT seems to have successfully advanced many of these possible objectives. The battered and largely outcome-free Indo-Pakistan peace process remained suspended until the summer of 2011, when foreign-minister-level talks resumed. The brief Indian military build-up that followed the attack provided some temporary respite to the Pakistani forces that swung away from their operations against Pakistani militants in the west. However, the attack critically resuscitated the relevance of Pakistan's conventional conflict against the backdrop of enduring internal security operations and provided continued justification for Pakistan's conventional purchases rather than investments in equipment and training (as well as doctrinal reorientation) for counterinsurgency operations. The selection of the operation's targets jettisoned LeT out of its regional basis and has fostered a notion that LeT is an al-Qaeda ally despite the evidence for this claim. Whether embarrassing the civilian leadership and reminding them of their vulnerable (and subordinate) position vis-à-vis the army and the ISI was the purpose of the attack, it certainly had this effect. Then Prime Minister Geelani and President Zardari were both held responsible for a policy they could not control.

The attack, while advancing several strategic goals, has imposed several negative outcomes as well. Whereas LeT was, according to one U.S. official, a "niche specialty" within the U.S. government, it is now a major concern.[66] Second, the proximity of the LeT to the ISI, along with continued revelations about ISI assistance to the Afghan Taliban, remind the United States and others that the Pakistani government continues to fight a selective war on terror while preserving those militant groups that service the state's foreign-policy goals. This has catalyzed widespread cynicism about Pakistan's role and the sense of continued U.S. military support. This has been no doubt been facilitated by the rise of the effective and well-resourced Indian lobby in Washington as well as the electoral pressure of influential Indian Americans. The attack has also convinced many within India's official establishment and across India's polity that Pakistan cannot be trusted and will remain a constant threat to the state. As one prominent Indian journalist explained to the author, many of the Indians scarred by partition are growing old and dying; the new generation of Indians does not recall partition. Rather, they know Pakistan only as a state dedicated to killing Indians.[67] While this appears to advance the goal of sustaining tensions between the two states, it undermines the goals of the political establishment in Pakistan to secure some modus vivendi with India to advance commercial and other ties beneficial to the populace and, over time, to reduce the influence of the Pakistani army. It has also been a boon to those within India's defense and political establishments who argue for a more offensive military capability to emerge with an ever-more reckless and dangerous Pakistan. This attack, coming upon the heels of dozens of others, has motivated the Indian armed forces to generate new doctrinal and operational concepts that will allow India to impose costs upon Pakistan through limited military action that will not prompt a conventional military response or threaten escalation to the nuclear threshold.[68]

———

Pakistan's insouciance towards LeT/JuD and the threat the organization poses strongly suggests that while the Pakistani state may have joined the fight against al-Qaeda and prosecutes a selective fight against elements of the Pakistani Taliban, LeT/JuD remains a tool of the Pakistani state. Indeed, Pakistan seems confident that it can rely upon these elements safely under its nuclear umbrella. With the United States nearly completely dependent upon Pakistan for logistical supplies for the conduct of the war in Afghanistan and given the paramount interest in remaining engaged in Pakistan to obtain information about it military and the evolution of its strategic systems, the U.S. government has been loath to exert punitive pressure upon Pakistan to persuade it to abandon terrorism as a tool of foreign policy. Indeed, as India continues to consolidate its national power and exert its influence in the areas surrounding Pakistan, Pakistan is likely to become more reliant—not less—upon militancy as a tool of foreign policy. India, too, seems to have few disincentives to render such asymmetric tactics more costly given the nuclearization of the subcontinent.[69]

Since Pakistan is unlikely to determine that LeT/JuD and similar groups are no longer useful in advancing its strategic interests, and neither India nor the United States has the space or tools to compel Pakistan to do so, the only likely option is a well-crafted strategy to contain the militant threat emanating from Pakistan.

For India—the principal target thus far—this means investing much more financial, human, and political capital to tackle its deficient internal security apparatus. Such capabilities should allow Indian authorities to eliminate militants once they enter, detect cells that have been established, and even deter their entry in the first place. The challenges to fortifying India are numerous. Its state police forces are to varying degrees rife with corruption and infiltrated by mafia and militant groups, and they have been politicized to serve the interests of the political class. India lacks a federal investigative agency of any consequence, and intelligence moves awkwardly—if at all—between external and internal intelligence and law-enforcement agencies. While defending India's massive coastline may be a heroic effort, virtually all agree that it is critical to devote more resources to protecting the coast. Indian officials are well aware of the state's numerous internal security deficits, but few leaders seem able to muster the political will to make important changes. However, with a dedicated threat from Pakistan-based groups, India's failure to protect its citizenry with modern internal security structures is a serious shortcoming.[70]

For others—including the United States—a more robust threat-containment strategy needs to be conceptualized and implemented. As containing Pakistan per se is not feasible, the United States, India, the United Kingdom, and other states victimized by LeT and similar groups should forge closer cooperation on intelligence and counterterrorism initiatives. Greater contacts must be forged with immigration, treasury, and other government agencies in those states used by LeT/JuD for logistical purposes. Currently, LeT moves people and funds through the Persian Gulf, Bangladesh, Nepal, Sri Lanka, and other states, and it has a robust fund-raising network throughout the Pakistani diaspora. This will not be an easy task; however, other, more feasible options do not appear to be available.

While India struggles with fortifying its internal security and while the international community attempts to erect a robust containment strategy for Pakistan-based terrorism, national and multilateral institutions (e.g., the U.S. Department of Treasury, the United Nations Security Council, the European Union) should work to target specific individuals within the militant organizations in question, as well as individuals within the Pakistani state found to be supporting these groups. Admittedly, the latter may be awkward. In the case of the UN Security Council (UNSC), this may mean working to forge coalitions with Pakistan's key supporter on the UNSC, China. More generally, the United States will have to reach out to Pakistan's friends—as well as foes—to forge a consensus on the best way to help Pakistan help itself. Indeed, Washington will need to develop a broad-based engagement strategy of all countries relevant to Pakistan (e.g., Iran, Saudi Arabia, UAE, China) to help forge a parallel if not convergent threat perception of Pakistan and develop policies to best address it. All of these options seem inordinately difficult given the political priorities of the United States and other critical countries. However, such engagement is necessary to increase the transaction costs of using terrorist organizations as proxies for the state. Until such an effective strategy is developed, neither the Pakistani state nor individuals within it face any serious disincentive to pursue this policy.

NOTES

1. Pakistan has long tolerated anti-Shia groups and even Shia pogroms at different parts of its history. This in because of efforts of Zia ul-Haq to promote Sunni Islam and to contend with a militarized Shia response sponsored by Iran. While Pakistan

has episodically cracked down on these groups because they have overlapping membership with key Deobandi religious institutions and with groups fighting in India/ Kashmir and Afghanistan, Pakistan has been reluctant to put them down decisively. See, C. Christine Fair, "The Militant Challenge in Pakistan," *Asia Policy* 11 (January 2011): 105–37; Vali R. Nasr, "International Politics, Domestic Imperatives, and Identity Mobilization: Sectarianism in Pakistan, 1979–1998," *Comparative Politics* 32 (2000): 170–91; International Crisis Group, *The State of Sectarianism in Pakistan*, Crisis Group Asia Report no. 95 (Brussels, Islamabad: International Crisis Group, 2005), 12, 19–20; A. H. Sorbo, "Paradise Lost," *The Herald* (Karachi) (June 1998): 31; Muhammad Qasim Zaman, "Sectarianism in Pakistan: The Radicalization of Shi'i and Sunni Identities, *Modern Asian Studies* 32 (1998): 689–716.

2. See Ashley J. Tellis, *Pakistan and the War on Terror: Conflicted Goals, Compromised Performance* (Washington, D.C.: CEIP, 2008), 5. Tellis makes a factual error in attributing all of these groups to the Deobandi interpretive school, however. Also see, among numerous other sources, Ahmed Rashid, *Descent Into Chaos: The U.S. and the Disaster in Pakistan, Afghanistan, and Central Asia* (New York: Penguin, 2009); Husain Haqqani, *Pakistan Between Mosque and Military* (Washington, D.C.: CEIP, 2005); Hassan Abbas and Jessica Stern, *Pakistan's Drift Into Extremism: Allah, the Army, and America's War on Terror* (New York: M. E. Sharpe 2004).

3. Praveen Swami, *India, Pakistan, and the Secret Jihad: The Covert War in Kashmir, 1947-2005* (London: Routledge, 2007).

4. This section draws from C. Christine Fair, "Pakistani Attitudes Towards Militancy and State Responses to Counter Militancy," unpublished essay, written while the author was a Luce Fellow at the University of Washington in 2009. Also see Fair, "The Militant Challenge in Pakistan," and Fair, "Militant Recruitment in Pakistan: Implications for Al-Qa'ida and Other Organizations," *Studies in Conflict and Terrorism* 27 (2004).

5. This taxonomy is deduced from author fieldwork in Pakistan from 2002 to 2009. See C. Christine Fair, "Who Are Pakistan's Militants and Their Families?," *Terrorism and Political Violence* 20 (2008): 49–65. Also see Arif Jamal, *Shadow War: The Untold Story of Jihad in Kashmir* (Hoboken, N.J.: Melville House, 2009); Muhammad Amir Ranan, *The A to Z of Jehadi Organizations in Pakistan*, trans. Saba Ansari (Lahore: Mashal, 2004); Amir Mir, *The True Face of Jehadis* (Lahore: Mashal Books, 2004), Amir Mir; *The Fluttering Flag of Jehad* (Lahore: Mashal Books, 2008). For an excellent synthesis of the sprawling Pakistani literature on the varied militant groups based in and from the country, see Nicholas Howenstein, "The Jihadi Terrain in Pakistan: An Introduction to the Sunni Jihadi Groups in Pakistan and Kashmir," Pakistan Studies Research Unit, Bradford University, February 2008, available at http://www.humansecuritygateway .info/documents/PSRU_JihadiTerrain_Pakistan.pdf; "Tehrik-e-Taliban Pakistan (TTP)," *Jane's World Insurgency and Terrorism*, July 1, 2009, available at http://wjit.janes.com (by subscription only); Manzair Zaidi, "Pakistan's Taliban Warlord: A Profile of Baitullah Meshud," *The Long War Journal*, September 30, 2008, www.longwarjournal.org

/archives/2008/9/pakistans_taliban_wa.php; "Pakistan's Most Wanted: Baitullah Mehsud," *Jane's World Insurgency and Terrorism*, February 8, 2009, available at http://www4.janes.com; Rahimullah Yusefzai, "Profile: Nek Mohammed," *BBC News Online*, June 18, 2004, available at http://news.bbc.co.uk/2/hi/south_asia/3819871.stm; Hassan Abbas, "A Profile of Tehrik-i-Taliban Pakistan," *CTC Sentinel* 1 (2008): 1–4; Abbas, "Tribal Tribulations: The Pakistani Taliban in Waziristan," *Jane's Terrorism and Insurgency*, January 13, 2009, available at http://www.janes.com.

6. See comments made by National Intelligence Director John Negroponte, quoted in "Al-Qaeda 'Rebuilding' in Pakistan," *BBC News Online*, January 12, 2007, available at http://news.bbc.co.uk/2/hi/south_asia/6254375.stm; K. Alan Kronstadt, *U.S.-Pakistan Relations* (Washington, D.C.: Congressional Research Service, 2008), available at http://fpc.state.gov/documents/organization/115888.pdf.

7. See Senator Carl Levin, "Opening Statement of Senator Carl Levin, Senate Armed Services Committee Hearing on Afghanistan and Pakistan," February 26, 2009, available at http://levin.senate.gov/newsroom/release.cfm?id=308740; Ian Katz, "Gates Says Militant Sanctuaries Pose Biggest Afghanistan Threat," *Bloomberg News*, March 1, 2009, available at http://www.bloomberg.com/apps/news?pid=20601087&sid=aehmlRXgKi2o&refer=home; Barnett R. Rubin, "Saving Afghanistan," *Foreign Affairs* (January/February 2007), available at http://www.foreignaffairs.org/20070101faessay86105-p0/barnett-r-rubin/saving-afghanistan.html.

8. Nasr, "International Politics, Domestic Imperatives, and Identity Mobilization"; International Crisis Group. *The State of Sectarianism in Pakistan*, 19–20. Also see Sorbo, "Paradise Lost," 31; Zaman, "Sectarianism in Pakistan," 689–716.

9. Zaidi, "Pakistan's Taliban Warlord"; Zaidi, "Pakistan's Most Wanted"; Yusefzai, "Profile: Nek Mohammed"; Abbas, "A Profile of Tehrik-i-Taliban Pakistan"; Abbas, "Tribal Tribulations: The Pakistani Taliban in Waziristan."

10. Declan Walsh, "Pakistan Sends 30,000 Troops for All-Out Assault on Taliban," *Guardian*, October 17, 2009, available at http://www.guardian.co.uk/world/2009/oct/17/pakistan-sends-troops-against-taliban.

11. Author fieldwork in Pakistan in February and April 2009.

12. See C. Christine Fair, "Antecedents and Implications of the November 2008 Lashkar-e-Taiba Attack Upon Mumbai," testimony presented before the House Homeland Security Committee, Subcommittee on Transportation Security and Infrastructure Protection, March 11, 2009.

13. C. Christine Fair, "Lashkar-e-Tayiba and the Pakistani State," *Survival* 53, no. 4 (August 2011): 1–23.

14. Stephen Phillip Cohen, "The Jihadist Threat to Pakistan," *The Washington Quarterly* 26 (2003): 7–25.

15. Stephen Tankel, "Lashkar-e-Taiba: From 9/11 to Mumbai," *Developments in Radicalisation and Political Violence* (April/May 2009), available at http://www.icsr.info; Jay Solomon, "U.N. Security Council Sanctions Lashkar Members," *Wall Street Journal*, December 10, 2008, available at http://online.wsj.com/article/SB122895332614496341.html.

16. This section draws in part from Fair, "Antecedents and Implications."

17. See Yoginder Sikand, "The Islamist Militancy in Kashmir: The Case of the Lashkar-e-Taiba," in *The Practice of War: Production, Reproduction, and Communication of Armed Violence*, ed. Aparna Rao et al. (New York: Berghahn Books, 2007), 215–38; Mariam Abou Zahab, "I Shall be Waiting at the Door of Paradise: The Pakistani Martyrs of the Lashkar-e-Taiba (Army of the Pure)," in *The Practice of War*, 133–58; Saeed Shafqat, "From Official Islam to Islamism: The Rise of Dawat-ul-Irshad and Lashkar-e- Taiba," in *Pakistan: Nationalism Without a Nation*, ed. Christophe Jaffrelot (London: Zed Books, 2002), 131–47.

18. In 1998, the United States bombed several al-Qaeda/Taliban training camps in retaliation for the al-Qaeda attacks on U.S. embassies in Africa. Militants of several Pakistani Deobandi groups were killed, including operatives of HUJI and HuM among others. See Barry Bearak, "After the Attacks: In Pakistan, Estimates of Toll in Afghan Missile Strike Reach as High as Fifty," *New York Times*, August 23, 1998. Also see Dexter Filkins, "'All of Us Were Innocent,' Says Survivor of U.S. Attack on Camp," *Los Angeles Times*, August 24, 1998, available at http://articles.latimes.com/1998/aug/24/news/mn-16045.

19. See Sikand, "The Islamist Militancy in Kashmir"; Abou Zahab, "I Shall be Waiting at the Door of Paradise"; Shafqat, "From Official Islam to Islamism," 7.

20. According to the South Asia Terrorism Portal, the Muridke Markaz (center) comprises a "madrassa (seminary), a hospital, a market, a large residential area for 'scholars' and faculty members, a fish farm and agricultural tracts. The LeT also reportedly operates 16 Islamic institutions, 135 secondary schools, an ambulance service, mobile clinics, blood banks and several seminaries across Pakistan." See South Asia Terrorism Portal, "Lashkar-e-Toiba 'Army of the Pure,'" available at http://www.satp.org/satporgtp/countries/india/states/jandk/terrorist_outfits/lashkar_e_toiba.htm (accessed July 25, 2009).

21. Business card of Yayha Mujahid, spokesperson of JuD, provided to the author during a meeting at the Pearl Continental in Lahore Pakistan in 2005.

22. The author has visited the Lahore office in Char Burji.

23. South Asia Terrorism Portal, "Lashkar-e-Toiba."

24. For more detailed information about LeT/JuD leadership, see South Asia Terrorism Portal, "Lashkar-e-Toiba." This source suggests the following structure: "the LeT leadership consisted of: Hafiz Mohammed Saeed (Supreme Commander); Zia-Ur-Rehman Lakhvi alias Chachaji (Supreme Commander, Kashmir); A. B. Rahman-Ur-Dakhil (Deputy Supreme Commander); Abdullah Shehzad alias Abu Anas alias Shamas (Chief Operations Commander, Valley); Abdul Hassan alias MY (Central Division Commander); Kari Saif-Ul-Rahman (North Division Commander); Kari Saif-Ul-Islam (Deputy Commander); Masood alias Mahmood (Area Commander, Sopore); Hyder-e-Krar alias CI (Deputy Commander, Bandipora); Usman Bhai alias Saif-Ul-Islam (Deputy Commander, Lolab); Abdul Nawaz (Deputy Commander, Sogam); Abu Rafi (Deputy Divisional Commander, Baramulla); Abdul Nawaz (Deputy Commander, Handwara); Abu Museb alias Saifulla (Deputy Commander, Budgam)."

25. For more information about this, see Ranan, *The A to Z of Jehadi Organizations.*

26. See U.S. Department of State, Office of the Coordinator for Counterterrorism, "Terrorist Organizations," in *Country Reports on Terrorism 2007,* chap. 6, April 30, 2008, available at http://www.state.gov/s/ct/rls/crt/2007/103714.htm. Note that many other details in the State Department write-up do not accord with knowledgeable sources on the organization. For example, it claims that most of the recruits come from madrassas, which is not confirmed by the analysts with deep familiarity of the organization who are cited throughout this article.

27. South Asia Terrorism Portal, "Lashkar-e-Toiba."

28. The author has collected LeT poster work and written materials since 1995.

29. Sikand, "Islamist Militancy in Kashmir," 219. Also see discussion of LeT in Ranan, *The A to Z of Jehadi Organizations,* 324.

30. Richard Norton-Taylor, "Britain Aided Iraq Terror Renditions, Government Admits," *Guardian,* February 26, 2009, available at http://www.guardian.co.uk/world/2009/feb/26/britain-admits-terror-renditions.

31. Recently, during a trial of several men plotting to attack the United States from Sydney, a participant (a Korean American Muslim convert) alleged that an Australian citizen known as Abu Asad trained with Lashkar-e-Taiba at a camp in Pakistan in 2001. See Geesche Jacobsen, "Australian in Training Camp Named," *Sydney Morning Herald,* January 13, 2009. For information on another collective of Australians trained in LeT camps, see Ashok Malik, "Lashkar Link in Aussie Terror Net," *Indian Express* (New Delhi), June 12, 2004. Perhaps the most famous Australian to train at a LeT camp is David Hicks, who was recently freed from Guantánamo. See "David Hicks: 'Australian Taleban,' " *BBC News,* May 20, 2007.

32. See, for example, "Lashkar Training in US, Canada, UK, Australia," *Rediff.com,* December 10, 2008, available at http://www.rediff.com/news/2008/dec/10mumterror-lashkar-training-in-us-canada-uk-australia.htm.

33. Abou Zahab, "I Shall be Waiting at the Door of Paradise," 138.

34. For a more thorough discussion of the connections between militancy and education, see C. Christine Fair, *The Madrassah Challenge: Militancy and Religious Education in Pakistan* (Washington, D.C.: USIP, 2008).

35. Abou Zahab, "I Shall be Waiting at the Door of Paradise," 140; Shafqat, "From Official Islam to Islamism," 142.

36. Farhat Haq, "Militarism and Motherhood: The Women of the Lashkar-i-Tayyabia in Pakistan," *Signs* 32 (2007): 1023–46.

37. See Sikand, "The Islamist Militancy in Kashmir"; Shafqat, "From Official Islam to Islamism."

38. Praveen Swami, "Terror Junction," *Frontline* 24, no. 11 (2007), available at http://www.hindu.com/fline/fl2411/stories/20070615002303500.htm.

39. Praveen Swami, "Lashkar-Trained Indian Terrorists Pose Growing Threat," *Hindu* (Chennai), December 19, 2008, available at http://www.hindu.com/2008/12/19/stories/2008121956141200.htm.

40. Praveen Swami, "Road to Unimaginable Horror," *Hindu* (Chennai), July 13, 2006, available at http://www.hindu.com/2006/07/13/stories/2006071303420800.htm.

41. In May of 2006, Mohammad Iqbal, a LeT activist from Bahawlpur (a city in southern Punjab in Pakistan), was shot dead by Delhi police. Iqbal had worked through mafia-linked traffickers to ship a consignment of explosives through Gujarat that was used in the February 2006 attack on an Ahmedebad (Gujarat) train platform. See Swami, "Road to Unimaginable Horror."

42. See Praveen Swami and Anupama Katakam, "Investigators Shut Down Terror Cells Tasked with Executing Strikes in Gujarat, but the Threat Remains," *Frontline* 23 (2006), available at http://www.thehindu.com/fline/fl2310/stories/20060602006109700.htm.

43. According to Mohammed Ajmal Amir, the only surviving militant, the assault was originally scheduled for September 27 but was postponed. The group of ten stayed in Karachi until November 23 under strict observation.

44. Angel Rabasa et al., "The Lessons of Mumbai," RAND Occasional Paper, 2009. The inventory of weapons of the team varies in different accounts. According to the lone survivor, "Each man was carrying an AK-47, two magazines, eight grenades and a mobile phone. Some also carried explosives." See "Mumbai Gunmen Identified—Kasab's Pak Nationality Confirmed," *Indian News Online*, December 15, 2008.

45. He is most frequently referred to as Ajmal Kasab which is not technically correct. Kasab refers to his caste (which means literally butcher) not his family name. Thus the author uses his family name, not his caste name.

46. Rabasa et al., "The Lessons of Mumbai."

47. "The Confession," *Indian Express* (Mumbai), July 24, 2009, 9; "Kasab's Confession—How the LeT Trained Mumbai Attackers," *NewKerala.com*, July 20, 2009. http://www.newkerala.com/nkfullnews-1-77027.html.

48. See "Mumbai Gunmen Identified."

49. Rabasa et al., "The Lessons of Mumbai"; "Mumbai Gunmen Identified."

50. Rabasa et al., "The Lessons of Mumbai"; "Mumbai Gunmen Identified."

51. The commandos, based in Agra, had no dedicated air assets and took nearly half a day to arrive. NSG commandos had (and indeed have) no presence throughout India. See Rabasa et al., "The Lessons of Mumbai."

52. Rabasa et al., "The Lessons of Mumbai."

53. Author fieldwork in Afghanistan between June and October 2007; Kathy Gannon, "Pakistan Militants Focus on Afghanistan: Jihadist Groups Are Increasingly Attacking U.S., NATO Forces in Afghanistan," Associated Press, July 14, 2008.

54. Yair Ettinger, "Mumbai Attack Sends Shock Waves Through Chabad Community Worldwide," *Haaretz* (Tel Aviv), November 29, 2008, available at http://www.haaretz.com/hasen/spages/1041785.html; Anshel Pfeffer, "Nine Dead in Mumbai Chabad House Attack; Israel to Help Identify Bodies," *Haaretz* (Tel Aviv), November 30, 2008, http://www.haaretz.com/hasen/spages/1041834.html.

55. On December 10, 2008, the United Nations Security Council placed financial sanctions on four members of LeT (Muhammad Saeed, whom the UN names as the group's leader; Zaki-ur-Rehman Lakhvi, described as LeT's chief of operations; Haji Muhammad Ashraf, its finance chief; and Mahmoud Mohammad Ahmed Bahaziq, described as a financier for the group). The four face an assets freeze, a travel ban, and an arms embargo. In addition, the Security Council amended its 2005 blacklisting of LeT to include the charitable foundation JuD after Pakistan banned LeT. President Asif Ali Zardari of Pakistan said that he would ban JuD if given conclusive evidence of its links to the Mumbai attack. Solomon, "U.N. Security Council Sanctions Lashkar Members."

56. "Faces of Terror," *OutlookIndia.com*, December 9, 2008, available at http://www.outlookindia.com/article.aspx?239184.

57. "The Confession"; "Kasab's Confession; "Mumbai Gunmen Identified."

58. "The Confession."

59. "The Confession"; "Kasab's Confession"; "Mumbai Gunmen Identified."

60. See the author's discussion of "Implications," in Rabasa et al., "The Lessons of Mumbai," 13–19.

61. Military and intelligence ties have in many ways formed the backbone of the Indo-Israeli relationship, and Israel is now India's preeminent arms supplier. For an early account of the emerging relationship see P. R. Kumaraswamy, "Strategic Partnership Between Israel and India," *MERIA Journal* 2, no. 2 (1998), available at http://meria.idc.ac.il/journal/1998/issue2/jv2n2a6.html. See Embassy of Israel, New Delhi, "Indo-Israel Relations," available at http://delhi.mfa.gov.il/mfm/web/main/document.asp?SubjectID=2010&MissionID=93&LanguageID=0&StatusID=0&Document ID=-1; P. R. Kumaraswamy, "Indo-Israeli Military Ties Enter Next Stage: A US$2.5 Billion Indo-Israeli Defense Project Marks a New Phase in the Two Countries' Relations," International Relations and Security Network, August 3, 2007, available at http://www.isn.ethz.ch/isn/Current-Affairs/Security-Watch/Detail/?ots591=4888CAA0-B3DB-1461-98B9-E20E7B9C13D4&lng=en&id=53611; Efraim Inbar, "The Indian-Israeli Entente," *Orbis* 48 (2004): 89–104.

62. This judgment is based upon numerous visits to Pakistan since the discussion of the deal emerged.

63. Andrew Buncombe and Omar Waraich, "Mumbai Siege: 'Kill All the Hostages—Except the Two Muslims': Phone Conversations Between Mumbai Attackers and Their 'Pakistani Handlers' Cast Chilling New Light on Massacre," *Independent* (London), January 8, 2009, available at http://www.independent.co.uk/news/world/asia/mumbai-siege-kill-all-the-hostages-ndash-except-the-twomuslims-1232074.html.

64. C. Christine Fair and Peter Chalk, "United States Law Enforcement Assistance to Pakistan," *Small Wars and Insurgencies* 17 (2006); C. Christine Fair and Peter Chalk, *Fortifying Pakistan: The Role of U.S. Internal Security Assistance* (Washington D.C.: USIP, 2006).

65. See the author's discussion of "Implications," in Rabasa et al., "The Lessons of Mumbai," 13–19.

66. Conversations with officials in the U.S. embassy, New Delhi, July 2009.

67. Conversations with journalist, New Delhi, July 2009.

68. Walter C. Ladwig III, "A Cold Start for Hot Wars? The Indian Army's New Limited War Doctrine," *International Security* 32 (2008).

69. Ashley J. Tellis, C. Christine Fair, and Jamison Jo Medby, *Limited Conflicts Under the Nuclear Umbrella—Indian and Pakistani Lessons from the Kargil Crisis* (Santa Monica, Calif.: RAND, 2001); C. Christine Fair, "Time for Sober Relations: US-Pakistan Relations," *The Washington Quarterly* 32 (2009).

70. After the 1999 limited war in the Kargil-Dras sector, the Kargil Review Committee Report produced a number of important recommendations to enhance India's domestic and external security. Nearly ten years later, few if any have been implemented. For a critical discussion of this, see K. Subrahmanyam, "Report of the Kargil Review Committee: An Appraisal," *CLAWS Journal* (Summer 2009): 18–27. Since the 2008 attack, the Indian government has announced a number of reforms aimed at addressing these various shortcomings. See Rama Lakshmi, "Indian Official Unveils Plan to Strengthen Security," *Washington Post*, December 11, 2008. However, few security analysts in India interviewed by this author in July 2009 have any optimism that these will be operationalized either. See full discussion in Rabasa et al., "The Lessons of Mumbai."

[25]

The 2010 Suicide Attacks in Kampala

ANNELI BOTHA

l-Qaeda's East African cell, responsible for the United States Embassy bombings on August 7, 1998, in Nairobi and Dar es Salaam, and the attack on an Israeli-owned hotel on November 28, 2002, in Mombassa, was implicated in the attacks in Kampala on July 11, 2010. While instability in neighboring Somalia since 1991 enabled al-Qaeda to enhance its operations in the region, the two suicide bombings that targeted innocent people—who were watching the final FIFA World Cup match between Spain and the Netherlands—and claimed eighty-one lives were a new blow for people in Eastern Africa. Although a Somali-based jihadist organization claimed responsibility for the attacks in the capital of Uganda by means of a communiqué, al-Qaeda's involvement was unmistakable. An analysis of the influence of al-Qaeda in the Kampala bombings needs to include reference to the U.S. embassy bombings twelve years earlier and the conflict in Somalia that provided al-Qaeda with a relative safe environment to operate in and around the Horn of Africa.

INFLUENCE OF AL-QAEDA IN EASTERN AFRICA

On August 7, 1998, suicide bombers almost simultaneously detonated two truck bombs, targeting the United States embassies in Nairobi, Kenya, and Dar es Salaam, Tanzania. These were the first recognized suicide attacks in Africa, and they killed 224 people and injured 5,000. The attacks displayed the hallmark of Osama bin Laden and al-Qaeda, which the world would soon become accustomed to. Although terrorism analysts were well aware of its existence, these attacks were the first al-Qaeda executed after its well-known fatwa, or rather declaration of war, from February 23, 1998.

Al-Qaeda gradually extended its reach in the Horn of Africa while Sudan hosted Osama bin Laden between 1991 and 1996, when he returned to Afghanistan. Using the hospitality of Sudan and instability in Somalia to his advantage, bin Laden established the East Africa cell that would be responsible for the attack on the West, in this case, the United States. Al-Qaeda operated in Nairobi since at least 1993, and in Mombassa since 1994.[1] Bin Laden wanted to accomplish several goals before shifting his focus to the attack. The establishment of safe houses for cell members and others who were passing through became the first priority. In addition to facilitating illegal movement across borders in the region, Kenya also serves a gateway to the Gulf, the Middle East, and South Asia. Second, al-Qaeda operatives opened small businesses and relief organizations to subsidize and conceal their activities. For example, in 1993, Khalid al-Fawwaz, who would later became a spokesman for Osama bin Laden in Britain, started a business in Nairobi called Asma Limited, which was later transferred to Abu Ubaidah al-Banshiri, a military commander. Wadih el-Hage, who American investigators said had served as bin Laden's personal secretary (el-Hage moved to Kenya in 1994 to help run the cell), established another business there, called Tanzanite King, and a relief organization, called Help Africa People. In August 1994, Mohammed Saddiq Odeh, a Jordanian member of al-Qaeda who had been trained in the camps in Afghanistan, arrived in Mombassa. That same year Mohammed Atef, the head of al-Qaeda's military committee who would later be killed in the bombing in Afghanistan, visited Odeh in Mombassa and gave him a fiberglass boat to start a wholesale fishing business for al-Qaeda. Under the arrangement, Odeh could take whatever money he needed to cover his expenses and give the rest to al-Qaeda. Finally, the African al-Qaeda cell recognized the importance of providing training. In a letter by a member of the East Africa cell that U.S. officials seized in Nairobi in 1997, the writer warned that the United States knew that Osama bin Laden's operatives in Kenya helped train the fighters who attacked American troops in Somalia in 1993. The letter was found at a home in Nairobi belonging to Wadih el-Hage.

Although the East Africa cell initially involved "foreigners," such as Wahid el-Hage (Lebanese), Anas al-Libi (Libyan), and Mustafa Mohamed Fadhil (Egyptian), the need to use local nationals to take over operations was immediately recognized. Most important were Fazul Abdullah Mohammad (Abdul Karim), Fahid Mohammed Ally Msalam, Issa Osman Issa, and Sheikh Ahmed Salim Swedan from Kenya, who formed the future core of al-Qaeda in East Africa. Fazul Abdullah Mohammad traveled in and out of Kenya since the early 1990s while Osama bin Laden was based in Sudan. Msalam, according to his uncle, had become religious after spending time in Yemen and Pakistan; Swedan (who grew up in Mombassa) did a basic training course in Afghanistan after he dropped out of school. Foreign nationals were also assimilated into al-Qaeda's new cadre. For example, Mohammed Saddiq Odeh, originally a Palestinian national, was granted Kenyan citizenship and settled in Witu, near Malindi, where he ran a carpentry business.[2] Early on, al-Qaeda's cell in Eastern Africa learned an important lesson that would prove useful when it planned the 2010 Kampala bombings: any successful operation planned or motivated beyond the target country requires some form of local assistance. Local nationals, for example, will not attract as much attention when renting an apartment or vehicle, and so local assistance, knowing or unknowing, is essential in keeping the planned attack secret for as long as possible.

In addition to using local nationals, al-Qaeda also used local circumstances to its advantage to such an extent that its operatives were able to settle in the region and evade capture, which raised concern among security experts. Al-Qaeda established itself in East Africa over six years and used local knowledge to operate with relative ease.[3] The men in the cell lived among Kenya's Muslim population, married into the local community, set up cover businesses, and used locals to help with their new lives. Additionally, many of the al-Qaeda associates who went to Somalia in 1993 and later to Kenya knew one another from the Afghan camps. There has been a particular focus on Somalia following claims by the CIA that al-Qaeda members have been smuggled into Somalia via the port city of Ras Kamboni, on the border with Kenya. According to United Nations investigators that monitor the arms embargo on Somalia, seventeen mobile training centers were found in Kenya in 2005 under the control of organizers who are believed to be veterans of training camps in Afghanistan.[4] However, the terror groups became inactive immediately after the 1998 bombings. Since then, members of al-Ittihad al-Islam and al-Takfir wal Hijra have established sanctuaries on the Kenyan coastal strip and in North Eastern Province. In Somalia, bases were established in Puntland, Kismayo, Mogadishu, and Bosaso, and in Ethiopia they operate from Ogaden and Gedo.[5]

It was, however, poor socioeconomic conditions that secured the acceptance of al-Qaeda operatives within local communities. Siyu village on Pate Island was identified as an area of concern that also provided insight into the strategy of foreign terrorists in the planning and execution of acts of terrorism. The population, approximately 1,500 people, is extremely poor and lacks basic necessities such as running water. This close-knit Islamic community welcomed Fazul Abdullah Mohammad as a Muslim and generous provider of relief from these dire economic conditions. When Fazul arrived on the island in 2002, he married Amina Mohammed Kubwa, the daughter of Mohammed Kubwa. Mohammed Saddiq Odeh married a Swahili woman from Witu Village, along the Mombassa-Malindi highway; Saleh Ali Nabhan (who before the U.S. embassy attacks facilitated direct communication with Osama bin Laden) married Fatma Ahmed Talo from Lamu.[6]

Fazul Abdullah Mohammad, Saleh Ali Nabhan, and Issa Osman Issa were later implicated in the November 2002 suicide attack at the Paradise Hotel in Mombassa, which killed fifteen people and injured forty, and the attempted surface-to-air missile attack on an Israeli passenger airplane in Mombassa. Saleh Ali Nabhan was the ringleader of the Mombassa cell under the supervision of Fazul Abdullah Mohammad.[7] In addition to facilitating communications with Osama bin Laden, Nabhan later served as the chief military strategist for al-Shabaab al-Mujahideen.[8] In other words, the actual links among al-Shabaab, al-Qaeda central, and the al-Qaeda cell in East Africa were facilitated by a small group of individuals, most notably Nabhan and Abu Talha al-Sudani (also known as Tariq Abdullah, al-Qaeda's ideological and strategic leader in East Africa and implicated in the 1998 bombings).[9] Further, Nabhan played a central role in securing the link between Sheikh Robow (the former deputy commander of the Islamic Courts Union, the deputy leader of al-Shabaab and its former spokesperson) and the al-Qaeda cell in East Africa.

ALLEGIANCE BETWEEN AL-QAEDA AND AL-SHABAAB

The origins of al-Shabaab, or "The Youth," can be traced back to al-Ittihād al-Islāmiyya (AIAI) and Ittihād al-Mahākim al-Islāmiyya, commonly known as the Islamic Courts Union (ICU). In 2006, a coalition of local sharia courts and Islamists in Mogadishu defeated the Alliance for the Restoration of Peace and Counter-Terrorism (ARPCT). The ICU comprised both moderate and extremist elements and included radical elements within al-Shabaab.

Earlier, following the defeat of AIAI by Ethiopian and Puntland forces in 1997, several of its members who would found al-Shabaab went to Afghanistan for training, including Aden Hashi Farah (alias Ayro, the leader of al-Shabaab till he was killed in a U.S. airstrike in Somalia, on January 1, 2008, and replaced by Ahmad Abdi Aw Muhammad Godane), Godane (alias Sheikh Mukhtar abu Zubayr); and Sheikh Mukhtar Robow Ali (alias Abu Mansur). Following the attacks on September 11, 2001, they returned to Somalia and established a training camp in Mogadishu under the protection of Sheikh Hassan Dahir Aweys (a senior leader in al-Shabaab and previously the head of Hizb al-Islam until the group's merger with al-Shabaab in December 2010).[10] Additionally, after the U.S. embassy bombings in Nairobi and Dar es Salaam in August 1998, members of the al-Qaeda cell settled in Somalia, most notably Fazul Abdullah Mohammad, Saleh Ali Nabhan, Abu Talha al-Sudani, and Issa Osman Issa.

Ayro was recruited by Sheikh Hassan Dahir Aweys (who at the time was the military commander of AIAI) to go to Afghanistan, establish relations with al-Qaeda, and receive additional training. According to available information, he returned to Somalia in 2000 or 2001 to become the leader of a militant group in Mogadishu. In September 2006 Ayro was appointed by Sheikh Dahir Aweys as the head of al-Shabaab, a position he held till May 1, 2008, when he was killed in a U.S. airstrike. Ayro was replaced by Godane, one of the original founders of al-Shabaab.

Although the ICU refrained from aligning directly with either al-Shabaab or al-Qaeda, the earlier allegiance with key members with al-Qaeda and the involvement of foreigners in its operations were unmistakable. For example, in July 2006 Sheikh Yusuf Indohaadde (an ICU leader implicated in weapons smuggling) was featured in a video that showed "Arab fighters preparing for a major battle on the northern outskirts of Mogadishu. Arabic anthems and poetry play on the audio track urging Muslims to join the global holy war to advance Islam and defeat its enemies."[11]

On September 18, 2006, the first suicide bombing in Somali history targeted President Abdullahi Yusuf outside the parliament building. The blast and a subsequent gun battle killed eleven people, including the president's brother.[12] Within weeks, the ICU declared a jihad on Ethiopia. Since this attack, Somalia's Transitional Federal Government (TFG) has lost a number of high-ranking security officials and political leaders. In contrast to AQIM in Algeria, al-Shabaab used suicide attacks in Kenya, Tanzania, and Somalia before its allegiance with al-Qaeda.

The invasion of Somalia by Ethiopian troops, backed by the United States, in 2006 prompted an outcry among the Somali diaspora worldwide. Within Somalia, a foreign enemy provided al-Shabaab with a new resolve. Under Abu Mansur, who served as a military commander and spokesman for al-Shabaab, the group began to post propaganda videos on the Internet. Through this platform al-Shabaab managed to connect with hardcore Somalis within the diaspora, leading to radicalization and eventually recruitment. In one weekly forum in September 2008, Abu Mansur claimed that the establishment of the "Islamic Emirate of Somalia" would be "imminent."[13]

Despite the withdrawal of Ethiopia from Somalia in January 2009, al-Shabaab continued to aggressively recruit foreign fighters through its Internet-driven propaganda network. Al-Qaeda used the replacement of the Ethiopians by African Union peacekeepers from Uganda and Burundi to enhance its influence in Somalia and beyond, claiming that this external interference was a Christian invasion of a Muslim country. This sentiment attracted members of the Somali expatriate communities to return to Somalia to fight for the "liberation" of their homeland. Among the foreigners who executed some of the most devastating attacks was Shirwa Ahmed of Minneapolis, who on October 28, 2008, participated in simultaneous suicide bombings in Hargeisa, the capital of Somaliland, that targeted the presidential palace, the UNDP compound, and the Ethiopian embassy. At least twenty people were killed, and more than thirty others were injured. At the same time, the intelligence service in Bosaso, Puntland, was attacked by two other suicide bombers.

On September 17, 2009, two suicide bombers—among them Omar Mohamed Mahmoud, a Somali American who lived in United States until 2007—targeted the headquarters of AMISOM. Among those who died was the AMISOM deputy commander, Major General Juvenal Niyonguruza, who was about to complete his tour of duty in Somalia, and the Ugandan general Nathan Mugisha, was among the wounded. The death toll rose to twenty-one, including seventeen peacekeepers. Al-Shabaab confirmed that the attack was in retaliation for the death of Salah Ali Nabhan (linked to the U.S. embassy bombings), who was killed in southern Somalia on September 14, 2009, during a raid by U.S. Special Forces.

On December 3, 2009, Abdulrahman Ahmed Haji, a Danish Somali who moved to Somalia in 2008, disguised himself as a woman and attacked a graduation ceremony attended by forty-three medical, engineering, and computer science students of Benadir University in Mogadishu. The incident took place at the Shamo Hotel as the graduation ceremony was about to start. Among the twenty-two people killed in the attack were the ministers for health (Qamar Aden Ali), higher education (Ibrahim Hassan Adow), and education (Ahmed Abdullahi Wayeel). Among the 200 injured was Sports Minister Suleyman Olad Roble, who later also died.

In addition to circumstantial evidence of al-Shabaab's allegiance with al-Qaeda, Abu Zubayr (Godane) issued a communiqué in June 2008 through the Global Islamic Media Foundation, al-Qaeda's media outlet, in which he stated that the movement was fighting within the framework of the global jihad. He additionally sent his greetings to Osama bin Laden, Mullah Mohammad Omar, and Abu Omar al-Baghdadi. On September 2, 2008, Ali Saleh Nabhan issued a twenty-four-minute video titled *March Forth* that was featured on four of al-Qaeda's Web forums: al-Ekhlaas, al-Boraq, al-Hesbah, and al-Firdaws.

This was the eighth video produced by al-Shabaab since January but the first to feature Nabhan. He first greeted bin Laden:

> My greetings to the courageous commander and my honorable leader: Sheikh Osama bin Laden (may Allah protect him and his followers). I hope from Allah the highest . . . that this salutation reaches you while you are in ease and good health. Allah knows how much we long for your meeting and the delight of your gentle voice. . . . My sheikh! The heart offers you thousand greetings combined with my love and

humility. My salutation is nostalgia and my love is permanent, filled with the truth of the emotions of the poets.

Recognizing other conflict areas, Nabhan continued:

> I greet the lions of the forest in Iraq and Afghanistan, the lions of war in Palestine and Chechnya, and the army of Tawheed in the Maghreb and elsewhere. My salutations to you and to every free man who for the sake of the religion offers the worldly life and the swords of the swordsmen have been drawn like an emerging lightning follows by thunder. And to every fighter who carries the sword in the face of the cross, to my companions of the path, to the intimates of my road, to the targeted Islamic nation, my love for you is not hidden. How could it be while every eye expresses with the love of Allah the exalted I love you. Love which illuminates the sides of my heart.

The video also encouraged Muslims beyond Somalia to participate in the jihad in Somalia:

> Oh Muslim youth everywhere, don't forget the calls of your brothers in Somalia . . . What are you waiting for if you do not wage Jihad now? When will you wage Jihad? Oh Muslim youth! Free your brothers from the nightmare of oppression and the hammer of punishment. Seek death so that you will be offered life, come forward to Jihad so that you will be granted dignity in this life and in the next. . . . I say, people of Kenya, Tanzania, Nigeria, Uganda and Chad! Will you not take your share of the Jihad? Will you nut rush to the help of your brothers in the army of difficulty? We are waiting for reinforcement from Sudan and Yemen, of wisdom and faith. Rise up from your seats in the house of your mothers and join in the caravan of the protectors of Tawheed in the forests of glory and dignity and be among those who raise the black banner in Somalia, the first time after the invasion of the Abyssinian rabble.[14]

Ayman al-Zawahiri acknowledged al-Shabaab in video distributed on November 19, 2008, calling them "my brothers, the lions of Islam in Somalia. . . . Rejoice in victory and conquest and hold tightly to the truth for which you have given your lives, and don't put down your weapons before the Mujahid state of Islam and Tawheed has been set up in Somalia."[15]

Further evidence came in June 2009 when Sheikh Mustafa al-Yazid, a senior al-Qaeda leader suggested that al-Qaeda had personnel in Somalia training and operating alongside al-Shabaab. Additionally, a number of rumors in 2010 suggested that, al-Qaeda's East African cell under Fazul, assisted by foreign jihadists, was playing an increasingly influential role within al-Shabaab, most notably by assisting the ideological hardliners within al-Shabaab, especially Godane and Sheikh Fuad Muhammad Khalaf (alias Shangole), to formally align al-Shabaab with al-Qaeda.[16] In addition to the already-mentioned "foreign" suicide attackers, a number of non-Somalis and Somalis that had a long jihadi pedigree are found in the top structure of al-Shabaab, most notably the Saudi-born Shangole, financier; Abu Suleiman al-Banadiri, a Somali of Yemeni descent who was trained in Afghanistan and is considered to be an adviser to Godane; Abu Musa Mombassa, a Pakistani, who arrived to replace Saleh Ali Nabhan after he was killed and is in charge of security and training; Mohamoud Mujajir, from Sudan, in charge of recruitment of suicide bombers; and Abdifatah Aweys Abu Hamsa, a Somali national trained in Afghanistan, who is commander of the Mujahidin of al-Quds.[17]

Because of Somalia's close proximity to Yemen, the threat of closer ties with al-Qaeda through al-Qaeda in the Arabian Peninsula (AQAP) only increases. For example, the association with Abu Mansur al-Amriki, who also appears in a number of al-Shabaab propaganda videos emphasizes this observation. On May 13, 2009, Godane classified the Somalia jihad as part of a broader campaign: "We will fight and the wars will not end until Islamic Sharia is implemented in all continents in the world and until Muslims liberate Jerusalem."

Following the death of Saleh Ali Nabhan, by a U.S. strike off Baraawe, in September 2009, Godane expressed al-Shabaab's growing allegiance with al-Qaeda in a video, affirming the organization's loyalty to Osama bin Laden. The video featured a large crowd waving their guns and chanting, "Here we are Osama! We are your soldiers Osama!" as well as audio clips from a previous bin Laden video in which he said, "Fight on O Champions of Somalia."[18] It was also after the death of Nabhan that Osama bin Laden appointed Fazul Abdullah Mohammad as the leader of al-Qaeda in the Horn of Africa (previously he served as al-Qaeda's operational chief and intelligence chief for the ICU). At his acceptance speech during an open ceremony in Kismayo, Fazul said, "I will honestly perform my duties following my appointment to this new big position by Sheikh Osama bin Laden (Allah save him)." Fazul also made clear his intentions to target neighboring countries: "Praise be to Allah, after Somalia we will proceed to Djibouti, Kenya, and Ethiopia." Godane then praised Fazul's skill in training Somali jihadis.[19] It was therefore not a surprise that the cell that was responsible for the Kampala bombings was referred to as the Saleh Ali Nabhan Brigade. The killing of Nabhan also set in motion the plans to attack Kampala.[20] In other words, the attacks avenged the death of a central figure in al-Qaeda's East Africa cell and important role-player in al-Shabaab.

Then later, in February 2010 Sheikh Hassan Turki, commander of the Kamboni militia (aligned to Hizbul Islam), and Godane from al-Shabaab issued the following statement: "We have agreed to join the international jihad of al-Qaeda. . . . We have also agreed to unite al-Shabaab and Kamboni mujahideen to liberate the Eastern and Horn of Africa community who are under the feet of minority Christians."[21]

After establishing its allegiance to al-Qaeda, al-Shabaab executed its first attack outside Somalia's borders on July 11, 2010.

THE ATTACKS ON JULY 11, 2010

As the rest of the world watched the FIFA World Cup final between Spain and the Netherlands, Uganda experienced one of the worst terrorist attacks in its history. Two suicide bombers detonated their devices at approximately 10:25 p.m. at the Ethiopian Village Restaurant and at 11:15 p.m. at the Kyadondo Rugby Club. In the first attack at the Ethiopian Village, situated in Kabalagala neighborhood, fifteen people were killed. The second attack, which consisted of two explosions, at the Kyadondo Rugby Club in Nakawa, resulted in the death of forty-nine people. Initially sixty-four people died (later rising to seventy-four) and an additional fifty-seven were admitted to various hospitals. While the majority of the casualties were Ugandan nationals, six Eritreans, one Ethiopian, an Indian, an Irish national, and an American national were among the fatalities.[22] After the blasts, an unexploded vest and a mobile phone were found in a Makindye discotheque.

Two contributing factors explain why Uganda was targeted (and not Ethiopia or Kenya as previously warned). First, Uganda contributes an estimated 2,700 peacekeepers to Somalia and replaced Ethiopia since its withdrawal from Somalia as one of al-Shabaab's primary enemies. Al-Shabaab considers AMISOM as its only obstacle in finally overthrowing the Transnational Federal Government.[23] Although this is considered to be its first attack outside Somalia, al-Shabaab made previous threats against Uganda, for example, threatening to attack Kampala and Bujumbura in Burundi during the 2009 festival season.[24] This was followed by a call from Abu Mansur, on July 5, 2010, to Islamist fighters around the world to attack the embassies of Burundi and Uganda: "We tell the Muslim youths and Mujahideens wherever they are in the Muslim world to attack, explode and burn the embassies of Burundi and Uganda in the world."[25]

Second, al-Shabaab and Hizbul Islam were very vocal in condemning and even banning any form of entertainment, including cinemas, DVDs, and playing and watching football. According to Sheikh Mohamed Abdi Aros: "We are warning all the youth of Somalia not to dare watch these World Cup matches. It is a waste of money and time and they will not benefit anything or get any experience by watching mad men jumping up and down."[26] On June 13 members of Hizbul Islam raided houses in Afgoi, arrested thirty-five, and killed two brothers for following the World Cup.[27] In another example, on July 7 at least two men were killed and three more injured after assailants hurled a grenade at a house in Mogadishu. Those inside were targeted for watching the Spain-Germany match.[28]

By targeting the World Cup final, those behind the attack made sure that they would not only cause massive casualties but also maximize the propaganda value of the attack. The symbolism of the date, the eleventh, should also not be ignored.

CLAIMING RESPONSIBILITY AND IDENTIFYING THE PERPETRATORS

Even before al-Shabaab claimed responsibility, many expected that the group was behind the attacks. For example, two days before the bombings, Abu Mansur had called for militants to attack sites in Uganda and Burundi. Immediately following the attack, Sheikh Yusuf Sheik Issa, an al-Shabaab commander, indicated that he was happy with the attacks in Uganda (while refusing to claim responsibility): "Uganda is one of our enemies. Whatever makes them cry, makes us happy. May Allah's anger be upon those who are against us."[29] Sheikh Ali Mohamud Rage, al-Shabaab's spokesman, announced on July 12: "We warned Uganda not to deploy troops to Somalia; they ignored us. . . . We warned them to stop massacring our people, and they ignored that. The explosions in Kampala were only a minor message to them. . . . We will target them everywhere if Uganda does not withdraw from our land."[30]

At the time of the attack, al-Shabaab was under the leadership of Godane, alias Sheikh Mukhtar Abu Zubayr; Fazul Abdullah Mohammad, who served as al-Shabaab's commander in chief; and Abu Musa Mombassa (a Pakistani national), its head of security. Abu Zubayr and Fazul in particular planned the Kampala bombings. Mohamood Mugisha, arrested before the attacks, confirmed in a press conference while in custody that the order came from Abu Zubayr. He also admitted that he joined al-Shabaab in 2008 and was tasked with renting a house to be used as an operations base. He initially rented a house in Nakulabye, a suburb in Kampala that al-Shabaab decided was too close to Ugandan soldiers.[31] In addition to the involvement in planning the attack of senior al-Qaeda members based in Somalia, the attack involved individuals in Kenya, Tanzania, and Uganda.

According to an organigram provided by security officials in Uganda following the attack, Fazul was the leader of the network. A person known as Omar Badrudin, identified as al-Qaeda's head of intelligence in Nairobi, reported directly to him, as did an individual called Bilal el-Berjawi, whose exact responsibilities were not provided. Omar Awadh Omar (alias Abu Sahal),[32] identified as Fazul's number two (currently detained in Uganda) was in contact with Badrudin in Nairobi and also with Hamid Mohamed Suleiman (alias Abu Zeinab, part of the Nairobi cell) and Hussein Hassan Agade (alias Gogo La Tanga or Prof or Muhadir, formerly known as Alex Lishama Agade), both in custody in Uganda. The following individuals reported to Hamid Mohamed Suleiman (alias Abu Zeinab, of the Nairobi cell): Yahya Suleiman Mbutia (alias Yasul), Musa Hussein Abdi (alias Musa Dheere), Habib Suleiman Njoroge (alias Bibu), and Abu Aiman Mzee (alias Mzwanda, in custody in Uganda).[33]

Issa Ahmed Luyima (alias Abu Zargawi), Sheikh Magondu (alias Doctor, formerly known as Christopher Magondu)—both detained in Uganda—and two individuals identified as Mohamed Ali and Jabir formed the second tier of the Uganda network. Mohamed Ali and Jabir were in contact with Hijjaar Nyamadondo Selemani Salim Hassan Ali (alias Salim King) and Abubakar Batemyeto (alias Nsimbi). Jabir was implicated as the bomb builder and on July 6 traveled to Uganda to make the final adjustments to the suicide vests and bags. He also taught a Somali boy how to fix detonators and test whether they were operational. Jabir left Uganda on July 8 on a Gateway bus. It is also suspected that during this time, Jabir gave Issa Ahmed Luyima an unknown amount of money for the expenses of the suicide bombers, to purchase two extra mobile phones and to vacate the safe house. Jabir (at the time of the bombing) was the only suspect allowed by al-Qaeda to escape to Somalia.[34] According to the organigram, Abubakar Batemyeto was responsible for the two suicide bombers. Although the identities of the two suicide bombers cannot be verified, they are suspected to have come from Somalia and Kenya.

The cell directly responsible for the attack included Issa Ahmed Luyima, Haruna Hassan Luyima, Idrisa Nsubuga, and Mohamood Mugisha. Issa Ahmed Luyima, the cell's leader, confessed that the suicide vests came from Somalia. He fought earlier for al-Shabaab in Somalia. He had also studied at Brilliant and Kawempe High School in Kawempe before working at Kampala International University. In a press conference, Issa Ahmed Luyima admitted that he recruited his brother (Haruna Hassan Luyima) as well as the Somali and Kenyan bombers and he examined the target places. "My rage was against the Americans whom I deemed were responsible for all the sufferings of Muslims around the world. Our aim was to kill Americans. I did not want to work with my brother but recruiting other people was very risky, so I manipulated him."[35] Luyima passed through Kenya to enter Uganda, delivered the suicide vests to his brother, and returned to Kenya before the attacks were executed.[36] According to investigations, Hassan Luyima, Issa Luyima, and Idrisa Nsubuga visited the three intended targets on July 9 to assess security. Issa arrived in Nairobi on the morning of July 11 and met with Jabir, who was with Mohammed Ali. Issa then left for Mombassa.[37]

Haruna Hassan Luyima, a businessman based at Majestic Plaza in Kampala, admitted that he took the Kenyan suicide bomber to Kabalagala and an explosive device to Makindye House in Kampala. According to him, Issa Luyima and Edrissa Nsubuga met him on July 10 and took him to Issa's home in Namasuba, where he met the Somali and a Kenyan suicide bomber. Issa also gave him the device he was supposed to take to Makindye House. On July 11, Haruna, along with the Kenyan suicide bomber, took a motorcycle to Kabalagala. He dropped the suicide bomber and proceeded to the Ethiopian Village Restaurant. He took the other device to Makindye but did not detonate it.[38]

Edrissa Nsubuga, a businessman at Pioneer Mall in Kampala and a bachelor of commerce student at Makerere University, was identified as the third suspect directly involved in the attack. Nsubuga confessed he took the Somali suicide bomber to Lugogo and detonated the second bomb: "On July 11, we took a boda boda to Lugogo. I put a laptop bag that contained one of the bombs on a stool under a table. When a scuffle ensued over a phone, we used the opportunity to get in. Before the Somali joined other revelers, he showed me his clock, which had the time 23:15 when the bombs were to go off. I got out and later, a blast went off. I used the phone I had to set off the second bomb." Asked why he did it, he said: "I was unemployed. I was emotionally distressed. I had problems, a lot of misunderstandings with my wife."[39]

On August 17, 2010, Joan Kagezi, the Ugandan state attorney confirmed that thirty-two suspects from Kenya, Tanzania and Uganda were charged for their suspected involvement in the bombings. Suleiman Hijar Nyamandondo, a Tanzanian national, was extradited to Uganda by the Tanzanian government soon after his arrest in July 2010. Mohamed Mohamed, a Kenyan national who was detained in Tanzania in January 2011, was also extradited to Uganda.[40]

At the end of 2012 judicial proceedings against the majority of those arrested were ongoing. But the influence of al-Qaeda through its East Africa cell was unmistakable. Although Fazul Abdullah Mohammad was killed in Mogadishu, on June 7, 2011—eliminating the last of the primary role-players in the al-Qaeda East Africa cell responsible for the U.S. embassy bombings in 1998—al-Qaeda had established a foothold in East Africa. Finding a lasting solution to instability in Somalia is central to minimizing the growing reach of al-Shabaab in countries in the broader region. That the terrorist groups can present the conflict as religious (Muslim Somalia invaded by Christian countries) and countermeasures are often religiously insensitive, adds to the volatility of the situation, particularly considering that Ugandan intelligence officials also hinted at the possible involvement of the Allied Democratic Forces (ADF) in the operation. In Kenya observers are growing more concerned about growing radicalization and al-Shabaab recruitment efforts in the coastal regions. In summary, although al-Qaeda might have lost its core in East Africa with the death of Fazul Abdullah Mohammad, al-Qaeda has not lost its appeal.

CONCLUSION

The U.S. embassy attacks in 1998, followed by the attack in Mombassa in 2002 and the Kampala bombings on July 11, 2010, were planned and executed through al-Qaeda's network in region, stretching back to Osama bin Laden's presence in Sudan. Because of instability in Somalia, al-Qaeda operatives have found a safe area to operate and launch attacks from since 1991. Al-Shabaab's allegiance secured a new base for al-Qaeda, which manifested through the Kampala attacks.

Notwithstanding its clear regional intentions, it is expected that al-Shabaab will continue to use Somalia as the hub of its activities, from recruiting Somali expatriates from Western countries—such as the United States, Canada, the United Kingdom, Sweden, and the Netherlands—to attracting fighters who participated in Iraq, Afghanistan, and Pakistan. But with Burundi and Uganda's participating in AMISOM and Kenya and Ethiopia's engagement in Somalia in 2011 and early 2012, al-Shabaab is under increasing pressure. This has led not only to the withdrawal of al-Shabaab from Mogadishu but also rumors within the organization that the group might change its name to reflect the organization's new focus.

To conclude, Somalia presents a valuable lesson to those studying the development of terrorist organizations: unresolved domestic challenges might seem unimportant for the international community, but they can provide a means of manipulation. Therefore the conflict in Somalia, which initially attracted little international attention, has consequences for the region and beyond.

NOTES

1. Marc Lacey and Benjamin Weiser, "After Attack, Kenya Traces Qaeda's Trail in East Africa," *New York Times*, December 1, 2002.

2. Wambua Sammy, "Coastline, Porous Borders Expose Kenya to Terrorists," *All Africa*, December 4, 2002.

3. Andrew England, "FBI's Most Wanted Leader of Al-Qaeda Cell Indicted for U.S. Embassy Bombing Escaped," Associated Press, June 13, 2004.

4. Daniel McGrory, Richard Ford, and Xan Rice, "Search for Bombers Centres on East Africa Connection," *Times* (London), July 26, 2005, available at http://www.timesonline.co.uk/tol/news/uk/article548062.ece.

5. "Kenyan Report Says 3 May Somalia Bombing Linked to Terror Networks," *BBC Monitoring Newsfile*, May 10, 2005.

6. Awadh Babo, "Small Village with a Reputation for Terrorism," *All Africa*, March 8, 2004, available at http://allafrica.com/stories/200403080455.html.

7. Global Jihad, "Profile: Saleh Ali Saleh Nabhan," October 18, 2007, available at http://www.globaljihad.net/view_page.asp?id=497.

8. Nick Grace, "Shabaab Leader Sanctioned as Zawahiri Responds to Group's Oath of Loyalty," *The Long War Journal*, November 21, 2008, available at http://www.longwarjournal.org/archives/2008/11/shabaab_leader_sanct.php.

9. Bill Roggio, "Senior al Qaeda Operative Killed in Somalia," *The Long War Journal*, September 1, 2008, available at http://www.longwarjournal.org/archives/2008/09/senior_al_qaeda_oper_1.php

10. Will Hartley and Matthew Henman, "JTIC Country Briefing—Somalia," Jane's Terrorism and Insurgency Centre, September 1, 2010.

11. Bill Roggio, "Al Qaeda in Somalia," *The Long War Journal*, July 5, 2006, available at http://www.longwarjournal.org/archives/2006/07/alqaeda_in_somalia_u.php.

12. Somali Leader Escapes Attack," *New York Times*, September 18, 2006, available at http://www.nytimes.com/2006/09/18/world/africa/18iht-capital.2851800.html (accessed March 14, 2011)

13. Grace, "Shabaab Leader Sanctioned."

14. Nick Grace, "Shabaab Reaches Out to Al Qaeda Senior Leaders, Announces Death Al Sudani," *The Long War Journal*, September 2, 2008, available at http://www.longwarjournal.org/archives/2008/09/shabab_reaches_out_t.php#ixzz1TxMJA9G6.

15. Ibid.

16. Hartley and Henman. "JTIC Country Briefing—Somalia."

17. "Foreign Jihadists Now Run Al Shabaab Militia—Intelligence Reports," *East African*, July 26, 2010.

18. "It's Official: Al-Shabaab Ties the Knot with Al Qaeda," *Investigative Project on Terrorism*, September 2, 2009.

19. Bill Roggio, "Al Qaeda Names Fazul Mohammed East African Commander," *The Long War Journal*, November 11, 2009, available at http://www.longwarjournal.org/archives/2009/11/al_qaeda_names_fazul.php#ixzz1U8FnRBEN.

20. Bill Roggio, "Uganda Attack Carried Out by Shabaab Cell Named After Slain Al Qaeda Leader," *The Long War Journal*, July 15, 2010, available at http://www.longwarjournal.org/archives/2010/07/shabaab_cell_that_ca.php.

21. "Somalia's Rebel Groups Unite, Profess Loyalty to Al-Qaeda," *Daily Star* (Beirut), February 2, 2010.

22. Phillipa Croome, "Eritreans Lost Six of Their Own but They Soldier On," *Daily Monitor* (Kampala), July 11, 2011, available at http://www.monitor.co.ug/SpecialReports/-/688342/1198672/-/uvsro9/-/index.html.

23. "UPDF in Somalia Hit by Strange Disease," *All Africa*, July 29, 2009, available at http://allafrica.com/stories/200907300007.html.

24. "African Union Envoy Says Al-Qa'idah Training Fighters in Somalia," BBC, December 21, 2009.

25. "Somali Islamist Leader Calls for Uganda, Burundi Embassy Attacks," Xinhua General News Service, July 5, 2010.

26. "Inevitable World Cup Thread," *Libcom*, June 15, 2010, available at http://libcom.org/forums/libcommunity/inevitable-world-cup-thread-07062010?page=2.

27. "Somali Islamists Kill Two for Watching World Cup," Reuters, June 16, 2010.

28. "Two Killed for Watching World Cup," *Africa News*, July 8, 2010.

29. Max Delany and Jason Straziuso, "Sixty-Four Die in Uganda Attacks During World Cup," Associated Press, July 12, 2010.

30. Max Delany and Jason Straziuso, "New Al-Qaida Threat: Somali Group Claims Blasts" Associated Press, July 13, 2010.

31. "Kampala Blasts Four Main Suspects," *Global Jihad*, March 6, 2011.

32. Awadh is a well respected businessman in Kenya who also has several businesses across East Africa that range from transport to tourism. According to Kenyan authorities he is suspected providing logistic support to both al-Shabaab and al-Qaeda's cell in East Africa. Awadh also allegedly facilitates the travel and training of new al-Shabaab recruits in Somalia, coordinated by the Nairobi cell. During the week before his arrest in Uganda, he allegedly acquired eighteen different mobile phones and eighteen SIM cards, which he used to communicate with al-Shabaab operatives in Uganda.

33. Barbara Among, "Uganda: Police Foil Another Bomb Attack in Kampala," *African Crisis*, September 27, 2010, available at http://www.africancrisis.co.za/Article.php?ID=83511&.

34. Steven Candia, "Uganda Detains Top Al-Shabaab Commander," *New Vision*, September 23, 2010, available at http://www.newvision.co.ug/PA/8/12/732933.

35. "Kampala Blasts Four Main Suspects."

36. Andante Okanya, Edward Anyoli, and Angela Nalumansi, "Kampala 7/11 Bomb Suspects Confess," *New Vision*, August 10, 2010, available at http://www.newvision.co.ug/D/8/12/728385

37. Candia, "Uganda Detains Top Al-Shabaab Commander."

38. "Kampala Blasts Four Main Suspects."

39. Ibid.

40. "Tanzania Allows Kenyan Kampala Bomb Suspect Extradition," *All Africa*, July 2, 2011.

Conclusion

BRUCE HOFFMAN AND FERNANDO REINARES

Three main conclusions emerge from this volume on the evolution of the global terrorism threat in the decade following the September 11, 2001, attacks. First and foremost is that from the time of those transformative events and bin Laden's killing a decade later, al-Qaeda remained a clearly defined and active terrorist organization with an identifiable leadership and chain of command. Further, al-Qaeda embraced a goal-oriented strategy that was repeatedly communicated and explained to its enemies and adherents alike. Although its core leadership was eroded progressively by death or capture and its operational capabilities were commensurately degraded, the fact remains that, during this period, al-Qaeda continued to consistently plan and sometimes successfully execute terrorist attacks in a variety of countries and expanded into a global terrorism structure with decentralized and autonomous territorial extensions.

Second, global jihadism or global jihadist terrorism as a whole became a polymorphous phenomenon—not an amorphous one. Although the jihadist movement posed a less cohesive threat during the decade following the September 11 attacks, at the same time it transformed into a dynamically heterogeneous collection of both radicalized individuals and functioning terrorist organizations. Command and control of these entities was uneven, but the al-Qaeda senior leadership nonetheless appeared to have had a direct hand in the most important and potentially high-payoff operations.

Finally, the evolving global terrorism threat coming from these varie-gated jihadist actors also differed remarkably across nations and regions of the world, though in general terms it can be characterized as diverse but often composite in nature: adhering to a shared ideology and a common mind-set serving and respecting the same preeminent leader—Osama bin Laden.

GLOBAL JIHADIST TERRORISM AS A POLYMORPHOUS PHENOMENON

When U.S. Navy Seals killed bin Laden in the Pakistani town of Abbottabad on May 1, 2011, he was still al-Qaeda's indisputably and preternaturally active emir. Despite all of the constraints imposed by the national and international counterterrorism initiatives adopted after the September 11 attacks, al-Qaeda continued to function as an organized entity, exercising core command-and-control responsibilities, and—in contrast to the conventional wisdom of the time—it had not been reduced to a mere ideology or hollow shell. In the post–September 11 era, al-Qaeda relied on the continued resonance of its ideology and appeal of its brand to like-minded jihadists worldwide in order to ensure its survival and compensate for its own diminishing material and human resources.

Decentralizing, allowing the formation of its own territorial extensions or branches, often referred to as franchises, was a critical component of al-Qaeda's adaptive move and its conversion to a global terrorism structure. In the early case of al-Qaeda in the Arabian Peninsula (AQAP), the group emerged from preexisting structures in the region. Al-Qaeda in Iraq (AQI) and al-Qaeda in the Islamic Maghreb (AQIM), on the other hand, were formed through agreements of mutual convenience with preexisting and geographically dominant jihadist organizations. AQI thus resulted from a deal with al-Tawhid wal-Jihad that brought that group within the broader al-Qaeda framework; AQIM emerged from a pact concluded by al-Qaeda's senior leadership with the Salafist Group for Preaching and Combat (GSPC), an offshoot of the more locally focused Armed Islamic Group of Algeria (GIA). Both al-Tawhid wal-Jihad and GSPC disappeared following the formal establishment of AQI and AQIM, respectively.

Al-Qaeda also adapted to the constrained post–September 11 operational environment that the U.S.-led global war on terrorism imposed on the core organization by fostering and strengthening ties with other new and existing jihadist groups. In some cases, this process led to the formal merger of existing entities with al-Qaeda. More often, however, the process involved a reinforcement of associative exchanges as opposed to actual mergers or formal alliances, such as between al-Qaeda and established organizations like the Islamic Emirate of Afghanistan (the Afghan Taliban) alongside the establishment of new affiliates from also recently created organizations such as the Tehreek-e-Taliban-e-Pakistan (TTP) and al-Shabaab in Somalia. Al-Qaeda leaders also cultivated ties with a number of smaller entities of the same Salafi jihadist ideology and orientation that had either existed before September 11, 2001, or emerged during the following decade.

Additionally, al-Qaeda leaders tried, with limited success, to promote—primarily through the organization's audiovisual propaganda—the mobilization of self-selected, independently constituted cells of self-radicalized individuals and so-called lone wolves, or people operating completely on their own, in many countries of the world, but most especially in the West. Inspired by al-Qaeda's ideology, both categories generally lacked significant, much less actual connections with existing terrorist organizations. But, by inspiring, motivating, and animating this array of self-trained, auto-radicalized jihadists, al-Qaeda could capitalize on their ideological affinity and exploit their violent inclinations simply by providing sufficient encouragement to carry out jihad. In other cases, however, independent jihadist individuals and cells look to establish a connection with al-Qaeda core or with al-Qaeda's territorial extensions or associate entities.

Thus, by the time of Osama bin Laden's death in 2011, the phenomenon of global jihadism—or global jihadist terrorism—comprised four separate but interconnected components:

Al-Qaeda Central or al-Qaeda Core

Al-Qaeda central comprised the remnants of the pre–September 11 al-Qaeda organization. Although its core leadership was progressively weakened as a result of the U.S. drone campaign and the number of its members decreased considerably, this hardcore nucleus continued to be based in or around Pakistan. It remained active in the ideation, planning, and preparation of major terrorist attacks in and outside the West throughout the period covered in this book, that is to say, from September 11, 2001, to the killing of Osama bin Laden in May 2011. Bin Laden's hope to perpetrate Mumbai-style attacks in some European cities, which was aborted late in 2010, is a good example. Al-Qaeda core also maintained some coordination and, in some cases, command capabilities over organizations belonging to other components of global jihadist terrorism, in terms of ordering attacks, directing surveillance, and collating reconnaissance of potential targets, planning operations, and approving their execution.

Al-Qaeda's Territorial Extensions or Branches

This component of global jihadist terrorism included AQAP, AQI, and AQIM. Interaction between al-Qaeda central and the territorial extensions or branches varied depending on the latter's antecedents, organizational history, leadership and commanders, internal dynamics, operational circumstances, and capacity to function independently of the parent organization. Regardless, a distinctive, often exclusive bond was forged between al-Qaeda's general command and its territorial extensions. The leaders of AQAP, AQI, and AQIM all pledged the *bayat*, or oath of allegiance, to the emir of al-Qaeda core, first to bin Laden and, following his death, to al-Zawahiri. Al-Qaeda's territorial extensions or branches can develop mutual interactions and establish links with other affiliated entities. Together with al-Qaeda core, they evolved into a global terrorism structure.

Entities Affiliated and Associated with al-Qaeda

This component includes formally established insurgent or terrorist organizations that over the years have benefited from bin Laden's largesse or spiritual guidance or have received training, arms, money, and other assistance from al-Qaeda core or from al-Qaeda's territorial extensions. This component is heterogeneous and includes groups like the Afghan Taliban, TTP, al-Shabaab, Lashkar-e-Taiba (LeT), Harakat ul-Mujahideen (HuM), Jemaah Islamiyah (JI), the Islamic Movement of Uzbekistan (IMU), and the Islamic Jihad Union (IJU), for example, all of which have aligned closely with al-Qaeda. Between 9/11 and the killing of Osama bin Laden other such affiliated and associated groups were active but disappeared by merger or exhaustion, such as the Libyan Islamic Fighting Group (LIFG) or the Moroccan Islamic Combatant Group (MICG).

Independent Jihadist Cells and Individuals

This fourth component incorporates two categories: On the one hand, jihadist adherents, active inside cells or isolated, who have had some terrorism experience as part of previous jihadist campaigns, such as those in Algeria, the Balkans, Chechnya, and, perhaps more recently, Iraq; they may also have been trained in an al-Qaeda facility in Pakistan, Yemen, Sudan, Somalia, or elsewhere. Their distinguishing characteristic is that there is some kind of previous connection with al-Qaeda. On the other hand, this last component of global jihadist terrorism includes Islamist radicals who have no direct connection with al-Qaeda (or any other identifiable jihadist terrorist organization) but nonetheless are prepared to carry out attacks in solidarity with or support of al-Qaeda's jihadist agenda. These individuals belong to no organized terrorist group, nor are they part of any terrorist chain of command.

Therefore, in the years following September 11 it was no longer possible to equate the global terrorism threat solely with the threat posed by al-Qaeda central. As it evolved into a polymorphous phenomenon, the global terrorism threat diversified both geographically and organizationally. Acts of jihadist terrorism became frequent in a variety of South Asian and Middle Eastern countries such as Afghanistan, Pakistan, and Iraq; somewhat frequent in Northern and Eastern African countries such as

Algeria and Somalia; and more sporadically occurring in places as diverse as Kenya, Turkey, Saudi Arabia, Morocco, Spain, and the United Kingdom. Organizations including the Islamic Emirate of Afghanistan (IEA), TTP, and AQI have presented the most serious and sustained threats in the countries in which they operated, often in alliances with other terrorist or insurgent groups active in those same areas.

At the same time, though, it is clear that, even as al-Qaeda evolved into a different organizational entity than existed on September 11, it continued to pursue a core strategy that embraced of six key components.

First, it sought to overwhelm, distract, and exhaust its adversaries, especially at a time of growing global economic difficulty. Al-Qaeda asserts that its ultimate victory will not be achieved militarily but rather by undermining the economies of its opponents, exhausting their finances, and wearing out their militaries. This strategy of attrition has been tightly woven into the al-Qaeda's narrative. In bin Laden's last videotape message, released just days before the American presidential election in 2004, he claimed credit for having spent the comparatively modest sum of half a million dollars to implement the September 11 attacks against the United States. By comparison, bin Laden argued, the United States has had to spend trillions of dollars on domestic security arrangements and foreign military expeditions. He therefore speciously claimed credit for America's economic travails and the fiscal developments that led to the fall of the U.S. financial juggernaut. Such assertions were, of course, completely divorced from reality. However, propaganda does need not to be true to be believed; it just has to be effectively communicated. Al-Qaeda's message in this respect acquired greater resonance than ever in light of the real and continuing economic troubles in the United States and the West.

Second, throughout this time period al-Qaeda actively sought to create, foster, and encourage divisions within the global alliance arrayed against it. This accounted for its focus on either encouraging or mounting attacks within the territory of close U.S. allies in Western Europe, such as the United Kingdom, Spain, the Netherlands, and Germany. This entailed the selective targeting of coalition partners in the U.S.-led war on terrorism both in the actual theaters of these operations (i.e., attacks directly specifically against perceived "weaker" NATO partners committed to the International Security Assistance Force in Afghanistan, such as the British, Canadian, Dutch, German, and Italian contingents) and at home—through attacks on mass transit and other "soft" targets in the national capitals and major cities of European countries allied with the United States (e.g., the 2004 Madrid and 2005 London bombings and the terrorist plots with links back to Pakistan foiled in 2007 in Germany and 2008 in Spain).

Third, al-Qaeda continued to prosecute local campaigns of subversion and destabilization where failed or failing states provided new opportunities for the movement to extend its reach, consolidate its presence, or forge close relations with local jihadist organizations. Afghanistan, Pakistan, Somalia, and other areas of East Africa, North Africa, and, especially, Yemen fell within this category.

Fourth, al-Qaeda actively continued to provide guidance and assistance to local affiliates and associated terrorist movements. This support enhanced local and regional terrorist attack capabilities and strengthened the resilience of these groups, thus presenting more formidable challenges to national and local police, military forces, and intelligence agencies. Al-Qaeda thus actively worked behind the scenes in these theaters as a "force multiplier" of indigenous terrorist capacity in terms of both kinetic and essential non-kinetic operations—including information operations, propaganda, and psychological warfare.

Fifth, al-Qaeda continued to seek out citizens or legal permanent residents of enemy countries, especially converts to Islam, who possessed "clean" passports and could deploy for attacks in Western countries without necessarily arousing suspicion. In other words, these people, whose passports retained their birth names rather than an adopted religious name, were intended to provide al-Qaeda with the ultimate "fifth column"—individuals whose appearance and names would not arouse the same scrutiny from immigration officials, border security officers, and national police, security, and intelligence services as people from Muslim countries with distinctly Muslim names might.

Finally, al-Qaeda remained as opportunistic as it was instrumental. In this respect, while its leaders planned and encouraged international terrorist attacks, they also continued to monitor al-Qaeda's enemies' defenses: identifying gaps and vulnerabilities that could be transformed into opportunities and quickly exploited for attack.

EVOLVING GLOBAL TERRORISM THREAT IN THE WEST

Between September 11 and the death of bin Laden, the global terrorism threat to Western countries diversified. Al-Qaeda's involvement in both executed and thwarted attacks continued, albeit at varying levels and degrees. New and old organizations, including al-Qaeda's emerging territorial branches, carried out attacks sometimes, but not always, in conjunction with the core al-Qaeda organization. The Internet also grew as a recruitment tool, inspiring participation in global jihad by independent cells and lone individuals alike. The diversity of the al-Qaeda universe and the means that facilitated its emergence and growth in the decade following the September 11 attacks are apparent throughout this volume.

In chapter 1, Lorenzo Vidino focused on the changing nature of the global terrorism threat facing the United States since the September 11 attacks. He cogently notes that until mid-2003, virtually all conspiracies to execute a jihadist terrorist operation on American soil had been planned by al-Qaeda core. However, its failure to replicate its spectacular success of September 11 resulted in a shift from sophisticated, remotely controlled and directed operations to the encouragement of homegrown and amateurish plots that were planned independently by cells or by individuals acting entirely on their own. The new counterterrorism measures adopted by the United States after September 11 combined with the loss al-Qaeda's sanctuary in Afghanistan account for this change. Al-Qaeda, accordingly, scaled down to smaller operations, using perpetrators with "unique" characteristics (speaking English, Western passports, etc.). Although this produced a remarkable decrease in the sophistication of al-Qaeda operations compared to the pre–September 11 period, it nonetheless demonstrated al-Qaeda's ability to produce a new generation of competent operational leaders and personnel capable of planning operations entirely on their own—even if their execution remained flawed, uneven, and, in some cases, completely inept. This process, however, was neither rigidly adhered to nor linear. It changed course dramatically in September 2009, for instance, with the arrest of Najibullah Zazi and two other confederates who were subsequently convicted of a plot to replicate the July 7, 2005, bombings of the London Underground with identical suicide attacks on the New York City subway. Their direct connection with al-Qaeda's remaining leadership in Pakistan marked a worrisome return to centrally planned and directed attacks against al-Qaeda's external enemies.

The diversity of the sources of global terrorist threats in Western Europe is clearly revealed in chapter 2. Fernando Reinares explains that the coordinated March 11, 2004, train blasts in Madrid were a particularly complex example of al-Qaeda's successful infiltration of that region in the years both before and after the September 11 attacks and the sophisticated operational capabilities it had developed by the early part of the twenty-first century. In this case, al-Qaeda's North African affiliates, especially the now extinct MICG, were heavily implicated in the planning and preparation of the bombings, thus demonstrating the salient operational role that al-Qaeda affiliates had come to play in the movement's strategy and continuing efforts to wage global jihad.

Bruce Hoffman's analysis of the July 7, 2005, suicide bombings in London in chapter 8, on the other hand, shed important light on how al-Qaeda's senior leadership clearly exercised command, control, and communication over the recruitment, training, and direction of local operatives enlisted to carry out the coordinated attacks on that city's mass-transit system. Besides al-Qaeda's involvement, the assistance of its Pakistani jihadist allies was enlisted in addition to local British operatives. Lindsay Clutterbuck's analysis of Operation Rhyme in London in chapter 3 and Peter Neumann and Ryan Evans's examination of the London Crevice Operation in chapter 4 highlight the dispersion of al-Qaeda's ideology throughout Western Europe. In both operations, terrorists who were well integrated into al-Qaeda's chain of command returned to London with orders to recruit local radicals and establish terrorist cells to carry out attacks there. These three cases all involved British nationals who traveled to Pakistan to receive training at al-Qaeda camps and then plotted to carry out mass-casualty attacks back in the U.K. using local violent jihadists. Indeed, the Hoffman, Clutterbuck, and Neumann and Evans chapters demonstrate a pattern of al-Qaeda operations in Britain that emanated from Pakistan but were implemented by radicalized locals who were trained and guided by al-Qaeda core.

In addition to the London plots and attack, al-Qaeda's senior leadership was deeply connected to a number of disrupted plots in Western countries between 2006 and 2011. Some of these, following the London model, aimed at the execution of major acts of terrorism centrally directed and orchestrated by al-Qaeda from its hub in Pakistan. The disrupted August 2006 plot to blow up at least seven North America–bound transatlantic airplanes departing from Heathrow airport was no less ambitious in scope and complexity than the September 11 attacks. This case is examined by Paul Cruickshank in chapter 9. It was a plot that again involved considerable hands-on involvement by senior al-Qaeda leaders. It also clearly demonstrated al-Qaeda's continued preoccupation with targeting commercial aviation. It is significant, too, that al-Qaeda was neither daunted nor deterred from attacking this specific target set despite the tremendous improvements in aircraft security generally and passenger screening in particular, as well as the extensive intelligence and security resources devoted to securing air travel in the years since September 11. The 2006 airline plot also further underscored al-Qaeda's intention and ability to recruit Western-based operatives along with the regeneration of the organization's global attack capabilities despite the setbacks resulting from the 2001 U.S. and allied invasion of Afghanistan and al-Qaeda's expulsion to Pakistan.

Additional plots, including the 2006 Toronto 18 incident analyzed by Stewart Bell in chapter 6, identified the role that al-Qaeda propaganda played in inspiring local terrorist activity in the West. In this chapter, Bell argues that the Toronto group is a prime example of how terrorist propaganda constitutes an effective form of leadership as it inspires activity in the absence of any direct command and control from al-Qaeda. A small number of Canadian citizens thus became increasingly radicalized and dedicated to jihad following the September 11 attacks. The Internet played a major role in this process. Al-Qaeda provided neither training nor guidance and exercised no direct control over the Toronto cell. Instead, a dangerous mind-set emerged among the plotters to avenge the West's persecution of Muslims and invasion and occupation of Muslim lands that was heavily influenced by al-Qaeda's online propaganda.

Other jihadist conspiracies in Western Europe were more akin to the Madrid model, with al-Qaeda playing a variable role over time depending on which affiliate or allied organization it was working with. For example, Javier Jordán's study of the foiled 2006 attacks in Italy in chapter 10 shows that although they were planned by al-Qaeda's senior leadership, AQIM and AQI working in tandem assumed responsibility for their execution. The Italian operations were conceived before the 2006 general election in that country and therefore bear a striking similarity to the 2004 Madrid commuter-train bombings. They appear to have originated within the GSPC/AQIM hierarchy among men who also had close ties to AQI and were responding to a suggestion from bin Laden communicated through Abu Hamza. Indeed, Abu Hamza continued to serve as the key interlocutor between the AQIM and al-Qaeda senior leadership. The slow, careful, and security conscious communications between the plotters and al-Qaeda via Abu Hamza meant that the senior leadership exercised broad strategic direction of the actual planning and other tactical dimensions of the plot delegated to the AQIM and its local, homegrown sympathizers. The fusion of local, homegrown radicals with the directing hand of an al-Qaeda affiliate connecting to the core in Pakistan would become an enduring feature of post–September 11 international terrorism.

This was the pattern evident in the so-called "Sauerland plot," involving a group of radicalized individuals who planned a series of attacks on the Sauerland region of Germany in September 2007. They had close ties to the Islamic Jihad Union (IJU), based in North Waziristan, which in turn had direct links to al-Qaeda's senior leadership. As Guido Steinberg recounts in chapter 11, like those in Spain in 2004 and Italy in 2006, this terrorist plot was calculated to affect a major political event—in this case the 2007 Bundestag elections. Some years earlier, a pattern of Turkish-Arab terrorist cooperation had emerged, which the IJU was able to exploit by sending recruits to Germany to carry out attacks. Once again, we see a leader-led operation, managed by a key al-Qaeda affiliate with close liaison to the al-Qaeda core. Finally, in this same category, there are the thwarted attacks on the Barcelona Metro in January 2008 organized by the Tehreek-e-Taliban-e-Pakistan (TTP), another close al-Qaeda ally, from its base in the FATA. Although the attacks were planned by individual jihadists, as Fernando Reinares shows in chapter 13, there was a direct al-Qaeda connection to these incidents as well. Each of these cases illustrates how al-Qaeda remained active in the ideation, planning, preparation, and execution of serious acts of terrorism in Western Europe. Indeed, as evidenced in U.S. declassified documents SOCOM-2012-0000015 and SOCOM-2012-0000019, letters written by Osama bin Laden from Abbottabad shortly before he was killed in May 2011 had dispatched al-Qaeda's external operations commander, Yunis al-Mauritani, to the Middle East and North Africa to carry out attacks in Western countries.

Not all of the global terrorist attacks and conspiracies in Western Europe between September 11, 2001, and bin Laden's death in 2011 were a product of al-Qaeda, however. Unaffiliated individuals and local cells with no demonstrated connection to al-Qaeda's senior leadership or any other related terrorist organizations abroad were an important part of the jihadist threat. Indeed, Beatrice de Graaf analyzes the November 2004 murder of filmmaker Theo van Gogh in chapter 5, noting that homegrown jihadism, inspired locally and domestically and without direct involvement from al-Qaeda, grew in the Netherlands between 2002 and 2004. De Graaf ultimately concludes that the development of jihadism in the Netherlands was a function of the internal and external pressures among diaspora communities. Government countermeasures played a pivotal role in this respect: during times of high counterterrorism activity by Dutch law-enforcement agencies, aspiring jihadists were more motivated to carry out attacks. Similarly, in chapter 12 Michael Taarnby discusses the evolution of Islamic radicalism in Denmark over the past two decades and the foreign influences on homegrown cells that impelled them to seek out the guidance and direction of the al-Qaeda core in Pakistan.

In chapter 14, Jean-Pierre Filiu examines the range of terrorist incidents that occurred in France in 2005 and 2006, concluding that the networks responsible for the attacks initially formed in reaction to the U.S.-led invasion of Iraq but later embraced mostly domestic motivations for their violence. Filiu shows how a new generation of jihadists emerged in France following the 2003 invasion and became associated with anti-Western violence. In this respect, Iraq provided local and regional militant networks, such as those of the GIA and Ansar al-Fatah, with an opportunity to mobilize for jihad. A similar case from Australia is recounted by Sally Neighbour in chapter 7, where al-Qaeda- and LeT-trained individuals formed an autonomous, homegrown group and conspired independently of senior al-Qaeda leadership to plot a series of attacks. These militants were clearly inspired and motivated by al-Qaeda—and, moreover, three had actually trained in al-Qaeda and LeT camps—but there is no evidence of any outside guidance or direction provided by terrorist leaders elsewhere. The Melbourne cell, for instance, was made up of youths from Lebanese immigrant families. As with the Toronto 18, the Internet replaced traditional training and indoctrination.

In sum, while al-Qaeda was clearly the driving force behind much of the terrorist activity that took place in the West between 2001 and 2011, several independent terrorist cells, groups, and broader networks also emerged to carry out or attempt to carry out violence inspired by al-Qaeda but motivated in these instances by parochial, locally generated grievances.

THE GLOBAL TERRORISM THREAT OUTSIDE THE WEST

The increasing diversity of the polymorphous global terrorism phenomenon was likewise manifested in other parts of the world. Global terrorism grew in both majority-Muslim societies and other non-Western countries, particularly where armed conflict was (and, in many case, remains) pervasive and acts of jihadist terrorism frequently emerged amid broader expressions of rebellious violence. The chapters devoted to cases of terrorism in South Asia, which arguably remains the epicenter of global terrorism, undeniably illustrate this. In Afghanistan, for example, acts of terrorism are often part of the local insurgency repertoire. Evidence suggests, however, that al-Qaeda, from its base in the Tribal Areas across the border in Pakistan, has played an important role in the insurgency. Despite al-Qaeda core's diminishing capabilities because of the sustained campaign of drone attacks since 2007 in the region, Seth Jones argues in chapter 15 that al-Qaeda has nonetheless continued to act as a force multiplier by coordinating with local affiliates such as the Taliban and the Haqqani network, helping to improve their tactical and operational capabilities. Across the border in Pakistan, the TTP forged close ties with al-Qaeda and other jihadist organizations active in South Asia to sustain a series of parallel, highly destructive terrorist campaigns. Jones further notes that al-Qaeda's resurgence in Afghanistan since 2007 was the result of carefully orchestrated relations between the organization's core leadership and allied regional networks. In this respect, al-Qaeda re-created itself as part of a complex, adaptive insurgency, embedding its fighters in multiple existing terrorist and insurgency organizations. All of these organizations, moreover, had different fundamental goals and objectives that al-Qaeda was able to lend support to and show solidarity with. In this respect, al-Qaeda provided these other groups with money, intelligence, training, and planning assistance that appreciably improved their tactical capabilities (especially with regard to suicide terrorist attacks). Al-Qaeda was thus able to enhance and improve the capabilities of these local allies, supporting combat operations commanded by local leaders, and through this low profile gain invaluable influence and obtain an assured sanctuary in the lawless territory along the Afghanistan-Pakistan border.

Al-Qaeda, however, does not figure prominently in the activities of the Pakistani militant jihadist organization LeT. Originally created to fight for control of the contested state of Kashmir, which is divided between India and Pakistan, the group has become increasingly international and anti-Western in its orientation and ideology, though not in its operations. The LeT, as C. Christine Fair reveals in chapter 24, has a notorious quasi-military apparatus along with a well-developed chain of command and divisional and district intra-organizational substructures. It was responsible for the November 26, 2008, attacks on multiple targets throughout Mumbai that lasted over sixty hours. The fact that a senior LeT commander in Kashmir masterminded the Mumbai operation, Fair points out, does not eliminate the possible implication of the Pakistani intelligence agency in the plot. Indeed, the Inter-Services Directorate (ISI) has historically provided guidance and support to LeT. Its alleged role in the planning and preparation for the attack provides a stunning example of state-led jihad as a form of leader-led jihad.

Rohan Gunaratna makes it clear in chapter 16 that JI in Southeast Asia was linked to al-Qaeda from its inception. Indeed, al-Qaeda's influence empowered JI to think and operate regionally rather than narrowly in Indonesia and to strike more lethally, with mass-casualty suicide attacks such as the 2002 bombings in Bali. JI's most senior operational leaders were trained in Afghanistan between 1985 and 1995, thus showing deep ties with the al-Qaeda core that pre-dated even the September 11 attacks. Al-Qaeda's influence on JI's ideology and mind-set was pivotal in its development as a dangerous regional terrorist adversary seeking to create a militant pan-Islamic state embracing Indonesia, the Philippines, Malaysia, and Singapore.

An analytically similar threat landscape emerged in Iraq, though jihadist terrorist activity in the region has varied greatly in extent and intensity since the U.S. invasion. Indeed, since 2003 AQI has been waging a systematically planned and executed campaign of sectarian terrorism, particularly by means of suicide bombings, primarily against Shiites. Interestingly though, as emphasized by Mohammed Hafez in chapter 18, AQI's strategy was created independently from the al-Qaeda senior leadership in Pakistan by the founding leader of the Iraqi branch of al-Qaeda, Abu Musab al-Zarqawi. This development challenges any simplistic view of al-Qaeda as a monolithic organization operating with a single strategy on multiple fronts. It also was far more sectarian than bin Laden and al-Zawahiri preferred; they both came to view AQI's anti-Shiite focus as counterproductive given the adverse effect that Muslims killing fellow Muslims had on global support for al-Qaeda. Significantly, the violence in Iraq, Hafez also shows, was demonstrably leader-led, evidencing a top-down leadership structure supported by a bureaucratically well developed organization.

The level of coordination between al-Qaeda core and its affiliates and associates seems to vary based on location and time. For instance, the detailed study of the May 2003 bombings in Riyadh by Thomas Hegghammer in chapter 23 illustrates that senior al-Qaeda leaders consistently overruled and micromanaged local AQAP commanders during the spasm of terrorist violence that occurred in Saudi Arabia. The attacks prompted a massive governmental crackdown by Saudi authorities that not only crushed the al-Qaeda presence in the kingdom but also fundamentally changed government and popular attitudes toward religious extremism there. Accordingly, five years later when the U.S. embassy in neighboring Yemen was bombed, al-Qaeda core's influence in the peninsula had been reduced, and the senior leadership provided little more than ideological inspiration. The two attacks are consistent with the assessment that al-Qaeda central's ability to operationally guide its various local branches decreased during the first decade of the twenty-first century. Even so, the center of gravity for al-Qaeda on the Arabian Peninsula successfully migrated southward to Yemen, where the organization was revived with AQAP's founding in early 2009. Its founder and leader, Nasir al-Wahayshi, had once served as bin Laden's personal secretary. While imprisoned in Yemen, he painstakingly mapped the infrastructure for a new al-Qaeda—a regional affiliate that would actively embrace the principles and managerial style of its parent organization but at the same time absorb and learn the lessons from past mistakes and missteps that had undermined the movement and sapped its strength. Al-Wahayshi created a clone of the al-Qaeda organization he had known in Afghanistan, selecting local emirs, or commanders, who were made personally beholden to him and would be responsible for implementing his battle plan across the country. AQAP, accordingly, is now widely regarded as posing the greatest terrorist threat both to the United States and international security—all while not adhering slavishly to the dictates of the al-Qaeda core leadership.

The Istanbul bombings of November 2003 are similarly significant in illustrating the polymorphous character of global terrorism after September 11. According to Guido Steinberg and Philipp Holtmann's analysis in chapter 19, al-Qaeda central and al-Zarqawi's AQI network played equally important but different roles at different stages of the Istanbul plot, even as relations between them became uneasy and local bombers began making their own operational choices. Nonetheless, the external influence on local jihadists in the multiple bombings is palpable. In chapter 20, Ami Pedahzur and Holy L. McCarthy conclude that the 2004 bombings of tourist targets in the Sinai Peninsula would never have occurred if al-Qaeda's ideology had not played a pivotal inspirational role.

Across Africa, the decade after September 11 similarly offered ample evidence of the evolution of the global terrorism threat. The coordinated attacks in Casablanca in May 2003, much like the incidents of March and April 2007 in the same city, involved various cells belonging to al-Qaeda affiliates in Morocco, as Jack Kalpakian describes in chapter 21. He explains how al-Qaeda gained sympathy in Morocco even as the organization's overall operational capacity progressively diminished. Although the two sets of attacks were carried out by local groups, they nonetheless conformed to a strategic decision communicated through the al-Zarqawi network. The attacks convinced the government that Salafi jihadists posed a serious threat to Morocco's security. In Algeria, the April 2007 suicide attacks in the capital, Algiers, highlighted the expanded regional ambitions of the GSPC and its merger with al-Qaeda to form and develop regionally as AQIM. This merger, which established an organization again equipped with a central command authority and divided into operational zones, implied important changes for al-Qaeda in methods and focus, though Anneli Botha observes in chapter 22 that AQIM planned and executed the April 2007 attacks in Algiers completely independent from al-Qaeda's senior leadership in Pakistan. Nonetheless, bin Laden's influence was seminal as he had encouraged the split in the GIA that resulted in the GSPC and the jihadist movement in North Africa's transition from a local, near-enemy focus to a far-enemy, more global orientation. AQIM's adoption of hallmark al-Qaeda attacks such as suicide bombings is a case in point, even if the adoption of that tactic ultimately backfired by undermining local popular support. It was perhaps for this reason that the group turned to kidnapping Western hostages for large ransoms—which served to fund not only the nascent AQIM but eventually other al-Qaeda allies elsewhere, as well.

Finally, a comparison between the November 2002 attacks in Mombassa and the July 2010 bombings in Kampala illustrates the polymorphous and increasingly composite nature of the emerging global terrorism threat. The Mombassa attacks, analyzed by Jonathan Fighel in chapter 17, involved two experienced, senior al-Qaeda commanders supported by a local terrorist network. Planning for the operation had commenced some two years before, and the attack unit was trained in Somalia before deploying to Kenya. It was financed by a long-time al-Qaeda operative based in the Sudan and planned and executed by al-Qaeda's senior leadership. The attacks were meant not just to kill and injure but to inflict economic damage to the Kenyan and Israeli economies by targeting tourism between the two countries, as well as to strike at easily accessible, soft targets (a hotel and a chartered passenger jet) and thus enhance the chances of the operation's success. Nearly eight years later, the suicide bombings in Uganda's capital emerged as a deadly expression of the allegiance between al-Qaeda and Somalia's al-Shabaab and the legacy of al-Qaeda's long-established presence in East Africa, as Anneli Botha shows in chapter 25.

In sum, between the September 11, 2001, attacks on the U.S. homeland and the killing of Osama bin Laden in May 2011, global jihadism became a polymorphous phenomenon with three broad components. First, al-Qaeda and its territorial affiliates emerged as a result of an adaptive decentralization strategy following global counterterrorism efforts and the U.S.-led invasion of Afghanistan. Second, a heterogeneous array of articulated jihadist organizations, which can be broadly considered as al-Qaeda-affiliated or -associated entities, emerged throughout this time period. Finally, proliferating independent jihadist cells and individuals completed the global terrorism threat. Additionally, as this volume demonstrates, while significant al-Qaeda-inspired terrorist activity occurred in the aftermath of the September 11 attacks, just as consequential were the proliferation and durability of its jihadist ideology. Local grievances, often in response to the treatment of Muslims in the West, inspired the formation of local networks or cells of like-minded, radicalized individuals seeking to change Western policies toward the Muslim world through the pressure of terrorist attacks. In many cases, these networks solicited al-Qaeda's assistance and sought closer relations with al-Qaeda in order to supplement their often meager resources and limited expertise while still maintaining significant independence and freedom of action in the planning and execution of their terrorist operations. Some grew to rely on al-Qaeda for ideological inspiration and guidance but developed independent leadership structures and strategies. Others were or became constituent parts of the al-Qaeda movement: nodes in elaborate transnational command, control, and communications networks adhering to the guidance or following the direct orders of al-Qaeda's senior leadership. Finally, another category comprised self-selected, entirely self-radicalized individuals inspired and motivated by al-Qaeda but who acted entirely on their own.

AL-QAEDA'S DISQUIETING LEADER-LED TRAJECTORY

Osama bin Laden, the cofounder and leader of al-Qaeda, is dead. Key lieutenants have similarly been eliminated. The fourfold increase in targeted assassinations undertaken since 2009 by the Obama administration has killed some three dozen key al-Qaeda leaders in Pakistan, as well as more than two hundred fighters, thus setting the core organization, in the words of a 2011 U.S. State Department analysis, "on a path of decline that will be difficult to reverse."

Although one cannot deny the vast inroads made against al-Qaeda core in recent years because of the developments described above, the al-Qaeda brand and ideology has proven itself as resilient as it is attractive to hardcore militants and Salafi extremists around the globe, as this volume has shown. For more than a decade, too, the core al-Qaeda command structure has consistently shown itself capable of adapting and adjusting to even the most consequential countermeasures directed against it, having, despite all odds, survived for nearly a quarter century. In this respect, weakened though it currently is, the core al-Qaeda organization has astonishingly withstood arguably the greatest international onslaught directed against a terrorist organization in history. The al-Qaeda organization has lasted longer than the overwhelming majority of contemporary terrorist movements, thus suggesting that its final elimination may take years, if not decades more to achieve.

The repercussions of the "Arab Spring" and the ongoing unrest and protracted civil war in Syria at the time of this writing have also endowed the al-Qaeda brand and, by extension, the core organization with new relevance and status that, depending on the future course of events in both that country and the surrounding region, could potentially resuscitate al-Qaeda's waning fortunes. The fact that the remnants of the al-Qaeda core continue to remain entrenched in South Asia, coupled with the planned withdrawal of U.S. forces and ISAF troops from Afghanistan, further suggests that it may well regain the breathing space and cross-border physical sanctuary needed to promote its aims and perhaps even ensure its continued existence.

Throughout its history, al-Qaeda has depended more than anything on its possession of or access to physical sanctuary and safe haven. In the turbulent wake of the Arab Spring and the political upheavals and instability that have followed, al-Qaeda has the potential to transform the toeholds that it has established over the past few years in the Levant and perhaps in the Sinai and in North and West Africa into footholds— thus complementing its established outposts in Pakistan, Afghanistan, Yemen, and Somalia.

Al-Qaeda's obituary has been written many times since the September 11, 2001, attacks, only to be proven to be wishful thinking. At the time, these views fit neatly with the prevailing consensus among government officials, academics, and pundits that al-Qaeda had ceased to exist as an organizational entity and had become nothing more than a hollow shell— an ideology without a command structure or the leadership to advance it—a leaderless entity of disparate individuals unconnected to any central authority. Bin Laden was also believed to be completely estranged from the movement he created; isolated from his fighters, sympathizers, and supporters; and unable to exercise any meaningful role in the movement's operations and future trajectory. The threat, it was argued, had therefore become primarily "bottom-up" and not "top-down"—to the extent that terrorist organizations were regarded as anachronistic and the command-and-control functions that they had traditionally exercised were said to no longer matter. Instead, it was argued, the real threat now came from self-radicalized, self-selected "lone wolves" and "bunches of guys" and not from actual identifiable terrorist organizations.

Then, just to focus on the U.S. case, the 2009 plot to stage simultaneous suicide attacks on the New York City subway system, to coincide with the eighth anniversary of the September 11 attacks, came to light. The ringleader, an Afghan-born green-card holder who lived in Queens named Najibullah Zazi, testified that he and two fellow conspirators had been trained at an al-Qaeda camp in Pakistan. Three senior al-Qaeda core commanders—the late Rashid Rauf and Saleh-al Somali, who were killed in U.S. drone strikes in 2008 and 2009, respectively, together with Adnan al-Shukrijumah—had overseen and directed the plot, which was also linked to two other ambitious sets of attacks planned for April 2009 in Manchester, England, and July 2010 in Scandinavia. Hence, the profoundly simplistic notion that al-Qaeda had ceased to exist as an operational entity and the myth that the only terrorist threat that still mattered was that posed by self-radicalized, self-selected individuals were effectively shattered.

May 2010 brought additional refutation, to continue with the American experience, of the "bottom-up" argument when a naturalized U.S. citizen of Pakistani birth named Faisal Shahzad nearly succeeded in staging a massive car bombing in New York City's Times Square. Shahzad had been recruited by the TPP, a close ally of al-Qaeda core. Shahzad, like Zazi, trained in bomb making at a terrorist camp in Pakistan before being sent back to the United States for his mission.

In sum, al-Qaeda core has stubbornly survived despite predictions or the conventional wisdom to the contrary and has persisted not only in providing ideological justification and guidance to the broader jihadist movement but also in the actual direction and implementation of terrorist operations. Indeed, virtually every major terrorist attack or plot against either the United States or the United Kingdom, for instance, during the period between September 11, 2001, and bin Laden's killing emanated either from al-Qaeda core or from close allies and associates often acting on its behalf—at a time when it was claimed that al-Qaeda central had ceased to exist. This calls into question many of the assumptions and arguments that gained currency throughout that long decade.

In this respect, while bin Laden's death inflicted a crushing blow on al-Qaeda, it is still unclear that it has been a lethal one. He left behind a resilient movement with an ideology that remains compelling and a brand that is still attractive even if the organization behind both has seriously weakened. Despite its systematic attrition as result of the U.S. drone campaign, for example, al-Qaeda has nonetheless been expanding and consolidating its presence in new and far-flung locales, including North and West Africa, the Levant, and Iraq in particular. Al-Qaeda has thus been able demonstrate a remarkable ability to replenish its ranks with new recruits and adherents; project a message that still finds an audience in disparate parts of the globe, however modest that audience may be; and articulate a strategy that continues to inform both the movement's and the core's operations and activities and that today is championed by bin Laden's successor, al-Zawahiri.

Since 2002, al-Qaeda has followed a path that, as this book has shown, enabled it to survive by becoming a decentralized, networked, transnational movement rather than a single monolithic entity. In the midst of the group's expulsion from and defeat in Afghanistan, al-Zawahiri charted a way forward for the movement—at a moment, it is worth recalling, when everyone else believed it was on the brink of annihilation. His treatise, published in the London-based Arabic language newspaper *Al-Sharq al-Aswat* in December 2001 and titled *Knights Under the Prophet's Banner*, explained how "small groups could frighten the Americans" and their allies. It equally presciently described how "the jihad movement must patiently build its structure until it is well established. It must pool enough resources and supporters and devise enough plans to fight the battle at the time and arena that it chooses." At the heart of this approach remained al-Qaeda's enduring strategy of conceptualizing its struggle in terms of "far" and "near" enemies. The United States, of course, was the "far enemy," whose defeat was a prerequisite to the elimination of the "near enemy"—the corrupt, reprobate, and authoritarian anti-Islamic regimes in the Middle East, Central Asia, South Asia, and Southeast Asia that could not remain in power without American support. In light of the Arab Spring, that strategy has now assumed an almost hybrid character, and the movement by necessity has focused almost entirely on the "near enemy," local struggles, while remaining characteristically poised to take advantage of any opportunity to attack the "far enemy" that presents itself.

Today, the conventional wisdom argues that, much like bin Laden's killing, the Arab Spring has sounded al-Qaeda's death knell. However, while the mostly nonviolent, mass protests of the Arab Spring were successful in overturning hated despots and thus appeared to discredit al-Qaeda's longstanding message that only violence and jihad could achieve that end, in the years since these dramatic developments, evidence has repeatedly come to light of al-Qaeda's ability to take advantage of the instability and upheaval across two regions to reassert its relevance and attempt to revive its waning fortunes.

The final chapter of al-Qaeda's long and bloody history has yet to be written. This volume has chronicled the phase of its evolution and development that lasted from the immediate aftermath of the September 11, 2001, attacks to the killing of bin Laden in 2011. It reveals a highly resilient organization capable of adaptation and adjustment that, despite grievous leadership losses and diminished resources, was still able to harness the energy of its constituent parts and marshal the powerful narrative and ideology that sustain the collective movement to carry on the struggle proclaimed by bin Laden in 1988. These characteristics ensure both that the final battle against al-Qaeda has not yet been fought and that in coming years the movement may assume new and different forms that cannot be anticipated or predicted and that will require an entirely different approach to finally eliminating it.

Contributors

BRUCE HOFFMAN is currently the director of the Center for Security Studies and the Security Studies Program at Georgetown University's Edmund A. Walsh School of Foreign Service and a senior fellow at the U.S. Military Academy's Combating Terrorism Center. He was director of RAND's Washington, D.C., office and scholar in residence for counterterrorism at the Central Intelligence Agency from 2004 through 2006; an adviser on counterterrorism to the Office of National Security Affairs, Coalition Provisional Authority, Baghdad, Iraq, in 2004; and in 2004 and 2005 an adviser on counterinsurgency to the Strategy, Plans, and Analysis Office at Multi-National Forces–Iraq Headquarters, Baghdad. Professor Hoffman is the author of *Inside Terrorism* (1998, 2006).

FERNANDO REINARES is professor and chair of political science and security studies at Universidad Rey Juan Carlos, as well as senior analyst on international terrorism at Elcano Royal Institute. He was a public policy scholar at the Woodrow Wilson Center in Washington, D.C., in 2011 and has been adjunct professor at Georgetown University since 2014. He is the author of several books, including the Spanish best-seller *Patriotas de la muerte. Quiénes han militado en ETA y por qué* (2001); *¡Matadlos! Quién estuvo detras del 11-M y por qué se atentó en España*; and many articles and chapters. He served a term as senior adviser on antiterrorist policy to Spain's minister of the interior following the 2004 Madrid train bombings. He received the Cross of Military Merit in 2009 and the Cross of Police Merit in 2012.

STEWART BELL is a Canadian journalist who writes about terrorism and security issues for the *National Post* newspaper. He is the author of *Bayou of Pigs*, *The Martyr's Oath*, and *Cold Terror*. His awards include the Amnesty International prize for a magazine article about child soldiers in West Africa and the South Asian Journalists Association Award for his coverage of the Sri Lankan conflict.

ANNELI BOTHA is a senior researcher on terrorism at the International Crime in Africa Programme in Pretoria. She joined the ISS in 2003 and has a specific interest in research on the underlying causes of terrorism, radicalization, and counterterrorism strategies. Anneli is currently working on a Ph.D. dissertation titled "Radicalisation and Suicide Terrorism in North Africa: From a Political Socialisation Perspective."

LINDSAY CLUTTERBUCK is a research leader at RAND Europe in Cambridge, U.K., currently engaged in a range of projects relating to terrorism, counterterrorism, insurgency, and counterinsurgency. He is a member of the European Experts Network on Terrorism. He coauthored "Exploring Patterns of Behaviour in Violent Jihadist Terrorists: An Analysis of Six Significant Terrorist Conspiracies in the UK" (2010).

PAUL CRUICKSHANK is an investigative reporter specializing in international security, a CNN terrorism analyst, and an alumni fellow at the Center on Law and Security at New York University's School of Law. He has written about al-Qaeda and Islamist groups for a variety of international publications and produced several documentaries on al-Qaeda for CNN.

BEATRICE DE GRAAF is professor of conflict and security in historical perspective at the Centre for Terrorism and Counterterrorism of the Hague–Leiden University and a research fellow at the International Centre for Counter Terrorism, the Hague. She is a member of the editorial board of *Studies in Conflict and Terrorism, Perspectives on Terrorism, Journal of European Intelligence Studies*, and the *Zeitschrift für Auswärtige und Sicherheitspolitik*.

RYAN EVANS is a Ph.D. candidate at the King's College London War Studies Department and an associate fellow of the International Centre for the Study of Radicalisation and Political Violence (ICSR). Evans served as a social scientist in Helmand Province, Afghanistan, for the U.S. Army's Human Terrain System in 2010 and 2011.

C. CHRISTINE FAIR is an assistant professor at Georgetown University's Center for Security Studies within the Edmund A. Walsh School of Foreign Service. She served as a senior political scientist with the RAND Corporation, as a political officer to the United Nations Assistance Mission to Afghanistan in Kabul, and as a senior research associate at the Center for Conflict Analysis and Prevention, United States Institute of Peace. She has authored, coauthored, and coedited several books.

JONATHAN FIGHEL is a senior research scholar and director of the Intelligence Assistance for Terrorism Prosecution Department at ICT, IDC Herzliya-Israel. He served in various operational and field positions in the Intelligence Gathering and Research Department of the Intelligence Corps of the IDF. Col. Fighel is an expert on Palestinian terror organizations, counterterrorism, and Middle East affairs.

JEAN-PIERRE FILIU is professor of Middle East Studies at Sciences Po, Paris School of International Affairs. He has held visiting professorships at both Columbia and Georgetown Universities. The French History Convention awarded him their main prize for his book *Apocalypse in Islam* (2011). His books on the contemporary Middle East have been published in a dozen languages, including *The Arab Revolution* (2011).

HOLLY L. McCARTHY holds a degree in security studies from Georgetown University and degrees in Middle Eastern studies and radio, TV, and film from the University of Texas, where she is currently studying for a Ph.D. in the history of the British Empire and the modern Middle East. She has traveled extensively throughout Africa, Europe, Southeast Asia, New Zealand, and the Middle East, and she lived and worked as a scuba diver in the Sinai desert.

ROHAN GUNARATNA is head of Singapore's International Centre for Political Violence and Terrorism Research. He is also professor of security studies at the S. Rajaratnam School of International Studies, Nanyang Technological University, Singapore. He is the author of *Inside Al Qaeda: Global Network of Terror*, an international best-seller and the lead author of *Jane's Counter Terrorism*, a handbook for counterterrorism practitioners.

MOHAMMED M. HAFEZ is an associate professor of national security affairs at the Naval Postgraduate School in Monterey, California. He specializes in Islamic social movements, Middle Eastern and North African politics, and violent radicalization. He is the author of *Suicide Bombers in Iraq: The Strategy and Ideology of Martyrdom* (2007); *Manufacturing Human Bombs: The Making of Palestinian Suicide Bombers* (2006); and *Why Muslims Rebel: Repression and Resistance in the Islamic World* (2003).

THOMAS HEGGHAMMER is senior research fellow and director of terrorism research at the Norwegian Defence Research Establishment. He has previously held fellowships at the Institute for Advanced Study at Princeton and at Harvard, Princeton, and New York Universities. He is the author or coauthor of several books, including *Al-Qaida in Its Own Words* (2008), *Jihad in Saudi Arabia* (2010), and *The Meccan Rebellion* (2011).

PHILIPP HOLTMANN is researcher on conflicts and conflict resolution in the Middle East and a freelance journalist. He specializes in social media and communicative strategies of extremists on the Internet. He has worked with the Stiftung Wissenschaft und Politik in Berlin, the University of Vienna, Harvard University, King's College London, and the Interdisciplinary Center in Herzliya, among others.

SETH G. JONES is a senior political scientist at the RAND Corporation and adjunct professor at the U.S. Naval Postgraduate School. He served in several positions at U.S. Special Operations Command. His book *In the Graveyard of Empires: America's War in Afghanistan* (2009) won the 2010 Council on Foreign Relations Silver Medal for Best Book of the Year. He has published articles in a range of journals, newspapers, and magazines.

JAVIER JORDÁN is associate professor of political science at the University of Granada and codirector of the master's in terrorism and counter-terrorism studies at the International University of La Rioja (Spain). Presently he is leading the research project "International Terrorism's Organizational Structure: Analysis of

Its Evolution and Implications for the European Security," funded by the Spanish Ministry of Science and Innovation.

JACK KALPAKIAN holds a doctorate in international studies from Old Dominion University, Norfolk, Virginia. He specializes in security studies, international political economy, and the Middle East/North Africa region. He teaches at al-Akhawayn University Ifrane—a Moroccan university following the American tertiary education pattern. Originally an immigrant from the Sudan, Kalpakian is a native speaker of Arabic and a naturalized United States citizen.

PETER R. NEUMANN is professor of security studies at the Department of War Studies, King's College London, and serves as director of the International Centre for the Study of Radicalisation. He has authored or coauthored five books as well as numerous peer-reviewed articles and policy reports. He is a member of the advisory boards of numerous think tanks and institutions.

SALLY NEIGHBOUR is an investigative journalist and the author of two books, *The Mother of Mohammed: An Australian Woman's Extraordinary Journey Into Jihad* (2009), which was short-listed for the Walkley nonfiction book award, and *In the Shadow of Swords: On the Trail of Terrorism from Afghanistan to Australia* (2004), which won the 2005 NSW History Prize and was named by *The Economist* magazine as among the best books of 2005.

AMI PEDAHZUR is a professor at the Department of Government at the University of Texas at Austin. His latest books include *The Triumph of Israel's Radical Right* (2012), *Jewish Terrorism in Israel* (2009, with Arie Perliger), and *The Israeli Secret Services and the Struggle Against Terrorism* (2009). He is currently working on a book manuscript entitled "Super-Soldiers: The Evolution of Israel's Special Forces."

GUIDO STEINBERG is a senior fellow specializing in Middle East and Gulf affairs at the German Institute for International and Security Affairs (Stiftung Wissenschaft und Politik) in Berlin. He has worked as a research coordinator at the Free University Berlin (2001) and as an advisor on international terrorism in the German federal chancellery (2002–2005). He is a frequent expert witness in German terrorism trials and a regular commentator on Middle Eastern affairs and terrorism.

MICHAEL TAARNBY is research associate at the University of Central Florida. The author of frequent publications in Danish and English, he is also a frequent speaker at international conferences on terrorism-related issues. He has presented his findings for the EU, NATO, OSCE, EUROPOL, the U.S. State Department, and the RAND Corporation and at think tanks and universities.

LORENZO VIDINO is a senior fellow at the Center for Security Studies, ETH Zurich, and a lecturer at the University of Zurich. He previously held positions at the RAND Corporation, the Kennedy School of Government, Harvard University, the U.S. Institute of Peace, and the Fletcher School of Law and Diplomacy. He is the author of two books and frequent articles in prominent newspapers and academic journals.

Index